AF411634

Stanford University Press
Stanford, California

Printed in the United States of America on acid-free,
archival-quality paper

Library of Congress Cataloging-in-Publication Data
Kraay, Hendrik, 1964– author.
Days of national festivity in Rio de Janeiro, Brazil, 1823–1889 /
Hendrik Kraay.
pages cm
Includes bibliographical references and index.
ISBN 978-0-8047-8526-6 (cloth : alk. paper)
1. Festivals—Political aspects—Brazil—Rio de Janeiro—History—
19th century. 2. Political customs and rites—Brazil—Rio de Janeiro—
History—19th century. 3. Brazil—Anniversaries, etc.—Political
aspects—History—19th century. 4. Holidays—Brazil—History—
19th century. 5. Brazil—Politics and government—1822–1889. I. Title.
GT4833.R5K73 2013
394.26981'5309034—dc23
2012049305

ISBN 978-0-8047-8610-2 (electronic)

Typeset by Thompson Type in 10/12 Sabon

Contents

Map, Table, and Figures

Map

Table

Figures

Currency, Orthography, Names, Pseudonyms, and Note Conventions

During the nineteenth century, the Brazilian currency was the mil-réis, 1,000 réis (singular, real), written 1$000; 1,000 mil-réis was known as a conto, and was written 1:000$000. The mil-réis fluctuated considerably in value from 1822 to the end of the century, although it averaged around US$0.50. To make rough comparisons possible, I provide U.S. dollar equivalents for the mil-réis figures mentioned in the text.[1]

Portuguese orthography has undergone a number of changes since the nineteenth century; following convention, I have modernized the spelling of names and book and newspaper titles in the text, retaining the original spelling in the notes and bibliography, except when, by convention, the archaic spelling is used.

No clear rules governed nineteenth-century Brazilian naming practices. Individuals were often known by a distinctive part of their first or last names. I provide the full names on first mention of people in each chapter, after which I use the portion of the name by which they were most commonly known.

Many of the newspaper articles cited in the following pages were published anonymously or under pseudonyms. If the author is known, I provide his name after the pseudonym in the note.[2] All italics and other emphases in quoted passages appeared in the original. Unless otherwise indicated, all of the newspapers cited were published in Rio de Janeiro. Many articles, particularly editorials, appeared without headlines or titles. Where there was a title or headline, I have included it (but not the subtitle). After the title, I sometimes indicate the section of the newspaper in which the article appeared; unfortunately, I did not collect this information systematically at the start of my research, so my information is incomplete.

Acknowledgments

Many people and institutions contributed to this project. A Standard Research Grant from Canada's Social Sciences and Humanities Research Council in 1999–2002 supported my efforts to turn myself into a historian of Rio de Janeiro. A Professor Visitante Estrangeiro fellowship from the Brazilian Ministério da Educação's Coordenação de Aperfeiçoamento de Pessoal de Nível Superior, held in the Programa de Pós-Graduação em História Social at the Universidade Federal do Rio de Janeiro (UFRJ) in 2004, gave me another six months in Rio de Janeiro. Serious writing began with a Killam Resident Fellowship at the University of Calgary in 2006 but inevitably took much longer than anticipated. The University of Calgary's generous policy on research and scholarship leave provided me with regular sabbaticals since I began this project. I thank all of these institutions for their support.

Numerous audiences in Brazil and North America listened to my early ideas and provided helpful feedback. I thank students and colleagues at the Pontifícia Universidade Católica do Rio de Janeiro; Universidade Federal de Minas Gerais; University of California, Los Angeles; Oliveira Lima Library and University of Maryland; Universidade Federal Rural do Rio de Janeiro; Universidade Federal do Rio Grande do Sul; Universidade Estadual de Santa Cruz; and York University (Toronto). I tried out chapters at eight conferences and received helpful feedback from panel commentators and audience members. The students in my 2004 graduate course on civic rituals and monuments at the UFRJ, several of them now colleagues, surely taught me more than I taught them.

Several colleagues contributed much to this book. Besides sharing many months of research in Rio de Janeiro and many hours of conversation about this project, Bert J. Barickman read the entire manuscript for Stanford University Press, as did Jeffrey D. Needell, who saved me from many oversimplifications about Brazilian politics. Roderick J. Barman also aided in numerous ways. Several Brazilian colleagues have been invaluable interlocutors, especially Elisabete Leal, Marcello Basile, Marco

Morel, and Paulo Knauss. Many more colleagues must be thanked for their assistance in ways large and small: Álvaro Pereira do Nascimento, Camillia Cowling, Celso Castilho, Daryle Williams, Eduardo Silva, Erik Steiner, Flávio dos Santos Gomes, Ian Read, James Green, José Celso de Castro Alves, José Murilo de Carvalho, Judy Bieber, Jurandir Malerba, Karen Racine, Keila Grinberg, Kirsten Schultz, Lúcia Maria Paschoal Guimarães, Marco Pamplona, Maria Angela Leal, Orna Levin, Renata Figueiredo Moraes, Renato Lemos, Richard Graham, Ronaldo Pereira de Jesus, Sandra Lauderdale Graham, Thomas Holloway, Vitor Izecksohn, the late Wiebke Ipsen, and Zephyr Frank. To all, a big thanks. My wife, Judith Elaine Clark, accompanied this book from the beginning and put up with my many absences. Viewing theater galas from her playwright's perspective shaped Chapter Seven. This book is for her.

I mostly resisted publishing portions of this book as articles for fear (often justified, as it turned out) that I would be obliged to modify my interpretations in light of subsequent research and analysis. Parts of Chapters Four, Six, and Seven appeared in " 'Let Us Be Brazilians on the Day of Our Nationality': Independence Celebrations in Rio de Janeiro, 1840s–1860s," in *Negotiating Identities in Modern Latin America*, ed. Hendrik Kraay (Calgary: University of Calgary Press, 2007), 27–48. Parts of Chapters One and Two appeared as "Nação, Estado e política popular no Rio de Janeiro: Festas cívicas depois da Independência," in *Nacionalismo nas Américas*, ed. Marco Antônio Pamplona and Don Doyle (Rio: Record, 2008), 329–54. A section of Chapter One was published as "A invenção do Sete de Setembro, 1822-1831," *Alamanack Braziliense* 11 (May 2010): 52–61; while parts of Chapter Ten appeared as "Alferes Gamboa e a Sociedade Comemorativa da Independência do Império, 1869–1889," *Revista Brasileira de História* 30:61 (2011): 15–39.

*Days of National Festivity in
Rio de Janeiro, Brazil, 1823–1889*

Introduction

In 1826, during its first session, the new Brazilian empire's parliament instituted five national holidays or "days of national festivity," a literal translation that better captures what deputies and senators understood as these days' purpose. Four of them were closely connected to Emperor Pedro I (1822–31): 9 January (the date of his 1822 decision to stay in Brazil in defiance of the Portuguese parliament that had called him to Lisbon); 25 March (the day on which he swore his oath to the constitution that he had granted in 1824); 7 September (the date of his Grito do Ipiranga [Cry or Shout from the Ipiranga (River)], his 1822 declaration of "Independence or Death," which had been constructed as Brazil's independence day in the previous years); and 12 October (his birthday and the date of his acclamation as emperor in 1822). The fifth day of national festivity, 3 May, commemorated the annual opening of the legislative session, mandated by the constitution for that date.[1]

The institution of national holidays was, of course, one of the many symbolic attributes of statehood. Throughout the Americas, the newly independent countries produced their own flags, coats of arms, and currencies, and they designated days on which to celebrate their independence and sometimes also their principal political institutions. Through this invention of national traditions, to paraphrase Eric Hobsbawm and Terence Ranger's familiar phrase, Brazilian senators and deputies, like their counterparts in Spanish America, sought to perpetuate the collective memory of their nation's institutional origins or to create what Pierre Nora has called *lieux de mémoire*, or memory spaces, to anchor the new nation.[2] Nation, for them, meant a political community. As José Antônio Pimenta Bueno (the future Marquis of São Vicente), the great jurist of nineteenth-century Brazilian constitutional law, put it in 1857, "the empire of Brazil" was synonymous with "the Brazilian nation"; both terms referred to "the civil and political society of a free American people."[3] The men who had assembled as the Brazilian nation's representatives understood the creation of what Benedict Anderson calls the "imagined community" of the nation in this political sense.[4] The insights encapsulated in Hobsbawm's and Ranger's and Anderson's compelling phrases (though not the latter's limited and misleading empirical work on Latin America) have stimulated a vast literature and a broad consensus that all traditions are in some way or another invented and that all nations are imagined, fostered by the state.[5] Certainly for Latin America, no serious scholar argues for the existence of primordial ethnic nations, and approaches that stress the rise of national feeling before independence have largely been discredited.[6]

Moreover, to understand nation in its early nineteenth-century political sense moves discussion about Brazilians' collective memory to the political realm. Condy Raguet, the U.S. minister and a keen observer of Brazilian politics, well understood this when he reported that parliament had instituted five "days of political festivity."[7] This was no slip of the pen—Raguet knew Portuguese and understood Brazilian politics too well for that. Rather, it reflected his judgment that the days of national festivity were and would be politically controversial. Four of them celebrated the actions of Pedro I, while the chamber of deputies had insisted on adding 3 May to underscore parliament's importance, thus foreshadowing the tensions between emperor and chamber that would contribute to his decision to abdicate in 1831. In fact, only two of these days of national festivity (25 March and 7 September) would endure until the end of the imperial regime in 1889.[8]

Following Raguet's insight, my central argument in this book is that the celebration of days of national festivity served as the occasion for Brazilians to debate the meaning and nature of the political institutions of the constitutional monarchy established in 1822–24. Each of the principal days of national festivity—25 March, 7 September, and 2 December (Pedro II's birthday, celebrated starting in 1831)—spoke to key aspects of imperial Brazil's institutions. Pedro I's declaration of independence could be interpreted as the act of a heroic prince who created the nation (in the sense of a political community), but there were many ways to downplay his role and seek other origins for Brazil. The constitution, which endured until 1889, established the rules of the political game and was either a product of its authors' great wisdom and foresight or a document hopelessly vitiated by its origins and by its terms, which centralized power in the monarch's hands (the charter had not been passed by a constituent assembly; rather, Pedro I granted it after forcibly closing the assembly). To celebrate the emperor's birthday meant considering his role in government, for he was no mere figurehead; the moderating or regulating power charged him with maintaining the balance among the other three powers, one of which—the executive—he also held.

Thus, in the following pages, I present a political history of the Brazilian empire as seen through the commemoration of its days of national festivity (and a few other civic rituals) in the capital of Rio de Janeiro. Some of the story is generally familiar; at other times, my reading of civic rituals has led me to unexpected conclusions. I provide a history of both "official" and "popular" celebrations on days of national festivity and study the debate over these days' meaning. The contemporary distinction between official and popular celebrations is an important one. Official festivities, organized by the state, involved mostly the court, members of government, and the armed forces, with the populace primarily cast as spectators. Popular festivities, by contrast, were organized by private groups—sometimes political parties, other times apparently apolitical patriotic associations. Somewhere in between stood the entertainment for the populace provided by the authorities.

The periodic surges of popular celebrations reveal a significant engagement with the state and the political system on the part of broad swathes of the urban population. Sometimes this derived from political conflict as parties and other groups mobilized their followers in the streets. At other times, the "popular" celebrants displayed greater autonomy from political parties, and then the popular festivities followed their own logic. The sometimes bitter debate about the significance of days of national festivity and their civic rituals—or better, the institutions celebrated on these days—reveals these festivities' importance to politics and highlights the very different understandings of the imperial regime in the capital. In other words, the regular celebrations of days of national festivity on Rio de Janeiro's streets and in the palace, the imperial chapel, and the theater, as well as the often lively discussion about these rituals in the press, formed integral parts of imperial Brazilian politics and may well have brought more people into politics than did voting or other political activities.

RITUAL AND POLITICS

Many scholars have pointed to the importance of ritual in politics, even in modern societies. In so doing, they have moved away from the structuralist or functionalist approaches to ritual exemplified in the work of classical anthropologists and sociologists typically based on small-scale societies. To be sure, the successful performance of a ritual builds what Victor Turner called *communitas* (social solidarity), defines the boundaries that mark inclusion or exclusion from a community, and legitimates authority by visibly enacting social and political hierarchies or associating them with the divine (Émile Durkheim's insight). It may also provide a socially sanctioned release of tensions or the occasion to enact stylized conflicts resolved in ways that uphold social hierarchies.[9] The centrality of ritual to demonstrating power holders' authority has been observed in numerous societies, perhaps most boldly by Clifford Geertz in his study of the so-called Balinese theater-state; he argues that this state "was a device for the enactment of mass ritual. Power served pomp, not pomp power."[10]

Such approaches to ritual can leave little room for politics; Geertz's analysis of Negara, for instance, implies an unchanging, broadly accepted culture and does not allow for change or contestation. Analyzing rituals (civic or otherwise) outside of their political context misses the key point that every ritual, every collective celebration, amounts to a claim that can be (and often was) contested. This contestation frequently remains muted, even invisible to historians. The surviving accounts of medieval and early-modern rituals in Europe and those in the colonial Americas consist mostly of what Helen Watanabe-O'Kelly has called "festival books," a genre of description whose tropes leave little space for conflict and much less for challenges to the assumptions and values that structured these celebrations. Indeed, on these grounds, one medievalist has forcefully cautioned against anthropological readings of these texts that use them as raw data for analysis of rituals.[11] Those who promoted a ritual or benefited from its message usually managed to control the public accounts of it and to present it in congenial ways, especially before the Age of Revolution.

While it is relatively easy to determine the purposes of those who promoted civic rituals, normally power-holders but sometimes also opposition groups, it is much more difficult to determine how the intended audience received these messages. The poststructuralist insight that rituals, both civic and others, have multiple meanings to promoters, participants, and observers moves the question away from simply determining what a ritual's promoters intended or what social function it served but does not offer a ready way to determine whether, for example, the celebration of a Brazilian emperor's birthday awed the populace or left observers unconvinced of his magnificence and the legitimacy of his authority. Ritual efficacy and the implication that rituals can fail remain difficult to elucidate on a theoretical level except by recourse to the larger external context, which ultimately reduces ritual to a variable dependent on, in the case of civic rituals, the political context.[12] For civic rituals, especially in the contested political environment after the Age of Revolution, this is a workable theoretical formulation and one that avoids circular functionalist or structuralist analysis.

On some basic level, the civic rituals discussed in this book undoubtedly reinforced state power (it is inconceivable that authorities would have continued them if they had undermined state power). They likewise certainly contributed to the population's self-identification as Brazilians and subjects of the monarchy. However, Brazilians extensively debated the nature of their nation or political community. The questioning of the monarchy that periodically surfaced and gathered strength in the 1870s and 1880s meant that assessments of the regime's civic ritual changed significantly. In this sense, civic ritual, however much it may seek to present the image of an enduring political order, is very much dependent on the political strength of those in power and their ability to impose their hegemony or at least secure acquiescence to their rule.

Much of the civic ritual analyzed in this book had a long history in the Western world. A medieval burgher, an early-modern European townsman, and even a citizen of the Roman Empire would have found much that was familiar in imperial Rio de Janeiro's public life. Politics in medieval and early-modern Europe was intensely ritualized. A vast literature examines how medieval and early-modern towns constructed their civic identities through rituals, how monarchs asserted authority through ceremonies, and how seemingly arcane and petty squabbles over protocol constituted integral parts of power struggles.[13] The rediscovery of the classics during the Renaissance, and particularly the accounts of Roman triumphs, offered rulers new celebratory forms through which to assert their authority. Ephemeral triumphal arches and processions entered the Western civic ritual lexicon where they would remain centrally important to the end of the nineteenth century.[14] Absolutism did away with civic autonomy; the rituals that demonstrated it, such as the *joyeuse entrée* (joyous entry) of French monarchs into Paris (last held in 1660 for Louis XIV), disappeared or lost their political importance.[15] The French Sun King created a lavish court and divulged a carefully designed image that exalted his power, even if court ceremony did not always proceed as smoothly and effectively as its organizers desired. Nevertheless, Versailles served as a model for monarchs throughout Europe.[16]

The eighteenth century saw a decline in ritual and a certain desacralization of European monarchy. Enlightened monarchs sought to escape the stifling confines of royal ceremony; the very concept of ritual gained connotations of emptiness and insincerity, part of the larger questioning of the value of outward forms.[17] Louis XIV's successors could not stomach Versailles's oppressive formality; the English kings George I, II, and III abandoned the sacral aspects of monarchy and adopted a more modest, domestic style.[18] Public ceremonies, however, continued to thrust "representations of Church and monarchy before the populace" of eighteenth-century Toulouse and countless other cities; proposals to do away with France's ancient coronation ceremonial in 1775 failed, but their very existence indicated that much was changing.[19] Eighteenth-century Iberian court and civic ritual has drawn little attention from historians. There are indications of elaborate ceremonies surrounding royal weddings, accessions, and entries; flush with Brazilian gold, Portugal's

João V (1707–50) emulated the Sun King, but his successors could not afford his lavishness, especially when faced with the costs of rebuilding Lisbon after the 1755 earthquake.[20]

Colonial American versions of early-modern European royal, Church, and civic ritual flourished in Mexico City and other Spanish-American capitals, although on Corpus Christi and in other festivals, space was made for Indians and other social groups not present in Europe, a reflection of their (subordinate) membership in the colonial body politic.[21] The viceregal entries echoed the royal entries into European towns and allowed municipal elites both to express their devotion to the monarchy and to demonstrate their privileges and their claims to autonomy. They gained "cultural capital" from these manifestations of power in ostentatious ritual.[22] The occasional celebrations of monarchs' accessions (and the funerals of their predecessors) served much the same purposes. The vibrant and rowdy popular diversions that surrounded these civic rituals increasingly troubled eighteenth-century reform-minded Bourbon bureaucrats and Church authorities dubious about the prospects for salvation through baroque Catholicism, but they found it extraordinarily difficult to do away with these manifestations of popular culture.[23] Indeed, despite Enlightenment reformers' best efforts, these ritual aspects of early-modern culture persisted longer in the Americas than in Europe.

The French revolutionaries' attempts to transfer sacrality to a new nation born of revolution through civic festivals, as traced by Mona Ozouf, foundered on the rocks of local cultures and values but also failed because of the eighteenth-century weakening of the association between rulers and the divine.[24] As numerous historians of France have traced, civic rituals and symbols became sites of explicit political conflict after 1789 as the French fought over the Revolution's legacies. Napoleon I's empire, the restoration monarchy, Louis-Philippe's bourgeois kingdom, the short-lived Second Republic, Napoleon III's empire, and finally the Third Republic wrought dramatic changes in France's civic ritual culture as they sought to impose their symbols, rituals, and court ceremonial (in the case of the two empires and the restoration).[25] As Peter Burke has put it, after the Revolution, regime after regime found it necessary to "persuade the people," now "the main targets of propaganda."[26] Persuasion through civic ritual, however, requires the populace's acceptance of the claims to authority enacted in these ceremonies. Opponents of the established order turned their backs on the rituals or found ways to subvert them. In this sense, civic ritual depends on the larger political context; it is not an autonomous realm, capable of creating reality, however much its promoters desire that their message be accepted (and sometimes go to great lengths to foster the illusion of acceptance).

In their efforts to create a new ritual calendar for France, the revolutionaries of the 1790s presaged in an extreme form the invention of new national traditions and political rituals that would take place through-out the nineteenth-century Atlantic World, adapting past traditions to new needs and inventing new ones. Newly independent states found it necessary to celebrate their founding. Many scholars have shown how celebration and public ritual, as well as the extensive press discussion about them, constituted integral parts of party politics and helped forge national identifications strongly mediated through politics in the United States. Early celebrations of 4 July often looked like "boisterous rallies for the party faithful" as Federalists and Democratic-Republicans struggled to define the nation.[27] David Waldstreicher emphasizes that national celebrations have long demonstrated "that America's common political culture consists of a series of contests for power and domination, contests over the meaning of the Revolution, the development of the United States, and who counted as truly 'American.'"[28] In these respects, the celebration of Brazilian days of national festivity was no different. The senator who, in the 1826 debate about the institution of days of national festivity, held up the enthusiastic celebration of 4 July as an example for Brazilians to emulate failed to recognize just how contested early republican U.S. civic ritual was.[29] And many aspects of North American politics were also conducted through rituals. Through parades and other public demonstrations that follow the forms of civic ritual, members of ethnic groups, workers, and other social groups displayed their identity and their public claims for recognition and incorporation into the nation.[30]

COLONIAL PORTUGUESE AMERICAN RITUAL

Like early-modern cities throughout the Catholic world, Portuguese America's towns had an annual cycle of sacred and secular celebrations, punctuated by the occasional nonrecurring celebration of important events in the lives of the royal family. Processions on saints' days and Corpus Christi brought together all members of the community and were sometimes the occasion for conflicts over precedence among competing authorities. Over the course of the eighteenth century, as this ritual life flourished in growing towns, Church and state sought to control the popular celebrations that accompanied these rituals.[31] Many aspects of colonial Brazilian civic ritual remain obscure. Because of the ban on publishing in Brazil, only lifted in 1808, there are few examples of festival books, and much analysis has focused on a handful of well-documented celebrations, such as those in honor of the future João VI's 1786 marriage to Carlota Joaquina promoted by Viceroy Luís de Vasconcelos e Souza in Rio de Janeiro. Thanks to a manuscript description, complete with sketches of the allegorical floats drawn through the city, we know much about this celebration, which José Ramos Tinhorão describes as the direct descendant of the "fifteenth-century Florentine *trionfi* [triumphs]."[32] The celebrations also included a stage at the Passeio Público (the public park) for dances, illuminated ephemeral structures, and equestrian displays (*cavalhadas*) in a specially constructed arena. The remarks about this civic ritual in a nineteenth-century history of Rio de Janeiro indicate that it was a singularly elaborate affair that lived on in popular memory; folklorist José Vieira Fazenda reported in 1901 that an octogenarian had once told him that no nineteenth-century celebrations could compare to Vasconcelos's "festival at the Passeio."[33]

The Portuguese monarchy's flight to Rio de Janeiro in 1807–08 to escape the French occupation prompted an intensification of monarchical ritual in the empire's new capital; in 1878, Joaquim Manuel de Macedo described the decade after the monarchy's arrival as "almost entirely [filled] with official and popular festivities."[34] Prince-Regent João (King João VI after 1816) sought to create what Manoel de Oliveira Lima called a "tropical Versailles" in what had hitherto been a colonial backwater.[35] The metaphor is, in fact, somewhat misleading, for European monarchs had already long abandoned the Versailles model, and João's modest court fell very far short of Louis XIV's ideal. Nonetheless, royal ritual and commemoration were now much more immediate, visible, regular, and spectacular than they had been before 1808, especially in 1817–18 when João was formally acclaimed king and his son, Pedro, married Leopoldina, an Austrian princess. Furthermore, it was much better documented. The new *Gazeta do Rio de Janeiro*, the first newspaper published in Brazil, devoted ample space to royal rituals; memoirists documented them in detail, and the genre of festival books flourished. The so-called French artistic mission of 1817 brought unemployed artists associated with the Napoleonic regime to Brazil; they produced elaborate ephemeral architecture and allegorical paintings for royal ceremonies and designed stage sets for theater galas. The historical painter Jean-Baptiste Debret, highly conscious of his role, not only contributed to these festivals but also documented them in watercolors that he later lithographed and published.[36]

Historians have devoted considerable attention to this efflorescence of royal ritual in the Brazilian capital and have shown that it drew on the early-modern traditions of the Portuguese monarchy adapted to the American environment and modified by the influences of Napoleonic neoclassicism brought by the French artists. Wealthy merchant-planters financed much of the ephemeral architecture, particularly the illuminated triumphal arches and allegorical façades, thereby associating themselves with the monarchy. The city council also actively promoted these celebrations. Such festivities offered spectacular sights and sounds to the populace, as well as entertainment such as bullfights and equestrian displays.

They invariably included a Te Deum and a reception in the palace at which the royal *beija-mão* (hand-kissing) ceremony took place and always ended with a gala in the large São João theater, opened in 1813; fireworks, military parades, and processions of allegorical floats were also essential elements. Portraits of the monarchs, classical imagery, and representations of America figured prominently in these celebrations, which presented Rio de Janeiro as the center of a renewed and glorious imperial regime, a status formally granted to Brazil when the prince-regent raised it to the status of a kingdom equal to Portugal in 1815.[37]

In more mundane ways, too, the monarchy made its presence known in Rio de Janeiro society. João's wife, Carlota Joaquina, insisted that her subjects kneel when she passed in her carriage. Outriders, nicknamed the *largura* (width) for their aggressive occupation of the entire street, compelled subjects to pay their respects in this way.[38] Foreigners chafed at this obligation, and several gleefully reported the 1815 diplomatic incident caused by the U.S. ambassador's refusal to dismount and kneel before Carlota. Instead, he drew a pistol on her entourage, compelled the outriders to back down, and even managed to return to João's good graces, for the future king was more casual about these matters than his irascible wife.[39] The *beija-mão*, a traditional demonstration of respect for the monarch, also brought the king into close contact with his subjects. People of all classes thronged the palace for his regular public audiences, at which all subjects could pay their respects through the *beija-mão* and present their petitions.[40]

The royal rituals of the 1810s visibly affirmed the social and political hierarchy, associated it with the divine, provided entertainment to the populace, and served as the occasion for members of the elite to link themselves to the crown. Given that João's regime remained an absolute monarchy, there is little direct indication that his subjects questioned the expense or the message of these rituals, although some residents occasionally failed to comply with obligations to whitewash their façades before processions or to illuminate their windows at night. One Portuguese-born civil servant muttered privately that, even if he had not been sick, he would not have gone to the theater gala for Pedro and Leopoldina's wedding, because such spectacles were, in his opinion, "of no value"; disdainful of Brazilians, he also sometimes judged the celebrations unworthy of the monarch.[41] João's regime, of course, stood precariously between the revolutionary winds that had swept Europe (and were still sweeping Spanish America) and the Holy Alliance's reaction. The 1817 republican revolt in Pernambuco, a rejection of both absolutism and the centralization of power in Rio de Janeiro, demonstrated that Brazil was not immune to revolution. This rebellion was quickly and brutally repressed, and the elaborate royal celebrations of 1817–18 in the capital have been seen as a direct monarchical response to the Pernambucan patriots.[42] The successful completion of these rituals demonstrated (or sought to demonstrate) that social hierarchies and the political order remained intact.

THE POLITICS AND RITUALS
OF BRAZILIAN INDEPENDENCE

The complex history of Brazilian independence, interpreted and reinterpreted since the 1820s, is difficult to summarize in a few paragraphs, largely because of the intertwining of Brazil's political emancipation with the establishment of a liberal and constitutional regime.[43] While many, even in the nineteenth century, looked for indications of anticolonial stirrings in the eighteenth century, and the 1789 conspiracy against colonial rule in Minas Gerais (the Inconfidência Mineira) was eventually incorporated into Brazilian history as the first step toward independence, the process that led directly to independence began with the arrival of the Portuguese monarchy in Rio de Janeiro in 1808. The opening of the ports to free trade with friendly nations ended Portuguese America's colonial status, and the establishment of government institutions in Rio de Janeiro gave Brazil a both real and symbolic political center and, more important, oriented powerful planter economic interests in the new capital's hinterland toward the monarchy.

While João VI's government had effectively dealt with the Pernambucan rebels, its confidence was shaken, and it could mount no effective opposition to the 1820 liberal revolt in Portugal. This movement's Rio de Janeiro supporters forced João to accept the still unwritten Portuguese constitution in February 1821; the new Portuguese Cortes (parliament) called the king to Lisbon, and he sailed in April, leaving government in the hands of his son and heir, Pedro. The Cortes envisioned a unitary, liberal government for the Portuguese nation. It welcomed representation from the empire's far-flung provinces but sought to dismantle the state apparatus in Rio de Janeiro. Some Brazilian provinces, particularly Pernambuco, seized this opportunity to escape control from Rio de Janeiro, but powerful economic and political interests in the capital and its hinterland refused to submit to Lisbon's directives. Articulated by city council president José Clemente Pereira, a petition signed by more than 8,000 men convinced Pedro to defy Lisbon's orders to return to Portugal, an action known as the "Fico [I'll Stay]," on 9 January 1822.

In the next weeks, Pedro freed himself from the coercion of Portuguese military units stationed in Rio de Janeiro and appointed José Bonifácio de Andrada e Silva to the posts of minister of empire (interior) and minister of foreign affairs. Originally from São Paulo, José Bonifácio had served as inspector of Portugal's mines for many years until his return home in 1819. He represented what Roderick Barman has called the Luso-Brazilian party, a group of educated men, familiar with Enlightenment ideas but more loyal to monarchy than to newfangled liberal notions.[44] Pedro increasingly defied the Cortes and invited the provinces to send representatives to a council of delegates to advise him on government, but the wording of this convocation upset radicals because it did not recognize popular sovereignty. Radicals pressed Pedro to adopt the title of "permanent protector and defender of Brazil"; he rejected "protector" for its republican connotations but accepted the title of *defensor perpétuo* (permanent defender) on 13 May. The council of delegates finally convened in early June, and radicals on it, notably Joaquim Gonçalves Ledo, pressed Pedro to convene a constituent assembly, which he did on the 3rd.

On 7 September 1822, while returning from São Paulo to deal with a political crisis there, Pedro received dispatches from Lisbon that convinced him that there was no further possibility of maintaining transatlantic Luso–Brazilian political ties. On the banks of the Ipiranga River, where his party had stopped because he was feeling unwell, he dramatically announced that, henceforth, his watchword would be "Independence or Death!" On returning to Rio de Janeiro, Pedro and José Bonifácio quickly instituted the trappings of nationhood, including the flag with the national colors of green and yellow. These were, respectively, the colors of the Bragança and Habsburg families, but they soon became understood to represent Brazil's spring (and tropical vegetation) and the country's gold.[45] The new coat of arms featured coffee and tobacco leaves, and Pedro instituted the *tope nacional*, a badge with the words "Independence or Death" to be worn until recognition was secured. It was soon resolved that he take the title of emperor, rather than king, and the city council set his acclamation for 12 October (also his birthday). The title of emperor, with its connotations of election and popular sovereignty, partially satisfied radicals, but José Bonifácio ensured that the ceremony included no direct reference to the constitution, the prior acceptance of which would have dramatically reduced Pedro's authority. Instead, Pedro accepted the title of "constitutional emperor and permanent defender" proffered by the city council. Later that month, José Bonifácio moved against the radicals and effectively destroyed them as a political force. Ledo fled into exile while José Clemente and others were deported. On 1 December, in a demonstration of the divine origins of Pedro's sovereignty, he was crowned and anointed or consecrated.

Both Pedro's acclamation and his consecration have been the subject of considerable analysis. On the one hand, they represented, at least in form, a continuation of old-regime rituals; on the other, they marked an important break with the past. The acclamation, which traditionally marked Portuguese kings' investiture through symbolic recognition by the people, took place outdoors, on the Campo de Santana, on the reviewing stand that had been built for João VI's acclamation. Likewise, the public rituals looked just like those of the 1810s.[46] The closed indoor ceremony of consecration and coronation, however, has continued to puzzle observers. Portuguese monarchs had never been anointed, nor had they been crowned since Sebastião had lost the kingdom's crown at the disastrous battle of Alcácer-Quibir in 1578. The 1822 ceremony has been associated with that of the Holy Roman Empire or with Napoleon's coronation; in either case, it both broke with Portuguese tradition and emphasized the providential nature of Pedro's authority, placing him above the nation.[47] This tension between radically different sources of authority would bedevil the emperor for the rest of his reign.

To focus, as I have done, on the rituals and ceremonies by which the Brazilian government asserted its independence is not, however, to suggest that this regime was a Lusophone version of Geertz's Balinese theater-state. Participation in rituals that associated the social and economic elite with the monarchy strengthened the ruling class's local and national position. A host of scholars have analyzed the Brazilian empire's class basis. Sugar and coffee exports, produced by slave laborers supplied by a slave trade largely under the control of Rio de Janeiro–based merchants, gave the Brazilian capital an economic dynamism that, incidentally, conforms poorly to interpretations that stress colonial Brazil's economic dependency.[48] This economic strength and autonomy gave rise to political power; as we have seen, merchants welcomed the exiled court in 1808, and they and their planter allies (often also their relatives) formed Brazil's dominant class and effectively controlled the Brazilian state through their lock on local politics and mechanisms of patronage.[49]

Such a focus on the Brazilian state's class basis does not, of course, obviate the need to pay close attention to the intricacies of partisan politics, as Jeffrey Needell has emphasized, and to the subaltern politics that, far more often than not, ended in defeat.[50] Much of the new political history of the Brazilian empire produced in the first decade of this millennium by historians associated with Universidade de São Paulo's Projeto Temático (founded by the late István Jancsó) and the Rio de Janeiro–based Centro de Estudos do Oitocentos (Center for Study of the Nineteenth Century) seeks to accomplish exactly this.[51] In my analysis of one more of the many still-unexamined aspects of the imperial Brazilian state—civic rituals—I cast light on some of the linkages between state and society, the cultural process of state formation,[52] and the ways in which politics incorporated significant portions of the urban population.

From the perspective of Rio de Janeiro, Brazil was effectively independent as of late 1822. To be sure, some three years would pass before foreign recognition was secured, the constitution remained to be written, Portuguese troops held out in Salvador, and governments in Pernambuco and some other provinces of the North maintained a wary autonomy vis-à-vis Pedro I. Nevertheless, already in 1823, discussions about how and when to commemorate independence began in the capital, the subject of Chapter One. Before addressing this question, however, we must introduce the setting of imperial Rio de Janeiro.

IMPERIAL RIO DE JANEIRO

Most of the events analyzed in this book took place within a rectangle of Rio de Janeiro urban space, about three kilometers long and two kilometers wide, that stretched from Guanabara Bay roughly westward on flat land between the hills that dominated the city's topography (Map I.1).[53] By following an imaginary nineteenth-century foreign visitor on a walking tour through this area, we can outline the locations that figure prominently in the following pages. Twentieth-century urban reform projects, notably the removal of two large hills that provided the landfill to expand the city into the bay and the construction of two wide avenues, changed much of this area and erased some of the places important to imperial civic rituals. It is a relatively small space, still easily traversed by foot, so long as one can tolerate the tropical heat (and dodge the traffic).

Arriving by sea, travelers normally landed at the Palace Square, known officially as Dom Pedro II Square after 1870, on the city's eastern shore (Figure I.1). To travelers' left stood the city palace, the viceregal residence built in 1743 and taken over by Prince-Regent João on his arrival in 1808. To their right, past hotels that did a brisk business catering to visitors, northward along the docks, which were gradually extended into the water over the course of the century, stretched a large vegetable and fish market. The construction of a market building in 1834–41 sought to bring some order to this chaotic area.[54] Its exotic sights and smells both attracted and repelled foreigners.[55] Straight ahead, on the other side of the square, stood the Carmelite convent and the imperial chapel (formerly the Carmelites' church), the former connected to the palace by a gallery as of the 1810s and the latter linked to the convent by a similar gallery in 1841.[56] For most of the empire, the downtown palace was used for ceremonial and administrative purposes; this was where the levees and other formal court ceremonies normally took place. Part of the palace housed government departments, and after 1849 the Instituto Histórico e Geográfico Brasileiro (Brazilian Historical and Geographical Institute, founded in 1838) functioned in one of its rooms.[57]

To our traveler's right, the wide Direita Street (Primeiro de Março after 1870) beckoned northward. Government offices and commercial

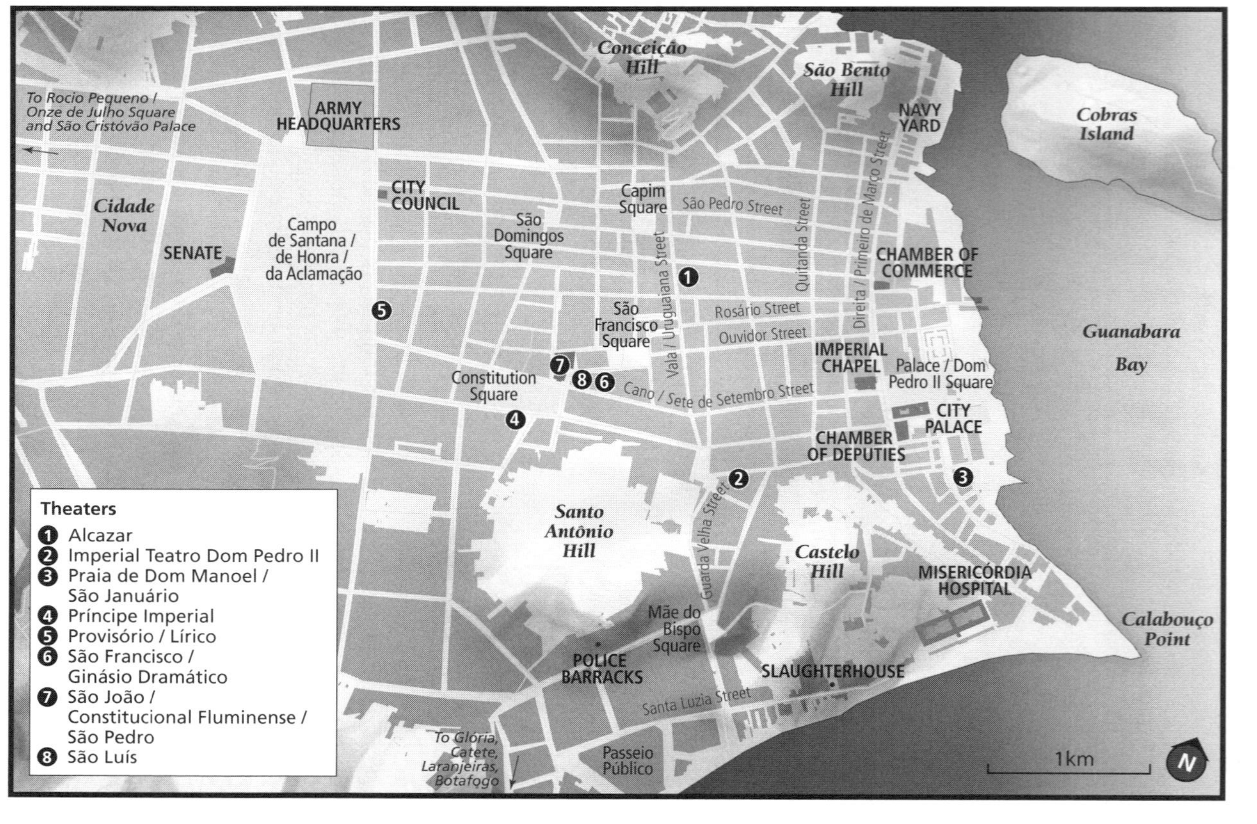

MAP I.I.
Imperial Rio de Janeiro.

Sources: Barreiros, *Atlas*; E. & H. Laemmert, "Nova planta da cidade do Rio de Janeiro," 1867, Library of Congress, Geography and Map Division; E. Gotto, "Plan of the City of Rio de Janeiro," 1866, CECULT, UNICAMP. Cartography by Erik Steiner, Spatial History Project, Stanford University.

FIGURE I.I.
The Palace Square, ca. 1820.
Source: Debret, *Voyage*, vol. 3, plate 1.

houses, including the Praça do Comércio, or Chamber of Commerce, lined this street. West of it stretched several blocks dominated by small-scale commerce. Direita Street narrowed as it approached the access to the navy yard at the foot of the São Bento Hill; this was where the emperors landed for their ceremonial entries into the capital after their journeys. Travelers would not likely have ventured this far, however, for to their left, only a block or so after the imperial chapel, they would have been drawn to Ouvidor Street by its numerous attractive shops and restaurants, as well as by the lively crowds normally found here. Closed to daytime vehicular traffic in 1867, Ouvidor was the principal shopping district, the gathering place for elite men (and some women), the Rue Vivienne of Brazil, as French travelers called it after Paris's main retail street; French modistes, in fact, had come to dominate the fashion industry in the late 1810s.[58] Later in the century, major newspapers' editorial offices also crowded into this street. Here could be seen the leading journalists, politicians, and writers; many described Ouvidor Street as the heart of Brazil's political and cultural life. A Belgian diplomat called it "the open-air club" to highlight the many functions that it served.[59]

After about 500 meters, Ouvidor terminated in the small São Francisco Square. To the left stood the large church dedicated to the saint who gave the square its name; after 1872, a small statue of José Bonifácio stood in the middle of the square. Early in the century, visitors could see the unfinished cathedral, begun in 1749, on the square's west side. When its construction was definitively abandoned, a large school building was erected on the site in the 1830s; it served as the military academy until 1851 and then as a technical school, the Escola Central (Escola Politécnica after 1874). Following the short street that exited the southwest corner of the square, our traveler would very quickly arrive at the northeast corner of Constitution Square (known as the Rocio until 1821), where the São Pedro Theater stood. Originally erected in 1813 as the Real Teatro São João (Royal Saint John Theater) and rebuilt after fires in 1824 and 1851, this was the city's principal theater venue until 1852; here the gala performances that concluded days of national festivity took place. Constitution Square, so named in honor of João VI's adoption of the still-unwritten Portuguese constitution in 1821, was dominated after 1862 by the massive equestrian statue of Pedro I. To the square's south, Santo Antônio Hill loomed over this area of the city. When the theater was constructed, this square marked the "edge of the original city," but "some rich proprietors" soon built "attractive houses" there; in the latter part of the nineteenth century, this square's environs turned into a center of bohemian nightlife.[60]

Both of the streets that exited west from Constitution Square led to the large Campo de Santana (Saint Anne's Field). Dubbed the Campo da Aclamação (Acclamation Field) in 1822 after Pedro I's acclamation as emperor of Brazil, it was finally developed into a chic urban park in the late 1870s. Until then, however, it was a rather desolate place, suitable for military parades (the main army headquarters was located on the square's north side). For João VI's acclamation, gardens were laid out, and a so-called *palacete* (little palace) was constructed to serve as a reviewing stand; a fireworks explosion destroyed the building at the time of Pedro II's coronation in July 1841. The washerwomen who labored around a large fountain normally dominated this square, which also sometimes served as a garbage dump.[61] As this area of the city developed, several important institutions came to surround this square. Starting in 1826, the senate met in a converted private mansion on the square's west side. In 1852, a temporary opera house was built on the square's east side; intended as a short-term replacement for the São Pedro, which had been destroyed by fire, this new Teatro Lírico (Lyric Theater) became the city's principal theater venue until 1871. North of the theater, the city council constructed its new building in 1825 (and rebuilt it in 1882), and the Dom Pedro II railroad station opened west of the army barracks in 1858.

Beyond the Campo da Aclamação stretched the Cidade Nova, or New City, whose straight streets and large lots made this an attractive area for members of the middle and upper classes to build new houses in the first half of the nineteenth century, especially after drainage projects eliminated the swamps that had formerly made this an unhealthy area.[62] From this district to the northwest the main road led to the São Cristóvão palace, donated to Prince-Regent João by a wealthy merchant in the 1810s. Located on a small rise that afforded a pleasant view of the bay, this was Brazilian rulers' principal residence while they were in the city. It was gradually expanded over the course of the nineteenth century but never became a truly impressive palace, at least by the standards of European visitors who measured it against Tuileries, Buckingham, or Schönbrunn.

Several straight and roughly parallel roads led back toward the downtown from the Campo da Aclamação, all north of the route that our traveler took from the Palace Square. The principal of these was São Pedro Street, which led past São Domingos and Capim Squares; this street, located in the middle of the present-day President Vargas Avenue, was the most common route that the imperial procession took on its way into the city on days of national festivity. Further to the north, a line of low hills separated this area from the sea. It gradually developed into lower-class neighborhoods; the Valongo slave market was located here until its closure in 1831.[63] Following São Pedro Street, our traveler would eventually reach Direita Street and the Palace Square.

Immediately south of the palace stood the hall in which the chamber of deputies met after 1826. Further south stretched a strip of flat land with small narrow streets that terminated at the army arsenal located on a sharp peninsula, Calabouço (Prison) Point. The steep side of Castelo (Castle) Hill marked the limits of this neighborhood, in which the São Januário Theater (1834–68) was located.[64] In the colonial period and in the very early nineteenth century, the three streets that led up to the Castelo peak and the squares on its top were desirable residential addresses that enjoyed refreshing breezes, but new, more distant upper-class neighborhoods developed over the course of the nineteenth century.[65] Our traveler could circle around this hill via Santa Luzia Street, which led past the Misericórdia Hospital (opened in 1852) and the slaughterhouse (moved in 1853 to the city's outskirts) to the Passeio Público, a public park opened in 1779 and renovated in 1861 (this was the site of the long-remembered 1786 celebrations).[66] Beyond the Passeio, Glória Street followed the bay shore and gave access to Glória Church, a favored subject for foreign artists because of its charming location on a sharp rise overlooking the bay.[67] From here, there was easy access to Catete, Laranjeiras, and Botafogo, neighborhoods that remained distant elite suburbs until streetcars intensified their development after midcentury.[68]

One block inland from the Passeio, the police barracks abutted the south side of Santo Antônio Hill. Mãe do Bispo Square filled the narrow gap between Castelo and Santo Antônio hills, and heading north from here our traveler would arrive at the Carioca fountain, supplied by waters from Corcovado Hill via the spectacular eighteenth-century aqueduct that linked Santa Teresa and Santo Antônio hills. The waters of this fountain, allegedly the best in the city, gave rise to the nickname by which residents of Rio de Janeiro are known today, although in the nineteenth century *Fluminense* was a more common designation for people from the Brazilian capital (today *Fluminense* refers to residents of Rio de Janeiro state, outside of the city). As one long-time foreign resident put it, *Carioca* had the connotations of *Cockney*.[69] Nearby, after 1871, stood the massive Imperial Teatro Dom Pedro II, in which galas on days of national festivity took place in the 1870s and 1880s. From here, a number of narrow streets led back to the vicinity of the palace.

By most measures, nineteenth-century Rio de Janeiro was a major Atlantic World metropolis. Thanks to the large influx of Portuguese exiles who abandoned the mother country in 1807–08, the arrival of numerous foreigners after Brazil's ports were opened to free trade (1808), and the booming slave trade that brought tens of thousands of Africans to the port each year, the population of the city's seven urban parishes grew significantly to 86,323 in 1821. To judge by the four enumerations completed between 1838 and 1890, population growth was steady, if uneven, although this may simply reflect inconsistencies in the censuses (Table I.1). Most of the 1,300,000 slaves imported into southern Brazil between 1811 and the early 1850s, when new legislation and effective enforcement of laws that had banned the trade back in 1831 put an end to it, passed through Rio de Janeiro.[70] Early in the century, most were transshipped to the sugar plantation districts northeast of the city or to Minas Gerais; as coffee gained importance as an export crop in the 1820s and 1830s, the plantations located in the Paraíba Valley north and northwest of the city became the principal destination for newly arrived slaves.

The 1850s marked a major turning point in the city's demographic development. From around 40 percent of the city's population, the proportion of slaves fell to less than half that in 1872. As slave prices soared in the aftermath of the trade's closure, many masters found it profitable to sell their human property to labor-hungry coffee planters. Free immigrants, mostly Portuguese, became an increasingly important part of the urban workforce; the 1872 census counted 45,497 Portuguese men (but only 10,441 Portuguese women) in the city, accounting for fully three-quarters of the city's foreign-born.[71]

Besides the monarchy, numerous other national institutions were concentrated in the capital. A Portuguese journalist remarked in the 1890s on Rio de Janeiro's "amazing power to centralize everything, from commerce to the arts," and his observation applies equally to earlier decades.[72] The Instituto Histórico e Geográfico Brasileiro brought together the country's intellectual elite under imperial patronage; its members produced an official national history that highlighted unity as the Brazilian monarchy's supreme achievement.[73] The best secondary education in the country was had at the Dom Pedro II School (opened in 1838), but university-level education was decentralized, with Rio de Janeiro having only one of the country's two medical schools (the two law schools

TABLE I.I.
Population of Rio de Janeiro (Urban Parishes), by Legal Status, 1821–1890.

Year	Free	Slave	Total
1821	45,947	40,376	86,323
1838	60,025	37,137	97,162
1849	127,051	78,855	205,906
1872	191,176	37,567	228,743
1890	422,756	—	422,756

NOTE: The 1849 free population includes 10,732 freedpeople enumerated separately.
SOURCE: Soares, "*Povo*," 363, 364, 368, 373, 382.

founded in 1828 that trained much of the country's political and administrative elite were located in São Paulo and Olinda, the latter transferred to Recife in 1854). After 1826, the imperial parliamentary session normally ran from May to September each year (the cool months), bringing deputies and senators from all across the country. Government investment in theater and the other arts was concentrated in Rio de Janeiro; seekers of public office and patronage flooded the capital, as did those who sought concessions for railroads and other development projects. The city was, in short, a "Mecca" for Brazilians, as another foreign observer put it.[74]

Foreigners too regularly made their way to the Brazilian capital, and not just the Africans forced to labor or the poor Portuguese immigrants seeking to better their lives. A significant diplomatic corps served in Rio de Janeiro; in 1844, twenty-four countries maintained diplomatic or consular representatives in the Brazilian capital, a figure that rose to thirty-five in 1864 but fell to twenty-six in 1884 (German and Italian unification eliminated separate representation for the new countries' constituent states).[75] The Brazilian Braganças had close ties to some European royal houses, and Pedro I's claim to the Portuguese throne after 1826 briefly made him an important player in European politics. Rio de Janeiro was the best American port in the South Atlantic. The ships attached to the major powers' naval stations regularly called at the port, which offered the only large dry-dock facilities in the region after the completion of the Dique in 1861. Those venturing around Cape Horn invariably stopped at the Brazilian capital for water and supplies. The numerous travelers' accounts of shorter or longer visits to Rio de Janeiro published in Europe and North America testify to the city's prominence.[76]

Foreigners' descriptions of Rio de Janeiro frequently dwelled on the large number of slaves on the streets, especially before the 1850s. In the first half of the century, this was a city in which slaves did all of the physical labor; households of even modest means could not do without their human property. Slavery was widespread in society; as long as their supply was plentiful, slave ownership offered a route to social mobility even for free people of color. The end of the slave trade in 1850 sparked a significant rise in slave prices, which prompted owners to sell their human property to coffee planters and made it more difficult for individuals of modest means to acquire slaves. Slavery profoundly shaped social relations in the city. The occasional concern about slave revolt (although no major violent slave uprisings took place), the highly visible private violence that masters meted out against their slaves, masters' insistence on deference from their slaves (and indeed from all those whom they considered their social inferiors)—all had their roots in the constant power struggle that characterized slavery. To be sure, manumission was a real possibility for urban slaves, especially those who labored on their own account (often women) or those who built close relations to their masters. Women and children were thus most likely to be freed.[77]

While racial hierarchies profoundly shaped Brazilian society, members of the Brazilian elite had long learned how to make exceptions in the interests of preserving the larger social order. In law and in practice, the Brazilian empire saw African-born slaves as aliens, ineligible for citizenship should they gain freedom, but Brazilian-born freedmen enjoyed a limited citizenship. By the terms of the 1824 constitution—a color-blind document—their freeborn descendants had full citizenship rights, provided that they met the income requirements mandated by the charter.[78] Fully three-quarters of Afro-Brazilians were free as of 1872. This lack of congruence between race and the legal status of slavery, as well as the evidence of extensive racial mixture, even among the wealthy and powerful, puzzled many an observer imbued with nineteenth-century U.S. racial ideologies or the scientific racism that came to dominate North Atlantic thinking about race in the latter part of the century, but it indicates that class (and culture) were often as important as race in shaping the social hierarchy.[79]

Accelerating in the 1850s, urban improvements gave Rio de Janeiro an air of progress and modernity. The first gaslight was inaugurated in 1854, and these street lights soon offered a spectacular view to those who approached the city by night.[80] Mule-drawn streetcars appeared in 1859, and their rails quickly reached even remote points like the Jardim Botânico (Botanical Garden). Known as *bondes*, after the bonds that English and North American companies issued to finance their construction, streetcars quickly replaced horse-drawn omnibuses and made possible the expansion of distant suburbs and consequently an increasing spatial segregation.[81] Returning to Rio de Janeiro in 1873 after twelve years, one traveler remarked that the *bondes* had wrought an enormous change in city life. Formerly, "people seldom moved more than they were obliged to move; now the tram-cars are full all day with people going in every direction and numbers of clerks and men of business are enabled to sleep in the lovely suburb[s] amid groves of oranges and gardens full of brilliant flowers instead of being cooped up in the city itself."[82] Many foreigners also remarked on the *bondes*' "democratic characteristic"—people of all classes rode side-by-side, and the only barrier was footwear; barefoot people were not admitted, a prohibition that derived from the denial of shoes to slaves.[83] Telegraph lines connected Rio de Janeiro with Petrópolis (the court's summer residence) in 1856 and in 1867, during the Paraguayan War (1864–70), linked the Brazilian capital to its southern provinces. In 1874, the first transatlantic cable reached Brazil.[84] Among the middle and upper classes, the latest European fashion predominated, to the point that heavy dark suits were de rigueur for men, as Auguste François Biard discovered to his embarrassment in 1858 when he went out in a more comfortable white coat.[85] Pianos proliferated in middle- and upper-class households after midcentury, and at this time some of the latest operas made it to Rio de Janeiro within a year or two of their European premières.

Like other Atlantic World cities, Rio de Janeiro remained an unhealthy place. The 1855 cholera epidemic took thousands of lives, and after midcentury endemic yellow fever claimed a regular harvest of victims every summer.[86] One army officer lamented the "heat and filth" and mused that living in Rio de Janeiro amounted "to having a shorter life, more full of sickness" than elsewhere.[87] Efforts to install a sewage treatment system in the 1860s made the city a pioneer in this area, but the system was inadequate.[88] Despite the growing popularity of sea bathing, beaches remained a common place to dispose of garbage and even human waste. The water supply could not keep up with a growing population, and many poorer neighborhoods often went without water for days.

The material symbols of European modernity and civilization coexisted with a vibrant popular culture, heavily African in origin, that increasingly embarrassed members of the Brazilian elite. Indeed, as historians have recently argued, Rio de Janeiro must be understood as "one of the largest African-Atlantic cities," at least until midcentury. An annual cycle of religious festivals brought together Catholic European popular culture and African practices. African religions flourished, albeit less visibly than the saints' festivals promoted by Catholic brotherhoods.[89] Practitioners of the Afro-Brazilian martial art of *capoeira* annoyed authorities, who seemingly could do nothing to control this expanding lower-class activity and the gang violence associated with it. Efforts to replace the boisterous pre-Lenten *entrudo* celebrations with a modern and "civilized" carnival likewise had only limited success.[90]

The evolution of this complex and vibrant city profoundly shaped the civic rituals analyzed in this book. Civic ritual cannot be understood apart from the society in which it took place. While Fluminenses of all backgrounds often disagreed profoundly about the meaning of the annual cycle of civic rituals or the occasional special celebrations mostly associated with the monarchy, they could not escape these displays. Highly visible on the streets, prominently debated in the press, and no doubt extensively discussed privately, civic rituals were an integral part of imperial Rio de Janeiro's life.

SOURCES AND METHODS

Key aspects of my approach to the study of imperial Brazilian civic rituals emerged only gradually as I gained familiarity with the sources and the material that they offered. That Brazil had officially designated days of national festivity after 1826 gave my research a focus; the analysis of these days' annual celebration forms this book's backbone. As I discovered the scale and salience of the other imperial festivals, like the periodic celebrations to welcome emperors Pedro I and II back to the capital after their journeys throughout Brazil and abroad, these rituals, with their ancient pedigree, joined the days of national festivity. The inaugurations of the monuments to Pedro I (1862) and José Bonifácio (1872) likewise stood out by their scale and controversial nature; through these ceremonies, Brazilian debated the same issues about the origins of their nation to which days of national festivity spoke.

Civic rituals are necessarily urban events—rural areas lack the concentrations of population required for collective celebration—and Rio de Janeiro was Brazil's political and cultural capital. The volume and density of sources for Rio de Janeiro, particularly the burgeoning and vibrant periodical press, also urged a focus on this city. The result is a book that unashamedly focuses on Brazil's center, the Corte (Court) as it was known, and it runs the risk of taking Rio de Janeiro for all of Brazil. Still, the Corte constituted Brazil's political, cultural, and social heart, and influences generally flowed outward from the city to the provinces. That no scholar had systematically examined civic ritual in imperial Brazil's capital suggested that it was a good place to start; in the conclusion, I briefly consider how imperial civic ritual played out in the provinces.

Two major categories of sources provide most of the evidence for the civic rituals analyzed in this book. Around each officially designated day of national festivity, I examined a few days' worth of virtually all of the surviving newspapers and periodicals, about 400 titles, ranging from ephemeral periodicals that failed to make it past their first issue to long-running dailies like the *Diário do Rio de Janeiro* (1821–78) and the *Jornal do Comércio* (which has published continuously since 1827 and whose coverage of civic rituals I read until 1890). Much of the analysis is shaped by the press's evolution. From its hesitant beginnings with the

Gazeta do Rio de Janeiro, founded in 1808 when Prince-Regent João lifted the prohibition on publishing in his American domains, the periodical press developed rapidly after the establishment of constitutional rule in the Portuguese empire in 1821. The partisan political periodicals of the early 1820s were soon joined by what we would today recognize as newspapers, whose circulation expanded steadily, until by the end of the imperial regime Rio de Janeiro supported several major dailies with circulations in excess of 10,000 copies, joined by a score of periodicals that appeared weekly or several times per week.[91] Over the course of the following pages, I comment on major aspects of the press's evolution, much of which still requires systematic historical analysis.

Newspapers commented extensively on civic rituals and the politics surrounding them, and they frequently published editorials explaining the meaning of the anniversary celebrated on the day of national festivity. In this respect, as Waldstreicher observes for the early United States, "Newspapers transformed the very rituals that they seem to merely describe."[92] Even apparently objective reports on civic rituals often interpreted the celebrations through partisan political lenses. What most surprised foreigners (and what makes the press the essential source for this study) was the freedom that journalists enjoyed after about 1830. A remarkably wide range of views appeared in print, and Pedro II protected this freedom to such a degree that some historians have concluded that press freedom was greater in the empire than in most of Brazil's subsequent republican regimes.[93]

Many foreigners commented on imperial Brazilian civic rituals, and their writings constitute the second major source for this book. Both travelers and diplomats left lengthy accounts of the ceremonies that they saw or, in the case of diplomats, in which they participated. I have examined the writings of about 225 travelers who visited nineteenth-century Rio de Janeiro. To be sure, many scholars have pointed out that travelers' observations of foreign societies are riddled with prejudices and shaped by imperialist or Romantic conventions, but they often described things that Brazilians took for granted.[94] Casual research in the newly available full-text searchable databases of U.S. periodicals turned up some invaluable correspondents' reports from the Brazilian capital. The diplomats accredited to the Portuguese and Brazilian courts implicitly acknowledged civic ritual's importance by frequently reporting on it, and in the 1820s they (and travelers) provide the only glimpses of the discordant voices that lingering censorship kept out of the press until 1830.

Other sources include festival descriptions and other publications such as poems, plays, and sermons produced for days of national festivity. Some of this material also appeared in the press. The festival description literature draws on the colonial and early-modern tradition of producing festival books to impose a certain interpretation on a given celebration and to win social and political prestige for its promoters. Here it is important to reiterate that the published description of a civic ritual was often more important than how the ritual was actually conducted. Government and opposition newspapers often reported completely different things about the same civic ritual and particularly about the populace's response to it. Juxtaposing the competing press coverage and comparing it with other accounts, such as those of foreigners not engaged in Brazilian partisan politics, provides a check on these inevitable biases in the sources.

Parliamentary debates about the designation or elimination of days of national festivity offer indications of what legislators had in mind when they set the civic calendar. There are only limited archival sources on civic rituals and consequently few indications of how the state organized the aspects of civic ritual for which it was responsible. Even fewer sources are available on those who organized the popular festivities analyzed in Chapters Six and Ten, for these private associations tended not to leave records. Occasionally, disputes about the organization or administration of celebrations made it into the press, and the ensuing discussions offer some indications of how Fluminenses organized themselves to celebrate days of national festivity.

The significant and often rapid changes in imperial Brazilian civic ritual and in the discussion about it underscore some of the key themes that run through recent literature on civic rituals.[95] Although there may be a seemingly unchanging core to a ritual, its meaning to participants and observers may change significantly. This was certainly the case for the relatively stable core of imperial official ritual, which gradually became simpler yet over time was subject to more and more criticism for its costly ostentation. When all of the elements of civic ritual on the Brazilian empire's days of national festivity are considered, it becomes clear that Brazilians were as inventive as any other people and that new forms of celebration could become considered "traditional" after only a very few years. Often the debate and discussion about the ritual mattered more than what actually happened on the street, in the theater, or at the palace (although I can usually come reasonably close to reconstructing the "facts" whose interpretation sparked controversy).

The first five chapters of this book follow a roughly chronological order as they trace the development of the Brazilian empire through its civic rituals. Chapter One examines the civic ritual of the seven years after December 1822, when Pedro I was duly crowned and consecrated as emperor of Brazil. Much of this chapter describes the relatively quick process by which Pedro's Grito do Ipiranga (7 September 1822) came to be identified as the moment of Brazil's independence, and the debate about which other dates should be celebrated as days of national festivity. Major monarchical festivals punctuated this period, notably Pedro's reception back into Rio de Janeiro after his trip to Bahia and the celebrations surrounding his 1829 wedding to Amélia de Leuchtenberg. Much of the politics that lay behind these days of national festivity concerned the question of the origins of Pedro I's authority and its extent. Did his power derive from divine right or from popular acclamation? Was he beholden to the nation, or did he stand above it?

Exaltados (radical liberals) rejected anything that smacked of divine right or imperial authoritarianism; in a dramatic symbolic challenge, they took to the streets on 25 March 1830 to celebrate the constitution that Pedro had granted six years earlier and, more important, to insist that he abide by its terms as they understood them. This, along with the freeing of the press, led to several years of intense debate about civic rituals described in Chapter Two, as Brazilians argued and fought over the nature of the state and the nation. Pedro's unexpected abdication on 7 April 1831 threw open Brazilian politics; Moderados, or moderate liberals, prevailed and ensured the monarchy's survival by establishing a regency on behalf of the young Pedro II, then five-and-a-half years old. They decentralized power somewhat and completed several key liberal reforms that had been in the works since the late 1820s, including the citizen militia, the National Guard, and the jury system.

The perception that these reforms were leading to anarchy, largely due to the provincial rebellions that broke out in the mid-1830s, sparked a reaction to the liberal reforms of the early regency, the so-called Regresso of 1837, whose leaders eventually undid many of the reforms in the interest of centralizing power and strengthening the state. One of the Regresso's key features was its investment in the symbols and rituals of monarchy, the subject of Chapter Three. Although the Regresso's triumph was not a smooth one, and all parties fought over control of the monarchy, the result was the exaltation of the young Pedro II's persona as the symbol around which all Brazilians could rally. Extensive efforts went into celebrating his birthday (2 December) in 1837–39 and, after his premature acclamation in July 1840, his coronation, finally held a year later. This was certainly the single largest civic ritual conducted in the imperial Brazilian capital, and it marked the apogee of the Regresso's investment in monarchical symbolism.

Chapter Four covers a much longer period as it traces the patterns of official civic rituals from the early 1840s to the early 1860s. As politics turned to other questions and in the 1850s moved toward the Conciliação (Conciliation) period, during which Pedro II sought to reduce partisan politics by constructing cabinets of moderates, civic rituals became more peaceable and routine. The 1848 reduction in the number of days of national festivity to only three simplified the Brazilian civic calendar but turned it into a clearly defined commemoration of the empire's principal institutions, the monarchy founded on 7 September 1822 and celebrated in the person of the current emperor on his birthday (2 December), and the constitution, to which the nation had sworn its oath on 25 March 1824. So long as general acceptance of these institutions prevailed, there was little controversy about their celebrations on days of national festivity, and for much of this time civic rituals took on an air of perfunctory routine. A flurry of anti-Portuguese nativism and radical liberal activism on 7 September 1848 echoed the politics of the early 1830s but proved to be short lived, while the weddings of Pedro II and his two sisters in 1843–44 and his receptions back into Rio de Janeiro in 1846 and 1847 echoed the monarchical ritual of 1837–41.

The March 1862 inauguration of the long-planned equestrian statue of Pedro I is the subject of Chapter Five. This was the largest civic ritual since the coronation, and the monument embodied the official interpretation of Brazilian independence, but a new generation of radical liberals mounted a vigorous attack on its premises that Pedro I had won independence and had given the nation its form through the constitution that he had granted. The campaign for the monument dated back to the 1820s and had gone through numerous iterations until the monument's inauguration. The official ritual was successfully carried out, albeit five days late because of heavy rains, but the press debate of March and April 1862 undermined the monument's message. Rich and dense sources on this highly symbolic moment provide a revealing look at how politics was conducted through a civic ritual.

The next two chapters pause the narrative to examine two key aspects of civic ritual. Chapter Six begins with an examination of a sudden, unexpected, and still largely inexplicable surge of what were known as popular festivities on 7 September during the late 1850s. Led by a few associations with some Liberal Party ties but soon joined by many others without evident partisan affiliations, these patriotic societies promoted street celebrations on 7 September. These popular independence celebrations embodied an understanding of the Brazilian nation that excluded many, and the societies appear to have been primarily middle- and upwardly mobile working-class associations. Their sudden appearance may have been linked to other cultural changes, notably efforts to civilize and modernize elements of popular culture. This chapter concludes with a discussion of middle- and upper-class sociability on days of national festivity, a social history of civic rituals.

The theater galas with which all days of national festivity ended (except those that occasionally fell during the Holy Week theater closing) are the subject of Chapter Seven. Here I trace the culture of theatergoing, midcentury government efforts to promote and control theater and opera, the evolution of the programs (particularly the rise of opera and the largely unsuccessful efforts to create a national opera and a national theater in the 1850s and early 1860s), and the extra program elements that turned a regular theater evening into a gala on days of national festivity. These included the cheers to the emperor, the performance of the independence or national anthems, poetry readings (sometimes scripted and planned, sometimes spontaneous and unexpected), and the special musical, dance, or theatrical pieces performed before the principal work on the program. An analysis of these dramatic laudations (*elogios dramáticos*) reveals how the impresarios and the government that fostered and censored their work sought to portray the Brazilian nation.

The last three chapters focus on what can broadly be viewed as the imperial regime's decline, as seen through its civic rituals. Chapter Eight examines the celebration of days of national festivity during the Paraguayan War (1864–70) and presents the unexpected finding that the war saw a significant reduction in the celebration of days of national festivity. If the war fostered Brazilian nationalism, as many have argued, it did not show on these days. Just before the war, the popular festivities of independence had diminished notably, and the government had cut theater subsidies. Popular victory celebrations in 1870, however, adopted all of the traditional forms of civic rituals, and, through them, the Liberals whom Pedro had removed from power in July 1868 challenged the Conservative government. The official celebration of the war's end in July 1870 was a great fiasco; the contrast between this official festival and the earlier popular victory celebrations reflected these political divisions.

Chapters Nine and Ten cover different aspects of civic ritual from mid-1870 to the monarchy's fall in November 1889. Chapter Nine begins with the decline of official festivities. Pedro gradually did away with the already limited ritual apparatus that surrounded his regime, and contemporaries noticed these changes. The discussion of the three days' meaning included more and more criticism of the imperial regime, and by the 1880s republicans were constructing a different interpretation of Brazilian independence, one that focused on a series of conspiracies and rebellions against the colonial and imperial monarchy that they interpreted as evidence of Brazil's republican vocation. In the 1880s, they began celebrating 21 April, the anniversary of the 1792 execution of Tiradentes, the martyr of the 1789 conspiracy in Minas Gerais that they saw as the key republican precursor of independence. Still, on occasion, the imperial regime could stage impressive celebrations that seemingly belied its decline, notably to welcome back Pedro II in April 1872 after his first journey to Europe, to inaugurate the statue of José Bonifácio on 7 September of that year, and to receive the emperor after another foreign journey in 1877.

Alongside this decline of official ritual, new forms of popular celebration of Brazilian independence emerged in the early 1870s, the subject of Chapter Ten. The lower-middle-class leadership of the Sociedade Comemorativa da Independência do Império (Society for the Commemoration of the Empire's Independence) organized popular celebrations around the equestrian statue of Pedro I that soon became a fixture in the capital and attracted large numbers of lower-class celebrants. This society had no evident political connections, and journalists' attitudes toward it gradually evolved from favorable to critical. In the 1870s and 1880s, the increasing presence of *capoeiras* who disrupted public celebrations came under regular criticism. Moderate abolitionists turned days of national festivity into vehicles to promote their cause through public manumission ceremonies organized by the city council in the mid-1880s, while more radical abolitionists took to the streets. All of these developments contributed to a reaction to the popular 7 September festivities that began in 1887 when a new group, closely connected to the city government and led by a senator, sought to take over the Comemorativa and to impose control over the plebeian patriots. They promoted schoolchildren's parades as a more appropriate (and orderly) form of commemoration. The four days of national festivity between abolition (13 May 1888) and the monarchy's fall (15 November 1889) and the celebrations of Pedro's return in late August 1888 reveal considerable tension between popular supporters of the monarchy and members of an upper class increasingly ready to jettison a royal family in which they no longer had confidence. Several incidents suggest that many of the forms of civic ritual in which members of the elite had participated at midcentury were gradually taken over by members of the lower classes in the 1870s and 1880s, at which point they became unacceptable to the elite, a process of appropriation visible in other aspects of Rio de Janeiro's popular culture.

In the Epilogue, I analyze the republic's new civic calendar, which repudiated the monarchy, and examine the celebration of the new holidays in the early 1890s. Republican civic ritual rejected the popular festivities of the late empire and sought to impose new forms of celebration. This attempt to institute a new civic order failed to efface the empire altogether, and republican governments eventually made peace with the monarchy. A brief look at twentieth-century Brazilian civic rituals follows in the Conclusion, after which I turn to imperial civic ritual outside of the capital and compare Brazil to contemporary Spanish America. Here, as indeed elsewhere, civic rituals formed an integral part of politics as people debated the origins, nature, and meaning of their political institutions on what Brazilians called days of national festivity.

CHAPTER ONE

Constructing the Monarchy, 1823–1829

The last years of João VI's reign in Rio de Janeiro left imperial Brazil a vibrant tradition of commemorating the birthdays, weddings, and accessions of monarchs and other members of the royal family with illuminations, ephemeral architecture, Te Deums, military parades, fireworks, theater galas, and artillery salutes. Late-colonial ritual forms suited the monarchy that Pedro I sought to establish, and little distinguished imperial civic ritual from its colonial predecessor until early 1830. However, the new regime was a constitutional monarchy—Pedro stressed that his power derived from both the people and from divine grace—and this lent a different tone to the celebrations of the new empire, especially given the nagging doubts about Pedro's commitment to the charter that he granted in 1824.

From 1823 through 1829, civic ritual presented Pedro I as a legitimate monarch, founder of the nation-state, and grantor of the constitution. Few discordant voices can be heard in the documentation from these years, largely because de facto press censorship and the more general repression of Pedro's critics after 1823 limited the scope of political debate until the late 1820s.[1] Foreign observers, both diplomats and travelers, did not face these restrictions, and in this chapter, their observations and assessments provide an essential counterpoint to official rhetoric. Independence was intimately connected to the issue of the form of government—indeed, one historian has recently pointed out that, in the parlance of the day, *independência* meant not just autonomy from Portugal but also an antiabsolutist political position.[2]

Until the mid-1820s, it was not entirely clear on which days the new empire's foundation should be celebrated. Several dates (celebrated with some regularity in the capital) and the elaborate rituals associated with Pedro's return from his journey to Salvador in 1826 underscored a monarchical interpretation of independence. Shortly after these festivities, during parliament's first session, legislators designated five "days of national festivity" and thereby established a calendar of civic commemorations that lasted until 1831. The legislators' civic calendar partially challenged the monarchical interpretation of independence by designating the date of parliament's opening as a day of national festivity. In the late 1820s, 7 September and 12 October (the former constructed as the date of his definitive declaration of independence and the latter the date of his acclamation, both in 1822) emerged as the empire's principal civic celebrations. Pedro's marriage to Amélia de Leuchtenberg in October 1829 was his last chance to bask in the full glory of imperial civic ritual. In early 1830 radical liberals attempted to seize control of Rio de Janeiro's civic ritual, thereby ushering in several years of intense conflict over the meaning of independence and the empire's political organization (Chapter Two).

While this chapter focuses on the principal recurring civic rituals and several moments of nonrecurring monarchical celebrations, it should be noted that the calendar was full of additional gala days and that births and deaths in the imperial family were celebrated and mourned throughout Brazil. Moreover, the monarch was a constantly visible presence in the capital, sometimes magnificent and distant, other times earthy and accessible. Pedro I's modest court was fully integrated into the city.[3] He directed Brazilian diplomats to study restoration France's court protocol and etiquette, but there is no indication that he attempted to reform the Brazilian court along the lines of Charles X's court, described by one historian as a "golden age" of French court life.[4] Pedro and his people came into frequent contact. Foreigners often remarked on his "affable" manners and the unusually "familiar contact with royalty" granted to his subjects in the regular audiences held at the palace, "when the humblest individual in society may in person claim redress," and during Pedro's outings into the city. The *beija-mão* or hand-kissing ritual of fealty, moreover, required that subjects come into direct physical contact with the emperor.[5] Robert Walsh saw a "droll forward fellow of the lower ranks" tell the emperor a joke after mass at Glória church, much to the amusement of Pedro and his attendants.[6] This accessibility continued the practices established by João VI in the 1810s.[7]

To prepare for his visit in 1828–29, Walsh had read James Henderson's 1821 *History of Brazil*, and he was surprised to see none of the "oriental homage" that Henderson had described when the royal carriage passed through the streets in the 1810s. Brazilians merely doffed their hats when royalty passed, and no one bothered him when he neglected this small courtesy. Jacobus von Boelen, who visited Rio de Janeiro two years before Walsh, by contrast, saw outriders with whips to remind people to take off their hats; he added that people had to remain standing while the monarch passed by.[8] Disrespect of the monarchy was, however, another matter, and in 1829 a carpenter was arrested for whistling in the emperor's presence.[9] With either shock or prurient curiosity, foreigners also recounted what they learned about Pedro's mistresses. Eduardo Theodoro Bösche suspected that Pedro had capped the celebrations in honor of his birthday and acclamation in 1825 with "some amorous conquest," while another foreigner proclaimed that the honors conferred on Domitila de Castro, his principal mistress during the mid-1820s, outdid "the age of Louis XIV."[10]

After the establishment of constitutional rule back in 1821, "the press began to teem with periodical publications," as John Armitage put it; most of these were not newspapers in the modern sense but rather "political journals" whose editors enjoyed considerable influence.[11] Alongside these journals, the *Diário do Rio de Janeiro*, founded in 1821, served the business community by publishing mostly advertising and commercial notices; the populace soon dubbed it the "butter daily" for its listing of food prices.[12] The *Jornal do Comércio*, established in 1827, also served these purposes; both it and the *Diário* later developed into major daily newspapers.[13] Pedro and José Bonifácio de Andrada e Silva's crackdown on the radicals in late October 1822 included an imposition of censorship that the emperor and his principal minister relaxed while the constituent assembly met (May–November 1823). Pedro again muzzled the press when he closed the assembly (by this time, he had also broken with José Bonifácio, who soon went into exile).[14] As far as Armitage was concerned, this "all but annihilated" independent journalism; in 1826, he judged the government-controlled *Diário Fluminense* to be little better than the colonial *Gazeta do Rio de Janeiro*.[15]

A gradual liberation of the press permitted the appearance of new newspapers over the next years, including Evaristo Ferreira da Veiga's *Aurora Fluminense* (in December 1827), "the most decided and liberal," according to Walsh; and João Clemente Vieira Souto's *Astréia* (in June 1826), published by what João Loureiro called "a gang of liberals" in 1829. Several other newspapers maintained close ties to the government, including both the *Diário do Rio de Janeiro* and the *Jornal do Comércio*, as well as *Analista* and the French-language *Courier du Brésil*.[16] That the traveler Walsh and the Brazilian Loureiro offered details about these newspapers' government or opposition connections indicates that these ties were widely known. Full press freedom returned in 1830, but legislation of that year established a complex procedure of jury trials for those accused of abusing this liberty.[17]

There is no indication of periodical circulation in the 1820s and little direct information on their readership, but it is clear that these newspapers were widely available, sold in many shops and by subscription, and read in public, which made them accessible to some of the illiterate.[18] Indeed, politics retained an important oral dimension; Johann Moritz

Rugendas, who had been in Rio de Janeiro from 1821 to 1825, recalled how "people of all classes gave themselves over to political conversations." They included "churchmen, officers, merchants, and workers," all of whom followed politics with "great interest, good sense, and eagerness."[19] Others made their views known in different ways that reveal the lively political culture. Night-time police patrols were necessary "to keep down placards" in early 1826, but they could not stem the tide of "seditious" documents. By August, reported Condy Raguet, the U.S. chargé d'affaires, "caricatures in charcoal ha[d] appeared upon the walls of white houses, pronouncing the treasonable and revolutionary expression 'Morra o Imperador [Death to the Emperor],' 'Viva Bolivar [Long Live {Simón} Bolívar],' and representing His Majesty as riding to destruction in a carriage driven by the Viscountess of Santos," his mistress Domitila (he had granted her the title in 1825 and would promote her to marchioness on his birthday in 1826).[20] Such graffiti indicate a significant, if normally invisible, political underground that rarely manifested itself directly on days of national festivity.

While civic rituals no doubt afforded an occasion for Brazilians throughout the far-flung empire to imagine themselves as fellow subjects of the Bragança monarchy, fellow Brazilian citizens, and members of the nation, imperial civic rituals placed little emphasis on the nation in this abstract sense. There are no indications of a Romantic nationalism during these years, and civic rituals turned overwhelmingly on the political arrangements of the new state. Tellingly, as we noted in the introduction, the well-informed Raguet called the holidays instituted by parliament in 1826 "days of political festivity," even though he certainly knew that the law designated them "days of national festivity."[21] Civic ritual's central political dimension ultimately facilitated the adoption of many of its forms by Pedro I's opponents in 1830, the subject of the next chapter.

IDENTIFYING INDEPENDENCE

Today every Brazilian schoolchild learns that Pedro I proclaimed Brazilian independence on 7 September 1822 on the banks of the Ipiranga River in São Paulo. In that year, however, the historical meaning of his actions was not quite so clear cut; at least for the rest of 1822, contemporaries attributed little significance to the date and the Grito do Ipiranga (Pedro's cry of "Independence or Death") as they busied themselves with the emperor's acclamation (12 October) and his coronation (1 December). De facto autonomy from Lisbon had been achieved well before 7 September 1822; in the early August manifestos written by José Bonifácio, Pedro had already claimed independence for Brazil.[22] The resulting lack of attention to 7 September has led to a historical consensus that it took some time to construct it as Brazil's independence day. In fact, 7 September was recognized as Brazil's independence day in 1823, and its commemoration quickly gained prominence in Rio de Janeiro, although 12 October remained a more important day of national festivity for much of the decade.

In 1860 Gottfried Heinrich Handelmann observed about 7 September that, "at first, not as much importance was given to it as later," but he offered no sources for this assertion. A number of other historians have recently noted the limited attention to the events of 7 September 1822 in the Rio de Janeiro press of later that year, the absence of the date from a list of court gala days published in December, and Hipólito José da Costa's failure to comment on the date in his *Correio Brasiliense* (among other things), all of which appear surprising in light of the later importance attributed to 7 September.[23] In a 1995 article, Maria de Lourdes Viana Lyra argues that the construction of 7 September as Brazil's independence day began in the mid-1820s and was only complete by 1830, with the publication of José da Silva Lisboa's *História dos principais sucessos do Império do Brasil* (History of the Principal Events of the Empire of Brazil, 1825–30).[24] In this official history, the Viscount of Cairu (Lisboa received the title of baron in 1826 and viscount the following year) presented Pedro as "the Hero of Brazil," responsible for its "elevation . . . to the rank of Empire," an assessment that, as Lyra notes, fully suited a conservative monarchy. On 7 September 1822 the prince-regent's "Herculean blow against the Lisbon Cortes" annihilated its "usurped Sovereignty over Brazil," and he thus proclaimed the "BRAZILIAN NATION'S COMPLETE INDEPENDENCE," declared Cairu in sections of the book published in 1830.[25]

This was a conservative interpretation of independence; as Lyra explains, Cairu was responding to the debate about the origins of Pedro I's sovereignty: The reformist and conservative position held that it derived from his royal lineage, while the revolutionary view held that only the people—the Brazilian nation—had the right to acclaim Pedro as their ruler and invest him with power. Pedro had to formally give up his claim to rule based on popular sovereignty in the 1825 treaty that resulted in Portuguese recognition, which in turn necessitated a reconstruction of the history of independence to emphasize that it came directly from Pedro's actions on 7 September 1822 and not through his acclamation by the Brazilian nation, which Cairu duly supplied.[26]

Lyra's elegant analysis, however, misses the extent to which Cairu's interpretation came into question, especially after radical liberals took to the streets on days of national festivity in 1830. Moreover, a closer look at the celebrations held on 7 September starting in 1823 reveals no doubt that it was already considered Brazil's independence day. Rather, the key issue was whether independence as proclaimed on 7 September was as important as Pedro's acclamation on 12 October (or even the other events that laid the groundwork for the imperial political order). To judge by the celebrations held in Rio de Janeiro, 7 September was, for a short time, overshadowed by 12 October, but by the middle of the decade it had caught up to the latter date. A second issue, vigorously debated in 1830 and 1831, was the nature of Pedro's role on 7 September 1822; many, in fact, rejected Cairu's view and argued that Pedro's call for independence responded to the nation's desire to be free, a view that subordinated him to the Brazilian nation or political community.

The events of the second half of 1822 that led to the creation of an independent Brazilian empire offered two major alternatives from which to date the new regime's founding: Pedro's Grito do Ipiranga on 7 September or his acclamation on 12 October, also his birthday. Pedro himself thought the latter most worthy of commemoration. A December 1822 decree mandating the court protocol for gala days failed to mention 7 September and, perhaps even more interestingly, identified no day as commemorating independence (12 October was described as Pedro's birthday and his acclamation).[27] Earlier that month, however, Pedro had decreed that "given that it is appropriate to commemorate the glorious era of Brazil's Independence and its elevation to the status of Empire . . . the number of years elapsed . . . should be counted from the memorable day of 12 October of the current year."[28]

The following year, however, 7 September quickly gained prominence. During the throne speech that opened the Constituent Assembly on 3 May 1823, Pedro alluded to the date as his first declaration in favor of full independence.[29] In early September, the assembly resolved that the day be considered, for the moment, a national holiday, for it was the "anniversary of Brazilian independence," and its members sent a large deputation to congratulate Pedro.[30] Much to Raguet's surprise, 7 September 1823 "was celebrated with all the parade, military, civil, and religious appropriate to so important a festival." He speculated that the ceremony had something to with the increasingly acrimonious politics surrounding the assembly and wondered whether he had been wrong to see the acclamation (12 October 1822) as "the true day of the declaration of independence."[31] Baron Wenzel de Mareschal, the Austrian representative, was apparently not surprised and simply reported that "a military festival is being prepared for 7 September, as the day on which independence was proclaimed in São Paulo."[32] The sole Rio de Janeiro press reference to this year's commemoration of 7 September was a sonnet in *O Silfo* that concluded: "Thou art independent . . . Oh! What remains for thee / Courage Brazil! Constitution or Death," a call for Pedro to let the constituent assembly complete its work.[33] What Raguet referred to as the "military, civil, and religious" elements of the celebration were the constituent parts of official civic ritual at that time—artillery salutes from forts and warships, a military parade, a Te Deum in the imperial chapel, a levee in the city palace (with the obligatory *beija-mão*), an evening theater gala, and nighttime illumination of the city.

A month later, deputies likewise designated 12 October as a day of national festivity, but they had some difficulty in deciding what they were proposing to celebrate—Pedro's acclamation, his birthday, or as Nicolau Pereira de Campos Vergueiro (a deputy from São Paulo) put it, "the anniversary of the empire's acclamation or of its creation." In their congratulatory message to the monarch, deputies stressed the empire's constitutional nature, reflecting the growing tensions between that body and Pedro.[34] The day was celebrated much like 7 September, and some took notice of the other day of national festivity. At the theater gala, José Pedro Fernandes recited a laudation in which he identified the Grito do Ipiranga as Brazil's founding moment: ". . . suddenly there appears / Mighty Nation, healthy Empire / In response to Pedro's voice, to the shout of 'INDEPENDENCE' / That thundered on the Ipiranga's banks," a view that would have been music to Cairu's ears.[35] That year, and on most subsequent celebrations of 12 October, Pedro issued promotions in the armed forces and granted titles of nobility and other rewards to his subjects, the so-called *despachos*.

In a ruling issued on 23 October, Pedro declared 7 September and 12 October to be equal days of national festivity, thereby sanctioning the constituent assembly's intent. The ruling described 7 September as the day "on which the said August Lord took the sublime decision to proclaim, for the first time, Brazil's independence at the place [known as] Piranga [sic]," while 12 October was the "auspicious anniversary of His Majesty the Emperor's acclamation." A few weeks later, another ruling clarified that 12 October also celebrated "Brazil's grandiose elevation to the category of Empire and . . . the birthday of the same August Lord."[36] Rio de Janeiro's city almanac for 1824 listed both as days of grand gala and explained their significance as outlined in the two decrees.[37]

During the night of 11 to 12 November, Pedro forcibly closed the constituent assembly; he subsequently pledged to grant a constitution twice as liberal as the draft on which the deputies had been working. As a result, celebrations of the coronation (1 December) became an important test for his government. The *Estrela Brasileira*, closely tied to the government, published a detailed account of the ceremonies, which Otto von Kotzebue also witnessed.[38] This Russian naval officer awoke to the "thunder of cannon"; when he went ashore, he saw the Palace Square full of people and soldiers, "a cheerful throng" that included "Negroes, released from labour." At 11:00, the emperor and the empress arrived in a "magnificent carriage" to attend the Te Deum, after which the vicar of Jacarepaguá preached on Pedro's virtues, comparing him to Peter the Great of Russia, a sermon that the *Estrela's* editor judged "excessively inclined toward servility." Raguet later explained that the priest naïvely believed that "such eloquence in favour of absolute government" would please Pedro; in fact, he so offended the "constitutionality of his auditor" that the government publicly reprimanded the priest.[39]

After the levee, Pedro reviewed 4,500 handsomely dressed troops on the Campo da Aclamação; the soldiers and onlookers loudly cheered him and the "constitutional system" as he personally directed the troops in parade maneuvers before the empress, who watched from the *palacete*, or little palace, the structure built for João VI's acclamation that served as a reviewing stand for parades on the Campo. At the "suffocatingly full" São João Theater, Pedro received cheers from the audience and an actress recited a prologue in his praise, which stressed unity. Kotzebue understood little of the performance but watched Pedro give audience to "many of his subjects, the interview always beginning with the homage of kissing hand on the bended knee." The *Estrela's* editor, by contrast, had nothing good to say about the melodramatic comedy or the "grotesque" ballet that followed. The tense political environment of late 1823 evidently eluded Kotzebue, while the *Estrela's* editor was clearly constructing an account that served Pedro's political interests by portraying a successful, well-conducted ritual. The British minister, Henry Chamberlain, more knowledgeable than Kotzebue, was unimpressed. No "marks of public joy" could be seen, and the monarchs were coldly received at the theater: "Many boxes were unoccupied, which has never happened before."[40]

By this time, the committee designated by Pedro to draft the constitution was hard at work, and in early January the text was ready for approval by the city councils of Brazil's provincial capitals. All of them dutifully complied, although some expressed cautiously worded reservations about a few clauses. After this formality, Pedro was ready to swear his oath to uphold the new charter. Great efforts, including the publication of printed programs, went into the preparations for the ceremony, so much so that normal government business was completely suspended by mid-March.[41] Foreign diplomats reported indications of considerable opposition to Pedro; "the republican party" posted placards denouncing him as a traitor. In response, Pedro resolved to move the date of the oath from 4 April (the birthday of Maria da Glória, his daughter and the future queen of Portugal) to 25 March in order to "remove public doubts of his constitutionality," but on the 24th, "placards of a more violent and incendiary nature" appeared.[42] Pedro swore to uphold the constitution during an indoor ceremony before "a multitude of citizens" at the imperial chapel; the day began with an elaborate parade into the city, along streets lined with soldiers; the buildings facing the streets were "all decorated with good taste and perfection." According to the *Estrela Brasileira*, the emperor and empress "were received amid deafening cheers, and with the greatest of enthusiasm" at the theater. Pedro himself led cheers to the constitution, the orchestra played the independence anthem, and the audience settled in for an oratorio on the life of St. Hermenegild. Minutes after Pedro left the building and as the audience was filing out, a backstage accident involving a fallen candle sparked a fire that completely destroyed the theater (the audience stragglers, actors, and crew all escaped unhurt).[43]

The next day, a large military parade took place on the Campo da Aclamação, at which the troops swore loyalty to the monarch and to the charter. Chamberlain commented that "considerable pains had been taken to make it [the ceremony] an imposing spectacle, and much splendour was displayed, but it was remarked that the people did not show much enthusiasm," a view that Raguet seconded.[44] An allegorical print produced at this time as part of Pedro's campaign to win over the Holy Alliance reveals the political message as clearly as any of the printed rhetoric: Pedro defends a helpless female Brazil from a man with African features and a serpent (Figure 1.1).[45]

The complex constitution that Pedro granted responded to contradictory impulses. In some respects, it was a highly liberal document, yet it also contained numerous undemocratic features. It set up a parliamentary system of government, with an elected chamber of deputies, and an appointed senate (for each vacant senate seat, provinces would elect three candidates, one of whom the emperor had to select). Only a modest income requirement limited the franchise, but elections were indirect; the men who satisfied the requirements to be voters merely cast ballots for electors (who had to meet a higher income requirement and had to have been born free). In addition to the legislative, executive, and judicial powers, the constitution established a fourth power, the regulating or moderating power, which gave the emperor broad responsibility for overseeing all aspects of government and securing harmony among the other three powers. Because the monarch also constituted the executive power and cabinet ministers were directly responsible to him, the charter ensured a strongly centralized government and the emperor's political predominance; his power to dissolve the chamber of deputies at will placed him above the other institutions of government. However, in thirty-five paragraphs, Article 179 specified an elaborate bill of rights, modeled on that of the French Revolution, which included equality before the law for all citizens, protected property rights, and promised freedom to communicate via the press (leaving journalists responsible for abuses of this freedom). Slavery was nowhere mentioned in the document (except indirectly by the restrictions on freedmen's citizenship).[46]

The detailed descriptions of civic rituals from 1823 and early 1824 highlight the forms of official festivities—in other words, the civic ritual organized by the government—which changed little over the next seven

FIGURE I.I.
"Hail Beloved Brazilian Day, 25 March 1824."
Source: Gianni, "Salve querido brasileiro dia 25 de março
de 1824," BN/SI, pg. 782. Courtesy Acervo da Fundação
Biblioteca Nacional—Brasil.

decades. Artillery salutes greeted the sunrise and punctuated the day. In
the morning, the emperor entered the city in a procession from São Cristóvão. This was followed by a Te Deum in the imperial chapel, a levee
in the downtown palace, a military parade, and an evening theater gala
(liberally sprinkled with opportunities to cheer the monarch). It is not
difficult to read these ceremonies. The military parade regimented the
citizenry in orderly fashion. The Te Deum associated the monarch with
the divine; to make this point clear, the emperor's tribune stood beside
the imperial chapel's main altar and his throne towered over the bishop's
seat.[47] The theater gala provided an occasion for emperor, court, and
the city's elite to express loyalty to each other. The venerable custom of
showing obeisance to the monarch by kissing his hand was a major part
of the levee and the less formal interaction between Pedro and his subjects. Invariably, the theatre gala began with an ode, laudation, or some

other poetic encomium in honor of the monarch. José Pedro Fernandes, a civil servant in the ministry of empire, reliably produced a fawning verse for virtually every occasion between 1823 and 1828.[48]

Brazilian sources from this period say little about the levees held in the downtown palace; Brazilians commonly called the entire function the *beija-mão*, or hand kissing, an indication of its principal purpose. Several foreigners who attended this function during the 1820s describe an efficiently conducted ritual. Maria Graham found the 12 October 1823 levee to be a casual affair, with "little form and no stiffness," but later levees were more formal functions. Soldiers in dress uniforms surrounded the palace and lined the steps up to the chamber, while a military band played the "Emperor's national hymn"; most of those in attendance were members of "the Brazilian nobility, officers, public functionaries, and distinguished ecclesiastics, in all the respective costumes of their orders."[49] Once the emperor arrived, a receiving line formed; people filed in to greet the emperor, bowed twice on their approach, kissed the emperor's hand, bowed once, and walked backwards for ten or twelve steps (protocol forbade turning one's back on the emperor). Walsh struggled to do so in his clerical garb on 2 December 1828, as did many a Brazilian priest.[50] Most accounts of these levees add that large crowds gathered outside the palace to witness the monarch's arrival and departure and to see him and his family in the palace windows. In other ways, too, the ceremony could not escape the city in which it took place. Boelen complained about the "intolerable stench" that wafted into the palace from trash in the square. During interludes in the music at the levee on 4 April 1829 in honor of Maria da Glória's birthday, Charles Samuel Stewart heard "the clanking of the chains of a gang of miserable galley slaves," as their work went on outside the palace despite the ceremony.[51]

While such civic rituals likely meant little to slaves, citizens took part in various ways. Those who lived on the parade route decorated the façades of their houses "with tapestry and richly-embroidered silks," as Chamberlain observed of the "great National Festival" of 12 October 1824.[52] Streets were usually strewn with fragrant leaves to mask the city's stench; on 12 October 1825, Bösche (one of the German mercenaries) paraded through streets covered in orange blossoms and laurel leaves, while showers of flowers rained down on the troops.[53] Crowds flocked downtown to the Palace Square to see the monarchs' arrival and departure from the Te Deum and levee (relatively closed ceremonies). The theater gala, with which "all the important days" ended,[54] was, in contrast to the levee, a relatively open ritual, as tickets to the floor sold for modest prices. Kotzebue noted the social distinctions laid out in the theater: The boxes held only white gentlemen and ladies, the latter "tastefully arranged in the Parisian fashion." The "pit" had a "singular appearance," for "every possible shade from black to white" appeared there, "although the darker tints had greatly the preponderance." He also contrasted the "decorum and politeness" of the boxes with "the noisy and coarse vulgarity of the pit," from which women were excluded.[55]

Finally, such ceremonies were important barometers of the political mood, but only foreigners enjoyed sufficient liberty to put critical assessments into writing. Chamberlain, who noted the empty boxes on 1 December 1823 and the lack of enthusiasm on 25 March 1824, judged 12 October 1824 to have been a more successful ceremony: "The people were in their holiday dress, and joy and gratification were present on every countenance." Less sympathetic to monarchies, Raguet muttered: "The elements of a despotic government were most fully displayed, not only in the troops, but in the immense and unusual concourse of people covered with gold and baubles (said to be 800) who flocked to the court to bend their knees to His Majesty and to kiss his imperial hand."[56]

Notwithstanding the 1823 ruling that mandated equality between the two days of national festivity, 7 September remained subordinate to 12 October during the next two years. In 1824, Raguet reported that 7 September had been "announced and celebrated as the second anniversary of the Declaration of the Independence of Brazil, but certainly not with the pomp . . . and magnificence" of 12 October, adding that, "in these [latter] celebrations *the people* have no part." *O Espectador Brasileiro* likewise proclaimed 7 September to be the "Anniversary of the Political Independence of the Constitutional Empire of Brazil," but no newspaper described the 1824 celebrations. In fact, there was little to describe; Mareschal reported that, for unspecified reasons, there had been no *beija-mão* while bad weather forced the military parade's cancellation.[57] By contrast, *O Espectador Brasileiro* looked forward to the "brilliant celebration" being prepared for 12 October and hoped that the day would be commemorated throughout the empire.[58] The minister of war made preparations for artillery salutes up and down the coast of Rio de Janeiro and ordered the province's militia to parade as well, all in honor of Pedro's "Glorious Acclamation and of his Birthday."[59] I have, unfortunately, found no descriptions of these celebrations, but as usual, Pedro issued numerous *despachos*.[60]

Three rulings regarding protocol on gala days issued by the war ministry between March and September 1825 have been taken to indicate continuing doubts about 7 September's importance, but they may well just reveal bureaucratic bumbling. In March, the ministry ordered that 7 September be celebrated in the same way as 25 March (the anniversary of the oath to the constitution); in other words, on these grand gala days, forts should hoist banners and fire three rounds of twenty-one salutes. This decree, however, omitted 12 October. In August, 7 September was reduced to the rank of "lesser gala," to be commemorated only with flags, while 12 October was designated a "grand gala day," to be marked with three salutes of 101 shots and a great parade. Ten days later, 7 September was promoted back to the rank of grand gala, to be celebrated as mandated in the March ruling.[61]

In 1825, the announcement of Brazil's recognition by Great Britain was made on 7 September, which prompted Carl Schlichthorst to declare that it was "the most important date in the history of imperial Brazil."[62] Pedro personally handed out copies of the treaty from the palace windows before the levee and publicly removed the badge of "Independence or Death" that he had worn since 1822.[63] French and Austrian diplomats reported little enthusiasm for these celebrations, however, for the treaty's terms in fact undermined the principle of Pedro's position as emperor by popular acclamation.[64] The usual celebrations took place on 12 October, reported Mareschal, while Raguet referred to "great pomp" and Chamberlain mentioned the "unprecedented concessions of favors, comprehending titles, honors, and promotions, to a degree that might almost be termed lavish."[65] Schlichthorst claimed that 10,000 troops paraded on the Campo da Aclamação but noted that this was the last of these great military exhibitions, for most of the soldiers were shortly thereafter dispatched to Montevideo, the outpost that Brazil would lose after the Cisplatine War (1826–28).[66]

This exposition of the available sources on the commemoration of 7 September, 12 October, and other important dates in 1823–25, much of it not available to those historians who have written about the origins of 7 September commemorations, clearly reveals that, if the day had little importance to contemporaries in 1822, it quickly emerged as Brazil's independence day, although it remained subordinate to 12 October. The meaning of both days, however, remained unstable. Both of course focused attention on Pedro as monarch and the hero who had proclaimed independence, yet both also could be read as embodying popular origins for the empire. Pedro's acclamation by the people on 12 October profoundly upset the conservative Holy Alliance and complicated Brazil's search for international recognition. But the day could also be celebrated as merely Pedro's birthday or as the date on which Brazil became an empire, less problematic concepts. For 7 September to serve as Brazil's founding moment, the shout of "Independence or Death" had to resonate among the nation, or from the Amazon River to the River Plate, a recurring trope in 7 September rhetoric that drew on colonial geographical imagining of Brazil as an island, separated from the rest of South America by the two rivers, which allegedly shared a common source.[67] More important than geography, however, the key question was whether the nation as a political community existed before the Grito do Ipiranga or whether Pedro's actions brought it into being. Ultimately, 7 September more readily offered a popular or populist vision of independence than 12 October, but this distinction did not become clear until 1830.

A ROYAL ENTRY, 1826

From February to April 1826, Pedro visited the province of Bahia, a long-promised journey to thank Bahians for their sacrifices during the war to expel Portuguese troops from Salvador.[68] Contemporary assessments of this royal tour differed significantly. The tightly controlled Rio de Janeiro press judged it a spectacular success. The *Atalaia da Liberdade* reported that the imperial family had been "received in the arms of the generous Bahians with the greatest of possible satisfaction, amid demonstrations of universal jubilation."[69] *O Verdadeiro Liberal* went further and declared that Pedro "had won over the hearts of all and firmly established the bases of his constitutional throne. Everywhere Liberty raises her Standards, and there the name of Pedro I is written; civilization advances with giant strides, order is established in all branches of [public] administration, commerce takes on new vigor."[70] This newspaper's editor, one Pierre Chapuis, a radical "notorious in Europe by the violence of his political views," who had recently arrived in Rio de Janeiro, apparently tried to mask his liberalism with "fulsome adulation of the emperor, and admiration of the constitution." Most saw through this ruse, and Pedro had him summarily deported.[71]

After Pedro's return, however, news "leaked out by degrees" that the visit had been less than a great public success. Courtiers who accompanied the monarch never saw the inside of a house, Raguet heard from a British diplomat, which amounted to "a total failure of hospitality" on the part of Bahia's elite that the U.S. diplomat could only ascribe "to political causes." He also heard that only "a crowd of blacks" had cheered Pedro on his arrival in Salvador.[72] More cautiously, the Austrian minister reported that "the enthusiasm and public joy demonstrated in Bahia at the moment of the sovereign's arrival was not sustained and the departure was a bit cold."[73]

During Pedro's absence, the courtiers left behind in Rio de Janeiro lamented the "insipidness and sadness" of life without their monarch, and the capital's population anxiously awaited his return. The police intendant organized a "great subscription to hold an elaborate celebration for His Majesty's arrival." On 21 March, the city council invited the population to illuminate the fronts of their houses for three days after the emperor's arrival; workers hastened to complete the new São Pedro de Alcântara Theater for the festivities.[74] Not only did the intendant promote the celebrations, he also ensured that they would be recorded for posterity by arranging for the publication of a detailed account of them. The preface proclaimed that "the testimonials of love and respect offered to monarchs by a free people will never be confused with the obsequious flattery, characteristic of enslaved nations that surround their thrones with incense so as not to be crushed by their weight." It further stressed the celebrations' peaceful nature, notwithstanding the "extraordinary concourse of people," and hoped that foreigners would read the book to learn "how our permanent defender is esteemed by [us] Brazilians."[75]

This was the first of many ceremonial entries that Rio de Janeiro would also stage for its emperors in 1831, 1846, 1847, 1860, 1865, 1872, 1877, and 1888. Like the commemoration of days of national festivity, these entries followed a form that changed relatively little over the next six decades. They echoed the medieval, renaissance, and early-modern entries of European monarchs into cities, the latter of which had been influenced by the rediscovery of classical accounts of Roman triumphal entries. Through such rituals, monarchs staged their claim to rule over cities, while city elites publicly expressed their understandings of the relationship between municipal and monarchical authority. Absolute monarchs undermined city liberties, and the entries had lost most of their political significance by the eighteenth century, but the celebratory forms persisted for royal visits.[76] In imperial Rio de Janeiro the issue was less one of city liberties than that of the larger relationship between the emperor and the Brazilian nation as represented by its capital city.

Artillery salutes marked Pedro's ceremonial disembarkation on 2 April, and fireworks punctuated his formal landing at the navy docks (he had secretly come ashore as soon as his ship arrived to sleep in the comfort of the São Cristóvão palace and to hear a private mass in the Glória church).[77] En route to the imperial chapel, he passed under several triumphal arches; further artillery salutes and fireworks marked the start of the Te Deum. After the sermon, Pedro held a levee at the city palace.[78] That night, "the most splendid illumination ever seen" transformed the city: "Arches, façades [decorated] with elegant taste . . . pyramids, artificial fountains, all spread a brilliance that appeared to detain the day [and] to dispense the night from taking its turn."[79] The poetry of the occasion presented Pedro as the source of all of Brazil's good fortune.[80]

The celebrations continued for several days, and the police intendant's *Relação dos públicos festejos* (Account of the Public Celebrations), a typical example of the early-modern festival book, lovingly details the dozens of temporary monuments and decorative façades erected throughout the city. The Corpo do Comércio (Chamber of Commerce) raised an eighty-four palm (seventeen meter) high faux-marble obelisk on the

Campo da Aclamação, lit by more than 4,000 lamps. A square structure surrounded its base and was decorated by representations of the "memorable episodes in the establishment of the Brazilian empire." Government corporations (the city council, the intendant's office, army battalions and police units, and the military college) also raised such allegorical structures, as did some wealthy individuals. In front of his house, the intendant erected a "rich and magnificent illuminated ephemeral monument," which featured a transparent portrait of Pedro I with a text that proclaimed him greater than all of the Roman emperors. Allegories showing "the legitimacy of Sovereigns" flanked this portrait; they included a classical monarch "crushing the figure of anarchy at his feet" and a figure of Justice, holding her sword and scales, with "the fury of jealousy and calumny" prostrate before her.[81] On the night of 3 April, Pedro and Empress Leopoldina toured the illuminations by carriage, followed by "an extraordinary concourse of people" who maintained perfect order.[82]

At a theater gala on 4 April the audience saw Rossini's *Tancredo* (or at least part of the opera). A group of French naval officers arrived as the audience stood in silence listening to Francisco Muniz Barreto, a Bahian second lieutenant recently posted to Rio de Janeiro, recite an ode to Pedro and Maria da Glória (whose birthday it was). The poet concluded that the emperor was:

> The envy of the nations! Fortunate Brazil
> It is not thy extent, thy grandeur
>> And the riches that thou hast
>> That give thee fortune
> Thy happy destiny is alone made by
> PEDRO, MARIA, and THEIR AUGUST PROGENY.

Copies of the poem fluttered to the floor from the second-class box in which Muniz Barreto stood. Pedro left halfway through the opera; much to the Frenchmen's surprise, the performance did not resume after his exit.[83] On 5 April, the Chamber of Commerce paid for a Te Deum in the São Francisco de Paula church; Jean-Baptiste Debret's watercolor (Figure 1.2) shows Pedro's arrival at the church amid a volley of rockets. Buildings around São Francisco Square are decorated; an ephemeral façade stands before a building on the square's north side, while a temporary monument obscures the unfinished cathedral to the west. A fireworks display on the Campo da Aclamação followed later that day.[84]

All the official accounts of these celebrations stressed the population's spontaneous and generalized happiness at their monarch's return, and Debret drew the requisite crowd cheering the emperor. These sources led Iara Lis Carvalho Souza to characterize this event as Pedro's last successful ceremonial entry into the capital.[85] Pedro may have managed to control the public discourse about the entry, but foreigners like the

FIGURE 1.2.
Fireworks and ephemeral architecture, São Francisco Square, 5 April 1826.

Source: Jean-Baptiste Debret, "Le 4 [sic] avril 1826: Fête du retour de S. M. de la Bahya,"
MEA 0458, Museus Castro Maya. Courtesy Museus Castro Maya—IBRAM/MinC.

German mercenary, Schlichthorst, saw something quite different. At his landing, he was "very coldly" received with "scarce cheers," and he looked "very unhappy." The ephemeral monuments were "roughly constructed" and poorly lit, while the slogans amounted to the "most exaggerated flattery."[86] Raguet concurred with this assessment, particularly the cheers "shouted in limited measure" at the landing.[87] In contrast, the public accounts of Pedro's journey to Bahia and the celebrations on his return to the capital highlighted the ideal monarch—mighty, magnanimous, just, glorious, and beloved by his subjects. Today, of course, we recognize this as propaganda, but it formed an essential part of the mystery of monarchy, that capacity of old-regime royalty to awe their subjects. In this respect, indeed, little distinguished Pedro from his Portuguese ancestors. At the same time, though, such rituals expressed ideals that monarchs had to live up to, a none-too-easy task, especially given that, once parliament convened, Pedro also had to abide by the constitution that he had granted in 1824.

DEFINING DAYS OF NATIONAL FESTIVITY

Shortly after this spectacle of loyalty to the emperor, parliament finally convened. During that session, legislators designated five days of national festivity, four of which were directly connected to Emperor Pedro I: 9 January (his 1822 decision to stay in Brazil, the Fico), 25 March, 3 May (the opening day of the annual legislative session), 7 September, and 12 October.[88] This law set the civic calendar's core for the rest of the imperial regime, but the debate about "days of national festivity" reveals the profound disagreements about the new regime's nature that would come to a head in 1830–31 and prompt Pedro's abdication. Indeed, senators and deputies had very different views about the empire's political nature.[89]

In the senate, the Viscount of Nazaré proposed on 10 May that the 13th be declared a "national holiday" (on that date in 1822, Pedro had accepted the title of "permanent defender"). This motion—not passed— led to a bill that proposed eight "days of national festivity": 9 January, 22 January (the empress's birthday), 25 March, 13 May, 7 September, 12 October, 1 December (Pedro's coronation), and 2 December (the birthday of the heir apparent, the future Pedro II). Nazaré justified his bill on the grounds that "all nations have always recommended to posterity the notable days of their institutions." Eight holidays were too much for the Viscount of Barbacena, who noted that all of them referred in some way to Pedro I, so he proposed retaining only 12 October. Noting that the constituent assembly had proposed three holidays (9 January, 7 September, and 12 October),[90] the Viscount of Caravelas defended 7 September as "the day on which the Emperor broke our prisons, the chains that tied us to Portugal, on which he declared independence, and his voice was followed by all of Brazil"; he also called for the retention of 25 March.

In the second reading, Barbacena's view prevailed: 12 October, he explained, "has the virtue of combining the most glorious Brazilian events." Nazaré, who had missed this session, lamented in the third reading that his fellow senators had "mutilated" his bill. To Barbacena's argument, he retorted that a single holiday celebrating every act of Pedro I would be a "mere fiction" and that many holidays were needed so that "future generations, hearing the salutes, seeing the flags and banners, and other demonstrations of joy appropriate to such days, will remember the glorious events that took place on them." Only with many celebrations would Brazilians remember the history of their nation, added Caravelas (now supporting Nazaré), for few men in Brazil read history books; unlike the ancients, Brazil had no public monuments, so festivals that the population could see were essential. In the end, the senators compromised on a list of four holidays (9 January, 25 March, 7 September, and 12 October), but Nazaré, Caravelas, and four other senators recorded their votes against the bill.

The bill then went to the chamber of deputies where, amid rousing cheers, Rio de Janeiro's Manoel de Souza Franco called for the addition of 3 May, the date on which, according to the constitution, parliament convened. The legislature, he stressed, was at least as important as the executive (the monarchy) celebrated in the senate's bill. São Paulo's Vergueiro—known for his strong liberal views[91]—proposed an amendment dropping 25 March and 7 September and adding 3 May on the grounds that the legislature was more important than the constitution and that 7 September was only the proclamation of independence in a single province. Bernardo Pereira de Vasconcelos retorted that 3 May was to 7 September as a pygmy to a giant. Independence, he continued, was proclaimed on 7 September, fully ratified on 12 October, and sealed on 25 March with the constitution; the legislature's opening merely depended on the other three days. Moreover, adding a holiday amounted to pandering to the civil servants, who would get another day off. Other deputies forcefully defended 3 May for, as one put it, independence and the constitution would have been worthless "if the national representation had not been instituted." Such arguments carried the day, and 3 May joined the senate's four monarchical days of national festivity. This debate reveals that 7 September had not yet been fully accepted as Brazil's independence day—Vergueiro, a deputy from São Paulo, could characterize it as merely a provincially significant day—but neither he nor any other legislator offered an alternative independence day. For the senators, the monarchy was more important than the legislature, a view that deputies contested with their addition of 3 May.

The 1826 law modified the practice of civic rituals in Rio de Janeiro, and for the next few years, 7 September and 12 October were celebrated side-by-side with all of the same elements as in the early years of Pedro's reign. Newspapers repeatedly stressed that these two days of national festivity commemorated Pedro's creation of the Brazilian nation and his political organization of it on a constitutional basis. His was the "regenerating voice that created a Nation" on 7 September 1822, declared *O Espectador Brasileiro* in 1826. On 12 October 1829, Brazilians celebrated much more than just the birthday of an "absolutist King," explained the *Aurora Fluminense*; rather, they recalled "the triumph of the doctrines proclaimed by civilization [which] were sanctioned by the descendant of twenty monarchs."[92]

Significantly, the other three days of national festivity designated by law in 1826 saw little commemoration. Parliament duly convened each 3 May, but residents of the capital did not celebrate this day. Robert Walsh marveled at the "little interest" in parliament's opening in 1829—the

FIGURE I.3.
The opening of Parliament, 3 May 1829.
Source: "The Opening of the Senate House," in Walsh, *Notices*, vol. 2, facing p. 416.

lithograph in his book shows but a few people watching the emperor's procession arrive (Figure 1.3)[93]—while the anniversary of Pedro's decision to stay in Brazil passed almost unnoticed. Nor are there indications that 25 March received more than cursory attention. In 1829, the *Aurora Fluminense* noted the day with an editorial that stressed Brazil's good fortune at having a "Monarch, whom the People have chosen, [who] did not hesitate to offer up for Brazilians' approval a liberal Code, in which are engraved all of the sacred rights" that had cost so much blood to achieve elsewhere. The 1824 charter was, according to Evaristo Ferreira da Veiga, this newspaper's liberal editor, "the most liberal of all Monarchical-Representative Constitutions." But there was apparently no public commemoration of this day other than artillery salutes.[94]

THE IMPERIAL WEDDING, 1829

On 11 December 1826, Empress Leopoldina died while Pedro was in the South to rally Brazilian forces in the ultimately unsuccessful war to retain the Cisplatine Province (modern-day Uruguay). By all accounts, she had been personally popular and utterly devoted to her often undeserving husband.[95] Elaborate rituals of mourning took place throughout the country; in Rio de Janeiro, Raguet reported that 15,000 to 20,000 people attended her funeral. Pedro's continued dalliance with Domitila, even during the official period of mourning, scandalized many.[96]

After some difficulty due to Pedro's reputation as a womanizer who consorted far too openly with his mistresses,[97] Brazilian diplomats arranged a marriage to Amélia, daughter of the Duchess of Leuchtenberg and a member of the Bavarian royal house. A proxy wedding was held in Munich on 2 August 1829, and the new empress arrived in Rio de Janeiro on 14 October. She soon "enchant[ed] her new subjects and predispose[d] everyone in her favor."[98] Her ship had made an exceptionally rapid Atlantic crossing, and preparations for her reception were not quite complete. Despite torrential spring rains, Amélia landed on the 17th and immediately proceeded to the imperial chapel for the blessing of her marriage to Pedro. Over the next two weeks, the capital staged celebrations that closely resembled those for Pedro's return in 1826. Besides the usual artillery salutes, levee, theater galas, Te Deum, and military parade, city streets and squares were once again filled with triumphal arches, obelisks, and illuminated façades financed by corporations, merchants, and subscriptions among private citizens.[99]

For the Palace Square, the Guarda de Honra (Honor Guard), led by Francisco Gomes da Silva, Pedro I's influential (and controversial) private secretary, raised more than forty contos (US$39,200) to build a "masterpiece that, because of its elegance, purity of style, harmony with the subject [of the celebration], and favorable impression that it made on the imagination, deserved to have been constructed of marble and granite." Fully 220 men labored for a month on this project.[100] Designed by the architect and member of the 1816 French Artistic Mission Auguste Henri Victor Grandjean de Montigny, it was an amphitheater or gallery supported by twenty-two Doric columns containing a throne room and bleachers for "the people," all of which faced a "temple of Hymen," the Greek goddess of marriage. Allegorical statues of Valor, Loyalty, Prudence, Love, Fidelity, and Constancy stood prominently along the steps to the throne, while a statue of Hercules on the cupola held a banner with the imperial couple's initials.[101] Voluminous poetry in various languages and brass bands stationed at many of the monuments, enjoyed by the usual peaceful and joyous crowds, figured prominently in the accounts of these celebrations.[102] The Marquis of Barbacena, who had been instrumental in arranging the match, wrote on 21 October: "For now, all is celebration and more celebration."[103]

Francisco Pedro do Amaral, head of the imperial household's decorations, repainted the imperial coaches, which had originally been used for João V's coronation in 1707 and had been brought to Rio de Janeiro in 1815. His imagery was, like that of the amphitheater, entirely classical. A "white man [*branco*]" represented the spirit of Brazil on a panel that featured the nineteen provinces united around a temple of Minerva (the Roman goddess of wisdom). The second coach highlighted Brazil's four main rivers—the Amazon, the Tocantins, the São Francisco, and the

Plate—as well as the dragon that symbolized the house of Bragança. In the artist's published explanation of the allegories, there is no indication of how the rivers were represented, but they are the only concession to local color.[104] In this respect, the coaches looked quite different from the oft-analyzed allegorical theater curtain painted by Jean-Baptiste Debret for the 1822 coronation in which tropical nature, Indians, and slaves joined European symbols of monarchy.[105]

Unlike the accounts of previous civic rituals in the capital, those of the marriage celebrations also mentioned significant popular elements: "Companies of costumed revelers . . . danced and frolicked in the squares, and stages for this were constructed," while "diverse and very well-designed dances" were performed for the monarchs on the stage at the Palace Square.[106] There is no indication of the type of dances performed here, but on a stage at the Campo da Aclamação Pedro and Amélia watched the dance of the Moors and Turks and that of the Velhos. The former was an old Iberian tradition that celebrated Christian triumphs over the Muslims.[107] Constitution Square turned into the site of a street festival. There, the Corpo do Comércio Nacional (National Chamber of Commerce)—likely an organization of Brazilian-born merchants and traders (Debret dismissed them as "an *association of grocers* [*vendeiros*], counting among their number many capitalists, although [they] often [wear] clogs")—built an artificial garden with eight lanes radiating out from a central circle in which stood an Ionic temple that also served as band shell. Bamboo fences and palm trees bearing lights instead of coconuts lined the lanes; at night, the internal spaces between the lanes turned into "dance halls for the grocers' families." Fireworks and cannon shots from four artificial fortresses in the square's corners punctuated the celebration.[108] Debret's dismissive comments indicate that he saw this as lowbrow entertainment, promoted by men of modest means, who sought unsuccessfully to emulate the great merchants who had contributed to the amphitheater.

The wedding celebrations continued until 1 December when the temporary monuments were again illuminated and, despite nighttime rain, "dances and numerous people filled the streets."[109] This is the only indication that I have of coronation celebrations in the late 1820s, and they were likely seen as a continuation of the wedding festivities. By this time, the temporary monuments must have looked worn by their exposure to the elements. Indeed, one man complained a few days later that the Palace Square had returned to its usual state: It was covered in "piles of filth that gave off such a pestiferous stench that I found myself immediately obliged to return home with a massive headache."[110] Vestiges of the monuments remained visible in February and March 1830, when municipal authorities had to remind those who had built them to remove their remains and to fill the holes that they had made in city streets and squares.[111]

To the end of 1829, Brazil's civic rituals offer relatively little of interest. Their origins in early-modern European and late-colonial Luso-Brazilian monarchical celebrations are clear, as is their message: Pedro I proclaimed independence, created the nation, gave it its political form through the constitution granted in 1824, and stood ready to preserve the Brazilians' liberties. Indeed, this message appeared in many forms. In 1830, the *Gazeta da Bahia* advertised newly arrived prints of the emperor. One showed him holding a sword "as a sign of determination, and pressing the constitution to his breast, to signify that he spontaneously and voluntarily bestowed on his people a new social pact."[112] These were top-down, tightly controlled rituals, in which there was little room for improvisation, independent popular participation, or criticism of the regime. They publicly and visibly validated the monarch's might and majesty and provided opportunities for the elite to associate with the court or with symbols of the monarchy. A history of Pedro's reign written on the basis of official accounts of civic rituals would entirely miss the political tensions of 1823–24 and the looming challenges to his rule late in the decade, not to mention the periodic social unrest that swept Rio de Janeiro.[113] This was, of course, official ritual's goal, and in this respect, it masked the regime's weakness by giving the comforting illusion of a stable social and political order in which all knew their place and duly performed it during civic rituals.

The occasional breaches of protocol, such as the absences from the theater boxes on 1 December 1823 or Pedro's cool reception on his return from Salvador, point to the importance of civic rituals as political spaces whose significance all those in the know recognized. However, given the press censorship that lasted until 1830, foreigners were far freer than Brazilians to comment on these political tensions. That foreigners' accounts sometimes differed dramatically from those that appeared in the Brazilian press and the festival description literature reveals the effort that went into controlling the discourse about civic rituals. Given their wider reach, the printed accounts may well have been more important than the actual ritual itself. Regardless of what they thought about the empire's rituals, foreign diplomats knew that they were important; despite his Yankee republican disdain for monarchical trappings, Raguet carefully studied the poetry that appeared in the days before 12 October 1825 in an attempt to gauge Pedro's view on the origins of his authority.[114]

Together, such civic rituals no doubt reinforced the sense of being part of a new nation, particularly in their repeated reference to Pedro as Brazil's emperor and to his creation of a constitutional regime. To be sure, it is next to impossible to prove such an assertion about the effect or the effectiveness of civic ritual, but in 1826 parliamentarians considered rituals an important way to teach national history to an unlettered populace. Some foreigners, by contrast, judged the pomp and circumstance an empty sham. John Armitage, who arrived in Rio de Janeiro in 1828, commented that "parades and processions were provided for the people with as great a zeal, as though within the phrase *'panem et circenses,'* were contained alike the cares and attributes of constitutional government"; more ominously, Walsh suggested that Brazilians' "fondness for show and display" was "fast wearing away" in the late 1820s.[115] Schlichthorst explained that, although Pedro highly prized these manifestations of "the people's love," he knew that the poetry and speeches were "royally paid, although each of the singers in these laudatory choirs personally receives very little. 'Only two *tostões* [200 réis or about ten cents]!' joked one of these unfortunate" performers. This mercenary also recorded—quite possibly from popular comments—that the female figure in the allegory of Pedro granting the constitution (Figure 1.1) so closely resembled Pedro's mistress Domitila that she might well have posed for the artist.[116] Others merely ignored the official messages. Bösche, who marched in the 12 October 1824 parade, found the elegantly dressed "beauties of Rio" who viewed the spectacle from their decorated balconies to be "the most interesting part of the celebrations." That evening, he added, many people took advantage of the holiday to get drunk.[117] No doubt, many of his fellow soldiers, Brazilians and foreigners alike, shared his interests. However, political ritual should not be so easily dismissed, for in 1830–31, liberal opponents of Pedro I boldly bid to seize control of it.

CHAPTER TWO

The Radical Challenge, 1830–1837

On the night of 25–26 March 1830, Rio de Janeiro's civic rituals changed dramatically when, for the first time, citizens celebrated the constitution separately from the official festivities. This demonstration against Pedro I's government launched four years of intensely politicized rituals as Brazilians, deeply divided over the great political questions concerning the nature of the imperial regime, struggled for control over the ritual spaces established during the previous years. The press freedom gradually instituted in the late 1820s allowed partisan journals to flourish in the 1830s; they described the celebrations of days of national festivity in considerable detail and intently debated their meaning or, better, the nature of the institutions established in 1822–24 and celebrated on days of national festivity.[1]

The politics of 1830–37 remain difficult to elucidate. An explosion of often ephemeral partisan newspapers whose language is obscure to modern readers, rapid turns in political fortunes, and dramatically different political trajectories in the provinces combine to make this, as João Manoel Pereira da Silva wrote in 1888, "unquestionably the most interesting, dramatic, and instructive [period] of Brazilian history."[2] While Pereira da Silva sought to draw lessons about the dangers of extreme partisanship and popular mobilizations, modern historians are more likely to celebrate the participation of broad sectors of the population in politics (although they sometimes exaggerate the degree of autonomy that the popular classes enjoyed). Simple distinctions between liberals and conservatives, constitutionalists and absolutists, Brazilians and Portuguese, or blacks and whites do justice neither to the partisan political positions nor to the innovative political practices pioneered by all factions. Broadly speaking, the conflicts pitted first "Brazilians," "patriots," or "constitutionalists" against Pedro I and his "Portuguese" or "absolutist" supporters (also known as "Colunas"), and then radical liberals (Exaltados), moderate liberals (Moderados), and conservative restorationists (Caramurus) against each other.[3]

The key political event of this period took place on 7 April 1831, when Emperor Pedro I unexpectedly abdicated. For the previous year and a half, he had been under increasing pressure from a diverse group of parliamentarians, journalists, and their supporters to appoint a ministry that had the full confidence of the "liberal" group in the legislature. For these "Brazilian" and "patriot" opponents of Pedro's "absolutist" and "Portuguese" supporters, the goal was an extension of constitutional rule beyond the limits envisaged by the monarch in 1824. Pedro refused to bow to these demands; abdicated in favor of his five-year-old son, Pedro II; and sailed for Europe. This set off a bitter struggle between Moderados and Exaltados—allied until April 1831—and between the former and Caramurus. Key issues included control over the regency and the young emperor, the degree of centralization (or federalism), and liberal institutional reforms such as the code of criminal procedure and the citizens' militia (the National Guard), some of which had been in the works since the 1820s. In 1834, the so-called Ato Adicional (Additional Act) devolved important powers to the provincial governments and established provincial legislatures. Significant popular unrest, both on the capital's streets and in the provinces, worried many, as did the willingness of radicals on both left and right to take up arms. Finally, during these years, an increasingly vigorous partisan political press expanded the scope of political debate and brought broad sectors of the urban population into the political process.[4] Indeed, one contemporary later recalled that, during these years, Brazilians lived "more in the public square than in their very homes . . . in an essentially political . . . atmosphere."[5]

From 1830 to 1833, bitterly contested civic rituals were central to political struggles. In 1830–31, patriots—a term that had specific associations with radical liberalism—adopted a series of political symbols that defined them as Brazilians. Their struggle continued after the abdication until the end of 1833, when Moderados finally won a precarious—even Pyrrhic—victory in Rio de Janeiro. This led to a sudden diminution in the intensity with which newspapers debated days of national festivity in 1834. After Pedro I's death (24 September 1834) removed the principal obstacle to a rapprochement between erstwhile Caramurus and conservative elements in the Moderado camp, a reaction gathered strength. Its triumph came in the so-called Regresso of September 1837; the new government revitalized monarchical ritual, the subject of Chapter Three.

RITUAL AND POLITICS, 1830–1831

The night of 25–26 March 1830 marked a major change in Rio de Janeiro's civic rituals.[6] Liberals resolved to celebrate the constitution's sixth anniversary with "spontaneous" festivities to demonstrate their loyalty to "the political system that rules us in law, but not in fact."[7] After the usual official celebrations, a large crowd gathered at Constitution Square (in front of the theater) to cheer the monarch. Then, led by bands, they dispersed to their home parishes, singing patriotic hymns and cheering "the objects of our public devotion." These included the constitution; the "great Pedro, constitutional emperor"; independence; and parliament. Ladies watched these demonstrations from the windows of their houses, waving white handkerchiefs and throwing flowers on the marchers. Most residents of the city placed lamps in their front windows, despite the fact that no authorities had issued instructions for illuminating the city.[8] To be sure, the "spontaneity" of this festival was relative. A conservative newspaper later complained that Exaltados had collected contributions from even those "who liked this function as much as Mohammed liked bacon"; many of these individuals paid only to avoid Exaltados' insults.[9] The city council's vote against inviting residents to illuminate their façades likely derived from councilors' doubts about their jurisdiction in light of the 1828 law that defined municipalities' responsibilities and, among other things, prohibited them from spending money on festivals; no journalists accused the council of seeking to prevent celebrations.[10] Nevertheless, for the first time during Pedro I's reign, a public civic ritual had taken place without government direction.

Rio de Janeiro's newspapers and foreign observers disagreed deeply about the significance of these events (and even about what happened). The Kingdom of the Two Sicilies' chargé d'affaires saw it as part of a rising tide of anti-Portuguese agitation and wrote about the "large band of madmen, among them a large number of mulattoes, all shouting death to Colunas, that is to say absolutists or Portuguese, and forcing the illumination of houses." Others were more sanguine. The *Jornal do Comércio* commented that it was "difficult to explain the enthusiasm that possessed Fluminenses" and marveled that "good order prevailed amid so much confusion!" For João Clemente Vieira Souto's *Astréia*, the celebrations demonstrated Brazil's support for the constitutional order; *Voz Fluminense* declared that they made clear the "impossibility of perpetuating [the] savage despotism," of which radical liberals had been accusing the ministry. Joaquim José da Silva Maia, the editor of *O Brasileiro Imparcial*, lamented that the celebrants had cheered "liberty in a country in which unfortunately exist slaves, which might inspire new Spartacuses to imitate those of ancient Rome, or even those of Haiti." Moreover, they had insulted the owners of houses that were not illuminated. By contrast, explained *Astréia*, the failure to illuminate houses demonstrated that their owners were "enemies of the [constitutional] system and therefore enemies of Brazil." A few days later, Silvério Mariano Queveda de Lacerda's *A Luz Brasileira* lashed out at the palace cliques who wanted peaceful citizens to be punished for their legitimate celebrations of the constitution.[11]

Four days after the celebrations, Evaristo da Veiga weighed in with his *Aurora Fluminense*. He stressed that the participants were "in general decently dressed" and hailed the youthful celebrants, raised on "the milk of the new doctrines," who "swear that they will never be slaves, who will always know how to maintain the human race's dignity [and] the rights of their beloved country." On 31 March, Evaristo published a two-page editorial to rebut Maia. To be sure, he preferred cheers to the constitution over those to liberty, for the former "presented . . . a clearly defined idea" but it was hardly criminal to hail liberty. He dismissed the "customary jeremiad about Saint Domingue" and the accusations of insults against unilluminated houses by "some hotheads," condemning those who had "railed . . . against the number of black men and boys [*moleques*]" who accompanied the bands. Some, of course, had followed the "no small number of decently-dressed citizens," but such riffraff appeared at every public celebration and often formed the largest part of the audience. In any case, 25 March had been celebrated with "much moderation," and "the few excesses that took place were committed by one or another isolated unknown individual [and] neither imitated nor supported by the majority."[12]

As 7 September approached, liberals sought to repeat their public successes of the previous March. A worried police intendant turned down a request from Exaltado journalist Ezequiel Corrêa dos Santos to hold nighttime celebrations at the Passeio Público.[13] The intendant exhorted "Brazilians" to maintain the peace and to moderate their celebrations' tone by not speaking "hurtful words, offensive to any individual, class, or nation," and called on justices of the peace and other authorities to maintain vigilance in their jurisdictions during the celebrations, for which Exaltado newspapers roundly condemned him.[14] Army bands received orders not to accompany paraders, something that they had apparently done on 25 March.[15] Months later, *Astréia* characterized all of this as the "antinational government's" effort to "obstruct this festival."[16]

The celebrations themselves passed without incident. The usual official rituals took place, perfunctorily described by the newspapers that sought to maintain their neutrality. Some "Fluminense citizens" had managed to obtain authorization from the city council to erect "a large band shell" on Constitution Square, where a band played and where citizens sang a hymn to 7 September and recited poetry.[17] The city was, once again, illuminated, and Evaristo described the "brilliant and numerous concourse of men and ladies" who remained on the square "from dusk on the 7th until the next day's dawn."[18] Unlike on 25 March, the celebrants refrained from marching around the city, although they had originally planned to parade with "decorated floats" and musical instruments (evidently, the ban on parading by army bands had its effect).[19]

On the street and in the press, radical liberals' rhetoric reached new heights and almost entirely ignored Pedro I (despite his central role in the events of 7 September 1822). Ezequiel declared that the anniversary of nations' independence "has always been counted by them as the only day that truly belongs to the people." *Astréia* similarly ignored the emperor and declared that Brazilians' attention to 7 September demonstrated the degree to which the constitutional system had taken root and the deep love of the *"pátria's* [homeland's] liberties and Brazilianism [*brasileirismo*].*"*[20] The *Aurora Fluminense* suggested that Pedro had followed Brazilians' lead on 7 September: "He willingly embraced our cause, declared himself [to be] also Brazilian, defied the fury of those who sought to fetter us with gilded chains on the pretext of a liberty that meant nothing to us, and thus made himself worthy of reigning over Brazilians by the unanimous choice of our new political association."[21] Pedro still had his defenders. In *O Brasileiro Imparcial*, Maia exhorted his readers to show themselves worthy of the independence and the institutions granted by "the most magnanimous of monarchs." At the Candelária church, Canon Joaquim Pereira dos Reis preached on Exodus 12:14, comparing Pedro to Moses; both led their people out of foreign captivity, and Pedro had granted "a constitution . . . as generous as the world's first charter, given on two tablets to the loyal Moses."[22]

The anniversary of Pedro's acclamation and his birthday came five weeks later. Already in mid-September, *Voz Fluminense*'s unknown editor had heard rumors of subscriptions to outdo the Exaltado patriots of 7 September. What Maia's *O Brasileiro Imparcial* described as a voluntary subscription promoted by "some enterprising and generous citizens," Ezequiel's *Nova Luz Brasileira* dismissed as a forced levy on armed forces personnel and underpaid civil servants so that "vile *corcundas* [literally hunchbacks, an allusion to their allegedly servile posture before the emperor] and big shots can have festivities in opposition to independence and the constitution" (thereby mirroring Maia's complaint about 25 March).[23] However this subscription was conducted, it raised a significant sum, and the organizers constructed an enormous wooden monument on Constitution Square, the same place where the

7 September band shell had stood. Designed by army engineers and decorated by Francisco Pedro do Amaral (the artist who had repainted the coaches for Pedro's wedding), it took the form of a round temple with an imperial crown at its peak, atop a cupola supported by eight Corinthian columns. It stood thirty-five palms (seven meters) high, and its outer portico formed a circle 140 palms (twenty-eight meters) in diameter. In the spaces between its columns, transparent paintings showed the main events of independence and represented the empire's provinces with their principal products. The entire structure was liberally decorated with verses in honor of the emperor and garlands of flowers, and was illuminated with no less than 11,126 lamps. Atop the monument, large capital letters proclaimed its meaning: "TO PEDRO FROM THE GRATEFUL *PÁTRIA*." Underneath the structure, bands played the national anthem and other appropriate music. According to *O Verdadeiro Patriota*, a "countless multitude of people of all ages, statuses, and ranks gathered to see this illumination; houses were also illuminated, and joy reigned over all."[24] The usual imperial civic ritual took place, and the brilliantly lit theater staged a lengthy gala, whose program included poetry readings, a symphony, Gioacchino Rossini's *Gazza Ladra* (The Thieving Magpie), a dance intermezzo, and an allegorical tableau that showed Pedro's auspicious future. Nymphs representing the Brazilian provinces brought offerings to the hero (Pedro), and Iris, the messenger of the gods, showed him a temple with statues of the great men of history. One pedestal was empty, reserved for the "Founder of the Empire of the Southern Cross." Throughout, the audience repeatedly cheered their monarch.[25]

For about a week, Maia's *O Brasileiro Imparcial* and *Voz Fluminense* debated these celebrations' meaning. For the monarchist newspaper, 12 October was "no doubt Brazil's most brilliant and majestic [day]; without it, there would be no empire, independence, or constitution," to which the Exaltado journal responded: "So long as the monarch lives up to the conditions under which he ascended to the throne, 12 October does not need the ridiculous flattery of *Imparcial*'s party." Two days later, Maia retorted: "The true constitutionalist must adore a generous prince, the model for those of his century, who by grinding old prejudices under his heels [and] joining the enlightened of his century, was the first to proclaim our independence, and [is] perhaps the only truly constitutional monarch." Fed up with the debate, *Voz Fluminense* condemned the "fury of the colonizing absolutists" who could not tolerate the "Brazilian patriotism" manifested on 25 March and 7 September. Hence, they resolved to turn 12 October into the "instrument for venting their rage." The celebrations of Pedro's birthday required no such elaborate monument; for 12 October to remain magnificent, all that was needed was "the inalterability of the constitutional ruler in his oaths, which he must uphold faithfully."[26]

March 1831 brought the last round of civic rituals of Pedro I's reign, his formal entry into the city on returning from his politically unsuccessful trip to Minas Gerais (15 March) and the celebrations of the constitution on the 25th. Pedro arrived on the 10th and the *Correio Mercantil* laconically described the official celebrations, for which the "Chamber of Commerce and other civil and military corporations" had raised eighteen contos (US$8,280): "The city was almost entirely illuminated on the 11th, 12th, and 13th in honor of His Majesty the Emperor's arrival. Quitanda and Direita streets stood out, not only for their illumination but also for their fireworks and bands."[27] On the 15th, the emperor and the empress

performed their public entry into this Corte [Court—the city of Rio de Janeiro], and after having attended the Te Deum in the imperial chapel, they held a *beija-mão* in the city palace. The diplomatic corps and a large suite of all classes attended. Their Majesties received salutes from the garrison's troops, who paraded before their persons. Ouvidor Street, through which Their Majesties passed, was magnificently decorated with curtains and flags, and the repeated cheers . . . demonstrated the esteem in which the nation holds them.[28]

O Verdadeiro Patriota, Pedro's principal defender after Maia's death in late 1830 or early 1831 put an end to *O Brasileiro Imparcial*,[29] went further: "It is not easy to describe the neatness and luxury with which houses were decorated." It estimated the crowd at 20,000 people and declared that they all manifested deeply felt "enthusiasm."[30] After this entry, the British minister judged that Pedro could still "reckon upon the support of a great majority of the inhabitants."[31]

Antônio Borges da Fonseca, who had quickly emerged as a leading Exaltado since his arrival from the North in October 1830,[32] saw something quite different, a partisan demonstration that reduced Pedro to emperor of the Portuguese:

I never saw a more beggarly accompaniment, and on purpose one could not have delivered a better insult to the emperor, who that day appeared to be the ruler only of *marinheiros* [literally, sailors, a pejorative nickname for Portuguese]. Four or five hundred *marinheiros* led the imperial coach; some were in short coats [*jaquetas*], some in waistcoats [*rodaques*], some in tailcoats [*casacas*], and all wore sandals, and many [were] raggedly dressed. Aside from the troops obliged by duty to attend, not one Brazilian could be seen; all were *marinheiros* and black boys [*molecagem*], who gave very ragged cheers and whose behavior must have embarrassed the emperor.[33]

With the benefit of hindsight, John Armitage concurred with Borges da Fonseca, as did other observers.[34] Critics declared that those who had

raised funds for these celebrations were not the distinguished corporations of the *Correio Mercantil*'s account; rather, the subscribers were
"men who do not belong to Brazil, neither by birth, nor by love," or
"naturalized Brazilians, and some natives, branded by the iron of servility."[35] No contemporary critic noted that the eighteen contos raised was
less than half of the sum collected for Pedro's 1826 entry. Several observers reported that the entry was marred by a certain Francisco Soares, a
Portuguese man and reportedly the brother of one of the emperor's mistresses, who rode "like a madman before the imperial carriage and hit
several Brazilians with the back of his sword" (or with a whip) because
they had cheered Pedro "so long as he is constitutional" or failed to
shout "Long live the emperor, death to Repúblico" (Borges da Fonseca's
nickname, derived from his newspaper's title). Soares and Francisco das
Chagas de Oliveira França almost came to blows when the editor of *O
Tribuno do Povo* tried to amend Soares's cheers of "Long live the emperor" with shouts of "constitutional." "Without this we do not want
him," declared Chagas.[36] Although the ritual entry was completed, deep
disagreement existed about its political meaning, and the public newspaper and pamphlet discourse about it revealed these conflicts. Unlike in
1826, Pedro could not control the printed rhetoric about this civic ritual.

These differences had emerged even more clearly on 13 March, during
the Noite das Garrafadas (Night of the Bottle-Blows), in which Exaltados disrupted the celebrations of Pedro's return in the so-called Cidadela
(Citadel), a downtown district dominated by Portuguese-born merchants
and clerks and a center of support for the emperor. Here partisanship
dominated; *O Novo Censor* reported that the "large number of people . . .
most enthusiastically repeated cheers to His Imperial Majesty and to the
constitution as granted by the emperor and sworn to by Brazil, and to
independence."[37] As far as Exaltados were concerned, this was a repeat
of the 12 October 1830 celebrations, and some confronted the Cidadela's
celebrants; gathering at Constitution Square, a group of about 200 men
resolved to "go to Quitanda Street to see the lamps and to give constitutional cheers."[38] Led by the editors of *O Repúblico* (Borges da Fonseca)
and *O Tribuno do Povo* (Chagas), they paraded through the street "giving cheers to the emperor so long as he is constitutional, to the sovereign
Brazilian nation, to its independence, and to Brazilians."[39]

This symbolic challenge soon turned violent, and the sequence of
events is impossible to disentangle from the conflicting partisan accounts.
Armitage blamed Exaltados' "imprudence" in putting out the celebrants'
bonfires, while Borges da Fonseca claimed that his party was provoked
by Padre Malheiros, editor of *O Novo Censor*, who cheered "His absolutist Majesty," which obliged a "citizen" to seize him and make the
priest hail "His Majesty so long as he is constitutional." At that point,
according to *O Repúblico*'s editor, the traitors to Brazil rained broken

bottles on the protestors from the upper windows; someone fired shots, and men armed with sticks and clubs drove the demonstrators back.[40] Malheiros, for his part, blamed the "revolutionaries [and] anarchists" for forcing the "people to cheer the federal system of government" and for throwing the first bottles and torches at those who looked on from the windows.[41] The violence escalated, and armed bands sallied forth from the Cidadela to exact revenge on the patriots. A number of patriot properties were sacked, and Evaristo da Veiga suffered insults at the door of his house, for he had not illuminated his front window. The police failed to stop the violence, and only a sudden thunderstorm dispersed the crowds. The following night, the police stood idly by as a group of "vandals" attempted to destroy two shops on Constitution Square where patriots customarily gathered. Amid shouts of "long live the Portuguese, long live the emperor, death to the liberals," they also attacked men who wore the "national ribbon [*laço nacional*]."[42] In a strongly worded petition, liberal deputies protested the government's inaction and called on Pedro to preserve the "constitutional throne" and public order, but Malheiros pointed out that Borges da Fonseca and his "*sans-culotte*" followers had been the first to disrupt legitimate celebrations.[43]

In these celebrations' aftermath, Pedro appointed a cabinet composed of men sympathetic to the opposition (on 19 March), but this move failed to placate his more radical opponents. As 25 March approached, observers feared a repeat of the Garrafadas' violence, and worried justices of the peace urged citizens to keep order.[44] Nevertheless, Evaristo da Veiga called on his compatriots to celebrate, once again, 25 March and invited "all Brazilians, friends of their country, the land where they were born or which they adopted as their *pátria*" to attend an evening Te Deum in the São Francisco de Paula church, funded by a subscription that raised 3,362 mil-réis (US$1,714). The charter was, he explained, "for Brazil the source of happiness, a sure guarantee of liberty."[45] Chagas's *Tribuno do Povo* sought to raise the stakes on 24 March by running a letter from "a Fluminense *caibra* [*cabra* or dark mulatto]" who called on "all that are Brazilian" to wear the "*tope nacional*," the badge with the words "independence or death" that had been used back in 1822–25. The writer also declared that "perverse men" were saying that the constitution existed only "because of Pedro's will," while in fact, his oath to the constitution was the nation's exercise of sovereignty over the monarch: "It was the nation that spontaneously decided to adopt it, regardless of the reasons that forced the acceptance of a less perfect work than that which would have come from the constituent assembly dissolved by force of arms."[46]

As in the major civic celebrations of previous years, authorities staged the standard official ceremonies. At night, there was a "brilliant and general illumination" of the city, as well as a "splendid illumination and fireworks on the Campo da Aclamação," which had been prepared for

Pedro's entry but had apparently not been used. Newspapers concur that these celebrations took place without the slightest disorder.[47] Latent tensions nevertheless manifested themselves. Eduardo Teodoro Bösche reported that all Brazilians wore badges with the national colors and that even ladies sported green-and-yellow ribbons. In an eruption of Exaltado enthusiasm published too late to affect the course of events, *O Brasileiro Ofendido* lamented Pedro's control by "furious Lusitanians" and hoped that "our *cabras* can take advantage of such a fine occasion to, with their customary bravery, once again win the independence of Rio, as they did with Brazil, teaching a lesson to those despicable foreigners and their protectors." Four days later, this newspaper carefully distinguished between the evening Te Deum in the São Francisco de Paula Church and the fireworks display at the Campo da Aclamação. The latter was "a remnant of the arrival from Minas," while liberals, "sporting the national symbol, and many of them with our comfortable straw hats," gathered at the church, elegantly decorated for the occasion.[48]

In a characteristically dramatic gesture, Pedro I arrived at the church without having been invited. Contemporary accounts of this episode vary. Armitage described a worried monarch who "scarcely appeared to be conscious of what he was saying" in response to cheers for Pedro II (the five-year-old heir apparent), and the French and Austrian ministers reported a fearful monarch who barely disguised his disdain for the ceremonies.[49] By contrast, Borges da Fonseca, no friend of the emperor, admitted that Pedro "won considerable popularity by procuring a green-and-yellow leaf, which serves on these great days as the nation's badge." A citizen kissed his hand and exclaimed: "Long live the emperor as long as he is constitutional!" to which Pedro responded, "I have always been, and will always show, that I am [a constitutional ruler], so much so that, without being invited to your function, here I am." Another citizen retorted: "As the first citizen, it is your obligation to come without having been invited." Amid the crowd, Borges heard nothing of the sermon, but he witnessed Pedro listening to patriotic poetry after the service (and applauding it): "He remained for a long time among the people who cheered the Brazilian nation, the nation's sovereignty, the constitution, liberty, the general assembly, and freedom of the press" but not the emperor himself. Only when he finally left "were cheers given to the emperor so long as he is constitutional."[50] *O Verdadeiro Patriota* condemned this "vulgarity, even an insult, that implies that the monarch's constitutionality is in doubt," and lamented that authorities had not done more to maintain order and respect for the royal person.[51]

The sermon that Borges da Fonseca missed expressed a moderate liberal interpretation of the day's meaning. Francisco de Monte Alverne preached that Brazil wanted neither "pure democracy" nor rule by a despot, and that the constitution, along with subsequent innovations such as the jury system and the elected justices of the peace, guaranteed Brazil's happiness. He declared that "one single sentiment unites all Brazilians in defense of the hereditary constitutional monarchy; the most sublime interest awakens in all hearts the love of this constitution, in which rights, guarantees, and social advantages are securely established," and concluded with an appeal to reject both those who preached "the horrible and execrable doctrine of absolutism" and those who flattered Brazilians with "notions of a liberty without limits" to drown the country in "the horrors of anarchy."[52] After the Te Deum, Borges da Fonseca and some friends visited the artillery battalion whose officers, "true defenders of Brazil's liberty and of the constitution with its federalist reforms," had prepared "spectacular illuminations" that featured the slogan "Independence or Death." There, Francisco Muniz Barreto improvised verse on the constitution and on independence, much to the celebrants' acclaim.[53]

Pedro's concession of 19 March and his symbolic gesture on the 25th failed to stem the opposition tide. On 5 April, he resolved to fight back by appointing a cabinet composed of loyalists, which the opposition perceived as the prelude to a coup. Armed Exaltados gathered on the Campo de Aclamação, and military units joined this direct challenge to the monarch. Instead of negotiating or capitulating, Pedro I abruptly abdicated during the night of 6–7 April. A hastily assembled regency took the reins of government and arranged an acclamation of the young Pedro II. As many as 20,000 people, according to a British merchant, Joseph William Moore, turned out to cheer the young emperor during his public entry into the city, which was followed by a Te Deum, a military parade, and Pedro II's presentation to the people from the palace windows (Figure 2.1). While Moore saw a worrisomely large accompaniment of armed "blacks, mulattoes and canaille," Evaristo praised the "more than five hundred citizens, all well dressed," who paraded "arm in arm as a sign of their firm unity."[54]

Such unity proved ephemeral, and the abdication threw open Brazilian politics. Although some hailed "the glorious revolution" and declared that it had definitively secured "Brazil's independence and liberty" in exemplary peaceful fashion,[55] others quickly became disillusioned, for the abdication had not, in fact, resolved the political issues that divided Brazilians. The Moderados who controlled the regency ultimately triumphed over both republican Exaltados and restorationist Caramurus; for the former, who had provided the shock troops in the campaign against Pedro I, 7 April amounted to a *"journée des dupes,"* a day of dupes.[56] Moderados' hour of glory came in 1831–32 when they held the country together and preserved the monarchy. Increasing divisions in their ranks after mid-1832 rendered their position more tenuous, and political conflicts repeatedly manifested themselves in civic rituals.

FIGURE 2.1.
Pedro II's acclamation, 7 April 1831.
Source: Debret, *Voyage*, vol. 3, plate 51.

Before addressing these developments, however, we turn to the political symbols that had emerged in Rio de Janeiro's civic ritual during the last years of Pedro's reign.

THE SYMBOLS OF POLITICS

The accounts of civic ritual in 1830 and early 1831 offer numerous indications of political symbols whose meaning is today not necessarily transparent. Through particular dress—especially straw hats—patriots identified themselves as a distinct group; they also donned badges that proclaimed "Independence or Death," sported green-and-yellow leaves and coffee sprigs (or flowers), and spoke of themselves and their enemies in racial language. They proclaimed Brazil to be their *pátria* (homeland) and sang new anthems and listened to patriotic poetry that expressed their political ideals. Such symbols of identity and affiliation made politics more accessible to larger sectors of society and served as markers of membership in the nativist and liberal opposition to Pedro I, which some called the Brazilian party.

Of all of these symbols, the racial language with which so many described street politics is the most difficult to elucidate, for it involved both more or less objective description of people involved and a politicization of racial terms that infused them with new meanings. Foreign observers repeatedly worried about the mobilization of "blacks and mu-lattoes" on 7 April and in subsequent weeks, while the press had vigor-ously debated the role of nonwhite participants on 25 March 1830.[57] Likewise, historians have emphasized the racial (and class) basis of the March 1831 Garrafadas incidents. Gladys Sabina Ribeiro, the most re-cent student of these events, focuses on underlying social tensions be-tween the largely nonwhite patriot protestors (repeatedly described as *pardos* [browns], *cabras, negros* [blacks], and even slaves in the police investigation and by the newspapers) and Portuguese immigrants. The two groups had long "fought over the workplace, residence, and sur-vival," and the attack on the Cidadela "was an attempt to demolish a symbol of power, oppression, and ruling-class exclusivity."[58] People "of color"—slave and free alike—"always united," she continues, fought for "liberty" as they understood it, and the conflict cannot be reduced to a struggle between two nations (Brazilians versus Portuguese) or a con-flict between radical liberals and conservative absolutists.[59]

Ribeiro's interpretation, although suggestive, relies on a mechanistic reading of social divisions. The racial terms used in accounts of events like the Noite das Garrafadas were far from "objective" labels, and Exaltados' enemies had every incentive to label them blacks and slaves; indeed, one contemporary called racial terms "epithets."[60] In a particularly revealing incident, a self-described white man, wearing "the Brazilian ribbon" on his hat, was insulted by what appeared to be (Portuguese) store clerks who called him "goat [*bode*], *cabra*, and other such insults," and many other sources note this use of racial slurs that challenged claims of white-ness.[61] *O Novo Censor* described the patriots who entered the Cidadela as "a few white men mixed with many blacks [*negros*], and some slaves." Its editor went further in this association of patriots with slaves by describing their cheers as "howls of the fugitive-slave [*quilombeiro*] *República*."[62] To interpret these as racial slurs rather than as descriptions of the people involved is not to argue that nonwhites were uninvolved in this unrest or that they merely acted as unwitting tools of the Exaltado leadership. Ribeiro rightly criticizes Thomas Flory's dismissal of racial rhetoric as merely an expression of conventional partisan politics, but the records left by the Noite das Garrafadas offer precious little information on what the rank-and-file protestors meant by their cheers.[63] Their actions, in any case, cannot be divorced from the Exaltados' political aims. Moreover, as Ivana Stolze Lima has observed, there was a "racial language of poli-tics" at this time, in which "citizens' color" meant much more than simply skin color.[64] Exaltados adopted racial terms (despite their negative con-notations) as positive affirmations of Brazilian-ness, most famously in an oft-cited Bahian broadside that proclaimed the blond-haired and blue-eyed Pedro II to be "*cabra* like us," a view that *O Tribuno do Povo's* Chagas shared when he hailed the child-emperor as a "Brazilian *cabra* [*caibra*] . . . , our compatriot."[65] Likewise, as we have seen, *O Brasileiro Ofendido* identified Brazilian patriotism with the *cabras* whom its editor had called on to win a new independence for their country.

Brazilian and Portuguese did not merely connote birthplace, although this was certainly an important element; rather, it involved political choices. Evaristo directed his invitation to the 25 March 1831 Te Deum not only at Brazilians but also at those who had adopted Brazil as their *pátria*. Thus, in mid-March 1831, *Astréia* explained that the government was not "national" but "Portuguese," adding that this was the view of "all constitutional Brazilians, friends of their *pátria*." For its editor, Vieira Souto, being Brazilian was inseparable from a constitutionalist political position.[66] Two U.S. ministers took pains to explain that Portuguese and Brazilian were the labels of political "parties" (as had the Two Sicilies' envoy in early 1830). For William Wright, the "Portuguese" were "friends of absolute monarchy" and the "Brazilians stern advocates of the constitution." His successor, Ethan Brown, explained:

Two parties divide the public . . . by the appellation of the 'Portuguese' and the 'Brazilians.' The latter in general advocate opinions and measures as liberal as in any way can be consistent with monarchy. The former [is] in favor of more power in the monarch and less popular influence in the government.[67]

The association of absolutism with Portugal was further reinforced by Miguel, Pedro I's brother, who ruled Portugal as an absolute monarch from 1828 to 1834, when he was deposed by the former Brazilian emperor.[68] To be sure, such finer political points were often lost on those who blamed their problems on foreigners. Carl Seidler remarked on the irony of Portuguese-born fathers and Brazilian-born sons divided by this rhetoric (one suspects that conservative fathers' disdain for youthful flirtations with radicalism were more important than petty nativism in such conflicts).[69] Others pursued class conflict through lusophobia: Expropriating Portuguese shopkeepers could easily be presented as a patriotic act.[70] Sometimes anti-Portuguese rhetoric took even more extreme forms, attributing inhuman or monstrous characteristics to Portuguese. On the eve of the abdication, *O Brasileiro Ofendido* lashed out at the likes of Padre Malheiros: "Brutish, prideful, hungry for fortune, they only know the base motives of ambition and personal interest. They were masters and today are guests, and hated guests. . . . They want to drink our blood."[71]

The term *pátria* (homeland or fatherland) turned up regularly in patriot rhetoric, generally reflecting the concept's extension to all of Brazil, rather than to the local community or place of origin to which it also referred. As Lacerda explained in *Nova Luz Brasileira*, the "narrow" definition of *pátria* encompassed the "city, town, or place" where a person had been born, while the "broad" definition referred to the "nation or province to which a man belongs."[72] All those whose uses of the term are cited thus far in this chapter closely connected *pátria* to Brazil, and this underscored the affinity between the concept and that of the nation or political community, at least in the view of those contesting Pedro's claims. Much the same usage of *pátria* appears in the anthems, poetry, and other rhetoric discussed in the following pages, all of which stressed the primacy of loyalty to the political community of Brazil (the Brazilian nation) as radical liberals understood it. And, as Evaristo noted in his 25 March 1831 invitation, one could choose to join a *pátria* or a political community.

The accounts of the Noite das Garrafadas reveal the emerging repertoire of patriot symbolic practice. Competing cheers and disruption of the Cidadela celebrations are one indication of the degree to which street politics was patterned or ritualized behavior, at least until the bottles flew. One of the armed groups set out from the Cidadela to Constitution Square, accompanied by "a band playing," to "finish off the republicans and the federalists"; no sneak attack, this was a public counterdemonstration.[73] A witness at the Cidadela saw the Exaltado attackers waving a small green-and-yellow flag, and another reported that they left behind republican and federal banners.[74] In March 1831, patriots resumed wearing the *tope nacional*, a flower-shaped badge with a yellow triangle and the slogan "Independence or Death." This latter symbol had been instituted by Pedro I in 1822 as a patriotic Brazilian device and a mark of Brazilian citizenship to be worn until international recognition was achieved. When this came in 1825, the *tope* was discarded, but it assumed new meaning in 1831 as the symbol of the "Brazilian party" in its fight against the "recolonizing faction." Shortly after the Garrafadas violence, Evaristo da Veiga declared that he now considered Brazil's independence to be under threat and recommended that all Brazilians wear the *tope*; the city council seconded him.[75] Patriots who wore these symbols risked having them violently removed by their opponents, especially during the Garrafadas.[76] One newspaper claimed that "ribbons of a different color . . . on the hats of a certain class of people . . . [were] a sign of seditious gatherings."[77]

Other symbols of patriot identity also emerged in these months. In early April, *O Brasileiro Ofendido* reported that Brazilians faced hostility from the "Cidadela's dictators" for wearing straw hats, considered the "new federal or republican emblem"; two employees had been recently barred from entering the post office while wearing them. The editor explained that the use of straw hats as political symbols first appeared in Bahia and that people in Rio de Janeiro subsequently copied the custom "for comfort and patriotism." Straw hats were far cheaper than imported headgear, he added, and local industry should be encouraged.[78] More condescendingly, Jean-Baptiste Debret attributed slaves' adoption of straw hats painted yellow and green to their work on the decorations and monuments for public festivals.[79] Through 1832, the appearance of "straw hat men," as Moore picturesquely put it, marked the start of Exaltado demonstrations.[80] Straw hats were both an assertion of economic independence and an effort to identify with the common people who could not afforded imported head gear.[81] There are even hints that, in the heady days of April 1831, patriots rejected foreign textiles and sought to wear domestically produced clothing.[82]

Along with straw hats and the *tope nacional*, patriots adopted the green-and-yellow leaves of the *Croton variegatum* (which the U.S. minister called the "constitution tree") as a symbol of their cause; hence the significance of Pedro I's act of donning such a leaf on 25 March 1831.[83] William Ruschenberger visited the botanical garden on 7 September 1831, where gardeners stopped him from breaking twigs on a specimen of this bush, "the national tree"; instead, they gave him a few leaves to take.[84] At the time of the abdication, coffee leaves briefly joined croton in the patriot symbolic repertoire. Debret's rendering of Pedro II's acclamation shows patriots bedecked with "boughs of flowering coffee bearing fruit" in addition to croton sprigs (Figure 2.1).[85] His sketches for a projected painting of patriots on the Campo da Aclamação show soldiers even more heavily bedecked with coffee branches.[86] Although coffee was still not Brazil's main export, it figured on the country's coat of arms (along with tobacco, which did not have civic ritual significance), so this use was clearly an allusion to this national symbol.[87]

In addition to wearing their affiliations on their heads or on their sleeves, patriots also sang, much more so than did Pedro I's supporters. Accounts of patriot civic ritual repeatedly refer to new hymns and anthems. The *Aurora Fluminense* published a new 7 September anthem in 1830; apparently it had been sung during the liberals' celebration of that day.[88] Just before 25 March 1831, one publisher distributed free copies of an anthem to be sung after the Te Deum at the São Francisco church; at least one other anthem was also published for that day.[89] At that time— and indeed for the rest of the empire—Brazil had no officially proclaimed national anthem, but what is today known as the "Hino da Independência" (Independence Anthem) whose lyrics were composed by a young Evaristo da Veiga in 1822 under the title of "Hino Constitucional Brasileiro" (Brazilian Constitutional Anthem), served as a national anthem during civic rituals. Its first stanza and chorus runs as follows:

> Thou canst, sons of the *pátria*,
> See the gentle mother in happiness;
> Liberty has dawned
> On Brazil's horizon.
>> Brave Brazilian people!
>> Away with servile terror.
>> Either the *pátria* becomes free
>> Or we will die for Brazil.

With its emphasis on liberty and freedom, these verses could readily be interpreted as a patriotic (constitutionalist) declaration.[90]

Evaristo's lyrics were, however, sung to two different tunes, one composed by Marcos Antônio da Fonseca Portugal, the other written by Pedro I himself, allegedly on 7 September 1822.[91] According to music historian Aires de Andrade, Marcos Portugal's tune was normally played on 7 September and Pedro's tune on the other days of national festivity during the 1820s.[92] Regardless of the tune, this anthem was not normally sung collectively; during the 12 October 1825 theater gala, for example, Bösche noted that the Italian opera company sang the lyrics, with the audience on floor joining in only for well-known lines (presumably the chorus).[93] Its words were nevertheless sufficiently familiar that, as Carl Schlichthorst observed, "The Portuguese make ridiculous mockeries of it."[94] Many versions of these parodies have been collected, including "*Cabra*-colored Brazilian people / [Descended] from Guinea[-coast] gentiles / Who quit the five wounds / For the coffee sprigs," an allusion to the Brazilian arms and flag that replaced the five shields of the Portuguese standard (understood to represent Christ's five wounds) with coffee (and tobacco) leaves.[95] The racial slurs are consistent with race's politicization in this period, while the parody indicates the anthem's importance to Brazilian patriots.

Patriot anthems, like their poetry, echoed the standard tropes in their rhetoric—liberty, the obligation to defend the country and the constitution (even to death), and hatred of tyranny. These were explicitly political anthems, with few signs of a Romantic nationalism or of identification with place. Sometimes they contained contemporary political allusions; in 1830, the new 7 September anthem recalled Portuguese efforts to enslave Brazil and noted that the former mother country "today in chains envies / our constitution," an allusion to the absolutist government of Pedro's brother, Miguel.[96] Francisco de Paula Brito's 25 March 1831 anthem concluded: "Long live the *pátria*, Brazilians / Already safe from the black abyss / Down with the nefarious mob / That idolizes despotism."[97]

The abdication prompted the production of several new anthems.[98] Ovídio Saraiva de Carvalho e Silva's "Ao grande e heróico dia sete de abril de 1831" (To the Great and Heroic Day of 7 April 1831), set to the tune of a march by Francisco Manoel da Silva that military bands played on that day, gained sufficient popularity that it eventually became recognized as Brazil's national anthem.[99] Carvalho e Silva's words hailed the expulsion of the "monsters" who had sought to "enslave" Brazil and lauded the ensuing dawn of liberty in the country. He called on patriots to reject all that had to do with ". . . Lusitanian / Monsters that always sought to betray / Us . . ." and appealed to old prejudices against Jews and Moors, from which the barbarous Portuguese had allegedly descended. He further called on Brazilian women to raise good sons who would sustain popular sovereignty and reminded patriots that there was still much to do, although "A prudent regency / A Brazilian[-born] monarch / Happily promise us / The most pleasing future." The chorus expressed an image of a Brazil that extended to its natural frontiers ("From the *pátria*, the cry / There it rises / From the Amazon / To the Plate"), notwithstanding the loss of the Cisplatine Province (Uruguay) in 1828, which had cut Brazil off from the southern river.[100] Carvalho e Silva's lyrics did not take, but Francisco Manoel da Silva's march—usually without lyrics—came to serve as the country's national anthem; along with the independence anthem, it was often used in later civic rituals.

The poetry of occasion, recited at theater galas, declaimed on the streets, and published in newspapers incorporated many of the anthems' themes. In style, patriot poetry varied widely. Domingos José Gonçalves de Magalhães, the leading light of Brazil's first generation of Romantic poets, hailed 25 March 1831 in formal verse:

> Holy Constitution! I will not falter
> > Gift of the benign heavens
> Thou art my shield, thou my safeguard
> > For thee I will give my life
> Thus the entire Nation wants it, and orders;
> Thus it swore, thus will I swear to it.[101]

Other poets sought to express their political messages in more accessible ways. Muniz Barreto kept it simple on 25 March 1831, preparing a rondel on the catchy and expressive lines: "To defend patriotic homes / To uphold the constitution, / To sustain Independence / Is our obligation."[102] Much the same sentiments appeared in an anonymous poem published in *Astréia*:

> Oh my *pátria*
> Beloved *pátria*
> Thou art insulted
> By a traitor!
> > If thou suffers, *pátria*
> > Who will want to live
> > It is beautiful, sweet
> > To die for thee
> >
> > . . .
> But whoever insults thee
> May he fall wounded
> Let from among us rise
> Thy avenger.[103]

Like the visible symbols of political affiliation, anthems and poetry brought political messages within easy reach of the population. While relatively few residents of Rio de Janeiro could read newspapers (although of course they could hear them read aloud), many more could pick up the abbreviated political messages of the patriot anthems and poems. The music and the repetition of phrases facilitated their commitment to memory. Through these various practices, patriots—Exaltados in particular—defined themselves as Brazilians, true defenders of the constitutional regime, to which Pedro I had been insufficiently committed, at least in their view. This, indeed, suggests how we can interpret what Seidler dismissed as the exaggerated pride of "every bedraggled mulatto" who proudly declared "I am a true Brazilian."[104] Rather than a declaration of abstract nationalist sentiment, it was a political statement. With the monarch's departure, however, neither Exaltados nor the other political factions had a clear vision of how to proceed, and this uncertainty dominated politics and civic ritual in 1831–33.

RITUAL AND POLITICS, 1831–1833

In the first years of the Regency, cash-strapped Moderados, facing challenges from both left and right, struggled to keep control of civic celebrations. The war over control of public, civic space was waged on many fronts as Brazilians debated four major political issues, each raised by a different day of national festivity: the constitution (25 March) and independence (7 September), and the abdication and the monarchy, the focus of the two new days to be celebrated (7 April and 2 December, Pedro II's birthday).[105] Neither 9 January nor 3 May received much attention, although they remained on the books as days of national festivity. Civic rituals were some of the most public and visible manifestations of the political issues over which Brazilians struggled in these years.

Under the banner of constitutional reforms, Exaltados sought a more decentralized system of government; in addition to federalism, some desired a republic. With little parliamentary presence but strong support among the free poor, a vocal press, and a willingness to take to the streets (as demonstrated in March 1831), Exaltados posed a serious threat to the more moderate liberals who held power. Moderados staunchly defended the monarchy and eventually oversaw a number of key institutional changes, including the creation of a citizens' militia (the National Guard, established in September 1831), a new code of criminal procedure (1832), and the Additional Act of 1834, which modified the constitution to strengthen provincial governments and to make provisions for a single elected regent. Moderados organized Sociedades Defensoras da Independência e Liberdade Nacional (Societies for the Defense of Independence and National Liberty) to advocate for their cause, published newspapers (Evaristo's *Aurora Fluminense* remained their principal mouthpiece), and precariously dominated civic ritual during the early 1830s. By early 1832, conservative opponents of the Moderados organized themselves around a program of opposition to constitutional reforms—and therefore a defense of centralized government—and calls for Pedro I's return. Like the Moderados and the Exaltados, they formed societies and published newspapers, notably, O *Caramuru*, from which they received their moniker (the name recalled Diogo Álvares, a fifteenth-century Portuguese castaway incorporated into Tupi society and known to them as Caramuru, who was instrumental in founding the first Portuguese settlements in Bahia). Unlike Exaltados, Caramurus had a considerable base in parliament, especially in the senate, from which they blocked early constitutional reform proposals. Caramurus also had influence via José Bonifácio de Andrada e Silva, whom Pedro I had appointed guardian of the young Pedro II (the two men had reconciled after José Bonifácio's return to Brazil in 1829). They managed to win Rio de Janeiro's municipal elections on 7 September 1832 as well as to elect justices of the peace in urban parishes. Unlike the Moderados and like the Exaltados, some Caramurus were willing to mobilize the lower classes in violent movements against the government.[106]

A narrowly defeated Exaltado revolt in July 1831 brought to power the strongest Moderado ministry, dominated by Diogo Antônio Feijó as minister of justice. Accordingly, the 7 September 1831 celebrations were an unmistakably partisan demonstration, controlled by the Sociedade Defensora, characterized by its most recent historian as an alliance among divergent political groups whose goal was to "brake the insurrection" that had accompanied Pedro's abdication.[107] The Sociedade paid for a Te Deum in the São Francisco de Paula church to give thanks, as "a patriot" put it, for the "divine protection" that freed Brazil from the "anarchists' ambition" and a "foreign despot's tyranny."[108] Surplus funds from the Sociedade's subscription were designated for the construction of Rio de Janeiro's new prison, of which one newspaper heartily approved, "for it is certainly by promoting good habits and public morality that one best works on behalf of national liberty."[109] There were some doubts about how best to celebrate the day. While admitting that Pedro I had placed himself at the head of the independence movement in 1822 only "to better enjoy its fruits and to not lose such a rich crown," the *Jornal do Comércio* nevertheless declared that 7 September 1822 marked the "first step toward liberty." For this reason, "7 September will always be a day of jubilation for good patriots."[110] In the same vein, Evaristo da Veiga called on "all Brazilians who love the *pátria*," "regardless of their political principles," to "embrace each other in brotherly fashion" on the day.[111]

Despite these calls for nonpartisan unity, 7 September 1831 was, at its core, a Moderado celebration. The regents, senators, and deputies all attended the Sociedade Defensora's Te Deum, where they heard a "brief and eloquent discourse" by Canon Narciso da Silva Nepomuceno.[112]

Two hundred uniformed Municipal Guards (the short-lived forerunner to the National Guard) stood outside the church, and Evaristo later praised the "handsome troop of citizens" who held Brazil's destiny in their hands. With nothing to gain from disorder or despotism, they were the "great secret for having liberty without anarchy, [and] order without oppression on the part of those who govern."[113] Apparently neither military parade nor Te Deum in the imperial chapel were held, but the *Jornal do Comércio* reported numerous "private dinners" at which "many patriotic toasts were raised in honor of this memorable day, to independence; to liberty; to the Brazilian monarch, our angel of peace; to the national congress; to the Regency; [and] to the fraternal unity of all Brazilians." Both this newspaper and another lamented that the celebrations were not greater, for "the spirit of evil" had spread "terror" among residents of the capital by announcing a massacre or "disorder" for 7 September.[114] Indeed, Feijó had earlier reported to the British minister that he had "positive intelligence" of a "formidable attempt . . . to overthrow the government," involving "a large body of mulattoes."[115] Nothing came of this, but *Astréia* published a complaint about the "youth in straw hats" at the theater on 7 September. After the performance, they "broke into shouts" that upset the "decent" people in attendance.[116]

Moderados' control of the 7 September celebrations through the Sociedade Defensora represented a blurring of the distinction between official and popular celebrations, popular in the sense of not state run; these unmistakably partisan festivities had largely supplanted the official ones. The 1831 independence celebrations' limited scope and the prison project demonstrated Moderados' larger concern to gain control over civic symbols and public space. The Sociedade Defensora petitioned the legislature to issue a decree standardizing the *tope nacional*'s form; parliament did so, and at the same time the finance minister dismissed employees who failed to wear the symbol "that the nation had adopted." The new *tope* consisted of a green circle with a five-pointed yellow star in the middle, to be worn either on hats or on coats.[117] Several municipal regulations sought to impose tighter control over the theater and the plays that could be produced.[118] The São Pedro Theater was renamed the Teatro Constitucional Fluminense (Fluminense Constitutional Theater), while the Campo da Aclamação became the Campo de Honra (Field of Honor), as physical locations in the city received the new regime's imprimatur.[119] Iconoclasts destroyed the coats of arms and effigies of Portuguese kings on the Passeio Público's gates, forced the painter who had decorated the imperial chapel with "images of royal personages" to erase his work, and obliged the city council to take down the portrait of Pedro I that hung in its chamber.[120] Although apparently no formal act abolished it, the *beija-mão* and much other court protocol disappeared with the abdication. An Exaltado later approvingly commented on the end of this "ridiculous ceremony . . . [an] act of abject servility."[121] Others welcomed the disappearance of a "lavish court," wryly adding that "French modistes" could now no longer make their fortune from courtesans' need for gala dress.[122]

Only at the very last minute did legislators remember that the days of national festivity had been established by law back in 1826. On the eve of 12 October, the chamber of deputies hastily passed a bill that abolished the date of Pedro's acclamation (and his birthday) as a day of national festivity, instituting 7 April and 2 December (Pedro II's birthday) as replacements (the other four days approved in 1826 remained unchanged). The abdication was politely described as the day on which the crown devolved to Pedro II.[123] The senate received the chamber's bill on 11 October and suspended its debate on law school regulations to deal with the pressing issue of whether to celebrate the upcoming day of national festivity. Most agreed that it was imprudent to mark Pedro I's birthday, but several senators (the Marquis of Barbacena, the Marquis of Caravelas, the Viscount of Cairu, and Nicolau Pereira de Campos Vergueiro) pointed out that 12 October was also the date of the empire's creation and therefore, as Caravelas put it, "must endure as long as the empire endures." When Antônio Gonçalves Gomide asserted that the empire had been founded on 7 September, Caravelas explained (correctly) that the form of government—kingdom or empire—had not been decided on that day. Cairu, no advocate of popular sovereignty, nevertheless added that 12 October was the "first explicit act of the nation's sovereignty." Such finer points of constitutional history were lost on the "rustic people," lamented Vergueiro, and the populace would simply see any celebration of 12 October as a restorationist demonstration. Senators said much less about adding 7 April to the roster of days of national festivity. Cairu opposed it on the grounds that no monarchy had ever celebrated an abdication, but Gomide stressed that the bill proposed celebrating Pedro II's acclamation, not Pedro I's abdication, which in fact took place late on 6 April. The bill passed, and senators returned to the regulation of legal education.[124] The formal decree to this effect only appeared on 25 October, so 12 October thus technically remained on the books in 1831. While there were no official celebrations in the capital, one contemporary reported that some "private dinners" complete with "cheers to Pedro I" were held.[125]

The Sociedade Defensora played no formal role in the celebration of 2 December 1831. The young emperor received the diplomatic corps, nobility, clergy, military officers, and a "large number of citizens" in the downtown palace. The newly organized National Guard paraded, and at night Pedro and his sisters attended the theater gala, at which "true Brazilians" were much pleased by the "allegorical drama" that featured "the spirits of North and South America, which joined hands

with [the spirit of] Brazil as a sign of complete union and friendship"
and their opposition to the colonial yoke's reimposition. In its editorial,
the *Jornal do Comércio* hoped that the "cause of reason and humanity
will triumph in this rich and important portion of the great American
continent, in spite of the factions and the devious intrigues of the anarchists and the ambitious," adding that the strong center of the monarchy
would allow Brazil to surpass even the United States, whose temporary
monarchy (the presidency) was inferior to Brazil's hereditary one.[126]

The civic rituals of 1832 and 1833 took place amid considerable political tension. Unable to push an authorization for constitutional reform
through parliament, Feijó and his cabinet resigned in late July 1832, as
the prelude to a parliamentary coup plotted by supporters of radical
constitutional reform. The maneuver failed and brought the deep divisions between reformist and conservative Moderados to the fore. An
unstable Moderado cabinet dominated by Aureliano de Sousa e Oliveira
Coutinho and Antônio Pinto Chichorro da Gama held office until January 1835 and won constitutional reform power for the 1834 legislature
(to be elected in 1833); late in the 1832 session, it also passed the code of
criminal procedure. The threat of a restoration—the Caramurus' principal aspiration—kept the Moderados together. They handily won the
March 1833 elections, in which Evaristo da Veiga played a key role in
organizing slates for Minas Gerais and Rio de Janeiro provinces; Feijó
still had enough support to become senator for Rio de Janeiro. In December 1833, the cabinet managed to disrupt Caramurus' extraparliamentary activity by disbanding their key institutions and by removing
José Bonifácio from his post as Pedro II's guardian. The 1834 chamber
passed the Additional Act, which has been called the "highwater mark
of liberal reform" in this period. It decentralized power by instituting
elected provincial assemblies and endowing them with considerable
powers; the three-man regency was replaced by a single elected regent.
The unelected Council of State was abolished, but the senate remained.
Fear of a restoration helped secure support for the Additional Act, which
Moderados saw as the best way to prevent a return to despotism. As far
as Exaltados were concerned, these reforms did not go far enough, while
Caramurus thought them dangerous innovations.[127]

In 1832 and 1833 the standard official rituals (military parade, Te
Deum in the imperial chapel, palace reception, and theater gala) took
place on 25 March, 7 September, and 2 December, while 7 April apparently saw no official celebrations; the latter date was too controversial.
The Sociedade Defensora usually held a separate Te Deum in the São
Francisco church on 25 March, 7 April, and 7 September, but not on
2 December. The importance of this ritual to the Defensora is clear from
the amount of money that it spent. The 7 September 1834 Te Deum cost
almost 642 mil-réis (US$506) and accounted for more than 60 percent

of the society's expenditures that trimester. In addition to the usual costs for priests' honoraria, candle wax, decorations, music, and fireworks, the society spent 60 mil-réis (US$47.40) on what must have been an impressive "tray of sweets for His Imperial Majesty."[128] No doubt the candies were more interesting to the nine-year-old monarch than the sermons that he had to sit through.

The political sermons that followed these Te Deums were clear statements of Moderados' views. On 25 March 1832, Manoel Álvares preached on "the advantages of the constitutional system" and declared that the 1824 charter "contains within it all that is needed to make the population's liberty effective."[129] Later that year, "after having shown the excellent results of 7 September," Canon Januário da Cunha Barbosa "concluded by inviting Brazilians to [join in] brotherhood, in the union that the good of the *pátria* and the presence of so many dangers urge."[130] On 7 April 1833, Monte Alverne preached that "the love of liberty and of the *pátria* is not incompatible with religion"; Cunha Barbosa returned to the pulpit on 25 March 1833 to argue "that, by Brazilians' oath to the constitution, independence and liberty, as well as the constitutional representative hereditary throne, were secured." The charter was "the most certain guarantee of the preservation of so much of value, and [the] source of so much good."[131] In their descriptions of these Te Deums, Moderado newspapers stressed that the church was handsomely decorated, that numerous citizens attended the peaceful gathering (at which even "enemies of the current order" were welcome).[132] More commonly, Caramurus stayed home; their newspaper lamented the aggressive posture of armed Moderado partisans at the 25 March 1832 Te Deum.[133]

The Sociedade Defensora's balls were, like their Te Deums, public demonstrations of allegiance and disdain for their opponents. On 6 April 1832, Evaristo da Veiga proclaimed that "good citizens' demonstrations of joy would not be interrupted by shouts from the rabble, directed by low-born ambitious people," a reference to the abortive Exaltado rising of three days earlier. He later recalled that society members declared "that they would dance . . . even if it were with weapons on their shoulders."[134] The 7 April 1832 ball was, according to Evaristo, a great success. A large number of citizens, some with their families, gathered at the war ministry building for an evening of speeches, anthems, and dancing. An army band played outside the building for the "multitude of people" who had gathered to watch the spectacle. At these balls, Moderados honored their leaders. On 7 April 1832, war minister Manoel da Fonseca Lima received a laurel wreath for his services in 1831; the following year, the celebrants honored Evaristo himself.[135] Bernardo Pereira de Vasconcelos's *O Sete de Abril*, mouthpiece of the conservative Moderados, questioned the custom of holding balls when there were more important things to do, while a Caramuru newspaper mocked the Chimangos (literally, falcons)—a pejorative nickname for Moderados—who could not stop boasting about their celebration; they were just like the tiresomely loquacious organizers of religious brotherhoods' festivals.[136]

Moderados' emphasis on private Te Deums and balls indicates their insecurity and points to their inability to control other civic ritual spaces. The Moderado press repeatedly alluded to the actions of "agitators" who "sought to embitter spirits and incite brothers against brothers." On 2 December 1832, "the libertine sect," which had lost its access to patronage, reportedly planned to assassinate Pedro II.[137] *O Caramuru* reported two incidents on that day. A handbill posted on the museum door announced that the government planned to proclaim a republic on Pedro II's birthday, and the police arrested a man carrying sonnets that included illegal content, but the justice of the peace released him.[138] On the eve of 25 March 1832, another handbill condemned the *"Aurora [Fluminense]'s* despicable editor" for his efforts to establish a dictatorship, an allusion to his support for constitutional reform.[139] Such rumors and counterrumors, provocations and counterprovocations, underscore the intense political struggle conducted in the civic ritual space. Others lamented the "retrograde . . . *moleques* who nowadays appear . . . at all public events, upsetting the order [and] insulting the peaceful free citizens."[140] Caramurus also staged demonstrations. On 7 September 1832, they honored the "patriarch of independence" and guardian of the young Pedro II, José Bonifácio, by then strongly identified with that party, which prompted much critical comment in the Moderado press.[141]

Newspaper editors also squabbled over whether the city had been properly illuminated, which served as an indication of support for the ideals expressed in the celebration and its promoters' political position. A Caramuru newspaper denied Moderados' assertions that the city had been illuminated on 7 April 1833 and claimed that scarcely one in a hundred homeowners had put out lamps or candles that night, evidence that, for many, the abdication's anniversary was "a night of gloom darker than the very darkness." By contrast, 7 September of that year saw spontaneous illuminations throughout the city, at least according to another Caramuru newspaper.[142]

The theater galas were likewise important occasions for political groups to test their strength. On 7 September 1832, one newspaper reported "cheers to independence; to liberty; to the *pátria's* martyr, Dr. [Cipriano] Barata [de Almeida, the Bahian radical liberal champion]; and to Pedro II," while another complained that the justice of the peace had tolerated the reading of "anarchist and seditious verses." He reported "a tirade of bad verse . . . in praise of the [emperor's] guardian [José Bonifácio], in which vile epithets were launched against the chamber of deputies" and noted that "similar anarchical shouting normally opens the way to disastrous agitation and serious disorders."[143] The following year, calls for cheers to the patriarch of independence (José Bonifácio) and the constitution as sworn were shouted down by repeated cheers to "the patriot [Diogo Antônio] Feijó," recently appointed to the senate, and "the constitution with its legal[ly instituted] reforms." In his account of these demonstrations, Evaristo added that "some poetic compositions were also recited, all in favor of the April revolution and the existing order of things." In the face of this show of support for the Moderados, the organizers of a parade "to applaud the most excellent guardian and 3 April [the date of an abortive Caramuru rising], and to insult liberals" prudently decided not to march through the square in front of the theater. Evaristo went on to lament that Caramurus only knew how to demonstrate their "patriotic joy [by] promoting disorder and unrest in the country, trying to discredit the government, sowing discord among citizens, and conspiring against the existing regime."[144] Caramurus, however, dismissed the cheers to Feijó as nothing more than the shouts of a half-dozen bedraggled "scoundrels" who had been paid to do so.[145]

Amid these tensions, not surprisingly, there are indications from both sides of the political spectrum that civic rituals ran less smoothly than in previous years. The Caramuru *O Catão* lamented that cabinet ministers had failed to don formal dress (or dress uniforms) for the levee on 7 September 1833. Such disrespect was indicative of Brazil's march toward "complete social disorder."[146] On 2 December 1832, all but one cabinet minister wore clothes more suitable for a country festival. The editor of *O Exaltado*, Padre Marcelino Pinto Ribeiro, thought that they looked like "little grammar students" and wondered whether this was a new "republican" style. That day, at the National Guard parade on the Campo da Honra, a "*pardo* youth" tried to lead a cheer to the young emperor but inadvertently hailed Pedro I, quickly correcting himself so that his cheer amounted to "long live Pedro the first, second."[147] Seidler was likewise unimpressed at the "parades . . . processions, balls, theatrical performances, and all other sorts of celebrations, on the occasion of which the little emperor was displayed to the people like a pretty doll" (see Figure 2.1, in which Pedro II stands on a chair during his acclamation). Worse yet, "there were always many thousands of blacks and mulattoes who raised their discordant chorus of 'Long Live Pedro II!'" while "the city's distinguished people rarely turned up at these pompous functions, no doubt for fear of these bastards' clever tricks and their well-sharpened knives."[148] If the success and effectiveness of a civic ritual lay in carrying it out in a properly dignified fashion, at least from the perspective of those who organized it, then clearly these rituals fell short. The presence of so many members of the lower classes and their active participation points to the expansion of politics during these years. It also indicates that political groups were willing to use lower-class thugs to intimidate their rivals.

Debates about the great political questions of the day dominated the press discussion of civic rituals. On 25 March, the most important issue was the decentralizing constitutional reforms eventually embodied in the 1834 Additional Act. In 1833, for example, after the Sociedade Defensora's Te Deum, Caramuru opponents allegedly cheered the "constitution as it was [sworn]," for which the justice of the peace, "fanatical about the reforms," arrested two of them.[149] Celebrations of the abdication raised key political issues. For Moderados like Francisco de Sales Torres Homem, editor of *O Independente*, 7 April was "our second political regeneration," won not through violent revolution but "through moderation, through the rule of reason and an enlightened civilization."[150] Others proclaimed that 7 April was the "true triumph of national sovereignty" by which the free people of Rio de Janeiro regained their *pátria*'s liberty but lamented in 1832 that the spirit of unity manifested in 1831 had disappeared.[151] Several newspapers vigorously attacked Pedro I in 7 April 1832 editorials. He was "Brazilians' oppressive tyrant," a man who considered the constitution a "document offensive to his glory."[152] Those who refused to celebrate the abdication were nothing more than the "slaves who crawled about the palace at Pedro's feet." Such men lacked "nobility"; all that they could do was gather "in their caves to celebrate the anniversaries of their slavery." Free men, by contrast, eagerly celebrated 7 April.[153] As far as Caramuru newspapers were concerned, only Chimangos could call "glorious the source of so many disasters"; moreover, they cast "all sorts of insults and calumnies upon the august person of the Brazilian empire's magnanimous founder."[154]

For Moderados, 2 December embodied their hopes for the future. Unlike 12 October, it was no "eunuchs' feast" nor a day of "promotions for the numerous band of Brazil's enemies." Rather, the monarchy guaranteed Brazil's "free institutions" and the country's unity; republics such as those proclaimed in Pernambuco in 1817 and 1824 "produced only lamentable catastrophes." In Spanish America, two decades of republican liberty had resulted in nothing more than "anarchy and military despotism."[155] Brazil's future lay in the monarchy as embodied in Pedro II and regulated by a revised constitution to prevent despotic rule.

Independence celebrations allowed Caramurus to focus on the empire's founder. What a small group in Rio de Janeiro had done in 1831, explained one newspaper, did not mean that the "general mass of Brazil" had forgotten Pedro I's services in winning independence and granting the constitution; Brazil's liberty was thus due to him alone.[156] The Moderado government therefore perceived even modest celebrations of the first emperor as dangerous. *O Catão* complained that, on 7 September 1833, "true patriots" dared not celebrate publicly and stayed home, but domestic celebrations landed an employee of the navy department in trouble. When he returned to work on 8 September, his supervisor accused him: "You had a portrait of Pedro in your house, hung up with pink ribbons; you drank tea at night, lit a bonfire at your door as people usually do on the eve of this saint's day; therefore you are a restorationist and cannot be scribe in the navy intendancy." *O Catão* went on to point out that Pedro I's name was inextricably linked to 7 September and lamented that "despots" had used this innocent homage to the empire's founder as an excuse to insult an honorable Brazilian.[157] Evaristo retorted that *O Catão*, the Sociedade Conservador (Conservative Society) and the Sociedade Militar (Military Society) were sending "filial invitations to the hero to come and subjugate rebellious Brazilians at the head of foreign troops."[158] Until news of Pedro I's death reached Brazil in late 1834, fear of a restoration ran high in liberal circles, and in May 1834, the chamber of deputies voted overwhelmingly to sentence the former emperor to death should he set foot in Brazil (the senate, however, rejected the measure).[159]

Pedro I's image was, in fact, the flash point for the Caramurus' defeat in December 1833. News had just arrived of Antônio Carlos Ribeiro de Andrada Machado e Silva's secret mission to invite Pedro I to return (an offer that the ex-emperor declined). The Sociedade Militar—a Caramuru association—celebrated Pedro II's birthday by illuminating its building on São Francisco Square. The society opened its doors to the public and placed two band shells in the square to amuse the populace. Among its decorations was an allegorical transparent picture that included a shield with "Pedro II" written on it, a book labeled the constitution, and two Brazilian flags. Six army officers, dressed in uniforms of the different services, flanked the shield and the constitution, with the two nearest ones supporting the charter. From a distance, the officer dressed in the general staff uniform apparently resembled Pedro I.[160] Meanwhile, at the theater gala, according to the Kingdom of Two Sicilies' consul-general, an uproar took place, notwithstanding the emperor's presence. Evaristo da Veiga dismissed the significance of the cheers to José Bonifácio, for they were overwhelmed by cheers to Feijó. For *O Verdadeiro Caramuru*, these Moderado cheers were actually "the most atrocious insults . . . [of] long live and death to whomever [their] fury dictated."[161] At about 11:00 pm, what Caramurus described as "groups of Moderados, composed of professional troublemakers, paid assassins, anarchists and police soldiers disguised as civilians," left the theater and headed for the nearby São Francisco square where they stoned the Sociedade Militar building.[162] On receiving word of this violence, the justice of the peace (who had earlier judged the portrait inoffensive) hastened to the scene, where he found 300 people shouting "long live Pedro II, the constitution with its reforms, the glorious day of 7 April, the permanent regency, and the current government; and down with the slaves of the Duke of Bragança [the title that Pedro I took after his abdication] and the Sociedade Militar." He convinced members of the Sociedade to remove the offending picture, in the course of which it fell to the ground. On the crowd's insistence, he took the panel to his home to prepare a formal report on its content.[163] Three days later, the regime acceded to demands that the Sociedade Militar be closed, allowing crowds to sack the building and to destroy two presses that published Caramuru newspapers, which effectively put an end to this group's organized activities.[164]

Bösche, who conflated the events of 2 and 5 December, nevertheless caught the political implications: "The Sociedade Defensora da Liberdade e Independência . . . took" the Sociedade Militar "by storm."[165] On 15 December, the cabinet completed the work of dismantling the Caramurus by removing José Bonifácio from his post as guardian of Pedro II on the grounds that he was plotting a coup from within the palace.[166] The Caramurus' defeat, along with the Exaltados' marginalization, closed the cycle of politicized days of national festivity that began on 25 March 1830. To be sure, politics was not absent from civic rituals in subsequent years, but those in power imposed more effective control over days of national festivity and the discussion of their meaning.

RITUAL ROUTINE, 1834–1837

In 1834, the rhetoric surrounding civic rituals cooled significantly, and the volume of press coverage likewise diminished. Some lamented the population's apparent disengagement from the commemoration of days of national festivity, but the lack of debate about civic ritual reflected the silencing of those who rejected the Moderados' point of view. With their Caramuru enemies cowed and parliamentary Exaltados supporting the bill that resulted in the 1834 Additional Act, the Moderado cabinet and its supporters could portray that year's celebrations as consensual. Such festivities could still attract significant crowds, as could the routine celebrations of 1835–37, but now the people were more spectators than active participants.

With a few exceptions the Sociedade Defensora continued to promote its celebrations alongside the usual official ritual. Vasconcelos's *O Sete de Abril* lamented the lack of a Te Deum on 25 March and the limited illuminations in honor of the charter; by the end of the decade the day would be completely forgotten.[167] On 7 April the Sociedade Defensora again failed to put on a Te Deum but held its largest ball to date, much to Vasconcelos's annoyance.[168] According to Evaristo, however, foreigners who had attended similar functions at European courts considered it "proper and splendid." Fully 700 men and 150 ladies, including the emperor and his sisters, demonstrated that "liberty is not rural and rustic; it is fully compatible with all the good things in social life."[169] *O Sete de Abril* noted early in the month that the society had enrolled many new members and wryly suggested that "the love of and desire to defend liberty and national independence increase as the ball approaches, [in] a direct correlation."[170]

Rain on the night of 6–7 April 1834 prevented the society from holding an outdoor public celebration, which was postponed until 12 April. According to Evaristo, fully 8,000 people gathered at the illuminated Passeio Público, where bands played patriotic anthems and a "brilliant" temporary monument had been erected at a cost of just over two contos (US$1,656). This peaceful celebration and the decorations, according to some elderly participants, compared favorably to those of Viceroy Luís de Vasconcelos e Souza (1779–90), while even Caramurus judged that, "in the time of the late Pedro, nothing was done that was so beautiful, so well-designed, and so popular."[171] Evaristo's comparison of the Sociedade Defensora's ball to European court celebrations and the outdoor gathering to colonial festivals and those of the former emperor is indicative of the rightward drift of many erstwhile Moderados who would eventually join in the conservative reaction, the Regresso, of 1837 (Evaristo himself, however, withdrew from politics in 1835 and died before the Regresso).

The date on which the Ato Adicional passed (12 August 1834) was designated a "day of national festivity" and celebrated with artillery salutes, a special session of the city council during which its president read the new law aloud, a Te Deum that Pedro and his sisters attended, and nighttime illuminations and a theater gala.[172] Despite the day's designation, this was clearly a partisan demonstration. A few weeks later, the Sociedade Defensora once again put on a 7 September Te Deum at the São Francisco church. The usual official rituals also took place, and a group of patriotic citizens, led by Antônio Ribeiro Fernandes Torbes, prepared a "brilliant illumination" for the Passeio Público. Several thousand citizens thronged the park at night, including "elegantly dressed ladies," and "sweet harmony" reigned among the "immense number of people of all classes," who watched a balloon ascend and enjoyed the "best symphonies" performed by groups of musicians stationed at both ends of the park. A Sardinian naval officer added that the park had "allegorical transparent images" and that fireworks were set off. The emperor, his sisters, the regency, and cabinet ministers attended part of the festivities and viewed them from a specially constructed stage. This was apparently Pedro II's first public appearance at an outdoor nocturnal civic festival, and his presence no doubt reflected the government's confidence that nothing untoward would mar the celebrations. Neither newspaper account of this event indicates that any opposition political manifestations took place; there are also no mentions of cheers for the monarchs nor reports of the reading of patriotic verse.[173] The success of this celebration moved Evaristo to declare that the "good people of Rio" had turned a deaf ear to the anarchists "who only find pleasure in public agitation," whether to restore a regime "that will never again return" or to establish "a dreamed-of republic that in Brazil would only be a synonym for anarchy and the provinces breaking away."[174]

Moderados' ability to control civic ritual was but short lived. News of Pedro I's death reached Rio de Janeiro in late November 1834; this removed the threat of a restoration, one of the key factors that held the Moderado cabinet together. To be sure, in the elections held on 7 April 1835, Feijó won election to the post of regent by a small plurality, but he was an increasingly controversial figure; without a strong mandate, he was personally reluctant to accept the post. Rebellions that broke out in Pará in the north and Rio Grande do Sul in the south demonstrated both the danger to the social order of a rising from below (in Pará) and the threats to the empire's political integrity when sectors of provincial elites rejected the imperial state (as in Rio Grande do Sul). Feijó's unwillingness to move decisively against the southern rebels reflected his vision of a Brazil composed of provinces (themselves legitimate *pátrias*), which had freely joined the nation of Brazil (and could therefore choose to leave it). This, in turn, alienated a growing reactionary block composed of erstwhile Caramurus and conservative Moderados, which eventually proclaimed itself the Party of Order.[175]

Civic rituals during 1835–37 settled into a routine. Torres Homem lamented the loss of the enthusiasm that had characterized earlier celebrations and, as the opposition usually did, blamed it on the government, but others welcomed the disappearance of the "parties that have so shaken the foundation of the structure of national prosperity."[176] Still, routine rituals drew large crowds. The National Guard parade—now normally held downtown on the Palace Square—could scarcely be seen on 7 September 1835 because of the populace that surrounded the citizen-soldiers.[177] One newspaper estimated that more than 3,000 people watched the 2 December 1835 parade.[178] The Guard commander led cheers to Pedro, the princesses, and the regent on 2 December 1836: "The people responded with considerable enthusiasm, principally to the first two, clearly revealing some coolness toward to the third," an indication of Feijó's increasingly difficult position.[179] The downtown palace's audience chamber regularly filled with officials, citizens, and diplomats who paid their respects to the monarch. The British squadron's commander noted that the grave young emperor—still a child—was not allowed to speak. On occasion, his elder sisters "did not behave well" or made faces during the ceremony, much to the amusement of "serious people" on 2 December 1835.[180] The evening theater galas took place without incident, although on 7 September 1837, the cheers pointedly omitted Regent Feijó.[181] Eleven days later, he resigned and turned power over to the conservative Pedro de Araújo Lima.

Newspaper rhetoric of these years stressed a small number of themes. Because Pedro I's death in September 1834 had removed the threat of a restoration, he could be presented as the empire's founder without the implication that he might return to reclaim his throne. The *Jornal do Comércio*'s report on his funeral exequies in Rio de Janeiro concluded that "regardless of his caprices, he always was the champion of independence, the empire's founder, and the grantor of the charter."[182] The constitutional monarchy that he had established was the "guarantee, and at the same time, the augury of order and true liberty's consolidation," as the chamber's orator put it at the 7 September 1837 levee.[183] Pedro I's premature death after leading Portuguese liberals to victory against his absolutist brother helped cement his constitutional image. Thus, 25 March was certainly Brazil's second greatest day, after 7 September.[184] Vasconcelos's *O Sete de Abril* warned against further tampering with the charter lest changes in the political system cause Brazil to succumb to the fate of its Spanish-American neighbors.[185] Not all welcomed this recovery of Pedro I's image. In mid-1835, Feijó lamented privately that "nowadays, Pedro I is spoken about favorably and enthusiastically, and it is already becoming ignominious to have been a Moderado and something to boast about to be, or to have been, a Caramuru."[186]

The abdication and consequently 7 April proved increasingly difficult to celebrate. *O Novo Caramuru* proclaimed in 1835 that Pedro's constitution was "more liberal," "less burdensome," and "better than all that has been legislated" since 7 April 1831—a jibe at the amendments passed in 1834—and called on "the great Pedro I" to look down with pity on Brazil.[187] The sons of 7 April had failed to march in harmony and to focus on the common good, lamented some, and for Vasconcelos, 7 April's only redeeming feature was Pedro II's accession.[188] He looked forward to 2 December 1843, when the emperor's majority would put an end to Brazil's orphan condition.[189] To commemorate 2 December 1836, his newspaper published one of the few anthems not associated with radical liberals:

> A light touch of his scepter
> Will maintain in UNITY
> The provinces inclined
> To separate from the center.
> Oh Day! Thou art all
> For the monarchists.
> Vile anarchists
> Do not like thee.

> Thy name alone can
> Expel from the South to the North
> The bloodthirsty factions
> That seek to kill the *pátria*.
>
> From the Amazon to the Plate
> All will obey
> The son of the Hero
> Who granted us Independence.
>
> . . .
>
> The empire's integrity
> [And] HOLY RELIGION
> Will be the firm bases
> Of the Brazilian nation.[190]

This anthem exemplifies as clearly as any political document the views of those who would come to power as the result of Feijó's September 1837 resignation.

When Exaltados took to the streets on 25 March 1830, they broke the mold into which Pedro I's regime had cast its civic ritual. For the next few years, political "parties" competed for control over civic rituals as politics poured out into the streets and incorporated broader and broader sectors of the capital's society. This transformation of civic ritual has largely passed unnoticed by historians; those who do note it have failed to recognize the degree to which the intense civic rituals of 1830–33 drew on the legacy of monarchical ritual of 1823–29, even as Exaltado and Moderado celebrants sought to impose their interpretations of the institutions celebrated on days of national festivity.

Much of the literature on civic rituals has implicitly or explicitly focused on their role in creating nations. To be sure, it is almost impossible to demonstrate that rituals had the effect intended by their organizers, and thus scholarship on civic ritual has tended to opt for an analysis of the message intended by those who controlled the celebrations. In Rio de Janeiro's civic rituals of 1830–37, the key theme was not loyalty to an abstract nation; rather, these celebrations were an extension of partisan politics into the streets. What was at stake was not Brazil or its "national identity" but the appropriate political organization of the state, which as far as most were concerned, ought to remain a monarchy. As might be expected, no one in the capital advocated dismembering the empire (although many favored the devolution of some power to the provinces). Brazil, after all, was their *pátria*. On some level, all of this stress on Brazil contributed to what one historian has called an "incipient national identity,"[191] but that identity was powerfully mediated through partisan politics, a partisan politics that mobilized broad segments of Rio de Janeiro society.

CHAPTER THREE

Monarchical Reaction, 1837–1841

On 18 September 1837, an embattled Diogo Antônio Feijó resigned his post as regent; Pedro de Araújo Lima, the minister of empire (interior), succeeded him as acting regent and immediately appointed a new cabinet. These events marked the beginning of what became known as the Regresso, the reaction to the liberal reforms of the previous decade that rolled back many of them in the early 1840s. The Regresso grew out of an alliance of disgruntled Moderados and former restorationists who built a firm power base among planters in Rio de Janeiro province in the mid-1830s. As Jeffrey Needell has shown, these reactionaries gradually won over a parliamentary majority whose opposition made Feijó's position untenable. This self-proclaimed "Party of Order," as it became known in the 1840s, offered a program of strengthening the state, safeguarding the supply of slaves, and securing a representative constitutional monarchy. Liberal reforms had only promoted disorder, such as the rebellions that were then wracking Rio Grande do Sul and Pará (and the one that would break out in Bahia shortly after news of the Regresso arrived there, the Sabinada), and only a stronger central state could address these threats to Brazil, Regresso advocates argued.[1]

The new government invested heavily in the presentation a monarchical view of the Brazilian nation. From 2 December 1837—the first civic ritual of the Regresso—to Pedro II's coronation on 18 July 1841, Rio de Janeiro experienced an intensification of monarchical ritual that included the restoration of traditional customs like the *beija-mão*. This was no consensual process, and many rejected the Regresso and envisaged a very different sort of monarchy from that espoused by the new government. Nevertheless, this investment in the monarchy and its ritual marked an important stage in the creation of the Brazilian empire, a regime that would, for the next five decades, be indelibly marked by not only the character and personality of its monarch, as Roderick Barman has argued, but also the image of the monarchy, created and recreated through its rituals and the debates about their meaning.[2]

This chapter begins with a detailed examination of the celebrations of 2 December 1837 and the restoration of the *beija-mão* ceremony on that day. The celebrations of other days of national festivity before the coronation likewise emphasized the monarch's importance, and this investment in monarchy culminated in the costly coronation of July 1841. While the elaborate ritual surrounding the emperor during these years can be read in quasi-anthropological terms to reveal Brazilians' understandings of monarchy, we must be careful not to read them as manifestations of the ideals or culture of a unified elite, as Lilia Moritz Schwarcz tends to do.[3] Although there was considerable respect for the monarchy and a broad consensus among the political elite about constitutional monarchy as the appropriate form of government, deep partisan divisions shaped the surge in monarchical ritual during these years. As one keen observer of (and participant in) the era's politics, the conservative journalist Justiniano José da Rocha, remarked in 1841, "Given the level of angry [rivalry] that our *pátria*'s parties have reached, it is absolutely impossible that a national festivity brings together the enthusiasm of all citizens."[4] Those in power—and we must note that there were very important ministerial changes in 1837, 1839, 1840, and 1841—certainly found the monarchy to be a useful symbol. With the exception of the most radical of radical liberals, those out of power did not reject the monarchy; rather, they lamented their lack of control over this symbol and plotted to regain it. In this sense, ritual cannot be an autonomous realm, divorced from conventional political questions. Rather, it formed one more field on which Brazilians conducted politics.

2 DECEMBER 1837

Rain threatened on Pedro's twelfth birthday, much to Admiral Graham Eden Hamond's disappointment, for the new government had gone to considerable trouble to make the day's festival more elaborate than those of previous years.[5] In the days leading up to the festival, the city council had called on residents of São Pedro and Direita Streets to decorate the fronts of their houses in honor of the monarch, who would enter the city along this traditional route. The inspector of Santana Parish added that residents should ensure that the streets in front of their houses were "perfectly clean" and sprinkled with "fragrant leaves."[6] If the weather held, the emperor would use the "very lavish coaches that have just arrived from England," the *Jornal do Comércio* promised its readers, and they were not disappointed.[7] The imperial procession left São Cristóvão Palace at 3:45 pm; at the Rocio da Cidade Nova (modern-day Praça XI), it was received by "lively acclaim from the immense concourse anxiously awaiting it." As the procession entered São Pedro Street, four children costumed as angels threw flowers on the imperial coaches, and ten children dressed in white with green ribbons released doves. Both this street and the Direita Street were "richly adorned" and the windows facing the street crowded with "beautiful ladies and gentlemen."[8] The Palace Square was packed when the emperor arrived—Hamond had never seen it so full— and both the Te Deum and the levee were better attended than they had been for some time.[9] The National Guard paraded and shouted cheers before the emperor and his sisters, who reviewed the citizen-soldiers from the palace balcony.[10] The day ended with an elaborate theater gala, at which Manoel de Araújo Porto Alegre's controversial *Prólogo Dramático* (Dramatic Prologue) was performed (see Chapter Seven).

Editorials stressed that, with Pedro steadily approaching his age of majority, "the future is losing its uncertainty," as Justiniano's *O Cronista* put it.[11] But exactly what the future held in store for Brazil remained unclear. Bernardo Pereira de Vasconcelos's *O Sete de Abril*, a strong advocate of the Regresso, explained that the enthusiasm manifested on 2 December demonstrated that, "in many ways, the current administration is calming fearful spirits," while *O Parlamentar* looked forward to 2 December 1843 as the day on which the new monarch would ensure that the "constitution triumphs forever."[12] Some in the government evidently worried that an opposition political demonstration would mar the festival. The National Guard commander ordered that his men repeat "without the slightest alteration" the prescribed cheers to "the Constitution and the Ato Adicional," the emperor, and "the regent acting in the emperor's name."[13] The Guard's parade in the crowded Palace Square was the largest public gathering on days of national festivity and the one that was the most difficult to control, for the citizen-soldiers had an active—if limited—part to play in cheering the monarch.

While none of the newspapers reporting on the 2 December 1837 levee mentioned it, two cabinet ministers and many other officers and civil servants kissed the emperor's hand, a restoration of the *beija-mão* or hand-kissing ceremony that *O Cidadão* later condemned as one of "the most ridiculous and outrageous travesties!" Brazilians, this newspaper fumed, would never stand for the restoration of such "feudal" customs.[14] The *beija-mão*'s restoration derived from Regent Araújo Lima's public gesture of kissing the emperor's hand at a church festival the day before.[15] According to Justiniano, it caused a "great sensation . . . of exultation in some, of indignation in others, [and] of surprise in all."[16] The next day, many, but not all, followed the regent's example at the levee.

When parliament convened in May 1838, Teófilo Benedito Otoni questioned the ministry on whether it had replaced the "honorable custom" of the previous years with the *beija-mão* and whether it had "prostrated itself before the throne in oriental fashion," as some newspapers had claimed. If so, this proved the ministry's intention to restore the practices of "ancient despotism."[17] Leading figures of the Regresso responded. Honório Hermeto Carneiro Leão denied that there had been any ministerial intervention in the *beija-mão*'s restoration and added that it was hardly an Oriental custom. Rather, it was a worthy tradition handed down by their forefathers, restored now that the monarch was older and the security concerns of the early Regency had passed.[18] Vasconcelos, the minister of justice and of empire, asked Otoni to repeat his question, which the radical liberal did, adding that the *beija-mão* "seems to me a bit improper for free citizens." Spectators tried to shout Otoni down; when order was restored, Vasconcelos denied any ministerial involvement.[19] Although no supporter of the Regresso leadership, Antônio Carlos Ribeiro de Andrada Machado e Silva concurred with Honório that kissing "the hand of the entire nation's father" was no Oriental custom. To be sure, the monarch's "young age perhaps makes it appear that there is some sort of contradiction, but nonetheless he is the father of the entire nation."[20]

Such denials were, of course, partisan assertions, but it was true that no law or decree mandated the *beija-mão*'s restoration, a point that Vasconcelos would reiterate in 1840.[21] Still, the *beija-mão* was controversial, and even government supporters like Justiniano wondered whether the custom was appropriate.[22] Its firm reestablishment at the levee on days of national festivity apparently took a few years.[23] The published invitations for National Guard, army, and navy officers to attend levees in 1838, 1839, and 1840 merely referred to paying respects (*cumprimentar*) or congratulating (*felicitar*) the emperor. In 1841 and for most of 1842, these invitations occasionally mentioned that officers would have the "honor of kissing His Majesty's hand"; not until 2 December 1842 did all three corporations' invitations mention the *beija-mão*. From then on, reference to the custom was de rigueur in these notices.[24] Foreigners' observations of the levee likewise confirm the *beija-mão*'s gradual reestablishment. Charles Wilkes, who attended the 2 December 1838 levee, did not mention the hand kissing. Otherwise, he noted, it resembled the ceremony described by Walsh in the 1820s; travelers in 1843 and 1844 observed the *beija-mão* during levees.[25] Newspapers only rarely referred to the levee as a *beija-mão* until well into the 1840s; rather, they called it a *cortejo*.[26]

While it exemplified the Regresso's determination to strengthen the monarchy, the *beija-mão* remained controversial. Teófilo Otoni maintained his intransigent position against the custom and refused to subject himself to its protocol, while his brother, Cristiano (then a teacher at the military school) ceded to the pressure in 1839 but only after a difficult discussion with Teófilo; a third brother, Eloi, refused to kiss Pedro's hand during his medical school graduation ceremony.[27] Just how controversial the *beija-mão*'s restoration was can be inferred from a document prepared by Francisco de Lima e Silva in anticipation of Pedro's majority. The senator and former regent recommended that Pedro begin his reign with, first, the traditional monarchical prerogative of an amnesty. Second, he recommended "a decree to prohibit the *beija-mão* custom, a barbarous habit that nineteenth-century progress repudiates and which is not followed in European courts, today not even in Portugal."[28]

The celebrations of Pedro's birthday in 1837 underscored the Regresso's vision of a Brazil in which traditional authority and hierarchies would be firmly upheld, but the controversy over the *beija-mão*'s restoration indicates that not all agreed with this view. There was deep disagreement about the monarchy's meaning as a symbol, or better, very different political purposes for which that symbol could be used. However much the rhetoric of the monarchy's ritual reconstruction emphasized Brazilians' unity around the throne, it barely papered over the bitter partisan politics that led to Pedro's premature majority on 23 July 1840 and his coronation on 18 July 1841.

THE RITUAL CONSTRUCTION OF MONARCHY, 1838–1841

The Regresso's investment in Pedro's birthday continued through 1840 and culminated in the coronation. The celebrations, ever more elaborate, partially masked the intensely partisan politics of these years. The main issue was the reconstruction of the imperial state and the recentralization of power through an interpretation of the Additional Act and the creation of a centrally controlled judicial police apparatus that would marginalize the elected justices of the peace. Even as the Regresso ministry's position weakened over the course of 1838 and early 1839 (it fell in April), a consensus around its core policies emerged. The continuing difficulties in securing control over rebellions in the North and the South and the perception that social order was in danger contributed mightily to this consensus. Given that the young Pedro appeared to demonstrate a precocious maturity, proclaiming him of age prematurely became increasingly conceivable as a way to secure authority in the country. As centralization and the emperor's early majority became inevitable, politics turned into a bitter and inelegant struggle for power. The proclamation of the majority, on 23 July 1840, thus amounted to a coup—or even a "revolution," as the U.S. minister reported—by which an opportunistic alliance of opposition leaders removed Regent Araújo Lima and a ministry closely identified with the Regresso by prevailing on Pedro to take power immediately, rather than at some future date (perhaps his fifteenth birthday on 2 December), as the ministry had been planning. With the terse declaration, "*Quero já*" (I want it now), Pedro accepted the offer of an immediate majority. Leading figures of the Regresso cabinet, including Vasconcelos, opposed this until the very end.[29]

At a hastily organized theater gala on the night of 23 July, Francisco de Paula Brito recited a poem in which he called on the "beloved prince" to select a ministry of "Men who can sustain the splendor / Of thy regal throne in all Europe / Men who prize even more than their lives / Their honor, [my] lord, and thy glory."[30] The city was illuminated for several nights, while "musical bands circulated through the streets, accompanied by the people, giving numerous and repeated cheers to the majority." Apparently these demonstrations were generally peaceful, although Vasconcelos's windows were smashed and Mary Hunter described one such group on 29 July as "a mobbish procession going towards the Palace waving torches [and] firing rockets."[31]

The ministry that Pedro appointed on 24 July 1840 was far from the disinterested body of loyal servants that Paula Brito had called for. Rather, the emperor rewarded the leaders of the majority campaign, and this cabinet would become famous for overseeing the exceptionally violent "cudgel elections" late in the year as it coerced voters to secure a majority in the legislature scheduled to meet in 1842.[32] The senate's reception of a proposal by supporters of the majority in the chamber of deputies to have 23 July proclaimed a day of national festivity reveals something of this partisanship. Manoel Dias Toledo presented the bill, which the chamber approved on the same day, 24 July; the original bill referred to the day on which "Pedro II was raised to the throne." The Bahian deputy and supporter of the majority, Francisco Gê Acaiaba Montezuma, successfully amended it to have it read "acclaimed of age," and a proposal to have 7 April deleted from the roster of days of national festivity failed, even though one deputy considered 23 July redundant, for Pedro's acclamation had happened on 7 April 1831. A few wondered whether the country was getting too many holidays.[33]

In the senate, the opposition, led by Vasconcelos, sought to amend the chamber's bill to describe 23 July as the day on which Pedro "began to exercise his authority." Vasconcelos argued that to describe the day as an acclamation was a bad precedent, for it implied approval of the principle that existing laws (in this case, the constitutional provisions regarding the emperor's coming of age) could be overturned by an acclamation. In so doing, he pointed out the uncomfortable fact that the hasty proclamation of Pedro's majority had, in fact, violated the constitution's terms. For three days, senators bickered about arcane constitutional points and argued about each other's roles in supporting or opposing previous governments and the campaign for the majority.

Vasconcelos's amendment ultimately failed, the bill passed, and 23 July joined the existing days of national festivity.[34]

Regardless of the political nature of the coup that led to Pedro's majority, his premature assumption of personal power flowed logically from the Regresso's emphasis on monarchy as the solution to Brazil's ills. The 2 December celebrations of 1838–40 reveal a massive investment in the monarchy's ceremonial aspects; William Hunter, the U.S. minister, discerned a "system of surrounding [the emperor] with pomp and splendour," which he judged "perhaps useful."[35] Likewise, the historian João Manoel Pereira da Silva explained the regent's efforts "to surround the young emperor with respect" as a deliberate challenge to the harmful "democratic" customs of the previous years that he had abhorred as a young Regresso partisan.[36] Pedro's birthday celebrations in 1838 differed from the already elaborate 1837 festival only in the construction of several temporary monuments, including a "magnificent arch" at the intersection of São Pedro and Direita streets, a structure that featured the imperial arms, "several inscriptions in honor of the emperor and his birthday, as well as the eighteen provinces' names." Other arches stood at Valongo Street and Capim Square; all three included space for bands to entertain the crowds. After the theater gala, Pedro and his sisters toured the city to see these monuments in what *O Despertador* described as a "truly triumphal promenade."[37]

Year after year, Brazilian and foreign observers alike insisted that the 2 December celebrations would outdo or had outdone those of the previous year.[38] In 1839, there were more temporary monuments for Pedro to visit after the theater gala; in 1840, the celebrations stretched over three nights with Pedro touring the city on the evening of the 3rd. During his entry into the city on 2nd, he counted seven arches en route. Most of these temporary monuments were apparently funded through popular subscriptions, like the one that the electors of Engenho Velho parish oversaw to put up an arch at Mataporcos.[39] Pedro liked the arch but not the "adjoining illumination" which "was good for nothing." It featured Pedro and his sisters on a rocky outcrop and his parents "blessing them from among the clouds with arms reaching out and looking like four very badly painted sticks." Most of these monuments offered music, "a principal thing," as Pedro put it, and like the Mataporcos arch, featured the emperor in some sort of allegorical context, along with verse to make their message clear. Sometimes this verse was what the studious monarch recognized as "Latin . . . well composed, a hexameter and a pentameter," but most was in Portuguese.[40] The poetry was of indifferent quality but clear enough in its message. Beneath the effigy of Pedro I that stood at the intersection of São Pedro and São Domingos streets in 1839, figures of "Concord and Peace [were] caressing the spirit of Brazil." Verses explained that the monarch, aided by the two, would bring:

> Holy laws, and valor, patriotism
> Enrich the arts and commerce
> Letters and science will rival each other.
> Thou art our hope, and our desire
> Our shelter, shelter of Brazil
> Our honor, duty, glory, and devotion.

Unfortunately, the description does not indicate how the spirit of Brazil was represented in this allegory.[41]

This outburst of enthusiasm for his persona scarcely moved Pedro, and he twice described his duties in December 1840 as an interminable "bore."[42] Few, however, publicly criticized these spectacles, for the consensus around the monarchy was too strong; indeed, Barman writes of a "general euphoria" surrounding the monarchy in 1840.[43] A family visiting the capital from Campanha, Minas Gerais, ensured that their seven-year-old son saw and heard everything from the dawn artillery salutes to the evening theater gala on 2 December 1839. The lad particularly loved the parade and envied Pedro's cocked hat.[44] A certain "Antiquário" (antiquarian) could not muster the boy's enthusiasm and observed in 1838 that it had never been the custom to celebrate monarchs' birthdays with the illumination of citizens' front windows; that custom had always been limited only to royal births, but the "Regresso gang" had extended it to birthdays: "Those hypocrites do not just want the Regresso, they want what eluded even the most servile and low toadies in the days of the king our lord!"[45] With the controversial restoration of the *beija-mão* and the heavy investment in celebrating the emperor's birthday (as opposed to the other days of national festivity whose commemoration remained perfunctory during these years), it certainly looked as if Brazil was returning to a traditional past. But it bears repeating that the rituals and symbols of this traditional past fell under the control of specific political groups. Justiniano later described the 2 December 1840 arches as the handiwork of the Andradistas (both Antônio Carlos and his brother, Martim Francisco Ribeiro de Andrada, held portfolios in the cabinet thanks to their leadership of the coup that had produced Pedro's majority).[46]

While the 2 December celebrations far exceeded those of the other days of national festivity in 1838–40 and one newspaper lamented the decline in the other days' celebration, the press continued to debate their meaning.[47] Indeed, such editorials were virtually de rigueur for Brazilian newspapers at this time. Several salient themes emerge from these editorials and reveal the broadly held values among members of the political classes, as well as some key points of difference regarding independence, the monarchy, and the constitution, the country's major political institutions.

The first day of national festivity each year, 9 January, received almost no attention at all. In the only editorial published about that date during this time, the *Gazeta dos Domingos* lamented that the day would pass almost unnoticed, notwithstanding the historical importance of Pedro I's decision to stay in Brazil.[48] Likewise, 3 May, the date on which parliament convened, scarcely received any coverage as a day of national festivity. Although the ritual of the throne speech to the joint session of the chamber of deputies and the senate took place in the capital, editorials focused on political issues and what was to be expected from the upcoming legislative session.[49]

The constitution (celebrated on 25 March) was, as progovernment newspapers repeatedly stressed, Brazil's "anchor" in stormy seas. It was the necessary complement to independence, and Pedro I's dissolution of the original constituent assembly saved Brazil from anarchy and resulted in a charter that placed Brazil safely between despotism and anarchy, securing the people's rights and the government's authority. Only "insane Brazilians" would want to replace such a constitution with the "chimerical republican-sabinian independence," a reference to the 1837–38 Sabinada Rebellion in Salvador whose leadership rejected the Regresso.[50] By this time, it was no longer possible to criticize the charter; rather, opposition newspapers chided governments for their failure to adhere to its principles.[51]

Pedro I's abdication (7 April) was an event whose consequences were, as several newspapers noted in 1838, "perceived in the most diverse of ways"; the date served as a "mighty weapon with which the parties constantly assail each other."[52] Many newspapers lamented the disorder that took place in the aftermath of 7 April but took comfort in the fact that the reaction to these troubles ultimately demonstrated Brazilians' unswerving loyalty to the constitutional monarchy.[53] Justiniano's *O Cronista* noted on 7 April 1838 that the key lesson to draw from the events of 1831 was the danger to a government "that does not hear the people's voice."[54] Anti-Regresso newspapers went much further, declaring that 7 April, "a truly national act . . . [,] restored the perpetual alliance that must link the throne and liberty." They condemned the new cabinet for seeking to undo the gains of 7 April: Brazilians wanted a "constitutional throne and liberty, without the gothic elements of discredited feudalism, [or the] traps set by tricky statesmen who thus dig their own grave, even as they seek to dig that of true constitutionalists."[55]

Editorials on 7 September developed a small number of common themes. Pedro I's Grito do Ipiranga echoed from North to South, and, as one, Brazil arose from colonial torpor, shook off its chains, and emerged as a free nation. The nation then embraced Pedro and the charter; the constitutional monarchy gave the nation its political form and secured its unity. These editorials naturally lamented subsequent divisions, such as the embrace of the "chimerical liberty of the celebrated republican regime" by "degenerate" Brazilians, and they called on their compatriots to embrace each other and form "a people of brothers" so that the country could be "great and powerful."[56] The recovery of Pedro I's posthumous reputation continued, and his portraits reappeared in public buildings; in 1837 the city council restored and rehung the painting that had been removed in 1831.[57] Some radical newspapers, like their Exaltado counterparts of a decade earlier, downplayed Pedro's role in independence. *O Filho da Sentinela da Monarquia* declared that Brazilians owed their political emancipation "to ourselves, to Brazilians"; Pedro and the Andrada brothers may have aided in this achievement, but they did not lead it.[58]

Editorials on 2 December repeated all of the themes that we have already noted in the commemoration of Pedro's birthdays. Not only had the monarchy served as the instrument of Brazil's salvation since 1831, it was the country's hope for the future, for it was the "symbol that personifies order and liberty." With some regularity, editorialists noted that the young emperor descended from illustrious kings but that, born in Brazil, he was a true American.[59] Opposition newspapers condemned the Regresso government's abuses in 1838 and looked forward to Pedro's majority when he "would free us from the inferno into which the squanderers [*devoristas*] have put us."[60] In 1839, one commented that, contrary to what had been happening, 7 September ought to be no less celebrated than 2 December. To focus solely on the monarch, this newspaper implied, was to ignore the "majestic day in which our beloved *pátria* first figured among the nations."[61] In its lengthy editorials on 2 December 1840, *A Regeneração* sought to equate Pedro II's "Quero já" (I want it now) with his father's declaration of "Fico" (I'll stay) on 9 January 1822, for both had saved the country from anarchy. However much the editor insisted that 2 December was not a "day of [political] parties," his praise of the majority clearly revealed his support for the cabinet that had resulted from the coup of 23 July 1840.[62]

The poetry of these years hailed Pedro as the instrument of Brazil's salvation; recited at theater galas and other functions, stenciled onto temporary monuments, and published in newspapers, such verse made abundantly clear the dominant rhetorical view about the young emperor's importance. One typical sonnet will suffice. J. G. S. Louzada hailed the emperor in 1839 and hoped for great things from his imminent majority:

> I adore thee, oh sacred day of Pedro!
> Of December, the second, oh desired day!
> Thy enemies firmly and bravely
> Thou defeatest with extraordinary happiness.
>
> For Brazilian hearts, thou art the day
> Of hope, of love, sacred day
> With sincere joy thou art celebrated
> With gentle harmonious canticles.

> Receive, thus, oh happy prince!
> The tribute of a people who celebrates
> Its innocent [and] generous monarch.
>   The people of Brazil, contentedly desire
> That their government be sufficiently honorable
> Jupiter I beseech, respond "so be it."[63]

Such poetry, an integral part of the rhetoric surrounding the monarchy, which included newspaper editorials, allegorical monuments, and even ritual practice itself, revealed Brazilians' hopes and fears for the future, in which the monarch would certainly play a major role. Attentive readers and listeners could readily discern the poet's political sympathies or infer them from the context in which the verse appeared.

All of this monarchical commemoration and the political struggle over the control of Pedro II's majority furthermore shaped his coronation. It is important to recognize the extent to which such civic ritual was an integral part of politics and the extent to which politics shaped Brazilians' views of civic rituals. While the members of the Brazilian ruling class shared much in their vision of society, they remained deeply divided into rival political factions that no amount of ritual could entirely paper over. Pedro II's coronation was no exception to this. Indeed, while preparations for the coronation were well underway, the cabinet that had resulted from the majority collapsed amid infighting among its leading members. The new ministry (23 March 1841), composed of men closely associated with the Regresso, oversaw the passage of the major institutional changes that centralized power in the country and also presided over the coronation.[64]

THE CORONATION, 1841

Pedro II's coronation, which finally took place on 18 July 1841, was certainly the largest civic ritual of the Brazilian empire. Relatively little has been written on it, in comparison to his father's acclamation and coronation, which were intimately connected to the politics surrounding the Brazilian empire's creation. The ceremony retained Pedro I's innovations of a consecration and a coronation, but I know of no analysis of the thinking that lay behind these ancient rituals, novel in the Luso-Brazilian world. Rather, scholars have focused on the coronation's larger social functions. Schwarcz argues that it was a "ritual [done] by the elites . . . and for the elites" but provocatively asserts that the "ritual's lavishness and the force of its divulgation led to an outburst of the popular imagination" that included a significant rereading of the monarchy.[65] Treating the coronation in isolation from politics and from the surge in monarchical ritual of the previous four years leads her to exaggerate its significance in this regard, and she cannot prove that a wave of popular monarchism directly resulted from the coronation. What is clear, however, is that authorities quietly made significant efforts to exclude the popular classes from the central spaces of celebration as they organized a ritual that was undoubtedly for Brazil's elite.

With the proclamation of Pedro's majority, a first order of business was to set a date for the coronation. Pedro initially proposed 2 December 1840, his fifteenth birthday, but in August the cabinet convinced him to delay it until early May 1841, when parliament would be in session.[66] In March, there was talk of delaying the coronation until 23 May or even until June on the grounds that preparations were not proceeding rapidly enough. The British minister, William Gore Ouseley, added that such delays would conveniently give the government more leverage over parliament.[67] Considerable uncertainty reigned in early May until 18 July was announced as the definitive date.[68] This decision gave rise to "general dissatisfaction," for many had already come to Rio de Janeiro for the ceremony and now had to choose between remaining in the expensive capital or returning home and repeating the journey.[69] In June, there was talk of a further postponement to September.[70]

The coronation itself was a costly affair, and the government did not release its accounts; Ouseley estimated an expenditure of "several millions of mil-réis."[71] Much later, a republican calculated that the country had spent nearly 554 contos (553:912$002 or US$337,886), almost four times the 147 contos (US$89,644) voted by parliament (both figures fall far short of Ouseley's estimate).[72] The principal ephemeral structure, a veranda on the west side of the Palace Square, designed by Manoel de Araújo Porto Alegre (who also oversaw its construction at a lavish monthly salary of 250 mil-réis [US$152.50]), alone cost at least 61:276$169 (US$37,378), exclusive of the expenses that would be incurred to dismantle it. In the course of presenting his monthly accounts, the project's treasurer admitted that he could not estimate its final cost.[73] The city council likewise threw budgetary caution to the winds and requested authorization to spend as much as was needed for its contribution to the celebrations.[74] It was expected that diplomats would likewise spare no expense.[75] Mary Hunter, the U.S. minister's wife, noted that her husband was "much troubled" about the cost of hiring a suitable carriage, for unlike other members of the diplomatic corps, he lacked an allowance for such expenses. Worse yet, she would have to spend "between 3 and 4 hundred mil-réis" (US$183–244) on a "black velvet dress with a train," which she judged a "decidedly improper" expense.[76] In April, William Hunter complained that "the extortion already commenced by shopkeepers, tailors, livery stablemen, etc., etc. [was] shocking." He and Ouseley enviously reported the large sums that their counterparts from Portugal, Denmark, and the Holy See had received to defray their expenses.[77] Hunter eventually billed the State Department US$380.68, but he estimated that the whole affair had actually cost him US$1,000, which included "female expenses extraordinary"—the frugal Mary apparently could not avoid getting the dress—as well as a new uniform and clothing for himself that could not be charged to Washington.[78] No doubt many Brazilians were likewise forced to dig deeply into their pockets to present themselves appropriately.

Much effort also went into preparing the Palace Square for the ceremony. The city assigned more workers to the landfill project at the docks to enlarge the square to accommodate the expected crowd.[79] More important, the popular classes who normally occupied the market on the northeast corner and dock side of the square, especially the African or Afro-Brazilian food sellers (*quitandeiras*), had to be moved out of sight, as the Candelária parish inspector recommended. One anonymous wag, however, commented that it was easier to stop rivers from flowing into the sea than to prevent such people from infiltrating crowds during public festivals.[80] Apparently the police also took pains to keep slaves away from the celebrations, to judge by a later ironic commentary in Paula Brito's popular satirical magazine, *A Mulher do Simplício*. Thanks to these efforts, ". . . before the monarch / Large numbers of slaves / Did not go shouting cheers / In the city streets."[81] In his later account of the coronation, folklorist Alexandre José de Mello Moraes Filho reported the presence of slaves among those watching the ceremony.[82]

One G. Neuville repeatedly requested authorization to construct bleachers on the bay side of the Palace Square to accommodate 1,200 people; for a price not to exceed two mil-réis (US$1.22) per person, families would enjoy "a more decent place" and be "spared the discomfort caused by the multitudes." Despite the great demand for such accommodation, the city council denied all of Neuville's requests.[83] Those who wished to enjoy the spectacle and distance themselves from the crowds could rent a table in the Hotel do Império's *varanda*, its windowed hall that overlooked the square, but, as the anonymous wag observed, this luxury would be enjoyed only by those "who, to feast their eyes, did not worry about emptying their wallets." Perhaps because it sought a windfall profit and charged too much, the hotel still had seats available on 14 July.[84]

City streets were carefully prepared for the imperial procession into the city. On 14 July, a letter to the editor proposed wetting the roads from São Cristóvão to São Pedro Street to prevent the procession from arriving "indecently covered in dust, as has happened more than once on gala days."[85] In fact, the city council had already requisitioned the necessary pumps from the army and naval arsenals. Furthermore, parish inspectors received orders to spread mango leaves on the streets through which the emperor would pass; if there were not enough leaves available close by, they would be brought by carts from the botanical garden (slaves did the predawn labor of spreading them).[86] In May, the owners of properties along these streets received reminders to whitewash their façades, while residents of the entire city were invited to illuminate their front windows for nine nights, starting on 16 July.[87] The chief of police banned private fireworks during the emperor's procession into the city, likely to ensure that the horses were not startled.[88] A detailed traffic plan directed the flow of carriages through the streets around the Palace Square, designated places where passengers could be dropped off, and assigned distant parking areas. This amounted to government-run valet parking, as soldiers would be on hand to fetch coaches when people wanted to leave.[89]

Proposals for public entertainment during the coronation posed some difficulties for the city council. The owner of a private natural history museum wanted to construct an "attractive gallery" on the Palace Square to display his exhibits. It would be "scientific, and appropriate for entertaining the public, and in accordance with what is done on similar occasions in foreign courts. . . . The view of rare and interesting objects . . . will constitute an appropriate celebration of this great country so rich in natural products." The council approved this request, but Porto Alegre felt that the space could not be spared, so the gallery had to be erected on the Campo da Aclamação.[90] The museum proposal matched the image that the council sought to present during the coronation, but a man who proposed to erect a five- by ten-meter structure covered with pine boughs to house "Olympic and other sorts of games"—presumably acrobatics—on the Campo da Aclamação, received a warning that his structure be "elegant, well-lit," and constructed in a spot designated by the parish inspector. The Benard brothers requested a license to set up a stand for "hydraulic games," both for the Holy Spirit festival (Pentecost, which fell on 30 May in 1841) and for the coronation. Their license was approved only for the former.[91]

While authorities could readily agree on the need to present a respectable image on city streets, other issues were less easy to resolve. Francisco de Sales Torres Homem's *O Maiorista*—the title announced his political affiliation with those who had proclaimed Pedro's majority—regularly criticized the ministry for weighing everything to do with the coronation "on the scales of their petty passions." Some worthy individuals failed to receive invitations to coronation functions. The presence of José Clemente Pereira, then minister of war, in the 18 July procession (he was originally slated to carry the sword of Ipiranga, with which Pedro I had proclaimed independence in 1822) gave a prominent role to the "head of the recolonizers of 1829," in other words, the cabinet of 15 June 1828 to 4 December 1829 composed of strong supporters of Pedro I; it would have been better to give the honor to one of the

Andrada brothers.[92] The Andradas, however, were out of power, and *O Maiorista* could only rail against José Clemente, repeatedly the target of radical liberal attacks since his return to politics as one of the most effective members of the 1828–29 cabinet (back in October 1822, he had been purged by José Bonfácio de Andrada e Silva, along with Joaquim Gonçalves Ledo and other radicals). When the list of those assigned to carry the imperial insignia was finally released, the Marquis of Barbacena received the honor of carrying the Ipiranga sword and José Clemente the emperor's sword. For those familiar with the political history of the 1820s, the substitution mattered, for Barbacena had been a leading figure in the 4 December 1829 cabinet, which took a more tolerant approach to the opposition.[93]

Inevitably, the distribution of titles in Brazil's nonhereditary nobility and other honorifics led to numerous complaints. While Justiniano had called for a very limited distribution of honors, the government was more generous, and *O Maiorista* perceived the notable "exclusion of the majority's supporters." Even the progovernment Justiniano judged that excessive partisanship had guided the distribution of honors.[94] He also chided the *Andradistas* for dismantling the arches that they had raised for 2 December 1840. While in power, they had resolved to leave them standing until the coronation (with minor touch-ups, they would have been perfectly serviceable). Once out of power, however, the *Andradistas* did not want their monuments associated with a festival that others would control, so they took them down.[95] An inelegant squabble between the bishop of Rio de Janeiro (who also served as the imperial chaplain) and the archbishop of Bahia (Brazil's metropolitan) over who had the authority to administer the consecration rite was finally resolved in favor of the latter, but hard feelings lingered, as is evident from the lengthy pamphlets that both published to justify their positions.[96]

Despite these difficulties, nothing marred the magnificent spectacle that began on Friday, 16 July. Eighty-five private coaches joined the imperial household's ten in an elaborate procession into the city. Mary Hunter thought the first vehicles too "shabby" for such an august affair, but the ones closer to the imperial household were "much handsomer." The *Jornal do Comércio* subsequently published the names of their owners, and the list amounted to a veritable "who's who" of imperial society.[97] While Schwarcz suggests that this procession served to intimidate the population as well as seduce them by its magnificence,[98] the almost complete absence of military personnel from it is notable. The ceremonial palace guard of halberdiers, the army general staff, and a cavalry picket were the only manifestations of state coercive power on display (and only the latter might be expected to use force if necessary). In this instance, power rested on magnificence and spectacle, as well as respect for the monarchy and those of the elite who led the procession.

The consecration and coronation took place on Sunday, 18 July, an uncharacteristically hot winter day.[99] Daniel Kidder judged the entire ceremony "magnificent beyond the expectations of the most sanguine," a view shared by foreign diplomats.[100] It began at 11:00 am, when Pedro gave the order to begin the procession from the palace to the imperial chapel.[101] Outside, the National Guard formed up in the Palace Square, and the massive crowd that had gathered saw nothing of this procession and the imperial insignia (whose bearers' selection had been so controversial), for it followed the palace halls and the galleries that connected it to the imperial chapel (the last gallery had been constructed for the occasion).[102] Volleys from the National Guard and strains of the independence anthem marked Pedro's progress to the chapel. Those onlookers who had spent the 320 réis (US$0.20) required to purchase the guide to the celebrations (complete with a description of the imperial regalia) could at least follow the ceremony, even if they could not see it.[103] Inside the chapel, the consecration and coronation ceremonies took place before a select audience. The abbot of the Benedictine monastery preached a lengthy sermon on 1 Kings 1:39 (Zadok's anointing of Solomon) and 1 Kings 2:12 ("Then sat Solomon upon the throne of David his father; and his kingdom was established greatly."). He exhorted Pedro and his subjects to live up to their mutual obligations: "We owe thee obedience, respect, fidelity, and even our lives; but thou owest us goodness, clemency, justice, and piety." Monarchy was firmly established in scripture, stressed the abbot, notwithstanding the efforts of the "modern politicians, having recourse to a thousand hypotheses and imagining compacts, social pacts, and many other things to prove the human origin of society." Nevertheless, the benefits that would accrue to Brazilians from loyalty to their country and their sovereign, as well as their obedience to the constitution and the law, were all material ones. After a long list of them, he concluded: "Brazil, in addition to [being] mercantile and agricultural, will be a country of artisans and manufacturers, [a] manufacturing [country]."[104]

Duly consecrated and crowned, struggling under the weight of his regalia, Pedro was then presented to his people. At the top of the stairs leading up to the veranda, the standard-bearer announced: "Hear ye, hear ye! The most high, and most powerful prince, the Lord Dom Pedro II, by the Grace of God and the Unanimous Acclamation of the People, Constitutional Emperor and Permanent Protector of Brazil, is consecrated. Long live the Emperor!" The noise of the crowd was so loud that he could not repeat this declaration three times as the program specified, and Pedro ordered the National Guard to begin firing salutes. Despite the canopy's shelter, Pedro could not remain outside for more than one volley and headed for the veranda's throne room where, seated beside the missal and the constitution, he held a *beija-mão*. This

FIGURE 3.1.
Crowds viewing the coronation on the Palace Square, 18 July 1841.
Source: Louis Auguste Moreau and Abraham-Louis Buvelot, "A coroação e sagração
de D. Pedro II," Lithographed by Heaton and Rensburg, AHMI, 02-2670.
Courtesy Museu Imperial/IBRAM/MinC.

was followed by a formal banquet, and at 8:00 pm the veranda was
opened to the public; the *Jornal do Comércio* estimated that 12,000 to
15,000 people filed through the structure. The one contemporary image
of the outdoor ceremony apparently shows the moment when Pedro was
presented to the people. Artist Louis Auguste Moreau and lithographer
Abraham Louis Buvelot nicely highlighted the centrality of the National
Guard and its orderly placement in the square in a lithograph sold in
early August, but they probably reduced the size of the crowd to make
the ceremonial apparatus more visible (Figure 3.1).[105] According to the
Diário do Rio de Janeiro, Direita Street and the Palace Square "could
scarcely contain the numerous concourse of people."[106]

The veranda, whose cost we have already noted, stretched for
310 palms (sixty-three meters) along the west side of the Palace Square
(Figure 3.2). It consisted of a middle temple and two side pavilions that
housed allegorical figures representing the Amazon and the Plate, the
two rivers that rhetorically marked Brazil's geographical limits. The temple, ninety-six palms (nineteen meters) high, contained the throne room.
Magnificently decorated, its ceiling featured a painting of Pedro I giving
the crowns of Portugal and Brazil to his two children. A massive allegorical painting presented the young emperor, "exercising his constitutional
rights," while "the calamities, the crimes that rent the empire asunder

FIGURE 3.2.
The coronation veranda, July 1841.
Source: "Descrição do Edificio construido para solenidade da coroação e sagração [de]
S. M. o Imperador D. Pedro II," BN/SI, ARC.16.1.1(7). Courtesy Acervo da
Fundação Biblioteca Nacional—Brasil.

during the abnormal and anarchic state of the minority, flee in terror to the inferno from which they emerged. . . . As the vices retreat, the sciences, the arts, [and] the civic virtues take their place, and under the throne's shelter, labor for the prosperity and the glory of the emperor and of the monarchy." The two side galleries featured the names of numerous "illustrious men, the meritorious of Brazil." All were deceased, and they included Pedro Álvares Cabral (the discoverer of Brazil), Antônio Vieira (the great Jesuit missionary), Henrique Dias (the black hero of the wars against the Dutch), and Catarina Paraguaçu (the semilegendary Indian woman who aided the first Portuguese settlers in Bahia). The last name was Cláudio Manoel da Costa, the poet involved in the 1789 Minas Gerais conspiracy against colonial rule, the Inconfidência Mineira. The structure's design, and presumably also the allegories' content, was the handiwork of Porto Alegre and his students at the fine arts academy. The author of the veranda's published description praised its beauty and workmanship, lamenting that it was but a temporary structure.[107] As it was going up, the anonymous wag judged it to be a perfect symbol for the age, a time of "political constructions made of wood, inspired by momentary enthusiasm for immediate use, to be shortly dismantled and consumed by the fires of revolt and revolution!"[108]

The coronation celebrations continued for another week with fireworks, music, and illuminated temporary monuments throughout the city, a theater gala on July 19 and a massive ball in the downtown palace on the 24th.[109] On more than one evening, Pedro and his sisters toured the city to view the public celebrations, making it as far as Laranjeiras on the 23rd.[110] On the 20th, the *Jornal do Comércio* devoted its first page to a portrait of Pedro in full regalia and a view of the veranda, apparently the first illustrations published in a Brazilian newspaper.[111] The only incident that marred the celebration took place on the morning of the 22nd, when a massive fireworks explosion destroyed the *palacete* (little palace) that stood at the center of the Campo da Aclamação, then being used as a pyrotechnic depot. It apparently started when sunlight, refracted through a glass lamp, ignited fireworks laid to dry outside the building. Three died, including the man in charge of pyrotechnics for the celebrations; two free employees and four slaves were injured. The blast broke windows around the large square.[112]

For several days, the *Jornal do Comércio* published descriptions of the numerous allegorical monuments that had been raised throughout the city. In its first issue after the coronation, it admitted that a written description would not do them justice and urged its readers to see for themselves the "beauty that they offer to the eyes."[113] Fortunately for us, a series of lithographs of the principal ephemeral monuments has survived and allows us to glimpse something of what Brazilians saw during the celebrations.[114] As one art historian has argued, the veranda and these other ephemeral monuments were one of the few ways that artists like Porto Alegre could use their skills and talents to reshape public space, albeit only temporarily. Not only did they exalt the monarchy, but they also presented public representations of conventional artistic ideals of beauty.[115] Furthermore, they reprised the Renaissance and early-modern adoption of the Roman triumphal arch; indeed, the 1841 coronation arches would not have been out of place in seventeenth-century Lisbon or Paris or many a fifteenth- and sixteenth-century town. That their inscriptions were mostly in the vernacular Portuguese, and not Latin, however, distinguishes them from their predecessors.[116] Throughout the nineteenth-century Western world, constructing arches and other ephemeral structures was one of the ways in which cities and towns continued to welcome royalty and other distinguished visitors. While they can be interpreted as markers of liminal space—by passing through an arch, the visitor (or in this case the monarch to be crowned) is symbolically made an honored member of the community—I know of no nineteenth-century Brazilian who reflected on these cultural meanings. Rather, as one historian has put it in another contemporary context, building arches "was one of those many things that goes without saying"; arches and other ephemeral structures would continue to be built in Rio de Janeiro for major civic rituals until well after the empire's end.[117]

The "Temple of Harmony" that stood at the intersection of São Pedro and Direita Streets (Figure 3.3) consisted of a classical temple atop a triumphal arch. Statues of Hercules and Mars (symbolizing "strength and valor") flanked the arch's opening, while the temple was actually a cleverly designed band shell. The imperial arms and a statue of Victory topped the structure, whose text proclaimed: "Long live his majesty the

FIGURE 3.3.
The arch on the corner of Direita and São Pedro Streets, July 1841.

Source: "Illuminação da Rua Direita canto da de S. Pedro," in Rafael Mendes de Carvalho, "Collecção das principaes Illuminascõns nos dias da Coroassão do Sn.ʳ D. P. 2.º" BN/SI, Arm. 20.3.1. Courtesy Acervo da Fundação Biblioteca Nacional—Brasil.

FIGURE 3.4.
The arch on Direita Street, July 1841.

Source: "Illuminação da Rua Direita," in Rafael Mendes de Carvalho, "Collecção das principaes Illuminascõns nos dias da Coroassão do Sn.ʳ D. P. 2.º" BN/SI, Arm. 20.3.1. Courtesy Acervo da Fundação Biblioteca Nacional—Brasil.

emperor of Brazil."[118] Another arch, prominently placed where Direita Street joined the Palace Square, featured portraits of Pedro (wearing a laurel wreath) and his sisters (Figure 3.4). Carefully painted to resemble the finest marble, it included portraits of Pedro Álvares Cabral and Martim Afonso de Souza (the discoverers, respectively, of Brazil and of

Rio de Janeiro) inside the arch. Allegorical figures of peace and abundance supported the imperial arms, while the dragons represented the House of Bragança and the reclining figures, only one of whom is visible in Figure 3.4, symbolized the Amazon and the River Plate.[119]

Many more such monuments stood throughout the city, and the *Jornal do Comércio* carefully listed the citizens who had raised the funds to construct them and who had organized the celebrations around them (but tactfully said nothing about their partisan affiliations). All were lit at night by hundreds or thousands of candles and oil lamps, and music entertained the visitors. Some were simple, like the modest obelisk on the Largo do Machado, which did not rate a description in the *Jornal do Comércio*. Others involved more creative designs, such as the Chinese pavilion on Constitution Square or the arch at the intersection of São Pedro and Quitanda Streets, which rested on forty elephants. Corporations such as the city council, army units, the police, and the fine arts academy also put up allegorical monuments or decorated the façades of their buildings.[120]

Both the *Jornal do Comércio* and its principal competitor, *O Despertador*, paid special attention to the elaborate monument put up by the residents of Rocio da Cidade Nova, then the entrance into Rio de Janeiro's built-up area on the road from the São Cristóvão palace. It consisted of a "sumptuous structure" in gothic style, with fourteen windows and a "grand portico" in which stood an effigy of Pedro II wearing his crown and the imperial cape, surrounded by spirits offering him laurels. A twelve-stanza poem inscribed on the structure focused on the theme of Pedro ("descended from noble blood, born in America") bringing order to Brazil and driving Discord and Anarchy back to their dens. Then industry, navigation, and the arts would flourish. A second story supported the imperial arms, vases of flowers, and garlands of roses held up by spirits. Including the attached gardens and pyramids, the entire structure extended for 630 palms (128 meters).[121]

O Maiorista could not muster the enthusiasm for the monuments manifested by the other major newspapers. It grumbled that the columns surrounding the Chinese temple on Constitution Square featured too much of the Portuguese colors and not enough of the Brazilian green and yellow. Moreover, one of its principal texts began: "On this limpid day, oh Pedro, the God of Ourique / Joyfully offers thee the crown." This invocation of the 1139 victory over the Moors that led to the Portuguese kingdom's founding (the battle of Ourique) and the legend that Jesus Christ himself had intervened on behalf of Afonso Henriques (who became Portugal's first king as a result) no doubt intended to highlight Pedro's illustrious European lineage (and perhaps also claim divine right for him). As far as *O Maiorista* was concerned, the monument might just as well have served for Miguel or Maria, Pedro's uncle and sister, rulers of Portugal. It would have been better, declared the editor, to invoke the "God of Ipiranga."[122]

The poetry and anthems published for the coronation repeated the themes that we have already seen in the previous four celebrations of Pedro's birthday. His reign would bring peace and prosperity; poets exhorted the young emperor to embody the virtues necessary for a successful monarch, urged him to uphold the constitution, and pledged their lives to his service. They lauded his illustrious ancestry and called on him to complete the work of his father by protecting Brazil and upholding its institutions. One poet went a bit further than most and declared that "The heavens do not make kings, the people do" and reminded the emperor of the fate that befell bad kings, like the one who lost the battle of Waterloo; he called on Pedro to serve the cause of liberty and to secure monarchy in the Americas.[123] Francisco Manuel da Silva composed a coronation anthem, with words by João José de Souza e Silva that expressed hopes for the future: "May sweet ties of concord / Link Brazil together / Under Pedro's reign / The *pátria* will flourish" ran one of its verses.[124] For the occasion, Ovídio Saraiva de Carvalho wrote new and innocuous lyrics for Francisco Manuel's 1831 march that had become the de facto national anthem. He retained, however, the chorus of "From the *pátria*, the cry / There it rises / From the Amazon / To the Plate."[125] This, along with the many other representations of these two rivers as Brazil's natural frontiers, led Ouseley to remark that the River Plate was to Brazilians what the Rhine had been to the French under Napoleon.[126]

Schwarcz has rightly stressed that the coronation was the occasion for a widespread divulgation of Pedro's image.[127] His portrait appeared, as we have seen, on the temporary monuments in the capital and even in the *Jornal do Comércio*. Institutions like the city council updated their official portraits (by early 1841, the council's old one no longer bore any resemblance to the rapidly growing boy emperor).[128] Newly arrived lithographs, produced in Paris, were advertised as far superior to those made in Brazil and especially suitable for government offices by virtue of their large size.[129] Relatively inexpensive medallions bearing Pedro's image were coined; as late as the early twentieth century, they still circulated as small change. One of them featured Brazil as an Indian simultaneously trampling a dragon (presumably representing anarchy or despotism) and crowning Pedro.[130] Only gold coins, however, bore his image, for silver and copper currency was considered too base for his likeness; likewise, Brazil's postage stamps, first issued in 1843, did not bear Pedro's image on the grounds that it should be reproduced "only in objects that are durable or worthy of veneration," as the head of the mint put it.[131] Notwithstanding the medallion with Brazil represented as an Indian, the dominant theme in the portrayals of the new monarch

FIGURE 3.5.
Pedro II in full imperial regalia, 1841.
Source: "Dom Pedro Segundo Imperador Constitucional e Defensor
Perpetuo do Brazil, em corpo e trajes magesticas," BN/SI, 4/G5.
Courtesy Acervo da Fundação Biblioteca Nacional—Brasil.

stressed his European origins. To be sure, his imperial regalia included
the famous toucan-feather mantle, but it appears as merely a minor concession to local color in coronation portraits (Figure 3.5).

How Brazilians received Pedro's coronation is difficult to elucidate.
Throughout the far-flung empire, they celebrated it with greater or lesser
pomp as local elites sought to enhance their power by connecting themselves to the monarchy.[132] News of the repeated changes in the date set
for the ceremony apparently failed to reach some parts of Brazil on time,
and the city of Porto Alegre, in Rio Grande do Sul, celebrated the coronation on 23 May; the province of Sergipe also did so.[133] Congratulations

to Pedro from city councils and corporations throughout the country poured into the capital and filled newspaper columns. In Salvador, difficulties in preparing for the celebrations prompted the government to combine them with independence celebrations on 7 September.[134]

It is even more difficult to determine how ordinary Brazilians responded to this elaborate monarchical ritual. There is much evidence to suggest that it lived on in popular memory. In 1888, a newspaper recalled how "our forebears enthusiastically and warmly recounted to us the celebrations of his majesty's majority and his coronation."[135] Two decades later, José Vieira Fazenda wrote about an old tailor and former National Guard sergeant by the name of Polidoro, a radical liberal ("a partisan of [Teófilo] Otoni and [Joaquim] Nunes Machado," a leader of the 1848 Praieira Rebellion), who could nevertheless recount in great detail the festivities of July 1841 which he considered "the greatest and best [days] of his life."[136] Pereira da Silva later recalled the intense days of celebration when "everything seemed to be swimming in jubilation," and a young judge who managed to get leave from his post in remote Caravelas, Bahia, to attend the coronation later told his children: "I never had a better time in my life, nor attended more magnificent celebrations."[137]

Some slaves too gave thought to the ritual's significance. The manager of a plantation adjacent to the imperial Santa Cruz estate complained in May 1841 that the emperor's slaves were saying that "all the slaves would become free" on his coronation.[138] This rumor, consistent with those that circulated widely at the time of independence (slaves then believed that liberty for Brazil would lead to their freedom), was not an entirely unreasonable expectation. Pedro had freed some slaves to celebrate his birthday in 1840; at the end of July, he would free twenty slave musicians who had played or sung during the ceremonies, but the Santa Cruz laborers remained in captivity.[139] The press accounts of the coronation offer no indications of what urban slaves or other members of the lower classes may have thought; rather, they suggest that either authorities succeeded in securing the capital's streets or that newspapers simply ignored the popular festivities that may have taken place in the interest of presenting a successful and orderly ritual. This points to the difficulty in grasping the popular understandings of monarchy about which Schwarcz and others have speculated.[140]

The investment in monarchical ritual that began with the Regresso culminated in the coronation. As Kidder explained, "It was thought to be an object of first importance to surround the throne with such a degree of splendor as would forever hallow it in the eyes of the people."[141] Justiniano assessed the coronation in much the same way, hoping that it would lead to unity and the forgetting of party differences, but he had to conclude on a pessimistic note: "This hope of ours may be chimerical."[142] Kidder, who left Brazil not long after the coronation, wondered whether the spectacle would "beget a morbid fondness of scenes of extraordinary ceremonies, which would only be satisfied with their frequent repetition."[143] However much Brazilians may have enjoyed the spectacles of monarchy staged from late 1837 to mid-1841, no civic rituals would approach their scale and magnificence for many years. Just as Exaltado and Moderado enthusiasm for celebrating the constitution and independence petered out by the mid-1830s as these movements weakened, so the ritual elements of the monarchical reaction rapidly lost their prominence after the coronation.

In contrast to Clifford Geertz's formula of politics and the state in the service of ritual, in Brazil, imperial ritual served the political interests of those who controlled the state.[144] While it was still (barely) possible for Pedro I to control civic ritual and the descriptions of it during the first years of his reign, the much larger and much freer press of the 1830s and 1840s meant that political questions would continue to be debated through civic ritual press coverage. What is clear from newspapers is that, starting on 7 September 1841, the celebration of days of national festivity settled into a routine that maintained their well-established forms but failed to elicit the political passion and enthusiasm that has been the central story of this and the previous chapter.

CHAPTER FOUR

Official Festivities and Politics, 1841–1864

With Pedro II duly crowned as of July 1841, official celebrations on days of national festivity settled into a modest routine for most of the rest of the decade. To be sure, critics occasionally raised questions about the course of the Brazilian state, but this fell far short of the Exaltado challenge of the early 1830s discussed in Chapter Two. A brief surge of radical liberal activism in 1848–49 did not reverse the long-term trend toward outwardly consensual official festivities, sometimes quite elaborate, but not particularly controversial until the early 1860s. In 1848, with almost no debate, parliament cut the number of days of national festivity from seven to the three that would endure until the end of the monarchy (25 March, 7 September, and 2 December). This reduction, however, turned the remaining days of national festivity into a more coherent monarchical story about the Brazilian empire's creation and effectively ratified the practice of the previous decades, in which these three had emerged as the principal days of national festivity.

Two important exceptions to the pattern of perfunctory ritual stand out. Considerably more effort went into celebrating the important, but occasional, events that that marked the imperial family's life—the weddings of Emperor Pedro II and his sisters in 1843–44 and the baptisms of Pedro and Teresa Cristina's four children in 1845–48—and Pedro's return to the capital after a journey to the South in 1846. These were, in effect, echoes of the coronation festivities, and they presented much the same monarchical message. Late in the decade came another round of politicization of civic ritual, closely connected to the September 1848 ministerial change that brought to power a long-lived Conservative or Saquarema ministry and put an end to several years of Liberal rule. Once again, partisan rhetoric flourished around days of national festivity, but the radicals had less success in putting people in the streets to gain control of the civic ritual space than they had had in 1830, nor did their critical rhetoric overwhelm official discourse about the days of national festivity. Nevertheless, radical liberals continued their campaign for a constituent assembly, other political reforms, and the nationalization of retail commerce until the early 1850s, and this was reflected in the press coverage of days of national festivity.

The 1848 reduction in the number of days of national festivity laid the groundwork for a simpler, but clearer, official interpretation of their meaning in the 1850s. Independence, the constitution, and the monarchy together laid the country's political foundations. Each day's full significance derived from its relationship to the institutions celebrated on the other two days of national festivity. By the mid-1850s, profound criticism of the institutions commemorated on the days of national festivity was almost impossible, although there was always room for the opposition to lament the government's failings. Only in the early 1860s did fundamental criticism of the monarchy return to the political agenda; it was particularly visible at the time of the inauguration of Pedro I's equestrian statue in March 1862 (Chapter Five). Nevertheless, the empire successfully carried out two elaborate nonrecurring monarchical celebrations, the 1860 reception for Pedro after his journey to the North and the 1864 weddings of Pedro's two daughters, Isabel and Leopoldina.

National politics in the 1840s saw a series of abrupt shifts in party fortunes. In early 1842, Pedro dissolved the legislature elected in 1840 (in the so-called cudgel elections) before it could meet in May. This action effectively supported the Party of Order and prompted future Liberals in São Paulo and Minas Gerais to take up arms. The rebels were quickly defeated and gained the nickname of Luzias (after the site of their final defeat at Santa Luzia). During this time, parliament, dominated by the Party of Order, passed a series of reforms that increased state power in reaction to the destabilizing reforms of the Regency period. These included the interpretation of the Additional Act that strengthened the central government and legislation that reduced the power of elected justices of the peace and instituted a police hierarchy of appointed delegates and subdelegates that reached into every parish. In a few years, Pedro pardoned the Luzias and called some of them back to power; a succession of relatively weak Liberal cabinets held power until 1848. They presided over the negotiated settlement of Rio Grande do Sul's Farroupilha Rebellion in 1845 and also oversaw the reestablishment of order in Pará. In September 1848, Pedro called on the Saquaremas to take office, inaugurating a long-lived and highly effective ministry. Radical liberals in Pernambuco rejected this in the 1848–49 Praieira Revolt, which was quickly defeated.[1]

By 1852, the Saquarema government had resolved the major issues that faced the country, notably the British pressure that forced the ending of the transatlantic slave trade and the conflicts in the Rio de La Plata region, in which the empire emerged as a hegemonic power after helping to depose Juan Manuel de Rosas in 1852.[2] A new political phase began in 1853 with the appointment of Honório Hermeto Carneiro Leão (now the Marquis of Paraná) as president of the council of ministers in what became known as the Conciliação (Conciliation) cabinet. Pedro wanted a ministry that would move beyond partisanship and so excluded Saquaremas and most Liberals; the moderate Conservatives and apolitical imperial servants in this cabinet advocated *melhoramentos*, improvements or reforms and economic development. Pedro's advocacy of a nonpartisan cabinet weakened the legislature and strengthened his personal power.[3] The Conciliação gave way in 1857 to a series of relatively weak Conservative governments, which faced a resurgent Liberal Party, particularly successful at mobilizing middle- and even working-class voters in Brazilian cities. In the 1860 elections, the Liberals swept Rio de Janeiro under the banner of nationalism, federalism, and individual freedoms—a victory that Joaquim Nabuco later called "a true political hurricane"— although they fell far short of a majority in parliament. Pedro worked hard to exclude the more radical liberals such as Teófilo Benedito Otoni from power; as Jeffrey Needell has emphasized, he increasingly intervened in parliamentary government. In 1862, the emperor handed power to the Liga Progressista (Progressive League), an unwieldy alliance of dissident Conservatives and moderate Liberals that handily won the 1864 elections. Doctrinaire Conservatives (Saquaremas) who rejected the Progressistas were known as Puritanos (Puritans) or Vermelhos (Reds). Frequent ministerial changes between 1857 and 1868 (when Pedro returned the Conservatives to power), on average about once per year, made this a period of considerable instability, during which Pedro's political role increased significantly.[4]

During these decades, the number of newspapers grew significantly, their size and circulation expanded notably, and the variety of articles published in them increased. The most important of these new kinds of articles for our purposes was the *crônica*, a periodic (usually weekly) column about life in the city. Frequently occupying the bottom quarter or so of page one, the location of the *folhetim* (the serialized novels known in French as *feuilletons*, from which *folhetim* derives), such *crônicas* began as theater reviews but soon evolved into broader discussions of culture, mores, politics, and society.[5] Their authors were known as *cronistas*, a term that might be translated as "chronicler" or "columnist," but neither English word captures the full meaning of *cronista*, so we will continue to use the Portuguese term. They included well-known figures such as playwright Luís Carlos Martins Pena, novelist José de Alencar, José Maria da Silva Paranhos (the future Viscount of Rio Branco), and novelist Joaquim Maria Machado de Assis, but many more remain anonymous, hidden behind cryptic titles and arcane pseudonyms.[6]

While a wag once commented that *crônicas* were as useless as men's ties, yet equally de riguer for newspapers as restrictive neckwear was for well-dressed gentlemen,[7] scholars now take them much more seriously. Recent work on *crônicas* has focused on those of a later period, but the analysis applies equally to the mid-nineteenth-century *cronistas*. As Amy Chazkel has observed, *crônicas* "present both a gold mine of insights into the daily life of the past and a minefield of authorial biases, distortions and idiosyncracies."[8] Many have pointed out that *cronistas* "both gave shape to and [were] intimately part of the transformations taking place in early twentieth-century society,"[9] but this applies equally well to their forebears who, particularly in the mid-nineteenth century, lived in a period of accelerating social and economic change. Some *crônicas* were closely connected to the newspaper's editorial line, while other *cronistas* insisted on their independence. Alencar, for one, stopped writing his "Ao correr da pena" (As the pen flows) *crônica* in 1855 when the *Correio Mercantil*'s editors sought to impose direction on his commentaries.[10]

Foreigners regularly marveled at the extent of press freedom in Brazil (not to mention the large number of personal attacks that appeared—often anonymously—in the paid sections of the major dailies). Benjamin Vicuña Mackenna was surprised that Antônio Borges da Fonseca could, in 1855, legally publish a frankly republican journal in the empire's very capital.[11] Both government and opposition strove to influence the press through direct and indirect subsidies, which occasionally led to controversy, such as in 1855 when Justiniano José da Rocha broke with the Conciliação cabinet and denounced the very subsidies that he himself had received.[12] Only the *Jornal do Comércio* sought to maintain a position of neutrality in party politics, although this led the French radical expatriate, Charles Ribeyrolles, to lament that this newspaper's only program appeared to be that of filling its cash box. Under its absentee Franco-Brazilian ownership, the *Jornal*, as it was known, was in fact a successful and profitable business; in 1863, it had fully 3,000 regular subscribers throughout Brazil.[13] This press freedom, strongly supported by Pedro himself, ensured that a considerable range of views about civic ritual—and indeed the imperial regime itself—could find public expression.

A final periodical occasionally cited in the next pages, the *Folhinha Laemmert*, first published in 1839, may also have been highly influential. This annual almanac, normally produced in several slightly different versions, contained a host of useful information, as well as a chronicle of the previous year's principal events, alongside miscellaneous content like satires, charades, medical advice, maxims, and plays. One traveler judged it more valuable "for the diffusion of useful knowledge among the masses" than Laemmert's well-known *Almanaque*, the massive city directory. In 1857, fully 80,000 *Folhinhas* were sold "throughout the empire" for a mere $320 (US$0.17) each.[14] The publisher advertised sixty different versions in 1863 and claimed that the 110,000 copies (printed in twenty-five variations) made it the empire's largest publication in 1889.[15]

The variety of newspapers and other periodicals, the diversity of articles within them, and the well-established press freedom meant that the press spoke with many voices about days of national festivity and about the political questions that crystallized on these days. The amount of press coverage of days of national festivity ebbed and flowed, and the intensity with which Brazilians debated these days fluctuated in response to larger political issues and the balance of forces among the political parties. Nevertheless, the cacophonous press clearly reveals the importance of days of national festivity and, more important, that Brazilians continued to debate their political institutions on these days.

OFFICIAL FESTIVITIES, 1840S–1860S

After the coronation, the tide of monarchical ritual ebbed rapidly. It was as if the country's appetite for ritual had been sated (instead of whetted, as Kidder had worried). Over the next quarter-century or so, with a few important exceptions, the commemoration of days of national festivity settled into a routine. Newspapers increasingly recorded that these days were celebrated "in the customary way," with no further elaboration. In 1843, one claimed that the *Jornal do Comércio*, by then emerging as the capital's newspaper of record (it had just contracted to publish government decrees), saved and republished festival descriptions from one year to the next, "for there is no difference among them."[16] Another commented in 1848 on the decline in the custom of publishing "obligatory articles" that "commemorated the most notable events of our political history" in which "their causes are analyzed and their effects discussed." In 1849, an ephemeral journal lamented that ordinary people seemingly "ignored days of national festivity," and a traveler remarked that gala days were "so common here that even the natives [did] not keep the run of them."[17] While such laments and observations exaggerated the decline of Rio de Janeiro's civic rituals, they nevertheless suggest that much had changed since the previous decade. In 1847, Martins Pena wrote in one of his weekly theater columns that, "on Wednesday, 7 April, a great gala day because it is the one on which, etc., and etc., we had the same old stuff."[18] Fifteen years earlier, no day of national festivity could have been so easily dismissed.

The routine official celebrations continued year after year. On days of national festivity, Rio de Janeiro awoke to artillery salutes from forts and warships, which were repeated at noon and at dusk. The foreign men-of-war that made the Brazilian capital a regular port of call while in the South Atlantic were expected to join the Brazilian batteries and vessels. Daniel Noble Johnson, of the U.S. Navy, regularly reported firing salutes during his frequent stops in Rio de Janeiro (and other Brazilian ports) in 1841–44, although by the end of his diary—which he evidently expected to publish some day—he merely commented: "I have neglected to mention the firing of numerous salutes, on various occasions since our arrival, but the reader is, no doubt, already surfeited with such remarks, and will therefore excuse my neglect in this instance."[19] As the sound of artillery salutes reverberated through the hills surrounding Rio de Janeiro, some lamented the waste of gunpowder. In little more than three weeks in August 1857, the Austrian frigate *Novara* participated in 432 salvos and consumed "about 5250 rounds of gunpowder."[20]

On 7 September 1842, Prussian Prince Adalbert accompanied Pedro II for the entire day and provided a lengthy description of the capital's official celebrations, which could easily stand for any day of national festivity during the next quarter century or so. He watched the green-and-yellow-uniformed National Guard form up on the "somewhat desolate-looking" Campo da Aclamação. That day, Pedro laid the cornerstone for an orphanage, after which Adalbert accompanied him in the procession into the city. Building façades were decorated with "crimson silk shawls." The streets were "filled with people; at all the corners were gathered groups of black slaves, to greet the emperor; all shades of colour were here seen collected, from the negro and mulatto to the half-brown or white dandy." After the Te Deum in the imperial chapel, Pedro reviewed the troops from the downtown palace's balcony as they filed by and fired salutes (Figure 4.1). This was followed by a levee, during which "the military and civil authorities . . . advanced in different corps to kiss the emperor's hand." The official celebrations ended with a theatre gala, which Adalbert also attended (see Chapter Seven).[21]

A certain amount of planning went into staging these rituals. The police imposed one-way traffic flows in streets near the Palace Square to avoid traffic jams as coaches dropped off their passengers for the Te Deum and the levee.[22] The city council routinely issued orders to clean the streets along which the emperor would enter the city.[23] The National Guard had to be called up and supplied with blanks for its salutes, and its marching order had to be established.[24] The parades put significant numbers of men into the streets; on 2 December 1849, 3,536 men mustered for the emperor's birthday. P. J. Forde, a U.S. Marines officer and *The New York Herald*'s correspondent, estimated the 7 September and 2 December 1854 parades at 4,000 and 6,000 men, respectively.[25]

Other more important events might require changes to festival routine. When 25 March and 7 April fell during Holy Week, the celebrations were often postponed; thus, in 1841, the Te Deum and levee for

FIGURE 4.1.
A 2 December parade, ca. 1850.
Source: "Parada no Dia 2 de Dezembro, no Largo do Paço," AIHGB, Icon. M.1 Gav. 2, No. 32.
Courtesy Instituto Histórico e Geográfico Brasileiro.

Pedro's elevation to the throne were moved to 12 April, while in 1864, the official celebrations of the constitution took place on Easter Monday, 28 March. Two years later they were moved to 2 April.[26] In 1860, when Palm Sunday fell on 25 March, Pedro cancelled the parade and merely held a levee; because of the Holy Week theater closing, there was no gala, and he returned to the cooler climes of Petrópolis (his summer retreat in the hills north of Rio de Janeiro) that afternoon.[27] Elections for city councils and justices of the peace, held every four years on 7 September, required the cancellation of the National Guard parade so that the citizen-soldiers could fulfill their civic obligations. By the 1850s, cancellations of the great parade due to bad weather—rain or heat— were common and were usually presented as a magnanimous gesture on the emperor's part.[28] In the 1840s, the government had apparently not been so indulgent. On 2 December 1848 Rio de Janeiro's guardsmen slogged through "flooded" streets, and in 1843 they (and the American minister, who returned home "much exhausted") spent four hours outside in the "intense" heat. Eight years after the fact, one newspaper recalled the 2 December 1842 downpour that struck while the Guard was forming up. The rain ruined uniforms (which the guardsmen had to acquire at their own expense), sickened the citizen-soldiers, and even led to some untimely deaths.[29] The cholera epidemic that started in mid-July 1855 prompted the 7 September parade's cancellation.[30]

As on 7 September 1842, inaugurations of public works often took place on days of national festivity. On 7 September 1851, Pedro opened a new waterworks amid congratulatory rhetoric about Brazil's progress; not even London, explained one *cronista*, had as sophisticated a water system.[31] Further extensions of the water system were opened on Pedro's birthday in 1854 and 1857.[32] Gas street lights were first lit on 25 March 1854.[33] On his birthday, Pedro laid the cornerstone of the art gallery in 1854, and he opened the first national exposition in 1861, the latter not without some controversy, for the exhibits were far from ready.[34] Evidently, the organizers could not pass up the opportunity to associate the exposition with the monarch.

Pedro's birthday was also the regular occasion for promotions in the armed forces and the distribution of decorations, titles of nobility, and other symbolic rewards that were the monarch's prerogative; the list of such *despachos* regularly filled several newspaper columns on or after 2 December. Many years later, André Rebouças recalled that his commissioning as second lieutenant had come on 2 December 1856; that same day, all military personnel serving short sentences for disciplinary infractions received imperial pardons.[35] The long-anticipated rewards for services rendered during the cholera epidemic of 1855–56 were finally announced on 2 December 1858, leading to a lively press debate about the merits of the more than 400 people who had received decorations, as well as about those whose services had been overlooked.[36] For the *Jornal do Comércio*'s *cronista*, "the *despachos* to reward services during the time of cholera produced a true invasion of choler" which made it look like services of 1855 and 1856 had been done out of "interest." "To those overlooked," he recommended "patience. To those upset [*coléricos*]: less fuss."[37] As one newspaper put it, days of national festivity were "the eve of martyrdom for the cabinet," during which the *despachos* received careful critical scrutiny. In 1845 Pedro's long-serving steward lamented that the lack of *despachos* provoked "discontent. As soon as they are issued, [the recipients'] merits are compared and discontent reappears." Pedro himself also disliked the system of honors, redolent of the patronage that he sought to overcome through the Conciliação, and he once complained privately about the "disagreeable" task of reviewing the candidates.[38]

Unannounced changes to the festival routines sometimes elicited critical comment. On his birthday in 1849, Pedro refused to enter the city via São Pedro Street, reportedly because of its "shabby and damaged condition." One ephemeral newspaper commented on the "offense" felt by its residents, who had gone to the trouble and expense of preparing to salute the monarch as he passed (and pointed to the city government's failure to fulfill its obligations regarding street maintenance). This last-minute change was impolitic and demonstrated a lack of respect for the people.[39] On 7 September 1850, Pedro once again entered his capital via the "nauseating Rosário Street" whose warehouses and "greasy tripe-sellers" made it an inappropriate place for families to greet him. Not until his birthday that year did he return to the traditional route.[40] On one occasion, the small cavalry picket that accompanied the procession bore carbines, which prompted critical comment from all quarters, for the troopers normally went unarmed.[41]

At the levee, the most senior diplomat read a brief congratulatory address, as did delegations from major institutions. Usually the diplomat's speech was an innocuous bit of rhetoric. On 7 September 1848, Buenos Aires's representative, Tomás Guido, proclaimed that "Brazil's independence, won by Your Majesty's august father and by the national spirit, was greeted in both hemispheres as a triumph of reason. This independence opened up a magnificent future for the new empire." Ten years earlier, his predecessor, "dressed in a flaming red Rosa[s] coat," ensured that his address would "offend no one for it was inaudible."[42] On 25 March 1843, however, the papal nuncio caused a minor scandal among his diplomatic colleagues by speaking only of the Virgin Mary and not of the constitution (on 25 March, the Church celebrates the Archangel Gabriel's annunciation to her of Jesus Christ's birth).[43] Delegations from the city council, the Instituto Histórico e Geográfico Brasileiro (Brazilian Historical and Geographical Institute), and the Instituto Episcopal Religioso (Episcopal Religious Institute) paid their respects on 2 December 1857.[44] Every 7 September (when parliament was normally completing its session and legislators still in the capital), delegations from the senate and the chamber of deputies—drawn by lot—also attended the levee and offered short addresses. After these formalities came the *beija-mão* from which, of course, foreign diplomats were exempt.

Diplomats sometimes mustered little enthusiasm for this aspect of their duties, as is clear from an incident related by the U.S. envoy extraordinary and minister plenipotentiary, Henry A. Wise. On 8 January 1845, he received a note from the Austrian minister, his immediate senior, requesting that he deliver the address on the following day. Wise was most surprised, for this meant that the papal nuncio and the ministers from Britain, Russia, Montevideo, and Buenos Aires (all of whom outranked the Austrian) would not attend (the French minister was then absent from the city). Arriving at the palace with his address in hand, the dutiful Wise found only the Spanish minister in attendance. Gamely, he read his congratulations, despite the embarrassment of speaking for the entire diplomatic corps when only two representatives had bothered to show up. The following day, the papal nuncio visited Wise to explain "that the

Corps Diplomatic did not approve of so many fête days, and they wished to make the court feel it—he pleaded the thermometer at 90° and the trouble and heat of preparation so often in such a climate." Wise refused to join this boycott, and as the nuncio took his leave, the navy minister arrived to thank him personally for his "attendance and address on the 'Fico' day."[45] Wise soon lost his enthusiasm for attendance at court, and when he was excluded during an 1846–47 diplomatic squabble between Brazil and the United States, he wrote disparagingly of the levees "where the only reward for going and waiting for hours on a hot day in a hot uniform, is to make three bows forward and three bows backwards, then bob out of [the] Imperial presence."[46] Indications that diplomats feigned illness or otherwise sought to escape their obligation to attend court on days of national festivity and other gala days recurred over the following decades. On 25 March 1862, the newly arrived U.S. minister, James Watson Webb, who made a point of attending court, was the only diplomat to bother to come down from Petrópolis (where foreign representatives increasingly resided after midcentury). Efforts on the part of some diplomats to reduce their protocol obligations had "led to a bad state of feeling between many of them and the court," he reported.[47]

Pedro himself likely sympathized with the diplomats. On 2 December 1849, Francisco de Paula Brito saw the emperor in the palace window; the monarch's green-and-yellow velvet cape highlighted his "grave and magnificent bearing." This dyed-in-the-wool monarchist journalist and publisher wondered whether Pedro enjoyed the thousands of ceremonial days in which he had to participate.[48] He might have been surprised to learn how little enthusiasm Pedro in fact had for what Walter Bagehot called the "dignified parts" of monarchical government.[49] In his diary entry for 23 July 1842, the teenaged emperor grumbled about "the Very Slow, instead of Very Reverend" bishop's intonation of the Te Deum, lamented how much a levee galled him even if it was "a sign of gratitude from [his] beloved subjects" for whom he had to put on "a happy face," and judged the theater gala "a waste of time."[50] Of course, such an outburst might be expected from a sixteen-year-old, and Pedro, who eventually destroyed most of his diaries, soon learned to keep his feelings to himself, but he once privately confessed his boredom at Te Deums and fireworks displays. Not surprisingly, he wrote nothing about the celebrations of his birthday in 1862, the sole full year for which his diary has survived.[51]

Pedro demonstrated considerable disdain for the outward trappings of royalty, and his biographers have noted his failure to establish a true court—a social and cultural center for the Brazilian elite and a venue for informal politics.[52] Even as newspapers and parliaments became central venues for political life, courts retained their importance in nineteenth-century European monarchies, so much so that Maximilian devoted considerable effort to planning his ill-fated Mexican court.[53] Pedro's palaces failed to impress well-traveled foreigners. Many turned up their noses at the modest downtown palace and its proximity to the market; nearby piles of rubbish "afford[ed] fine fun to dogs of mangy appearance and carrion-crows," according to an English visitor, while Édouard Manet called it a "real dump."[54] The São Cristóvão palace, where the imperial family normally resided, sometimes garnered faint praise as a "pleasant country house."[55] More seriously, one foreigner judged the palaces unworthy of a monarch who ruled over a territory larger than that of Europe west of Russia and another thought them laughable: "The smallest private palace in Italy is much more sumptuous," declared Juan Bautista Alberdi.[56] Likewise, the palace at Petrópolis, where the court began spending summers in the late 1840s, looked little better than a rich merchant's house, at least in one foreigner's estimation.[57]

On occasion, Brazilians shared foreigners' concern about the monarch's style. According to Ribeyrolles (in exile because of his opposition to Napoleon III [1852–70], one of the more notoriously extravagant midcentury monarchs), some held that "a bourgeois lifestyle does not look good among princes" and that "the throne's splendor is necessary for business." These were at least in part the self-interested remarks of tailors, dressmakers, and architects (who wanted to design a new palace). Proposals to build a new palace in 1848 and in 1862 apparently went nowhere in the face of Pedro's resistance to expenditures on what he considered unnecessary luxury.[58] Pedro increasingly presented himself as a citizen-king or a bourgeois monarch, as Lilia Moritz Schwarcz has shown, roughly analogous to Louis-Philippe of France (1830–48), and he eschewed anything that smacked of Napoleon III's style.[59]

There are some indications that those who bemoaned the decline in the celebrations of days of national festivity had good reason for their laments, at least in the 1840s, but other such complaints were standard opposition tropes. In 1843, *O País* explained that "it no longer behooves the people to celebrate national days, let the police celebrate them," and in 1846 *O Mercantil* lamented that "the greatest national festivities are almost entirely ignored amid public indifference."[60] Such jeremiads, particularly in the politically tense years after the coronation, were an opposition rhetorical tactic to demonstrate the government's unpopularity. Thus, regarding 7 September 1841, Francisco de Sales Torres Homen's *O Maiorista* explained that "good Brazilians took little or no part in these celebrations of hypocrisy ordered pro forma by an administration of Brazilians by birth, and Lusitanians in spirit." In contrast to the previous year, 1841's 2 December "was celebrated coldly and without the slightest enthusiasm." There were no subscriptions to raise temporary monuments, few illuminations, and unenthusiastic responses to the cheers to the monarch at the theater.[61] These were clearly partisan assertions by supporters of the disparate alliance that had staged the coup that had resulted in Pedro's majority but had lost power in March 1841. Nevertheless, the volume of civic ritual coverage in Rio de Janeiro's newspapers diminished notably after the coronation.

The official core of commemorations, with the monarch and government officials at its center, arguably differs little from the rituals that all political leaders engage in. Those who hold power in most societies find it necessary to surround themselves with rituals that demonstrate their claim to legitimate rule. The emperor's importance underscores his centrality to the Brazilian monarchy's political order, even if he declined to develop his symbolic role to its fullest possible extent.

DEFINING DAYS OF NATIONAL FESTIVITY

Just as civic rituals settled into a routine of increasingly pro forma celebrations, so too the discussion about their meaning lost much of its fervor in the mid-1840s. The defeat of the Liberal risings in 1842 cowed the radical leadership, while the other rebellions' defeats highlighted the imperial regime's success. Over these years, it became clearer and clearer that 25 March, 7 September, and 2 December were the country's principal days of national festivity, and in 1848, with very little debate, the Liberal-dominated parliament abolished the other ones.

In the mid-1840s, newspapers placed more or less emphasis on Pedro I's actions in their assessment of 7 September but rarely questioned his role. They repeatedly proclaimed that 7 September celebrated both independence and the constitution. It was the day, explained one newspaper, on which "a magnanimous prince . . . inaugurated a [nation's] life of independence and liberty." Independence was, according to another, the "magnificent work of a truly liberal prince, aided in his heroic efforts by the patriotism and enlightened [actions] of many distinguished Brazilians."[62] Others echoed in moderate terms the old Exaltado argument that Pedro had merely followed Brazilians' lead in declaring independence; thus, in 1845, *O Mercantil* explained that Pedro had "adhered to Brazilians' ardent desires" in 1822.[63] By executive decree, the date of Pedro I's death, 24 September, was designated a day of mourning in 1842, and artillery salutes, flags at half mast, and masses regularly marked the day.[64] One foreigner thought it all a farce given that Pedro had been "compelled to abdicate." In 1849, Antônio do Coração de Maria e Almeida preached on the many virtues of the "hero of two hemispheres" who had established Brazil's independence on a liberal and constitutional basis and then resolved to drive despotism out of Portugal. Pedro I's willing abdication of two crowns demonstrated his noble disinterest.[65]

A common theme in discussions of days of national festivity's meaning was progress. In 1845, shortly after the negotiated end to the long-running Farroupilha Rebellion in Rio Grande do Sul, *O Mercantil* proclaimed on 7 September that Brazil, under its constitutional monarchy, now advanced along the "road of progress toward peaceful conquests in the arts, in civilization, and in moral and material prosperity." The inaugurations of public works exemplified this preoccupation with progress. Others might lament that Brazil had not progressed sufficiently. In 1843, *O Eco do Rio* declared that Brazil was still "very far from where she should be"; two years after its optimistic assessment of Brazil's prospects, *O Mercantil* lamented the lack of material progress and called on Brazilians to unite to raise their country to the status of the "cultured nations of Europe."[66]

Pedro's birthday was celebrated "with true enthusiasm," explained *O Mercantil* in 1844, for the day embodied "happiness, grandeur, prosperity, and progress for the country that we love with all our hearts." Pedro's education, "his benevolent soul, [and] the love that he has for the nation in which he was born, constitute the most perfect guarantee for our future prosperity," explained *O Social* in 1845.[67] Two years later, Fidelis Honório da Silva dos Santos Pereira, a poet who regularly produced laudatory verse in this decade, sang Pedro's praises:

> With thy government, opulence reigns
> Sweet peace finds a prosperous asylum.
> The law dominates, and reason has power.
> Virtue, and worthy merit
> Are rewarded with laurels.
> Gentle punishment, prompt and certain,
> Is the bitter scourge of evil crime.
> Science triumphs, and wholesome commerce.
> Through thy influence, happiness, glory
> Thy people enjoy, replacing
> The volcanoes of anarchy, and the vain plots
> Of intrigues and party passions
> Born of dust they expire in the same dust.[68]

Opposition newspapers could readily attack the government on 25 March by arguing that it had failed to respect the constitution. "How can a strangled constitution, without any power, without any authority, be celebrated?" asked *O País* in 1843. The year before, *O Constitucional* had called on Brazilians to don the *tope nacional* and to make 25 March 1842 into a new 7 April by removing "this debased ministry, traitorous and antinational, which they [the Portuguese] sustain with their gold to put an end to our liberty."[69] Both of these newspapers invoked the events of March 1831 and called for independent popular participation in civic rituals. In the context of the 1842 Liberal revolts in São Paulo and Minas Gerais and their subsequent repression, such appeals for popular involvement were clearly partisan, Exaltado manifestations, as were the laments about poorly attended celebrations that we noted in the last section.

The opening of parliament, normally on 3 May, received very little attention as a day of national festivity. Rather, newspaper editorials focused on the upcoming legislative session and on the following day analyzed the throne speech. With some regularity, foreigners described the rituals associated with the reading of the throne speech: the joint session of the chamber and the senate in the senate house on the Campo da Aclamação; the arrival of the monarch in formal imperial regalia, complete with his toucan feather robe, which Thomas Ewbank judged to be the "imitation of some ancient monarch's" dress; and the usually modest number of onlookers and the small honor guard.[70]

The two days of national festivity that celebrated Pedro II's coming to power contained political connotations that made them increasingly difficult to fit into an official discourse about civic rituals. Despite the designation of 7 April as the celebration of the day on which the crown devolved to Pedro II, foreigners marveled at the emperor's participation in a festival that commemorated his father's abdication "as if there had not been the least relationship between them." Justiniano José da Rocha wondered why such a "calamitous day" remained on the books as a festival day in 1845; it commemorated, of course, the "elevation to the throne of Brazil's guardian angel," but in 1848 the only people who took note of it were those who attended the levee, the civil servants who had the day off, and the schoolchildren who did not have to attend class.[71] The celebrations of Pedro II's majority were likewise difficult to disentangle from partisan considerations, especially in 1842 when some of those who had supported the majority had taken up in arms against the government. Others seemed to forget what the day was all about. In 1848, the last year in which 23 July was celebrated as a day of national festivity, the *Diário do Rio de Janeiro* wrongly described it as the anniversary of Pedro II's coronation (which had taken place on 18 July 1841, not a day of national festivity)![72]

Early in the 1845 legislative session, a bill to reduce the seven days of national festivity to three—25 March, 7 September, and the emperor's birthday—came to the senate floor. Because its sponsor (curiously, not mentioned in the records) was not present that day, the bill was not debated. A senator failed to have it discussed in 1846, and the bill was revived only in 1848. Francisco de Paula Souza e Melo spoke in favor, arguing that the country had too many holidays that hindered public service. Moreover, "it is appropriate that the days on which the monarch appears before the country be few, so that they can be accompanied by the solemnity that they require." The three proposed days were the right ones to celebrate, he added; 7 September was "no doubt a day of great celebration," while "this independence became real through the constitution" and "the monarch is the symbol of unity [and] of the nationality." The Saquarema-dominated senate passed the bill and sent it to the Liberal-controlled chamber of deputies, whose members approved it without recording any debate.[73]

In contrast to the impassioned parliamentary debates about days of national festivity recorded in 1826, 1831, and 1840, the elimination of most of the country's days of national festivity prompted no significant opposition. Two of Rio de Janeiro's three major dailies duly noted the decree's promulgation, but none offered any comment on it.[74] The sole criticism of the measure that I have found came from the sarcastic pen of the Bahian poet, Francisco Muniz Barreto, who regaled his fellow employees at the Salvador customs house with a "poetic apologia" dedicated to the law that had reduced the number of holidays. In catchy rhyme, he lamented the decline of traditional customs and the pressure to speed up work that came from English merchants. Soon employees would have to labor on Sundays, saints' days, and moonlit nights: "And on this, the erudite agree / For only in these evenings / Will revenue really increase / And allow those who give orders to demonstrate / The great zeal that they have."[75]

Notwithstanding the complaints of those deprived of their holidays, the law merely sanctioned what had become more or less customary practice. Neither 9 January, 7 April, 3 May, nor 23 July had rooted itself as a day of national festivity. Pedro I's decision to stay in Brazil was, by then, an increasingly remote event, an arcane historical detail that did not have the evident significance of 7 September. While the opening of parliament was certainly a major innovation in 1826, 3 May had never become an important day of national festivity. As the annual legislative session became a routine and expected event, it made less and less sense to celebrate its beginning. Both 7 April and 23 July (Pedro II's acclamation and his majority) lent themselves too easily to partisan interpretations. The 1848 law on days of national festivity thus set the days that would be celebrated throughout the country with greater or lesser enthusiasm for the next four decades.

WEDDINGS, BAPTISMS, AND ENTRIES, 1843–1848

Although the official celebration of days of national festivity had settled into a generally perfunctory routine after the coronation, echoes of the monarchical enthusiasm of 1837–41 continued in the celebrations of Pedro and his sisters' weddings to European royalty, the births and baptisms of Pedro and Teresa Cristina's children, and Pedro's entries into

Rio de Janeiro after journeys to the South and Rio de Janeiro province's interior. To be sure, none of these celebrations approached the scale of the 1841 coronation, but they presented much the same message. On the whole, they were not controversial; rather, they provided the occasion to celebrate the monarchy as the guarantee of Brazil's future, and thus they reveal the monarchy's continued strength as a symbol that all Brazilians could support (even as they disagreed about much else).

In the short space of a year (May 1843 to April 1844), Rio de Janeiro saw three imperial weddings: Princess Francisca married the Prince of Joinville (son of Louis-Philippe, king of France) on 1 May 1843; on 4 September, Pedro wed Teresa Cristina, sister of Ferdinand II of Naples; the following year, on 28 April, Princess Januária celebrated her marriage to Luigi, the Count of Áquila and Teresa Cristina's brother. Neither the politics of securing these matrimonial alliances for the Brazilian Bragança family nor Pedro's unfavorable first impression of his bride (she was not the royal beauty that he had been led to believe) need detain us here as we focus on the public celebrations.[76] Both the *Diário do Rio de Janeiro* and *O Brasil* explained the central importance of Pedro II's wedding for securing the dynasty, the principal symbol for Brazilians.[77]

These were festive months in the capital. Johnson, the U.S. naval officer who dutifully recorded artillery salutes, was on hand for the first two weddings and described the elaborate naval protocol as the French and Neapolitan squadrons competed with the Brazilian navy in salutes, decorations, maneuvers, and courtesy calls.[78] Other ships joined in, and to welcome Teresa Cristina on 3 September, U.S.S. *Columbus* alone consumed more than forty barrels of gunpowder. Much more powder went up in smoke and thunder on the day of the wedding itself—"a few hundred barrels," estimated Johnson—but on the 5th, when the Brazilians and Neapolitans began the day with still more salutes, none of the other warships joined them in this "very wasteful and fully unnecessary expenditure of powder." Midshipmen on another U.S. vessel got so accustomed to these salutes that they slept through an entire salvo even though their bunks were immediately below the gun deck. On shore, the Count of Castelnau, who spent July to September 1843 in Rio de Janeiro, slept less well amid Brazilians' "extreme . . . mania for celebrating festivals." The noise of fireworks, musicians stationed in band shells on the main streets, the shouts of crowds, "grand fireworks displays," and the incessant ringing of church bells may have demonstrated their "national zeal," but they left him suffering from "insomnia and nervous irritation."[79]

Preparations for the emperor's wedding celebrations had consumed many months; the published program specified nine nights of illuminations and other festivities after the ceremony. On 23 August, Johnson saw close to 100 workers laboring on the "splendid arched Colo[n] nade" that spanned the Rua Direita, the largest of the temporary monuments. They had, he estimated, about a week's work left, but other such monuments were already complete. Earlier that month, the city council authorized varied popular entertainment for the first days of the celebration, including music on the Campo da Aclamação and the Largo da Lapa, a regatta on Botafogo Bay and, for the third evening, "grease poles" complete with prizes for those who managed to scale them. Street cleaning and preparations to spread leaves on city streets were also on the council's agenda.[80] As during the lead-up to the coronation, tailors were hopelessly overworked, and Johnson could not "get a single article of clothing made until after the marriage." Although he should have had plenty of clothing left over from the coronation, the U.S. minister, William Hunter, was caught off guard by Teresa Cristina's unexpectedly early arrival; he had no carriage engaged, his dress coat was at a tailor shop for new buttons, and his new breeches had still not been delivered.[81]

The wedding day itself dawned "threatening rain, inauspicious for the great event," according to Mary Hunter (the U.S. minister's wife), but the occasional showers did not disrupt the festival.[82] Amid the thunder of cannon, Pedro went out to meet his bride on the Brazilian frigate that had brought her to Rio de Janeiro; together they landed at the navy yard, decorated with "a quite elegant pavilion" and "a vast amphitheater filled with women in gala dress," according to Castelnau.[83] Johnson landed soon after Pedro and saw "the grand triumphal entry," which included, he claimed with no small exaggeration, "at least one thousand coaches," including the costly imperial vehicles (according to the commander of the Neapolitan fleet, there were only about a hundred coaches). The streets that Pedro and Teresa Cristina would follow from the docks to the Campo da Aclamação and back were covered with mango leaves and building façades decorated with banners and garlands of roses.[84] The imperial party briefly stopped at the downtown palace and, at about 3:30 pm, proceeded to the imperial chapel, where Mary Hunter and other dignitaries had been waiting since 11:00 am. Johnson could hear nothing of the marriage ceremony in the crowded church, after which the newlyweds retired to the palace, followed by the dignitaries who expected that a levee would take place as announced; given that the ceremonies were far behind schedule and that "the Emperor was not quite well," it was finally announced to the assembled diplomats that there would be no levee. Both Hunter and Johnson remarked on Teresa Cristina's white dress and diamond jewelry.[85]

As the unhappy newlyweds headed for the São Cristóvão palace where there was to be a formal dinner, the city "was brilliantly illuminated," and the arches looked like "so many vast pyramids of fire." Johnson also remarked on the "splendid bands of music," including those from the foreign warships, stationed throughout the city. "Immense crowds" gathered around each of the arches, but his eye was drawn to the numerous "beautiful damsels" whom he had never seen out in the streets. For the next days, he carefully watched the festivities. On 6 September, he went ashore and saw the preparations for another procession through the city. The leaves being sprinkled on the streets caused the normally "filthy city, to emit something like an endurable flavor." That day he also received a reminder of the empire's social hierarchies. On Alfândega Street he saw "a Negro slave in the last stage of a foul disease"; passersby ignored the man's "piercing, heart rending groans"; on returning to the spot, Johnson saw that "death had put an end to his sufferings," although no one had yet bothered to remove the body.[86]

On 7 September, Pedro and Teresa Cristina "paraded through the city with great ceremony," a procession that was followed by the postponed levee, a review of troops from the palace balconies, salutes, and cheers; that evening there was a theater gala. This was, of course, the usual program for a day of national festivity, but curiosity about the new empress ensured an especially large attendance at the levee and in the streets.[87] By the 10th, the festivities were visibly on the decline; on the last day, the 13th, rain let up in the late afternoon; once again, the illuminations were "brilliant" until about 9:00 pm when a "tremendous shower" doused them all, leaving the city "dark, damp, and dirty." From the comfort of his ship, Johnson was much amused "to behold men, women, and children scampering in every direction" to seek shelter. Perhaps because it had expected more rain, the city council did not illuminate its building that night, for which it was roundly criticized.[88]

After some doubts about Pedro's virility and his acceptance of Teresa Cristina as his wife,[89] the emperor and empress produced four children over the course of 1845–48. The two sons—Afonso Pedro and Pedro Afonso—died in infancy, leaving Isabel as heir to the throne, followed by her younger sister, Leopoldina. Each birth was heralded "by rockets and artillery, and was followed by a grand fête day at court . . . and by illuminations and displays of various sorts and public rejoicings," to quote the U.S. minister's report on Afonso Pedro's birth on 23 February 1845.[90] Considerable preparation went into ensuring that news of the birth was quickly transmitted to the Brazilian and foreign warships to fire salutes.[91] The day after the births, Pedro received congratulations at the São Cristóvão palace. After Isabel's birth on 29 July 1846, the roads were "thronged with parties hastening to leave their salutations for 'her serene highness, the imperial princess'"—all for "a lady one day old!" marveled Ewbank. The levee at São Cristóvão on 19 July 1848 (after Pedro Afonso's birth) was more splendid and better attended than any since the proclamation of Pedro's majority, declared one *cronista*.[92]

The baptisms came a few weeks after the births. These were primarily closed ceremonies in the imperial chapel, to which the public was admitted only after the religious rite had been completed.[93] In the evenings, and for some nights afterward, public buildings were illuminated and decorated, while private citizens placed lights in their windows. Thus, instead of the usual nighttime darkness and quiet, after Afonso Pedro's baptism on 25 March 1845, Rio de Janeiro's streets displayed a "pleasant appearance and extraordinarily large crowds."[94] Fireworks displays entertained the crowds after Pedro Afonso's baptism.[95] For Afonso Pedro's baptism, a "gigantic structure" on the Rocio Pequeno could not be completed on time, which apparently led the government to refuse payment to Manoel de Araújo Porto Alegre, who had designed the temporary monument and, despite his ill health, had completed four enormous paintings for it.[96] Apparently these structures—a band shell that could hold 150 musicians, a reviewing stand, and "a very high column" with the names of the provinces in gilded letters—were finally finished and used on 6 May to celebrate the prince's presentation to parliament. A similarly large band shell was raised in 1848—funded by a popular subscription—for Pedro Afonso's baptism.[97]

Ida Pfeiffer described Isabel's christening on 15 November 1846 as "the most brilliant of the public festivals" that she had seen. She watched the honor guards form up around 3:00 pm and saw the elaborate procession of officials in splendid uniforms from the palace to the chapel. Pedro presented his daughter to the people from the chapel's steps; the act of baptism itself "was announced to the whole town by salvos of artillery, volleys of musketry, and the discharge of rockets." After the hour-long ceremony, the procession returned to the palace, and the chapel was opened to the public. Pfeiffer did not attend the levee, but she enjoyed the evening, when the main public buildings were "covered from top to bottom with countless lamps, which look exactly like a sea of fire."[98]

As might be expected, the rhetoric surrounding the birth and baptisms stressed that the princes and princesses secured the dynasty's future. Afonso Pedro's birth fulfilled Brazilians' "sweetest hopes for peace, unity, and stability," preached Januário da Cunha Barbosa. The new prince was the "firm guarantee of our liberty, and or our independence, so gloriously identified with the constitutional monarchy." With the pacification of Rio Grande do Sul earlier in the year, the empire stood on the verge of a new era of peace and prosperity, he added. On the occasion of Isabel's birth, Archbishop Romualdo Antônio de Seixas drew parallels between the monarch's "domestic happiness" and that of the Brazilian nation now at peace.[99] Such rhetoric appeared in the press, in the congratulations that poured into the capital from the provinces, and in the poetry distributed by those responsible for the monuments.[100]

Few Brazilians questioned these celebrations. One member of the city council suggested that, instead of celebrating Isabel's birth "with the rumble of rockets prohibited by municipal bylaws" or with "smoky illuminations promoted by calculating monarchists, which last but an instant," he and his colleagues promote a subscription to support the construction of docks to be named after the new prince or princess. The motion and its critique of festival culture apparently did not pass.[101] In 1847, Justiniano took the Liberal ministry to task for announcing that, to "better celebrate" 7 September, Leopoldina would be baptized that day. In other times, the celebration of independence would have been more than sufficient to lend luster to the baptism, but under the current regime, Brazilians needed more motivation to celebrate.[102]

Just as the festivities surrounding the imperial births and baptisms celebrated the monarchy, so did the receptions of Pedro on his return to the capital from his travels. They were, however, much less elaborate (and less controversial) than those staged for his father in 1826 and 1831. From October 1845 to April 1846, Pedro and Teresa Cristina undertook a tour of Brazil's southern provinces, politically important given the recent pacification of Rio Grande do Sul. Their absence from Rio de Janeiro, as Roderick Barman has shown, also helped secure Pedro's independence from the courtiers who had dominated his life since the 1830s. Journeys in 1847 and 1848 took the emperor through Rio de Janeiro province, the heartland of the established sugar-planter and the emerging coffee-planter oligarchies that were so important to the imperial state.[103]

Considerable effort went into Pedro and Teresa Cristina's reception back in the capital on 26 April 1846. As during previous monarchical celebrations, coaches and flowers were in "fierce demand," and Ewbank reported much discussion among ladies and gentlemen about the appropriate dress, as well as complaints about expensive and overworked tailors. "A stately and massive arch" was raised on Direita Street, capped by a "colossal" equestrian statue of the monarch.[104] On the invitation of the city council, property owners along this street, from the navy arsenal to the Palace Square, decorated and illuminated their façades. The monarchs landed at 4:00 pm; despite the light rain, the procession followed the prescribed route to the imperial chapel where a Te Deum was sung. Along the way, forty schoolchildren showered the imperial couple with flowers. The remainder of the day was filled with a *beija-mão*, a military parade, and a theater gala.[105]

This was a much more modest celebration than the one staged for Pedro I in April 1826 and, of course, a much less controversial one than the first emperor suffered through in March 1831. Nevertheless, Wise described it as "most extravagant." Even less pomp and circumstance greeted Pedro after his return from Campos on 30 April

1847—fireworks, artillery salutes, and a reception at the arsenal by civil and military authorities, as well as a "large number of citizens of all classes" who cheered his arrival. In late February 1848, when Pedro returned overland from his journey through the coffee plantation districts of Rio de Janeiro province, no ceremonies marked his return.[106]

The occasional monarchical rituals of the years 1843–48 partially contrast to the decline in the celebration of days of national festivity. They also partially contradict Pedro's disdain for pomp and circumstance; reluctantly perhaps, he subjected himself to these dignified aspects of his role. These celebrations were very much official rituals and affairs of the Corte—the capital of Rio de Janeiro—and focused squarely on the monarch and his dynasty. There was little criticism of them, for the monarchy remained a powerful symbol that virtually all respected, even as they disagreed about much else.

RITUAL AND RADICAL POLITICS, 1848–1850

The year 1848 brought a new round of radical politics to civic rituals. The key political event was the change of ministry on 29 September that brought to power the long-lived Conservative (Saquarema) administration and sparked the Praieira Rebellion in Pernambuco. These were tense years. The British minister reported worries about the French monarchy's fall (particularly because Pedro's sister, Francisca, had married into Louis-Philippe's family) and noted the commercial panic early in the year, which "set in motion all those unquiet spirits to be found in great cities." Rumors of revolts and insurrections circulated widely, and the "escort of the emperor when he opened the chambers was immensely increased" as a precautionary measure.[107] A wave of short-lived radical liberal and virulently anti-Portuguese periodicals in 1848–49 heightened tensions.

By 7 September 1848, the Liberal ministry's grip on power was tenuous at best; in the capital, it made strenuous efforts to secure victory in the elections for city councilors and justices of the peace. The cabinet was particularly eager to prevent the election of the Portuguese-born José Clemente Pereira, an erstwhile liberal during the early 1820s, viewed as "turncoat" to the radical liberal cause since 1828, and now a committed Saquarema whose participation in the coronation had been controversial back in 1841. In both the chamber of deputies and the senate, opposition parliamentarians bitterly denounced the violence that took place around the polls and the government's efforts to prevent Conservatives from voting.[108]

For our purposes, however, what is most interesting about these events (and the debates about them) is the merging of electoral contest and patriotic celebration on Rio de Janeiro's streets in ways that reprised the celebrations of the early 1830s and those of Pedro's majority in July 1840. The official civic rituals were much attenuated that day. Pedro was suffering from an attack of erysipelas, and the levee was not held in the city palace but at São Cristóvão. There was apparently no Te Deum, and in view of the municipal elections, no National Guard parade.[109] While the ministers were attending the theater gala, a Conservative newspaper reported that "the night's silence was broken by sinister shouts of 'long live' and 'death to' by a torchlit mob of rabble." Apparently the demonstration had been planned in advance, for the protesters had arranged for bands to accompany them as they paraded through downtown parishes. The following day, this turned into isolated nativist attacks on Portuguese nationals.[110] The moderate Liberal *Correio Mercantil* claimed that the crowd simply cheered "the objects of our veneration" on 7 September, condemned the "imprudent shouts," and denied that anti-Portuguese agitation was justified. A few days later, this newspaper lamented that the government had invoked a law that banned illicit gatherings in order to "disperse those who were celebrating 7 September with cheers and music," a view that ephemeral radical liberal newspapers expressed much more vigorously than the *Correio*.[111] The British minister described the 7 September demonstrators as "principally mulattoes" and saw the hand of radical liberal Luzias like Deputy Joaquim Nunes Machado behind the violence.[112]

During raucous senate and chamber sessions, Conservatives demanded explanations from the government; in both houses, the government eventually managed to stifle debate, but not before Conservatives had thoroughly aired the issues.[113] Senator José Pedro Dias de Carvalho, the minister of empire, denied that 7 September had been celebrated "with blades, fire, and blood." Rather, that night "a group gathered on Constitution Square to celebrate that day," a perfectly normal occurrence that had never been prohibited: "It is customary on such days for the people to parade with music through the streets, giving cheers to independence." To be sure, there were some "imprudent shouts," but on days of "public festivity" it was common for "one or other man from the lowest social class" to take advantage of the enthusiasm "to insult someone."[114] The Conservative Antônio Luís Dantas de Barros Leite described how, at 11:00 pm on 7 September, he heard "much shouting to the sound of music." He thought it was "some demonstration of joy for the anniversary of independence," but on opening his window he heard anti-Portuguese and anti-Saquarema shouts and saw the mob break into a shop. So much for the alleged peaceful 7 September![115] Dantas's Liberal colleague and neighbor, José Joaquim Fernandes Torres, heard nothing of what Dantas described, but earlier in the evening he had seen some citizens go by his window. They "said that there would be music that night [and] that they were gathering to accompany the band." Torres added: "As a Brazilian, I even rejoiced that on that day there were demonstrations in favor of the empire's independence."[116] For the police to have banned patriotic manifestations, which the opposition suggested that the government should have done (street parades with bands required a license), government spokesmen insisted, would have been wrong: "Who can prevent Brazilian citizens from demonstrating in one way or another in honor of such a sacred day for Brazil?" asked Urbano Sabino Pessoa de Melo, another radical liberal deputy.[117]

Although deputies and senators divided along strictly partisan lines in this debate, all implied that some sort of popular street celebration of 7 September was a normal occurrence. For radical liberals like Urbano Pessoa, such activities were welcome manifestations of patriotism, much as they had been in the early 1830s, but even for Conservatives like Dantas, late-night music and shouting on 7 September were expected. By contrast, no other sources from the 1840s indicate that such street celebrations took place on independence day. Indeed, in early 1849, *O Brado do Amazonas* lamented that citizens no longer "paraded . . . as if enchanted, bedecked with the leaves that symbolize our flag," implying that this had been the case for some time. Formerly, they had thus "circulated through the streets, giving cheers in honor of the great days" of 7 September, 25 March, and 3 May. This "criminal indifference" only served to perpetuate the despotism of the "gang of evil Luso-absolutists that, to the country's dismay, surrounds our adored emperor." This occasional periodical looked back at Pedro I's reign through rose-colored glasses, recalling a nonexistent freedom to celebrate days of national festivity that had prevailed during the late 1820s. Its editor, Inácio José Ferreira Maranhense, the so-called Bard of Bacanga, was a mediocre poet whose satires and attempts to make money from unsolicited poetry were well known in Rio de Janeiro.[118]

For the Conservatives who would come to power three weeks later, such popular manifestations were deeply worrisome; they heralded a breakdown of the social order that Saquaremas had sought to secure since the Regresso. The next days of national festivity were celebrated without incident, but a new crop of radical liberal opposition periodicals—fully forty-four appeared in 1849, according to one count—tried to undermine the government by demonstrating that civic rituals were poorly attended and only by unenthusiastic citizens.[119] *O Farricoco* declared that 2 December's celebrations were marked by the "coldness and indifference with which the National Guard, and even the regular troops, behaved at the moment of the cheers" and by poor attendance at the levee. Worse yet, the new blue and scarlet uniforms worn by the fusiliers and the police echoed the colors of the troops who had fought for Pedro I's absolutist brother, Miguel, in Portugal in the early 1830s. This journal's editor feared that Brazil would soon be reduced to the status of Portugal's Ireland.[120] On 25 March 1849, progovernment newspapers described the "numerous and enthusiastic" citizens who watched the official celebrations, despite the rain, which demonstrated the nation's confidence in the constitution, adding that the people eagerly crowded around the emperor to kiss his hand as he left the imperial chapel: "They seemed to want to climb over each other" in their eagerness "to have such a great honor."[121] The moderate Liberal *Correio Mercantil* limited itself to observing that even the most liberal constitution could not prevent the "most severe despotism" when ordinary laws and regulations were not consistent with the charter's principles.[122] *O Grito Nacional* went further on 7 September, emphatically declaring that "for INDEPENDENCE to be effective, free institutions must be maintained in practice." On Pedro's birthday, this radical liberal newspaper declared that the soldiers and guardsmen on parade demonstrated a remarkable "despondency" and lack of enthusiasm for the obligatory cheers. Saquaremas had turned 2 December into a "day of sadness" despite Brazilians' love for their monarch.[123]

Joaquim Feliciano Gomes, *O Grito Nacional*'s editor, carried on this campaign through 1850, lashing out against the "vile Portuguese influence" on 7 September, which meant that independence was but "nominal." He particularly condemned the constitution's "monstrous" fourth article, which had granted Brazilian citizenship to natives of Portugal who had remained in Brazil and did not oppose independence. Thanks to this clause, an "evil man" like José Clemente wielded excessive influence.[124] By contrast, Justiniano described the "unanimous cheers . . . to the Brazilian nation, to its constitution, to its monarch, [and] to the imperial dynasty" during the theater gala as evidence of the nation's support for the established institutions. As he made clear in his 2 December editorial, Gomes never rejected the monarchy. Rather, in what amounts to classic long-live-the-king-and-death-to-bad-government rhetoric, he lamented that people could not demonstrate their enthusiasm for the monarch "when, in his name, ministers who betray him and the nation are governing."[125]

The politicization of civic rituals in 1848–50 repeated the pattern seen in the early 1830s and in 1840. When political issues spilled onto the streets, patriotic mobilization was a powerful political tool. More important, when Brazilians were divided over the issues raised by days of national festivity—the constitution and the monarchy (both also implied in celebrations of independence)—then civic rituals became important venues for politics, whether in street celebrations or in impassioned newspaper accounts. Of course, the politicization of civic ritual in 1848–50 fell far short of the much deeper debates of the early 1830s. Despite the noisy rhetoric, Brazilians debated political questions within the framework of the nation-state as represented by the days of national festivity, a telling indication of the imperial regime's secure establishment by midcentury. And both Liberals and Conservatives loudly proclaimed their support for the emperor.

THREE DAYS OF NATIONAL FESTIVITY
AND THEIR MEANING, 1850s–1860s

In the early 1850s, the partisanship stimulated by the 1848 change of ministry declined as Brazilian politics moved toward the Conciliação. The number of partisan broadsheets diminished notably as a proportion of the total number of newspapers. Some radical liberal firebrands gave up the fight. In 1854, Joaquim Feliciano Gomes's *O Grito Nacional* turned into a staunch supporter of the Conciliação ministry, encouraged by a subsidy,[126] but Antônio Borges da Fonseca had already taken up the radical standard with *O Repúblico* (1853–55). These developments gradually narrowed the range of rhetoric about the three days of national festivity to a predominantly official interpretation, which in turn reduced the opposition to laments, not about Brazil's institutions themselves but about details of their functioning or about officials' failure to uphold constitutional precepts.

As newspapers regularly noted at this time, the three days of national festivity—25 March, 7 September, and 2 December—presented an integrated whole, much as parliamentarians had apparently intended when they had eliminated the other four days of national festivity in 1848. The constitution, independence, and the monarch were, as the *Jornal do Comércio*'s *cronista* put it in 1858, "three great elements dependent on each other, mutually supporting each other, perpetuating each other by [their] glory and by the interest of all, and resulting in Brazil's grandeur and prosperity." To continue with this bit of official history:

The Brazilian nation was formed and made glorious by independence; it was ennobled by the constitution; it was fortified and tranquilized by the throne.

Independence secured the nation.

The constitution secured liberty.

The throne founded in the constitution guarantees order.[127]

Needless to say, such an interpretation of Brazilian history and the origins of the country's institutions ignored the bitter conflicts that had taken place at the time of independence and the constituent assembly closed by Pedro I in late 1823, not to mention the first emperor's abdication, the tumultuous regency, and Pedro's controversial early majority.

Given the fate of so many contemporary constitutions, it is understandable that the regime's ideologues—and this is how we should understand many of the journalists writing in the capital's newspapers—praised the charter as "a political constitution that, in its wisdom and in its democratic principles, still exceeds many of the liberal constitutions of Europe."[128] By 1852, it was the oldest existing written constitution in the world, save that of the United States; moreover, it was "more liberal" than that proposed by the constituent assembly, explained the *Correio da Tarde*. Others pointedly recalled recent political history. Had the "demagogic party's" constitutional reforms (the Ato Adicional of 1834) not been rolled back by the counterreforms of the 1840s, instead of "liberty and representative institutions . . . we would be in the arms of a demagogic-federalist republic" like that of Argentina under Rosas (recently deposed with the assistance of Brazilian troops).[129] Praise of Brazil's liberal institutions, critical comments about neighboring Hispanic republics, and arguments that the constitution laid the groundwork for Brazil's future "prosperity" and "opulence" recurred on 25 March. As the *Jornal do Comércio* explained in 1858, "the constitution is the monarchy with liberty; it is progress with order; it is peace with glory and national honor."[130] Even José Antônio Pimenta Bueno, author of the leading study of constitutional law, slipped into rhetoric that could have been lifted straight from the press in his remarks about "the wise constitution that governs the empire; every one of its beautiful articles is a summary synthesis of the most luminous principles of public law. . . . It will always be, as it has been, our covenant ark during storms and dangers; it is and will always be the firm basis of our power."[131]

Editorials on the emperor's birthday repeatedly praised his "incontestable virtues" as a faithful husband (a sharp contrast to his father, a notorious rake); a generous patron of the poor and of the arts, culture, and industry; a pious and just ruler; and a virtuous citizen. Paula Brito's *Marmota Fluminense* concluded this list of virtues with the assertion that Pedro was "the best of all monarchs."[132] Given his centrality in the constitutional order and his place as the single untouchable symbol of Brazil, Pedro "is not just a man. . . . He is the guarantee of order; he is the *pátria's* treasure of good fortune; he is the one responsible for the country; he is the shield against which crumble in rage both demagogy's fury and the audacity of the noisy struggles of civil wars originating in deranged dissensions of passion," explained another newspaper. For the *Correio da Tarde*, he was the "supreme representative of Brazilian society's great interests." Another theme in these editorials was the monarch's importance in upholding the constitution and maintaining the far-flung empire's unity, repeatedly contrasted to Spanish America. While a united Brazil was "fearlessly and hopefully progressing, tranquil and ennobled by liberty," thanks to the emperor's virtues, explained the *Jornal do Comércio* in 1860, "those so-called republics tear themselves apart in interminable or successive civil wars."[133]

Editorials on 7 September highlighted Pedro I's role in winning independence and thereby creating the nation. He was "the magnanimous prince [who] shouted the words that founded . . . the nationality." In response to his Grito do Ipiranga, "Independence or death, our forefathers shouted enthusiastically, and the improvised patriotism created a nation that goes on advancing in civilization to fulfill its great destiny."[134] Moreover, Pedro's actions resulted in a peaceful independence—desired by all Brazilians—and ensured liberty and order, as well as unity among Brazilians. The author of a 7 September proclamation called on his fellow countrymen, "Let us be Brazilians on the day of our nationality," and the *Jornal do Comércio*'s *cronista* explained that it was "the day to remember the most beautiful achievement; [the] day on which all party divisions disappear . . . [the] day in which all are true brothers in the *pátria*."[135]

The official interpretations of days of national festivity's meaning did not go uncontested in the press. Respect for the emperor's person was still sufficiently great that newspapers rarely questioned the celebrations of his birthday, and virtually none attacked him personally. By the late 1850s and early 1860s, the most critical comments on 2 December were polite appeals to the monarch to make changes to the ministry or to rely more on youth than on the old guard.[136] In 1862, the radical liberal *A Atualidade* lamented that no significant progress had taken place during Pedro's reign: "Everything remains to be done. That which did not retrogress, or which was not made more difficult with complications or compounded with mistakes, is in the same state that it has remained since the start of the new order of things."[137]

One of the few journalists who dared to launch a frontal attack on the monarchy was Borges da Fonseca. In 1853, this stalwart of radical liberal politics returned to Rio de Janeiro after having been pardoned for his involvement in the Praieira Revolt. He resumed publishing his *O Repúblico* and engaged in bitter polemics with other journalists; authorities watched him closely but let him publish.[138] After 2 December 1854, Borges da Fonseca reviewed the other newspapers' editorials. As usual, Paula Brito's *Marmota Fluminense* placed the monarch "on God's throne." The *Jornal do Comércio* and the *Correio Mercantil* were strangely silent that day, while the *Diário do Rio de Janeiro* wrote about the mutual love between Brazil and its protective emperor. Parodying the rhetoric of monarchist editorials, he concluded: "The monarchy alone is the solid base for the ruination of a state through the corruption of its customs." As if to prove his point, the emperor and empress attended the São Pedro Theater's much-applauded production of Shakespeare's *MacBeth* that evening: "A king was poisoned by his valet, hand in hand with the queen," he remarked. "The choice [of play] is remarkable!"[139] A year earlier, Gomes's *O Grito Nacional* had seen a similar message in Pedro II's attendance at the Teatro Provisório's performance of Verdi's *Nabucco*, about "this so barbarous and inhumane king, who was condemned by God to eat grass for seven years."[140]

The constitution's celebration on 25 March increasingly became the occasion for criticism as the Conciliação broke down. With growing confidence, opposition newspapers lamented the government's failure to uphold the charter, the lack of protection for constitutional rights, and corruption. Popular indifference to the constitution's anniversary, many newspapers stressed, demonstrated Brazilians' understanding of the government's failure to live up to its ideals.[141] In 1860, the *Correio Mercantil* reprised a more substantive critique of 25 March commemorations by reprinting an article from *O Império* that argued that the constitution was not "a donation" by Pedro I. Rather, he was forced to issue the charter by resistance from Bahia and Pernambuco; thus, it "was a conquest, which we expanded with the Additional Act." Here was the reappearance of an interpretation of independence and the establishment of national institutions that downplayed Pedro I's role and represented him as the (reluctant) follower of Brazilians' popular will.[142]

In typically irrepressible Brazilian fashion, *cronistas* more commonly used humor to score political points about the constitution. When some national guardsmen fainted during the parade on 25 March 1851, wags commented that this "symbolized some of the deformities from which the constitution has been suffering" (that day Pedro cancelled the rest of the parade to spare the troops more suffering in the heat). In 1855, José de Alencar wondered whether the Teatro Lírico Fluminense's dance intermezzo, entitled *O Remorso* (Regret), was a subtle critique: 25 March ought to be a day of remorse for government officials of all ranks, for they had all perjured themselves at one time or another by failing to uphold the constitution. For the *Jornal do Comércio*'s *cronista*, the heavy clouds meant that "the sun was as hidden as the constitution at the time of elections." In 1856, two *cronistas* compared the constitution to a woman; one described her as a "Chinese virgin": "they cover her with flowers, pompous encomiums, and costly decorations, but they break her feet." The other characterized the constitution as a run-down but still captivating beauty, "enchanting as the angels" but almost impossible to find when she was most needed. And he could not resist the observation that the evening's opera about "an invasion of barbarians" (Giuseppe Verdi's *Attila*) was especially suitable for the constitution's anniversary. Even the elements seemed to be shedding tears for the constitution during the heavy rains on 25 March 1859, at least according to the *Revista Popular*'s cronista.[143] In 1864, one of the new illustrated periodicals portrayed the constitution's grave, guarded by a Roman soldier, and hoped that the charter, like Christ, would be resurrected. Others had less hope. In his 1855 satire of imperial politics, *A carteira do meu tio* (My Uncle's Notebook), Joaquim Manoel de Macedo places the constitution in a tomb under the epitaph of "Here lies one who never lived" and repeatedly refers to the charter as "the deceased one [*defunta*]."[144]

On 7 September, opposition newspapers repeated familiar radical liberal themes of government despotism and anti-Portuguese nativism. The virulent nativism prominent in civic rituals in the early 1830s and again in 1848–49 was generally subdued during this period, although Gomes regularly published anti-Portuguese diatribes on 7 September until his conversion into a supporter of the Conciliação. For the 1852 elections, he called on his fellow citizens to vote against the Portuguese-born Roberto Jorge Haddock Lobo in favor of a list of "Liberals from the pure Brazilian party."[145] The *Correio Mercantil* reminded its readers to welcome "with all gratitude" the foreigners who might wish to join in celebrating 7 September 1857: "No more rivalry," it exhorted.[146] That same year, *O Tirano* denounced the violence visited on National Guardsmen by their officers, complained that the police arrested people indiscriminately "on the three nights in celebration of liberty," and lamented the fate of "poor citizens, slaves to despotism," incarcerated in the *presiganga* (prison hulk), itself decorated in honor of Brazilian independence. Condemnations of foreign (Portuguese) control of retail commerce and the lack of a free franchise were also wrapped in 7 September patriotism.[147]

In 1855, the *Correio da Tarde* published an essay about 7 September that interpreted Brazilian history as a long struggle for liberty, which began with the "notable event" in eighteenth-century Minas Gerais (a cryptic reference to the Inconfidência Mineira of 1789) and continued through the arrival of the Portuguese monarchy to the 1817 rebellion in Pernambuco, which proved the advance of liberal ideas. Finally came the prince who identified with Brazil; his Grito do Ipiranga "resounded with the greatest of enthusiasm in every corner of the empire," and thus 7 September was "our greatest day."[148] Both the 1789 and 1817 movements would figure prominently in the critical narratives about independence presented on days of national festivity after the 1860s. A loosely organized plot involving some of the wealthiest and most powerful men in Minas Gerais, the Inconfidência Mineira was betrayed, and after a lengthy trial, José Joaquim da Silva Xavier, known by his nickname of Tiradentes (literally tooth-puller, after one of his occupations), was executed; several other men received lesser sentences. The wealthy plotters feared that they would be ruined by government efforts to collect back taxes. They talked of independence and the creation of a republic but had made few concrete plans. Economic grievances also underlay the 1817 republican revolt in Recife, a largely urban movement that mobilized important sectors of that city's lower classes in an effort to break ties with the Portuguese monarchy recently established in Rio de Janeiro. This movement was quickly defeated and its leaders severely punished in what was probably an impolitic demonstration of royal power.

Modern historians have used the trials of those involved to investigate the influx of new ideas that led some to question the colonial regime, and these movements have long been seen as precursors to the Old Regime's collapse and to Brazilian independence.[149]

In the 1850s, however, their significance was far from clearly established. The Inconfidência and the 1817 rebellion occasionally turned up as precursors to independence in the 7 September editorials of newspapers broadly supportive of the imperial regime, but they were not well-known events. John Armitage only briefly mentioned them in his history of Brazil from 1808 to 1831, translated into Portuguese in 1837.[150] The Instituto Histórico e Geográfico Brasileiro did some research on the Inconfidência in 1839–40, and its members knew of Robert Southey's assessment of the movement "as a manifestation of revolutionary principles and practices" (although his *History of Brazil* was not translated into Portuguese until 1862).[151] This work likely lay behind the *Jornal do Comércio*'s 1840 editorial:

Twice Brazilian patriotism tried to hasten this glorious era [Independence]: In response to the shout of their fellow American brothers, people from Minas Gerais prepared to shake off the yoke; and years later, Pernambucans raised their voice in the name of Independence and the reorganization of society; but their efforts were premature, and were necessarily snuffed out.

However, continued the editorialist, these movements laid the groundwork for the independence that came in 1822.[152] In 1857, the *Correio Mercantil*'s *cronista* lamented that those who had paid "on the gallows or in exile for the crime of wanting to free themselves from an oppressive government" had been forgotten.[153] Ten years later, the *Diário do Rio de Janeiro* noted the 1789 and 1817 precursors of independence but credited Pedro I with breaking "with one stroke Brazil's political chains. Then a new future, a new horizon, a new course was opened."[154] What is important about each of these invocations of 1789 and 1817 is that Pedro I's Grito do Ipiranga achieved the conspirators' goals. These movements, in other words, could be incorporated into a monarchical history of the Brazilian state's origins, although they would soon come to form the historical basis of radical liberals' rejection of the imperial regime.

By contrast, Francisco Adolfo Varnhagen, the first Brazilian historian to deal at length with these movements, condemned both in his *História geral do Brasil* (General History of Brazil, 1854–57), usually seen as the culmination of the Instituto Histórico e Geográfico Brasileiro's project of writing an official history of the empire (although not written directly under its auspices). While he entitled his chapter on the Inconfidência "First Conspiracy on Behalf of Brazil's Independence," he concluded that, had it succeeded, it would have created at best a "petty republic, embedded in the majestic empire of the Holy Cross," which would have attracted the attentions of foreign powers. Providence spared Brazil this fate.[155] As far as the 1817 rebellion was concerned, the future Viscount of Porto Seguro wished that he could have ignored it altogether. Nothing in it could serve to "uplift the [common] people"; the petty personal ambitions of its leaders would have resulted in the destruction of Brazil's "integrity," the unity of Portuguese America that the imperial regime prized so highly.[156] In his view, there was no place for these movements in the imperial nation-state's triumphal narrative.

The press discussions of days of national festivity from the 1850s to the early 1860s closely followed the course of partisan politics. The interpretation of three mutually supportive institutions—constitution, independence, and monarchy—suited the Conciliação, but even as partisan politics resumed later in the decade, there was initially little criticism of these institutions; rather, the opposition sought to turn them to its advantage. While the celebrations of these years were dominated by the official, congratulatory rhetoric, opposition journalists and the irrepressible *cronistas* maintained a healthy, if often lighthearted, critical stance toward the regime. Nevertheless, the dominant tone of civic ritual coverage during these years is one of acceptance of the basic rules of the political game. Only a few diehard radicals like Gomes and Borges da Fonseca called for profound changes; the former was bought off and the latter remained in the capital only for a short while.

MORE MONARCHICAL CELEBRATIONS,

1860 AND 1864

From October 1859 to February 1860, Pedro visited the four provinces to the north of Rio de Janeiro along Brazil's coast, a journey that Barman describes as a "high point of his reign."[157] His entry into the capital was once again celebrated with considerable pomp, much as his 1846 return from the South. In 1864 the two princesses were married in ceremonies that echoed those of Pedro's 1843 wedding. These two rounds of imperial ritual indicate the monarchy's continued strength and popularity; few discordant voices were heard, and both celebrated the imperial regime.

The program for Pedro's reception on 11 February 1860 followed that of fourteen years earlier—artillery salutes and fireworks to greet his arrival, a landing at the navy yard (Figure 4.2), a procession along streets lined by the National Guard to the imperial chapel for a Te Deum, followed by a levee in the downtown palace and three nights of illuminations.[158] The major newspapers described the large crowds that had gathered on 11 February, despite the "blazing heat," which demonstrated "the love of a free people that knows how to recognize

FIGURE 4.2.
Pedro II's landing at the Navy Yard, 11 February 1860.
Source: "Desembarque de SS. MM. II. no Rio de Janeiro," AHMI, MI-337.
Courtesy Museu Imperial/IBRAM/MinC.

the monarch's great virtues," editorialized the *Jornal do Comércio*.[159] Numerous ephemeral monuments once again stood on major streets and squares, raised by institutions such as the Chamber of Commerce, the National Guard, and the city council, as well as neighborhood associations (Santa Rita parish's was one of the best, according to the *Revista Popular*'s *cronista*, while Santana parish's residents had gone to great lengths to decorate the Rocio Pequeno). The commercial crisis appeared to have been forgotten amid the eagerness to spend money on these structures.[160] Rain in the evenings of 12 and 13 February did not dampen the festivities, which on the 11th had turned night into day.[161]

The poetry of occasion focused on the public happiness at the emperor's return and avoided any specific commentary on the imperial regime.[162] Antônio José Nunes Garcia wrote a cantata (apparently not performed), in which he hailed Pedro: "Thou hast arrived, my lord, full of so much happiness / For having extended thy beneficent right hand / To thy people, / Who anxious to see thee, still bow / And venerate with a noble pride / Thy name!"[163] At the Te Deum put on by the city council on 13 February, Friar Antônio do Coração de Maria e Almeida preached on Brazilians' need to give thanks not just for Pedro's safe return but also "for his enlightenment . . . for the magnanimity of his soul that develops and supports the sublime theories of the [monarchical-constitutional] system that we have adopted."[164] The relatively new radical liberal opposition newspaper, *A Atualidade*, criticized the rest of the press's enthusiastic coverage and claimed that its writers "saw what they would want to have happen and not what really happened." The population "remained aloof," and took no part in this inconsequential "diversion" that, along with the costly trip, had not "improved the lot of the provinces, victims of centralization, [nor] put up obstacles to the devastating torrent of corruption."[165]

In October and December 1864, respectively, Princess Isabel married Gaston d'Orléans, the Count of Eu, and Princess Leopoldina wed Auguste of Saxe-Coburg-Gotha; both grooms were grandsons of Louis-Philippe.[166] The weddings themselves followed identical programs, and both were followed by the usual street ceremonies of public rejoicing.[167] A freak hailstorm destroyed all of the flowers being grown to decorate the chapel and the palace for Isabel's wedding, which some perceived as a bad omen (it also broke all of the city's west-facing windows).[168] Machado de Assis noted that there had been some complaint that the temporary monuments failed to live up to expectations, but he considered the pavilion on the Palace Square particularly "elegant."[169] Congratulations poured in from around the country, as did affirmations of support for the monarchy, and the imperial family made the appropriate magnanimous gestures; Pedro pardoned criminals, and Isabel freed ten palace slaves.[170] *O Constitucional* declared that the weddings secured "the national institutions, which constitute the country's glory and good fortune, [and which] are so closely identified with the dynasty of the founder of independence and the empire that all events that serve to perpetuate it are for this reason another hope for the nation['s future]."[171]

James Watson Webb, the U.S. minister, lamented that, unlike his European counterparts, he had no allowance for the extra expenditures that he would incur to make a respectable presentation at the wedding ceremonies, the levees, and the balls. Isabel and Eu's wedding alone cost him £200, but he consoled himself that "the senior lady of the diplomatic corps (Mrs. Webb) fairly represented the character and dignity of our country." He looked forward to the last ball on 28 December, after which the "expenses of those proceedings will close." The price gouging that he and his fellow diplomats suffered at the hands of livery stables and hair dressers particularly galled him. When he complained, he was curtly told that "the *corps diplomatique* must certainly be willing that all classes benefit on such occasions."[172] All that he could do was submit to this argument, which offers an indication of how some sought to turn these imperial rituals to their own benefit.

In the second half of the 1850s, the Brazilian monarchy stood at the height of its political success. The regime had weathered numerous crises, and its institutions had survived far longer than those of most other newly independent American states. It had developed an ideological justification for its existence, and, through the celebrations of days of national festivity, presented this interpretation to its population. By then, the Brazilian empire was four decades old, Pedro II had two decades of personal rule under his belt, and the constitution had regulated Brazilian political life for more three decades. Celebrated on the three days of national festivity—25 March, 7 September, and 2 December—that had been reaffirmed in 1848 and in the occasional imperial weddings, baptisms, and entries, these institutions had gained a level of legitimacy that placed them outside the scope of political debate. Instead of rejecting the emperor, many erstwhile Luzias wanted the monarch to rule through them. They saw much good in the constitution even if they wanted to improve it. And the Brazilian nation, created on 7 September, was likewise here to stay. Nevertheless, in the early 1860s, cracks were appearing in this consensus, and they manifested themselves most visibly in the vigorous criticism of the equestrian statue of Pedro I, inaugurated on 30 March 1862, to which we now turn.

CHAPTER FIVE

The Equestrian Statue of Pedro I, 1862

In March 1862, the long-awaited equestrian statue of Pedro I was finally inaugurated in Rio de Janeiro. The monument embodied the interpretation of independence that saw the first emperor's actions as central to the founding of Brazil's political institutions—empire, constitution, and dynasty. While the inauguration ritual was a success, at least in the sense of being effectively carried out, the statue became the lightning rod for criticisms of the imperial regime and indirect challenges to Pedro II himself. After a long campaign that, in different guises, dated back to 1825, the inauguration was Rio de Janeiro's largest civic ritual since Pedro II's coronation; unlike the coronation, it sparked bitter polemics as a new generation of radical Liberals joined old stalwarts to challenge the political assumptions that underlay it and the imperial regime more generally. The moderate Conservative government's failure to control the rhetoric surrounding the inauguration boded ill for the monument and, in some ways, presaged the imperial regime's decline.

The equestrian statue's inauguration and the debate that it spawned are extremely well documented in the press and in the many pamphlets issued at the time. Pioneering photographers recorded it and left the first photographs of the imperial capital's civic ritual. Newspapers filled page after page with densely written commentary and analysis. Thus, in addition to surveying the debates about the statue's inauguration—which reprised many of the themes that we have already seen in the discussion about days of national festivity—this chapter offers a more detailed look at midcentury civic ritual and at the politics that surrounded it. While broad sectors of society participated in this celebration of monarchy and the campaign for the equestrian statue was presented as the nation's effort to honor its founder, few failed to notice that it presented a specific interpretation of the nation-state's origins, one espoused most forcefully by conservative Saquaremas. While the equestrian statue has drawn considerable attention from historians, none has effectively addressed the political debate that erupted at the time of its inauguration. To be sure, most recognize its broad outlines—radical Liberals, now known as Históricos (Historicals), led by Teófilo Otoni, the critic of the *beija-mão*'s restoration back in 1838, rejected the monument's unsubtle message that Pedro I won independence and granted the constitution, which together founded the Brazilian nation—but do not examine its full complexity and give short shrift to the government's efforts to impose its interpretation.[1]

Numerous studies of public monuments have emphasized that the bronze and marble figures and busts that proliferated in the Western world during the second half of the nineteenth century offer distinct perspectives on politics. The "statuomania" of the French Third Republic expressed this regime's bourgeois values while the U.S. Civil War monuments aimed "to yield resolution and consensus" in a nation traumatized by the recent conflict (and did so by reinforcing racial hierarchies).[2] Monuments that celebrated recent political events or existing institutions were often particularly controversial—as indeed was Pedro I's equestrian statue for in a powerful symbolic way, they marked the tri umph of a specific group of power holders and its members' view of the recent past.[3] Not surprisingly, then, new regimes have often sought to remove their predecessors' statues, a fate that Pedro I's statue narrowly avoided in 1893, after the proclamation of the republic (see the Epilogue). A monument's success or failure is often difficult to predict from the enthusiasm for or opposition to its erection. Pedro I's monument, which began as an elite project and celebrated all that official ritual held dear on days of national festivity, never became part of official festivities on 7 September or 25 March, the days of national festivity to which it spoke most directly. Rather, as we will see in Chapter Ten, the monument and the square on which it was located became the center of popular independence festivities in the 1870s. The numerous proposals for a monument to Pedro I examined in this chapter's first section all claimed to speak for a united nation, but they were deeply embedded in politics as different groups struggled to control this homage to Brazil's founder. The inauguration's organizers likewise sought to present a Brazilian nation united around its liberator. While the ritual came off peacefully and impressed many observers, the Históricos' challenge to its message, expressed in the Liberal press, undercut the meaning that the government and the monument commission sought to give to the ceremony and the statue.

MONUMENT PROPOSALS

The massive monument raised in 1862 to honor Pedro I had a long history, intertwined with the first emperor's political fortunes and the fall and posthumous recovery of his reputation. Any homage to the first emperor inevitably raised all of the issues associated with the political institutions—constitution and monarchy—that he had founded in 1822–24. Thus, it was easier for Conservatives to contemplate a monument than for Liberals, although there were undertones of radicalism in some of the proposals, for the first emperor could be interpreted in different ways. As we have seen, a streak of radical liberalism sometimes tempered his authoritarian impulses.

Immediately after Pedro I made clear his intention to remain in Brazil and not to return to Lisbon as the Portuguese parliament had ordered—the "Fico [I'll stay]" declaration issued on 9 January 1822—the first monument proposal appeared. Manoel Dias de Oliveira envisaged that the prince would stand atop a globe symbolizing Portugal's worldwide empire, surrounded by figures representing unity, tranquility, and friendship (these three presumably all directed at Portugal), along with the kingdom of Brazil, represented as "a hero in armor ready to fight his enemies."[4] Events quickly overtook this proposal and its mix of pacific and bellicose messages; by the end of the year, Pedro was crowned Emperor Pedro I.

In April or May 1825, a year after Pedro had sworn his oath to the constitution, Brigadier Domingos Alves Branco Moniz Barreto, whom the British minister characterized as a sometime "republican" leader, called on civil and military officials to promote a subscription for an equestrian statue. Apparently to prevent this campaign from falling under control of a man closely associated with the radicals purged in late October 1822, Rio de Janeiro's city council moved in and took over the campaign, before Moniz Barreto could even hold his public meeting.[5] With Pedro's approval, the council launched the campaign in midyear. It was quickly decided that the statue should be raised on the Campo da Aclamação, on the site of the *palacete* (little palace) where Pedro had taken, "by the spontaneous decision of the people and for their happiness, the glorious title of Emperor of Brazil."[6]

In nine months, the subscription raised 27,417 mil-réis (US$28,788) in 263 individual donations and numerous collections taken up in military units, guilds, and other corporations; through early 1826, notices of contributions filled the press.[7] Individual donors expressed the monument's official interpretation. For João José Vahia, who contributed sixty mil-réis (US$63), it was "the most authentic testimony to posterity of our firm loyalty and perpetual gratitude to such an immortal sovereign who, [by] establishing an empire on the most edifying bases, ensured our happiness and his, and our, glory." City councils in the provincial capitals received invitations to raise funds; most initiated subscription campaigns in their parishes. Condy Raguet, the U.S. minister, judged that Pedro was "determined to have" the statue.[8]

The capital's municipal council submitted the monument proposal to the imperial government in September 1825. It would commemorate Pedro's great deeds on behalf of "Brazilian liberty and independence and the extraordinary political events of this empire." Pedro would be sculpted in military uniform and all the imperial attributes (crown, scepter, and robe). Holding the scepter, he would look forward, in an "unequivocal demonstration of the empire's stability and His Majesty's august character." The pedestal would refer to "the four most notable dates in the new era of the great empire of Brazil": 9 January 1822, 7 September 1822, 1 December 1822 (curiously described as the date of the creation of the first military order in Brazil, and not the date of Pedro's consecration and coronation), and 25 March 1824. Furthermore, the commission recommended major improvements to the Campo da Aclamação to make it worthy of the monument. Working from these guidelines, Auguste Henri Victor Grandjean de Montigny prepared two designs.[9]

As Pedro's popularity flagged, however, the campaign faltered. An anonymous 1862 history of the monument campaign published in the radical Liberal *A Atualidade* blamed this on Pedro's loss of interest after the death of his father in early 1826. Pedro then began to pursue his dynastic ambitions in Portugal and "could no longer desire a statue that would commemorate the fact of independence, which would not please the Portuguese." Manoel de Araújo Porto Alegre later blamed the Cisplatine War and those who promoted the "disastrous events of 1831." A contemporary historian and teacher at the Colégio Dom Pedro II, Manuel Duarte Moreira de Azevedo (1832–1903), likewise blamed the turbulence of 1831 for the campaign's failure.[10] While the campaign had raised significant funds in the capital, only nine provinces had contributed anything, Bahia the irrisory sum of 121$280 (US$119).[11] In early 1831, auditors found the campaign's books "almost completely abandoned"; worse yet, the Banco do Brasil (Bank of Brazil) account held only 21,665 mil-réis (now worth only US$11,049), although some documents indicated that more than twice this sum had been contributed. The auditors failed to put the books in order, and the finance minister appointed new ones in 1832.[12] Over the next years, deputies periodically called on the government to provide information on the funds' whereabouts.[13] A suspicious municipal council in Campos de Goitacazes asked for its money back in 1834, but Rio de Janeiro's council could find no trace of it. The chamber of deputies got involved in 1836 when another donor appealed for assistance in securing his reimbursement; the finance committee proposed that procedures be established so that all those who wished to receive their money could easily get it back.[14]

The first campaign's ignominious collapse also had much to do with Pedro's declining popularity. His reputation quickly recovered after his death in 1834; as the Brazilian empire's founder, father of the current ruler, and grantor of the constitution, he was fully reincorporated into official ritual by the 1840s, but an anonymous writer lamented in 1846: "Neither bust nor obelisk / Nor statues have we raised / To him who gave us liberty / To him whom we hail as hero."[15] To be sure, some radical Liberals continued to vituperate the first emperor, but they were increasingly isolated by the early 1850s.

In 1838–39, a new monument campaign that began with representatives from a range of political groups degenerated into personal and partisan bickering. It should have been a propitious time to promote a monument to Pedro I, given the heavy investment in monarchical symbolism at that time. We only have Porto Alegre's accounts of this committee's work; given his propensity for quarreling, they are no doubt biased. The committee initially included both Saquaremas like Antônio Peregrino Maciel Monteiro (the future second Baron of Itamaracá) and men who had closer ties with the opposition that would soon promote Pedro II's premature majority as a coup against Saquaremas (Paulo José de Melo Azevedo e Brito and Francisco Vilela Barbosa, the Marquis of Paranaguá). Porto Alegre, recently returned from studies in Paris, represented the artistic community. Paranaguá appears to have been the leader of this campaign, but Bernardo Pereira de Vasconcelos, in his capacity as minister of empire, removed him and appointed José Antônio Lisboa to chair the committee, a deliberate insult to the marquis, according to Porto Alegre.[16]

Despite this inauspicious start, the committee under Lisboa called for the erection of two monuments, an equestrian one of Pedro I and a pedestrian one of José Bonifácio de Andrada e Silva, who had guided the emperor to his break with Portugal in 1822. It invited donations of no more than two mil-réis (US$1.28) to increase the old subscription fund and proposed that teachers at the Academia das Belas Artes (Fine Arts Academy) design and execute the statues.[17] Apparently foreign artists were nevertheless considered, for the owner of a foundry that specialized in making bells angrily protested this, arguing that the use of foreigners "will only serve to discredit the nation, which is now beginning to distinguish itself before the civilized world, . . . [by] making it look like there is no one in Brazil who can or knows how to create such a work." He did not, however, help his case by asking for government aid to build a new furnace large enough for the work, thereby confessing his lack of experience with projects on this scale.[18] Despite Vasconcelos's approval of the subscription in December 1838, and later approvals of the design by his successor as minister of empire, neither foreign nor Brazilian founders got the commission, for this project was not carried out.[19] Leading artists could not agree on the budget. Zeferino Ferrez judged that both monuments could be produced in Brazil for forty-seven contos (US$30,080); Grandjean de Montigny and Porto Alegre disagreed vehemently, and in 1839 the latter calculated the cost of casting the two "colossal" bonzes in Brazil and setting them on Brazilian marble pedestals at more than sixty-eight and thirty-one contos (US$43,520 and US$19,840) respectively, more than twice Zeferino's estimate (both budgets included the cost of constructing a foundry, which indicates that there was serious consideration of producing the statues in Brazil).[20]

In 1844, José Clemente Pereira attempted to revive the campaign, but he apparently accomplished little.[21] Deputies occasionally tried to get the government to fund and build the monument. In 1846, Fernando Sebastião Dias da Mota presented a bill that called for the expenditure of forty contos (US$22,000) "or whatever is necessary" to raise the monument, but deputies were not interested in signing this blank check. Six years later, Pedro Rodrigues Fernandes Chaves tried to amend the budget to allocate one hundred contos (US$52,000) to the monument; in response, Venâncio Henriques de Resende (an old radical liberal who had moved to a conservative position) noted perceptively (and presciently) that "as long as the empire's independence and its constitution exist, a monument is raised to the memory of Pedro I . . . and when this edifice tumbles, this [proposed] monument will be good for nothing; perhaps there will be sacrilegious hands who determine to serve the country by destroying it." Neither measure passed, nor did another such bill proposed in 1854.[22]

To have a monument built with government funds of course cheapened it as a national gesture, and in the early 1850s calls to revive the subscription for the Pedro I monument reappeared. In December 1852 a city councilor, Domingos de Azeredo Coutinho Duque-Estrada, proposed that Rio de Janeiro resume collecting funds for a bronze equestrian statue of Pedro I on the Largo do Rocio, officially known as the Constitution Square (today Tiradentes Square), but the city shelved this proposal.[23] Two years later, Joaquim Norberto de Souza e Silva, a member of the Instituto Histórico e Geográfico Brasileiro (Brazilian Historical and Geographical Institute), called for three major monuments: one on the banks of the Ipiranga River, an imperial equestrian statue for the capital, and "a colossal and monumental cross" in Porto Seguro to commemorate the discovery of Brazil in 1500.[24] In a special session on 7 September 1854, the city council unanimously approved a detailed proposal for a Pedro I monument presented by Roberto Jorge Haddock Lobo. In his speech, the councilor recalled that independence began "on the fields of Ipiranga," from whence it spread "from the Amazon to the Plate," sparing Brazil the immense sacrifices that independence had cost other nations. Moreover, Pedro had granted the constitution, reducing his liberty "to give it to others." To commemorate these achievements, Haddock Lobo recommended an equestrian statue on a base whose bas-reliefs would consist of portraits of "all of the exalted prince's companions . . . who effectively collaborated in [winning] independence." These men were to be identified by the Instituto Histórico, and the monument would be erected on Constitution Square. To raise funds, a subscription would be conducted in the Corte and the province of Rio de Janeiro, this time accepting donations of up to 100 mil-réis (US$56).[25]

Press accounts of the council meeting emphasized the large number of spectators in the chambers, which demonstrated that this was "the national idea of an entire people."[26] Nevertheless, the proposal immediately elicited criticism. Miffed at his exclusion from the committee to oversee the campaign, Duque-Estrada grumbled that Haddock Lobo's proposal was "unjust and petty," for it excluded Brazilians from outside the capital from contributing: "Rio de Janeiro alone does not constitute Brazil," he declared. To this point, Justiniano José da Rocha replied that, in fact, this was a Rio de Janeiro project and that other provinces should raise their own monuments. Were the proposal a national one, he added, there would soon be complaints about the location of the monument in the capital and calls to construct it at Ipiranga. One journalist, in fact, recommended exactly this in October, as did another the following June, but these were isolated proposals in ephemeral periodicals.[27]

Jeffrey Needell has recently suggested that an important political subtext underlay this monument proposal and the campaign that followed. Although its launch coincided with the beginning of the Conciliação, leading figures of the Conciliação cabinet were not involved, and the resulting monument—an equestrian statue with Pedro holding the constitution—exemplified Saquaremas' commitment to constitutional and representative monarchy, a principle undermined by the Conciliação and even more so by Pedro's increasingly direct involvement in government in the 1860s. He adds that this "enduring statement" of the Party of Order's ideology amounted to Eusébio de Queiroz Coutinho Mattoso Câmara's last triumph (the Saquarema stalwart presided over the committee until the statue's inauguration in 1862).[28]

Saquaremas and Conservatives closely linked to the Rio de Janeiro merchant and planter class—the Saquaremas' power base—dominated the monument committee. João Antônio Miranda, a magistrate (and after 1855 senator for Mato Grosso), had been appointed president of Ceará by the Regresso cabinet (he had also proposed the 1854 bill to fund the statue).[29] José Francisco de Mesquita, the Baron and later Viscount of Bonfim, served as treasurer; he was a prominent merchant, but his political leanings are not clear. João Pereira Darrique Faro, the second Baron of Rio Bonito, was a "wealthy planter and respected merchant" and a moderate Conservative since his adherence to the Regresso.[30] Porto Alegre had had strong Liberal ties in the 1840s, but as director of the Academia de Belas Artes, he was a logical addition to the committee, and this monument was certainly consistent with his long-standing view that such public art should inspire patriotism; moreover, by this time, his loyalty to the monarchy weighed more than his political convictions.[31] Porto Alegre did not fit well in the committee, and he later recalled the "great vexation" that it brought him, for he had to deal with "a man of science without conscience," perhaps a reference to Polidoro da Fonseca Quintanilha Jordão. This colonel in the army engineers was likely included for his technical expertise; he would serve as war minister in the 1862–63 moderate Conservative cabinet.[32] The other cultural figure on the committee, Joaquim Norberto, was a long-serving civil servant, well known for his leading role in the Instituto Histórico and for his many historical and literary works.[33]

Changes in the committee in 1859 did not materially affect its political composition. When Porto Alegre received a diplomatic posting abroad (something of a dignified exile after his falling out with the first post Conciliação cabinet), he was replaced by João de Oliveira Fausto, president of the city council and a medical doctor.[34] Rio Bonito died in 1856 and was eventually replaced by Duque-Estrada, a recognition that this prominent doctor and proponent of homeopathic medicine had been an early advocate of resuming the monument campaign; he descended from an old landowning family.[35] In 1861, there were further changes to the committee. Isidoro Borges Monteiro, Rio de Janeiro's chief of police from April 1857 to February 1860,[36] replaced the deceased Miranda, and two new members joined the committee: Haddock Lobo, the doctor and conservative municipal politician who had presented the monument proposal in 1854, and João Afonso Lima Nogueira, a longtime civil servant.[37] In short, involving no prominent Liberals, the monument commission was broadly Conservative and Saquarema.

The new committee quickly set to work. At its first meeting, it prepared the terms of an international competition to be concluded before 12 October 1855; the call for designs specified an equestrian statue of Pedro I in the act of proclaiming independence, but it omitted the bas-reliefs of Pedro's collaborators. As Porto Alegre explained to the city council, too many people were worthy of inclusion on the pedestal, and no artist could pack them all in. Selecting only a few would inevitably lead to complaints, and he doubted that the Instituto Histórico would want to take on "such a difficult task."[38] While this decision may have been politic (a journalist noted that to let the institute make this decision opened up far too many political considerations because its members had known many of the leading independence-era statesmen), it also meant that the monument would focus entirely on the monarch.[39] Thus the artists were free to propose decorations or allegories for the pedestal; one of them, perhaps knowing of this uncertainty, proposed bas-reliefs representing key episodes in Brazilian history but offered to make whatever changes the jury desired.[40] The architect, Francisco Joaquim Betencourt da Silva, condemned the decision to invite foreign artists to participate in the competition as a "shameful insult" to Brazilians, an issue that would periodically crop up in discussions about the monument.[41]

In mid-1855, the thirty-five designs were exhibited in Rio de Janeiro, and the committee made its final decision in August.[42] First place went to João Máximo Mafra, a painting professor at the Rio academy. A German finished second, and a French artist took third place. Because Mafra had no experience in executing bronzes, the Frenchman, Louis Rochet, a sculptor of some renown and considerable experience with bronze statues, received the commission, provided that he follow Mafra's design. It envisaged an equestrian statue of Pedro I (as mandated by the competition's terms) but contemplated the emperor with the constitution in hand (a conflation of the events of 7 September 1822 and 25 March 1824). The pedestal would be surrounded by allegorical Indian figures representing the country's four main rivers: the Amazon, the Paraná, the São Francisco, and the Madeira.[43] Mafra's close ties to Porto Alegre led to rumors that the latter had actually prepared the design and that the two had secretly shared the 1,000 mil-réis (US$560) prize. Porto Alegre admitted having suggested to Mafra the "general idea" and privately condemned his "conceited and ignorant and lazy" colleagues for spreading such rumors.[44]

Despite these controversies, work proceeded steadily. On 12 October 1855, the city council laid the monument's cornerstone.[45] Rochet signed a contract with the committee's agents in Paris and promised delivery of the statue by July 1859 so that it could be inaugurated on 12 October of that year, all for a price of 670,000 francs (US$134,000). The sculptor visited Rio de Janeiro in September 1856 to view the site and recommended a European marble or bronze, rather than Brazilian granite, pedestal: "The granite, with which you pave your streets, is not worthy of my statue and of the illustrious man that it represents," he explained (he would eventually cast a bronze pedestal for the statue). The artist apparently also studied Brazilian Indians and flora and fauna for his design.[46] The committee recommended that the city council devise a plan to redesign and beautify Constitution Square, perhaps responding to criticisms that the statue was not appropriate for a square normally full of "gypsies, people of horrible traditions," and "coachmen, every last one very stupid and coarse, and many of them uppity slaves" (the square was a terminus for omnibus lines and a place where coaches for hire awaited customers, as well as an area where Romany had traditionally lived).[47]

I have found very little information on the fund-raising campaign. When the committee finally closed its books in 1866, it left no debt. More than 334 contos (US$177,397) had been raised (a total that included the funds from the 1825 subscription).[48] The proposal to limit donations to a maximum of 100 mil-réis soon fell by the wayside. Back in 1854, rumor had it that the Baron of Mauá had donated an "enormous quantity," and the Viscount of Bonfim, the treasurer, personally covered the last deficit of just over seven contos (US$3,710); Moreira de Azevedo later reported that several additional individuals had made substantial donations.[49] The first round of fund raising did not elicit sufficient monies, and in late 1860 the city council launched a new campaign.[50]

The monument to be inaugurated in 1862 thus had a long history, during which many of its features had slowly taken shape. That it would be an equestrian statue was clear by the 1830s; anything less would presumably have lowered Pedro's standing among monarchs too much. The connection of independence and the constitution (two events separated by a year and a half) made the monument somewhat allegorical but emphasized Pedro's centrality in creating the constitutional monarchy; it was certainly consistent with official civic rituals' message. The campaign's limitation to Rio de Janeiro reflected the empire's centralization, the Corte's importance, and the imperial regime's social base. During the long interval between Rochet's visit to Rio de Janeiro in 1856 and the arrival of the statue in late 1861, there were few references to the monument in the commemorations of 25 March and 7 September, the days of national festivity to which it spoke most directly.

INAUGURATING THE MONUMENT

The equestrian statue's inauguration on 30 March 1862 was probably the most intensely debated civic ritual in imperial Brazil. It came at a complex political juncture. The Conciliação had ended, and the Conservative cabinets that followed had difficulty containing the challenges from a reinvigorated Liberal Party and its radical wing. Moreover, the system of single-member districts instituted for the 1856 elections and changed to three-member districts for the 1860 vote made it more difficult for cabinets to control election results.[51] Some twenty-five Liberals won seats in 1856, as well as a similar number of independent Conservatives who rejected the Saquarema leadership.[52] About the same number of Liberals won election in 1860, but the most notable outcome of the vote in December of that year was the success of radical Liberals, now known as Históricos (Historicals), who swept Rio de Janeiro city with a popular campaign under Teófilo Otoni's leadership. A new generation of young Liberals rejected both the Conciliação and Saquaremas' understandings of the constitutional order. Their inspiration came from, as one of them later recalled, the defeated "revolutionary movements of Minas [Gerais], Pernambuco, and São Paulo." *A Atualidade*, founded in May 1858, served as the principal vehicle for their criticisms of the imperial regime, but they also published pamphlets critical of centralization and Pedro's use of the moderating power.[53]

Despite these successes, as Needell reminds us, Liberals remained a minority party, and the real winners in 1860 were the Saquaremas, who had drawn enough moderate Conservatives under their leadership to command a clear majority in the legislature. Pedro, however, continued to seek a version of the Conciliação and worked to exclude both Saquaremas and Historical Liberals from power. He appointed the Marquis of Caxias to organize a moderate Conservative cabinet in March 1861. Soon after the statue's inauguration, he would appoint the first (abortive) cabinet of what eventually became known as the Liga Progressista (Progressive League), a disparate alliance of moderates from both parties.[54] Although of course politics and ritual cannot be disentangled, this section focuses on the outward and visible aspects of the statue's inauguration. To be sure, newspaper writers viewed the monument through partisan lenses and, as was so often the case, saw completely different ceremonies, but this can be analyzed on the familiar level of government versus opposition. The much more fundamental debate set off by the inauguration began in late March with a Liberal press campaign against the assumptions about the imperial regime embodied in the monument. This polemic, which lasted well past the inauguration, is the subject of the next section.

The press reflected the major political divisions of this time. In the first months of 1862, five major newspapers were published in Rio de Janeiro. The *Jornal do Comércio*, the largest, maintained a generally neutral political stance even as it held a broadly conservative outlook. The Caxias administration subsidized the *Correio da Tarde* to serve as its mouthpiece, but when it launched its defense of the statue, it resorted to filling the paid section of the more widely read *Jornal*.[55] Three Liberal newspapers appeared daily or several times per week: *A Atualidade*, edited by Flávio Farnese, Lafaiete Rodrigues Pereira, and Pedro Luís Pereira de Souza; Joaquim Saldanha Marinho's *Diário do Rio de Janeiro*; and Francisco Otaviano de Almeida Rosa's *Correio Mercantil*. The biweekly *A Atualidade*, published by what Joaquim Nabuco later called "young republicans," was the most radical and the *Correio* the most moderate of the Liberal periodicals. No Saquarema journal was published at this time.[56] Henrique Fleiüss's illustrated weekly, *A Semana*

Ilustrada, founded in 1861, was rapidly gaining a wide readership for its cartoons, satires, and critical commentary. Fleiüss respected the imperial family but regularly criticized government policy and administrative acts.[57] About ten other minor political periodicals appeared for longer or shorter periods during the year. The major newspapers offered extensive coverage and commentary on the monument, the preparations for the inauguration, and the inauguration itself as they debated Brazil's political arrangements—monarchy and constitution—commemorated in the statue.

Rochet finished work on the statue in early 1861 and exhibited it at the Paris Salon of that year. Critics praised it, and one remarked that Rochet had been the first sculptor to produce successful images of "savages" in the Indian figures that served as allegories of the four rivers surrounding the pedestal.[58] In early September 1861, news reached Rio de Janeiro that the statue was being packed up for shipping. The 55,000 kilogram monument arrived in October, followed soon thereafter by Rochet, who oversaw its installation on Constitution Square.[59]

On 1 January 1862, work on the foundation began, after a ceremony to lay a second cornerstone, during which a time capsule was buried underneath the site. It included coins from Pedro I's reign and copies of the constitution and other documents, among them Pedro's major acts before 7 September 1822, the independence anthem, and the 1852 and 1854 monument proposals.[60] Eusébio de Queiroz spoke on behalf of the committee and described the statue as a symbol of "Brazilians' gratitude" for Pedro I's achievement of a peaceful independence and his granting of a "constitution so wise [that it is] still today the guiding light of peace for all Brazilians, regardless of [their] party [affiliations]." The *Correio da Tarde* proclaimed that the new monument honored a "liberal king" and would serve as an "example and incentive to the sovereigns of this country."[61] Pedro said nothing about the ceremony in his diary, but he was most pleased with the statue, which he carefully inspected at Rochet's nearby workshop.[62]

The *Jornal do Comércio*'s *cronista* looked forward to the inauguration, scheduled for 25 March, when Rio de Janeiro would finally have a monument worthy of showing to foreigners. His counterpart at the *Revista Popular* seconded this view, adding that the statue was a "monument truly worthy of a great capital." More was still needed, however, including cleaning the beaches surrounding the downtown core and a major project to turn the Campo da Aclamação from a "field of trash and [a place] for washing clothes" into a pleasant spot. Others pointed out that the monument would be placed amid the unattractive buildings that surrounded Constitution Square and the "rachitic trees" that managed to survive on the inhospitable site. Indeed, back in December 1861, rumor had it that Rochet thought the square "unworthy" of his statue, "thanks to its lamentable state," but efforts to improve it did not take place until after the inauguration.[63]

During the next three months, the work on Constitution Square attracted much interest. The site became the "meeting place for people of all classes of society," especially in the afternoons; people seemingly could not get a sufficient dose of stone and bronze and kept coming back for more, remarked the *Jornal do Comércio*'s *cronista*.[64] In late February, the whole square was covered with piles of stone as the gas company laid its lines for the lamps that surrounded the monument.[65] The construction of large ephemeral monuments added to the chaos. These included a simple triumphal arch and a Roman temple with a dome topped by a statue of religion and, behind it, space for musicians.[66] On 13 March, Pedro noted that the crews were behind schedule and that hard work was needed to be ready for the 25th. The equestrian figure was raised onto the pedestal on 21 March, and only on the 24th were the last allegorical figures set around the base.[67]

While Rochet oversaw the first stages in the statue's installation, the monument committee busied itself with drafting a program for the inauguration ceremony. In mid-December 1861, the committee submitted the draft directly to the imperial government, but the city council protested this on the grounds that it should have first approved the program, for it had originally appointed the committee. The monument committee responded that it had never sought prior approval from the council for any of its decisions and that it had been granted unlimited powers over the monument. What lay behind this squabble is not clear, but the Conservative monument committee perhaps sought to marginalize a Liberal-dominated council; the two councilors on the monument committee took the committee's side.[68]

The December program contemplated an elaborate ceremony, different in key ways from normal civic rituals. After the National Guard formed up on the square, the ceremony would start at 10:00 am on 25 March, with a procession from the city council building on the Campo da Aclamação to nearby Constitution Square. The program specified that the groups' placement in the procession did not reflect precedence, but it surely did not go unnoticed that police authorities would go first, followed by staff from other government departments. After that, the list included virtually every organized group in Rio de Janeiro: deputations from literary and cultural societies; schoolteachers; the Instituto Histórico, the bar association, and the college of physicians; clergy and brotherhoods; newspaper editors; banks; the court, the cabinet, and parliament; and finally the city council whose members would bear the canopy under which Pedro and Teresa Cristina would walk. There was also space for independence veterans. Once Pedro arrived at the São Pedro Theater's *varanda* (the windowed front hall that overlooked the square and would be reserved for the imperial family, the court, diplomats, and senior officials), the Guard troops would fire the customary salutes, and the statue would be unveiled to the sounds of the national anthem. The city council president would then lead the crowd in a cheer to national independence. The troops would present arms to the sounds of the independence anthem and artillery salutes from Santo Antônio Hill. Then the Te Deum would be sung and congratulatory speeches read. After this, the troops would parade around the statue and line the streets to the downtown palace, to which the procession would continue; for this final leg, the monument committee members would have the honor of holding up the canopy. At the city palace, Pedro would hold a levee; as usual, citizens would receive invitations to decorate their façades, and streets would be covered with fragrant leaves.[69]

This projected parade involved far more civil society groups than civic rituals normally did, and in some respects it resembles the characteristically North American parade as described by Mary Ryan. However, unlike the paraders in U.S. cities, these marchers had a specific destination (the monument) and a clear center (the emperor), neither of which figured in the American parade, which primarily involved the display of social groups. Rather, the 1862 procession most closely resembled the traditional Iberian Corpus Christi processions, which arranged all members of society in relation to the Host, the body of Christ, although in this case there was no religious connotation, and the program denied any significance to placement in the marching order.[70]

Critics were quick to question the decision to hold the ceremony at 10:00 am, which would require the hapless National Guard to shoulder arms in the full heat of the midday sun. The *Jornal do Comércio*'s *cronista* mocked this debate: To be sure, holding the ceremony in the middle of the day would be particularly unpleasant for bald-headed statesmen, but holding the ceremony after lunch would make it difficult for them to button up uniforms and walk for long distances. In any case, the atmosphere might well make the final decision by sending rain, and given the procession's length, the sun that burned bald heads might just be the one that dawned on 26 March![71] In mid-March, it was decided to move the ceremony to 4:00 pm, which meant eliminating the procession's continuation to the downtown palace. Pedro and the Council of State insisted on conducting the official rituals of 25 March—the Te Deum and the levee—before the monument's inauguration, even though Eusébio and the monument commission felt that the day of national festivity was more than adequately acknowledged by the statue's unveiling. Furthermore, given the large number of people expected in the square, it was decided that the guardsmen should not fire salutes.[72]

Other preparations were well advanced by late March. Two or three times per week, Francisco Manoel da Silva rehearsed the massive orchestra and choir of children from seven schools that would perform Sigismund Neukomm's Te Deum. José Vieira Fazenda (1847–1917), who sang in the choir, later recalled that the maestro conducted with an enormous cane, for his baton was too small to be seen by the 500 to 600 singers and the 263 musicians in the orchestra (enthusiastically beating time during one rehearsal, he broke the cane). For the young Vieira Fazenda and his fellow singers, the Sanctus was the most difficult part because it had to be coordinated with artillery salutes.[73]

As 25 March approached, it became clear that the inauguration would be a major social and political event, eagerly anticipated in all quarters; the *Jornal do Comércio*'s *cronista* expected that it would be the "greatest Brazilian festival" since the coronation.[74] Hundreds of societies, corporations, and municipalities from across the country appointed delegations to attend the ceremony or designated representatives in Rio de Janeiro. In early March, *Semana Ilustrada*'s *cronista* wondered whether there would be enough room on the square for all of the people.[75] Most of these institutions prepared congratulations that could not be read at the time of the inauguration; they were collected, and over the course of April the government paid to have them published in the *Jornal do Comércio*.[76]

There was much money to be made and numerous advertisements for formal wear and other items referred to the upcoming inauguration. The new railroad changed its schedule to bring passengers from its terminus to the city in time for the ceremony.[77] "Considerable contingents of neighboring populations" were in town on 25 March, and a jewelry store invited "Brazilian ladies from the province's interior" to view its "rich and varied stock," all at reasonable prices.[78] Another store advertised souvenir pictures of the statue.[79] The lucky property owners on Constitution Square earned "a fortune" by renting their front windows to spectators, while ladies struggled to decide what to wear to gain "*distinction* for beauty, to win the *title* of elegant, and display brilliant *graces*." Men too wanted distinctions, titles, and graces [*graças*], but of a different sort, continued this *cronista*, referring to the extensive discussions about whether there would be *despachos* (the issuance of noble titles and promotions in the honorific orders) on 25 March.[80]

In mid-March, the *Diário do Rio de Janeiro* mocked the eagerness for decorations by remarking that the government would grant a habit [*hábito*] to each traffic post [*frade de pedra*, literally translated, stone friar] on the square and raise them all to the rank of column, just as any João Fernandes could be made a baron, a marquis, or even a duke.[81] As it became clear that there would be no *despachos* to celebrate the inauguration, the opposition press's rhetoric shifted, and *A Atualidade* condemned the many contributors to the monument campaign who had allegedly donated only to secure themselves a decoration.[82] On the day that the inauguration finally took place, the *Correio da Tarde* railed against the "party of contradiction" for now saying that the lack of re-wards would hinder the campaign for the José Bonifácio monument. In that case, remarked the ministerial newspaper, nobody would contribute anything at all to a statue "of this illustrious citizen whom Mr. Otoni considers the first patriarch of independence"—a jibe at Tiradentes (see below).[83] Pedro agreed to induct Louis Rochet into the Ordem do Cru-zeiro (Order of the [Southern] Cross), but the minister of empire pushed for an officership in the Ordem da Rosa (Order of the Rose), for the artist reportedly expected "great rewards." Pedro apparently had his way on this point, and Rochet formally received his insignia on 20 April.[84] Op-position newspapers were quick to criticize the decision to honor only Rochet, and several writers cast it as an affront to the Brazilian artist Mafra, who had been responsible for the design. In fact, in late April, Pedro proposed honoring him, but the minister of empire reported that the monument commission "was not on good terms with Mafra because of his pecuniary demands."[85]

In mid-March, Liberal journalists caught wind of rumors that a revo-lution would take place on 25 March. *A Atualidade* made light of the minister of justice's investigative skill at discovering a plot that not even the alleged Liberal ringleaders knew about and connected the decision to eliminate the National Guard salutes from the program to the govern-ment's fears. The citizen-soldiers were so unreliable, in the ministry's er-roneous view, that they had not even received their new rifles and would have to make do with old weaponry. Further evidence of the cabinet's ridiculous fears lay in its reaction to a request from the Zuavos carnival society to join the procession. Instead of 200 members, the Zuavos were allowed only 100 paraders, and the police searched their clubhouse. No revolt would take place, the *Diário do Rio de Janeiro* assured the min-istry, for "the people will look impassively on the statue . . . considering it a simple decoration on Rocio Square." The *Correio da Tarde* retorted that the monument had been raised by the people's "spontaneous will"; Teófilo Otoni and the other radical Liberals wanted "disorder," but these "anarchists" lacked the means to carry out their plans. Within a few days, the rumors were the subject of mockery by the *Semana Ilustrada*'s *cronista*.[86]

A last-minute police order that only those "decently dressed" be admitted to the square on 25 March prompted another round of criti-cal comment. Did this mean "silk pants and coat, a decorated hat and sword"—courtiers' uniforms—asked *A Atualidade*? Its writer concluded with exaggerated weariness that, this time, the government was right, for the inauguration would indeed be no "people's celebration"; rather, it was "a royal festival," nothing more than the "adulation and hom-age of the wealthy and powerful to those currently in power; it would be a festival for big shots" and the people knew this.[87] The *Correio da*

Tarde defended the government's decision to control the space by noting that if *capoeiras* disrupted the ceremony, the opposition would accuse the ministry of incompetent policing. Joaquim Maria Machado de Assis, the *Diário do Rio de Janeiro's cronista*, claimed that the whole issue amounted to a "fine and clever trick." After the orderly and peaceful inauguration that he expected, the administration would attribute this success "to the terror [imposed] by [their] earlier measures." Much later, an ephemeral newspaper claimed that when authorities saw that the square was not full on inauguration day, they quickly abandoned their efforts to keep the canaille out; ministers and marquises smiled and said, "Let the [common] people enter, for today is their day; this festival is entirely popular," but there is no indication of this in the mainstream press.[88]

As the inauguration approached, Liberal newspapers published editorials critical of the monument and its political message, which we examine in the next section. They had no impact on the conduct of the ceremony itself; rather, the weather disrupted it, as the *Jornal do Comércio's cronista* had predicted. From the early hours of Tuesday, 25 March, until about noon it rained heavily, damaging the decorative structures erected around the monument; among other things, one of the arms of the statue of religion that topped the Roman temple fell off, and part of the dome caved in. Streets were hopelessly flooded (as usual, added some journalists).[89] Despite the rain, preparations for the inauguration began early in the morning. The gun crews trudged up Santo Antônio Hill and spent the day in the mud beside their batteries, much to the detriment of the soldiers' health. The future Viscount of Taunay (Alfredo d'Escragnolle Taunay) tried to ride into the city from his home at Cascatinha, but his horse slipped and he was thrown, breaking his arm.[90] At 10:00 am, Pedro was still determined to go ahead with the ceremony, but the cabinet finally persuaded him to postpone it to Sunday, 30 March. He insisted, however, that the inauguration should not take place on 7 April. Inaugurating a monument to the first emperor on the date of his abdication would have been completely contradictory. The *Diário do Rio de Janeiro* judged it appropriate that the anniversary of the constitution would now not be confused with the inauguration of a monument to the man who least respected it.[91]

Despite continued unpromising weather, the inauguration went ahead on 30 March, following the revised program (Figure 5.1). James Watson Webb, the U.S. minister who dutifully attended all court functions even though he resided year-round in Petrópolis, enjoyed the "imposing and brilliant procession" and judged the whole ceremony "superior to any thing of the kind [that] I have witnessed in Europe, except in the military display. That was quite unworthy of the occasion." Vieira Fazenda recalled that he and his schoolmates put on a spectacular performance (Pedro noted that the artillery salutes were perfectly timed with

FIGURE 5.1.
The Pedro I equestrian statue's inauguration, 30 March 1862.
Source: BN/SI, Fotos Arm. 6.4.2(11). Courtesy Acervo da Fundação Biblioteca Nacional—Brasil.

the choir's intonation of "Sanctus, Sanctus, Sanctus"). Immediately after the ceremony, however, a sudden downpour dispersed the crowd, and the schoolboy arrived home drenched, the white pants of his uniform deeply stained by mud and bootblack. Thanks to the rain and a poor choice of location from which to view the proceedings, a judge later recalled that he saw nothing.[92]

No travelers wrote about the ceremony, and partisan politics deeply colored the press accounts. All agreed that the celebrations came off peacefully and followed the program, but editors saw very different things. The ministerial *Correio da Tarde*'s editor had never seen "a ceremony so majestic, and at the same time so popular." Even many Liberals had joined the procession, he added. The moderate Liberal *Correio Mercantil*'s editor concurred that the crowds were large, but he judged the procession small; many societies and corporations were but poorly represented. The two more radical Liberal newspapers went much further. The *Diário* claimed that "complete indifference" was the dominant sentiment that day: "Each entertained himself in his own way."

A Atualidade went furthest: Only a third of the people appointed by city councils and corporations showed up to represent their constituents in the parade; half the square was empty, and the police kept out the "people in jackets." Those who claimed an enthusiastic response to the cheers were deluding themselves: "We saw nothing that resembled enthusiasm."[93] The *Semana Ilustrada*'s *cronista* added one further detail: "Monumental" chaos reigned as the procession formed up, and somehow, "the little blacks [*pretinhos*] commissioned by the brotherhoods of Saint Ephigenia, the Rosary, and Saint Benedict" (three black sodalities) wound up with a privileged position immediately after the canopy and the city council. The latter brotherhood had also prepared a congratulatory address in which it recalled its reception of Prince-Regent João in 1808 and pledged to pray for the empire's peace and prosperity, as well as for Pedro II's long life.[94]

Later accounts of the inauguration, such as those published in the 1863 *Folhinha Laemmert* and the last volume of Moreira de Azevedo's *Pequeno panorama ou Descrição dos principais edifícios da cidade do Rio de Janeiro* (Little Panorama, or Description of the Principal Edifices of the City of Rio de Janeiro, 1867) ignored these competing assessments of what took place and accepted the *Correio da Tarde*'s version.[95] Nevertheless, these slightly later accounts and the ministerial paper hinted at a bifurcated celebration. Moreira de Azevedo described a "festive camp" that surrounded the artillery park on Santo Antônio Hill. Affording an excellent view of the square, the hilltop was "packed with people"—fully 30,000, asserted (quite improbably) the *Folhinha*. It may be that those barred from the square climbed up the hill for a better look, leaving what Fleiüss portrayed as a well-dressed crowd to cheer the statue in the square.[96]

The numerous speeches and poems prepared for the day expressed the monument's official interpretation. No addresses were, however, read in Pedro's presence at the São Pedro Theater *varanda* after the unveiling. It was apparently too dark for the nearsighted Eusébio to read his address, so Pedro just thanked the commission and the city council for their work. In the published version of his speech, Eusébio stressed that the monument revealed Pedro on his greatest day (7 September 1822) but also underscored that it commemorated the constitution, which made Brazil the second-oldest constitutional regime in the world: "Many of the most civilized nations have not been able to achieve this last word in political wisdom." Pedro thought the speech "very well done," except for the exaggerated comparison of his father to Alexander the Great. Apparently no one remarked on Eusébio's historical slip when he declared that "this divine work of human wisdom," the long-sought "foundation of order through liberty," had been proclaimed thirty-eight years ago "on this very square." In fact, as we saw in Chapter One, no rituals involving the 1824 constitution had taken place on Constitution Square, whose name in fact dated back to March 1821 and celebrated João VI's acceptance of the then-unwritten Portuguese charter in February of that year.[97]

A flood of poetry inundated Rio de Janeiro. Scores of sonnets and other short verses, printed on colored sheets of paper, circulated widely. Francisco de Paula Brito's press produced the majority of these flyers, whose mostly indifferent verse hailed Pedro as the proclaimer of independence and the grantor of the constitution.[98] Other verses, including a long poem by Dr. Jacy Monteiro, were thrown from windows to the crowds below.[99] Some poets made a point of linking the two emperors:

> After PEDRO THE FIRST
> Follows Emperor PEDRO THE SECOND:
> The father creates the nation; the son makes it prosper;
> One made free citizens from vassals;
> The other [makes] citizens [into] happy men.[100]

One pamphleteer adopted this theme as well, predicting that a second monument would soon be erected: "Not far from this glorious monument another no less sublime will be raised. One will tell newcomers that Pedro I founded the Empire of the Holy Cross; the other, that Pedro II secured it through his wisdom and his virtues."[101]

Although the heavy downpour put an end to the outdoor ceremony, the festivities continued with an evening gala at the São Pedro Theater, and the square was illuminated with the new gas lamps. A beam of electric light focused on the statue from the theater *varanda* to particularly good effect in the rain; according to Pedro, it looked like a "luminous ray descended from the heavens." The celebrations continued for two more nights, during which the theater *varanda* was open to box holders to view the square from that vantage point. In the square itself, there was music for the populace.[102] On 1 April, the last day of the celebrations, the Sociedade Petalógica (a literary club) organized a procession to Rochet's house on Ourives Street and brought him back to Constitution Square in triumph. In front of the bookshop in which the society met stood a bust of Rochet produced by a Brazilian artist, to be presented to the Frenchman. The many people present sang Francisco Manoel's "Anthem to the Arts," and the usual round of speeches and poetry took place. Eusébio toasted Rochet, who reportedly could not hold back tears at this recognition.[103]

Almost four decades after the original proposal for a monument to Brazil's first emperor, the equestrian statue finally stood in the capital. Despite the earlier rumors about Liberal revolts, nothing but rain disrupted the conduct of the ceremony, which on the surface looked like a successful civic ritual, although the Liberal press predictably tried to deny legitimacy to the government by claiming poor and unenthusiastic attendance, a routine opposition trope. The *Correio da Tarde* retorted that the large numbers of people who went to the square amounted to a protest against the opposition's assertions.[104] Radical Liberals went much further, however, and directly challenged the monument's political message and the assumptions that had underlain the decades of work on it.

THE POLITICAL DEBATE

At the time of the decision to move the ceremony to the afternoon, Pedro confided to his diary that "my principal desire is that the inauguration of my father's statue not be the occasion for any incidents or criticism; my pleasure will be much greater if it is unanimous."[105] Such was not to be the case, for radical Liberals attacked the monument and its celebration of the Brazilian state's monarchical origins as a way of indirectly, and sometimes directly, challenging the entire imperial regime. As 25 March and the statue's expected unveiling approached, the debate heated up. The monument's message, of course, was unmistakable. It honored Pedro I as the monarch who proclaimed independence and granted the constitution. But Liberal journalists asked: Was he really worthy of such an honor? Some went further and suggested that others deserved credit for independence and the constitution.

The Caxias administration, deeply invested in the monument and the success of the inauguration ceremony and initially surprised by the effective attack, vigorously defended the statue through the *Correio da Tarde* and paid articles in the *Jornal do Comércio*. The inauguration's transfer to 30 March meant that the debate lasted longer than it might otherwise have, but the *Correio Mercantil* judged that its peaceful nature spoke well of Brazil's progress.[106] It is difficult to determine which side won the debate, but in key respects the monument emerged crippled, at least among the political elite, and there is much truth to Iara Lis Carvalho Souza's speculative observation that, almost at once, the statue came to be seen "by contemporaries and inside the very monarchical regime as a thing of the past."[107] The pithy summation that the statue was a "bronze lie [*mentira de bronze*]" eventually caught on, although the exact phrase does not, to my knowledge, appear in any published contemporary discussion of the inauguration.[108]

The *Correio Mercantil* led the Liberal attack with a three-part editorial published on 23, 24, and 25 March, likely written by Francisco Otaviano. It responded to two earlier publications and promised an impartial assessment of Pedro I, which amounted to a profound critique of the first emperor.[109] A people's independence should not be personified in the form of a prince who only adhered to the cause "so as not to lose a throne," nor should political liberty be celebrated in the form of a constitution that the monarch issued only under pressure from those in the South and the North who rejected his closing of the Constituent Assembly. In any case, Pedro failed to adhere to the charter and executed patriots sentenced in military courts. Thus, to honor him with a monument was "shameful flattery" that amounted to a condemnation of Brazilian forefathers' struggles for independence and liberty.[110]

The next day, Francisco Otaviano recalled the bloody suppression of the Rio de Janeiro electors who had attempted to write a constitution in 1821 and pointed out that the "liberal party" was less interested in independence per se than in the "structures that secured liberty"; many doubted that a prince raised in the traditions of Portuguese despotism would effectively uphold liberty. In any case, Pedro was hardly essential to independence; had he gone to Portugal as the Cortes had ordered, independence would have come regardless (and perhaps without the "centralization in Rio de Janeiro," which in fact had made some northern provinces reluctant to join the new country). While many argued that Pedro's presence had spared Brazil much bloodshed during the struggle for independence, the *Correio Mercantil*'s editor doubted this, for surely Providence did not make liberty dependent on the leadership of a prince; in any case, there was fighting in some places, and the provinces' desire for unity was undermined by Pedro's actions. At this point, the editorial returned to Pedro's motives and reiterated that his principal goal as emperor was to serve the Bragança family's interests; thus, 7 April 1831 was a "second national revolution." The inauguration, expected for the next day, would "perpetuate, not the false glory that [they] want to attribute to the first monarch, but rather the true glory of his son, before whom some of those judges who condemned the father will tomorrow beg pardon for having been unfaithful to the cause of despotism."[111] This last passage alluded to the many statesmen who had, in 1831, criticized Pedro I and contributed to his decision to abdicate, but subsequently supported Pedro II.

On 25 March, the *Correio Mercantil* focused on Pedro I and the constitution; the constituent assembly's closing amounted to an act of "treason against the Brazilian nation," and he granted the new charter only to save his monarchy, as the experience of the next seven years showed. Thus, the regents declared on 13 April 1831 that "Brazil, *today* free, will demonstrate what it is, very different from what it appears to be. *The Law begins to reign among us . . . we are free.*" The monument amounted to telling the world that the "revolution against Pedro I . . . was a crime and forcing the Brazilian nation into a solemn atonement."[112]

One day before the scheduled inauguration, Teófilo Otoni published a pamphlet in which he explained his refusal to take part in the unveiling ceremonies, despite having been nominated to represent several municipalities and provincial assemblies; all three Liberal newspapers reprinted it on 25 March.[113] Otoni argued that the statue implied that independence had been "a gift of the monarch," that the constitution had been granted by divine right, and that 7 April 1831 was "a crime of rebellion." In contrast, according to Otoni, independence was the product of several generations, beginning with Tiradentes and the 1789 Inconfidência Mineira, the conspiracy in Minas Gerais, for which the militia lieutenant and amateur dentist was executed on the very square on which the statue now stood. The republican rebellion in Pernambuco in 1817 continued Tiradentes's work, and Pedro merely responded to this well-established desire for independence. More important, he soon turned himself into a dictator by closing the constituent assembly and he granted a constitution only to placate the opposition from the North. Because he did not consider the pressure on Pedro to abdicate to have been treasonous, Otonoi did not feel the need to participate in this "atonement." In short, the radical Liberal leader rejected the entire political message of the monument, and he did so much more forcefully than the *Correio Mercantil*'s editor.

In addition to publishing Otoni's broadside, the *Diário do Rio de Janeiro* condemned the "festivities ordered by the government," which the people would simply ignore.[114] This newspaper also launched what turned into a four-part critical historical analysis of Pedro I that defended 7 April 1831 as a legitimate act that vindicated the blood shed by the many victims of Pedro's reign and restored "the nation's rights." The last installment appeared on 30 March.[115] *A Atualidade* observed that statues "do not always symbolize a people's recognition and admiration, nor revoke the inexorable decrees of history." Pedro I granted the constitution to deflect the challenges that he faced after closing the constituent assembly and his unswerving aim was to reunite Brazil and Portugal. Thus, 7 April 1831 was a national act that condemned both a tyrannical ruler and an enemy of the "*pátria*'s independence." The statue "will be an [act of] homage rendered to the living [that is, Pedro II] on the pretext of [commemorating] the dead [that is, Pedro I]; but [it] will never amount to the revocation of the sovereign people's solemn voice of judgment on the Campo de Santana" (using the old name for the Campo dissociated it from Pedro I).[116] In other words, the monument actually celebrated Pedro II, albeit indirectly.

The Caxias cabinet was apparently caught off guard by the Liberal onslaught, even though the minister of empire, João Ildefonso de Sousa Ramos, had, on 22 March, attributed *A Atualidade*'s critical articles about the preparations to Otoni.[117] Given that the inauguration did not take place on the 25th, the monument commission's view of the statue, as expressed in Eusébio and Haddock Lobo's congratulatory addresses, would not enter the public domain until after the 30th (they appeared in the press on the 31st). No effective rebuttals to the *Correio Mercantil*'s editorials of 23 and 24 March appeared on the 25th, except for a short paid article in the *Jornal do Comércio* that responded to the first one or two of the *Correio*'s editorials. Its author—likely Senator Firmino Rodrigues Silva, a leading Saquarema ideologue—declared that the *Correio*'s editors did not know their history and that their protest would have been more believable had they opposed the statue from the beginning of the campaign. To be sure, independence would have come, with or without Pedro, but he was central to the process as "a center of action and order." Without him, Brazil would have been "sliced up into republican states" and would have fallen prey to European intervention and "ambitious caudillos." This was, of course, the classic conservative defense of unity and order as the Brazilian monarchy's supreme achievements.[118] In its editorial on the 25th, the *Jornal do Comércio* declared that the inauguration celebrated "the two most important events of our history—Independence and [our] political organization." Pedro's central role in 1822 ensured that Brazil avoided "the atrocities of the New World caudillos, or the anarchy of democratic multitudes." No honest man could disagree that Pedro played the most prominent role in the movement for independence and that "the man's blemishes disappear before the citizen's and the prince's heroism."[119]

At the cabinet meeting at which the postponement was decided, Justice Minister Francisco de Paula de Negreiros Saião Lobato, "very angry," lamented that he could not personally respond to the Liberals' attacks; Pedro recommended that his ministers "criticize ideas with the necessary energy, but never insult" their opponents. He privately doubted the hotheaded Saião, the most "intransigent historical conservative, Red or Puritan," in the cabinet, could keep an even temper in the debate.[120] The administration quickly articulated a press campaign to rebut the Liberals and particularly Otoni, whose hand Pedro saw behind all three Liberal newspapers.[121] On 26 March, the *Correio da Tarde* reprinted a paid article from the *Jornal do Comércio*, and in its report on the constitution's celebration (whose official rituals had taken place), condemned the "ungrateful gang" whose members were now trying to portray the charter as "an imposition by the first soldier of independence."[122] A paid article in the *Jornal do Comércio* reiterated Pedro I's centrality in the struggle for independence, in which he served as the "north star to guide the Brazilian provinces in marching united," and praised his role as a liberal prince, grantor of the constitution. The monument expressed, moreover, the entire nation's will as evidenced by the numerous delegations to present congratulations.[123]

On 28 March, Senator Firmino published the first of three "communiqués" in the *Jornal do Comércio* to rebut Otoni. Firmino began by criticizing the Liberals for their last-minute attack on the statue; if they had disagreed with it, they should have done so eight years earlier. Moreover, it was wrong to use the events of 7 April 1831 to condemn Pedro's entire reign. To be sure, the first emperor had made mistakes, but this hardly justified retroactively denying his earlier achievements. To condemn them amounted to taking the side of the Portuguese Cortes, which had sought to reduce Brazil's de facto independence. The final installment of this essay, published on 30 March, systematically defended Pedro's actions as emperor. He maintained order in the country; although he dissolved the constituent assembly, he quickly granted a new constitution to which Brazilians swore their oath "in the midst of enthusiastic acclamations by the capital's residents." He abdicated the Portuguese crown in favor of his daughter and did his best to preserve the integrity of the empire through the Cisplatine War. Pedro always abided by his constitution; while in France in 1830, it was the king who violated the charter; in Brazil in 1831, "it was the people, in the full enjoyment of all political liberties—free elections, a free press, and free speech—who wanted one more right, that of imposing on the head of the nation, [through demonstrations] in the streets, the dismissal of a ministry in which he had confidence." At that point, Pedro sacrificed himself for the good of his country by abdicating. What followed was hardly a revolution, stressed Firmino, for abdication was entirely within the emperor's constitutional prerogative, and all of the country's institutions continued to operate. In sum, "Pedro I did everything possible to prove his good intentions, his commitment to the constitutional cause, [and] his love for Brazil; he did not do what was impossible—proclaim the republic to satisfy those who judged the monarchy to be an exotic plant in the Americas and be [himself] born in Brazil."[124] Pedro II apparently appreciated Firmino's efforts, which he judged "skillfully written," and he cast the senator a benevolent smile at the moment of the unveiling.[125]

Other critics of Otoni were less measured than Firmino. A communiqué in which Pedro recognized Saião Lobato's style condemned Otoni for his efforts to "corrupt [public] opinion" and "discredit the principle of [respect for] authority" and accused him of blasphemy in his attacks on the "Brazilian population's generous sentiments" and the "head of state, [Pedro I's] worthy son and successor."[126] The criticisms of Otoni quickly turned into personal attacks, as some blamed his rancor on Pedro's failure to select him for a senate seat (vacant senate seats were filled by the emperor who appointed one of the three candidates elected by the province; Otoni had twice topped the list from Minas Gerais, but Pedro had chosen others).[127] In the first week of April, accusations of insider trading in shares of his Mucuri colonization company further sought to discredit Otoni.[128] Several writers accused the Liberals of artfully constructing their campaign and propagating false rumors about the government's fear of a conspiracy in the days leading up to the inauguration; others recalled Otoni's involvement in the 1842 revolt in Minas Gerais.[129]

The debate quickly became repetitive, but several of its features merit further comment. Many appealed to history. The author of a five-part paid article proclaimed that his was "the voice of severe and rigorous history," an impartial judge of the "degenerate liberalism of recent origin" that sought to "disparage the heroic figure" of Pedro I.[130] On 29 March, the author of a paid article in the *Correio Mercantil* published the names of all the deputies and senators who had voted to ban Pedro from returning to Brazil on pain of death in 1834, a list that included more than a few supporters of the current administration and the monument.[131] On the 25th, *A Atualidade* published the section of John Armitage's *History of Brazil* on those who had sought to proclaim Pedro an absolute monarch back in the 1820s.[132] In response to the transcription of Evaristo da Veiga's relatively favorable obituary of Pedro I, *A Atualidade* reprinted a much more critical 1831 article from the Moderado leader's *Aurora Fluminense*.[133] Individuals who changed their political views were reminded of their past. Among them was Francisco de Sales Torres Homem, who had moved from radical liberalism as expressed in his 1849 pamphlet that condemned the repression of the Praieira Rebellion, *O libelo do povo* (The People's Accusation), to the Conservatives in less than a decade.[134] *A Atualidade* also juxtaposed Domingos José Gonçalves de Magalhães's laudatory poetry, "in which Pedro I, his statue, and the second empire [sic] are exalted to the heavens," with some of his Exaltado verse of thirty years earlier.[135]

In response to the Liberal newspapers' editorials on 7 April, which reiterated the attacks on the statue, the authors of two paid articles responded by pointing out that the date had been struck from the roster of days of national festivity in 1848 by a Liberal-dominated chamber.[136] In an unusual assertion, one Dr. França Leite praised Pedro I in a *Jornal do Comércio* paid article for his recognition that "Africa was Brazil's cancer," which led him to sign the treaty to end the slave trade and to promote European colonization to deal with the country's "lack of workers."[137] Only the most radical newspaper, *A Atualidade*, paid much attention to the martyrs of the Confederação do Equador, the resistance to Pedro I's government in Pernambuco and other northern provinces which coalesced into a short-lived republican confederation in mid-1824. Although allusions to such resistance as one of Pedro's motives for granting the constitution occasionally referred to this movement, the Confederação was difficult to fit into a smooth narrative of precursors to independence for, coming after 1822 and after Pedro had granted the constitution, it could be easily dismissed as a separatist movement.[138]

The space for compromise or moderate positions closed as the debate progressed. Luís Francisco da Veiga had little success in his efforts to distinguish between "the prince, who adhered to our independence, who established monarchy in Brazil, and granted us the most liberal of written constitutions"—worthy of the monument—and "the emperor, who thousands of times violated the constitution, who squandered state revenue, who launched the country into ruinous adventures, and never showed himself to be truly Brazilian." This pamphlet, published in late February, initially drew little commentary, but Veiga's insistence that the monument not be seen as a commentary on those who had been central to the events of 7 April 1831 (among them, his uncle, Evaristo) soon drew criticism from all quarters.[139] It was simply not possible to draw such fine distinctions—political figures could not be judged "on the basis of isolated facts in their lives," explained one writer—and at the time of the inauguration, both *A Atualidade* and paid articles in the *Jornal do Comércio* condemned the younger Veiga, though for very different reasons.[140]

Historians have made much of Otoni's invocation of Tiradentes as the first martyr of independence, and the contrast between the execution of a humble patriot and the erection of the monument, which allegedly took place on the same site, was a powerful image.[141] In addition to Otoni's pamphlet, the *Diário do Rio de Janeiro* published a sonnet dedicated "to the martyrs of Brazil's independence," among them Tiradentes, forgotten by "an inconstant and flattering group / . . . / Preaching only—Pedro I." The following day it published the sentence against the Minas Gerais conspirators.[142] *A Atualidade* joined in the poetic politics by publishing Pedro Luís Pereira de Souza's "O Tiradentes," which declared that "the blood of this Christ baptized the *pátria*," and contrasted this with Brazilians' response to the new statue:

> Brazil, crossing his arms,
> Bends his knees, contrite
> Before the mass of granite
> Of the first emperor.[143]

According to Salvador de Menezes Drummond Furtado de Mendonça (1841–1913), then a young journalist and contributor to the radical liberal press, this poem "filled the square" on 30 March and joined the other laudatory verse distributed that day.[144] José Murilo de Carvalho claims that the police seized copies of it, but there is no contemporary press indication of such heavy-handed action. In any case, the authorities could not prevent the poem's publication on 25 March in *A Atualidade*.[145] The poem soon became so well known that, in 1870, a writer judged it unnecessary to reprint the work, "for all repeat it," at least in the São Paulo student milieu about which he was writing.[146]

Nevertheless, in 1862, Tiradentes was far from a familiar figure. Radical Liberals sought to make him into their symbol, stressing the martyr's call for liberty, but he was not widely known. One journalist lamented that Charles Ribeyrolles, a French radical exile, rather than a Brazilian, had been the first to give notice of the Minas Gerais conspirator in his 1861 *Brasil pitoresco* (Picturesque Brazil).[147] This was, of course, something of an exaggeration, for Tiradentes was known in Minas Gerais, and back in 1821 Otoni's father had led the campaign to remove the marker of infamy that had been placed in Ouro Preto.[148] As we saw in the last chapter, the Instituto Histórico had done some research on the movement, and there were occasional references to it on 7 September in the 1840s and 1850s; Francisco Adolpho de Varnhagen had roundly condemned it. In April 1862, the Liberals of Diamantina held a mass for Tiradentes's soul; five years later, Saldanha Marinho, then president of Minas Gerais, presided over the ceremony of laying the foundation for a monument "to the conspirators' memory" in Ouro Preto.[149] For others, Tiradentes was merely a premature forerunner of independence; one of the laudatory poems distributed at the inauguration invoked him as a man who died for his *pátria*; Pedro I, however, fulfilled the dream: " . . . He proclaimed / What the unfortunate [Tiradentes] wished to see flourish here / And [the] *pátria* today calls itself independent."[150]

In short, the full implications of the competing invocations of Tiradentes had yet to be worked out. Otoni's critics did not seem to know how to respond to his view of Tiradentes as the independence struggle's first leader. Senator Firmino admitted that he would be the first to recognize Otoni's originality but said nothing more about Tiradentes in his lengthy rebuttal of the *Histórico*.[151] Likewise most of the other critics simply ignored this aspect of Otoni's pamphlet. The most effective conservative rebuttal of Otoni's invocation of Tiradentes came in the form of an anonymous paid article in the *Jornal do Comércio* on 30 March 1862. Tiradentes may have had the laudable goal of winning "liberty" for his country, but because Brazil was not ready his cry for freedom was especially dangerous. Nor was Brazil ready in 1817, and had either Tiradentes or the Pernambucan republicans succeeded, they would have left Brazil "a mountain of ruins, like the Spanish republics, our neighbors."[152] An anonymous Bahian pamphleteer who argued that independence had actually come in 1808 with the arrival of João VI and the establishment of Portuguese imperial government in Rio de Janeiro, and held that Pedro I merely sought to defend an existing independence from the despotic acts of the Lisbon parliament, resorted to an ad hominem argument and dismissed Tiradentes as a "man of low condition," perhaps even a "barber." The 1789 conspiracy, he added, was merely an effort to save Minas Gerais tax farmers indebted to the crown (a view not so different from that of some modern historians). Given that Brazil was already independent in 1817, the Pernambuco rebellion could not have been part of the process.[153]

In a brilliant satire of Tiradentes and the radical Liberals' use of him, Henrique Fleiüss portrayed a giant tooth, topped by a classically dressed figure wearing a Phrygian cap, pulling a tooth from a prostrate despotism. Caricatures of the major Liberal newspapers' editors in the form of Indian allegories like those of the equestrian statue sit between the tooth's roots. Among them, Otoni holds a smaller parrotlike figure labeled *Atualidade*. What amounts to simply a clever pun on Tiradentes (literally tooth-puller) carefully shies away from identifying despotism— Fleiüss, in fact, never criticized the monarchy in his cartoons—and also indicates that there was then no recognized way of portraying Tiradentes (the image of Tiradentes as a Christ-like martyr still lay far in the future).[154]

Other critics carped about the monument's design. At the end of January, a short-lived literary journal, *A Mocidade* (probably a student newspaper), had pointed out that the statue was chock full of historical anachronisms. On 7 September 1822, Pedro was merely prince-regent, so he could not have been wearing imperial insignia, and the constitution was not granted until 25 March 1824. The author ultimately judged the statue as "national in name and foreign in every other way."[155] *A Mocidade* evidently had a small readership, and not until the *Jornal do Comércio*'s *cronista* raised these questions were they more widely debated. He argued that the monument was internally contradictory. The pedestal should have retained the reliefs of the patriarchs of independence, rather than the Indian figures who represented savage, uncivilized lands instead of the civilized constitutional monarchy that Pedro I had founded. The base was more appropriate for a monument to Pedro Álvares Cabral, the Portuguese explorer regarded as Brazil's discoverer. And the journalist remarked on the historical anachronism of combining 7 September 1822 and 25 March 1824, noting further that Pedro I was not in full-dress uniform at Ipiranga. Responding to these critiques, Pedro II noted privately that the author appeared to want "historical accuracy to the point of putting my father in fatigues and mounted on a mule."[156] In a series of paid articles published in the first week of April in the *Correio Mercantil*, one Eurípides also pointed to the historical anachronisms and criticized the horse's pose, the "colossal, frenzied, and extraordinary hat" (some claimed that Mafra's design had contemplated Pedro waving his hat), and the color of Pedro's face (not white but bronze, just like the Indian figures).[157] Another wag thought that the position of the horse's tail made it look as if it was fleeing the noise of artillery salutes, while more than a few noted that Pedro held the constitution in the direction of the theater to indicate that the charter amounted to a "political comedy."[158] The shamelessly self-serving fictional politician who narrates Joaquim Manuel de Macedo's satire of imperial politics, *Memórias do sobrinho do meu tio* (Memoirs of My Uncle's Nephew, 1867–68), also thought the Indians "admirably executed" but noted that they "give no indication of understanding what is going on above them; they are an exact representation of the Brazilian people."[159]

Two years later, Alexandre José de Mello Moraes condemned the choice of Indians to symbolize Brazil's rivers; the original proposal to surround Pedro with "the architects of our independence" should have been maintained. The monument amounted to "a joke. So the emperor proclaims the constitution to Indians and crocodiles? What role did those Indians and crocodiles have in Brazil's independence or in writing the constitution?"[160] By contrast, Moreira de Azevedo praised the Indian figures as the most beautiful part of the monument. He joined others in questioning the choice to have Pedro wear a hat and lamented that a foreign artist had been contracted. As a result, the monument did not adequately demonstrate Brazil's progress.[161]

The debate about Pedro I and the equestrian statue reprised all of the familiar discussions about Brazil's constitutional monarchy that had long characterized days of national festivity. The Historical Liberals' sustained critique, however, was something that had not been seen for some time. How much impact it had in 1862 is not clear, nor is it clear how effectively the administration campaign had discredited Otoni. Machado de Assis suggested that few took the government's response seriously: "The country knows what the paid harangues in the *Jornal do Comércio*'s anonymous columns are worth."[162] In the 1862 session, the chamber of deputies failed to take up an 1861 senate bill to restore 12 October to the roster of days of national festivity, an indication that the first emperor's position had been undermined by the monument's critics.[163] At the time of the inauguration, the radical Liberals' view was that of a minority in the political class, but they first effectively articulated some of the themes that republicans would develop further in the 1870s and 1880s. Already in 1871 a young Rui Barbosa could claim that "there is no Brazilian who believes in the bronze lie [*mentira de bronze*]"; that year, the future abolitionist, José do Patrocínio, also used the phrase in one of his first published poems.[164]

By about mid-April, the three months of "hard-fought and heated discussion" had finally given way to silence.[165] The debate had, of course, not settled anything; as Machado de Assis remarked, it did not bode well for "a monument that claims to derive from the country's unanimous desire" to be caught up in such a "bitter debate."[166] To be sure, the statue remained a landmark in the capital, an obligatory stop on foreign visitors' itineraries. Although today it is overshadowed by unattractive mid-twentieth-century high-rises and three- and four-story

FIGURE 5.2.
The Pedro I equestrian statue, ca. 1870s.
Source: AHMI, II-5-1-N.º 2. Courtesy Museu Imperial/IBRAM/MinC.

late-nineteenth-century buildings, at the time of its inauguration the monument loomed over the modest structures around the square (Figure 5.2). To English-speaking residents, Constitution Square became known as "Statue Square," while according to one later folklorist, people dubbed it "Caboclos' Square," after the Indian figures around the pedestal (*caboclo* was then a synonym for Indian).[167]

Some limited improvements to the square came in the next few years, including a wrought-iron fence around the statue and new trees, although in 1867 Moreira de Azevedo thought that the square should have been left open to accommodate "large popular gatherings" or "magnificent ceremonies of the nation." He did not, however, repeat this suggestion in the substantially revised 1877 version of his book.[168] Over the next few decades, the area around the square gradually declined; it eventually became known more for prostitution and male homosexual cruising than for the lively night clubs, bars, and theaters in its environs.[169] The statue of José Bonifácio de Andrada e Silva, long contemplated as the counterpart to the equestrian statue of Pedro I, was not inaugurated on the nearby São Francisco Square until a full decade later (Chapter Nine), and this delay was no doubt what lay behind the *Folhinha Laemmert*'s prognosis for August 1867: "A subscription will be opened to receive cash donations for some monuments that will be concluded on Saint Never's day."[170]

Perhaps the most striking feature about the statue is how quickly the passions elicited by its inauguration faded. That the government made no effort to incorporate the monument into official celebrations on days of national festivity deprived radical Liberals of a target that might have encouraged them to reprise their criticisms of March 1862. Instead, as we will see in Chapter Ten, the square became the site for new forms of popular festivities on 7 September in the 1870s. The monument, once advocated in the upper reaches of Rio de Janeiro society, fell into the hands of plebeian patriots on independence day, perhaps the reason why Moreira de Azevedo dropped his call to use the square for national ceremonies from the 1877 edition of his book.

CHAPTER SIX

Patriots on the Streets and at Home, 1840s–1860s

Although political questions normally dominated the press discussions about days of national festivity and most of what took place in Rio de Janeiro consisted of official festivities, for a brief period starting in the mid-1850s, so-called popular festivities flourished on 7 September. What made them "popular" in the parlance of the day was their organization by, to use modern jargon, civil society groups known as "patriotic societies" and not the state. These popular 7 September celebrations generally lacked partisan political overtones, although there are some indications that their early organizers had close ties to the Liberals, and they attracted significant participation from a broad range of people, certainly broader than most of the official festivities. The first of these patriotic societies, the Sociedade Ipiranga, began celebrating independence in 1856; by the early 1860s, about twenty such associations had promoted independence celebrations in at least one year. Although this tide of popular festivities ebbed rapidly in the early 1860s, vestiges of these celebrations lingered through the decade, and they resumed in different form in the 1870s.

Public celebrations are inherently political; exclusion or inclusion marks the boundaries that celebrants draw between those who are part of the group—in this case, Brazilians—and those who cannot be members. Such micropolitics gains prominence in this chapter, in contrast to the last five chapters, which focused on the large political questions concerning the nature of the imperial Brazilian state. The popular festivities did not include all residents of Rio de Janeiro, and the celebrants distinguished between themselves and those who could not be part of the nation that they envisaged. They excluded the usual suspects of slaves, Africans, the disorderly, and many of the free poor. The "popular festivities of independence" were dominated by members of the middle and upper classes and a few groups in the working classes whose members sought to gain respectability, although the celebrants often claimed the mantle of the *povo*—the common people—for themselves. While *povo* could mean "people" in the sense of a nation, more commonly it referred to the masses, poor, nonwhite, and illiterate, who lacked the attributes of the civilization and culture in which the middle and upper classes took pride.

This assessment of these celebrations leads naturally into an examination of middle- and upper-class sociability during days of national festivity. Some of these questions have already been noted in passing in previous chapters, particularly from the perspective of foreign diplomats and travelers, but the density of Brazilian sources on the celebrations during these years makes it possible to examine this sociability systematically, without the distraction of the overwhelming partisan political rhetoric. The expansion of the press and the many new kinds of articles—particularly the *cronistas'* accounts of life in the city—offer access to the experiences of their middle- and upper-class readership. Although members of this elite normally enjoyed holidays on days of national festivity, they often had the obligation to participate in aspects of the official festivities. There are also indications of private, domestic celebrations, in which music and poetry figured prominently, and opportunities for families to venture out on the street.

The middle decades of the century saw important social and cultural changes in Rio de Janeiro. João Manoel Pereira da Silva (1817–98) recalled that the political peace of the 1850s "enlivened families' domestic life and social customs. Lyric and dramatic theater, balls and concerts repeated almost daily in the empire's capital, private gatherings to listen to music and song, dramatic soirées, [all] enlivened [life] and stimulated the desire for pleasant diversions."[1] In addition to underwriting the state's newfound strength and financing the construction of railroads and other improvements, coffee revenue paid for the import of European consumer goods ranging from pianos to fashionable dress.[2] The middle and upper classes whose members benefited most from these changes were also the principal readers of the newspapers that proliferated after midcentury. While one of the characters in Manoel de Araújo Porto Alegre's 1845 *Angélica e Firmino* grumbles that reading newspapers "wastes a lot of time," he nevertheless eagerly searches for the *Jornal do Comércio* in the "large bundle of newspapers" that a servant brings.[3] Such interest in the burgeoning press characterized middle- and upper-class life in Rio de Janeiro and sustained the steady growth in newspaper circulation.

POPULAR 7 SEPTEMBER FESTIVITIES,
1850S–1860S

Successful days of national festivity required popular participation or at least a popular presence, but the level and nature of the *povo*'s engagement is almost impossible to elucidate. The *Diário do Rio de Janeiro*'s anonymous *cronista* wrote in 1853 and 1854 about the crowded Palace Square and the vigorous cheers on 7 September; in 1853, he claimed that all could plainly see "the multitudes' happiness."[4] Such accounts cast the population as spectators who watched the official festivities and dutifully cheered when called on to do so (there are no indications that the government packed the outdoor crowds with "official shouters" or "cheerleaders" to ensure a good response, as did the French government of this time).[5] In the second half of the 1850s, however, a significant portion of Rio de Janeiro's population moved from being merely onlookers to participating actively in what the press described as the popular festivities of independence.

Although partisan politics was muted during most of the 1850s, and particularly during the Conciliação (1853–57), it was never entirely absent from the press's discussions of days of national festivity, in which journalists regularly claimed to speak for the people or to infer the people's views from their response to official commemorations. Commenting on newspaper coverage of 25 March 1859, the new radical liberal periodical, *A Atualidade*, contrasted the *Correio Mercantil* ("more of the *povo*") and the *Jornal do Comércio* ("always [on the] official [side]"). The *Correio* had reported "almost general indifference. . . . Besides this day's official celebration, it merited no other demonstration of joy." By contrast, the *Jornal do Comércio* "confused the movement of some imperial grandees' coaches, the display of some embroidered [court] uniforms, and the artillery salutes and musket volleys with the *povo*'s happiness, jubilation, and enthusiasm."[6] In December 1855, the Exaltado and sometime republican Antônio Borges da Fonseca reveled in what he saw as the "cold shoulder that all, *povo* and *big shots*, turned to these official days," while the viscerally monarchist Francisco de Paula Brito lamented the indifference to the three days of national festivity.[7] We must be careful not to take such assessments at face value, for all claimed to represent faithfully the people's true views. In 1861, the Conservative *O Regenerador* sought to discredit the opposition by explaining that articles lamenting the lack of popular participation in festivals and blaming it on the government always appeared in opposition newspapers on days of national festivity.[8]

Days of national festivity were more than merely referenda on those in power, whose outcome partisan journalists sought to influence, through their portrayals of the rituals, the predictable politicization of civic ritual coverage that appeared year after year. A careful reading of the press leaves no doubt that the three days of national festivity resonated in different ways with Rio de Janeiro's population. For reasons that puzzled contemporaries and that remain unclear today, 7 September turned into an elaborate series of citywide popular festivals in the second half of the 1850s, which declined abruptly in the early 1860s. Nothing comparable took place on 25 March or 2 December. The principal feature that distinguished such "popular festivals"—a term widely used in the press—was their organization by civil society. Official civic rituals were, as we have seen, essentially administrative matters. Orders went out to the Guard and army units to prepare a parade, requisitions for blank rounds went to the army and navy arsenals, invitations to the Te Deum and the levee were issued, theater impresarios fulfilled their contractual obligations to stage gala performances (see Chapter Seven), and government offices pulled out their lights to illuminate their buildings' façades. Large crowds might watch these rituals and could play a limited role by joining in the cheers to the objects of the festival, but this alone did not make for a popular festival. Nor did the political demonstrations that had characterized so many days of national festivity since the 1820s, although they sometimes had widespread support. "Popular festivities" were something else.

Despite the large crowds that the *Diário do Rio de Janeiro*'s *cronista* noted in 1853 and 1854, 7 September celebrations in the early 1850s apparently had little popular resonance. Two old stalwarts of Rio de Janeiro political journalism argued about the reasons for this in 1854. Borges da Fonseca reportedly lamented that the day had passed "with neither remembrance nor enthusiasm," to which the conservative Justiniano José da Rocha retorted that the radical liberal only saw as true national festivals those in which "disorderly mobs of *povo* run through the streets shouting, among cheers, death threats." Brazil had last seen such a festival on 7 September 1848, but now the nation recognized the need for peace and progress. Only when "revolutionary treachery convinced the youth that absurd recolonization plans were afoot was 7 September greeted with noisy demonstrations." Today, there were no such pretexts and not the slightest need for such manifestations.[9] Borges da Fonseca responded that Brazil was still not free of Portuguese and pointed out that the United States celebrated its independence enthusiastically, as did Bahians on 2 July. In Rio de Janeiro, "not a single lantern was set out, for this city belongs to the Portuguese."[10]

While the debate between Borges da Fonseca and Justiniano remained largely on the terrain of politics and amounted to refighting the battles of the 1830s and 1840s, a few sought to do something about the apathy that both journalists acknowledged. Before dawn on 7 September 1853, the poet and diplomat José Maria do Amaral "and some distinguished Brazilians" ascended the Corcovado peak and, at daybreak, resolved to found the Sociedade dos Cavaleiros do Ipiranga (Knights of Ipiranga Society), whose name invoked the locale in São Paulo where Pedro had proclaimed independence in 1822. Its purposes were to commemorate Brazil's independence each 7 September, to construct "a grandiose monument" in honor of independence, "to develop and sustain national sentiment," and to acquire documents and artifacts related to the "declaration of independence."[11] By the end of the year, Senator Aureliano de Sousa e Oliveira Coutinho, a Liberal who, as leader of the so-called court faction, had been enormously influential on Pedro II until 1848, was "Grand-Master of the new Knights of Ipiranga Order." Manoel de Araújo Porto Alegre—characteristically blunt—liked the "silliness, for it speaks to the heart at a time when the *pátria* is in the purse, and when people hide their feelings, and when national sentiment [is] down the toilet." He judged that Pedro II supported the order's establishment, but nothing more came of it.[12]

The abortive Ipiranga Order apparently led to the founding in 1855 of the Sociedade Ipiranga (Ipiranga Society).[13] Its first board of directors explained that its "patriotic and philanthropic aim is not limited to the puerile amusements of a *povo* without ideas, but rather [is] to preserve, year after year, through a meaningful act, the anniversary of the empire's independence, and in this way awaken patriotism, and with it, love of liberty and hatred of slavery." By September 1856, the society counted almost 900 members, each of whom had paid six mil-réis (US$3.36) in dues. It actively recruited members and prepared printed invitations for that purpose.[14] In its listing in the *Almanaque Laemmert* for 1857 (the only year that it appeared in this city directory), the Sociedade declared that its purposes were (1) to prepare "illuminations, band shells, and other public festivities" on 7 September, (2) to raise statues of the "great men who played major parts in the work of [winning] Brazil's independence," (3) to improve the lot of these men's descendents who lived in poverty, and (4) "to redeem slaves born in Brazil from captivity."[15] In this section we examine its first purpose, while the fourth is addressed later in this chapter. The second—monuments—amounted to very little as others ran the equestrian statue campaign, and I have found no evidence on this society's charitable work.

Immediately after its founding, the Sociedade Ipiranga took on the task of rejuvenating traditional forms of commemoration and instituting new traditions. In 1855 and subsequent years, it requested that residents once again illuminate the windows of their houses in honor of independence, a traditional custom that had largely disappeared.[16] In 1856 and 1857, the Sociedade prepared detailed programs for its celebrations. At dawn on 7 September, a band would play the independence anthem on

Constitution Square, the site designated for the equestrian statue of Pedro I. At the same time, fireworks from the city's hills would announce the start of the festivities, alongside artillery salutes from the forts and ships in the harbor. This would be repeated at 1:00 pm and at dusk. A deputation from the society would attend the levee, and at 4:00 pm the society would hold a Te Deum at the Ordem Terceira do Carmo's chapel. After this, the entire society would parade to the city council chambers to pay homage to the portrait of Pedro I. The society hired bands to play outside the council building and, in 1856, planned a fireworks display for after the theater gala. The following year, it planned fireworks for 9 September.[17]

Within a year or two, numerous other societies joined the Ipiranga in promoting similar celebrations. By 1864, newspapers had recorded fully twenty societies as active in at least one year. A handful of them merely added commemorations of independence to their other purposes, but most presented the celebration of 7 September as their raison d'être. The Sociedade Petalógica—an informal association of Romantic *literateurs* who met in Paula Brito's bookshop on Constitution Square—appealed to its "friends" and neighbors for funds to illuminate the square in 1859.[18] Founded in 1856, the Sociedade Independência Brasileira (Brazilian Independence Society)—300 strong in 1857—claimed São Domingos Square as the locale of its festival and raised temporary monuments in 1857, 1858, and 1859, by which time it was calling them customary celebrations; in 1857, it was composed "in its entirety of artisans."[19] The Associação Nacional dos Artistas (National Association of Artisans) constructed temporary monuments on the Palace Square in 1856, 1857, and 1858, and invited "all Brazilians who reside in this capital" to join their celebrations.[20] The Sociedade Festival 7 de Setembro (7 September Festival Society), founded in 1859 by "young Brazilian students," ran a bimonthly literary and scientific salon and organized annual 7 September celebrations.[21] The Sociedade Independência Juvenil (Youth Independence Society), which joined the Petalógica on Constitution Square in 1859, consisted of students in the military preparatory schools; likewise, the Sociedade 7 de Setembro (7 September Society) that appeared in 1861 enrolled students from several schools.[22]

A few of these societies appear to have been neighborhood associations like the Sociedade Setembrista Castelense (Castelo Setembrist Society), which celebrated 7 September on Castelo Hill in 1862, as did the newly founded Sociedade Independência (Independence Society) in 1863.[23] In 1857 and 1858, residents of Saco do Alferes, São Cristóvão, and Santa Rita parish put up band shells and temporary monuments and arranged for music and fireworks. The Santa Rita festival organizers constituted themselves as the Sociedade União e Independência (Union and Independence Society) and raised 600 mil-réis (US$324) in their first year.[24] Beyond these rather vague indications of occupation—artisans, students, members of the literary and cultural elite—or residence, there is little evidence about most of these societies' social composition.

In this regard, the Sociedade Ipiranga is better documented. Its membership dues, of course, would have excluded most of the city's population; indeed, in this sense, these societies were far from "popular" organizations. The abortive Ipiranga Order, the Sociedade Ipiranga's forerunner, had close ties to Liberals through Senator Aureliano; the diplomat, Amaral, later gained some prominence as a Liberal journalist. Likewise, Porto Alegre, who enjoyed Pedro's patronage, had been associated with Aureliano and the court faction in the 1840s.[25] None of these three men, however, were central to the Ipiranga's early work. By the time that the society was founded on 7 September 1855, Aureliano was sick (he died on the 25th), and Porto Alegre was busy with his new post as director of the Fine Arts Academy (an appointment that he received in 1854 from the Conciliação ministry).[26]

The Sociedade Ipiranga's first president, Luís Cipriano Pinheiro de Andrade, was a long-serving treasury and customs employee with no apparent political connections.[27] I have been unable to identify the other officers, but the thirteen *conselheiros* (directors-at-large) included Ezequiel Corrêa dos Santos, a pharmacist and editor, back in 1830–31, of the Exaltado *A Nova Luz Brasileira*. After the abdication, Ezequiel retired from politics and devoted himself to his profession.[28] He also paid for the publication of the society's statutes. The Baron of Suruí (Manoel da Fonseca Lima e Silva) served as war and navy minister in several regency cabinets (before 1837) and had been president of São Paulo in 1844–47 during the Liberal quinquennium. João Maximiano Mafra, winner of the design competition for the Pedro I equestrian statue, was a teacher at the fine arts academy (and had close ties to Porto Alegre), while Francisco Manoel da Silva may have been the national anthem's composer (although his name is sufficiently common that I cannot be confident about this identification).[29] Fifteen years later, Joaquim Pinto de Campos, the priest who celebrated the Ipiranga's Te Deums in 1856 and 1857, recalled that he had been invited to do so in the former year by one of the society's directors, Dr. Fernando Sebastião Dias da Mota, a lawyer and Liberal who had served in parliament and in the Rio de Janeiro provincial assembly in the 1840s.[30] Campos himself, however, partially contradicts the Ipiranga Society's Liberal complexion, for he had long been a Conservative, although apparently a moderate.[31]

Clearer evidence of the Sociedade Ipiranga's political orientation emerges from an examination of the fifty-two men who either served as *orador oficial* (spokesman) or joined the deputations that congratulated Pedro II on the society's behalf in 1856, 1857, 1858, 1859, 1860, and 1862. The list includes not a single prominent Saquarema, but numerous individuals associated at some point in their careers with the Liberals, such as Antônio Pereira Rebouças (1858, 1859, 1860), Porto Alegre (1856, 1858), and Suruí (1860). Six other men on this list had either been cabinet ministers during the 1844–48 Liberal period or would hold cabinet posts during the Progressista years (a seventh, the novelist and three-term Liberal deputy Joaquim Manoel de Macedo, turned down a cabinet post in 1864).[32] This evidence gives credence to the British chargé d'affaires's report that "more than usual enthusiasm on the part of the Liberal Party and the Brazilian people" characterized the celebrations in 1856,[33] a year of municipal elections. One short-lived radical Liberal newspaper called for citizens to vote against all of the Portuguese-born candidates, and especially Roberto Jorge Haddock Lobo (once again),[34] but there are no indications that Exaltados managed to mobilize their supporters in the way that they had done eight years earlier. Indeed, the elections were scarcely mentioned in the press coverage of the 7 September festivities.

A final bit of evidence for the Ipiranga's Liberal orientation comes from its exclusion from the Conservative-dominated equestrian statue campaign. The *Diário do Rio de Janeiro*'s *cronista* noted immediately after the campaign's launch that Brazil was entering the "era of monuments," given the revival of efforts to honor Pedro I and the Ipiranga's stated purpose of immortalizing the great men of Brazilian history in bronze.[35] As the society's official spokesman during the 7 September 1858 levee, Porto Alegre declared that the Ipiranga would contribute to the Pedro I monument, but there is no evidence that it actually did so.[36] When the statue was finally inaugurated, only two of the 7 September societies appointed delegations to represent their membership at the ceremony.[37] I have located no evidence that the Ipiranga did so, which is not surprising for by then it had fallen on hard times.

The artisan societies also had important Liberal connections. In 1857, the Sociedade Independência Brasileira held a Te Deum and, at its arch on São Domingos Square, honored Dias da Mota. He presented the society with its standard, and its members reciprocated with a "garland of coffee and tobacco [leaves], made out of Brazilian feathers." In his address to the society, Dias da Mota declared: "*Povo!* This day is yours, and no one will take it away."[38] At its formal session that year, the Associação Nacional dos Artistas honored the Pernambucan deputy, Francisco Carlos Brandão, for his efforts to "better the condition of the poor classes, the country's needy classes."[39] During that year's legislative session, Brandão had sponsored bills to require all "commercial establishments, workshops, and factories" to close on Sundays and other holy days and to create a commission to investigate exorbitant food prices. The year before, this representative of northern radical liberalism had also proposed measures to nationalize retail commerce by slapping a special tax on shops that employed more than one foreign (Portuguese) clerk.[40] While the Ipiranga apparently amounted to an association of a moderate Liberal elite, Dias da Motta's and Brandão's links to the artisan societies reflect the more radical Liberals' efforts to reach out to the urban working- and lower middle class, voters who would prove important to their 1860 electoral success in Rio de Janeiro.[41]

There is insufficient documentation on the directors, let alone the memberships, of the other societies to discuss their political orientation, and none took part in overt political demonstrations like those of the artisans in 1857. Given the very limited scholarship on associative life in nineteenth-century Brazil, it is impossible to set these patriotic societies into a larger social and political context. As in Buenos Aires, Mexico City, and Lima, the number of societies surged in midcentury Rio de Janeiro. The imperial government began to regulate societies in 1860, but only one patriotic association, founded in 1869, attempted to get its statutes formally approved (see Chapter Ten).[42] Like their counterparts elsewhere in Latin America, Rio de Janeiro's associations appear to have had internal democratic features, and joining such societies constituted a form of political involvement, just as did participation in civic rituals.

Newspaper accounts of these years generally suggest a broad, nonpartisan surge in popular celebrations. Whereas a *Jornal do Comércio cronista* judged the 1855 celebrations as "insipid, very insipid"—not surprising given the cholera epidemic—the following year he could barely contain himself as he described the "din of happiness," led by the Sociedade Artista Nacional and the Sociedade Ipiranga. The artisans constructed a triumphal arch on the Palace Square, while the Ipiranga's members celebrated on Constitution Square. Numerous public and private buildings were illuminated. The usual official rituals took place, with the exception of the National Guard parade, but all eyes were on what newspapers called the "popular festivities."[43] The *Diário do Rio de Janeiro* concluded that, "in short, the celebration was complete; all took part happily and even enthusiastically."[44] In 1857, explained the *Jornal do Comércio*'s *cronista*, Rio de Janeiro enjoyed "three nights of illuminations, salutes, girandoles, and rockets until we couldn't stand them any longer, philharmonics in band shells and on the streets, dinners and patriotic gatherings, and finally, a fireworks display in front of city hall, in their imperial majesties' presence."[45] His counterpart at the opposition *Correio Mercantil* was a bit less impressed, suggesting that most people on the streets were merely observers, no more engaged in the celebrations than if they had been for the independence of Timbuktu, but he conceded that the crowds were large. The rain that fell on 8 September reduced the festivities somewhat.[46]

Rain also hampered preparations for 7 September 1858, but the *Correio da Tarde* announced that at least seven different locations in the city would feature illuminated temporary monuments. The weather held, and the entire imperial family visited many of these street festivals on foot.[47] "The fervent enthusiasm with which the Brazilian people celebrated their independence" deeply impressed Altève Aumont, a French journalist, who found it impossible not to join in and shout "Long live the independence of Brazil" like a native; his friend and compatriot, Auguste François Biard, was less impressed and dismissed all of this as the shouts of ignorant slaves who did not understand the words.[48] The celebrations began even earlier in 1859. At midnight, hundreds of girandoles lit up the sky; "thousands of citizens of all classes and positions" rose well before daybreak "to hail the dawning of the first national day." On Constitution Square, the Sociedade Petalógica had constructed a fountain, topped by a bust of Pedro I and supported by the four great rivers of Brazil (the Amazon, Plate, Tocantins, and São Francisco), surrounded by twenty pillars with stars representing the provinces. Other societies likewise put up ephemeral allegorical structures. Bands and delegations from patriotic societies circulated through the streets, visiting each other's celebrations and attracting crowds.[49] The *Courier du Brésil*'s editor judged this the greatest celebration that he had seen in his eight years in Brazil. The Constitution Square festivities were such a success that Leuzinger published a lithograph of the "brilliantly illuminated square" that showed the "large concourse [of people] that was there during the festival's three nights."[50]

At the same time, neighborhood committees began raising funds and organizing 7 September celebrations. In 1858 and 1859, residents of several districts requested permission from the city council to construct monuments and fireworks platforms in public streets; others set up band shells and arranged for music.[51] Criticism of the neighborhood committees' efforts occasionally surfaced; in 1857, "O Oprimido" (The Oppressed One) complained that too many of these subscriptions were organized by city councilors and other officials who, backed by a detachment of municipal guards, intimidated residents into contributing to the celebrations.[52] Still others worried that the proliferation of celebrations was diluting the commemorations, while a satirical newspaper mocked the monument mania by announcing in 1859 that a triumphal arch would be erected between the Santa Cruz and São João forts, located on opposite sides of the entrance to the bay![53]

For no apparent reason, this outburst of patriotic commemoration declined almost as abruptly as it had burst onto the scene. The celebrations of 1860 were "less brilliant" than those of previous years, but the *Jornal do Comércio*'s *cronista* consoled himself with the peaceful elections of that day, proof of the country's orderly progress. The *Diário do Rio de Janeiro* opined that the elections had absorbed all of the previous years' enthusiasm.[54] In 1861, the *Revista Popular* declared that "sad and dispirited, the greatest Brazilian day has descended into the abyss of the past." Those who, only a few years earlier, had doubted the durability of the "false flame of improvised patriotism" had been right when they dismissed it as a short-lived "infatuation [*fogo de palha*]."[55] The following year, things were little better. One newspaper castigated the Sociedade Ipiranga for doing little more than putting up two band shells beside the newly inaugurated equestrian statue and hastily dismantling them the next day. More charitably, another reported that a few die-hards from this society and the Sociedade Festival Sete de Setembro rose early to greet the statue at dawn. Even Emperor Pedro II marveled at the "indifference with which today was celebrated this year, in light of the enthusiasm of a few years ago." The *Diário do Rio de Janeiro* judged that independence had been "celebrated in an almost ridiculous way" and called for the city council to rejuvenate the festival.[56] José Maria do Amaral's *O Espectador da América do Sul* agreed with Pedro's assessment in 1863: "We no longer have those popular festivals of independence in which, formerly, [members of] the *povo*, all heart, remembered, almost with tenderness, the birthday of their collective mother." That year, the Sociedade Ipiranga ceased to collect dues and announced that it would not promote any commemorations.[57] Clearly, much had changed since the societies' heyday of 1856–59.

Just as it is difficult to explain the rise of these popular celebrations on 7 September, so it is difficult to explain their decline. The popular festivities can be associated with the Conciliação and its emphasis on nonpartisan unity, but they only began in 1856, the last year of the Conciliação cabinet; although dominated by moderate Conservatives and apolitical imperial servants, this ministry reached out to urban Liberals. In its 7 September 1857 editorial, the *Diário do Rio de Janeiro* attributed the new celebrations to the development of civilization and industry; as progress "lights the way to the future, the *povo* awakens, takes heart, feels and understands this great idea of a free nation winning a distinguished place in the civilized world through its own intelligence. . . . A country must have arrived at the age of improvements to recognize that it is strong, independent, [and] sovereign to appreciate its nationality."[58] Such rhetoric characterized the Conciliação's emphasis on progress and material improvements. These themes also appeared in the sermon that Campos preached at the Ipiranga's 1857 Te Deum, although the priest lamented that "in these days of cheers and triumphs for material progress, God is forgotten in this confused laboratory for the perfection of [all] things" and emphasized that the Church had an important role to play in fostering moral progress.[59]

The popular festivities of independence can also be connected to the concurrent changes taking place in Rio de Janeiro's festival culture, notably the new forms of carnival celebrations that involved parading by elite societies. These are usually interpreted as the product of middle- and upper-class efforts to impose a model of orderly and civilized celebrations on the rowdy pre-Lenten festivities of the *entrudo*.[60] In 1857, the *Jornal do Comércio*'s *cronista* saw both 7 September 1856 and 1857's carnival as parallel celebrations that demonstrated the populace's orderly nature.[61] At about this time, the traditional popular festivities of the Divino Espírito Santo (Holy Spirit or Pentecost) went into steep decline, which Martha Abreu attributes to these efforts to civilize the population of Rio de Janeiro.[62]

The *Diário do Rio de Janeiro*'s *cronista* drew an important distinction in 1858 between the *povo*—the common people—"motivated by the desire for distraction, entertainment, and novelties," and the true believers in this new patriotism. The societies were gradually replacing the old veterans of independence as "a part of the youth . . . rises in protest against the weakening of such glorious recollections." These young people were not engaged in mere "patriotic nonsense [*patriotadas*]," added the *Correio Mercantil*'s *cronista*. They were a new generation that held dear the "land of [their] cradle."[63] Certainly the patriotic societies' activities, especially the nocturnal vigils and parading, required the energy of youth (as did the new carnival celebrations). Some further indications of the social ambitions (and social composition) of the celebrants—both the societies and the members of the *povo* who joined them—can be teased out from the newspaper coverage. The Associação Nacional dos Artistas and the new Sociedade Independência Nacional (National Independence Society), also composed of artisans, sought respectability in their 1857 morning gathering held at the São Pedro Theater. Before a portrait of Pedro II, its members heard an "eloquent speech" (presumably about 7 September), received a report about membership and finances, and listened to music. Their motto, "Work, Unity, Morality," underscores their efforts to bid for respectability, and Brandão congratulated the artisans on their devotion to "labor and morality," as well as to "national traditions."[64] The *Correio da Tarde* marveled in 1857 that even "families" joined the crowds at dawn on Constitution Square, and we have already noted a number of references to people of all classes and positions who joined the nighttime celebrations, including even the imperial family.[65]

On the last day of 1862, a long-simmering diplomatic dispute over British claims on Brazil boiled over when the irascible British minister, William Dougal Christie, ordered the Royal Navy to seize Brazilian vessels in Rio de Janeiro harbor as security for British claims.[66] For about a week, the port was effectively blockaded. A wave of patriotic indignation swept the country. Dionísio Cerqueira and his fellow students at the Escola Central marched to the palace and offered their services; they then joined other patriots in anti-British demonstrations. Dias da Motta led a "popular demonstration" in early January that filled the palace lobby with a "multitude" demanding the emperor's presence.[67] Pereira da Silva later recalled the "furious mobs, shouting, threatening vengeance against the English"; the police eventually had to move in to control the "rebellious plebe's furor."[68] Poets fanned the flames with rousing declamations against the British, and the future Baron of Capanema marveled at the number of "unmilitary heroes" who were eagerly joining volunteer battalions; others hatched suicidal plans to attack the British frigates with harbor barges.[69] From across the country, donations for strengthening coastal fortification and acquiring warships poured into government coffers. Teófilo Otoni, the radical Liberals' undisputed leader, headed up a Chamber of Commerce committee to raise funds for rearmament.[70] Pedro II took a leading role in this campaign, according to Roderick Barman, to outcompete the radical Liberals who sought to use the incident to discredit the moderate Conservative administration that paved the way for the first durable Progressista cabinet; another historian suggests that this episode marked the peak of his personal popularity.[71]

Curiously, however, the Christie Question, as the affair became known, had little visible impact on the celebrations of days of national festivity in 1863, even though the conflict led to a break in diplomatic relations between the two countries that lasted until September 1865. The patriotic enthusiasm to defend the country against British outrages did not spill over into the celebrations of 25 March, 7 September, or 2 December 1863. The Liberal *Diário do Rio de Janeiro*, then run by Joaquim Saldanha Marinho, praised Pedro on 25 March and hoped that he would soon establish true constitutional rule, the traditional radical liberal demand.[72] The Christie Question did not arrest the popular independence celebrations' decline, although the *Diário* claimed on 7 September that "the chords of patriotism have never vibrated so strongly in the nation's breast." That day, Dias da Motta launched a campaign to present Pedro with a medal in honor of his patriotic defense of the nation.[73] There are indications of a slight recovery of 7 September celebrations in 1864 (a year of municipal elections), but nothing connects this to the by then waning diplomatic dispute. The *Jornal do Comércio* noted the programs of fully six societies in 1864, and the *Correio Mercantil* described streets and squares packed with people as the societies and their bands passed.[74] The Conservative opposition's *Constitucional* remarked that, despite these societies' efforts, people were at a loss to find "a reason for distraction"; few would willingly leave home just to see "illuminations," of which there were actually few. Moreover, only the Petalógica had put up a band shell to provide entertainment on Constitution Square. In his *Diário do Rio de Janeiro crônica*, Joaquim Maria Machado de Assis praised the Petalógica's efforts and described the city as "splendid and elegant," thanks to the illuminations and the "*povo*" that crowded the streets, the bands, and the early-morning cheers."[75]

The Christie Question's limited impact on days of national festivity's celebration is surprising, but, as we will see in Chapter Eight, much the same took place in 1865, when the outpouring of bellicose patriotism in response to the November 1864 Paraguayan invasion of Mato Grosso had no discernible impact on the celebration of days of national festivity. What this suggests, in fact, is that the patterns of popular commemoration on days of national festivity followed their own logic, sometimes connected to partisan politics, sometimes inexplicable to contemporaries, and not necessarily connected to the events that we would usually expect to foster patriotic enthusiasm. Thus, although folklorist Alexandre José de Mello Moraes Filho (1844–1919) described the popular 7 September celebrations in a manner consistent with the press record (in an article originally published in 1887), he wrongly attributes their decline to the Paraguayan War.[76] In fact, as we have seen, the decline preceded the war by four or five years.

RESPECTABILITY, ORDER, AND SLAVERY

While 7 September celebrations in the late 1850s were popular festivals in the sense of mobilizing large sectors of the population, the community envisaged by patriotic celebrants remained limited in significant ways. Those who organized the popular celebrations, the Sociedade Ipiranga and the many other such associations, envisaged respectable, orderly, and civilized celebrations. They, along with the police, actively excluded a significant proportion of the population from the spaces of celebration, often disdainfully dismissing them as the "*povo*." In this sense, the contemporary characterization of these festivals as "popular" is confusing to modern ears.

Indications of the class to which these celebrations appealed—and thereby the limits of the nation envisioned in them—can easily be found in the newspaper coverage. Above all, the press stressed that the celebrations were orderly and peaceful. Scarcely a year passed without newspapers commenting that the large crowds had behaved in orderly fashion, a backhanded indication of how worrisome such gatherings could be. Moreover, the *Correio da Tarde* noted that there were no manifestations of the "dangerous theories of a poorly understood liberalism" on 7 September 1858.[77]

Closely related to the concept of order was that of respectability. Nighttime street celebrations required major changes to this public space, normally neither safe nor appropriate places for "respectable" middle- and upper-class members of society.[78] Light figured prominently in this transformation, and Joaquim José de França Júnior later recalled that "to conceive of Rio de Janeiro celebrating without lamps would be as absurd as imagining an election without police and broken heads."[79] The illuminations, both the temporary monuments and the practice of lighting candles and lanterns in front windows, made it possible for gentlemen and ladies (*senhores* and *senhoras*) to frequent the celebrations. Their impact in an era of inadequate street lighting was much greater than we might suppose. Celebratory illumination had a long history in the Western world and has been related to carnivalesque inversions, as the custom turned night into day.[80] It also required widespread participation to be effective. In the week leading up to 7 September, stores did brisk business in a lush variety of lamps carefully detailed in newspaper advertisements. Manoel Olegário Abranches's shop was the leading "innovator in good taste" to replace the "wretched oil lamp" with "elegant lights" like those used in Paris.[81] Most people, however, continued to use the traditional *copinhos*, small cup-shaped receptacles made of colored glass that held wax and a wick. In 1955, folklorist Vivaldo Coaracy described the work required to prepare these candles for setting along window and door frames to create a "very decorative effect."[82]

Accounts of experimental demonstrations of electric lighting reveal a fascination with new technologies that could turn night into day and underscore that only new and modern forms of lighting were acceptable.[83] Plans for massive bonfires on the hills surrounding Rio de Janeiro elicited a vigorous condemnation in 1856. The author of a letter to the editor denounced the "insane bonfire plan," for 7 September should never be celebrated, he concluded, "with bonfires like those [holidays] of savages or country bumpkins."[84] The writer need not have worried, however, for the "mountain holocaust" produced but "little effect"; nobody saw it, and only peculiar individuals would have preferred such blazes to the many attractive illuminations in the city. Nevertheless, worried the *Diário do Rio de Janeiro*'s *cronista*, if allowed to continue their work, this "arsonist sect" might suffocate the entire city with smoke.[85] Not surprisingly, such bonfires were never again lit during this period.

Closely related to the illuminations were the fireworks to which we have frequently alluded. Travelers remarked that Brazilians were "exceedingly fond" of pyrotechnics and judged them experts at designing sophisticated displays. One described how, before every holiday, people took up collections "for the purpose of purchasing rockets, and every other description of luminary materials," which they then set off all night long. Others launched rockets and crackers in broad daylight, in which case making noise was the principal purpose.[86] There must have been professional pyrotechnicians, like the man killed in the *palacete* explosion at the time of Pedro II's coronation, but they are scarcely mentioned in civic ritual coverage.[87] Municipal bylaws and other regulations sought vainly to restrict the potentially dangerous private use of fireworks (and to license their use during "religious and national festivals"), but there was relatively little concern about them, certainly nothing comparable to the campaign for a "safe and sane Fourth of July" in the early twentieth-century United States, which sought to put an end to the "day of carnage."[88] One long-time foreign resident explained that Brazilians were "adepts" at dodging errant rockets "flying in a horizontal direction."[89]

Other types of celebration that belied the image of civilization so painfully being constructed in Brazil's capital were unwelcome. As early as 1845, there were complaints that *capoeiras* had terrified citizens as they joined 7 September crowds in the capital. In subsequent years, *capoeiras* were occasionally arrested on 7 September and 2 December, although it is normally not clear whether they were actually disrupting the festivities.[90] The five *capoeiras* arrested in front of the First Infantry Battalion as the soldiers returned to their barracks after the 2 December 1864 parade were likely engaged in the swaggering displays that became much more common in the 1870s and 1880s (see Chapter Ten). Likewise, the "barefoot mulatto man [*pardo*]" who imprudently "amused himself by repeatedly going back and forth in front of the [artillery] pieces that fired the customary salutes" and "was wounded from his head to his knees at point-blank range" by a cannon blast on 25 March 1852 may also have been showing off his *capoeira* moves (the lack of shoes indicates his slave status).[91]

Authorities excluded other lower-class people from the festival space on days of national festivity in the interest of presenting a respectable celebration. Sometime before 2 December 1851, the chief of police put a stop to the practice of "black street urchins [*moleques*]" running alongside the imperial coach as it entered the city, "shouting cheers and attracting other *moleques* and dirty, bedraggled blacks, some with work baskets on their backs and others even selling fish" (some of the shirtless men running near the coaches in Figure 1.3 may have also been doing this). Those who lived and worked on the streets were also obstacles to respectable celebrations. The female food sellers (likely Africans) of Capim Square had to move in 1858 to make way for a 7 September triumphal arch, and one newspaper hoped that the government would make their removal permanent.[92] Similar efforts had taken place at the time of Pedro II's coronation. What underlay these concerns was the fervent desire, as *A Semana* explained, that "the foreigners who share our enthusiasm have no reason to find fault with our knowledge, civilization, and progress."[93]

The transformation of public space was, however, only temporary and, during the early-morning liminal period as the celebrations wound down, the street returned to its former condition. Respectable celebrants who failed to return home on time ran risks. On 7 September 1857, a group of shop clerks insulted a woman as she was returning home with her husband.[94] Using canes and rocks, a group of revelers tried to break down the door of a café at 2:30 am on 8 September 1857 when the owner refused to reopen his closed establishment, located on Constitution Square. Others, including João Caetano dos Santos, witnessed the incident; the actor and theater impresario lectured the troublemakers, explaining "that such a *riot* was not proper on such a glorious day for our compatriots."[95]

A more serious incident took place two years later when the police arrested a Spaniard who had been making "offensive jokes" and insulting "ladies [*senhoras*]" leaving the celebrations on Constitution Square. He offended one "woman [*mulher*]" with an "indecent action"; before her escort could respond, police arrested the Spaniard. A crowd numbering about 200 people gathered, some shouting for the man's release, others cheering the police's actions. As the crowd dispersed, one group proceeded to vandalize the darkened fountain constructed for the celebrations, amid shouts of "death to the chief of police." Members of the Sociedade Petalógica, who had built the monument, were enjoying a late-night dinner at a nearby house and rushed to protect their handiwork. They failed to calm the mob by explaining that it was wrong to destroy "a structure raised in celebration of the *pátria*'s independence." Finally the police cavalry moved in and arrested twenty-five men: "thirteen Brazilians of low condition, ten unemployed Portuguese shop clerks, a Frenchman, and a slave." The *Jornal do Comércio* denied any political significance to the vandalism, explaining that it had been perpetrated by "vagrants and rowdies of the sort that abound in all cities in order to give the police something to do." Another ephemeral periodical, however, condemned the police's excessive use of force against the populace.[96] Regardless of the vandals' motives, these discussions make it clear that the Brazilian nation necessarily excluded many, who had to be controlled by the police.

The issue of patriotic manumissions also raised questions about the Brazil envisaged by the 7 September celebrants. Since independence, Spanish-American patriots had regularly freed slaves to commemorate independence or other important political occasions as they looked forward to the ending of slavery.[97] Brazilians too frequently manumitted slaves to mark important occasions but did so as individual masters with an eye to securing the new freedperson's dependence. After the slave trade's end in the early 1850s, it became possible to contemplate slavery's end. In 1855, the Sociedade Ipiranga's founders declared that they would promote love of liberty and hatred of slavery. At that time, no active antislavery movement existed in Brazil, although British subventions had made possible the publication of abolitionist newspapers, and some small antislavery societies had existed early in the decade.[98]

News that the Ipiranga planned to free slaves on 7 September 1856 caused a stir in Rio de Janeiro. Rumors spread among the "lowest classes" that all slaves would be freed that day.[99] Undeterred, the society drew five names by lot from the large number whose names had been proposed by the membership and whose owners were willing to part with them on easy terms. All were women, something that the society had stipulated, and three were identified as mulatto women (*pardas*); in these respects they were typical of the slaves who gained manumission.[100] Dubious about the proceedings, the *Correio da Tarde*'s *cronista* worried that, without continued support, the women would fall into prostitution. His counterpart at the *Correio Mercantil*, however, wholeheartedly supported the manumissions, for the newly freed would forever associate "the greatest day of their lives with the greatest day in a people's history," while the *Diário do Rio de Janeiro* judged these manumissions to be "one of the most beautiful honors rendered to the day of national independence."[101] Pedro II lent his support to the Sociedade Ipiranga by attending the Te Deum at which the freedom papers were distributed; the British minister judged this a demonstration of his abolitionist sympathies.[102]

Despite the controversies of 1856, the following year, the Sociedade Ipiranga and the parish committees that it organized managed to raise sufficient funds to free twenty-two slaves who, as the *Jornal do Comércio*'s *cronista* exulted, "thus entered into the great assembly of this nation, for which the philosophical and Christian dogma of brotherhood and human equality is not a theory questioned by prideful prejudice."[103] Responding to the concerns of the previous year, the Ipiranga's spokesman, the Viscount of Sapucaí (Cândido José de Araújo Viana) explained to Pedro II that his society sought to restore, "without undermining order or challenging legitimate interests, the most precious gift" of liberty to those slaves. After the society's Te Deum, Campos concluded his sermon on progress with a discussion of Brazilians' views of slavery. Since the ending of the trade, the emperor and "a great majority of Brazilians . . . support the generous ideal of washing the sad stains of subjection in the waters of the Ipiranga, the clear Jordan of the Americas. . . . The man who truly loves liberty does not want it just for himself, he likewise wants it for others."[104] The Sociedade Independência Nacional (National Independence Society) was founded that year for the express purposes of freeing slaves and promoting "popular festivities" on 7 September. Its president was Antônio Gonçalves Teixeira e Souza, the mulatto poet and close friend of Paula Brito usually associated with the radical strain of early Indianism that denounced racial discrimination.[105]

The enthusiasm of 1857, however, was not sustained, and patriotic manumissions would not become a major feature of the capital's civic rituals until the 1880s, when the abolitionist movement took to the streets to promote emancipations. No society, not even Teixeira e Souza's, freed slaves in 1858 or in the next three years (and only one newspaper commented on their failure to do so). The last 7 September manumission by a society in this period took place in 1862, when the cash-strapped Sociedade Conservadora Sete de Setembro (7 September Conservation Society) found itself with insufficient funds to put on a public celebration and opted to spend its last monies on freeing an "almost white" slave boy.[106] The following year, Dr. José Tomás de Aquino baptized and freed a slave infant "in remembrance of the great day of Brazil's liberty and independence," but his was an isolated, private action, and not untypical of Brazilian masters, who often freed infants.[107]

Given what we know about nineteenth-century Brazilian society, it is not surprising that Africans and slaves marked the limits of the Brazilian nation (but also that suitably subordinate native-born slaves could, through manumission, become part of the nation). Nor is it surprising that many worried about large crowds and the potential for violence during popular festivals or that members of the middle and upper classes sought to present a civilized image to foreigners. Nevertheless, it is notable how few references to actual incidents of disorder appeared in the press after midcentury. The 1859 destruction of the Petalógica's monument and another riot in 1877 (discussed in Chapter Ten) are the only incidents that approach the kind of disorder that Rio de Janeiro authorities and journalists apparently feared on days of national festivity.

MIDDLE- AND UPPER-CLASS SOCIABILITY

The emphasis on civilized and orderly celebration points to the class interests of those who sought to dominate the popular festivities on days of national festivity. The 7 September societies' social composition and their emphasis on respectable celebrations reveal that members of the middle and upper classes claimed control over civic rituals and membership in the nation more generally. The *cronistas*' commentaries on days of national festivity, directed at this newspaper-reading segment of the population, indicate how members of these classes spent their days and reveal how the festivities were incorporated into the routine of family life.

The *Correio da Tarde*'s "João Fernandes" awoke to the sound of cannon on 7 September 1855, on which he remembered what day it was.

He felt "enthusiastic happiness, recalling that it was on this day that a prince, endowed with heroic qualities, issued the shout of 'independence or death' on the Ipiranga's banks." Enjoying a cup of coffee brought by his servant, he contemplated the city from his window and reflected on his country's progress. A nearby window opened, and his neighbor poured "a large vat of waste water" into the street; a "terrible stench instantly rose [and] almost suffocated" him, putting an end to his higher thoughts and forcing him to "reflect on this filth of this capital." Because there was to be no parade (thanks to the cholera epidemic)—and therefore little interesting to see—he resolved to spend the day writing to his *compadre*, "Manoel Mendes."[108]

Not all enjoyed holidays on days of national festivity. Slaves of course had to keep working, and Adalbert saw "half-naked" slave washerwomen in the "clear rivulets" along the route into the city from São Cristóvão on 7 September 1842.[109] Likewise, some of the slaves who greeted Pedro on his birthday before 1851 were merely taking a break from their task of selling fish. Although the 1848 law had mandated that government offices close on the three days of national festivity, João Pandiá Calógeras, a middle-ranking civil servant, went to work early on 2 December 1864; he left at 1:00 pm, just in time to see the imperial procession into the city.[110] Some business went on as usual. On Pedro's birthday in 1853, Joaquim Feliciano Gomes condemned the army arsenal for requiring its laborers to work. Several auctions were announced for 25 March 1852.[111] At the height of the popular 7 September celebrations, clerks requested that owners keep their shops closed on 7 September so that they could "attend the celebrations of this great national day," thereby reiterating what Brandão had proposed in parliament earlier in the year.[112] With some regularity, newspapers did not publish on the day after days of national festivity, but not because they gave their staff a day off; rather, as they sometimes explained, no one was available to compose the pages for the next morning's edition because their typographers served in the National Guard and had to parade.[113] If the day of national festivity fell on a Sunday, then civil servants did not get an extra holiday.[114] Nonetheless, in the 1861 debate about restoring 12 October as a day of national festivity, one senator lamented that "a day of national festivity brings with it general idleness."[115]

In many households, days of national festivity began early as male family members prepared themselves for their duties. The Viscount of Taunay (1843–99) later recalled a childhood memory of his uncle, Admiral Teodoro Alexandre de Beaurepaire (1787–1849), who resided in distant Engenho Novo. On each day of national festivity, the admiral arrived in a large coach at the Taunays' downtown house, accompanied by slaves, so that he could put on his uniform and decorations before going to the levee. Dressing up and attending court was an onerous task, as we have seen in the diplomats' complaints of the 1840s and the 1860s. In 1853, Porto Alegre worried about whether he should attend on the levee on Pedro's birthday, given that he had been unwell for some time, but he assured his correspondents that he would make an effort.[116]

Younger men donned their National Guard uniforms and no doubt hoped for good weather or a quick decision to cancel the parade; if they were in the cavalry and did not have a suitable mount, they could rent one from a stable that advertised "good horses" at eight mil-réis (US$4.48) "for the day of the parade." Slaves might lighten the guardsmen's duties. At 1859's 7 September parade, Assier saw a throng of blacks behind the assembled guardsmen. He first thought that they were spectators, but when the parade ended, each of these slaves hurried to relieve his master of burdensome equipment and weaponry. This freed the "nation's brave defenders" to head for the nearest bars to recuperate, to recount their exploits, and to sing patriotic songs. Not all guardsmen could so easily avoid work on days of national festivity, and "cousin Lulu" came home on 2 December 1852, his hands blistered from handling the cannon.[117] This fictional character was more fortunate than the artillery guardsman "seriously hurt in the face and hand" on 7 September 1862. Assier remarked that artillery accidents were so common that nobody appeared surprised when a cannon blew up on 7 September 1859.[118] This lack of concern extended to the press, which rarely remarked on the number of soldiers and sailors injured or killed by accidents. Parliament regularly approved pensions to soldiers and guardsmen maimed on days of national festivity.[119]

Both the Guard parade and the levee were closely watched. Comments on the guardsmen's uniforms and presentation turned up with some regularity in the press.[120] José Maria da Silva Paranhos declared that, on 2 December 1851, "as a good citizen and an even better Carioca, I went to the palace lobby to see who was going in for the levee." The levee itself was at least partially visible from the square.[121] Indeed, all of the rituals that took place in and around the Palace Square were easily accessible to those who wore respectable dress. Charles Stewart and his companions got close enough to rub elbows with ministers on 2 December 1850; they could have conversed with the emperor during the parade, were that allowed. The *Correio Mercantil*'s *cronista* recounted in brutal detail the dress and demeanor of cabinet ministers and others during the levee. On 25 March 1851, one José Marques Lisboa "appeared all dressed in green" (likely a court livery); "by his size and color, he looked like a beautiful watermelon."[122] Others sought to draw political conclusions from the interaction among ministers during the Te Deum.[123]

As men left home for the parade and the levee, the *varandas* of houses along the parade route filled with women who would watch from the comfort of these windowed front rooms. The *Periódico dos Pobres*'s

Dom Matias, who lived on the traditional parade route, was frequently importuned by relatives who wanted to watch from his windows and ended up staying for dinner. Such banquets, in fact, contributed to the 25 percent increase in Rio de Janeiro's meat consumption recorded on "any day of celebration." The parade was the occasion for much flirting, as windows overlooking the streets were "packed with the fair sex" on 7 September: "It was all merriment [and] conversation, something about this or that fellow who marched by . . . or about fashion and courting, etc." Buildings along the parade route were, in 1851, "elegantly decorated with rich tapestries and very pretty girls dressed in their finest."[124] Other spectators lined the streets, forming the multiracial crowds that Adalbert observed on 7 September 1842.

There were other ways to watch civic rituals, but they cost money. The Hotel da França, located on the Palace Square, offered specials in its *varanda* for "respectable families" to watch 1856's 7 September "celebrations and magnificent illuminations" in security and comfort. A party of North Americans en route to California paid US$5.00 for the privilege of watching Prince Pedro Afonso's funeral from a hotel balcony in January 1850; for Pedro's return to Rio de Janeiro in 1877, windows along the procession route went for fully US$50.00, according to a North American visitor.[125] As we have seen, homeowners on Constitution Square profited handsomely from the rental of their windows for the inauguration of the equestrian statue of Pedro I.

The evenings of days of national festivity might be given over to domestic celebrations—even if the relations who stayed for dinner after watching the parade were not always welcome—but many members of the middle and upper classes went out. In 1850, a year in which the 7 September parade was rained out and therefore Dom Matias did not have to worry about visitors, he attended the levee, after which he and his wife had dinner with a "glass of good wine to toast Brazil's independence." Later that evening, he went to the theater gala, an important aspect of upper- and middle-class sociability on days of national festivity that we deal with in Chapter Seven.[126] For those who did not wish to attend the theater, some of Rio de Janeiro's patriotic societies of the 1850s and 1860s put on 7 September balls, as did private establishments and student associations.[127]

Respectable families might spend part of the evening out on the street. In an 1851 serialized novel, P. M. de O. Quintana Júnior describes the evening outing of a middle-class Rio de Janeiro family:

It was one of those poetic nights, in which the moon is so beautiful and melancholy in Brazil's majestic sky.

Rio de Janeiro seemed possessed by some kind of spell. Its houses were the magical homes of fairies, illuminated by thousands of lights.

It was a night of national festivity.

In every street through which the small group led by Senhor Rafael passed, enchanting music was heard, and then the music was enlivened by the addition of dancing.[128]

As Quintana emphasizes, the streets were well lit, both by the moon and the illuminations. Senhor Rafael nevertheless kept close watch over his family, whose members apparently did not join in the dancing, all of which underscores that the streets could be a respectable social space on those nights, but that there were limits to what a family like his would do. (This fictional account is, moreover, the only indication of street dancing that I have found for midcentury days of national festivity.)

Besides admiring the illuminations, enjoying the music, and watching the fireworks, it is not clear what else people like Senhor Rafael's family did. A few foreigners offer some hints. On 27 April 1846, Mary Hunter reluctantly went with one of her children and some friends to see the monuments raised for the emperor's return from Rio Grande do Sul. Her party slowly walked through the arch on Direita Street, "but in such a closely packed mob that [she] felt sick and frightened," for she could not get out "of this moving mass of human beings." No doubt the heat from the lights contributed to her claustrophobia and nausea, for she described her relief at getting a breath of fresh air "a little beyond the arch." Despite speaking of a mob, she noted the orderly and courteous behavior of the people of "all colours and sex and ages from decrepid [sic] age to infancy" who turned out as if "dressed for a ball"; a foreign correspondent marveled at the populace's sobriety on 7 September 1856, "a great contrast with what we would see under the same circumstances in the United States." Some engaged in window shopping. In 1865, *The Anglo-Brazilian Times* described people "admiring the brilliantly lighted shops" on Ouvidor Street, "with all their choicest wares elegantly displayed in tasteful forms," during the celebrations of Pedro's return from the South.[129]

Those who wanted to avoid the social mixing of the street celebrations could sometimes find an alternative at the Passeio Público, an enclosed public garden. Hunter described the scene there one evening during the 1841 coronation celebrations: music, illuminated buildings, and "a dense throng of Brazilians in ball dresses." She added that women outnumbered men by about ten to one, an indication that this space was considered especially appropriate for ladies.[130] The Passeio reopened on 7 September 1862 after renovations, and the police announced that they would keep out drunks, barefoot people, and those otherwise indecently dressed. Slaves, even if properly attired, would also be barred, unless they had charge of children. Rain reduced the attendance on the night of its reopening, but the foreigners who visited the Passeio in later years described it as a busy and attractive place.[131]

Others celebrated at home. As a child, Machado de Assis (1839–1908) knew a certain Major Valadares, who lived on Cano (Sewer) Street, patriotically renamed Sete de Setembro Street in 1857. Every independence day, he decorated his doorway with green-and-yellow satin, spread croton leaves on the sidewalk and in his house, and invited friends over.[132] The novelist could not recall whether Valadares also provided music for his guests, but music figured prominently in others' domestic celebrations. Advertisements for flute and piano scores, including variations on the independence anthem, a "triumphal march for piano" (complete with a portrait of Pedro I and dedicated to the Sociedade Ipiranga), the independence anthem scored for piano and voice, or an especially composed work dedicated to Pedro's return to Rio de Janeiro in 1846 all indicate that those who could afford pianos might celebrate at home.[133] Pianos, in fact, proliferated in Brazilian cities after midcentury and quickly became the center of a domestic musical culture (as well as an important status symbol), and travelers frequently commented on their ubiquity.[134] Many years later, José Vieira Fazenda (1847–1917) recalled that his family owned a luxurious edition of Francisco Manoel da Silva's anthem (the de facto national anthem), which was regularly played.[135]

While many households echoed with patriotic music on days of national festivity, it is not clear which independence anthem was played at this time, Marcos Portugal's or Pedro I's. In 1856, a *Correio Mercantil cronista* explained that the independence anthem played at the 7 September theater gala was Marcos Portugal's and added that he had only heard rumors about the existence of an anthem composed by the first emperor, which would have been more suited to the occasion. Likewise, Vieira Fazenda denied that he had ever heard Pedro I's composition at any of the 7 September festivals promoted by societies such as the Petalógica or the Setembrista Castelense. Only in 1862, at the time of the equestrian statue's inauguration, was Pedro's tune revived, and he recalled singing it in the mass choir assembled for the occasion.[136] That Pedro's tune fell into disuse after his abdication and was only revived for the monument inauguration would seem logical, but fully four travelers from the 1830s to the 1850s heard what they described as the "national hymn," "the national anthem," a "national air," or "Dom Pedro I's anthem" sung on different occasions. The first three all heard that the music and perhaps the words too were Pedro's, although the first, Daniel Kidder, noted that some attributed the lyrics to Evaristo da Veiga.[137] Marcos Portugal's and Pedro's tunes may have been so closely associated with Evaristo's anthem that the two had become interchangeable. To make matters more complicated, however, in 1856, an advertisement in the *Jornal do Comércio* offered a piano score of the "Independence Anthem" with "the original lyrics."[138] There is no indication of what these words were.

Poetry joined patriotic music as one of the distinctive 7 September sounds. Verse was the major artistic genre of nineteenth-century Brazilian civic culture, and newspapers regularly published sonnets, odes, and cantos in honor of days of national festivity, sometimes even on their front pages, ahead of what we would consider "news." After midcentury, poems more commonly appeared in the major dailies' paid sections; on 2 December 1856, one Custódio de Oliveira Lima ensured extra visibility for his sonnet to Pedro II by having it published in at least two newspapers.[139] Other poems were printed on separate sheets of paper, apparently for distribution in the theater or on the street. Still others were improvised on the spot. Although historians can assess only the printed poetry, it was intended to be read or recited aloud. A few poets specialized in producing longer works on days of national festivity. During Pedro I's reign, José Pedro Fernandes regularly churned out formal fawning laudations, odes, and other verse, as noted in Chapter One; in the 1840s, Fidelis Honório da Silva dos Santos Pereira provided much the same service for Pedro II. These two men shared a close association with the state; both were civil servants about whom little else is known, but they may be characterized as what Daniel Unowsky calls "professional patriots," "otherwise undistinguished" writers who specialized in producing texts for official occasions.[140]

Poetry was not, however, solely the preserve of specialists. Educated men were expected to have some skill in the art form. The future Baron of Paranapiacaba recalled that, when he was a law student in São Paulo at the time of Pedro II's visit in 1846, the school's director told him to write a poem to welcome the young emperor; the nervous student managed to produce some passable verse. Pedro II himself also dabbled in poetry but had little talent for it.[141] The deeply monarchist publisher, Paula Brito, himself a poet of considerable ability, described his activities on 2 December 1849. The rain of the previous days had cleared, and as he awoke to the sounds of the National Guard preparing for its parade, he resolved to commemorate the day by writing a sonnet. "To strengthen the muse," he had an early lunch with a friend, but he "ate so much that" he "became stupid." All that he could do was compose the first quartet and the last tercet. At noon, he gave up his literary efforts and went to the palace to see the parade. According to his biographer, Paula Brito "produced poetry with the same ease with which he spoke," so this *crônica* likely spoke to the many readers who had more difficulty composing verse.[142] *Cronistas*' comments also reveal poetry's ubiquity; because of the cloudy weather in 1854, "it seemed that the sun wanted to play tricks on the bards by taking away their invariable theme of the day's brilliant dawn."[143] The commemorative poetry on days of national festivity was, in many respects, merely a continuation of the well-established custom of marking important private occasions with verse.[144]

Poetry and music, the hustle and bustle of getting ready to go to the palace or to parade with the National Guard, visits of friends and relatives, the excitement of watching a parade and looking for familiar faces in the ranks of marching troops, a nighttime excursion through well-lit streets—these were central aspects of middle- and upper-class families' experiences on 7 September and, to a much lesser extent, the other two days of national festivity. Some of these activities, of course, have little to do directly with the object of the day's celebrations, but they were important elements of people's daily lives. As such, they deserve some attention alongside the politicized debates about the meaning of days of national festivity.

The three days of national festivity did not resonate equally among Rio de Janeiro's population. In 1858, the *Diário do Rio de Janeiro*'s *cronista* called on his compatriots to turn 25 March into a popular festival, much as they had recently done with 7 September. After all, "this brilliant triumph of modern ideas" merited such an honor. Members of the *povo*, however, were incapable of doing this on their own, for authorities had failed to explain the charter's meaning, presumably by their lack of adherence to its principles.[145] Despite his considerable personal popularity, Pedro II never became the object of significant "popular festivities" on his birthday. Government departments might provide a bit of public entertainment in the evening of 2 December in the form of military bands, but these were not "popular" celebrations.[146] In 1864, one newspaper reported unspecified "popular demonstrations of jubilation and gratitude" in addition to the usual official festivities, but there is no indication of what they were.[147] Three years earlier, a committee in Sacramento parish put on a Te Deum in honor of Pedro's birthday, but this is the only explicit indication of a 2 December civic ritual conducted independently of the state.[148] No doubt Pedro's personal modesty and dislike of ritual contributed to this lack of attention to his birthday. In short, only 7 September had significant "popular festivities," popular in the contemporary sense of not organized by the state, and then only for a few years.

Not all Brazilians paid attention to civic rituals. After leaving work early on 2 December 1864, Calógeras stopped at a pharmacy to take his bismuth and saw "by chance the imperial procession"; he thought it impressive but had to admit that, "Since I haven't seen such a ceremony for many years, I don't know whether the changes in court fashion have come gradually, or whether the emperor has just adopted this new luxury because of the princesses' marriages." He also managed to avoid going to the levee for Princess Leopoldina's wedding.[149] Calógeras appears to have been more skeptical and cynical about days of national festivity than many other Brazilians, but his comments are a useful caution against attributing too much importance to civic rituals in people's lives.

It is tempting to conclude this chapter's discussion of 7 September with remarks on how these popular festivities demonstrate that there was a strong identification with the imperial nation-state and its founding moment, Pedro I's Grito do Ipiranga. To be sure, 7 September was for a time the occasion for significant popular festivals that expressed what it meant to be Brazilian; as such, they could be analyzed as evidence of "popular" nationalism. However, the sources do not allow us to penetrate that far into people's consciousness; notwithstanding the denomination of "popular festivities," there were significant limits to the popular classes' involvement. Most important, the patriotic ardor was both relatively short lived and confined to 7 September. Other manifestations of patriotism, such as the anti-British demonstrations of 1862–63, had no significant impact on the celebration of days of national festivity.

Moreover, there were plenty of motives to celebrate other than patriotism or nationalism. Party politics sometimes mattered a great deal to celebrants in the streets. So did the presentation of an orderly and civilized Brazil, whether to those who failed to live up to these standards and were therefore (sometimes forcibly) excluded or to those who sought to maintain them. We can say even less, of course, about those who were excluded from these celebrations. What these days meant to *capoeiras* remains largely unknowable, although their presence in civic rituals would become much more prominent in the last decades of the imperial regime. For members of the middle and upper classes, days of national festivity provided an opportunity to socialize with members of their class; they offered interesting sights and sounds to all. For many, they may have been as much about entertainment as about patriotism and politics; for many, too, the celebrations afforded an opportunity to present themselves as members of a "modern" and "civilized" nation on the road of "progress." This mixture of diversion, socializing, politics, and patriotism, all in a "modern" and "civilized" environment, also characterized the theater galas, to which we now turn.

CHAPTER SEVEN

The Empire on Stage, 1820s–1864

Theater galas were central to the celebration of days of national festivity. No such day was complete without a gathering of several hundred or more men, a few elite women, the emperor and the empress, members of the cabinet, and other officials to see and to be seen, to cheer the monarch and the objects of the festival, to hear patriotic poetry, and to see an opera or a drama and perhaps a prologue or an afterpiece. Historians of Brazilian theater have tended to dismiss the "suffocating predictability" of these "official celebrations,"[1] as one puts it, but a close reading of gala programs and the press discussion about them reveals significant changes over the course of the empire. Some of these changes reflected larger developments in Brazilian theater, such as the rise and fall of subsidized grand opera from the 1840s to the 1860s; other aspects of theater galas offer insights both into the state-supported nationalist and Romantic project of Brazil's cultural elite and that midcentury project's reception in the capital.

Back in the 1810s, the theater had emerged as a key locus of political activity; although its importance diminished in the 1820s as parliament and a free press emerged, the theater gala remained a key barometer of the political mood.[2] While two historians of Brazilian theater have lamented that "the Corte's theaters seemed to serve less for gatherings of opera and comedy fans than for manifestations of politics or social relationships,"[3] this chapter focuses specifically on these political aspects and on the culture of theatergoing on days of national festivity. In this respect, it contributes to recent Brazilian scholarship on theater and music, which pays more attention to audience reception than did traditional literary or musical scholarship. Audiences were far from passive observers or auditors; rather, they actively engaged with what they saw and heard, interpreting it in their own ways. The ultimate failure of the midcentury cultural elite's didactic and nationalist projects reflects not the decadence of the arts in Brazil, as this elite's spokesmen would have it, but an expression of audience preferences for the other forms of entertainment that proliferated after the 1850s.[4] In its focus on the galas held on days of national festivity—some of the most exclusive theatrical spectacles in imperial Rio de Janeiro—this chapter parts company with the latest work on Brazilian theater, which focuses on the popular genres such as comic scenes, annual reviews, circuses, and musical theater that attracted broader audiences after midcentury, much to the cultural elite's dismay.[5]

We begin with a survey of theatergoing culture, drawn from travelers' accounts and from the extensive newspaper reporting on galas. The galas on days of national festivity amounted to considerably more than performances before a passive audience. Rather, they were elaborate rituals in which all those present played an active part. In this important respect, these galas elide anthropologist Victor Turner's distinction between ritual and theater.[6] As with the other aspects of civic rituals addressed in this book, little is known about the mundane business of organizing and staging galas, but it is clear that considerable effort and funds went into preparing these patriotic manifestations.

The narrow trail marked by the gala evenings on days of national festivity passes by all the major landmarks in mid-nineteenth-century theater history and offers distinct perspectives on them. The predominance of European operas on days of national festivity in the 1820s and again from the 1840s to the 1860s reflects the Brazilian elite's desire to partake in what its members understood as European high culture. In the 1850s a nationalist reaction to this European domination emerged, but it was curiously halfhearted in comparison to the efforts to create a national history and a national literature undertaken by the Romantic and Indianist poets and novelists connected to the Instituto Histórico e Geográfico Brasileiro (Brazilian Historical and Geographical Institute) and generously supported by Pedro II's patronage. Efforts to create a national opera resulted in a handful of poorly received works that could not displace the Italian favorites from the capital's gala programs. Only a smattering of "national plays"—that is, plays written by Brazilian authors—made it to the stage on days of national festivity before government pressure forced impresarios to commission "national-historical" plays. The resulting genre of mostly melodramas set amid important historical episodes took but limited root, even though it offered playwrights and impresarios a compromise between the popular genre of melodrama—always a box office success—and the serious dramas that some in the cultural elite sought. Through these works, playwrights reinforced official interpretations of the struggle for independence, highlighted Brazilians' patriotic unity, and occasionally commented on contemporary issues.

While the efforts to create Brazilian operas or plays for days of national festivity foundered, another genre of works unique to days of national festivity—the laudations and allegories that served as prologues or afterpieces to theater galas—flourished from the mid-1830s to the 1860s. Of at best modest literary, theatrical, and musical merit, these encomiums nevertheless reveal a vision of the Brazil desired by those in control of the gala programs, one in which harmony, order, and progress prevailed. Although these works expressed values broadly shared by the elite, theater critics regularly panned them in the 1850s and 1860s, and it is difficult to determine how audiences received them.

THEATERS AND THE CULTURE OF THEATERGOING

In 1839, one Vilela noticed that the São Januário theater was announcing "an interesting show" for 25 March, whose program would be revealed on billboards that evening.[7] He hurried to purchase his ticket and found the theater surrounded by people sweltering in the noontime heat. As it turned out, they were actors awaiting the director to begin rehearsals, not a good sign. At 8:00 pm, Vilela entered the theater, and a scalper trampled his foot in his eagerness to sell him a ticket. Much to his dismay, the announced plays were old and familiar works, *A Caridade de Santa Isabel* (Saint Isabel's Charity) and *A Penitência dos Monges de Toledo* (The Penitence of the Monks of Toledo); both, in fact, had been on the program on 7 April 1838.[8] Despite his misgivings, Vilela hurried to find a seat in the pit, so as not to have to remain standing as had happened to him on previous evenings. Bad luck struck again, and he found himself beside one of those "fools" who rarely went to the theater and seemed ignorant about the proceedings. While Vilela was admiring "the decorations' extravagance and perfection" and the people in the boxes, the fool asked him about the portraits above the curtain:

"Are those the portraits of folks from this house?"
   "Yes sir, they are," responded Vilela.
   "Then they are all foreigners, for their names are . . . just so strange. . . . I'd love to meet that Mr. Shakes Piare."
   "That Shakespeare is long dead, my friend . . . , and incidentally, he left £1,000 in his will to any Portuguese who can spell and pronounce his name."

At this point, the overture ended, the curtain rose, and an actress sang the national anthem, which was followed by the customary cheers. Vilela's newfound friend continued his questions:

"Now, tell me, sir, what is the name of this comedy?"
   "This is no comedy, it's the Brazilian anthem."

"And how many acts does an anthem have?"

"It has the devil, who can take it [*Tem o diabo, que o carregue*],"

retorted Vilela, as he sought a new place and the "weak, soporific, and uninspired play" began. He did not care for the ahistorical costumes, inappropriate for a drama set in 1319, and left before *Monges de Toledo* began.

Vilela's account of his misadventures, published in the form of a review in the *Jornal do Comércio*, reveals many aspects of theatergoing that provide a context for this chapter's analysis of galas on days of national festivity. Until the 1870s, theaters routinely announced some sort of gala for days of national festivity; sometimes, this amounted to nothing more than a performance of the national or independence anthem prior to the regularly scheduled show. For the major theaters, however, the gala normally included additional elements on the program; at the theater honored with the emperor's presence, audience cheers and poetry readings almost always took place. Curiously, Vilela did not mention the young Pedro II's presence at the São Januário; by this time, he and his sisters regularly attended theater galas, and on 25 March 1839 the larger São Pedro, where galas were then normally held, was closed for renovations.[9]

Before going further in the analysis of Vilela's misadventures, a brief survey of Rio de Janeiro's theaters is in order.[10] The independence-era galas took place in the Real Teatro São João, constructed in 1813 to give the exiled court a suitable venue for music and drama. It burned to the ground on 25 March 1824, but in three years the new Teatro de São Pedro rose to take its place on Constitution Square. Briefly known as the Teatro Constitucional Fluminense (1831–38), it reigned supreme as the city's principal venue until fire consumed it on 9 August 1851. The galas for two days of national festivity were shoehorned into the Teatro São Januário (on the Praia Dom Manoel) while the Teatro Provisório (Temporary Theater) was hastily erected on the Campo da Aclamação in time to be inaugurated on 25 March 1852. Opera productions moved into this temporary structure, and the rebuilt São Pedro devoted itself to drama. It burned again on 26 January 1856 but was quickly reconstructed. In 1854, the Provisório (originally projected to serve for only three years) gained the grander name of Teatro Lírico Fluminense (Fluminense Lyric Theater); notwithstanding its shoddy construction, it remained in existence until 1875, although its place as the largest theater venue was taken over by the massive Imperial Teatro Dom Pedro II, erected closer to downtown on Guarda Velha Street (today Treze de Maio), in 1871.

Most of the theater galas on which this chapter focuses took place in Rio de Janeiro's two main theaters (the São João/São Pedro/Constitucional Fluminense/São Pedro and the Provisório/Lírico), but smaller ones like the São Januário also occasionally hosted galas attended by the imperial family on days of national festivity. Located near the docks, this theater normally hosted cheaper entertainment and catered to shop clerks and others of modest means.[11] For historians of Brazilian theater, smaller venues such as the one on São Francisco de Paula Street, which began as a French-language theater in the 1830s, are also important, for they staged the work of Brazilian playwrights and produced much innovative work. This was particularly the case for the São Francisco theater in its incarnation as the Ginásio Dramático (1855–68), when it introduced Realism to Brazilian audiences.

While Vilela managed to avoid paying a scalper for his ticket, no doubt many in the audience had fallen afoul of this scourge of nineteenth-century Rio de Janeiro's theaters. In 1850, Dom Matias (another anonymous *cronista* whom we met in Chapter Six), grumbled that the São Pedro's box office was nothing more than a "fish-sellers' booth" whose staff "cheated the public" after he had to pay three mil-réis, instead of the advertised price of two mil-réis, to attend the 7 September gala (from 1830 to 1870, the mil-réis fluctuated in value around an average of US$0.54).[12] For the independence-day gala at the Teatro Lírico in 1867, scalpers drove a harder bargain; at that time, tickets to seats in the pit cost two or three mil-réis, but one disgruntled spectator complained that he had to spend five mil-réis in order to get a seat at 7:45 pm.[13] Gala after gala, box offices mysteriously sold out well before the performance, and the tickets turned up in the hands of scalpers who "swarmed the lobby" in plain view of the police who were supposed to put a stop to the practice.[14] Prices for prestigious boxes soared during periods of enthusiasm for civic rituals, particularly the Regresso-era 2 December galas and the coronation gala. On 1 December 1837, the *Jornal do Comércio* reported that boxes for the next day's gala at the São Pedro Theater were going for sixty mil-réis and, and Admiral Graham Eden Hamond heard that some had sold for as much as 100 mil-réis.[15] Boxes at the coronation gala on 23 July 1841 went for fully 600 or 700 mil-réis.[16] In the aftermath of the first São Pedro fire, the São Januário's limited capacity drove prices for third-class boxes to thirty mil-réis on 2 December 1851.[17]

How much theater tickets normally cost is difficult to determine, for advertisements typically indicated only that they would be sold for the customary price at the usual places. One evening in early March 1824, Ernst Ebel observed that the São Pedro's pit was full, despite the cost of one mil-réis for the cheapest seats; Carl Schlichthorst confirmed this price but added that ticket prices doubled "on important occasions." In the early 1830s, Carl Seidler reported that they sold for only 640 réis.[18] The first gala advertisements that list prices date from 1852. For the opening night of the new Teatro Provisório (25 March 1852), at which Giuseppi Verdi's opera *MacBeth* was performed, one could join Pedro II for as little as two mil-réis for a bench seat in the pit and twice that for a chair, prices that a *cronista* considered excessive (they had been, in fact, raised for the occasion, and for the second performance on the 27th, chairs and general admission tickets went for three mil-réis and 1$500 respectively). Only a handful of fourth-tier boxes were for sale to the public at eight mil-réis, for the rest of them then belonged to those who had invested in the theater's construction. Seats in the pit were then unnumbered, so, like Vilela in 1839, a spectator had to go early to secure himself a good place.[19] For those who did not want to go to the Lírico's opening night, the São Francisco theater advertised tickets at two and one mil-réis for seats in its orchestra for a performance of a play and a lyric drama, interspersed with a dance number and a duet.[20] On 2 December 1866, there was no opera, but theatergoers could join Pedro and Teresa Cristina for Luís Cândido Furtado Coelho's *O ator* (The Actor) at the Lírico Fluminense (formerly Provisório), while the São Pedro offered a recent Portuguese dramatic success, J. Ricardo Cordeiro Júnior's *Um cura de almas* (A Curate of Souls).[21] Seats in the Lírico's pit went for two or three mil-reis; those at the São Pedro for one or two mil-réis. Boxes ranged from five to fifteen mil-réis at the former, and from four to twelve mil-réis at the latter.[22]

Clearly, boxes were out of reach of the vast majority of Rio de Janeiro's population, and all contemporary accounts stress that they were the preserve of an elite. Some theaters had separate entrances for box holders and those with general admission tickets. The social mixing that took place as "families" leaving their boxes in the São Pedro jostled for the exits with people from the floor prompted complaints in the 1840s.[23] In most theaters, only an open railing fronted the boxes, which meant that spectators like Vilela had a full view of the dress and comportment of those in attendance.[24] Schlichthorst, the German mercenary of the 1820s whose fascination with Rio de Janeiro's women we have already noted, commented that "the enchanting Cariocas" in the boxes were usually much more interesting to watch than "what was performed on stage." All of the São Januário's boxes were full on 2 December 1838, with ladies and gentlemen in formal dress, an indication of the day's importance, according to *O Sete d'Abril*; by contrast, a *cronista* complained about the presence of "three inappropriately dressed women" in a second-class box on 2 December 1840. Altève Aumont, a French journalist, saw more elegant, diamond-bedecked ladies on 7 September 1858 than he had ever seen at the Paris Opera.[25]

Who attended the galas in the pit remains difficult to elucidate, at least in some respects. Until after midcentury, women were entirely excluded from the general admission seating, as several travelers noted during the 1820s and 1830s.[26] Thus, in 1851, Dom Matias went alone to the 7 September gala, after having dinner at home with his wife.[27]

A piano recital in 1855 reportedly marked the first time that women were admitted to the Lírico's pit, although other historians date this development to the 1860s.[28] By the 1880s, things had changed, and Carl Koseritz was surprised at the lack of "prudery" that prevailed in Rio de Janeiro's theaters, at least in comparison to his home in Porto Alegre; women and families sat in the pit and the galleries, and it was not considered shameful for a woman to sit beside a stranger if other seats were not available.[29]

Historians of Brazilian theater have not yet satisfactorily traced audiences' class composition. One foreigner remarked that "all classes" appreciated theater in the 1860s, but it is doubtful that anything other than a relatively small minority of the city's 205,000 residents (in 1849) frequented the theaters on which this chapter focuses.[30] Theater historians have noted that ticket prices were low enough that even skilled artisans could have theoretically afforded to attend theater spectacles, but they do not indicate that such members of the working classes actually did so. For a successful midcentury artisan who might make sixty mil-réis per month, or even an army captain who earned a base salary of sixty mil-réis after 1852 or one hundred mil-réis after 1873, two mil-réis for a cheap seat at a gala spectacle would have been an extravagance.[31] Theater audiences on gala days consisted of members of Rio de Janeiro's upper and middle classes, those who enjoyed sufficient financial security to afford respectable dress and the luxury of paid entertainment.

In Chapter One, we noted Kotzebue's observations about the racial composition of the audience in the pit on 1 December 1823, in which he saw "every possible shade from black to white" with a predominance of "the darker tints." Ruschenberger concurred in 1831 that "Negros and whites were promiscuously mixed" in the pit, but no other travelers that I know of commented on the racial composition of theater audiences; in keeping with nineteenth-century etiquette, Brazilians said little about race.[32] For those who aspired to middle-class status, silence about race was a way to claim an unmarked whiteness.[33] One incident underscores this in a backhanded way. On 7 September 1852, a *crioulo* (a Brazilian-born man of entirely African descent) and uniformed member of the National Guard was seen walking the Teatro Provisório's corridors, peeking through doors to catch a glimpse of the performance. Some English naval officers invited him to join them in their box, and a writer in the *Correio Mercantil* observed: "It was a nice contrast to see the very dark countenance of one of Henrique Dias's brothers among the affable Britons' white and ruddy faces" (Henrique Dias was a black hero of the seventeenth-century wars against the Dutch in Pernambuco).[34] A black man of evidently modest means—the guardsman apparently lacked money to buy a ticket—would have been an unusual sight in a theater box on any occasion. Had he had sufficient money to purchase a general admission ticket, however, he might well have blended into the audience.

How many people attended these galas is also difficult to determine. Assuming that the major theaters were full on days of national festivity—newspapers frequently reported that they were—by the 1850s, well over 2,000 people might be in attendance at galas in Rio de Janeiro. The Real Teatro São João could reportedly accommodate 1,020 people in its pit, although one traveler offered a much lower estimate of only 400. It also had 110 boxes in four tiers, but there is no indication of their capacity.[35] The Teatro São Pedro, built in 1824–27, could accommodate 1,266 spectators in 110 boxes (with five seats each) and in its pit, which had space for 716 people (although more could be packed in if necessary); several travelers commented that it was a large venue.[36] When constructed in 1851–52, the Teatro Provisório was designed for 1,326 spectators, 830 in the pit and 496 in 122 boxes.[37] Rebuilt after the 1856 fire, the São Pedro theater could hold 1,395 spectators in a similar configuration of boxes, chairs, and general-admission seating.[38] The capital's other theaters were, however, considerably smaller; in its incarnation as the Ginásio Dramático, the renovated São Francisco could accommodate only 256 spectators, while the São Januário's capacity was just over 600 people at the time of Vilela's visit.[39]

Theater galas on days of national festivity began when the emperor arrived at his box. The box's curtain was opened, the audience rose, and the orchestra played the national anthem or the independence anthem, while performers sang the words. During Pedro I's reign, and on 7 September after the mid-1830s, the anthem of choice was the independence anthem, which Schlichthorst called a "sort of national anthem."[40] By almost all accounts, the anthem was not sung collectively, although the words were certainly familiar enough to the audience, and in 1873 a foreign correspondent remarked that the audience joined in for the chorus.[41] Sometimes *cronistas* remarked critically on the fact that foreign opera stars sang the independence anthem with its lines, "Either win the *pátria*'s freedom / Or die for Brazil." Moreover, on 7 September 1855, the man who sang the line, "Brave Brazilian folk [*Brava gente brasileira*]," laughed as he did so—the "rascal" knew that, in Italian, the phrase "*brava gente*" could mean "imbeciles."[42] Enrico Tamberlick, the popular Italian tenor who sang the anthem the following year, had better patriotic bona fides; the audience erupted in cheers as he pronounced the words *pátria* and *independence*, for he had fought for Italian unification.[43] On other days of national festivity, galas began with the "national anthem," normally played by the orchestra. There are a few references to singing it, but there is no indication of which words were used for the anthem composed by Francisco Manoel da Silva back in 1831.[44] As we have seen, the original radical liberal lyrics quickly fell by the wayside, and the lyrics composed for the coronation were not often used thereafter. It is also possible that some simply called the independence anthem the national anthem. In any case, Brazil had no officially designated national anthem until after the proclamation of the republic; as late as 1876, a weekly gazette published new lyrics that it described as suitable for singing to the national anthem's music.[45]

Cheers, usually led by the chief of police or the theater subdelegate (the police authority directly in charge of theater comportment), followed the anthem. On 7 September 1850, the audience at the São Pedro theater unanimously hailed the Brazilian nation, the constitution, the monarch, and the imperial dynasty. Many contemporaries commented on these cheers, which amounted to an important barometer of the political mood.[46] On 7 September 1855, the audience repeated the "customary cheers" with but "little enthusiasm" while the omission of an independence-day cheer "to the venerable regent" in 1837 dismayed one observer (it was, however, a clear indication of Feijó's untenable political position and his imminent resignation). Aumont thought the anthem and the cheers on 7 September 1858 to be a magnificent scene, a manifestation of respect and unity the likes of which he had never seen in France.[47]

After the cheers (or sometimes even during them), hand clapping or shouts of "Here's some verse [*Lá vai verso*]" from one of the boxes or from the floor announced that a poet wanted to recite his work in honor of the day. *Cronistas* and theater critics uniformly panned the custom, but no one could put a stop to it. Theater regulations dating back to 1824 merely banned "reciting poetry unrelated to the day's celebration" and both Rio de Janeiro's first municipal ordinances and an 1833 regulation mandated that such poetry be approved in advance by the theater's police inspector.[48] On 7 September 1837, "an outburst of bad verse, full of much thunder, lightning, [and] storms, Jupiters and who knows what else," poured from one box. According to Pedro II, the 2 December 1840 poetry went from bad to worse.[49] A *cronista* wrote about 2 December 1851: "There in the second box of the second row [they're] clapping hands. . . . It's a bard who wants impose a torrent of his verse on the audience. The thing is long . . . very long . . . but just as everything in this world must end, he concludes." Then another clapped, but fortunately "this one had some pity on us; he only versified a sonnet, or a stanza of ten lines [*décima*], or one of eight [*oitava*], I don't know, but praise God, it was a short thing." In fact, as another *cronista* noted that day, the poets interrupted the actors who had already taken their places on stage, as also happened on 23 July 1842.[50] Many poets came to the galas prepared with printed leaflets that they tossed from their boxes. José de Alencar described the "rain of . . . verses [that] fell on the audience" on

2 December 1854: "There must have been people who received a ream of paper on their heads."[51]

Amid this lighthearted criticism came some more serious debate about the custom. After 2 December 1851, the *Correio da Tarde* recommended that poets restrain themselves and publish their work only in newspapers. The *Correio Mercantil*'s *cronista* went further and marveled at the emperor's toleration for this custom and noted that subjecting him and other "people of standing" to such verse exposed Brazil to the ridicule of foreigners.[52] The one foreigner who described this custom in the 1850s did not, in fact, criticize it; rather, Aumont noted that the audience listened carefully and applauded the two poets who recited on 7 September 1858. Another *cronista* enjoyed the much-maligned 2 December 1851 poetry and reproduced his favorite lines of the first and longest poem; written and recited by Manoel Afonso da Silva Lima, it ran to eighty-five lines, which helps explain the complaints about its length.[53] As one historian has noted, the custom diminished noticeably after the mid-1850s, but it did not disappear entirely. As late as 1877, the chief of police complained about the reading of "inappropriate compositions" from boxes, but he was not referring specifically to galas on days of national festivity; at the gala to welcome Pedro back from his 1876–77 journey abroad, the audience booed a poet who attempted to read a poem in honor of the occasion.[54]

Many of these poems later appeared in the press, but poetry was an oral genre and had far more impact when read aloud, at least as long as it was recited well. In 1842, the Prussian prince, Adalbert, who knew no Portuguese, nevertheless noticed that some of the five poets who recited verses at the independence day gala had "learned their task imperfectly."[55] On 7 September 1850, Dom Matias heard Antônio José Nunes Garcia's cloying sonnet:

> If our existence came from PEDRO
> Granting Brazil the sweet honeycomb
> Removing from our shores the condition of slave
> Giving us prestige, independence
> Preferring the condition of nation
> Separating from the Metropolis without damage
> Determined, courageous, and brave!
> [He] prepares emancipation with Providence['s help]
> Like Titus, Rome's father, [he] gave laws to the world
> And sought to better Portugal's condition.
> The son of PEDRO the Hero!! PEDRO the Second!!
> Brazilian monarch! Illustrious, mighty
> Of many virtues, of profound wisdom
> Will eternalize independence from South to North.

Garcia stumbled over his words, "but concluded very well."[56] As Garcia's sonnet suggests, the content of these poems, with their mix of adulation and advice, was no different from the poetry that we have analyzed in previous chapters.

With the anthem, cheers, and poetry done, the audience settled in for the evening's performance. "Settled in" is perhaps an exaggeration, for just as Vilela found himself having to put up with repeated questions from his seatmate on 25 March 1839, audiences did not necessarily pay much attention to the spectacle. With his characteristic sarcasm, Schlichthorst remarked that, in the 1820s, "Rio de Janeiro's truly distinguished society would consider it a serious gaffe to pay any attention to the stage." In 1828, Pedro I spent much of a theater evening "talking promiscuously to the ladies and gentlemen in the boxes on each side of him" and fanning himself to tolerate the heat; in 1843, Pedro II dozed off while his sister chatted with the Prince of Joinville during a theater performance. In 1887, another traveler commented that, despite the "interesting performance," "a large part of the audience" was "looking at each other." In short, the theater was a place to see and be seen.[57] Travelers had different views on whether the theater was uncomfortably hot. Schlichthorst thought the new São Pedro very well ventilated, but another traveler complained of the "very bad air and an infected odor" that permeated the building in 1830; later observers left equally contradictory assessments.[58]

People came and went during the performances, as Vilela did. On 2 December 1839, despite the investment in celebrating Pedro's birthday at this time, the abysmal performance prompted much of the audience to leave the São Pedro theater to view the "magnificent illuminations in the city, which were certainly worth something more than the . . . absurd mimicry and unintelligible declamations" on stage. There are a few indications that people might attend more than one gala on a single evening. On 7 September 1835, Pedro II saw the first half of the show at the Teatro Constitucional Fluminense and then went to the Teatro da Praia de Dom Manoel (later known as the São Januário) for the second half of its gala, apparently the only time that he did this. Perhaps out of a feeling of professional obligation, the *Jornal do Comércio*'s *cronista* spent the evening of 25 March 1855 shuttling between the Provisório and the São Pedro; he praised the "grandiose shows" that each put on. Lengthy intermissions provided opportunities for theatergoers to smoke or to purchase a cup of coffee, but foreigners sometimes grumbled that this meant that shows went on until the early morning hours.[59]

The 1824 theater regulations banned loud shouts or cheers and permitted audiences only to "demonstrate their pleasure or discontent in moderate ways" during performances, a rule reiterated in the municipal ordinances and the 1833 regulation.[60] On days of national festivity, however, it was customary not to applaud performers so that cheers be reserved solely for the glory of the day itself. This meant that, as mid-century theater critics sometimes observed, poor performances avoided well-deserved *pateadas* (foot-stamping), a customary way of showing disapproval.[61] It also meant that the rowdy fans of opera prima donnas, the so-called theater parties of the 1840s and 1850s, had to remain silent when their favorite singers performed. They normally did so, but on 7 September 1855, fans of the prima donnas loudly called for them to return to the stage after the performance of Bellini's *Norma*. The opera company's manager permitted them to do so and was immediately arrested by the police delegate, prompting a flood of letters to the *Correio Mercantil*'s editor. Some claimed that there had been a plot to have the manager, himself a Portuguese native, applauded, which would have been an insult to Brazilians.[62] The police intervention apparently succeeded in restoring the traditional custom of respect: On 2 December of that year, the performance of Bellini's *I Capulletti e i Montecchi* (Romeo and Juliet) deserved "a standing ovation," but the audience contained itself because of the "appropriate behavior that the police want and should uphold on nights of gala performances."[63]

Given everything that audience members had to put up with on days of national festivity, it is perhaps not surprising that, in 1852, the *Jornal do Comércio*'s *cronista* advised his readers to not go to theater galas, unless they were willing to pay for a box. Vilela, disappointed with his experience on 25 March 1839, would certainly have agreed with this advice and with what the *Correio Mercantil*'s *cronista* described in 1849 as a hard-and-fast axiom: "day of great gala, day of great bore in the theater."[64] Nevertheless, galas continued to attract audiences. Through this ritual, members of the Brazilian elite and the middle class associated with the monarchy in mutual demonstrations of respect. Furthermore, as Jeffrey Needell has detailed for a slightly later period, the opera theater was a central institution to the Rio de Janeiro elite, whose members flaunted their wealth and proclaimed their sophistication by attending. No doubt much serious politicking and business took place in quiet conversations in boxes and corridors during the performances and during the lengthy intermissions.[65] Galas on days of national festivity turned otherwise routine theater and opera evenings into significant social and political rituals by ensuring a larger and more select audience.

STAGING GALAS

Little is known about theater management and financing, but it is clear that, like the French governments of very different political persuasions that supported the Paris Opera,[66] the Brazilian empire promoted opera (and theater), at least for a time. This support came with strings attached, including the requirement that impresarios stage costly galas on days of national festivity and, particularly in the late 1850s, pressure to produce so-called national operas and dramas. Moreover, the police watched audiences' behavior and censors kept inappropriate works off the stage.

For most of the period covered by this chapter, Rio de Janeiro's principal theaters—the São Pedro and the Provisório (later Lírico Fluminense)—received indirect government funding, mostly in the form of lottery revenues, and sometimes also direct subsidies.[67] In return, the impresarios who contracted to stage operatic or dramatic seasons had the obligation to produce suitable galas on days of national festivity. Thus, in addition to the six opera performances per month that it was required to stage for 1857, the lyric company had to produce galas for 25 March, 7 September, and 2 December (as well as for 14 March, Empress Teresa Cristina's birthday); by the terms of his 1853 contract for the São Pedro, the actor-impresario João Caetano dos Santos was also required to produce galas for these same four days.[68] Subsidies for bringing in opera and ballet troupes were controversial; in the 1852 parliamentary session, opposition deputies questioned these expenses on the grounds that the country had more urgent needs.[69]

The complex management structure for Rio de Janeiro's public theaters included the government through the minister of empire (interior); the police, who had responsibility for censorship and audience behavior and for enforcing the ten-day closure of theaters leading up to Easter; the impresarios of the lyric, dramatic, and ballet companies, who hoped to make a profit; and sometimes a separate management for the theater buildings themselves. In the case of the newly constructed Provisório, investors also had a say in its management. Needless to say, such cumbersome administration led to frequent conflicts among all parties involved, which newspapers assiduously followed. On one occasion, the police reportedly had to intervene to secure payment for artists so that an opera would be performed on Pedro's birthday.[70] These conflicts became more complicated after midcentury as the campaign to nationalize the arts gathered strength.

Reasonably certain of attracting a respectable audience on days of national festivity and contractually obligated to celebrate the days, impresarios usually went to some trouble to put on a suitable gala, which earned them praise from newspapers. On 12 October 1828, the impresario rounded up 100 extras for a short ballet that one journalist judged to be a "true masterpiece." Despite the São Pedro's straitened circumstances after its 1839 renovations, it was lavishly decorated with flowers and silk banners for Pedro II's birthday; likewise, in 1846, the management "spared nothing to ensure a brilliant spectacle."[71] Two years earlier, one newspaper blamed the "manager's cutbacks" for the "no small number" of empty seats on 2 December.[72] Even though the emperor went to the Provisório on his birthday in 1853, the São Pedro featured "rich decorations," much to the credit of its impresario, João Caetano.[73] By then, he was an old hand at putting on gala spectacles; indeed he had made his reputation in this regard by organizing a "grandiose spectacle" in honor of the proclamation of Pedro II's majority on only forty-eight hours' notice.[74] This did not mean, however, that gala evenings would necessarily feature new or interesting operas or plays. In 1847, Luís Carlos Martins Pena observed that managers of the São Pedro theater had adopted the custom of putting on "the oldest play in the repertoire, for, supported by the day's celebration, it could still earn a few pennies."[75] Most impresarios were not so shameless, and an examination of the programs of the principal galas—those attended by the emperor—reveals both their efforts to put on a respectable gala, as well as the changing tastes in theater and opera and the nature of the Brazil envisioned by audiences and artists alike. We begin with opera, the most costly genre to stage.

EUROPEAN AND NATIONAL OPERAS

During the 1820s and again from 1844 to the mid-1860s, European operas dominated Rio de Janeiro's principal theater venue on days of national festivity. This repertoire reflected the Brazilian elite's fascination with what its members saw as an idealized European culture. For a time, government subsidies underwrote the capital's European opera culture, but by the end of the 1850s a small cultural elite attempted to create national—that is, Brazilian—opera, an effort that fell flat. The suspension of opera subsidies in 1864 put an end to the national opera, and for a time, opera performances on days of national festivity ceased.

On the whole, foreigners were unimpressed with these productions. In 1828, Victor Jacquemont reported that a "detestable Italian company, with a still more execrable orchestra, murder[ed Gioacchino] Rossini three times a week." Despite the popularity of Rossini's operas at this time, the first performance of *The Barber of Seville* (7 September 1826) "did not live up to the spectators' desires."[76] Given Rio de Janeiro's dependence on itinerant opera companies whose members had typically enjoyed no more than modest success in Europe, this is perhaps not surprising.[77] With the abdication of Pedro I, opera productions ceased; they resumed in 1844, and from then until the early 1860s the capital had a regular opera season with foreign, usually Italian, companies.[78] Some operas arrived very soon after their European premieres (Verdi's *Il Trovatore* less than two years after its first performance in Rome in January

1853), but operatic tastes ran to an older repertoire, and works of Rossini, Bellini, and Gaetano Donizetti continued to receive performances long after their heyday had passed in Europe; works by these men accounted for twenty-nine of the forty-nine opera performances that I have identified on days of national festivity between 1844 and 1864.[79] With five performances, *Trovatore*, however, was the single most frequently staged opera on days of national festivity in these two decades.

Typical of the midcentury repertoire was the notable series of operatic "fiascos" that began on 2 December 1851 with Donizetti's *Maria di Rudenz*. On 25 March 1852, Verdi's *Macbeth* (with which the new Teatro Provisório opened) amounted to the "drawn-out murder . . . of a long-promised opera"; on 7 September, the performance of Donizetti's *Betly* "was good for nothing" and narrowly escaped "a tremendous *pateada*" from the disgruntled audience (spectators contained themselves out of respect for the imperial family). On 2 December, Rossini's *Barber of Seville* "was strangled . . . in the most barbarous way possible."[80] This run of fiascos finally ended, and Verdi's *Attila* was more successful on 7 September 1853, as was *Trovatore* in 1854, but it is easy to find devastating reviews of opera productions in subsequent years.[81] More tactful than many of his colleagues, the *Correio Mercantil*'s reviewer opted not to say anything about Donizetti's *Marino Faliero*, which had its Rio de Janeiro première on 2 December 1849; "in honor of the day's celebration," he promised to review the second performance.[82]

The almost complete dominance of European opera in the principal gala on days of national festivity during the 1850s reveals an elite desire to make Brazil into a European and civilized country. "The lyrical genre," writes Gonzalo Aguilar, "mobilized different interests to determine gradations of civilization and contact with European or a universal culture."[83] Many Brazilians accepted these values and eagerly identified with European opera. Translations of opera libretti sold briskly and were sometimes even available for purchase in the theater lobby; Francisco de Paula Brito's publishing houses issued no fewer than forty-one libretti between 1848 and 1860.[84] Pedro II and his Neapolitan wife, Teresa Cristina, likewise set the tone by attending operas on days of national festivity. I can account for their evening activities on most days of national festivity from 1844, when opera resumed, to 1864, and it is clear that they never chose a play when an opera was available. They attended forty-nine opera performances (including the three Brazilian operas discussed in the following paragraphs) and one night that consisted of a medley of favorite opera tunes but only nine plays, all on evenings when no opera was sung.

Not all Brazilians shared this fascination with things foreign. Commenting on 7 September 1855, the *Correio Mercantil*'s *cronista* lamented that all of the city's theaters had put on foreign productions

and that most of the performers (including the prima donnas) were foreigners.[85] Indeed, back in 1852, the Provisório's manager had sought to
commission an opera on a Brazilian national theme, the restoration of
Pernambuco to Portuguese rule in 1654, for production on 7 September.
Manoel de Araújo Porto Alegre prepared a libretto, which Luis Vicente
De Simoni would translate into Italian and Gioacchino Giannini set
to music. It quickly became clear that the project was overambitious,
and the artists produced only a short cantata, finally performed in late
1856 during an opera intermission. Undeterred, the Provisório's manager commissioned a number of libretti for 2 December 1852, none of
which ever reached the stage.[86] De Simoni wrote another libretto, *Marília de Itamaracá ou a donzela da mangueira* (Marília of Itamaracá or
the Maid of the Mango Tree) in 1854, which the German expatriate
composer Adolfo Maersch scored for piano; it was never performed, but
it reflects the same concern to create a national opera that had motivated
the commissions of 1852.[87]

In the late 1850s, a diverse group of artists resumed the effort to create
a national opera. Led by José Amat, a Spaniard who had settled in Brazil,
they founded the Imperial Academia de Música e Ópera Nacional (Imperial Academy of Music and National Opera) in 1857. They included Giannini and Porto Alegre, then director of the Academia Imperial de Belas
Artes (Imperial Academy of Fine Arts), which he envisaged as the core of
a school devoted to developing all of the arts. The group quickly received
a government subsidy in the form of lotteries to develop Brazilian opera,
or at least opera sung in Portuguese. By the terms of its contract, the new
company received an eight-year monopoly on the production of "operas
in the national language" in theaters subsidized by the imperial government. It also had a mandate to develop Brazilian musical talent.[88]

The first and only major success of this initiative, which took the
name of Empresa de Ópera Lírica Nacional (National Lyric Opera
Company) in 1859, was the production of Antônio Carlos Gomes's *A
noite do castelo* (The Night of the Castle). It opened on 4 September
1861 (Pedro and Teresa Cristina's wedding anniversary) and was sung
again to considerable acclaim on 7 September, the first Brazilian opera
staged on a day of national festivity. The story, however, was taken from
a Portuguese poem set in the Middle Ages and concerns the romantic
intrigue that ensues when a count's daughter's betrothed—presumed
killed while on a crusade—returns on the eve of her wedding to another
man.[89] Other operas by Brazilian composers or librettists produced by
the Opera Nacional on days of national festivity were fiascos, including
Dois Amores (Two Loves), a lyric drama or operetta about pirates and
Turks in the Aegean Sea, performed on 2 December 1861. Although this
opera was presented as a Brazilian work and sung in Portuguese, *A Semana Ilustrada* pointed out that librettist Manoel Antônio de Almeida

had merely reworked Verdi's unsuccessful 1848 opera, *Il Corsaro*; the composer, Countess Rozwadowsky (apparently a European expatriate), however, had shown some talent in her score.[90]

The Italian lyric company's 1861 bankruptcy and Amat's difficulties in living up to the terms of his contract prompted the minister of empire to combine the remnants of both companies into a single one, run by Francisco Manoel da Silva, Antônio José de Araújo, and Joaquim Norberto de Souza e Silva, which had the obligation to produce 110 opera performances in 1863 and 1864; one-quarter of them were to be in Portuguese in the first year and one-third in the second. Each year, the new company was to develop two original national operas. Lottery revenues and free use of the Teatro Lírico building constituted the subsidy for this company.[91]

Under the new regime, Carlos Gomes's *Joana de Flandres* (Joan of Flanders), set in 1225 in Lille, was scheduled to be performed on 7 September 1863, but at the last minute it was replaced by Donizetti's *Maria di Rohan*; *Joana* opened a week later amid squabbles among the composer, librettist Salvador de Mendonça, and Amat.[92] The national opera's last production of a Brazilian work, Henrique Alves de Mesquita's semiserious melodrama, *O vagabundo ou a infidelidade, sedução e vaidade punidas* (The Vagabond or Infidelity, Seduction, and Vanity Punished), opened in late 1863 and reappeared on 7 September 1864 to devastating reviews that cut to the heart of the Opera Nacional's weakness.[93] The *Correio Mercantil* observed that the foreign performers who composed this so-called national opera company carried out this "barbarous assassination" because they did not know the language in which they sang; thus, the libretto amounted to an incomprehensible patois. Until Brazil developed its own opera singers, added another newspaper, the country would never have a true national opera (Figure 7.1).[94] Opera historian Luís Antônio Giron argues that the Brazilian operagoing public was not engaged in this project of creating a national opera; when the capital's audiences sought grand opera, they preferred European works[95] but not necessarily the latest in opera fashions, it should be added.

In 1864, the government resolved not to support any opera company, for prospective impresarios demanded excessive subsidies and the opera house—the old Teatro Provisório—needed extensive repairs.[96] By then, it had exceeded its projected three-year lifespan by fully nine years; wags had long dubbed it the "permanent temporary" theater.[97] In January 1865, when the last performances of the subsidized company took place, the government reiterated its decision, much to opera fans' disappointment.[98] Henceforth, Rio de Janeiro would have to make do with visiting opera companies and impresarios who took on the risks of bringing in performers; in the 1870s, regular opera seasons resumed under this regime of private enterprise.

FIGURE 7.1.
The incomprehensible National Opera, 1864.
Source: Semana Illustrada, 18 Sep. 1864.

Contemporaries also blamed the Ópera Nacional's failure on a major shift in taste toward operettas and light musical drama, which made it even more difficult to sustain opera companies without subsidies. The French impresario Joseph Arnaud sparked the craze for Jacques Offenbach's works when he opened the Alcazar Lyrique in 1859. While many condemned the Alcazar for its immoral performances and saw it as the principal cause of the decline of highbrow opera and theater, the new venue nevertheless became the center of the capital's risqué nightlife.[99] Porto Alegre saw even more serious dangers in the new theater. Just as Offenbach's comic operas undermined the French monarchy by sowing disbelief and driving away seriousness in favor of laughter, so the Alcazar was leading Brazil inexorably to "disorder, anarchy, defeat, and destruction." Joaquim José de França Júnior condemned Offenbach's oeuvre in 1868 as "a true *progressismo* in music," a jibe at the Progressistas (who had just lost power) on the part of this Conservative *cronista*. The enthusiasm once lavished on opera prima donnas now passed to Alcazar actresses like the "seductive Aimée," as the Viscount of Taunay later recalled her.[100] In 1867, John Codman reported the "Italian opera-house" and the São Pedro "closed for want of patronage," while crowds thronged "to two stifling little dens called the Alcazar and the El Dorado, where a company of strumpets exhibit themselves nightly for the public entertainment."[101] Of course, the Alcazar's popularity and, for that matter, the appeal of the French cocottes readily available there do not contradict the fetishization of things European manifested in the early opera craze. It had merely shifted to other cultural forms.[102]

Even as it became the center for Rio de Janeiro's bohemian nightlife, the Alcazar paid its respects to Brazilian patriotic culture. For its first 7 September, the management offered a free "portrait of His Majesty the Emperor, handsomely lithographed, to all people who attend the shows on these three days of celebration." During the next decade, it regularly began its shows on days of national festivity with the national anthem, and for Pedro's birthday in 1864 it announced that its hall would be especially decorated.[103]

Competition from the Alcazar, the ending of subsidies in 1864, and the Paraguayan War (1864–70) were not good for opera, and on 2 December 1865 Carl Maria von Weber's *Der Freischütz*, put on by an unsubsidized itinerant company, became the last opera to grace the Lírico's stage on a day of national festivity until, five years later, Carlos Gomes's *Il Guarany* (The Guarani [Indian]) received its Rio de Janeiro première.[104] It was, of course, the great nineteenth-century Brazilian operatic success, and it derived indirectly from the efforts to create a national opera a decade earlier, for the composer's early works had earned him a scholarship to study in Italy. There, he wrote his operatic adaptation of José de Alencar's Indianist novel, *O Guarani*, which had a successful première at Milan's La Scala in early 1870.[105] Rio de Janeiro's audiences responded enthusiastically to the opera. Carlos Gomes was called back eight or ten times for applause (the unique circumstance of a Brazilian opera that had gained success in Europe apparently justified this exception to the custom of not applauding on days of national festivity).[106]

Il Guarany's Brazilian success lay, as Cristina Magaldi and others have noted, in the fact that a Brazilian had produced an Italian opera as good as that of any European composer. Tunes from this opera quickly spread beyond the opera house's confines and entered the repertoire of Brazilian popular music.[107] Jean Andrews has noted that *Il Guarany* was the only popular nineteenth-century grand opera to portray a successful interracial relationship—between Ceci and the Indian, Peri—and Magaldi has commented on the "threatening situation of a 'savage' invading the sanctuary" of the elite, the opera house.[108] Such observations, however, fail to recognize the extent to which Indians—idealized and safely placed in the remote colonial past, as in Carlos Gomes's opera—were well established as symbols of Brazil. Indeed, as we shall see, "Indians" representing Brazil routinely appeared on stage in the dramatic laudations that were often also part of galas.

The predominance of European operas on the programs for galas held on days of national festivity demonstrates the Brazilian elite's cultural values. That the Brazilian operas staged before *Il Guarani* did not deal with Brazilian themes underscores this focus on Europe, as does the Alcazar's popularity, notwithstanding the condemnation of its lighter fare by members of the cultural elite. The national as envisaged in opera had to conform to European standards.

A NATIONAL THEATER

The campaign for a national opera had its counterpart in drama, and, like the national opera, the national theater had but limited success. It is more difficult to analyze the plays staged on days of national festivity, for the theatrical repertoire is far less well documented than opera. A variety of Portuguese melodramas and translations of French and Spanish works dominated the stages of secondary venues on days of national festivity. Romantics' efforts to create a national theater led to a number of plays that dealt with independence or other Brazilian themes and that reveal their authors' views of the nation. While the principal figures in Brazil's Romantic movement—both those who rejected the Indianism favored by Pedro II and those who espoused it—all wrote for the theater, they directed most of their energies to other genres; the leading contemporary historian of nineteenth-century Brazilian theater concludes that they failed to establish a theater tradition.[109] Nevertheless, the Romantic movement's project of creating a national history and a national literature set an important context for both the efforts to develop a national opera and the attempts to create a national theater. What Romantics saw as a cultural independence to go along with political independence, however, required that Brazil live up to European Romanticism's expectations; Indians thus came to stand in for the medieval past that the Brazilian nation did not have.

Conventionally dated to 1836 and the founding (in Paris) of the short-lived journal, *Niterói,* by Domingos José Gonçalves de Magalhães, Manoel de Araújo Porto Alegre, and Francisco de Sales Torres Homem (all then studying in France), Romanticism flourished in the 1840s and especially in the 1850s under the patronage of Pedro II. Romantics drew no clear distinctions between the purposes of literature and history and focused heavily on Brazil's indigenous and colonial past, as well as on the country's natural beauties. The Instituto Histórico e Geográfico Brasileiro, founded in 1838, provided a home for these men and fostered a national history suitable for the new empire.[110]

Poetry and literature were the Brazilian Romantics' favored genres, and the Indian, ennobled but safely placed in the remote colonial past, their symbol for the Brazilian nation (some, including Pedro II and José de Alencar, went so far as to study Tupi-Guarani). This aspect of Romanticism culminated in Gonçalves de Magalhães's massive *A Confederação dos Tamoios* (The Tamoyo Confederation, 1856), whose publication the emperor financed. This epic poem prompted a lengthy controversy in the press as Alencar led an attack on its literary merits.[111] The controversy is not especially important to our purposes, but it highlights some of the divisions within Romanticism. While Porto Alegre encouraged his art students to seek inspiration in Brazilian nature, he had little interest in the Indianism that characterized so much of the Romantic movement. Likewise, the historian Francisco Adolfo Varnhagen dismissed the "dangerous *caboclo* Brazilianism [*brasileirismo*]" and preferred to emphasize Brazil's Portuguese origins.[112] Nevertheless, the Romantics' fascination with Brazil's Indian past secured the idealized male Indian as a symbol for Brazil, even as many of their works, especially those produced during the midcentury Conciliação, seemed to suggest that Indians were doomed to disappear in the new nation, either by dying out or through miscegenation in which the Portuguese predominated. And the country continued to wage war against its indigenous peoples, a tragic irony that David Treece has stressed.[113] Finally, of course, it bears noting that the choice of the Indian as a symbol also implied the rejection of Africa and Africans as cultural symbols, unsurprising in a country so reliant on slavery.

Romantics' ideals certainly underlay the ill-fated efforts to produce a national opera. They also informed the periodic efforts to produce plays on national-historical themes for days of national festivity, even if leading Romantics themselves rarely contributed to this genre. The prevalence of foreign plays on days of national festivity in the 1830s and early 1840s meant that Brazil still fell far short of the cultural independence that the Romantics sought. During the early decades of the imperial regime, when there was no opera company available on days of national festivity, a Portuguese drama or the translation of a Spanish or French work was staged. What Vilela saw on 25 March 1839 was thus typical of that time, and one French observer condemned midcentury Brazilian audiences' lowbrow and old-fashioned tastes. Poor translations often marred these productions. One reviewer complained of the many Gallicisms in the performance on 2 December 1839 (this was, perhaps, one more reason for the audience to leave early to visit the illuminated monuments).[114] Other foreign works, however popular, were judged insufficiently uplifting for a day of national festivity. Thus, on 25 March 1851, Paula Brito observed that Eugène Sue's *Os Mistérios de Paris* (The Mysteries of Paris), which Pedro II was expected to attend at the São

Pedro, was "not right for the day, because the drama is a compilation of vices, in which the debauchees of Parisian society figure" prominently.[115]

As early as 1826, one newspaper hoped that the new São Pedro Theater would inspire Brazilians to write plays "so that we do not always have to beg foreigners for their comedies and tragedies."[116] The first Brazilian play staged on a day of national festivity was Camilo José do Rosário Guedes's *O dia de júbilo para os amantes da liberdade ou a queda do tirano* (The Day of Jubilation for the Lovers of Liberty or the Tyrant's Fall), performed to great acclaim on 3 May 1831, the day of parliament's opening and the first gala after Pedro I's abdication. *O Constitucional* praised Guedes for "having sketched an allegorical play that satisfied all," and another newspaper seconded this assessment.[117] Guedes had successfully appealed to the radical liberal patriotism of the early regency; incidentally, the actor who played the part of the tyrant felt obliged to publish a statement that he did not personally share his character's beliefs.[118] Although Guedes's *Dia de júbilo* was the principal work performed that evening, its characterization as an "allegorical play" suggests that it belongs to the genre of dramatic laudations analyzed in the last section of this chapter. Guedes's commitment to the Exaltado cause, incidentally, meant that no contemporary remarked on his Portuguese birth.

Theater historians conventionally consider Domingos José Gonçalves de Magalhães's *Antônio José ou O poeta e a Inquisição* (Antônio José or the Poet and the Inquisition), which opened on 13 March 1838, to be the first Brazilian drama, notwithstanding the fact that the story about a Brazilian-born playwright burned by the Lisbon Inquisition in 1739 takes place entirely in Portugal; nevertheless, the author called it a "national subject." His *Olgiato*, with which João Caetano's company reopened the renovated São Pedro on 7 September 1839, was probably the second Brazilian play staged on a day of national festivity in the capital. Like *Antônio José*, it was set outside of Brazil, in fifteenth-century Milan.[119] On days of national festivity, João Caetano and the other impresarios who managed the São Pedro during the 1840s staged none of the satires and comedies by the most popular Brazilian playwright of the 1830s and 1840s, Martins Pena. These works were, in all likelihood, seen as insufficiently serious for such solemn occasions.[120]

In his 1839 contract with the imperial government, João Caetano took on the task of staging a certain number of plays by Brazilian authors each season.[121] Under this regime, his company put on the first unambiguously Brazilian historical play on a day of national festivity, G. J. M. Pimentel's *A expulsão dos holandeses ou o heroísmo brasileiro* (The Expulsion of the Dutch or Brazilian Heroism), performed on 7 September 1840. This work had apparently been in the repertoire for some years, and Justiniano José da Rocha later described it as a bombastic "drama in which all that you see is cannon and more cannon, soldiers and more soldiers, bunches of Indians [*caboclada*] and more bunches of Indians."[122] The only information about the 1840 performance comes from a reviewer whose account suggests that the playwright had presented an interpretation that challenged Brazilian social hierarchies. The critic disliked the prominent role given to Henrique Dias, the black hero of these seventeenth-century wars in Pernambuco, for he was an African, and not a Brazilian, and because "some of the words that he says on behalf of blacks [*pretos*] . . . seemed a bit subversive." Moreover, the play portrayed Indians as uncorrupted until the arrival of Europeans. The critic declared that Brazilians were neither black nor Indian and thanked God for the "European blood" in his veins. Statements that the land belonged to Indians were tantamount to inviting Botocudo chiefs to come rule over Rio de Janeiro, a reference to an indigenous people against whom Brazilians had formally waged a war of extermination between 1808 and 1831. All of this, concluded the critic, was an insult to the imperial family, "whose grandeur and majesty derive entirely from its European lineage, illustrious and most ancient."[123] While nothing is known of the playwright, his ideas suggest that he belonged to the radical strain of early Indianism identified by Treece with Antônio Gonçalves Teixeira e Sousa and Antônio Gonçalves Dias.[124]

The establishment of the Conservatório Dramático Brasileiro (Brazilian Dramatic Conservatory) in 1843 marked the first major government initiative in the development of a Brazilian theater. Its mandate included "promoting the study of theater and improving the Brazilian stage so that it becomes a school of good habits and [proper] language."[125] It consisted of a committee of prominent literary and cultural figures who were charged with both censorship—judging whether a play was a danger to public morality—and with improving Brazilian theater's quality. On the Conservatório's recommendation, the chief of police licensed a play for production. During the two decades of its existence, the Conservatório focused most of its efforts on censorship and accomplished little in the way of developing Brazilian theater, largely because it never received more than token funding to do so, as the minister of empire lamented in 1862.[126] It was not a heavy-handed censor, however, especially in comparison to the regime of censorship that prevailed in the Restoration-era Kingdom of the Two Sicilies where Empress Teresa Cristina had grown up.[127]

That the theater could perform an important role in uplifting national culture was a widespread view that dated back to the Enlightenment.[128] Back in 1830, instructions to provincial presidents to establish censorship over plays explained that theater was recognized by "all cultured nations . . . as one of the most effective means of inculcating notions of virtue into the people, and of softening the rudeness and barbarity of [their] customs." At the same time, the state of theater's development was "the touchstone by which one knows a country's [level of] civilization and the nature of its inhabitants," as Paula Brito explained in 1851.[129]

The Conservatório made one halfhearted effort to stimulate the production of national-historical plays in 1843, when it proposed three sixteenth- and seventeenth-century topics for playwrights to address, but, to my knowledge, this did not result in any plays that were staged on days of national festivity.[130] In any case, with the resumption of opera seasons in 1844, there was no need for Brazilian (or foreign, for that matter) plays on days of national festivity. When opera productions moved to the new Teatro Lírico in 1852, the rebuilt São Pedro fell under the full control of João Caetano, whose interests in classical tragedies, foreign historical dramas, and profitable melodramas ensured a foreign repertoire on days of national festivity for most of the decade, although the contract that mandated the four gala productions also required him to produce at least three original dramas written by Brazilians (but not necessarily on days of national festivity).[131] At this time, however, the São Pedro was a secondary venue on days of national festivity, as evidenced by the imperial family's preference for the opera.

Not until late in the decade did João Caetano come under pressure to put on national works on days of national festivity. On 7 September 1858, his company performed Luis Antônio Burgain's 1843 *Fernandes Vieira ou Pernambuco libertado* (Fernandes Vieira or Pernambuco Liberated), a "drama in verse" that reprised the theme of Pimentel's *Expulsão*.[132] Several other national plays were staged at the São Pedro in subsequent years, including the double bill of Joaquim Manuel de Macedo's new works, *Cobé* and *Amor e Pátria* (Love and Homeland), on 7 September 1859. Characteristically, João Caetano showed his disdain for the Brazilian playwright's works by not taking a part in either play.[133] *Cobé*, a drama in verse, has received some attention from students of Romanticism and Indianism for Macedo's portrayal of the title character, the loyal Indian slave of Dona Branca, whose unrequited love for her leads him to murder her unwanted suitor and then to commit suicide so that she can find happiness with her true love. Favorably received at the time as a condemnation of slavery's evils—the young critic Joaquim Maria Machado de Assis hailed its "great democratic doctrine"—the play is now seen much more critically for offering suicide as the only solution for the Indian Cobé's dilemma.[134]

Macedo's *Amor e Pátria* is a lighter melodrama. Set in Rio de Janeiro in the first weeks of September 1822, the plot focuses on the family of Prudêncio, a timid Portuguese merchant and *ordenanças* (reserve militia) officer. His daughter Afonsina and adopted son Luciano are keen patriots, and they repeatedly urge their father to take a more active role in the "*pátria*'s regeneration and . . . independence." They are also betrothed. On the eve of the wedding, set for 15 September (the day that Pedro returned from São Paulo after the Grito do Ipiranga), Prudêncio's scheming Portuguese clerk, Velasco, convinces his employer that his patriotic adopted son has denounced Prudêncio as an enemy of Brazil. Prudêncio immediately offers Afonsina's hand to Velasco. In a series of unexpected plot reversals characteristic of these melodramas, Prudêncio reveals that Luciano is in fact his nephew and heir to his father's fortune, which he promptly gives to Luciano (much to Velasco's dismay). Luciano, in turn, refuses the inheritance and declares that he will win his own fortune in the newly independent Brazil. Another character then brings news that Luciano has, in fact, posted a bond to prevent Prudêncio's deportation and that the denunciation is Velasco's handiwork. At this news, the thoroughly chastened clerk scurries off, and the family breaks into cheers for the "immortal prince, the paladin of liberty" who arrives from São Paulo at that moment. Even Prudêncio joins in as Afonsina presents him with "the standard of your children's *pátria*," inviting him to "adopt as your *pátria* the Brazilian nation, which will achieve greatness in the world's eyes!" The play concludes with the national anthem.[135] The moral is obvious—good Portuguese can become part of the Brazilian nation.

João Caetano's halfhearted foray into national theater came to a bad end in 1861. That year, he commissioned a new work from José de Alencar, but, after a few rehearsals in July, he decided not to stage the play on 7 September. Set in 1759, on the eve of the Marquis of Pombal's order to expel the Jesuits from Brazil, *O jesuíta* (*The Jesuit*) is about Samuel, a Jesuit disguised as a doctor, who plots the independence of Brazil and envisages peopling the land with Indians (civilized by the Jesuits) and with gypsies and Jews (the two European groups without a homeland).[136] On the very day that João Caetano cancelled the play, Alencar, then a deputy and member of the chamber's budget committee, retaliated by taking the first steps to cutting the subsidy for João Caetano's company and the São Pedro Theater.[137] When questions were later raised in the chamber about whether João Caetano was going to put on a national play for 7 September, the impresario hastily assembled a production of Porto Alegre's *Angélica e Firmino* (Angélica and Firmino, 1845), a melodrama set in 1830. In this play, Firmino, a doctor and intellectual who writes about Brazilian issues under the pseudonym of Brasílio Elísio, finally realizes his love for Angélica and wins election to the chamber of deputies under the Conservative Party banner. The play ends with a demonstration of party faithful in honor of their newly betrothed deputy, all to the sounds of the national anthem, a patriotic and partisan trope.[138] Parliament nevertheless cancelled the subsidy, and both João Caetano and the São Pedro quickly fell on hard times. He died, embittered, in 1863, shortly after presenting a detailed proposal for a government-run Teatro Nacional (National Theater) and Escola Dramática (Drama School); an advisor to the Marquis of Olinda (president of the council of ministers), judged it "unrealistic to want to achieve much in this area right away" and recommended that impresarios put on "shows that please the public and turn a profit."[139] A long-time foreign resident concluded that "since his [João Caetano's] death, the [São Pedro] theater has completely fallen."[140]

Realism, a reaction to Romanticism and to the melodramas preferred by João Caetano (and by much of Rio de Janeiro's theatergoing audience), came to Brazil in 1855, and brought with it a renewed effort to develop a national theater. Joaquim Heliodoro's company took over the old São Francisco Theater, dubbed it the Ginásio Dramático, and introduced the French Realist repertoire to Brazilian audiences. Realism rejected the excesses of Romanticism and its focus on the past in favor of a realistic style and commentary on contemporary social questions. Its actors wore contemporary dress—hence the nickname "suit-coat dramas [*dramas de casaca*]"—and strove for a natural style in their acting, while playwrights abandoned the many unrealistic conventions of melodrama and Romanticism alike. Perhaps most important, Realism offered an opportunity for playwrights to provide moral lessons to their audiences and realize the full didactic potential of their art. In this sense, it was eagerly embraced by a sector of the capital's cultural elite, which saw in Realism the best way to create a national theater and to comment on social issues.[141]

Although it dutifully began its shows on days of national festivity with the national or the independence anthems, the small Ginásio remained a tertiary venue; Pedro never once attended a gala there, although he did frequent regular performances. Nevertheless, two plays that opened on days of national festivity at the Ginásio speak to the question of portraying Brazil on stage during civic festivals. José de Alencar's *Mãe* (Mother), which opened on 25 March 1860, is about a slave woman, Joana, who must deny her maternity so that her mixed-race son Jorge (who knows nothing about his parents) can find happiness. Like the Indian Cobé in Macedo's play, she must sacrifice herself to secure Jorge's future happiness as a white man. Contemporaries received *Mãe* favorably, perhaps because it lacked the heavy-handed moralizing of a *raisonneur*, the character in Realist plays who presents the lesson of the play to the audience. Some saw it as an abolitionist play, or at least a condemnation of the evils of slavery, but modern critics stress its conservative message that white Brazil would be better off by ignoring its slave past altogether.[142]

Valentim José da Silveira Lopes's drama *Sete de Setembro* (7 September), staged at the Ginásio on 7 September 1861, is a more explicitly abolitionist work. Set in the backlands of Rio de Janeiro province, the play concerns the orphan Maria, promised in marriage to Carlos, son of the humble farmer, Raimundo, who is also Maria's adoptive father. As it turns out, Maria is actually the slave of Jacinto, a rich planter, who has been looking high and low for her. On seeing Maria's distress at being returned to slavery, Jacinto laments the institution but declares that he cannot reduce himself to misery nor disinherit his son, Artur, by freeing his slaves. Artur, just returned from six years of study abroad, witnesses Carlos and Raimundo's efforts to buy Maria's freedom by turning over their farm to Jacinto. The day happens to be 7 September; Artur refuses the payment, returns Maria to Carlos, and declares that the sounds of artillery salutes and the strains of the national anthem heard in the background "express the desire of our brothers for the freedom of the *pátria* to which we all belong!" Not only will liberty characterize Brazil, but so will unity between Carlos, the "man of work," and Artur, the "man of science," who together "henceforth form a partnership that will excite the envy of foreigners."[143] Thus, the younger generation will both abolish slavery and secure a prosperous society free of class tensions.

The popular shift in taste toward light opera and musical theater that both undermined the national opera and contributed to the decline of grand opera in the last years before the Paraguayan War likewise emptied the Ginásio's seats. While writers like Macedo fulminated that "the Theater must not be solely an institution of public entertainment, ephemeral amusement, sterile and of no consequence for the future," in his defense of its didactic functions, such moralizing did not draw audiences.[144] As the most recent historian of Realism explains, these literati could not accept that audiences might have their own views of what they wanted to see, nor that a Brazilian popular theater was gradually emerging.[145] Instead, for decades, they and their successors lamented Brazilian theater's decadence.[146]

The national plays that received performances on days of national festivity were, on the whole, better received than the handful of Brazilian operas produced at this time. They did not, of course, look like second-rate imitations of European works, and they addressed Brazilian themes in ways that reinforced elite values such as unity between Brazilians and Portuguese (Macedo's *Amor e pátria*), progress and gradual abolition (Lopes's *Sete de Setembro*), or the overcoming of racial difference through the convenient, if tragic, sacrifice of the racial inferior (Alencar's *Mãe* and Macedo's *Cobé*).

MUSIC, LAUDATIONS, AND ALLEGORIES

Much less well known than the operas, which brought the Brazilian capital into European high culture, and the national-historical dramas of the 1850s and 1860s, a few of which have entered the Brazilian literary canon (less for their own merits than because their authors produced a much larger oeuvre), were the occasional new musical and dance numbers especially composed for the theater galas on days of national festivity, along with the *elogios dramáticos* (dramatic laudations or encomiums) and allegories that sought to make a political point or express patriotic values.[147] Commissioning and staging such works was one of the principal ways in which impresarios turned ordinary theater evenings into galas for days of national festivity. These works tended to follow strict conventions in their portrayals of Brazil and in their climaxes that featured a tableau unveiled to the strains of one of the anthems.

A survey of the programs for the galas attended by Pedro II before the Paraguayan War reveals the following musical novelties: a new symphony by José Pereira Rebouças, just returned from studies with Rossini (7 September 1837); a new anthem with words by Domingos José Gonçalves de Magalhães set to music by Saverio Mercadante and a new symphony by Cristiano Stockmeyer, based on themes from the independence anthem (2 December 1852); a cantata, entitled *Dois de Dezembro* (2 December), written by a certain Santos Neves (2 December 1857); Hugo Bussmeyer's *Grande fantasia sob motivos do hino nacional* (Grand Fantasia on Themes from the National Anthem, 2 December 1862); another cantata, *A manifestação do patriotismo* (The Manifestation of Patriotism), written by Joaquim Norberto de Souza e Silva and set to music by Carlo Bosoni (2 December 1863); a new waltz, dedicated to 7 September, by an anonymous but "distinguished Fluminense amateur" (1858); and another cantata entitled *Aurora do Ipiranga* (Ipiranga's Dawn, 7 September 1862).[148]

By the second half of the 1830s, prologues or afterpieces had become de rigueur at theater galas on days of national festivity, and *O Despertador* remarked on the failure of the São Pedro theater to produce a laudation for 2 December 1839 "as was customary."[149] The titles of the many such laudations produced in previous years offer some indication of their nature: *A coluna do imperador* (The Emperor's Pillar, 2 December 1836), *O despotismo fulminado* (Despotism Annihilated, 25 March 1837), *A glória do Brasil* (The Glory of Brazil, 7 April 1834, repeated on that day in 1837), and *O descobrimento do Brasil ou o vaticínio da Independência* (The Discovery of Brazil or the Prophecy of Independence, 7 September 1837).[150] Another such allegory, a *baile mímico* (wordless dance) prepared for 7 September 1847, was not staged because the lead dancer fell down the stairs at her home on the eve of the performance.[151] With the exception of the 1847 mime, these were apparently written in verse and recited by actors, who may have performed the parts in a limited way. An advertisement for the 2 December 1835 gala promised "a splendid dramatic laudation, which includes among its characters Jupiter (who will arrive in a chariot pulled by lions), the spirit of Brazil, Vulcan, Providence, Pluto, Discord, Anger, Cyclopes, Nymphs, etc.," without indicating its title.[152] Only a few such works saw publication, and many of their manuscript scripts and scores were likely consumed in the 1851 São Pedro fire, which destroyed "the dramatic and lyric companies' archives," as well as costumes, props, sets, and musical instruments.[153]

The most elaborate of these allegories was Manoel de Araújo Porto Alegre's *Prólogo Dramático* (Dramatic Prologue), which aroused a storm of controversy, likely because of the ways in which it departed from conventions.[154] Performed at the São Pedro on 2 December 1837, at the start of the Regresso's investment in monarchical ritual analyzed in Chapter Three, it is set in the center of the earth, where Satan resides in a flaming palace, surrounded by boiling lava. He and his choir of devils sing the praises of evil and vices and pledge to "Conquer / This Empire / That begins / So swiftly / To prosper."[155] Ambition, Egoism, Vanity, Discord, Intrigue, and Calumny all gather to receive Brazil, who arrives at the start of the third scene. Revelry dances around Brazil and finally presents him to Satan, who, in the course of a long discourse about the exaggerated benefits of progress, science, liberty, and other virtues, invites Brazil to drink from a cup that will seal his subjection. Brazil hesitates when Revelry offers the cup, and Satan alternates between threats and promises. As Brazil is finally about to take the cup, thunder, lightning, and trumpets announce the arrival of the Angel of Truth; Satan's throne disappears into a cloud, along with the devils and the vices. The spirits of Art and Science join the Angel of Truth, who concludes with a long speech about Brazil's glorious future under the reign of Pedro II.

While one reviewer praised this "ecstasy of the imagination" and claimed that it "thrilled the spectators, not just because of its novelty, extravagant action, and attractive decorations, but also because of the excellent and sublime messages displayed in it,"[156] others were much more critical. While admitting that "everything" in *Prólogo* "was new," Bernardo Pereira de Vasconcelos did not much care for the scenes involving Satan and Brazil's temptation; rather, *O Sete de Abril*'s editor much preferred the enthusiastic speech of the Angel of Truth, played by João Caetano, with lines such as:

> Brazil! Brazil! Thine is Eternity
> [Thou] wilt be great and powerful, God so orders
> In vain the Inferno seeks in thy future
> To launch the poison of tenebrous discord.[157]

For two weeks, Justiniano José da Rocha's *O Cronista*, whose questioning of the Regresso's enthusiasm for restoring rituals like the *beija-mão* was noted in Chapter Three, ran a series of articles and letters to the editor that mocked Porto Alegre's work. To be sure, prologues of this sort were a genre "of excesses, frivolity, and soporific compositions," but this one was the product of the "delirium of a *sick* imagination . . . *that does not understand the rules of reason and the maxims of good taste.*"[158] A visitor to the capital wrote that, amid the "infernal music," Brazil seemed close to enjoying the "diabolical *batuque* [African dance accompanied by drumming]." To have Brazil prevented from drinking from the cup by the timely intervention of an angel was scarcely a novel trope, although to have the angel sing Brazil's praises while still in Hell was an "entirely new and original idea." This writer concluded that he would return home to "belie all those who have extolled Corte's theater to me."[159] By the 16th, the criticisms of *Prólogo* had degenerated into ad hominem attacks on Porto Alegre, recently returned from France, who "wants to be a big shot in everything [and] came to Rio de Janeiro with the goal of putting things right, in other words, to force this rabble of stupid Fluminenses to erect statues in his honor."[160] On that day, Justiniano put a stop to the discussion by declaring that he would publish no more correspondence about the play. In all likelihood, this vicious attack on Porto Alegre derived from the personal and political enmity between the journalist and the artist.[161]

After its founding in 1843, the Conservatório Dramático paid careful attention to these works, to judge by the small number of its reports that have survived. Santos Neves's 2 December 1857 cantata contained "good ideas" that made it an appropriate work to stage, despite its "many metrification errors."[162] Censors found "many passages that could be [taken as] alluding to contemporary affairs" in a "Drama alegórico ou o dia 7 de Setembro" (Allegorical Drama or the 7th of September) scheduled for the São Pedro in 1853, which might lead to "disagreeable demonstrations" and forced changes to it.[163] In 1851, the Conservatório rejected two laudations, one because it appeared disrespectful to the emperor, and another because it was unworthy of the capital's audiences. The former was an unsolicited manuscript that João Caetano had no intention of producing. Two more were approved that year with minor changes, one to remove a passage that might be taken as an inappropriate reference to one of the recently deceased princes; the other was returned to its author with two mandated changes marked on the script's last page.[164]

Brief summaries of three more of these heavy-handed allegories and the reaction to them reveal the main features of the genre as it stood at midcentury. A collaboration between the two Italian expatriates involved in the earliest efforts to write a Brazilian opera, *A harmonia celestial no Brasil* (Celestial Harmony in Brazil), with music by Giannini and a libretto by De Simoni, performed on 2 December 1851, is better documented than most. For the benefit of the audience, a bilingual

(Italian-Portuguese) edition of the libretto was printed, and Giannini published a summary of the plot on the day of the performance. It amounted to an analogy between the arts and Brazilian politics. Just as in music, "the perfect, agreeable, and happy harmony of all things" appeared in Brazilian history, in which Divine Providence supplied the "element of general harmony" that kept the country united after 1831, namely the young emperor. Set in "a rural location in the environs of the city of Rio de Janeiro," the plot involved the Spirit of Brazil and the union between Affection and Reason proposed by Celestial Harmony. Once this was accomplished, a portrait of Pedro II appeared, and all of the actors broke into variations on the national anthem and cheers to the emperor.[165] Critics differed in their assessments. The *Correio Mercantil*'s *cronista* judged that it demonstrated the arts' progress in Brazil, even if the composer and the librettist were Italian expatriates.[166] Another critic called it a "risotto," and the *Jornal do Comércio*'s theater reviewer judged that the whole thing was too long and that it lacked any merit as allegory and poetry, although he liked Giannini's music.[167]

On 7 September 1853, the Teatro Provisório's performance of Verdi's *Attila* would be followed by a new "allegorical divertissement" or "allegorical dance," entitled *A glória do Brasil* (The Glory of Brazil, also advertised as *A liberdade do Brasil* [The Liberty of Brazil]). It featured a male Brazil and five female dancers playing the parts of Liberty, Philosophy, Ignorance, Treason, and Despotism, along with numerous furies and nymphs. The plot apparently involved Brazil being freed from the clutches of Ignorance, Treason, and Despotism by the timely intervention of Liberty and Philosophy, another transparent allegory of the imperial regime. The *Correio Mercantil*'s *cronista* derided it as "a ridiculous little farce"; the "strumpet" who played the part of Philosophy looked like one of those women who impoverished many a Brazilian man as she danced around Brazil "showing her legs and revealing a delicate little foot."[168]

José De Vecchy's *A união do Império* (The Empire's Unity), performed before the emperor on his birthday in 1860 was "intolerable, both because nobody understood it and because the audience took it on itself to embarrass the theater judge," presumably by stamping its feet.[169] De Vecchy published the "argument" of his allegory two days after the performance, but this was too late for the audience forced to sit through this wordless ballet. The large cast included Time, the Corte, Discord, Providence, Justice, Peace, Liberty, and Brazil's then twenty provinces. The provinces begin by complaining that Time favors only the Corte. Discord secretly encourages the provincial complaints until Providence descends to exhort the provinces to have faith, that their problems cannot be solved overnight, and that "strength is born from unity." Moreover, "the empire's capital is the heart of the social body:

From it emanate life and vigor. United, the empire will be respected; disunited, it will be the laughingstock of the whole world." Providence rises into a cloud amid music; now knowing that they can count on Justice, Peace, and Liberty, the provinces embrace the Corte as the orchestra breaks into the national anthem and a sign proclaiming "Long live the emperor" descends.[170]

With the exception of Porto Alegre, writers in this allegorical genre generally followed a number of strict conventions. Almost invariably, they set their works in idyllic, rural locales, a "fantastic garden" or the "Brazilian bush"; in another, the setting is described as the Uruguay River's banks.[171] Giannini's *Harmonia celestial* is the only work in this genre whose script mandates that human constructions appear in the scenery, in this case, "rural houses, representing a square in which a country festival is being prepared" for the emperor's birthday.[172] Rusticity, however, was not always appreciated. The 7 September 1840 production of Pimentel's *Glória do Ipiranga* (Ipiranga's Glory) was criticized for being no more elaborate than a "country celebration," with its smoky "wagon of Despotism" that looked no more sophisticated than rural pinwheel fireworks in honor of St. John's Day.[173]

The plot structure varied little. Giannini's *Harmonia* is unusual in its avoidance of any explicit conflict in which Brazil is threatened or tempted by evil figures such as the ones already noted—Ignorance, Treason, Despotism, and Discord—or Anarchy (played by a "disheveled woman with a torch in her hand" in Valle's *Elogio*) and a generic Spirit of Evil.[174] When Brazil faces a direct threat, he usually fights back, with the assistance of, to cite three different plays, Patriotism and Minerva (wisdom), Peace and Mercury (bringing a message that Jupiter is on Brazil's side), or Pallas and Jupiter.[175] The temptation of Brazil offered more scope for plot complexity and dramatic tension as Brazil could appear to be succumbing, as in Porto Alegre's *Prólogo Dramático*, before the intervention by positive allegorical figures.

Most of these works ended with the evil figures scurrying to their lairs or being cast into Hell, at which point an allegorical tableau is unveiled, and the cast and orchestra perform the national or the independence anthem. In Antônio José de Araújo's cantata, *O gênio benéfico do Brazil* (The Beneficent Spirit of Brazil), set to music by Giannini and hastily prepared before its performance on 3 May 1847, Discord and the Spirit of Evil descend into the earth, from which tobacco and coffee plants emerge, representing "the two principal sources of the empire's prosperity" (more likely, the author intended to represent the Brazilian flag, which featured tobacco and coffee leaves, for sugar was always a more important export than tobacco).[176] At the end of the allegory performed for the birthday of Pedro I's second wife, Amélia de Leuchtenberg, in 1830, the clouds in the backdrop part to reveal a Temple of

Immortality and an obelisk on which are inscribed the imperial arms and Pedro and Amélia's names, admired by Europe, Asia, Africa, and America; Minerva embraces the latter of these and points to the temple, while the spirits sing Pedro's independence anthem.[177] Many of these allegories ended with the appearance of a portrait of the emperor, the heir to the throne (as in Valle's *Elogio dramático* written for the 1848 baptism of Prince Pedro), or the constitution.[178] On 7 September 1840, Pimentel's *Glória do Ipiranga* ended with the independence anthem, during the singing of which an illuminated transparent equestrian painting of Pedro I proclaiming independence at Ipiranga descended. The critic who disliked this allegory complained that the portrait did not bear the slightest resemblance to the former emperor and lamented that the artist, Porto Alegre, was "such a clumsy portraitist."[179]

Rarely did the authors indicate how Brazil should be represented, but it is clear that he—I know of no female Brazil figures—was an Indian. One script mandated in its cast list that Brazil be "symbolized by an indigenous" man and, in another, the fact that Brazil mentions his bow and arrows indicates how the author intended him to be portrayed.[180] Departures from this convention elicited loud criticism that revealed what was expected. For his *Harmonia celestial*, Giannini dressed the Gênio do Brasil (characterized by two newspapers as a *caboclo*, then a synonym for Indian) in a metal helmet and a red Greek-style tunic. This nod to classical culture might have been excusable in Russia or China, but everyone in Brazil knew that the country's *caboclos* did not dress like this, declared the *Jornal do Comércio*'s *cronista. Album Semanal*'s *cronista* judged the criticisms of the costumes well-taken, for "*caboclos* . . . with helmets and Greek tunics, this was the first time that we have seen such a thing."[181] The Brazil saved by the leggy Philosophy on 7 September 1853 was played by "a big guy dressed in rags with tin handcuffs on his wrists and a rag on his head," another unconventional costume that drew critical comment. By contrast, the Brazil in Santos Neves's 2 December 1857 cantata was "richly dressed" and "well made-up," presumably therefore, a standard Indian.[182]

To represent Brazil as an Indian and to place him in the countryside reflected the aesthetics of Romanticism and Indianism, a nationalist literary identification with place and the country's first inhabitants. It also drew on long-standing European traditions of representing America as an Indian woman. What is striking, however, about Rio de Janeiro's civic rituals is the absence of appeals to an Indian past, the "indianesque nationalism" that Rebecca Earle has traced for Spanish America. Brazil had no great pre-Columbian civilizations like the Aztecs and the Incas to which Brazilians could trace their origins (although many hoped that evidence of such civilizations might be found).[183] The representation of Brazil as an Indian on the imperial stage echoed the allegories that appeared in some colonial civic celebrations, and a smattering of such portrayals of either Brazil or America appeared at the time of independence and Pedro II's coronation. Indeed, the female figure rescued by Pedro I in Figure 1.1 is wearing a feather headdress and skirt, although she appears to be a white woman.[184] Classical imagery, however, dominated in ephemeral architecture and in civic-ritual rhetoric.

There was, finally, a radical symbolic use of Indians, particularly in the *caboclo* that Bahian Exaltados made into the symbol of Dois de Julho, the celebration of the expulsion of the Portuguese from Salvador on 2 July 1823.[185] This usage had its echoes in Rio de Janeiro, most notably on the masthead of *O Grito Nacional* in the early 1850s, which featured a male Indian figure, with bow and arrow, trampling some sort of serpent or dragon and holding a flag that bears the newspaper's name.[186] The vanquished creature, understood to be despotism, marked this, like the Bahian *caboclo*, as a radical symbol, and Joaquim Feliciano Gomes, this newspaper's publisher, once celebrated 7 September by putting an image of "America trampling despotism" in his window.[187] This was, however, a minority interpretation, and the male Indian as a symbol of Brazil, without radical overtones, was well established in the genre of dramatic laudations by the 1840s, and further developed by cartoonists Henrique Fleiüss and Ângelo Agostini starting in the 1860s.[188]

The Indian's prominence as a symbol of Brazil in the allegories and laudations presented on the stage makes these works somewhat exceptional in the larger history of imperial civic ritual, which, as we have emphasized, focused on the regime's institutions and their founding in 1822–24, and not on the nation's distant origins. The larger lessons of these theatrical works are so transparent and so consistent with the overall message of official civic ritual as to require no further comment. These works, it should be added, were all produced by Brazilian authors or by foreigners long-established in the country, and they in fact accounted for the majority of the Brazilian work staged on days of national festivity.

Theater galas on days of national festivity served numerous purposes. Through these complex and multifaceted rituals, members of the middle and upper classes expressed their membership in the Brazilian nation—an orderly, monarchical, and civilized one. While the principal galas' programs changed significantly in the decades between independence and the Paraguayan War, their importance to Brazilian patriotic culture endured. To be sure, Romantic projects for a national opera and a national theater fell short, as ultimately did much of the Brazilian state's "civilizing mission," but they demonstrated the determination of a cultural elite to nationalize the arts along European lines.[189] The nationalist and Romantic project's failure, of course, underscores the limits of cultural politics and the rejection of these efforts on the part of their intended audience, even as the broader acceptance of European civilization's perceived superiority endured.

During the nationalist and Romantic cultural project's heyday, however, Brazilians debated their nation's nature. Issues such as slavery, the place of Indians in the nation, and the appropriate cultural forms for the nation were debated through the newspaper discussion about theater galas. No resolution, of course, was reached at this time. Notwithstanding *Il Guarany*'s success, Brazil would not become, in cultural terms, an American equivalent to an idealized Europe. Despite the condemnations of slavery, abolition remained a distant goal, even if slavery's eventual demise was inevitable after the slave trade's end in 1850. No Indianist seriously contemplated handing Rio de Janeiro over to the Botocudos, and most viewed the continued devastation of the remaining independent Indians with equanimity.

The prologues and afterpieces—however "hokey" they may seem to modern readers, one of whom remarks on the concluding tableaux's "circus-like atmosphere"[190]—perhaps best demonstrate the ideals that predominated in these theater galas. Their emphasis on harmony, order, and progress reveals the Brazilian elite's ardent desires. The dangers that Brazil might succumb to despotism or fall into anarchy were their greatest fears—very real ones during the 1830s and early 1840s. Their repetition during the galas of the 1850s and early 1860s suggests that, at least to some, the achievement of political stability and material progress still appeared tenuous, or that salutary reminders of past difficulties still had their place.

CHAPTER EIGHT

War, Patriotism, and Politics, 1865–1870

From late 1864 until 1 March 1870, Brazil (along with its allies of Uruguay and Argentina) struggled to defeat Paraguay and remove its president, Francisco Solano López. The war's relationship to Brazilian nationalism has long been the subject of debate, with some presenting the war effort as a patriotic national campaign and others focusing on the limits of that patriotism, quickly crushed by the violent impressment that fell disproportionately on the nonwhite lower classes.[1] An examination of wartime days of national festivity and the extended victory celebrations from February to July 1870 offers new evidence to address these questions. Surprisingly, the war years saw a marked decline in the celebration of days of national festivity. To be sure, as we saw in Chapter Five, the popular celebrations of 7 September had already diminished before the Paraguayan invasion of Mato Grosso in November 1864, but they continued their decline; more important, official celebrations also diminished during the war. The National Guard parade was effectively eliminated in 1865, thus dramatically reducing official civic ritual's visibility. The end of theater subsidies and government support for national opera meant that the theater galas lost much of their former importance. Furthermore, the celebrations of 25 March, 7 September, and 2 December that took place contained very few allusions to the war. Instead, they continued to focus on the institutions of the constitutional monarchy that the days of national festivity commemorated.

Of course, there were other ways for Brazilians to manifest their patriotism, and the enthusiastic celebrations with which they saw off their battalions in 1865 stand in sharp contrast to the diminished days of national festivity. This bellicose patriotism, already presaged during the Christie Question, faded after midyear, as eager volunteers gave way to hapless impressed men. Brazilian victories occasionally prompted celebrations, most notably after the much-hyped 1868 naval operation that isolated the Paraguayan fortress at Humaitá, but also after the victories later that year that cleared the way for the allies to occupy Asunción. The return of battalions in first months of 1870 sparked elaborate popular celebrations, as did news of López's death and the return of the Count of Eu, Pedro II's son-in-law, who had commanded the Brazilian forces during the last year of the war. However, the July 1870 official commemoration of the war's end proved to be a dismal failure. This contrast reflected the complex political environment as Liberals mobilized to celebrate Eu and to discredit the Conservative government's official victory celebrations. Thanks to these political disputes, more details about the organizing and financing of civic rituals entered the public domain, and in this chapter I occasionally digress to discuss these aspects of civic rituals, which are normally undocumented.

At the war's outbreak, the sole Liberal ministry between 1848 and 1878 held power; the "fervent and expansionist nationalists" in Francisco José Furtado's cabinet shared the emperor's sense of affront at the Paraguayan invasion of Mato Grosso. Furtado, however, lost a confidence motion at the outset of the parliamentary session in May 1865, and Pedro replaced him with the elderly Marquis of Olinda. Zacarias de Góis e Vasconcelos organized another Progressista cabinet in August 1866 and held power until the major political realignment of July 1868, when Pedro called the Conservatives back to power under a leading Saquarema, Joaquim José Rodrigues Torres, the Viscount of Itaboraí. Many have seen this exercise of his moderating power as a turning point in the imperial regime. Progressistas and Liberals condemned this as a coup, for the main issue was the role of the Marquis of Caxias, a Conservative and commander of the Brazilian forces in Paraguay. Caxias had accepted command in late 1866 after the advance into Paraguay had stalled, but by 1868 he saw the cabinet's hand behind criticisms of his handling of the war effort and threatened to quit if the Progressistas remained in office.[2]

In the face of what José Murilo de Carvalho has called "a second Regresso," the new opposition reorganized itself. Within days of their fall from power, leading Liberal senators formed the Centro Liberal (Liberal Center), which called for judicial, electoral, and political reforms, as well as the end of slavery. Some former Progressistas and radical Liberals (known as Históricos or Historicals) formed the Clube da Reforma (Reform Club) in April 1869, and the following month they began publishing *A Reforma*, a newspaper that would be a thorn in Conservative governments' side for most of the 1870s. The more extreme Históricos founded the Clube Radical (Radical Club) in 1869; some of the young men involved in this organization had been publishing *Opinião Liberal* since 21 April 1866 (a telling date—the anniversary of Tiradentes's execution in 1792—for the launching of their journal). Most of them eventually gravitated to the Republican Party, founded in December 1870. According to Carvalho, this was an especially fruitful period of political debate, during which Liberals of all stripes wrestled creatively with the problem of political reform.[3] This political context is particularly important for making sense of the celebrations at the end of the Paraguayan War, which all saw through partisan eyes.

WARTIME OFFICIAL AND POPULAR FESTIVITIES

While the Paraguayan War prompted a surge of patriotism and support for the nation's war effort—at least for the first half of 1865—the war years also saw important changes in the commemoration of days of national festivity: the elimination of the great parade and a substantial reduction in the scale and prominence of the theater galas. The remaining official festivities took place with their usual regularity on these days, but the debate about them had little apparent connection to the war—not surprisingly, given their focus on the empire's foundation.

In a recent and provocative analysis of nineteenth-century Latin American state and nation building, political scientist Miguel Angel Centeno argues that the caudillo conflicts of the time were the wrong sorts of wars for stimulating the expansion of state capacity and for fostering nationalism in support of state aims. Thus, the state-formation dynamic that Charles Tilly describes for Europe did not apply in the region. The few interstate wars get short shrift in Centeno's analysis, yet he appears to consider the Paraguayan War insufficiently large to have required Brazil to increase its state capacity.[4] Centeno's argument about a disengaged citizenry, however, goes too far, and the patriotic response to the Paraguayan invasion, as well as to the earlier Christie Question, certainly smacks of a deep-seated Brazilian engagement with the state or nationalism. This sense of Brazilian-ness, it is important to stress, preceded the war and shaped Brazilians' response to its outbreak.

The enthusiasm with which Brazilians flocked to the colors in early 1865 is well known, and the first battalions headed south amid all the apparatus of civic ritual culture. The future Viscount of Taunay recalled that Rio de Janeiro "trembled with enthusiasm and war fever" at this time.[5] Contemporary observers identified "kindlings of genuine patriotism" among the population; one noted that "the most humble classes, as well as the most opulent and distinguished Brazilian families," had sent their sons to the army and the navy in 1865.[6] Less taken with the enthusiasm around him, João Pandia Calógeras, the civil servant who paid little attention to civic rituals, prayed for God's protection over "these poor lads who, without being forced, are going to risk their lives motivated by a sense of love for the *pátria*." He was quite happy that his sons were not going.[7] Throughout Brazil, humble individuals presented themselves as volunteers. In Bahia, an African freedman's son, Cândido da Fonseca Galvão, later known in Rio de Janeiro as Dom Obá II, brought thirty volunteers from his home in Lençoes to the provincial capital and embarked as an *alferes* (infantry second lieutenant). A young woman from Ceará, Jovita Alves Feitosa, disguised herself as a man and enlisted. Her sex was soon discovered, but she quickly became a minor celebrity as she traveled with volunteers to Rio de Janeiro. Authorities prevented her from going to the front, and she lingered in the capital, where she committed suicide in 1867 after a failed romance.[8] For Eduardo Silva, these kinds of volunteers embodied a popular nationalism that historians have failed to recognize.[9]

Styling himself "the *pátria*'s first volunteer," Pedro joined this rush to the colors and personally oversaw the September Paraguayan surrender at Uruguaiana. His July departure from the capital was controversial, and he had to quietly threaten abdication to convince the Olinda cabinet to grant him leave, which it finally did when mollified by an early adjournment of parliament that allowed ministers to concentrate on prosecuting the war.[10] Pedro and his sons-in-law returned on 9 November to much the same ceremony that had greeted his earlier entries into the capital—the landing at the navy yard, a procession to the imperial chapel for private prayers, a levee in the palace, and a procession to the São Cristóvão palace late in the day, followed by three days of illuminations and other public celebrations.[11] Preparations were incomplete when he arrived—his ship had been expected on the 10th—but the major dailies agreed that the reception had been a great success and that the incomplete decorations merely served to highlight the people's "enthusiasm and cordial affection" for their monarch.[12]

Workers labored all night from 9 to 10 November to put finishing touches on Direita Street's decorations, which prominently featured Pedro's portrait and highlighted Brazil's military victories; once finished, they "were very handsome," according to the U.S. minister.[13] By the 11th, more of the decorations were ready, and "some band shells looked magnificent," but a critic remarked that some of the arches were not well lit (their lamps had gone out) and added that some of the light fixtures on the arches were "more appropriate for hanging sausages than for putting up colored lights."[14] That day, a Te Deum was held, followed by a formal levee in the downtown palace; in the evening, the imperial family attended the gala at the Teatro Lírico, at which "warm cheers were raised" to the emperor before the performance of Giovanni Pacini's 1825 opera, *The Last Days of Pompeii*.[15] On the 12th, the imperial family walked through the illuminated city amid "the greatest warmth and enthusiasm," noisy cheers, blasts of martial music, and rumbling skyrockets; merchants on Ouvidor Street presented Pedro with a laurel crown made of velvet leaves.[16] Treasury employees, celebrating in front of their offices, greeted Pedro with hackneyed verse that echoed the Pacini opera in comparing the Paraguayan capture of Uruguaiana to Pompeii's destruction by Vesuvius. In this case, however, God set matters right: "He sent his beloved angel / His beloved chosen one / Shining [star] of our nation / And there . . . there . . . humiliated / He saw the tyrant prostrate / Begging pardon. . . ."[17] A few neighborhood celebrations were postponed until after the main festivities downtown.[18] All told, according to the *Folhinha Laemmert*, "a more beautiful celebration of love and gratitude has never before been observed in Rio de Janeiro."[19]

There are some indications of conflicts during the preparations for these celebrations. The city council, which traditionally called on residents to celebrate their monarch's return and coordinated their efforts, did so only in late October, and some of those named to organize celebrations only learned of their appointments on 2 November, too late to prepare adequate decorations, especially once it became clear that Pedro would arrive within a week.[20] Other neighborhood or block committees had started raising funds before the city council began organizing the festival and demarcating the committees' areas of responsibility; those already at work refused to conform to the council's plan. Hence, the route that Pedro followed to São Cristóvão was unevenly decorated. One anonymous bard criticized the town council for seeking to control celebrations for which others were paying.[21] Protocol also caused officials some headaches. A city councilor protested that the ministry of empire's program, as published in the *Jornal do Comércio*, did not give the traditional precedence to the city council (its members were designated as the fourth and last group of men to bear the canopy); in Solomonic fashion, Pedro resolved this question by dispensing its use altogether.[22] In discussions about other protocol matters—in this case, the place for Princess Isabel and the empress's unwillingness to make any decisions about her husband's return—Pedro's long-serving steward, Paulo Barbosa da Silva, complained to Olinda that "it's not just the big questions of state that trouble ministers and stewards; the little things are like the birds that pursue the falcon and bother it."[23]

Such carping about the cost of celebrations and the complaints of officials struggling to handle members of the imperial family no doubt took place during the lead-up to other major celebrations, but they were rarely recorded. Their appearance at this time no doubt reflects the tense environment—the war was almost a year old, and there was no end in sight—and the political conflicts that would intensify over the next years. Still, these complaints did not detract from the overall impact of the welcoming celebration, which all of the press described in enthusiastic terms. It was perhaps the last manifestation of the early wartime patriotic enthusiasm, but of course it also drew on the memory of previous imperial entries, the last of which had taken place in 1860.

This enthusiasm for volunteering, seeing off the troops, and welcoming back the emperor had very little impact on the celebration of days of national festivity. The volume of press coverage on these days diminished notably from the levels of only a few years earlier. To be sure, most of the familiar official rituals took place, but there was much less passion in the discussion about these days' meaning, and even less enthusiasm for the celebrations. On 7 September 1867, the *Diário do Povo* listed the official celebrations that would take place, noted that four literary and musical societies would hold special sessions, and observed that there would be illuminations throughout the city, but added: "The current state of the country certainly does not admit the noisy customary celebrations." Other minor periodicals were still more emphatic about this decline. *A Guarda Nacional* correctly noted in 1866 that the decline of popular 7 September celebrations had preceded the Christie Question and blamed the lack of "popular celebrations" on the *povo's*—the common people's—recognition that "our independence was merely a distant echo from the past, stifled by the corruption and irregularities of the present." Under these circumstances, *O Futuro's cronista* expected in 1869 that 7 September would soon disappear from the calendar.[24]

Writers in the major dailies likewise noted little more than official celebrations on days of national festivity. In 1869, the *Diário do Rio de Janeiro* observed that "the most memorable day in the *pátria's* annals could not pass unnoticed by the Brazilian *povo*, [whose members] are above all distinguished by their civic virtues and patriotism," but it described only the standard official festivities. That this report appeared on 8 September indicates that the *Diário's* staff had been at work on the holiday (the previous year, they had the day off).[25] Joaquim Maria Machado de Assis described the constitution's anniversary in 1865: "The distinguished patient received official honors, the prescribed ceremonial, the Te Deum, the levee, the palace dinner, and the theater gala spectacle. Besides this, nothing more."[26] The illumination of public buildings, city council invitations to residents to light up their front windows, and official rituals made for perfunctory celebrations of days of national festivity, with little or no popular resonance.

The most visible change on days of national festivity was the elimination of the National Guard parade. No journalist commented directly on this, but the parade's abolition probably had to do with the lack of available military personnel in the capital during the war. Given that the National Guard had taken over routine garrison duties—a burdensome task for these unpaid part-time militiamen—additional parades would have added insult to injury. The program for Pedro's return in November 1865 contemplated a Guard parade, but he cancelled it, "no doubt to not unnecessarily tire the citizens [already] exhausted by garrison duties."[27] The parade's disappearance meant that far fewer citizens now had any involvement in the official celebrations. This must have been a great relief to many guardsmen, who no longer had to endure the heat, watch their uniforms be ruined by an unexpected rainfall, or suffer calloused hands from handling artillery, but it substantially reduced the scale of Rio de Janeiro's celebrations and made them considerably less visible. All that remained of a military presence on days of national festivity was the regular army guard that accompanied the emperor and the honor guard posted at the palace and the imperial chapel.

Impresarios still put on galas on days of national festivity, but the programs changed significantly and no longer regularly included operas—whether European or Brazilian—or works on Brazilian historical themes. Joaquim José de França Júnior observed in 1867 that major changes had taken place in Rio de Janeiro's theater scene. Italian operas were no longer sung, and the music of Rossini, Donizetti, and Verdi had fallen "into the keyboard's domain," as piano versions were the only operatic music heard in the city. No longer were the classical dramas preferred by João Caetano staged; instead, adaptations of Victor Hugo's and Pierre Alexis Ponson du Terrail's works dominated the repertoire.[28] Government funding for theater and opera had dried up just before the Paraguayan War, and it appears that, from 1866 to 1869, no foreign opera companies found their way to Rio de Janeiro. The expectation of galas remained. In 1868, the Teatro Lírico's manager complained that he received no subvention for the seven galas that he was obliged to produce (for the three days of national festivity and for four court gala days).[29]

After the opera *Freischütz* (2 December 1865), wartime galas attended by Pedro featured a steady succession of Portuguese and other foreign dramas and melodramas. They were usually held in the Lírico, with different dramatic companies contracted for the occasion. Three Brazilian plays, Luís Cândido Furtado Coelho's *Os voluntários* (The Volunteers, 7 September 1865); his drama, *O ator* (The Actor, 2 December 1866); and Joaquim Manoel de Macedo's comedy, *Luxo e vaidade* (Luxury and Vanity, 25 March 1870) were apparently the only Brazilian works staged during the main gala on a day of national festivity before *Il Guarany* later that year. *O ator* and *Luxo e vaidade* were successful Brazilian plays, and their performance had no particular significance; *Os voluntários* was apparently not published, but it likely spoke to wartime patriotism. The return to a mostly foreign repertoire on days of national festivity—and the lack of criticism of this—signaled the defeat of the Romantics' and the Realists' efforts to create a national theater.

Indeed, the repertoire during galas in the late 1860s looked little different from that of the 1830s and early 1840s, except that there were now more contemporary foreign works.

The Paraguayan War's outbreak spurred composers to new heights of bellicose patriotism; one music historian has identified dozens of new anthems, marches, and other compositions written during these years.[30] Among them was J. A. A. Albernoz's *O primeiro voluntário da pátria* (The Homeland's First Volunteer), an anthem set to piano music in honor of Pedro's return from Uruguaiana; proceeds from its sale would be donated to the old soldiers' hostel.[31] On 2 December 1865, Arcangelo Fiorito's cantata (originally written for Pedro's return but not performed then for lack of time to rehearse it), judged "a bit long" by the *Correio Mercantil*, celebrated Brazil's success in repulsing the invasion of Rio Grande do Sul. Its aria included the refrain: "Uruguaiana has already fallen / Soon will fall / With its inhuman folk / The famous Humaitá!"[32] The best known of these wartime compositions is Louis Moreau Gottschalk's "Grande fantasia triunfal sobre o hino nacional" (Grand Triumphal Fantasia on the National Anthem), composed in 1869 during the U.S. pianist's sojourn in Rio de Janeiro. It became an instant hit, and audiences insisted that he play it at every occasion. Preparations for an orchestral version that called for 650 musicians to be packed onto the Lírico's stage so exhausted the composer (already in poor health) that he collapsed during the performance on 26 November 1869; he died three weeks later. Notwithstanding the scale of Gottschalk's arrangement and his cachet as an international piano virtuoso, his work merely continued the well-established practice of incorporating Francisco Manuel da Silva's familiar tune into other patriotic compositions and using it in patriotic laudations and dramatic allegories, as we saw in Chapter Seven.[33]

Readings of patriotic poetry and the performance of a few allegories distinguished some wartime galas; most of these took place in 1865 and reflected the concurrent wave of bellicose patriotism. On 25 March 1865, a night when neither the Lírico nor the São Pedro was open and when Pedro apparently did not go out, the Ginásio Dramático, under Furtado Coelho's direction, put on two comedies and a "Patriotic Scene," written and performed by Francisco Correia Vasques, entitled *O Brasil e o Paraguai* (Brazil and Paraguay). It consisted of a monologue by Mr. Brazil about the "gang of bandits" that had attacked his house. Despite his generosity to his neighbors, they sacked his backyard, broke into his house, and slit the throats of his little children. Sword in hand, Mr. Brazil then calls his compatriots to arms, and the play ends with a "tableau vivant representing Paraguay crushed by Brazil." The curtain falls to the sounds of the national anthem. A series of puns and contemporary political allusions allowed the popular actor to give free reign to his comic talents even as he presented a serious message.[34]

On 7 September, while Pedro was in the South, this allegory received a second performance at the Lírico, when it followed Furtado Coelho's *Os voluntários*. Not to be outdone, the São Pedro staged scenes from the Brazilian naval victory, the battle of the Riachuelo (11 June 1865).[35] In addition to Fiorito's cantata, on 2 December 1865, *Freischütz* was preceded by the reading of José Tito Nabuco de Araújo's "heroic canto" dedicated to Pedro II. Subsequent galas occasionally included poetry on wartime themes, always part of the formal program and not the unscripted readings from boxes that had been so common just a few years earlier. On 25 March and 7 September 1868, a tableau vivant representing the Grito do Ipiranga was staged at the Lírico.[36] It is not clear, however, whether it made any allusion to the war, and there are no indications of other wartime laudations or special musical compositions at galas after 1865.

As we saw in Chapter Five, the tide of popular celebrations pioneered by the Sociedade Ipiranga in the 1850s ebbed in the early 1860s. A few of the prewar societies lingered on through the war years. In 1865 and 1866, the Sociedade Sete de Setembro held its *solenidade* (formal meeting) and paid for a Te Deum.[37] The student-run Sociedade Festival Sete de Setembro kept up its listing in the *Almanaque Laemmert* until 1870, declaring year after year that it always celebrated "Brazil's political emancipation" with Te Deums "and other celebrations" in addition to its biweekly literary sessions. Its members gathered before dawn on 7 September in 1865 and 1867 to parade with a band to the equestrian statue of Pedro I, where they hailed the "founder of our political liberty" and sang the independence anthem. Early in the evening, the society held its literary session. At dawn on 7 September 1867, the Sociedade Festival was in fact one of several that gathered at the statue, along with "some virtuous citizens desirous of seeing the [sun] dawn on the emperor's statue."[38]

Neighborhood celebrations of 7 September continued as well, but none approached the scale of those in the late 1850s. In 1865, the Sociedade Setembrista Castelense announced that its members would set off fireworks at dawn, sing the independence anthem, and parade through neighborhood streets. The Sociedade Clube Familiar (Family Club Society) sought permission in 1867 to construct an arch and set flag poles in the street in front of its building, as well as set off fireworks. Such organizations no doubt constituted some of the main customers of the stores that continued to advertise lamps, lanterns, and other decorations before 7 September.[39] So were the other societies that held literary sessions, balls, or other celebrations on this day of national festivity, such as the S. P. M. Monarquista Brasileira (Brazilian Monarchist P[atriotic] M[usical] S[ociety])—a "party" in 1866 and a "family gathering" in 1867 and 1869—or the Sociedade Brasileira Ensaios Literários (Brazilian Literary

Essays Society)—a lengthy evening program of poetry readings, music, and speeches in 1866 and 1867.[40] There are also a few indications that government departments or musical societies arranged for music in the street to celebrate Pedro's birthday.[41]

Some journalists commented on the popular celebrations' decline. In 1867, the *Correio Mercantil*'s editor remarked that he would have been happy to see celebrations like those of 1863, which he had then judged to have been much less elaborate than those of 1861 when "the city did not sleep in order to exult in jubilation" at the sun's first rays. Since then, the river of calamities sweeping the country had swelled to a veritable Amazon. To be sure, this assessment formed part of an opposition's newspaper's condemnation of the government, but the observations about waning popular festivities were widespread; others also recalled a long-past golden age of celebration.[42]

By way of conclusion to this section and as a transition to the next section's discussion of the meaning of wartime days of national festivity, let us give the last word to Confúcio (Confucius), an anonymous *cronista* in *Opinião Liberal*, the radical Liberal organ, whose analysis of 1866's independence day satirized the official celebrations and denied the construction of the Grito do Ipiranga as an heroic act. The writer explained that, were he a poet, he would "sing of the liberty imprisoned for three and a half centuries, and present on stage a muscular Indian crowned with feathers, the sad symbol of Brazil." The Indian's wrists would be bruised "purple from the *chains wrought in the vast furnaces of despotism*." All would shout "the customary cry" and await the "danseuse who, jumping, spinning, and skipping, performs the final pirouette and takes her position" (without comment he switched his role to that of playwright, author of a dramatic laudation). Were he a reporter, he would write about the speeches addressed to the emperor; the senate would pronounce "a cold, carefully thought-out speech, [every word] measured by a compass," while the chamber of deputies would be "more verbose" as befitted its claim of sovereignty. "With marginal notes, dates, and documents," the Instituto Histórico e Geográfico Brasileiro (Brazilian Historical and Geographical Institute) would present "a yellowed speech on old parchment, smelling of libraries from three leagues away." None of this proved anything other than that we exchanged "tyrannical domination from over there for [the same] from here." In any case, back in 1822 at Ipiranga, "the emperor returned from Santos dressed like a traveler and mounted on a handsome donkey." Witnesses said that he was ill—suffering from diarrhea, in fact—and that he needed to make frequent stops, so he fell behind the rest of his party, which only went to show that "the bronze horse is a big lie. . . . And the emperor, perhaps more afflicted by stomach pains, unleashed the great words of Ipiranga when he received the offensive dispatches from the Lisbon court. And the belly then spoke very loudly." Were it not for Pedro's upset stomach, Brazilians might well not have had a *Grito*, at least not on 7 September. He concluded:

> The belly irritated the prince's passionate spirit.
> The belly!
> From thence came all the troubles that today surround us.
> Since then we have been ruled by the belly.
> . . .
> New belly pains and a new war cry, Confucius thinks, are needed.[43]

This brilliant satire of official patriotic culture mocked some elements that were already falling out of fashion, reiterated the radical liberal critiques of the equestrian statue, and called for more profound change, calls which would become more strident after 1868. Nowhere in this *crônica*, however, is the Paraguayan War mentioned.

DEBATING DAYS OF NATIONAL FESTIVITY

The principal reason for the Paraguayan War's failure to leave significant traces in the celebration of days of national festivity lay in these days' commemoration of the empire's political institutions. Thus, instead of celebrating the nation or commenting on the war, the relatively few editorials published on these days during wartime focused primarily on the constitution and the monarchy, two institutions that increasingly came into question in light of Pedro's growing personal power. This was not unconnected to the conflict, for Pedro used all means at his disposal to prosecute the war to a successful conclusion, and in so doing he alienated many in the political class.

While the *Diário do Rio de Janeiro* (a Conservative newspaper under new editors since late 1867) declared in 1869 that the constitution was an "august and venerated monument to the wisdom of our legislators [and to] imperial magnanimity and gives homage to liberal principles and to the generous tendencies of the century," this reprise of Conciliação-era rhetoric stood out by its rarity.[44] It was far more common for those in power to remain quiet on 25 March, while the opposition trotted out the standard criticisms of those who failed to respect the constitution. In 1865, Alexandre José de Mello Moraes wrote that it "would truly be a national day, if the country's government, true to the oath that it took, kept in mind that the constitution that governs us, the best constitution that we know of, is like the Ark of the Tabernacle, which no one could touch without falling dead." Likewise, in 1867, the *Correio Mercantil* invoked religious imagery and lamented that "the official worship" of the constitution stood in sharp contrast to its practical application but at least demonstrated the respect that "all, government and *povo*," paid "to this sacred repository of the Brazilian citizen's civic and political rights." Recalling how the charter "has saved our political society during more than one crisis," it hoped that renewed respect for its rules would carry Brazil through the current tribulations.[45] To call for strict observance of the constitution, as the *Correio* again did in 1868, or the repeal of all laws that deformed it, as did the *Diário do Povo* that year, was naïve, according to *Opinião Liberal*, for the charter was "a work of imperialism [that is, the monarch's personal power]"; its "beautiful theories of constitutional law" were belied by the moderating power.[46]

Editorials on 7 September said little about the war or contemporary issues; to be sure, there were the occasional allusions to the lack of success against Paraguay that could be blamed on the government, as did some small radical liberal opposition periodicals in 1866.[47] That year, and again in 1868, the *Correio Mercantil* hailed the progress that Brazil had achieved since 1822; sensible Brazilians recognized the value of the country's constitutional order and would, at most, consider minor reforms.[48] In 1868, the *Diário do Rio de Janeiro* condemned the "Liberal Party's pettiness," for its members had failed to appreciate Caxias and Inhaúma's military victories earlier in the year. The general and the admiral were closely associated with the Conservative Party, and their incompatibility with Zacarias's cabinet had led to the change of ministry on 16 July. This jibe at the new opposition, however, was merely a prelude to criticism of the Liberals' newfound eagerness to tamper with the country's institutions.[49] The Liberal *Diário do Povo* lamented that "absolutist principles had spread under the false pretences of constitutional elements," which meant that the 1822 dream of those who desired a free nation had not come to pass. Brazil's "enormous constitutional apparatus . . . is nothing more than a cluster of ineffectual and sterile formulas, which the absolutist element manipulates at will."[50]

The *Diário do Povo*'s editor carefully refrained from identifying the emperor himself as the "absolutist element," but others were more direct. Given Pedro's growing influence and personal power over the government and his unwavering determination to see the war through to an absolute victory, 2 December editorials increasingly debated the monarchy's appropriate role. To be sure, there was still a great deal of respect for Pedro and his persona, as evidenced by *Semana Ilustrada*'s treatment of the man whom it called a "model" monarch, "a great prince, exemplary in civic and private virtue, enlightened, a zealot on behalf of his country's dignity and aggrandizement" (Figure 8.1).[51] Occasional advice to Pedro to rid himself of "mediocre administrations" composed of the "mediocrities, the ambitious, and the egoists who ruin nations" were nothing new and merely repeated the traditional distinction between crown and ministers.[52]

FIGURE 8.1.
"The monument raised by the first [Pedro] is preserved by the second,"
7 September 1867.
Source: Semana Illustrada, 8 Sep. 1867.

Others, however, went further. In 1866, the *Correio Mercantil* argued
that the *povo*'s rough-hewn intuition clearly distinguished between "the
good-hearted prince, motivated by the best of intentions" and the "head
of the executive power." The centralization of power in the capital and in
the emperor's hands meant that Brazil had achieved little in the previous
twenty-seven years. Critics of this editorial took two directions. *O Pandokeu* argued that Brazil had in fact accomplished much, building railroads

and telegraph lines, holding national expositions, and winning victories against the Paraguayans. The author of a paid article in the *Jornal do Comércio* declared that, given Brazil's constitutional regime, the monarch could not be tarred with the failures of the country's governments.[53] Such a denial of Pedro's direct influence on government was hardly credible in light of his use of the moderating power, yet it served as a convenient fiction.

After Zacarias's fall from power in July 1868, Historical Liberals and Progressistas struggled to redefine themselves. On 2 December of that year, the *Diário do Rio de Janeiro* criticized the newly founded Centro Liberal's program that called for democracy; worried that the Centro sought "absolute democracy, the republic," the Conservative newspaper offered a vigorous defense of constitutional monarchy and of Pedro's understanding of the "difficult and glorious mission of a constitutional sovereign," which "has contributed to the consolidation of liberty." The following year, the *Diário* went further and proclaimed that Pedro's "abstention" from political conflicts "peacefully resolves all of the crises that in other [forms of] government end either in anarchy or in despotism." While the Liberal *Sentinela da Liberdade* accepted the *Diário*'s defense of constitutional monarchy in theory, it declared that Pedro had violated the people's rights by forcing the recent ministerial change and the farcical elections that the Conservatives had won handily (the Liberals had, in fact, boycotted the vote). The divorce between the nation and its "first magistrate" would inevitably be fatal for both.[54]

Pedro's first birthday after the 1868 ministerial change was the occasion for a remarkable breach of protocol. In its paid section, the *Jornal do Comércio* published an indifferent poem that, on the surface, looked like a typical bit of empty adulation of Pedro and Teresa Cristina:

> Oh! sublime monarch, I salute thee!
> Just as the entire world salutes thee;
> The world, that knows of thy glories. . . .
> Brazilians, rise up, and with one cry
> Salute the monarch,—salute with anthems
> December's magnificent second day
> The day that brought us a thousand fortunes!
> Let the artillery roar at the break of dawn
> And seem to say in festive sound
> Empire of Brazil, sing, sing!
> Festival harmony reigns among all;
> The monarch's glories, his wholesome virtues,
> Let us watch over them, unceasingly sing their praises.
> The eminent empress, mother of the poor,
> Let us not forget to celebrate [her]
> On this immortal day which is for her
> The happy day on which was born
> The ever great immortal Pedro II.[55]

The *Jornal do Comércio*'s staff may well have failed to notice that the first letters of each line spelled out "*O bobo do rei faz annos* [The fool of a king is having a birthday]," for the French-language *Ba-Ta-Clan*'s *cronista* thought that the poem would have passed unnoticed had not someone inserted a paid article in the *Diário do Rio de Janeiro* to point out the insult.[56] *Opinião Liberal* gleefully reprinted the offending poem, while the *Diário*'s paid section included an acrostic poem that likened the offending poet to beetles and other noisome insects. The first letters of each line spelled out "*Bobo é quem fez o hino* [Foolish is the one who wrote the anthem]."[57]

Minister of Justice José de Alencar reportedly wanted to prosecute the *Jornal do Comércio*, but nothing came of this, and the poem's authorship remains a mystery. Contemporaries pointed to the republican, Salvador Furtado de Mendonça Drummond; the Liberal senator and accomplished poet, Francisco Otaviano de Almeida Rosa; and to the irreverent and witty Conservative journalist, Antônio Ferreira Viana, who had published a bitter polemic against the moderating power back in 1867 (when the Conservatives were out of power).[58] No one claimed responsibility. A later attribution of the poem to Luís Nicolau Fagundes Varela has been accepted by some and denied by others.[59] Less important than the poem's authorship, however, is the political context in which it was published; the change of ministry earlier in the year undermined Pedro's authority and pushed some into the more radical criticism of the monarchy that eventually led to the 1870 Republican Manifesto.

What is most striking about the wartime editorials on days of national festivity is the almost complete lack of references to the Paraguayan War. If Brazilians' "sense of nationality had been enhanced by the long and bloody struggle," as Roderick Barman argues,[60] it did not show on days of national festivity. A 7 September 1865 *Diário do Rio de Janeiro* editorial that asserted that the war had called Brazil to "the great period of [our] manhood" stands out by its rarity. Brazilians had risen to the occasion, declared the editorialist, and the battle of the Riachuelo had served as "the baptism of fire that we needed. We received it. We are now a true nation."[61] Such bellicose nationalism failed to take root, and already in 1871, a *cronista* lamented that Brazilians had forgotten the war.[62] No doubt this failure of the war to enter into Brazil's patriotic culture on days of national festivity derives from the conflict's length and high cost, the difficulties that Brazil and its allies had in defeating tiny Paraguay, and the poor treatment accorded to veterans.[63] In these senses, there is much truth in Alexandre José de Mello Moraes Filho's assertion that the war liquidated Brazilian patriotism.[64]

The Paraguayan War may not have been the right sort of conflict for fostering nationalism, but days of national festivity focused on the political institutions of the constitutional monarchy founded by Pedro I, none of which had much to do with the war. Conjunctural issues such as Pedro's use of his moderating power in 1868 were, of course, closely connected to the war (and to the monarch's determination to win it), but these were also the usual political issues that crystallized on days of national festivity, not the nebulous stuff of national identity. Thus, days of national festivity remained largely political celebrations during which Brazilians debated their country's institutions.

VICTORY CELEBRATIONS, 1870

Brazil's early victories were duly celebrated, but, as the war dragged on, patriotic enthusiasm declined, volunteers gave way to conscripts, and draft resistance increased. The allies' victories of 1866 secured them a toehold on Paraguayan soil, but they were costly, and they failed to bring the war to a satisfactory conclusion. The devastating defeat at the battle of Curupaiti (22 September 1866), when allied troops failed to take a line of Paraguayan fortifications, put an end to their advance, and the war turned into a lengthy stalemate, during which Caxias rebuilt the army. With less and less support from Uruguay and Argentina, Brazilian forces resumed the offensive in 1868. They gradually closed in on Humaitá and then steadily advanced toward Asunción, which they took on 1 January 1869. Caxias then quit his command, and Pedro reluctantly appointed the Count of Eu to lead the campaign against the remnant Paraguayan forces, which finally led to López's death on 1 March 1870.

The much-touted but militarily insignificant Passagem de Humaitá (the February 1868 operation by which the Brazilian navy finally forced its way upriver past the major Paraguayan fortification), the first bit of good news in some time, prompted a massive outburst of celebration throughout the country. Rio de Janeiro residents decorated their façades, illuminated their windows, and poured into the streets to follow marching bands; government departments likewise illuminated their buildings. Cheers to the army, the navy, and their commanders filled the air, along with poetry; Pedro discerned much happiness among the population.[65] The final occupation of Humaitá, abandoned by the Paraguayans in July, set off another round of celebrations. The U.S. minister thought it much exaggerated: "There is no end to the rejoicing; and the press assures the people that there is no such triumph on record in ancient or modern warfare." Taunay also recalled the "intense joy" and "splendid celebrations and illumination in Rio de Janeiro" after the December 1868 victories that led to Asunción's fall.[66]

Victory finally came, and the first months of 1870 amounted to one long sequence of celebrations in Rio de Janeiro. On the surface, it looked as if all of the difficulties of the previous five years had been forgotten and the country—or at least its capital—had reunited around the monarchy. One day after news of López's death reached Rio de Janeiro (on 17 March 1870), a committee of merchants proposed launching a subscription to fund an equestrian statue of Pedro in honor of "the constancy and tenacity that he always demonstrated in sustaining the struggle against the Paraguayan tyrant." The next day, however, Pedro let it be known that he did not want such a monument, and he requested that any funds raised for the purpose be applied to the construction of schools.[67] Pedro's refusal of this honor—consistent with his growing disdain for the outward trappings of monarchy and his interest in education—was well received, and the cornerstone for the first of the schools was laid on 7 September 1870. *Opinião Liberal*, however, pointed out that buildings alone would not ensure the "*povo*'s education."[68]

When the news of López's death reached Rio de Janeiro, the capital was already in the midst of homecoming celebrations for returning army units and the first demobilized *Voluntários da Pátria* battalions (volunteer units raised for the war's duration). How best to demobilize the fourteen *Voluntários* battalions that remained at the war's end had been extensively debated since the November 1869 agreement by the allies to draw down their forces in Paraguay. The Saquarema government appeared initially reluctant to organize celebrations for units organized by Furtado's Liberal and Olinda's Progressista cabinets in 1865; the lack of transports and the limited accommodation in Rio de Janeiro meant that the battalions would return individually rather than all at once. This also conveniently reduced dangers inherent in concentrating several thousand veterans in the capital.[69] Battalions en route to their home provinces in the North nevertheless stopped in the capital, where they participated in victory parades before resuming their journey.[70] Ângelo Agostini's spectacular illustration in *A Vida Fluminense* shows the 23 February parade of the first *Voluntários* battalion to arrive (Figure 8.2); the last landed on 24 July. As Marcelo Balaban notes, the image shows no black men among the troops and emphasizes the parade's orderly nature.[71] Lengthy speeches and poetry greeted the veterans, and the cartoonist suggested that these ceremonies were more difficult for them to face than Paraguayan grapeshot (Figure 8.3); that the men paraded for hours in the hot sun without receiving water or a snack caused some complaint.[72] Most accounts of these parades highlight the participation of Pedro and senior civil and military officials in the formal welcoming ceremonies, as well as the enthusiastic reception by the populace. As the late Wiebke Ipsen has noted, committees of ladies also figured prominently in these rituals.[73]

News of the war's conclusion added to the celebrations, and the U.S. minister reported:

FIGURE 8.2.
The *Voluntários da Pátria* parade, 23 February 1870.
Source: Vida Fluminense, 26 March 1870.

The entire population . . . turned out with demonstrations of great rejoicing and a universal excitement prevailed. The Emperor's carriage was drawn by his enthusiastic subjects through the streets of his capital, and the night following, the Emperor, Empress and Princess walked through Ouvidor and Direita, the two great streets of the city of Rio. Music and marches, banners, torch lights and illuminations continued on the grandest scale for three successive days and nights, and every manifestation indicated that there was but one feeling. . . . The masses seemed to have devoted themselves entirely to giving expression to their triumphant joy.[74]

The news of Lopez's death had, of course, arrived without warning, so this amounted to a spontaneous festival. There was no time to construct ephemeral monuments; people hastily pulled out their *copinhos* and other lamps to illuminate their façades, bands took to the streets, and fireworks were set off. In the intermission to a hastily prepared gala at the São Pedro Theater, the imperial family went to the *varanda* to receive cheers from the people who packed Constitution Square.[75] On 25 March, the city council held a formal Te Deum at the São Francisco church to celebrate the war's end.[76]

These celebrations gave way to another round of festivities at the end of April, this time to welcome back the Count of Eu. Because his arrival

FIGURE 8.3.
Patriotic poetry worse than Paraguayan grapeshot, April 1870.
Source: *Vida Fluminense*, 9 April 1870.

was expected, there had been time to prepare, and popular subscriptions turned the city into "one enormous triumphal arch, that begins at Mataporcos [Street] and ends at Guanabara [Street], in Laranjeiras," where Eu and Isabel resided.[77] No detailed program for his reception was published in the press, unlike for Pedro's reception in 1865; the author of one paid article wondered about this but concluded that the celebrations were not official: "The government will thus not publish a program; . . . these are popular festivities." The British minister also reported that "the authorities . . . abstained from taking any part in the arrangements."[78] Given that there was no formal program, residents of

FIGURE 8.4.
The Count of Eu and Pedro II struggling through the crowd, 29 April 1870.
Source: Vida Fluminense, 7 May 1870.

Riachuelo Street publicly requested that Eu visit their street "so that they [could] show how thankful they [were] to the eminent general."[79]

A Vida Fluminense's cronista judged Eu's reception on 29 April to have been "the most complete, most spontaneous, and most brilliant" that he had ever seen, although another illustrated newspaper thought the ephemeral architecture overly modest in size.[80] Julia Keyes, a Confederate exile, lamented that an outbreak of yellow fever made it too dangerous for her to go into the city from Bangu to witness the festivities, but her father "enjoyed the whole scene for the rest" and told her about the crush of people on Direita Street. Soldiers could not prevent them from blocking the road: "The mass became so dense [that] the emperor begged permission to pass, waving his hat imploringly, which he had taken off to cool his brow" (Figure 8.4). *The Anglo-Brazilian Times's* reporter described the crowd as a "waving river of restless life," from which "rolled on a mighty cheer" from the moment that Eu came into view until he disappeared into the imperial chapel. André Rebouças, who was in Eu's party at the landing, recalled the indescribable "delirium" and the procession's difficulty in making its way through the "compact and disorderly mass." After the Te Deum, he went home, "clothes soaked in sweat and wrinkled by the crush of people." He rejoined the celebrations that evening, when numerous commissions congratulated Eu and Isabel at their official residence and a 200-strong children's choir sang a new anthem; Rebouças noted that "a mob of the *povo*, who forced their way into the palace, disrupted this celebration's end," an indication that more than just the organized committees sought to participate. Later that night, he still had the energy to visit many illuminated streets and squares downtown.[81] Keyes's and Rebouças's accounts of the chaotic and enthusiastic reception are fully borne out by the press coverage, although no newspaper adopted Rebouças's disdainful tone for what *A Reforma* called the "*povo* who filled the palace gardens."[82]

The celebrations continued for several days with all of the usual elements of civic ritual, including a Te Deum, a theater gala (complete with complaints that the Lírico's management had raised ticket prices for that evening).[83] Until well into June, a steady stream of societies, corporations, and government departments sent delegations to congratulate Eu and Isabel at their palace.[84] On 11 May, the Sociedade Clube Fluminense held a ball in his honor. Neighborhood celebrations for the war's end and for Eu's return likewise continued until well into June, as did Te Deums in brotherhood chapels and parish churches.[85] These celebrations (and the receptions of the returning battalions) certainly belie assertions that "the victorious Brazilian army's homecoming parade was far from triumphant," as Peter Beattie has claimed.[86]

In mid-May, Alencar estimated that the sums spent on these "private celebrations" had exceeded 800 contos (US$360,000).[87] To judge by a few accounts published by organizing committees, a neighborhood or block festival cost only a few thousand mil-réis. Thanks to a squabble over the quality of the decorations on Ourives Street between Ouvidor and São Pedro Streets, the local festival committee judged it necessary to publish a full accounting of its work. Ninety-six donors contributed a total of 3:369$740 (US$1,516), most in small amounts of less than 20$000 (US$9.00). The major expenses were for the construction of a triumphal arch and platforms for the musicians (1:140$000), lighting (650$000), musicians for three nights (800$000), and assorted banners, flags, and poles (540$200).[88] The Estácio de Sá Square committee raised a similar sum (3:296$340) but spent more on the construction of an obelisk and its illumination (2:700$000) and apparently obtained musicians for free, for it only spent 96$780 on refreshments for them.[89]

The numerous paid articles published in the *Jornal do Comércio* in which "all boast about their street" reveal not just local pride and identification with neighborhood celebrations but also suggest a chaotic and uncoordinated citywide festival. The owners of the businesses located on an alley off Direita Street were dismayed to see the entrance to their street blocked by a band shell (constructed by the Chamber of Commerce), which meant that they could not decorate this space. Others complained that, despite their contributions to local campaigns, the decorations were located far from their residences.[90]

A considerable number of slaves were freed in honor of the count—at least thirty, according to the *Anglo-Brazilian Times* of 6 May.[91] Typographers raised funds to free two children and hailed Eu for his role in both freeing Paraguay from despotism and in ending slavery in that country. *A Reforma* ensured that its staff could participate in this presentation by not publishing on 30 April.[92] Between 30 April and 3 May, the *Jornal do Comércio* noted seven private manumissions in honor of the war's end and of Eu's return.[93] For the same reasons, the Baron of São João do Príncipe pledged to free the children henceforth born to his slaves and committed to raising them to adulthood (thereby anticipating the Free Womb Law that would be passed in 1871).[94] The Estácio de Sá festival committee applied its surplus funds to purchasing the freedom of a slave child and to assisting a slave woman in completing the sum that she needed for her manumission.[95] Even the Democráticos carnival society freed a slave child at its ball to celebrate Eu's return.[96] Notices of manumissions to commemorate the battles of Tuiuti and the Riachuelo, the safe return of sons, or simply the war's end continued to appear in the *Jornal do Comércio* until July.[97]

These manumissions were not merely a repeat of the traditional custom of commemorating important events by freeing slaves. In May and July, *The Anglo-Brazilian Times* described them as part of an "emancipation movement" that was rapidly gaining strength and had considerable support in parliament.[98] That Eu had ordered abolition in Paraguay—although it is doubtful that any slaves remained in that devastated country—indicated his support for abolition in Brazil, which Pedro had quietly been advocating for some years. The emperor's 1867 call to begin discussion of the issue forced it onto the public agenda, but the Council of State sought to postpone consideration until after the war. The reorganized Liberals had included abolition in their platforms in 1868–69, and Pedro's pressure was intensifying, but parliament and the two Saquarema cabinets of 1868–71 were reluctant to act, which belies the abolitionist English-language newspaper's assessment of legislators' views.[99]

Celebrating Eu's return with manumissions nonetheless highlighted Liberals' support for abolition and perhaps sought to drive a wedge between Saquaremas and those Conservative deputies willing to contemplate antislavery measures. More generally, it also conveniently undermined the Conservative Caxias's prestige.[100] Certainly the enthusiastic coverage of Eu's return in *A Reforma* offers many indications of this, and one incident explicitly reveals the festival politics. *A Reforma* criticized a group of "salaried officers" who had planned to "force the *povo* to cheer Mr. Caxias" on 2 May; these men had apparently roughed up a band stationed on Constitution Square when its members refused to "celebrate the duke's glories" and then tried to knock down a triumphal arch. Paid articles soon appeared in defense of Caxias's supporters: They merely wanted to recognize all of Brazil's generals, including the one who had led the army from Tuiuti to Asunción (Caxias). The paid articles denounced those who "hid themselves in the Corte's cafés and theaters" during the war and now dared to insult "a much-beloved commander."[101] A much later magazine also attributed the celebrations to the Liberals but added that they quickly became disillusioned with Isabel's consort. Devastated by his experience in the war, Eu was in no physical or mental condition to assume a political role, and Pedro soon packed him and Isabel off to Europe for ten months.[102]

Even as the echoes of Eu's welcoming reception continued, the Conservative government began preparing a final official celebration of the war's end. It would consist of a Te Deum in a specially constructed temple located on the Campo da Aclamação, followed by a National Guard parade, a levee in the downtown palace, an afternoon cantata performed in the temple, and nighttime illumination of the entire Campo. To accommodate the expected numerous spectators, the government contracted for the construction of large bleachers. This official festival, which looked like a government response to the welcome for Eu, was an utter fiasco when finally held on 10 July. Very few of the people who had received invitations bothered to show up, and the authorities were obliged to open the gates to the populace, who streamed in to fill the space.[103] A closer look at how this festival failure came about reveals much about the politics of official festivities and the tense postwar political climate.

In contrast to the popular festivities in honor of Eu and the returning battalions—popular in the sense of involving organized civil society groups (private associations, as Alencar called them)—this was an unabashedly official celebration and one whose cost was deeply controversial. It was originally set for 24 May (the fourth anniversary of the first battle of Tuiuti), and shortly after the legislature convened the government introduced a bill to open a supplementary credit of 200 contos (US$90,000) to the war ministry to finance it. Half of this allocation was for the construction of the temple, while most of the rest was destined for decorations, musicians, priests, and illumination. Alencar, who had quit the Itaboraí cabinet in January, spoke forcefully against the bill in the chamber of deputies; as far as he was concerned, it amounted to a colossal waste of money. Did the government plan to "set an official celebration against the popular festival" of earlier that month, he asked? Moreover, it would not be a national celebration, for there would not be sufficient time to invite representatives from distant provinces.[104] The war minister, the Baron of Muritiba, justified the expense on the grounds that Catholics had an obligation to "give solemn thanks to the almighty for the great benefit that he granted to Brazil." At most, the celebration would cost each of Brazil's estimated one million taxpayers a mere 200 réis (US$0.09), he added.[105]

The bill passed second reading handily (fifty-eight to eight) and was approved on 24 May, the date originally set for the celebration, but the government had already postponed it to an unspecified future date. The bill then went to the senate.[106] While the bill was still under discussion in the chamber, a large number of laborers were already hard at work on "the great cardboard temple," and *A Vida Fluminense*'s *cronista* joined Alencar in lashing out at the cost and the waste of money when disabled veterans went without aid. What sins had the government committed, he wondered, for it to budget 40:000$ (US$18,000) for priests?[107] One of its cartoons showed Muritiba gleefully handing out money to secure cheers to the cabinet, to Caxias, and especially to himself.[108] Other critics condemned the government for contracting foreigners to design the monument and oversee its construction; *A Reforma* later smelled nepotism when it learned that one of the Italian designers was Itaboraí's son-in-law.[109] Another writer complained in verse about the waste of public money on decorations when citizens went without water thanks to the city's precarious supply.[110]

The senate debated the measure during three sessions between 15 and 27 June. In the upper chamber, there was an organized opposition, and leading Liberals castigated the government for the unconstitutional expenditure of funds before parliamentary approval had been obtained, denounced the measure as a massive waste of money on ephemeral structures and fireworks that would just go up in smoke, and anticipated that it would run far over budget. Muritiba took responsibility for the decision to start construction and claimed that all of the monies already spent had come from his ministry's contingency fund.[111] The undisputed Liberal leader, José Tomás Nabuco de Araújo, recalled the popular celebrations of March and April and wondered whether the government was engaged in a "politics of diversion" to deflect attention from the country's many unmet needs. The 200 contos could have been better spent on supporting fallen soldiers' widows and orphans or on freeing slaves. Amid raucous cheers from his colleagues, Nabuco concluded that the "big shed" (as wags had dubbed the temple) demonstrated "outward glory" even as it revealed the parliamentary system's "decadence" and "degeneration" under the Conservative administration.[112] The Conservative majority secured the bill's passage, and it was promulgated on 8 July.[113]

FIGURE 8.5.
The temple on the Campo da Aclamação, 10 July 1870.
Source: BN/SI, 870518. Courtesy Acervo da Fundação Biblioteca Nacional—Brasil.

As it rose on the Campo the victory temple proved an impressive structure (Figure 8.5). Fully 124 Doric columns supported the 85-palm (17 meter) high round temple. The central cupola, 186 palms (38 meters) high, was topped by an angel of victory. The entire structure consisted of 43,000 square palms (178 square meters) of covered space, and the central chapel contained an altar and a cross that could be seen from the entire square. There was space for musicians and ample room for thousands of spectators.[114] The temple stood on the west side of the square, near the senate and in front of the mint (today the Arquivo Nacional), and bleachers lined the square's north, south, and east sides.[115]

It soon became public knowledge that the bleachers' construction left much to be desired. Already on 20 May, residents on the Campo thanked the contractors for blocking their view of the temple with one of the bleachers; instead, they would have a first-class view of its collapse (they would, in fact, be well placed to watch the fire that destroyed the bleachers a few days after the festival).[116] The city police and the war ministry dispatched engineers to inspect the structures, and both teams recommended significant reinforcements in June; in the first week of July, after the festival had been set for the 10th, they were still not satisfied and demanded additional structural work on one of them. The government published the engineers' reports in several newspapers on the day of the festival, but this probably served more to remind the populace of the construction problems than to allay concerns about the structures' soundness.[117] While the engineers now concluded that the three bleachers could safely hold 4,355 people, *A Reforma* claimed that they could bear the weight of no more than a few hundred spectators and advised its readers to stay away.[118]

In early July the government announced that the celebration would take place on Sunday, 10 July, and the debate heated up.[119] On the 4th, Alencar published a pamphlet in which he appealed to Brazilians to stay away from what he called the "burlesque festival." He reiterated his original criticisms, emphasized the unconstitutional way in which the government had financed it, and reserved sharp words for Pedro II's ostentatious modesty. The original plans had contemplated a large temporary statue of the monarch, which Pedro struck from the proposal (organizers replaced it with a statue representing peace). Such excessive modesty among kings was dangerous, Alencar concluded, for it usually disguised overweening ambition. By this time he had turned into an articulate critic of Pedro's personal power.[120] *A Reforma* noted that both the *Jornal do Comércio* and the *Diário do Rio de Janeiro* had refused to accept advertisements for the pamphlet. This pamphlet, along with another anonymous one, *Roleta italiana* ([The] Italian Roulette Wheel), judged one observer, contributed to the cabinet's unpopularity.[121]

The Liberal *A Reforma*, however, led the attacks on the official festival, now focusing on its exclusionary nature. The invitations to attend the celebration in the "big shed" specified gala dress, something that many recently returned military personnel did not have. Civilians in "suits" or "jackets" were normally admitted to Te Deums in the imperial chapel, but they were apparently being excluded from this service.[122] When the war ministry announced the categories of invited guests allowed to enter by each of the four gates to the temple, *A Reforma* added that the fifth gate would be reserved for the *povo*. There was of course no fifth entrance, and the Liberal newspaper's point was to criticize the elitist nature of the festival.[123] Those who did not receive invitations could, of course, purchase seats in the bleachers, but the cost put them out of reach for most people. A box for six spectators went for 50$000 (US$22.50), and single general admission tickets cost 5$000 (US$2.25), respectively comparable to the price for first-class theater boxes and the best seats on the Lírico's floor.[124] Others contrasted the fate of war widows who were still not receiving pensions with the "two hundred contos [spent on] the cardboard temple." Two authors of paid articles in the *Jornal do Comércio* lamented the temple's ephemeral nature and called for the construction of either a "magnificent cathedral" or a permanent war memorial. In late June, one wag proposed that the festival be set for 16 July, the Itaboraí ministry's second anniversary, for it was ultimately the cabinet's celebration.[125]

Despite the criticisms, Colonel Antônio Tibúrcio Ferreira de Sousa, recently returned as commander of one of the *Voluntários* battalions, expected "a great national celebration," another "great pretext to reproduce the frenzied delirium of this *peaceful and simple povo*."[126] On 11 July, readers of the *Diário do Rio de Janeiro*, the *Jornal do Comércio*, and the *Jornal da Tarde* learned that "everything came together so that the ceremony was conducted with the greatest of dignity," to quote the *Diário*. Both the *Diário* and the *Jornal* published lengthy descriptions of the temple and its decorations. The next day, the *Diário Oficial* added that the *povo* had cheered enthusiastically during the celebration.[127]

A Reforma and the illustrated newspapers vigorously contested these attempts to portray the celebration as a success, and their accounts indicate that it was an utter fiasco. While 8,000 invitations had been issued for the morning Te Deum, only 200 people showed up, and only fifteen people braved the bleachers, most of them members of the contractors' families (no other source confirms these figures). The Campo was "a great empty space" in which police and soldiers far outnumbered spectators (an assessment at least partially confirmed by Marc Ferrez's photograph, Figure 8.5). By 10:00 am, the imperial family had arrived, and bells announced that the Host was being brought from the nearby São Gonçalo Church to the temple. A large crowd followed the priests carrying the Host; instead of letting the Te Deum take place in an empty temple, Pedro ordered the gates thrown open to all who wanted to enter. This gave the celebration "a simulacrum of popular life," thanks to the "influx of the rabble of the city," noted *The Anglo-Brazilian Times*. Etelvino, a *cronista* in *Comédia Social*, added that the emperor did so out of compassion for Muritiba. *A Reforma* highlighted the social mixing that then took place: "Thus, alongside the Baron of Muritiba, were gathered the carter and the female food-seller [*quitandeira*], people in jackets and in bare feet [that is, slaves], and the other brothers in Jesus Christ whom he [Muritiba] had disdained in favor of blue pants and embroidered uniforms," references to officers' dress uniforms and court livery. One of Etelvino's friends, "perceiving the excessively democratic nature of the gathering," hastily stuffed his gloves into his pocket. The one foreigner who left an account of the Te Deum noted that "the extensive platform was only scantily occupied" and described "the outside public" as "very orderly" when they were admitted.[128] *Roleta italiana*'s anonymous author described the refusal to attend the festival as the *povo*'s exercise of sovereignty over the cabinet—"six inept [and] unpopular men, true enemies of the *pátria*, which they shamelessly sell"—and warned Pedro to break with all those who had promoted the celebration.[129]

Etelvino thought little of the Guard parade and returned to the Campo for the afternoon cantata, only to find that organizers were freely handing out tickets to the bleachers; he did not visit the square that night but heard that the illumination was unimpressive. *Semana Ilustrada* and *A Vida Fluminense* later mocked those few who had paid for seating when they could have been admitted for free.[130] For the next few days, *A Reforma* continued to criticize aspects of the festival, the temple's interior decorations that any "country village" could have improved on (even the *Jornal do Comércio* admitted that the chapel was "perhaps a bit cheaply decorated"), delays in paying the musicians, the 800 tickets to the gala that the police and the war ministry had given away. Its writers imagined the reaction of two female slaves admitted to the temple, one of whom declared: "Wow! . . . whitey don' know how to do thing right . . . Shed look like ole Injun hut [*Uê! . . . blanco não sabe faze cousa direta . . . Barraca está que parece tijupa velha*]." On 17 July, it compared the structure's imminent demolition to Samson's destruction of the Philistines' temple; nothing would survive of the government that had ordered its construction.[131]

The major newspapers hushed up the most serious incidents, which took place at the end of the official festival. Etelvino heard "vociferations against the minister of war" in the late afternoon, and *A Reforma* reported that, during the evening, "throughout the city was heard the cry of 'Down with the cabinet!'" A group of army officers paraded through the streets "hailing the emperor, the Count of Eu, and the imperial family, and shouting 'out with the cabinet of 16 July' and *death* to Muritiba." They prevented coaches from reaching the Teatro Lírico and the war minister, "for prudence's sake," retreated to the safety of the army barracks. Pedro may not actually have heard the demonstrators, for his coach had been held up by people presenting him with petitions. Tibúrcio, who offered the most detailed account of this incident in a private letter, condemned this criminal behavior on the part of soldiers whose duty it was to obey the law.[132]

As far as *A Reforma* was concerned, the official celebration's failure, a sharp contrast to the *povo*'s "delirious jubilation" in March, April, and early May, was entirely due to the government's handling of the preparations, its wasteful spending of "meager savings on family celebrations," its alleged exclusion of the *Voluntários da Pátria* and the navy from the celebration, and the invitations sent only to the rich and the powerful. The date of 10 July was the anniversary of Pedro's departure for Uruguaiana in 1865, but 24 May or even 11 July (the battle of the Riachuelo's anniversary) would have been more appropriate. By their absence, citizens "also protested against the government that tramples their liberty; denies them justice, bread, and water; and converts the *povo*'s blood into circus shows." Tibúrcio attributed the population's "solemn protest" to the "opposition press" and to festival fatigue.[133] Beattie has recently blamed the Rio de Janeiro elite's reluctance to attend the celebration on its members' disdain for the mostly lower-class and nonwhite soldiers who had fought in the war.[134] Such alleged racism, however, had not stopped Brazilians of all classes (including elite women) from celebrating the soldiers' return earlier in the year, and the explanation for the celebration's failure lies, as contemporaries recognized, in partisan politics and perhaps also in the decline in official festivities discussed earlier in this chapter.

The contrast between the successful popular or privately organized festivities that celebrated the war's end (and Eu's return) in early 1870 and the failed official celebration in July highlights the government's inability to control the reception of civic rituals. Widespread relief at the war's end and satisfaction with the return of family and friends no doubt contributed in important ways to the popular festivities that welcomed back the troops. So too did the Liberals' efforts to associate themselves with Eu in opposition to the Conservative cabinet and its support for Caxias. The arches and decorations may have been relatively modest, but these were celebrations with which many identified strongly, some even to the point of forcing their way into Isabel and Eu's palace. By contrast, the costly official festivities and the exaggerated temple, which stood forlornly on the Campo da Aclamação awaiting a decision on when the celebration would take place, smacked too much of waste, empty ostentation, and shameless promotion of the cabinet. The popular classes' exclusion from the festival space, and their eventual last-minute admission, also poses questions about their identification with the imperial regime, an issue that we will address further in Chapter Ten.

In Rio de Janeiro, the Paraguayan War ended much as it had begun, amid elaborate and often enthusiastic celebrations. Brazilian civic ritual culture had changed substantially during the war, and the country's victory would scarcely be celebrated in subsequent years. Whether the war had created a nation is of course unknowable. It may indeed have been insufficient to force major changes in Brazil, as Centeno implies, but the conflict came at a time when aspects of Brazilian civic ritual culture were well established, if already in decline. What the postwar celebrations demonstrated, however, was that Brazilians eagerly joined in popular festivities but rejected a clumsy and costly official attempt to celebrate one more time, months after the war had ended and long after most of the troops had returned and the *Voluntários da Pátria* battalions had been disbanded. Liberals certainly took advantage of this, but neither the enthusiasm for Eu's return nor the repudiation of the 10 July celebration can be attributed solely to partisan politics.

The war's most enduring symbolic legacy lay in the city streets and squares that received new names in 1865–70. Direita Street became Primeiro de Março (1 March) in honor of the war's end, and Pedro could not avoid the public recognition of having the Palace Square renamed Dom Pedro II Square. Other new names included Riachuelo Street (formerly Mata-Cavalos) and Uruguaiana (formerly Vala). The Rocio Pequeno became Onze de Junho (11 June) Square, and Caxias lent his name to the Largo do Machado.[135]

The limited attention to the war during the celebrations of days of national festivity is consistent with one of my central arguments, that civic rituals were ways of conducting politics and occasions to debate the empire's principal institutions—constitution and monarchy—founded by Pedro I. Wartime politics cast into sharper relief Pedro's personal power and strengthened the hand of his critics, but the monarchy was still a firmly rooted institution, and Brazil's belated victory did much to assuage discontent at the war's length and at Pedro's single-minded determination to defeat Paraguay. By the end of 1870, politics had turned to other issues, and the celebrations of days of national festivity entered a new phase, in which more questions were raised about the imperial regime.

CHAPTER NINE

Questioning Official Ritual, 1870s–1880s

After the noisy and enthusiastic popular celebrations of the Paraguayan War's end and the fiasco of the July 1870 official ceremony, civic rituals resumed the decline that had begun before the war. The war itself was almost never mentioned on days of national festivity in the 1870s and 1880s, and Pedro continued to dismantle the ritual apparatus that surrounded his persona, most notably with the *beija-mão*'s abolition in 1872. The theater galas, once key barometers of the political mood and widely discussed in the press, lost much of their former importance. Although galas were still held, fewer and fewer especially commissioned works were performed, newspapers paid less attention to them, and the emperor did not always attend. This simplification of official ritual coincided with what historians generally see as the imperial regime's drawn-out decline.[1]

Alongside this decline in official rituals, the debates about the constitution, independence, and the monarchy continued and even intensified. Editorials usually followed predictable party lines, but the Republican Party founded in 1870 offered more fundamental criticism of the imperial regime. Critics increasingly sought to incorporate the antimonarchical movements of 1789 and 1817 into their interpretations of independence, and in the 1880s republicans sought to make Tiradentes, executed for his role in the 1789 Inconfidência Mineira, into a national hero, greater than Pedro I, as Teófilo Otoni had already attempted at the time of the equestrian statue's inauguration. The result was a lively debate about the origins of independence.

Finally, this chapter examines a few nonrecurring civic rituals and the debate about them in the 1870s. Pedro's April 1872 return from his trip to Europe reprised many aspects of the 1846, 1860, and 1865 receptions. The September 1872 inauguration of the monument to José Bonifácio de Andrada e Silva, a long-contemplated counterpart to Pedro I's equestrian statue, served as the occasion for extensive debate about the meaning of independence and the imperial regime. In 1877, Rio de Janeiro welcomed Pedro as he returned from travels that had taken him to the United States, Canada, Europe, and the Middle East; this time, however, he openly rejected the festival. Nevertheless, these three rituals reveal that the imperial regime still had the capacity to put on large-scale official festivities in the 1870s.

Several developments in the press during these years shaped the discourse about civic rituals. The proliferation of illustrated newspapers provided a new genre for commenting on days of national festivity—caricatures and cartoons. The first successful and long-lived of these publications, Henrique Fleiüss's *Semana Ilustrada* (1860–76), maintained a respectful attitude toward the monarchy. Ângelo Agostini—the other great caricaturist of the time—was associated with several shorter-lived newspapers before founding the *Revista Ilustrada* (1876–98). He took a more critical view of the monarchy and advocated the abolition of slavery. About a dozen other illustrated newspapers joined these two leaders for longer or shorter periods.[2]

While there is considerable literature on the capital's illustrated newspapers, historians fascinated by these weeklies have left the much larger daily press relatively unstudied. The *Revista Ilustrada*'s circulation of 5,000 copies per week by the late 1880s was an impressive achievement that secured Agostini editorial and financial independence, but this figure paled in comparison to the major dailies' circulation, which expanded significantly as the press became a more competitive business.[3] Neutral in party politics but conservative in outlook, the *Jornal do Comércio*, with its large pages, fine print, and circulation of 15,000 in the 1860s and early 1870s was, according to Michael Mulhall, the "most important newspaper in Brazil or in all South America," a view that Émile Levasseur reiterated in 1889.[4] While Jeffrey Needell has observed that the *Jornal do Comércio* is an "acquired taste for the modern reader," Brazilians devoured its coverage of parliamentary debates, serialized novels and *crônicas*, correspondence from the provinces and abroad, pages of advertising, and ample section of paid articles, the so-called *a pedidos*. As soon as her train for São Paulo left Rio de Janeiro in 1882, Ina von Binzer observed that most of the male passengers hid themselves behind the *Jornal do Comércio*'s "enormous sheets."[5] Several other dailies took a variety of political positions, as did a number of shorter-lived party organs, and they accounted for the rest of the 30,000 or so newspapers sold daily in the capital in 1870, a figure that grew substantially by the end of the empire; in 1881, four dailies' collective circulation totaled 46,000. José Ferreira de Souza Araújo's *Gazeta de Notícias*, founded in 1875, was the first popular newspaper; sold for a modest 40 réis (US$0.02), it soon achieved a circulation of 24,000. At the end of 1886, *O País* also printed 24,000 copies daily, a figure that grew to 32,500 by 1889, when it proclaimed that it had "the largest circulation in South America."[6] Much of the expansion in circulation was facilitated by the street sale of newspapers, pioneered by the *Diário de Notícias* in 1870; the immigrant newsboy soon became a common sight on city streets.[7]

In the early 1880s, a wave of usually ephemeral political papers revived the old tradition of radical journalism, leavened with a heavy dose of scandalmongering and intemperate language; most of them were also republican and abolitionist. Fully 169 new periodicals were launched in 1881–83, but only about half of them produced more than a single issue. *Carbonário* (1880–90) and Apulco de Castro's *Corsário* (1880–83) endured for longer periods. The violent reaction to Apulco's murder in 1883 demonstrated that his critical comments on society and politics had earned him a following.[8] Several newspapers took up the cause of abolitionism, a topic addressed in Chapter Ten; the most prominent of these was the *Gazeta da Tarde*, under José do Patrocínio's direction from 1881 to 1887. Student newspapers and literary magazines also proliferated in the last decades of the empire; while usually short lived, they offer perspectives on the views of the generation born after midcentury that came of age in the last years of the monarchy.

The press continued to enjoy full freedom, and many foreigners marveled at the range of rhetoric that appeared in the paid section, whose anonymous articles often included personal attacks and amounted to "one of the worst abuses that exist in Brazil," according to Émile Allain.[9] Others recognized, however, that such paid articles served the important purpose of bringing "views before the public."[10] This was also the space in which the authors of patriotic poetry paid to have their work printed, although the volume of such verse had already diminished notably in the 1860s.

At the end of the war, Brazilian politics stood in flux. The July 1868 ministerial change had brought Saquaremas to power, and the Liberal boycott of the subsequent election ensured an overwhelmingly Conservative chamber. Liberals reorganized themselves and presented the first clear party program, calling for electoral and judicial reforms, decentralization, and greater protection for citizens' rights. A segment of the Liberals went further and, on 3 December 1870, issued the Republican Manifesto; for a few years, the new Republican Club published a newspaper, *A República*.[11] As Needell has shown, Pedro retained his suspicion of doctrinaire Conservatives (Saquaremas) and, in early 1871, handed power to the Viscount of Rio Branco (José Maria da Silva Paranhos), whom he charged with pushing the free womb bill through a reluctant legislature dominated by Saquaremas. This first step toward the final abolition of slavery—the law freed all the children henceforth born to slave women—provoked a constitutional crisis, for it was clearly the monarch's bill and did not emerge from the legislature. As the first major government intervention in slave–master relations, it also sparked bitter opposition from those who feared that the measure would undermine masters' authority.[12]

Subsequently, the long-lived Rio Branco cabinet undertook a variety of reforms, including the first census and an unsuccessful attempt to institute a draft lottery. In 1875, a cabinet headed first by the (now) Duke of Caxias and later by the Baron of Cotegipe (João Maurício Wanderley) continued this program.[13] From 1872 to 1875, a bitter Church–state conflict dominated the political agenda, as ultramontane bishops tried to exclude freemasons from the Church while Pedro insisted on his imperial prerogative to sanction papal bulls (he refused to do so for the antimason measures, but the bishops implemented them in flagrant disregard of imperial authority).[14] The Religious Question gave way to a debate about electoral reform in the late 1870s. Conservatives failed to institute substantial changes, not least because, according to one view, modifying electoral procedures required constitutional amendments, a potentially dangerous precedent. In January 1878, Pedro returned the Liberals to power, and they held office until 1885. During their tenure, Liberals instituted direct elections by law, after having first failed to do so by constitutional amendment. While the reform protected the rights of opposition candidates, it also reduced the electorate substantially by imposing a literacy requirement that eliminated most voters (those who had cast ballots for electors under the old two-tier system) from the rolls.[15] A number of erstwhile republicans, notably Lafaiete Rodrigues Pereira and Pedro Luís Pereira de Souza, both of whom had written for *A Atualidade* in the early 1860s, played important roles in these Liberal cabinets, which indicates the weakness of the republican movement, the strength of the imperial regime, Pedro's tolerance for what he saw as youthful flirtation with republicanism, and his efforts to win over critics.[16]

Not all of these political questions figured prominently on days of national festivity. Governments only halfheartedly implemented the Free Womb Law, and, given that no significant abolitionist movement had pushed for the law, there was no constituency for celebrating it in the 1870s, nor for associating it with days of national festivity, as abolitionists would do in the 1880s. In response to the abolitionist challenge, slaveowners then held the law up as the last word on abolition, despite having done their best to evade its terms in the 1870s. Progress remained an important theme for editorialists, but neither the Religious Question nor electoral reform stood out in the political debate on days of national festivity, which remained focused on the old questions of the imperial regime's origins and nature.

Historians generally see these decades as the time of the imperial regime's decline, especially after the mid-1870s. Pedro II's increasing disinterest in the minutiae of imperial administration—of which he was the linchpin—contributed to this, as did his health problems in the 1880s.[17] The decline in official ritual traced in the first section of this chapter suggests a regime that lacked sufficient self-confidence to publicly celebrate itself and its origins. Some further suggest that this decline alienated many of the popular classes, deeply imbued with monarchical ideals, an issue that we take up in Chapter Ten. What is clearer is that many in the intellectual elite rejected the regime. The so-called Generation of 1870 condemned the empire's narrow liberalism and the Romantic cultural ideals embodied in Indianism (critics also questioned the use of the Indian as a symbol of Brazil, but cartoonists like Agostini continued to deploy it).[18] The new generation embraced a diffuse positivism (and not usually its more rigorous orthodoxy), republicanism, and a scientific rhetoric that dismissed the imperial regime as an outdated institution, incapable of reform. Maria Thereza Chaves de Mello suggests that the spread of these ideas led by the 1880s to a broad, if diffuse, consensus that the empire's time was up, that reform was impossible under its aegis, and that only a republic could bring real progress to Brazil.[19] Cynicism about politics further undermined the regime. Establishment figures like the historian and Conservative Party deputy João Manoel Pereira da Silva contrasted the passionate and ideological but usually honest politics of the 1830s with the time in which he was writing (the 1880s) when "personal interests predominate, and society is therefore much more corrupt and demoralized, even if more peaceful and submissive." Popular figures like Dom Obá II echoed these views, lamenting that unlike their predecessors who entered office rich and left poor, modern Liberals "leave [office] overloaded with ostentatious wealth."[20]

Tempered with such cynicism, the new ideas underlay much of the criticism of the imperial regime in the discussion about the three days of national festivity's meaning and guided the search for new symbols and a nonmonarchical history of Brazil's origins, the subject of this chapter's second section. The three great official rituals of 1872–77 with which this chapter concludes, however, indicate that the regime still had the capacity to claim symbolic control over Rio de Janeiro's urban space. From 1877 to 1888 no comparable large-scale official celebrations took place, and the great festivities of 1888, analyzed in Chapter Ten, were very different from those of the 1870s.

OFFICIAL CELEBRATIONS:
DECLINE AND CRITICISM

While no day of national festivity passed without official commemoration in the 1870s and 1880s, these civic rituals continued the slow decline that had begun with the end of theater subsidies and the National Guard parade's wartime elimination. In 1872, Pedro removed the *beija-mão* from imperial protocol; over the course of these years, the theater gala lost much of its former importance. This simplification of imperial ritual can also be seen in the press, whose reports on civic rituals either became more perfunctory or manifested a more critical tone. The monarchy's more extreme critics, however, continued to lambaste the regime for its excessive pomp and ceremony.

During these decades, each of the three days of national festivity still had its official core—artillery salutes from forts and warships (the latter decorated with flags), the Te Deum in the imperial chapel and the levee (with the *beija-mão* until 1872) in the downtown palace, the illumination of public buildings at night, and the theater gala—but there is only one indication of an army or National Guard parade in Rio de Janeiro after the Paraguayan War, on 7 September 1870, when 3,000 guardsmen, "extremely well-turned-out, rivaling those of Europe," according to the *Diário de Notícias*, paraded on the Palace Square. Much less impressed, the Liberal opposition's *A Reforma* lamented that, "like plough oxen, hundreds of uniformed citizens . . . pulled enormous artillery pieces to embellish the official festivities."[21] No further parades took place on days of national festivity, and, on 2 December 1871, *A Reforma* commented that, as a result, hospital beds would see fewer sick soldiers who no longer had to declare, like Roman gladiators: "Hail Caeser, those who are about to die salute thee."[22] By 1872, a magazine could describe the "laborious movement of troops" on days of national festivity as another one of the old customs that had disappeared. The 1873 reform of the National Guard reduced it to a largely symbolic organization, exempt from service except in cases of foreign war or rebellion; as far as participation in civic rituals was concerned, the law merely ratified by then existing practice.[23]

In April 1872, Pedro II abolished the *beija-mão*. The decree that announced his decision explained that, because the hand-kissing custom had derived from "the old Portuguese monarchy's practices" and had been reestablished during his minority without any formal decree that it was an obligatory ritual, the emperor could simply abolish it as a personal decision.[24] Republicans like Francisco Xavier da Cunha, who had long considered the ritual a "servile adoration of brutal and despotic power, invented by the potentates of Asia," were unimpressed. Hardly an act of "democratic sentiment," it was a belated "bit of housecleaning"; Brazil required more profound change than simply abolishing the *beija-mão. A República*'s editors thought it shameful that the ritual had to be abolished by imperial fiat, rather than by Brazilians' refusal to abase themselves before the monarch.[25] According to the U.S. minister, some expected that the *beija-mão*'s abolition would lead to the abandonment of the "cumbrous ceremonial and theatrical display" at the legislature's opening on 3 May, but Pedro appeared in his usual formal regalia.[26]

In other ways, too, Pedro continued to let the dignified parts of his government decline; he never asked for an increase in his civil list (set back in 1840) and could afford to do little maintenance on his palaces, whose increasingly rundown appearance failed to impress either Brazilians or foreigners.[27] When he went out in full imperial regalia to open and close the legislature, he looked more and more old-fashioned, an image that cartoonists like Agostini regularly satirized.[28] By the 1870s and 1880s, Pedro showed less and less interest in the celebration of days of national festivity, especially 25 March. The steamship and rail connection to Petrópolis (the latter built in stages between 1854 and 1881) made it ever easier for him and the empress to return to their summer palace immediately after the levee, which meant that they skipped the theater gala.[29] In 1875 correspondence with the minister of empire regarding scheduling the constitution's celebration (25 March fell on Maundy Thursday that year), Pedro suggested moving the levee and the Te Deum—which he hoped would be short—to Easter Sunday morning so that he could attend Easter mass as well that day and still get to Petrópolis by late afternoon.[30] On his birthday in 1873, Pedro sent the honor guard back to the barracks when he arrived at the theater instead of requiring the soldiers to wait for his departure.[31]

Pedro's presentation of himself as a citizen-king or a bourgeois monarch along the lines of Louis-Philippe of France (1830–48) increasingly put him out of step with the late-nineteenth-century flourishing of monarchical pomp and circumstance in European courts. As historians influenced by Eric Hobsbawm and Terence Ranger's concept of invention of tradition have shown, this efflorescence of royal ritual helped, for a time at least, to give an image of stability and permanence to monarchical regimes increasingly threatened by social and economic change.[32] Lilia Moritz Schwarcz argues that the image of citizen-king meant that Pedro "no longer enchanted the local imaginary," an allusion to what she sees as the monarchy's declining popularity as a result of Pedro's abandonment of official ritual.[33]

Not all contemporaries would have agreed with Schwarcz. In 1872, a writer in *A Vida Fluminense* contrasted the simple celebration of Pedro's birthday with those in honor of Napoleon III (1852–70), which he had seen in Paris a few years earlier: The French empire staged eleborate military parades in Paris, opened theaters for free to the populace, and put on elaborate fireworks displays to entertain the masses. Pedro thought all of this a waste of money, continued the writer, and his simple manners were, in fact, the source of his popularity (perhaps not surprisingly, some of his European relations considered him a boor).[34] Pedro lacked the imagination or the interest to pursue a strategy of exalting the monarchy, analogous to the investment in imperial ritual during the years leading up to his coronation. This disinterest in fostering the magnificent aspects of the Brazilian monarchy (and more broadly Pedro's failure to articulate a justification for monarchy) had important consequences for the celebration of days of national festivity, particularly 7 September, which was increasingly dominated by lower-class celebrants, as we will see in the next chapter. Moreover, the remaining official rituals were taken less seriously and, despite their simplicity, increasingly condemned for their cost and grandeur.[35]

The importance attributed to the theater galas also diminished during these years, a process that began during the Paraguayan War. Pedro set the example with his absences on 25 March; newspapers said less and less about the galas that took place, and by the 1880s the secondary theaters often no longer bothered to have the anthem sung in honor of the day of national festivity. To judge by the comments about a few exceptionally well-attended galas, empty seats were the norm even at the theater that Pedro honored with his presence.[36] Nor was there much concern about fostering Brazilian opera or theater for days of national festivity. The Conservatório Dramático, reorganized in 1871, amounted to little more than an institution of censorship, an adjunct to the police, whose concern with regulating theater audience comportment continued.[37]

The poetry and adulation that had characterized the rhetoric on days of national festivity in earlier years gradually disappeared. A *cronista* marveled that not a single sonnet graced the *Jornal do Comércio*'s third page (where paid articles usually appeared) on 7 September 1870.[38] Between 1866 and 1878, José Rodrigues Teixeira, a customs clerk, paid the *Jornal do Comércio* for the publication of at least fourteen short articles on 7 September and 2 December in which he hailed independence and praised Pedro II's virtues (he also published one on 10 July 1870, one of the few people to hail the official victory celebration). In most of these articles, he did not identify himself nor did he request anything from the emperor (many published such paid articles in the hope of catching the monarch's attention).[39] Teixeira thus continued a long-standing tradition, but his efforts looked increasingly old-fashioned (tellingly, he published nothing in honor of 25 March). Antônio José Nunes Garcia, the poet who botched his recitation of a sonnet on 7 September 1850, periodically produced adulatory verse. To celebrate Pedro's return from Europe in 1877, he distributed a poem outside the palace in which he called on the monarch to regenerate Brazil. For Pedro's birthday in 1885 he published a commemorative leaflet entitled "A luz da verdade" (The Light of Truth) which consisted of a poem that compared Pedro to "the sun that shines today throughout the empire of Brazil." This old-fashioned imagery prompted José Ferreira de Sousa Araújo to mock the "bard's stupendous verses."[40]

To cast this discussion solely in terms of decline, however, runs the risk of missing what actually took place. Although diminished, the official rituals continued year after year and drew more and more critical comment. People still woke to "the most terrific cannonading," as one traveler put it on 2 December 1874. Indeed, what most caught the attention of the three foreigners who saw 1878's independence celebrations was the noisy artillery salutes (and the fireworks).[41] Late in the morning or early in the afternoon, Pedro and Teresa Cristina rode into the city accompanied by a small honor guard drawn from the cavalry detachment stationed at the São Cristóvão palace.[42] By this time, the state coaches acquired for the 1841 coronation looked shabby and out-of-date to observers (in 1882, one foreigner guessed that they dated to 1815, while Apulco de Castro called the emperor's coach "fantastically ugly").[43] There was very little press comment on the Te Deum. For *O País*'s *cronista*, 1886's Te Deum for Pedro's birthday amounted to an "exhibition of sniffling monsignors in capes that had been gilded back in the days of the Count of Irajá" (1798–1863, bishop of Rio de Janeiro and imperial chaplain after 1839).[44] A *New York Times* correspondent remarked that, on 7 September 1872, people "had little mind to spend their time in church." Those who did, noted a French traveler six years later, paid no attention to the service and the magnificent music, entering and leaving the church without kneeling or making the sign of the cross, instead greeting friends and chatting at will. Such a casual attitude toward church services was, however, characteristic of Brazilian Catholics.[45]

At the levee in the downtown palace, "there was a great display of uniforms and cocked hats" as officialdom arrived to pay respects to the emperor.[46] An honor guard in full-dress uniform was usually on hand, as was a military band to play the appropriate anthem. Newspapers offered more and more critical comment on this ritual. The small number of attendees at the 2 December 1871 levee (held by Princess-Regent Isabel while her father was in Europe) contrasted sharply with the crowds that normally packed Rio de Janeiro's theaters or the Fábrica de Cerveja (Beer Factory, a sort of brew pub or beer garden located on Guarda Velha Street). In the past, the great men of the empire had taken this ritual seriously, added *A Reforma*, but now many stayed home while others came in undignified rented carriages that plainly displayed the hack's vehicle number. "Any *Soulouque* of Haiti" could have done a better job at staging a royal ritual, he concluded. When a major and widely read opposition newspaper could compare the Brazilian monarchy to the reign of Faustin I of Haiti (1849–59)—even if in a light *crônica*— then clearly the empire was in trouble.[47]

O Mequetrefe pointed to the seemingly unchanging imperial ritual in 1879 and to Pedro's commitment to his routines: "This year, His Majestry, as per [his] habit, had a birthday on 2 December. Even in this the man is eccentric! He is incapable of changing even once."[48] Other critical commentators observed that little new ever appeared in the congratulatory speeches read before the monarch during the levee; in 1876, the most excitement at 2 December's levee reportedly occurred when three buttons popped from a foreign diplomat's ill-fitting uniform.[49] Buenos Aires's *El Nacional* claimed that Rio de Janeiro reporters had no reason to attend court celebrations to describe them, for the festivities were all the same.[50] Indeed, many of the notices about days of national festivity are suspiciously alike. The *Jornal do Comércio* repeated, word for word, its reports on 2 December for 1875, 1877, and 1878, changing only the reference to Pedro's age and the name of the theater that he attended.[51]

Critical commentary about the levee in the downtown palace emphasized the "people's indifference" in 1875 or suggested that the ritual merely served to highlight the regime's contradictions. As the *Gazeta de Notícias* explained in 1881, "Normally there are gatherings in the palace environs on gala and levee days." But these people could only watch, stressed *A Lanterna*, for the levee was "despotism's celebration"; those who saw it, however, would not forget the prideful arrogance with which those in attendance looked down at the people in the square. The writer for another short-lived newspaper watched the 2 December 1883 levee from the square and called on Pedro to flog some of those who served him, for "in your name they beat the *povo* and vex [its members] with taxes."[52] Apulco de Castro declared that he would not go to the 7 September 1883 "hand-kissing levee [*cortejo-beija-mão*]," for independence meant equality among men; therefore, he could not accept that "a bunch of individuals prostrate themselves like Oriental people, half-barbarous, before a clay idol, before a fetish like you [the emperor]."[53] The levee must have been one of the emperor's most boring duties, observed a *Gazeta de Notícias cronista*, a sentiment no doubt shared by many of those who had to attend. When he heard rumors that he was being considered for the honorific title of *conselheiro* (counselor), Cristiano Benedito Otoni declared that he would never line up in livery— "making a wall," as it was derogatorily known. Another *cronista* wondered what Pedro really thought about the "flattery" of some and the indifference of many others on his birthday.[54] In verse, a writer in *Carbonário* summed up what many felt when he called on Pedro to "Strike a blow at the levee / Which today is a joke."[55]

As earlier, those who watched the levee could draw conclusions about the cabinet's strength or take jibes at ministers in their accounts of the ritual. Lafaiete Rodrigues Pereira, justice minister in the 1878 Liberal cabinet and a man who had signed the 1870 Republican Manifesto, drew particular ire from *O Besouro* on 2 December 1878 as one of its writers described the "curve traced by the deteriorated republican corpse's spine" and Pedro's "smirk of a proud winner"; rumors that this sometime republican had kissed the emperor's hand, despite the *beija-mão*'s abolition, circulated the following year.[56]

Later in the day, there were often inaugurations of public works (the cornerstone of a school on 7 September 1870, the municipal library and new docks on 2 December 1874), the National Exhibition (2 December 1875) or the Exposição Histórica do Brasil (Historical Exhibition of Brazil, 2 December 1881), the new gardens on the Campo da Aclamação (7 September 1880), and the new city council building (2 December 1882).[57] In addition to the evening theater gala, government buildings were illuminated at night—although not always very well, if we accept Carl von Koseritz's observation on 7 September 1883 that the downtown palace "was illuminated only with sad little lamps."[58]

The baptism of Pedro, the Prince of Grão-Pará (Isabel and Eu's first son and consequently second in line to the throne), on 2 December 1875 left a particularly bad impression. It followed the formal protocol used for the baptisms of Pedro and Teresa Cristina's children, and a Belgian diplomat marveled at the pomp and the "Bragança house's detailed traditions of etiquette," which seemingly belied the emperor's reputation for bourgeois simplicity.[59] *A Vida Fluminense* respectfully published a two-page lithograph of the baptism, but one of *Semana Ilustrada*'s characters declared that he went neither to the levee nor to the baptism, for both were "just for magnates and somebodies."[60] *O Mequetrefe* condemned the government for making soldiers stand for hours in the pouring rain so that they could present arms when the imperial procession passed by, with the emperor and his entourage comfortably ensconced in their coaches.[61] *Brasil Americano* went furthest in its mockery of the program that took on "epic carnivalesque proportions" and "the prince's thousand names" (his full name was Dom Pedro de Alcântara Luís Felipe Maria Gastão Miguel Rafael Gonzaga). It parodied the adulatory rhetoric: "In the magnificent regions of royalty, another constellation arises. On the great tree of monarchy, another sprout appears: It is the growth of the perfidious manchineel [a tree that produces toxic sap] under whose sinister shade the Brazilian *povo* grovels, yoked to the ignominious post of its moral atrophy." Finally, this newspaper had sharp words for the authorities who closed the chapel's door on the people who sought shelter from the rain.[62]

The official celebrations of independence and Pedro's birthday almost always ended with a gala in the Teatro Lírico, the venerable São Pedro, or, most commonly, the massive Imperial Teatro Dom Pedro II (Imperial Pedro II Theater). Opened in 1871, this latter theater, with a capacity that may have reached 6,000, quickly became "one of the centers of cultural life . . . and elegant society."[63] At least thirteen of the nineteen celebrations of the constitution between 1871 and 1889 had no gala with the monarch's presence, most often because of his return to Petrópolis (after 1879, the lengthy Holy Week theater closing, much criticized by actors forced into unemployment, was reduced to the three days before Easter, so there were more galas on 25 March).[64] The galas began with a performance of the independence anthem (on 7 September), which the audience joined for the chorus in 1873, or the national anthem (on 25 March and 2 December).[65] From his box, the chief of police then led the audience in the usual cheers.[66]

In the early 1880s, there were frequent accusations that the police had packed the house to ensure a favorable response to the chief's cheers. On 2 December 1880, the enthusiastic response from three rows of second-class seats revealed that he knew "how to get things done." Rumors about this were already circulating before the gala; two days later, there were reports that the police had arrested some of those who had received tickets but failed to show up. The recipients of free tickets included senators, deputies, and "the empire's greatest nobles," at least one of whom was sufficiently offended at this shameless effort to pack the house that he gave the covering letter to the press. The *Gazeta de Notícias*'s *cronista* offered a long analysis of this episode. He blamed impresarios' lack of investment in gala productions for the poor attendance and wondered whether the custom of public cheers was still appropriate; perhaps the solution was to put on free performances on days of national festivity.[67] Despite the controversy, accusations that the police had packed the house recurred in subsequent years; for 7 September 1885, they reportedly purchased seven first-class boxes, forty first-class seats, one hundred second-class seats, and another one hundred general admission tickets for the upper galleries.[68] Likely as a result of these efforts, the cheers lost most of their political importance, and I have found only one newspaper that commented on the poor response to them, without however drawing explicit conclusions from this.[69]

The legislation that reestablished the Conservatório Dramático in 1871 mandated that impresarios submit their programs for days of national festivity two weeks in advance, but they gave censors little work, for the programs rarely offered anything new.[70] On twelve of the nineteen postwar 7 September galas, the monarchs attended a European opera, put on by visiting companies in town for the winter season (improvements in transatlantic transportation had made possible regular, short visits by foreign opera companies after the war). Verdi's *La Forza del Destino* was on the program in 1871, 1873, and 1882, while Meyerbeer's *Robert le Diable* was sung in 1877 and 1881 (and also on 25 March 1874); three other Verdi operas were performed once, as well as another Meyerbeer. The Italian opera company put on Carlos Gomes's *Il Guarany* in 1880, but Pedro was not impressed with the performance because the singers seemed tired.[71]

A single play with a Brazilian theme was performed at a gala that Pedro attended (2 December 1874). It was, however, the work of a Portuguese playwright, Francisco Gomes de Amorim's *O Cedro Vermelho* (Red Cedar), set in the Amazon region in 1837 and dedicated to Pedro II. Its plot turned on the encounter between "the two races, European and indigenous," representing civilization and savagery, and the emerging "third race" that drew both good and evil from each of its parent sources, as one newspaper announced. The death of the title character, son of a Juruna chief raised in the household of a National Guard colonel, before he can return to claim his birthright, marks the play's climactic moment. The other characters resolve to shroud him in the Brazilian flag. That the play had originally been written in 1856 for a Conservatório Dramático competition and that it contained many by-now old-fashioned Romantic Indianist tropes, not to mention some forced plot turns, ensured it a poor reception. Moreover, according to the *Jornal do Comércio*'s *cronista*, a foreigner could not write a good play about Brazil; he advised Amorim to stick to Portuguese themes.[72] And one Brazilian playwright, Joaquim José de França Júnior, had a work performed on Pedro's birthday, his operetta *Triunfo às avessas* (The Backwards Victory), in 1871.[73]

More dubious programs took place on days of national festivity, especially on 25 March and 2 December, when opera companies were often not in town. The *Diário do Rio de Janeiro* condemned the Fénix Dramática company for putting on Eduardo Garrido's version of *Ali Baba and The Forty Thieves* at the Teatro Lírico on 25 March 1873. Fortunately, "the respectable public had the good sense to not show up," and Pedro had returned to Petrópolis after the levee. On his birthday in 1881, however, "the always popular" play was put on to no critical comment.[74] The year before, this company staged the "fantastic opera," *Mil e uma noites* (A Thousand and One Nights), but three lines, "a bit inappropriate, about one character's birthday," were censored; Pedro thought the evening "very boring." On 2 December 1883, he took his grandsons for an evening cruise on a navy ship, reportedly because he thought the play scheduled for the Imperial Teatro Dom Pedro II, *Dona*

Juanita, to be "very lowbrow"; even the boring *Mil e uma noites* would have been preferable, suggested a newspaper.[75] The *Gazeta da Tarde*'s theater critic remarked that 25 March 1881 would feature two spectacles. The first was the "farcical" one of the cheers to the emperor, the constitution, and the monarchy, during which the audience, "standing hat in hand, fakes a respect and veneration that it does not have." Then the second spectacle would begin as Jacques Offenbach's "cancans, aphrodisiacal, exciting, nervous music" filled the air. During the performance—that night, it was *Madame Favart*—"the emperor is obliged to sit through it all, pretending that he doesn't get . . . the off-color puns, the spicy sayings, that Offenbach directs at him."[76]

The custom of producing allegories or laudations as prologues or afterpieces disappeared almost entirely, and critics had nothing good to say about the few that were staged. On 2 December 1871, a poem in honor of "this auspicious anniversary" was read before an "allegorical tableau," but there is no indication of what form it took.[77] The Conservative *A Nação* had sharp words for the São Pedro Theater's decision to stage an allegory entitled "O Brasil esmagando o Paraguai" (Brazil Crushing Paraguay), complete with "an artillery salute, cheers, multicolored fireworks, and the national anthem," on Pedro's birthday in 1873, for it would give foreigners "the most dismal ideas about our civilization and our common sense." After all, Brazil had not fought against the Paraguayan people but only against Francisco Solano López's despotic government, and the two countries were now allies.[78] At least Pedro would not see this performance, for he was expected to attend the Lírico, where the program would begin with Joaquim Jacome de Oliveira Campos's *O Brasil e o Paraguai, ou, A rendição da Uruguaiana* (Brazil and Paraguay, or The Surrender of Uruguaiana). The play, written soon after the Paraguayan surrender at the Rio Grande do Sul border town in 1865, featured all of the standard tropes of the prewar genre analyzed in Chapter Seven. The plot begins with a sleeping Brazil (costumed as an Indian), whom Paraguay, dressed in military uniform, threatens. When Brazil awakes, he condemns Paraguay's isolation; Fanaticism encourages Paraguay to attack Brazil. They fight, and Brazil disarms Paraguay, but he magnanimously refuses to kill his helpless enemy. The allegory concludes with an angel crowning Brazil in front of a portrait of Pedro II while a "celestial choir" quietly sings the national anthem. *A Nação*, which had received a copy of the script in advance, called it a "grotesque scene, which cannot help but provoke laughter among the small number of sensible people who will be present." The main piece on the program was a "fantasy drama" entitled *Vampiro ou Os demônios da meia-noite* (Vampire, or the Midnight Demons), hardly suitable fare for the emperor's birthday, added the Conservative newspaper.[79]

The poor reception of the 2 December 1873 Paraguayan War allegories, themselves conspicuous by their rarity, highlights the lack of attention paid to the war on postwar days of national festivity. Almost never mentioned, the conflict had no significance to Brazilian patriotism as manifested on these days. As suggested in Chapter Eight, this most likely had to do with the days' focus on the principal institutions of the imperial regime—constitution and monarchy. The failure to raise a Paraguayan War memorial in the capital underscores the war's absence from Brazilian civic culture. Pedro had set the tone with his ostentatious refusal of an equestrian statue in March 1870 (and his rejection of a temporary statue for the July 1870 official festival), but right after the war's end the city council approved a proposal for a "monument to commemorate our victories won in the republic of Paraguay" to be raised on the Campo da Aclamação. It launched a subscription campaign, and in mid-1872 a large maquette was displayed in Rio de Janeiro and widely debated in the press. The contract with Francisco de Azevedo Monteiro Caminhoá and Paul Bénard specified a sixty-meter column, and the two "architects" designed it to be topped with a female figure of Brazil crushing the "demon of tyranny" atop a globe with stars representing the provinces. The base included figures of victory, prows representing the navy, and fountains that alluded to Brazil's major rivers.[80] Fund raising went poorly, but on 14 March 1876 (Teresa Cristina's birthday) Pedro laid the cornerstone, even though he privately judged the monument "inopportune." Manoel Duarte Moreira de Azevedo, writing the following year, expected that the monument would soon be raised, but the project stalled. There is no indication in the Rio de Janeiro city archives of how much money was actually raised, but Caminhoá was still hopeful in 1890 that the monument would eventually be built.[81] It never was.

Much had changed in Brazil's culture of public civic rituals by the 1880s. The official ritual would still have been familiar to those who had lived in the 1850s, but the limited press attention to the rituals and the significant critical comment indicated a substantial shift in how the monarchy and its symbols were perceived, a shift in large part initiated by the monarch himself. While most recognized the decline in official festivities, radical critics still saw the remaining ritual as excessive. Furthermore, those "whose knowledge of such affairs ha[d] been derived from books," like Thomas A. Osborn, the U.S. minister who arrived in 1882, were impressed at the empire's pomp and circumstance, at least for a time. Both Osborn and his predecessor, Henry W. Hilliard, wrote lengthy descriptions of what Osborn called the "exceedingly interesting" ceremonies during their first months in Rio de Janeiro. The novelty soon wore off, however, and their later despatches contain no references to civic rituals.[82]

DEBATING THE MEANING OF DAYS OF
NATIONAL FESTIVITY

Most newspapers published some sort of editorial on days of national festivity. As one *Gazeta de Notícias cronista* explained about 7 September, these texts were "more or less optimistic, more or less pessimistic, according to the editor's disposition, according to what he had had for dinner, or according to how his mother-in-law treated him at the table." However, "in all of them there is no evident concern to say something, no saying what needs to be said."[83] While it was easy enough to make fun of these editorials, they continued to function as one of the venues in which Brazilians debated the nature of the imperial state and some of the great political questions of the day. The frequency of such editorials was greatest on 7 September and least on 25 March, in keeping with the latter date's declining importance. The discussions on Pedro's birthday steadily shifted from the adulation characteristic of midcentury commentary to a more critical view of the emperor's role. With the exception of a few radical newspapers, journalists maintained a degree of (perhaps grudging) respect for the monarch. None, for instance, called him "Pedro Banana" in print on a day of national festivity, although this was reportedly a widespread nickname for him.[84] While the constitution still had many defenders, criticisms of its illiberal terms—the moderating power, the Council of State, and lifetime senate appointments—were increasingly heard. On 7 September, Brazilians debated both the origins of independence and the empire's principal political institutions, for the constitutional monarchy's establishment derived from decisions taken in 1822–24. Critics of these arrangements looked to find the origins of independence outside of Pedro I's actions. The 1788–89 Inconfidência Mineira and Tiradentes evolved from premature precursors of independence to symbols of Brazilians' struggle for liberty (a liberty still to be realized) and a republic.

Through the 1870s, editorials on Pedro II's birthday still served up generous helpings of adulation. Journalists praised his wisdom and erudition (for which he was known around the world), his ability to promote Brazil's progress and civilization, his dedication to duty, his virtuous private life, his generosity, and his prudence and patriotism. Loved by his people, admired by foreigners, he ensured Brazil's constitutional monarchy.[85] While political passions might lead to criticisms of the emperor, declared the *Diário do Rio de Janeiro*—Conservative in the 1870s—on 2 December 1877, "History's calm and impartial judgment must recognize and proclaim that, if Pedro II was not [an exemplar] of PERFECTION, for this does not fall to man, he was no doubt a true constitutional monarch."[86]

Such adulation, of course, came from those who held power; opposition newspapers saw matters quite differently. During the Conservative Party's long tenure (1868–78), Liberals and republicans increasingly criticized the emperor. While republicans could easily reject monarchies as incompatible with democracy, for they inevitably degenerated into "personalist regimes, true autocracies disguised by democratic forms,"[87] the Liberal *A Reforma* steered a difficult course as its editors sought to answer the question of whether monarchy was "still compatible with liberty and with Brazil's prosperity." Without entirely rejecting the constitutional monarchy, they lamented the lack of electoral freedom, the centralization of power, the country's financial difficulties and its failure to develop industry, the lack of judicial independence, and high taxes. The blame for much of this lay with the emperor's moderating power, the newspaper concluded in 1874. *A Reforma*'s *cronista* went further in 1876 and pointed out that Pedro had begun his reign by violating the constitution (he had accepted the throne before the constitutionally mandated age of 18), from which point he began "not only to reign, but also to govern and administer." He hoped that the emperor would return from his travels in Asia to "make his empire less Byzantine."[88]

Ultimately, of course, there was no solution to the conundrum of Pedro's political role, and even the ministers who worked regularly with Pedro expressed increasing exasperation with their master's meddling in matters large and small.[89] In 1877, another Liberal newspaper claimed that the "mournful . . . appearance of the capital," where no one wanted to celebrate Pedro's birthday, reflected the monarchy's failure to strive for "Brazil's moral and material greatness." Only a change of ministry would resolve this problem. The change came a month later, and the Liberals returned to office. Commenting on Pedro's birthday in 1879, the Conservative Party's weekly noted more "indifference" than ever before: Only a handful of gawkers watched the levee, and newspapers failed to publish editorials. It hastened to add that the *povo* still loved the monarch, but the current Liberal administration, which had perpetrated so many injustices and imposed so many "terrible taxes," had made it impossible to celebrate.[90]

By the 1880s, unabashed adulation of Pedro II was increasingly rare, although it still occasionally appeared.[91] A few editorialists, like those in the *Jornal do Comércio* in 1887 and 1888, emphasized Pedro's patriotism; the mistakes that he may have made did not detract from the fact that he always desired the best for his country.[92] Others acknowledged the emperor's virtues or Brazil's achievements under his rule, while lamenting either that Brazil's constitutional regime did not leave governance up to the people or that the existence of the moderating power and lifetime appointments to the senate meant that Brazil "has not been able to keep up with the reformist spirit of these times."[93]

Radical newspapers went further. Patrocínio's *Gazeta da Tarde*, highly critical of the monarchy in the early 1880s, declared in 1883 that Brazil could not celebrate, for the country was in mourning because of all that had taken place during Pedro's reign. Three years earlier, just before Patrocínio assumed full responsibility for the newspaper, its *cronista* observed that Pedro's ministers hid from him the fact that he was not just the ruler of "whites [*brancos*]," but also of "blacks [*pretos*]" and "Indians [*caboclos*]," a rare appeal for racial equality on a day of national festivity. In 1880, Rodopiano Raimundo, editor of *Tagarela*, wished Pedro another half-century of life "so that he could see the disastrous consequences of his forty years of governing," while Apulco de Castro advised Pedro to take his family out of the country and leave Brazilians to deal with their own problems.[94] Two years later, he parodied the adulatory rhetoric and described Pedro as the greatest of all "heads of state, past, present, and future, since the first king that the first crooked businessmen in the world invented to aid in their plans, to the latest banker prince of Monaco, with stops along the way at Solomon and Nero, at Caligula and Tiberius, at Philip II and King Bobêche [a character in Offenbach's 1866 operetta, *Barbe Bleue*], at João VI and King Simon XL." And he broke another taboo by observing that Pedro had married a woman "who was not really a model of beauty," which prompted the creation of "the important post of head pimp." Little wonder that people eagerly, if furtively, read *Corsário*.[95]

Discussion of the constitution touched on a relatively small number of themes. The principal conservative arguments about the charter, then the oldest written monarchical constitution in the world, were effectively presented in the *Jornal do Comércio* in 1878. The charter's durability proved both the "highly liberal and progressive spirit of the prince who granted it" and "Brazilians' character, judgment and patriotism." It provided the perfect balance among powers, secured citizens all liberal and democratic rights, and ensured "the liberty and order necessary for development." In a series of editorials during the mid-1870s, the ministerial *A Nação* forcefully expressed these views as well, as did its predecessor, the *Jornal da Tarde*, which stressed the charter's perfect balance of "progress without precipitation, conservation without immobility, liberty without licence, and order without oppression."[96] The *Diário do Rio de Janeiro* pointed to all of the "social and political disorders and commotions that have taken place in all of constitutional Europe and in America," which Brazil had avoided, and warned against "remedies advised by demagogy and despotism."[97]

Critical commentary on 25 March returned to familiar themes. It was possible to support the charter but lament the failure of those who held power to uphold its principles, but this theme appeared most regularly in the illustrated press in which the constitution was often portrayed as

FIGURE 9.1.
The constitution saved by Dr. Semana, 25 March 1872.
Source: Semana Illustrada, 31 March 1872.

a young woman in need of protection. In 1872, *Semana Ilustrada*'s Dr. Semana saved her from the attacks of street children (*moleques*) who treated her like the Judas doll that was destroyed in rowdy celebrations on the Saturday before Easter (Figure 9.1). Lighter editorials and *crônicas* likewise described the constitution as a "pure virgin, so barbarously violated" by "savage courtesans." The week before it published Figure 9.1, *Semana Illustrada* ran an article about the upcoming birthday of Senhora Dona Constituição da Paciência Angélica (Mrs. Constitution of Angelic Patience), whose "startling . . . strength" allowed her to survive "sorrows and sickness, and even stabs." Those who "managed her affairs" considered her a virgin while those who formerly had charge of her "shout every day that Mrs. Constituição was violated." Although they respected her honor, they did not respect her face or ribs: "It is said that the venerable lady receives many kicks, even from her guardians," which they called "caresses."[98]

Such risqué light criticism followed no clear party lines, but for Liberals (especially when they were in opposition) and republicans, the charter was hopelessly "corrupted in its origins." The closing of the 1823 constituent assembly was a "great attack on national sovereignty," and no constitution granted by a monarch—even if under popular pressure—could be legitimate. For *A República*, the only solution was for Brazil to throw off the monarchy and join "America's common destiny."[99] In 1886, a conservative party organ acknowledged the constitution's questionable origins (an important concession to the Liberal and republican criticisms) but argued that it "has become historically legitimated by the benefits that it has brought us." Two years earlier, *Brasil* likewise noted the charter's durability and took a jibe at Lafaiete, now president of the council of ministers. The erstwhile republican had made a successful political career "under the very constitution that he wanted to subvert and replace. Sad republic, not to mention sad republicans." In 1881, Foreign Minister Pedro Luís Pereira de Souza, another "republican convert to the *moral order*," came in for similar criticisms.[100] Time had sanctioned the charter, and even republicans fell under its sway, or so its defenders argued.

At about this time—the mid-1880s—debate about the constitution on 25 March ceased. Slavery's abolition in the province of Ceará on 25 March 1884, a measure apparently timed to coincide with the constitution's anniversary, turned the day into an abolitionist festival. Until 1888, newspaper coverage and commentary on that day of national festivity focused on abolition, to which we turn in Chapter Ten, and paid almost no attention to the constitution. On 25 March 1889, the only celebration of the 1824 constitution after slavery's end, the *Jornal do Comércio* returned to traditional themes and stressed the "flexibility of our institutions, which accommodate all of the demands of progress and civilization and satisfy the *povo*'s legitimate interests, securely guaranteeing liberty and binding [the *povo*] with a chain of love to the supreme magistrate, stable like the nation in his independence and integrity."[101] Likewise, the Liberal Party organ praised the charter's "extremely liberal principles" but called for reforms to perfect them.[102]

Editorials on 7 September brought together the issues posed by 25 March and 2 December in their discussions of the Brazilian nation-state's origins. The *Jornal do Comércio*'s editorialists hopefully declared in 1881 that 7 September was "a national day par excellence" that all could celebrate, regardless of their political views: "From the palace to the most humble abode, wherever a Brazilian lives, 7 September will evoke noble sentiments and fond memories."[103] Such a declaration was, of course, a clear political statement, one that implied general satisfaction with the form of government established in the early 1820s, Brazil's development over the course of the previous six decades, and the existing administration. Many failed to muster the same enthusiasm for the imperial regime implicit in this declaration, and 7 September editorials served as a forum to debate contemporary political questions and to draw lessons from the past. In these discussions, Pedro I, the monarchy, the constitution, and the empire's administrative structures were widely debated.

Much turned on the motives and consequences of Pedro's actions on 7 September. A simple—even simplistic—conservative position held that the heroic Pedro I declared "Independence or Death," a cry that echoed from the Amazon to the River Plate, amid a jubilant population that thus gained its liberty.[104] Few, however, made this argument; a more common editorial interpretation held that Pedro recognized Brazilians' "most ardent aspiration for political independence, which had long developed among them." Pedro was perhaps not necessary for independence, but his involvement hastened it; moreover, emphasized the *Jornal do Comércio*, a leading exponent of this interpretation, he founded the empire and "granted it a constitution in which liberty . . . still finds effective guarantees." His errors as a ruler may have shortened his reign, but they hardly negated his achievements, which fully justified "Brazil's eternal gratitude."[105] Likewise, in an 1876 editorial, the *Diário do Rio de Janeiro* emphasized Pedro's centrality in winning independence; regardless of his later errors, he turned Brazil into a "free and independent nation" and left "his beloved son to free us from chaos and . . . from anarchy." *A Província de São Paulo*'s correspondent judged the author of this latter editorial either hopelessly naïve or a brilliant satirist.[106]

The *Correio do Brasil* chided republican critics of Pedro I in 1872 for their failure to recognize that his constitution had secured twenty-four years of "complete internal peace," a sharp contrast to Spanish America's disastrous experience that demonstrated "our forefathers's wisdom." Others added that Pedro and the constitutional monarchy ensured Brazil's political unity. In 1883, *A Folha Nova* called on Brazilians to celebrate on 7 September, for the country had won its liberty without the "bloody battles" that had wracked the United States or the "*caudillismo*" of Spanish America.[107] These arguments echoed the views of historians like Francisco Adolfo Varnhagen (whose history of independence was completed in 1875 but not published until decades later), Pereira da Silva, and Moreira de Azevedo, all of whom celebrated Pedro's achievements in facilitating independence and instituting liberal institutions. To be sure, the latter two historians recognized the first emperor's many errors and personal failings, but these did not detract from his achievements.[108] Others, however, saw this lack of struggle as the root cause of Brazil's ills, for it left a nation incapable of effectively demanding its rights when faced with an overweening monarchy.[109] Peace, order, and unity came at a price.

Ferreira de Araújo's *Gazeta de Notícias* said little about how liberty and independence were achieved and rather focused on Brazil's impressive material, political, and social progress. To be sure, there was always more to do, but railroads and telegraph lines exemplified the country's material achievements, while peaceful elections demonstrated its political maturity; "public opinion seeks to intervene in all the great questions, [and is] already accustomed to discern and reason."[110] Others offered more critical assessments of Brazil's situation than Ferreira de

Araújo's celebrations of progress. In 1879, the *Gazeta da Noite* simply lamented the country's lack of progress, but seven years later another newspaper declared that the internal peace secured by the monarchy more than compensated for the country's limited progress since then.[111]

There was always the opportunity to comment on current political issues in independence-day editorials. *Brasil Americano* condemned both impressment and the new draft lottery in 1875; *A Reforma* called for an end to centralization in 1877, for electoral reform in 1875, and for religious freedom in 1873.[112] In 1881, the *Diário do Brasil* looked forward to the institution of direct elections as a way to resolve the country's many problems, all attributable to Pedro's "narrow-minded and obscure despotism." The following year, however, Patrocínio's *Gazeta da Tarde* observed that the new electoral law had left only 130,000 citizens eligible to vote, of whom 66,000 were civil servants—this in a country of 11,000,000 inhabitants![113] In a rare critical editorial, the *Gazeta de Notícias* argued in 1885 that slavery, the established Church, "sterile party struggles," corruption in the civil service, the lack of public education, the failure to exploit natural resources, and unfair taxation all meant that Brazil's citizens were not truly independent.[114] Opposition newspapers regularly lambasted the government's failings on 7 September and often claimed that the lack of enthusiasm for the celebrations demonstrated Brazilians' recognition of this fact. *A Reforma* pointed to the lack of democratic rights of citizens in 1870 and the burdensome provincial debts in 1876 as reasons for Brazilians not to celebrate.[115]

Agostini vividly portrayed opposition criticisms in his *Revista Ilustrada* cartoons on 7 September, castigating Conservative and Liberal governments alike. Brazil, dragged down by the state and the Church in 1876, is forced to celebrate by a figure labeled "government" wielding a whip labeled "executive power" (Figure 9.2). From above, the equestrian statue looks on. Two years later a more regal Brazil—still an Indian, however—pays homage to a pensive Pedro I (the statue has come to life). Pedro tells Brazil to dispense with the formal speech and asks how the country is getting on with its independence. A statesman (perhaps João Lins Vieira Cansanção de Sinimbu, president of the new Liberal council of ministers) and a female figure labeled "politics" prompt Brazil to answer: "Well, thank you very much" (Figure 9.3).

Numerous radical newspapers characterized Pedro I as an opportunistic scoundrel, interested only in perserving his crown and his dynasty, hardly a liberal and constitutional monarch.[116] Others held that Pedro had, at best, grudgingly supported independence when faced with widespread popular pressure for it.[117] Brazil needed a new independence that, as the republican Francisco Cunha put it, would turn Brazilians from "the Bragança royal house's subjects" into a true nation.[118] In an 1881 editorial, *Carbonário* declared that the patriarchs of independence

FIGURE 9.2.
Chained to the state and the Church, Brazil is forced to celebrate
independence, 7 September 1876.
Source: Revista Illustrada, 9 Sep. 1876.

had erred in supporting a man who would betray his father and "in whose breast existed not a fibre, not an artery, not an atom of Brazilian blood"; he only followed "the cold calculus of a political egoist," for which he was wrongly immortalized "in bronze, in a colossal statue" raised close to the site where Tiradentes had been executed.[119] In 1888, *Novidades* went so far as to suggest that independence was solely the victory "of the Brazilian people, who had sufficient courage to throw off the metropole's yoke." Its editor did not mention Pedro I at all in this editorial, an omission of the monarchy that reflected this newspaper's role as the mouthpiece of the Rio de Janeiro planters adversely affected by abolition.[120]

The publication of Alexandre José de Mello Moraes's *A Independência e o Império do Brasil ou A Independência comprada por dois milhões de libras esterlinas* (Independence and the Empire of Brazil or Independence Bought for Two Million Pounds Sterling) in 1877 provided grist for the mill of Pedro I's critics by making more widely known the secret financial terms of the treaty by which Portugal recognized Brazil's independence. Mello Moraes further argued that, because Brazil had been a kingdom since 1815, the country's founder was João VI and not Pedro I. A *cronista* observed that the book undercut the equestrian statue's message. So did Luís Francisco da Veiga, who in 1862 had sought to

FIGURE 9.3.

Brazil tells Pedro I that all is well with independence, 7 September 1878.

Source: *Revista Illustrada*, 7 Sep. 1878.

distinguish between the heroic prince who had won independence and the emperor who had violated the constitution. In his 1877 polemical history of Pedro I's reign, Veiga concluded that only personal ambition had motivated the first emperor.[121] Amid this condemnation of Pedro I, José Ricardo Pires de Almeida's 1885 call for a monument to liberty, as embodied in the first emperor's actions on 7 September 1822, to be raised on the highest peak near Rio de Janeiro, stands out by its rarity.

The municipal archivist wanted Brazilian artists to design and build the monument by the centenary of Pedro I's birth (12 October 1898).[122] Needless to say, this proposal went nowhere.

In 1871, *A Reforma* declared that, while it had no desire to "undermine the prestige generally attributed to this day," all the 7 September glory should not go to Pedro; Brazilians should pay more attention to "liberty's known or unknown martyrs."[123] It did not, in fact, mention any of these martyrs in this editorial, but by then they were certainly well known, if not necessarily acknowledged by editorialists. If Pedro's Grito do Ipiranga had responded to Brazilians' long-standing desire for independence, then a nation must logically have existed before 1822, and its desire for liberation must have manifested itself. Two episodes presented themselves most prominently as candidates for this, the 1788–89 conspiracy in Minas Gerais, known as the Inconfidência Mineira, and the 1817 republican revolt in Pernambuco.

As we have seen, the Inconfidência Mineira could be—and for a time was—incorporated into the more or less official monarchical history of independence as a (premature) precursor to the independence proclaimed by Pedro I. In 1865, Joaquim Maria Machado de Assis proposed that the government organize an "annual ceremony" in honor of Tiradentes whose "crime" was no different from that of Pedro I and José Bonifácio: "He only wanted to speed up the clock."[124] As late as 1881, an emphemeral illustrated newspaper presented Tiradentes as the precursor to independence without any evident republican implications: On the scaffold, an angel shows the condemned man that his dream would be achieved on 7 September 1822 (Figure 9.4), an image that contrasts with other republican declarations in this periodical. Pedro himself visited the sites of the conspiracy during his 1881 journey to Minas Gerais, although one republican wondered why he had gone to "the house where Tiradentes held his republican meetings." Was it to recall that his throne was "stained with the blood of that martyr for liberty?" A courtier later recalled that, already in 1872, Pedro was quite knowledgeable about the movement.[125]

Varnhagen, as we saw in Chapter Four, rejected the Inconfidência, and in even more forceful terms, condemned the Pernambucan revolt as a threat to Brazil's unity. Pereira da Silva, whose *História da Fundação do Império Brasileiro* (History of the Brazilian Empire's Foundation, 1864–68) began in 1808, only briefly mentioned the Inconfidência. He characterized it as a halfhearted tax protest, easily suppressed, although he did note Tiradentes's noble goal of freeing his *pátria* and condemned the repression that befell the plotters. For the 1817 revolt, Pereira da Silva tried to strike a balance between those who "praise[d], exalt[ed], and rais[ed] to the heavens" the patriots of 1817 and those who reduced them "to the level of troublemakers and rabble-rousers." Instead, most

FIGURE 9.4.
Tiradentes's dream realized on 7 September 1822.
Source: O Binoculo, 10 Sep. 1881.

of the leaders were mediocrities, and the rebellion was but a chance event with no larger significance whose principal causes lay in the failings of local government officials.[126]

The Pernambucan rebellion was difficult to fit into a monarchical history of independence. The *Gazeta de Notícias* omitted the revolt from its long list of evidence to show in 1881 that 7 September was "a logical day . . . that had a centuries-long incubation period and would have dawned regardless of the circumstances." Struggles against outsiders dominated the list: hostile Indians in the sixteenth century, the Dutch in the seventeenth century, French pirates in the early eighteenth century. This patriotic sentiment turned into anti-Portuguese feeling in the struggle over control of the mines in the early 1700s and in the Inconfidência, all of which demonstrated that Brazil was ready for independence.[127] To include 1817 in this list would have called unwarranted attention to divisions among Brazilians. But 1817 could and did belong to the strain of radical liberalism (and eventually republicanism) exemplified by men such as Antônio Borges da Fonseca who, back in 1854, had hailed the movement as the precursor to Brazil's future destiny as an independent republic.[128] In 1882, Patrocínio lamented that the "condemned dynasty" attributed all the independence glory to itself, leaving nothing for Tiradentes and the martyrs of 1817; in 1889, the 1817 movement figured prominently in the republican *Diário de Notícias*'s list of precursors to independence.[129]

Other colonial protests, sometimes also presented in modern historiography as evidence of the colonial regime's decline and the desire for independence, were not unknown during the empire, but they rarely received mention on days of national festivity. A working-class newspaper and Mello Moraes added Salvador's 1798 Tailors' Conspiracy to the list of precursors to independence; the historian called the Bahian plot an "effort at independence" that developed out of the Inconfidência Mineira. A conspiracy of mixed-race artisans and soldiers, however, was far too dangerous a movement, and even Mello Moraes, who by then (1877) had completely rejected the official interpretations of independence, subordinated the Tailors' Conspiracy to the Minas Gerais plot.[130]

As is well known from the José Murilo de Carvalho's work, republicans ultimately seized control of the historical memory of the Inconfidência and especially Tiradentes, whom they constructed as a precursor, not just of independence, but also of a republic; as a symbol, the conspirator could serve many different purposes.[131] In 1872, *A República* declared 21 April (the anniversary of Tiradentes's execution in 1792) to be a day of mourning for the Republican Party and urged its readers to consider the fate of Brazil's recent monarchs. Maria I died insane, João VI was poisoned by his "dissolute wife," and Pedro I died in exile from Brazil. The writer wondered: What fate lay in store for the fourth generation?[132]

At this time, however, the republican interpretation of Tiradentes was far from secure. Joaquim Norberto de Souza e Silva, a leading member of the Instituto Histórico e Geográfico Brasileiro (Brazilian Historical and Geographical Institute), published his *História da Conjuração Mineira* (History of the Mineiro Conspiracy) in 1873. In this, the first book-length study of the plot, Norberto echoed Varnhagen in arguing that, if successful, the Inconfidência would have at best won the independence of Minas Gerais and a few neighboring captaincies, thereby dividing Brazil "which must always remain united and constitute a mighty empire. . . . Fortunately, the Grito do Ipiranga echoed from north to south, east to west," and a unified Brazilian nation won independence under Pedro I. Moreover, Tiradentes died, not as "a great patriot" but as a Christian, repentant and resigned to his fate, and he even asked to kiss his executioner's hands and feet.[133] The literary critic Sílvio Romero later judged that Joaquim Norberto's work helped reduce "the frightening proportions" that the "myth of Tiradentes" had attained. Needless to say, republicans rejected such interpretations of Tiradentes and Mello Moraes implicitly addressed these criticisms by connecting 1789 and 1798 to make the Minas Gerais conspiracy a more national plot by extending its reach into Bahia.[134] Joaquim Norberto's reference to Tiradentes' kissing the executioner particularly galled republicans, and someone attempted to erase this passage from the archival documents held by the Instituto.[135] In 1879, the Pernambucan deputy, José Mariano Carneiro da Cunha, introduced a bill to declare 21 April a day of national mourning. He described Tiradentes as "the glorious 1793 [sic] martyr of our *pátria*'s independence, the initiator of this great Mineiro enterprise, which later, in 1817, echoed in Brazil's north and shaped the achievement of our political emancipation." The bill was apparently buried in committee, but José Mariano clearly rejected Joaquim Norberto's interpretation, although he did not explicitly characterize Tiradentes as a republican.[136] One republican later condemned the efforts to make Tiradentes into a nonrepublican precursor of independence as the creation of "a bastard imperial Tiradentes, framed in green and yellow."[137]

Positivists added their distinct voice to the cacophony of critical commentary about 7 September. Raimundo Teixeira Mendes stressed in 1875 that the "Independence party" was entirely republican and that Pedro I had always opposed "our emancipation." In a 7 September 1881 speech, he constructed a more complex argument in which he interpreted Brazilian history in a positivist framework. In 1822, the day marked the end of the country's theological stage of development. Men like Tiradentes and the "heroes of '17," however, lacked the scientific knowledge that those of Mendes's generation now had, and he called on his fellow Positivists to work systematically to ensure the "advent of fraternity and universal peace."[138] Positivist-influenced republicans like Antônio da Silva Jardim saw Tiradentes as an important precursor to independence, itself a major step forward for the *pátria*, even if it left Brazil only "half-free." Now it was time to move Brazil to the historically necessary republic.[139]

Systematic commemoration of 21 April began in 1881 and revealed the great differences among republicans. That morning, as the self-proclaimed *caipira* (hick), author of a long-running *Jornal do Comércio crônica*, observed, Rio de Janeiro awoke to shouts of "*A Revolução* [Revolution]! Tribute to Tiradentes. Forty *réis*," as newsboys sold a paper with that provocative title. The tribute to Tiradentes amounted to a call for vengeance; to be sure, the ruler who had presided over his execution was already in Hell, but her descendents, "according to the laws of heredity, just as nefarious" as she was, remained in power: "You scarcely know, wretched king, that [members of] the *povo* are preparing for you the same fate that your ancestors gave to Tiradentes. . . . [W]e will laugh when your bloody head rolls from the guillotine." The *cronista* marveled at the extent of press freedom in Brazil—"Here everything is tolerated"—but consoled himself with the observation that this freedom was better than the alternative; it provided an essential "safety valve" for the "popular boiler."[140]

A more respectable gathering took place that evening at the Teatro Príncipe Imperial (Imperial Prince Theater), the first of republicans' annual commemorative meetings in honor of Tiradentes (no one re-marked on the irony of meeting in a venue named after an heir to the throne). The Clube Republicano de São Cristóvão (São Cristóvão Republican Club) organized 1881's function, a task that the Clube Tiradentes (founded that year) took on in later years. The stage featured Tiradentes's bust on an altar, and the program included lengthy speeches by republican leaders such as Quintino Bocaiúva, "frenetic applause and cheers to liberty and to the republic," poetry readings, and an enthusiastic rendition of the *Marseillaise* (although the independence anthem composed by Pedro I opened the evening); the stage also featured the Brazilian flag, with the imperial crown removed.[141] Patrocínio cautioned his fellow republicans to moderate their tone; declamation had gone out of fashion in 1848: By the 1880s, "republican rhetoric must demonstrate serenity [and] the keen [and] persuasive logic that shows the power and the capacity of the ideas that it advocates."[142]

In 1882, fully 2,000 people packed the São Luís Theater to honor the "great martyr of Brazilian liberty." They included a "good part of our literati and an extraordinary popular concourse."[143] That year, the Clube Tiradentes produced the first of its annual magazines in honor of its namesake.[144] Subsequent commemorations of Tiradentes closely followed the pattern set in the early 1880s (republicans no more innovated in their rituals than did the monarchy!),[145] and they evolved into a regular and almost legitimate part of late-imperial political culture. In 1885, three republicans won election to parliament, and the Clube Tiradentes reserved a box for them; the government-run orphanage provided a band to play the anthems, and even the *Jornal do Comércio* reported on the function (it would, however, ignore the republicans in 1886, 1887, and 1888).[146] One *cronista* described the 1885 function as "a peaceful and orderly meeting that does not shake institutions"; in its 1887 editorial, *O País* called the commemoration of Tiradentes "a national tradition" but also added that a republic, "sooner or later, will finally come to Brazil."[147] All of this underscores the relative moderation of most republicans and their affinity with Liberals, whose watchword since 1869 had been *reform*, not *revolution*.

I have found only one indication of efforts to suppress commemoration of Tiradentes, although republicans later claimed that the police watched them closely. In 1883, one of the *Gazeta de Notícias*'s *cronistas* mocked the medical school's director for banning a student meeting on the Minas Gerais conspiracy.[148] The students' interest in the Inconfidência points to the appeal of republicanism among youth, a development usually attributed to the empire's inability to absorb all of the country's graduates, the failure of patronage, and frustration with the country's lack of progress.[149] Much of the discussion about Tiradentes took place in normally ephemeral student newspapers and literary magazines (indeed the *Gazeta da Tarde* lamented that the mainstream daily press completely ignored the significance of 21 April 1886, which Patrocínio attributed to the monarchy's overwhelming power).[150] What emerges from these periodicals and the radical press is a complex, multivalent symbol that served many purposes, a complexity increased by the tendency for student newspapers and literary magazines to publish short works by different authors in their issues devoted to 21 April.

The single most common trope about Tiradentes was that of the "martyr of liberty," a conveniently abstract phrase that could place Tiradentes at the forefront of radical liberalism, in a long tradition that stretched from 1789 through 1817 and all of the liberal revolts against the empire.[151] Some of the allusions to liberty referred more narrowly to the independence of the *pátria*, Brazil, although they slid easily into a broader definition.[152] Still, as late as 1884, a contributor to a literary magazine could declare that "Joaquim José da Silva Xavier's blood was gloriously washed by the blessed waters of the Ipiranga."[153] For others, liberty meant a republic: "The drops of Tiradentes's generous blood will become rivers of liberty that will destroy the monarchy's pedestals and bronzes."[154] A few saw Tiradentes as an avatar of abolition, but this was a minority position, notwithstanding students' involvement in the antislavery campaign.[155] Finally, presenting Tiradentes as a martyr for liberty, independence, the republic, or abolition led occasionally to comparisons between him and Jesus Christ or to other Christian analogies: "This blood shed / By brutal despotism / Was the Brazilian *pátria*'s / Holy baptism," wrote one poet.[156] These themes also appeared in the few editorials published in the mainstream press on 21 April in the late 1880s.[157] As David Haberly points out, even critics of Tiradentes like Joaquim Norberto stressed his Christian resignation and thereby reinforced this view of him as a martyr.[158]

The radical-liberal and republican construction of independence as a movement that began with Tiradentes and continued through the 1817 rebellion led inevitably to reiterated criticisms of the equestrian statue. Many writers worked with what Carvalho has called the "powerful symbolism of the struggle between Pedro I and Tiradentes."[159] One pamphleteer expected that the statue would soon be thrown to the ground and a new one raised to the martyr, "amid the festive sound of anthems [and] cries of joy," and in 1884 the *Gazeta da Tarde* proposed smelting the equestrian statue and using the bronze to cast a monument to Tiradentes.[160] In the early 1880s, republicans also had easy targets in the form of Pedro Luís and Lafaiete, critics of the statue in 1862 and signatories to the 1870 Republican Manifesto now serving in the cabinet. Critics recalled these men's 1862 writings against the monument in *A Atualidade* or contrasted their participation in official rituals on 7 September with what they had written at the time of the statue's inauguration.[161]

By the mid-1880s, the debate about the meaning of Brazil's days of national festivity had evolved far from the discussions of the 1850s in which independence, constitution, and emperor had been presented as the three indispensable elements to Brazil's progress. Many now held that independence had left the country with creaky, outdated institutions in need of more than just reform; they sought a new history for Brazil to justify these changes. The last word in this section goes to an anonymous writer in *O Besouro* who observed in 1878 that, back in 1792, "the plump chicken on whose egg our national stability depended clucked for the first time, and the unfortunate one who went after it suffered execution and was exposed as a lesson for the future unfaithful." In 1817,

the fatal chicken clucked again and once more the indulgence of our grandfathers' rulers condemned to the firing squad the reckless ones who tried to put the bird in the incubator.

Finally, for the third time the deadly clucking was heard and this time a member of the royal family set out and managed to secure the chicken with such a frightful history.

To prevent further trouble he struck its craw with army bayonets, slit its throat in the Constituent Assembly's meeting hall, poured the boiling water of scandal on its body, plucked it as much as he could, and finally reduced it to the broth that today strengthens the body of Pedro II and our life as a civilized nation.

. . .

Long live the emperor and the broth![162]

Given Pedro's well-known fondness for chicken soup, the image of an all-consuming monarchy readily resonated with readers, especially those frustrated at the lack of change.[163]

IMPERIAL TRAVELS AND STATUES, 1872 AND 1877

Although the two decades covered by this chapter were characterized by a long decline in official civic ritual and a steady increase in critical commentary about the institutions celebrated on days of national festivity, Pedro's receptions in 1872 and 1877 and the inauguration of a statue of José Bonifácio de Andrada e Silva in the former year merit further consideration. These rituals suggest that, at certain points, my argument about the decline in imperial patriotic culture and the increase in critical commentary on the imperial regime needs to be nuanced. On 8 September 1872, *A República* declared that the previous day's inauguration of the statue honoring José Bonifácio (the long-contemplated counterpart to the equestrian statue of Pedro I) amounted to "new proof of the unpopularity into which the emperor has fallen." He should have expected this, for the "celebration in the Campo de Santana [da Aclamação] shed and the big bash [*festanças*] on his return from Europe" had already demonstrated this.[164] *A República*'s assessment of the two major nonrecurring civic rituals of 1872 was deeply colored by its rejection of the imperial regime, which it likewise saw in 1870's failed victory celebration. A closer look at Pedro's reception and the statue's inauguration in 1872 highlights the partial exceptions to this chapter's argument about the decline in official ritual, as does his welcome back in 1877.

On 31 March 1872, Pedro II returned from his first trip to Europe to an elaborate welcome that closely resembled those described in earlier chapters. Once again, government departments and corporations led the way in constructing arches and other allegorical monuments, while the city council coordinated street decorations and celebrations. The program was much like the earlier ones: the landing at the navy yard, a procession to the imperial chapel for a mass, artillery salutes and a parade of army troops (not the National Guard) that the monarchs would view from the downtown palace, followed by a procession to the São Cristóvão palace. Three nights of illuminations would follow, and on subsequent days there would be a theater gala, a levee, and an opportunity for the imperial family to visit the allegorical monuments.[165]

Rio de Janeiro spared no expense. Members of the city's elite pulled their best clothes out of storage, while modistes and tailors lost weight; they had so much work that they had no time to eat, explained a *cronista*. Even before the emperor had returned, some couples had divorced over the cost of new outfits, he added![166] By this time, the technology for gaslight had evolved to the point that almost all of the ephemeral monuments were connected to a gas main by special flexible piping that the gas company kept on hand for this purpose; permanent gas pipe arches over Ouvidor and a few other downtown streets could also be lit on any appropriate occasion. While its employees may have torn their hair out worrying about how to keep the system working, as a *cronista* remarked, the company realized a handsome profit of US$50,000 on sales approaching US$150,000, at least according to the calculations of two foreign correspondents.[167] The *Boston Daily Globe*'s correspondent estimated that the entire festival cost US$500,000 and described the illuminated arches, fifteen to twenty-one meters tall, as "temple[s] of living fire." The fireworks display "beggar[ed] all description," and he doubted that "La Belle France" had ever put on such an elaborate festival, a compliment that would have certainly pleased many a Brazilian. The foreigners' estimate of the total cost far exceeds that of a *cronista* who judged that the festival cost more than 450 contos (US$229,500). The U.S. minister enthused that it "offered sights and sounds not soon to be forgotten."[168]

FIGURE 9.5.
Crowds on Ouvidor Street welcoming Pedro II, April 1872.
Source: *O Mosquito*, 6 April 1872.

The arches and monuments expressed the themes that they usually did in such celebrations: the people's love of monarchy; values such as "civic virtue [*civismo*], wisdom, work, [and] gratitude"; commerce; Brazil's four main rivers; the four continents; and Brazil's provinces.[169] Massive crowds filled downtown streets, both on the day of Pedro's arrival and during the three nights of illuminations (or at least the two nights during which it did not rain). There are indications of efforts to impose social segregation on the festival space; on the night of 2 April, when Pedro and Teresa Cristina visited the celebrations, they were received by "a brilliant gathering of leading ladies" who filled a special seating area along Primeiro de Março (formerly Direita) Street.[170] Those who ventured out on foot faced a difficult odyssey, especially at the intersection of Ouvidor and Primeiro de Março, where the crush was so great that there were "swoons, fainting, fits of hysteria, punches, [and] pinches" (Figure 9.5). Attentive policing kept pickpockets under control but could not save citizens' clothes.[171] A commission of navy arsenal employees freed four slaves in honor of Pedro's return, while two private citizens each freed one.[172] Teixeira paid for the publication of a short article in which he proclaimed that the celebration "demonstrate[d] the indescribable joy that possessed us for the right and glorious motive of Their Majesties' arrival."[173]

The festivities ended with a theater gala on 3 April, at which the actor-impresario Francisco José Furtado Coelho recited two poems in honor of Pedro's return, a sonnet by Machado de Assis, and a larger work by Rozendo Moniz Barreto, who hailed Pedro as a "model king." A Portuguese playwright's adaptation of Molière's *Misanthrope* was the principal work, and while most critics agreed that the performance was exceptionally good, one *cronista* wondered whether critical conclusions about the imperial regime could be drawn from the play. By contrast, *A República* reported that only seventy-five people attended the performance, which provoked a "concert of yawns"; at the end of the second act, Pedro joined many others "and went to sleep."[174]

There was little critical commentary about the festival. No one raised his voice against the cost; indeed, *A Vida Fluminense* chided the city council for the modesty of its arch. A *Jornal do Comércio cronista* published a fable about the consequences of overweening ambition directed at the emperor, while Francisco Cunha lamented that nothing had changed as a result of Pedro's journey to Europe (he would, however, shortly abolish the *beija-mão*).[175] One *cronista* worried what ordinary people thought ("I confess that I understand nothing about this frightening problem called *povo*") but concluded that they held their monarch in high esteem. *A República* had a very different answer to this question: To be sure, members of the *povo* liked "to amuse themselves when given celebrations," but they "reserved their freedom to applaud or stamp their feet." In this case, the festival "did not please them," and all returned home disappointed.[176]

Since 1838, projects for the erection of an equestrian statue in honor of Pedro I had envisaged a second statue to honor José Bonifácio, the São Paulo statesman and Pedro I's principal minister and advisor at the time of independence. The plans for this pedestrian statue fell by the wayside during the campaign to raise funds for the monument inaugurated in 1862, but in mid-1861, the Instituto Histórico resolved to undertake a popular subscription for a monument to José Bonifácio, to be erected in the Largo de São Francisco, the square at the western end of Ouvidor Street. Little is known about this campaign, but the fact that Eusébio de Queiroz chaired this committee as well as that of the equestrian statue indicates the two campaigns' close alignment. In 1862, the committee apparently rejected a number of proposals by Brazilian artists in favor of a design by Louis Rochet, who proposed a white marble statue of José Bonifácio, surrounded by bronze figures representing Poetry, Science, Civic Virtue, and Strength. In addition, the monument would feature broken symbols of colonial servitude, the imperial crown, and nineteen stars representing the provinces. This competition took place while Rochet was still in Rio de Janeiro. The decision to contract him drew critical comment from those who felt that a Brazilian should produce a national monument.[177]

The committee expected to inaugurate the statue on 13 June 1863, the centenary of José Bonifácio's birth,[178] but fund raising went poorly, and the subscription ultimately raised only 60 contos (US$30,600), less than a quarter of the projected 250 conto (US$127,500) cost. Some questions were raised about the committee's failure to complete the promised monument,[179] but the project seems to have been largely forgotten. After the war, the committee was reorganized under the chairmanship of the Viscount of Bom Retiro, Pedro II's "closest intimate and friend"; it included two new members associated with the Liberals, Francisco Inácio Marcondes Homem de Mello and Joaquim Manoel de Macedo.[180] The committee's changed composition reveals Pedro's direct interest in the monument, as well as a more bipartisan approach than that of the equestrian statue campaign. During Pedro II's visit to Europe, Bom Retiro reopened negotiations with Rochet on the basis of a lower budget. On relatively short notice, the sculptor agreed to produce a monument for inauguration on 7 September 1872. A bronze figure of the independence patriarch would stand beside a bench with books, all on a square pedestal, with figures of Justice, Integrity, Poetry, and Science at the corners. In his hand, José Bonifácio held the pen with which he signed the 1 August 1822 Manifesto to the Nations (Figure 9.6).[181] *A República* noted that Pedro had strongly pressed for Rochet to make the statue, rather than a Brazilian artist who had offered to cast it for free, and presented this as one more example of the emperor's personal interference in matters of government.[182]

The inauguration was set for 7 September 1872, to take place immediately after the levee in the downtown palace. Authorities made the usual preparations for the ceremony. The police requested that people enter the relatively small square via Ouvidor and other streets on its eastern side and exit to the west in the direction of Constitution Square. Band shells were erected on both sides of the statue, and guards would be posted to keep the area immediately around the statue clear for the imperial procession, which would come up Ouvidor Street after the levee. Led by a band and the symbolic palace guard of halberdiers, the procession would include members of the court, participants in the levee, the city council, and members of the monument committee. These officials, along with José Bonifácio's descendants, were invited to meet in the Escola Central's front rooms. After the independence anthem, Pedro would return to the square to participate in the statue's unveiling amid cheers to "national independence" and the sounds of artillery salutes and fireworks. Then, back in the Escola, Macedo would deliver his address on behalf of the committee and the Instituto Histórico (as in 1862, other addresses had to be submitted in writing). The committee also

FIGURE 9.6.
The José Bonifácio de Andrada e Silva monument, 2011.
Source: Photo by Hendrik Kraay.

requested that residents of the square and nearby streets illuminate their façades on 7 and 8 September.[183]

Press accounts of the inauguration concur that the program was followed to the letter; the weather cooperated, and the square and surrounding streets were packed with onlookers, so many that the imperial procession had great difficulty making its way up Ouvidor Street; from the Escola Central, the *New York Times* correspondent saw "a sea of heads . . . down the whole length" of the street; "banners and flags were flying everywhere." His description of the festival's climactic moment—the statue's unveiling amid artillery salutes, ringing church bells, and "fireworks by the hundred"—approaches a sociological analysis of the celebration's impact: "It is impossible that the crowd can view all this and remain unexcited. So they give themselves up to enthusiastic cheering." That night and the following evening the statue was illuminated with electric lights, and large numbers of people visited the square, all in perfect order.[184]

One unscripted element took place during the ceremony. Some days before the inauguration, the construction foreman discovered that a certain Adão, one of the carpenters hired for the job, was a slave. He requested that the architect in charge, Francisco Joaquim Betencourt da Silva, take on the task of raising funds to free the man. Betencourt spoke to students at the Escola Central, and they took up a collection. On learning of this during the inauguration ceremonies, Pedro II immediately gave 600 mil-réis (US$306) to complete the sum needed to free the slave; according to the *Jornal do Comércio*, students then cheered "the citizen king."[185]

While the inauguration itself may have been a success, at least in the sense that it attracted significant crowds and that nothing untoward marred the program, the press debate about the ritual indicates that many did not accept the statue's meaning as explained by Macedo in his address. The novelist described José Bonifácio as "Pedro's guide, Brazil's strong arm, the heart of liberty, the blazing spirit of the independence revolution, and the spirit that inspired harmony among Brazilians. . . . [The] Brazilian empire burst out from his vision, electric, compact, independent, free, and strong."[186] For newspapers supportive of the cabinet and this interpretation of José Bonifácio's role in independence, the statue amounted to the repayment of a long-overdue debt of gratitude to the patriarch; future generations of Brazilians and foreigners would be able to see how, to cite the *Jornal do Comércio*, "the people pays its dues to the memory of one of the renowned men who helped it become free."[187] Machado de Assis weighed in with a bit of unabashed adulation of the ". . . distinguished and noble Andrada! / Thou, whose name, among those who gave the *pátria* / The baptism of beloved independence / Perpetually shines. . . . / Never did base interests stain thy name / Nor low passions." In his address, not read during the ceremony, Homem de Mello recalled José Bonifácio's 1824 call to end slavery, an obstacle to true independence, and proclaimed that the patriot's wish had finally been fulfilled for "the sun of 7 September no longer shines on slaves' cradles."[188] Such a connection of the Free Womb Law with the celebration of independence was, however, extremely rare at this time.

A República led the attack on the statue with an editorial entitled "A farsa imperial" (The Imperial Farce). Because Brazilians had already raised a statue to Pedro I, despite his reluctant support for independence, his closing of the constituent assembly, and his acceptance of the 1825 treaty whose secret terms obliged Brazil to pay 2,000,000 pounds sterling, it was only logical that the minister who collaborated with the emperor should also get a statue. The rest of the editorial recalled the many martyrs to liberty, including Tiradentes and Padre Roma (executed for his role in 1817), and particularly João Guilherme (John William) Ratcliffe, João Metrowich, and Joaquim Loureiro, three men involved in the 1824 Confederação do Equador, who had been hanged the following year in the very square on which the statue now stood.[189] A student newspaper likewise recalled Ratcliffe, and *A República* later praised the students' invocation of him, noting that this belied the cheers to the emperor attributed to students by the *Jornal do Comércio*.[190] Under the pseudonym of Esqueiros, Alfredo Moreira Pinto, a teacher at the preparatory school, published the trial of Ratcliffe and his fellow rebels; in the preface he called on those attending the inauguration to reflect on the fact that the ground on which they stood, "today covered with flowers and carpeted with velvet, was then sprinkled with the precious blood of the body of this sublime trinity," true "martyrs for liberty."[191]

Recalling those executed for their role in the 1824 resistance to Pedro I's imposition of the constitution sought to raise them to the same status as Tiradentes, executed on, allegedly, the very site of the equestrian statue. The juxtaposition, however, did not catch on, for the Confederação could not be construed as a step toward independence; too many saw it as merely a revolt against the first emperor and a movement that threatened to divide Brazil (moreover, two of those executed in Rio de Janeiro were foreigners). Thus, the Confederação's martyrs could not compete with Tiradentes or those of 1817, and I have found only one later attempt to link all three movements.[192]

In a short editorial published the day after the inauguration, the republican newspaper concluded that the "second bronze lie" now stood amid "the calm of indifference." As far as the inauguration ceremony was concerned, it was "as petty as the statue that the court ordered to be raised. Half the people wandered the streets to see the other half and to be in turn seen." Moreover, the inauguration left no lasting legacy; only a single slave gained his freedom, and no orphans or elderly would benefit from a new orphanage or hospice, while no children could look forward to studying in a new school.[193] *A Reforma* constructed a complex interpretation that dismissed the equestrian statue as a "bronze lie"; the first emperor had been a scoundrel, in contrast to José Bonifácio, who went into exile instead of seeking for himself the glories of a South American George Washington. In the second article, the newspaper described José Bonifácio as a defender of liberty and called on Brazilians to emulate him and take charge of their destiny. In this way, the Liberal newspaper used José Bonifácio to criticize the monarchy and the Conservatives who held power.[194]

According to *A Vida Fluminense*, public attention quickly turned away from the monument and to the municipal election results (the vote had also taken place on 7 September), but for about a week *cronistas* continued to debate the meaning of the statue and its inauguration, and their articles offer indications of what was said about it. One writer wondered why José Bonifácio was dressed in the uniform of a Portuguese court minister; others thought the statue small and remarked that the unfortunate patriarch would soon catch a cold, for he had no hat. Others wondered why he was standing beside a piano bench. And some thought that the statue did not resemble José Bonifácio. The *caipira* responded by pointing out that the original proposal had contemplated raising 250 contos; less than a quarter of that amount had been raised, and no doubt many of the critics had not contributed a single real.[195]

A few days after the José Bonifácio statue's inauguration, Dr. Pedro Bandeira de Gouveia, a signatory to the Republican Manifesto, announced the start of a campaign to raise funds for a statue in honor of Tiradentes. He sought to present it as a national effort with broad appeal by acknowledging that Pedro I and José Bonifácio deserved their statues; so did, however, Tiradentes, "the courageous Mineiro (native of Minas Gerais), the dauntless son of the *povo*, who was the first architect of this work . . . [and] the true hero of Independence." He had been executed "for the great crime of passionately loving his country." The campaign would accept no government money and invited donations of any size. Gouveia received a warm welcome in most newspaper offices, and only *A Nação*, the government mouthpiece, refused to publish his appeal.[196] Not all on the left agreed with the choice of Tiradentes, and "A Democrat" suggested that Ratcliffe or Padre Roma was a better candidate for a monument. They had died proudly for their beliefs, while Tiradentes had humbly kissed the hangman's feet before his execution.[197] The campaign sputtered along for some time, drawing editorial support from a variety of newspapers.[198] In early 1873, a photograph of a maquette designed by sculptor Cândido Reis was circulating in Rio de Janeiro; according to Joaquim Norberto, it portrayed Tiradentes in a martyr's tunic with a rope around his neck and thus looked more like a colonial "lesson of terror" than a patriotic monument.[199] Apparently nothing more came of this monument campaign; as the first wave of republicanism subsided (*A República* ceased publication at the end of February 1874), it was apparently forgotten; Gouveia's death later that year probably contributed to this. Later republican writers added that the publication of Joaquim Norberto's book also hindered the campaign.[200]

Without official support, a monument was beyond the means of political parties or private groups. Nevertheless, the campaign likely served to keep alive the republican criticisms of the José Bonifácio statue.

Although originally contemplated as a counterpart to the equestrian statue, José Bonifácio's statue failed to become a site for regular 7 September celebrations in the way that Pedro I's monument did (a topic that we will address in the next chapter). *A Reforma*'s *cronista* called for those who were not "courtiers" to celebrate independence around the new statue in 1873, but this effort to separate Pedro I and José Bonifácio did not take. That year, the statue was left in the dark on 7 September, as indeed it would be in many other years.[201] Mello Moraes's attacks on José Bonifácio as unworthy of the monument, first published in his *Brasil Histórico* in 1873 and much more fully developed in his 1877 *Independência*, likely also contributed to the monument's lack of success. As far as the historian was concerned, Rio de Janeiro now had "two bronze lies, one on horseback, showing the constitution to Botocudo [Indians], crocodiles, and tapirs; and the other on foot with his hand outstretched as a sign of repentance."[202]

In late September 1877, Pedro returned from his second journey abroad, which had taken him to North America, Europe, and the Middle East. He arrived to a welcoming ceremony that very closely resembled that of March–April 1872. There was the usual reception at the navy yard and the procession up Primeiro de Março Street; plans had been made for a Te Deum and a parade of army battalions; arches stood at prominent locations on city streets and squares (a massive one made Guarda Velha Street almost impassable); and a theater gala with Meyerbeer's ever-popular *Robert le Diable* and a newly composed march-anthem was held. Teixeira published a paid article in which he claimed that the "magnificent rejoicing" demonstrated the population's respect for "the noble virtues of the two diamonds," Pedro and Teresa Cristina. Frank de Yeux Carpenter estimated that US$250,000 had been spent to turn Rio de Janeiro into the "best-lighted city in the world" for three days.[203]

Lighthearted critics, like Agostini, compared the celebrations to a grapeshot blast that would overwhelm with monarch.[204] On landing, Pedro himself declared that, had he known that so much money was going to be spent on welcoming him, he would have requested that it be donated to relief for the victims of the drought then raging in Ceará.[205] Pedro further rebuked the ceremony's organizers by cancelling the Te Deum and dispensing the army parade; instead, he and Teresa Cristina prayed privately in the Imperial Chapel and took an open carriage to São Cristóvão after a quick lunch at the downtown palace (the Te Deum and a levee were, however, held two days later).[206] The crowds were massive, according to Carpenter, and, just as during Eu's arrival in 1870,

FIGURE 9.7.
Celebrations in the court and drought in the North, September 1877.
Source: Revista Illustrada, 29 Sep. 1877.

the procession quickly merged into the crowd, "and the bare-bosomed slave was rubbing elbows and trampling toes with the gold-laced nobility of the suite"; authorities could not prevent the crowd from surging into the imperial chapel just as Pedro and Teresa Cristina slipped away after saying their prayers. França Júnior also wrote about the massive crowds of people in their Sunday best, the inevitable pushing and shoving on Ouvidor Street, crying children separated from their parents, and the exhausted fathers carrying their drowsy offspring to streetcar stops when it was time to return home. More than a few swore that they would never again subject their families to the experience, reported the *cronista*.[207]

Many had, in fact, criticized the expenditures on the grounds that they were inappropriate at a time of massive suffering in the North of Brazil (Figure 9.7). One merchant made this point as he later also complained that the festival's organizing committee had put excessive pressure on donors to contribute.[208] *A República* (a new short-lived iteration of this newspaper) condemned the heads of government departments who obliged their subordinates to contribute to subscriptions and noted that city bylaw inspectors were targeting merchants who had failed to donate with fines for petty violations.[209] Others remarked that "the cardboard [structures], the lanterns, the stupid fireworks, [and] all this conventional homage inherited from the days of absolutism" amounted to a useless expense and that it would have been better to have freed some slaves instead (one woman, in fact, did so privately and liberated two women).[210] Agostini contrasted the sights that Pedro had seen on his travels with the "astonishing extravagances" of "Cardboard arches, famous arches / On Ouvidor Street." An even more heavy-handed writer in *Comédia Popular* mockingly declared that "no Roman victor [ever] had the likes of the Guarda Velha Street arch."[211]

Opinions were divided on whether the reception had been successful, and *cronistas* concluded that it depended on the observer's political position. The *caipira* thought it best to write two accounts of the celebrations. For Greeks, he wrote about the spectacularly successful festivities that demonstrated the population's deep love for their rulers; for Trojans, he wrote about the meaningless monuments and decorations and the wasted money that could have been better spent on drought relief.[212] He might have been thinking about the sharply contrasting editorials in *A República*, whose editor professed embarrassment at the shameless adulation in the celebrations, and those in the *Diário do Rio de Janeiro* and the *Jornal da Tarde* that stressed Pedro's centrality to "the grandeur and prosperity of Brazil's future destiny," to quote the *Diário*.[213]

Writing about 25 March 1887, *O País's cronista* reflected on the many changes that had taken place in the celebration of days of national festivity:

When we had the parade, the *beija-mão*, band shells and stages in the principal squares, the lyric theater with [Madame] Charton [one of the 1854 opera season's stars] and the dramatic theater with João Caetano; the honor guard with the brass band; the nobility in [theater] boxes with glittering diamonds and velvet tail[coat]s; cannon shots without the petty efforts to save powder; the Instituto Histórico's speeches full of tropes and flourishes [*bambinelas*]; a Te Deum with all the sniffling cathedral chapter; tapestries in windows; glass-windowed palace coaches that looked like giant jam-pots; lanterns, transparent illuminated images, and pyrotechnic talent; rains of gold and verses from behind theater curtains, etc., etc., etc.; when the great gala [day] offered all of these sights, the constitution's celebration was something to behold, as was any palace festival. . . .

But bit by bit, the palace's bourgeois ideals [*burguesismo*] suppressed these lovely treats.

The National Guard law came and swallowed up the parades; the trip to Europe came and wiped away the *beija-mão*; the patriotic societies' lack of money [*pindaíba*] came, and there went the band shells, the transparent illuminated images, and the fireworks; a disease of the tongue [*gogo*] came and dried up the enthusiasm of the bards and the event orators; cuts to opera subsidies put an end to the divas and the great Italian shows; João Caetano was not eternal, and the *Milagres de Santo Antônio* [Miracles of Santo Antônio] are contemporaries of the great artist; the velvet tail[coat]s lost their pile, and the nobles' diamonds fell into the hands of mortgage banks.

All that remained for us is the dying lantern, the dry salute, the parade of a few gentlemen in ungentlemanly hired coaches, the palace levee with an out-of-tune national anthem that almost [sounds like] a hurdy-gurdy.[214]

This lengthy passage summarizes, virtually point by point, this chapter's argument about the decline in official ritual on the three days of national festivity.

The author went one step further and drew political conclusions: "To not diminish institutions' prestige, as says Offenbach's Colchas, 'one must capture the people's imagination.'"[215] As we have seen, however, others thought that Pedro's bourgeois simplicity was the source of his popularity, and many condemned the remaining ritual apparatus as excessive. On occasion, as in 1870, 1872, and 1877, the government could still stage elaborate official festivities, although they were not necessarily well received in some quarters. None of this is especially surprising, although it adds another dimension to our understanding of the imperial regime and the changes that Brazil went through in the last decades of the nineteenth century.

The rapid growth in the number of newspapers meant that there was probably more printed debate about the meaning of days of national festivity at this time than ever before. Certainly there was more criticism of the government in these days' editorials and a broader range of opinion about the constitutional monarchy's principal institutions commemorated three times per year. By the end of the 1880s, republicans had developed a history of independence that largely bypassed Pedro I in favor of the Inconfidência and the 1817 Pernambucan revolt; in this interpretation, Pedro I's Grito do Ipiranga marked a detour on the road to a republic.

There is, however, more to this story than just declining official rituals and growing criticism of the imperial regime. On 7 September, important popular celebrations took place in the 1870s and 1880s. These popular festitivies, the topic of the next chapter, point to both the extent to which the debate about days of national festivity filtered down into urban society and the degree to which members of the *povo* reinterpreted these days of national festivity. An examination of these celebrations also allows us to address the question of the imperial regime's popularity, and to some extent, the reception of its civic ritual project. Furthermore, the abolition movement, a significant popular mobilization by the mid-1880s, also left its mark on the celebration of days of national festivity. It is to these questions that we now turn.

CHAPTER TEN

Popular Patriots and Abolitionists, 1870–1889

Alongside the decline in official celebrations on days of national festivity and the increasing criticism of imperial institutions during the 1870s and especially the 1880s, there is also considerable evidence that the monarchy—and perhaps even the imperial regime more generally—continued to enjoy considerable popular support. During the 1870s and the first half of the 1880s, popular independence celebrations involved significant numbers of Rio de Janeiro's lower classes (but few of the middle and upper classes). After the mid-1880s, the abolitionist movement mobilized broad sectors of the population and turned the three days of national festivity into integral parts of its antislavery campaign. Finally, in 1888–89, many blacks and mulattoes, some only recently freed, saw the monarchy as an institution attuned to their interests, or at least more sensitive to them than the major political parties. In this light, the monarchy's overthrow can be interpreted as the reaction to what some saw as a dangerously populist regime.

Nevertheless, the monarchy's popularity remains a controversial question. For some, there is no doubt that Pedro and Isabel stood at the pinnacle of their personal popularity in the aftermath of abolition, especially among the Afro-Brazilian lower classes.[1] Sidney Chalhoub suggests that the monarchy's retrospective popularity among the black lower classes was consolidated by the republic, whose first governments deported numerous *capoeiras*, demolished tenement housing, and instituted urban reforms that constituted an attack on the "black city."[2] Ronaldo Pereira de Jesus, by contrast, argues that the predominant popular view of the monarchy amounted to "indifference," punctuated by isolated violent outbursts such as the 1880 Vintém Riot and occasional pragmatic individual or collective appeals for patronage.[3] Lilia Moritz Schwarcz and Martha Abreu perceive a reciprocal relationship between the official image of the monarchy and reworkings of the concept of monarchy through popular festivals. They both argue that Pedro's abandonment of the apparatus of rulership and the cultural changes that led to the decline of these popular festivals undermined the monarchy's standing among the populace.[4] Others write of the "monarch's dessacralization," as critical cartoons and other satires proliferated in the 1880s.[5] Despite these developments, it is clear that Pedro himself continued to enjoy considerable goodwill from the urban population to the end of his reign. Schwarcz goes so far as to argue that his persona stood in much higher esteem than the monarchical regime in 1889.[6]

An examination of the "popular festivities" on days of national festivity—popular in the sense of not organized by the state—offers new ways to address the question of the imperial regime's popularity. Rather than seeking monarchism in often poorly documented popular culture, as Schwarcz and Abreu do, I focus on the better-documented popular celebrations on days of national festivity. A dynamic of support for the monarchy and reaction to this support appears in the history of the Sociedade Comemorativa da Independência do Império (Society for the Commemoration of the Empire's Independence), founded in 1869, which seemed to continue the patriotic street festival tradition of the late 1850s. From 1870 to 1885, the Comemorativa's nocturnal celebrations around the equestrian statue on Constitution Square, the principal popular festivities of independence, attracted thousands to a festival that drew more and more criticism both for its old-fashioned forms and plebeian participants and for its celebration of institutions and symbols that were increasingly being called into question. Efforts to marginalize the Comemorativa in the late 1870s failed, but the death of its founder and principal festival organizer in early 1886 made possible a top-down reorganization of the society in 1887. The new Comemorativa joined several other concurrent efforts to discipline Rio de Janeiro's lower classes and speak to concern about the *povo*—the burgeoning urban free lower classes—at a time when impending abolition heralded major changes in social relations.

The campaign to abolish slavery encroached on the celebration of days of national festivity in the 1880s. Ceará's abolition of slavery on 25 March 1884 pushed aside the constitution's anniversary and turned that date into an abolitionist landmark. Antislavery demonstrations, notably the city council's Livro de Ouro manumission ceremonies on 7 September and 2 December in 1885–87, added another widely debated semiofficial ritual to these days of national festivity. Abolitionists explicitly connected independence (freedom for the *pátria*) and abolition (freedom for the slaves) in their 7 September rhetoric and would continue to do so after slavery's end on 13 May 1888.

The monarchy's perceived centrality in the abolition of slavery contributed to its popularity in 1888 and 1889. The celebrations of Pedro's return from Europe in late August 1888 spilled over into that year's independence celebrations and demonstrated widespread support for the imperial family, if not for all aspects of the imperial regime. A massive demonstration of support for the emperor took place on 2 December 1888, as thousands of lower-class people thronged the palace to present him with the so-called *album popular* (popular album) in belated honor of his return to the capital. This little-studied episode and the celebrations of abolition's first anniversary marked popular monarchism's apogee, and the two days of national festivity in 1889 before the 15 November coup suggest receding support for the monarchy.

One of the central developments of the 1880s was the increasing political prominence of Rio de Janeiro's free lower classes. The 1 January 1880 Vintém Riot against an unpopular tax on streetcar fares marked the first time since 1848 that large-scale protests had taken place on city streets. The violent police reaction shocked Pedro, who prided himself on his good relationship with the populace.[7] Over the next years, the street became an increasingly important political space, and explicitly political demonstrations occasionally took place on days of national festivity. On 25 March 1881, for instance, protestors opposed to the new electoral law met outside the palace; Pedro received a delegation but referred its members to the minister of empire.[8] Street politics pulled in different directions, reflecting the range of political groups that sought to mobilize the urban population, many of whom were disenfranchised by the 1881 electoral reform.[9] Antislavery rallies and republican meetings shared the street with popular patriots, *capoeiras*, the Guarda Negra in 1888–89, and mass demonstrations in support of the imperial family in 1888. Some worried about the *povo* but for the most part Pedro continued his accessible style. A conservative Austro-Hungarian diplomat marveled at the lack of security around the emperor during his visit to Glória Parish's festival in 1882. In July 1889, a mentally unstable Portuguese immigrant easily got close enough to Pedro to fire a pistol shot at him as he was leaving the theater, but the assassination attempt was condemned from all quarters.[10]

This chapter begins with the Sociedade Comemorativa da Independência do Império's popular celebrations on 7 September; well documented, they indicate a significant engagement with the state that for some marked a disturbing level of popular support for the imperial regime. Nothing like this took place on the other two days of national festivity. After a brief look at the activities of *capoeiras* during these celebrations, this chapter turns to the abolitionist movement and its efforts to turn days of national festivity into antislavery demonstrations.

Attempts to suppress the popular independence celebrations followed the intensification of the extraparliamentary campaign against slavery (1883–85) and suggest a concern in some quarters with the povo's symbolic political activity. These efforts, led by the reorganized Sociedade Comemorativa in 1887–89, contrasted sharply with the demonstration of popular support for the monarchy on the last birthday that Pedro celebrated in Brazil. What emerges from this dynamic is an imperial regime that was at once popular, even tolerant of lower-class political manifestations, but also sought to shape the *povo*'s engagement with the state.

THE SOCIEDADE COMEMORATIVA DA
INDEPENDÊNCIA DO IMPÉRIO

As newspapers debated the meaning of the three days of national festivity (and thereby Brazil's principal political institutions) and published their increasingly critical commentary on the official rituals, popular celebrations also took place, especially on 7 September. The few patriotic societies that had continued their activities through the Paraguayan War, like the Sociedade Festival Sete de Setembro, disappeared in the early 1870s.[11] There are some indications of neighborhood independence celebrations later in the decade on Castelo Hill and in Glória Parish; the latter were sponsored by the streetcar company, which paid for the fireworks on the Largo do Machado.[12] In 1888, the police precinct commander in São Cristóvão arranged for the construction of two illuminated arches and secured bands and fireworks displays for what the press described as the first independence-day celebration in that neighborhood.[13] On Pedro's birthday, there was occasionally music at the Passeio Público.[14] Merchants on Ouvidor Street still illuminated their establishments, demonstrated electric light, and lit the entire street with arches of gaslights.[15] From 1870 to 1885, however, the principal street celebrations were those of the grandly named Sociedade Comemorativa da Independência do Império. This society's outdoor celebrations of independence became increasingly popular in the sense of drawing more and more lower-class participants and fewer representatives from the middle and upper classes. To judge by the gathering critical press commentary on these celebrations, the Comemorativa's control over independence-day festivities troubled many, albeit for very different reasons.

Alferes (Second Lieutenant) Américo Rodrigues Gamboa founded the society in October 1869; it met at the Liceu de Artes e Ofícios (a trades school), and its first president was the "most worthy citizen and notable architect," Francisco Joaquim Betencourt da Silva (who would shortly oversee the José Bonifácio statue's installation).[16] Initially the society appeared little different from the others that had preceded it, but its celebrations around the Pedro I equestrian statue on Constitution Square soon became the principal popular festival of independence. For 1870's 7 September, the Sociedade Comemorativa announced that it would launch fireworks every thirty minutes starting at midnight; at dawn, singers and military bands would perform the independence anthem. Two bands would play from 6:00 pm, and the statue would be illuminated by gaslight (indeed, the society apparently paid for the installation of gas lines to the statue and rented eight large candelabra, which it later purchased). Perhaps using Gamboa's army connections, the society arranged for a mobile artillery battery to be posted on Santo Antônio Hill, an unoccupied and brush-covered eminence overlooking the square, to join in the salutes from the city's forts and the ships in the harbor. Flags and banners would surround the statue, and the society invited residents of the square to decorate their façades and illuminate their windows.[17] The *Jornal do Comércio* judged the festival a great success.[18]

Very little changed in the society's celebrations over the next years. Its advertisements in the major newspapers, often headed by a small picture of the equestrian statue, reveal a few additions to its program. In 1871, it added artillery salutes to Princess-Regent Isabel when she passed by during her procession into the city for the Te Deum and levee (it appears that, henceforth, the imperial procession always made the short detour to Constitution Square on its way into the city on 7 September).[19] In 1872, the society obtained an honor guard of apprentices from the army arsenal for the statue during the evening of 7 September; their skill at drill much impressed one observer in 1873.[20] The Baron of Lorena (Estevão Ribeiro de Resende, the younger), who resided on Constitution Square in a house that had once belonged to José Bonifácio and had joined the society's board of directors, opened his home to fellow directors and their families in 1874. He offered them light refreshments, and they exchanged several toasts. That year, the society had sufficient funds to put up two "elegant band shells."[21] Curiously, none of the early accounts of the Sociedade Comemorativa's festival refer to Gamboa or someone else leading the crowd in cheers after the singing of the anthem; such cheers are only noted in reports from the 1880s.[22] Newspapers generally had favorable comment on the Sociedade Comemorativa's "modest and cheerful popular festivities"; in 1872, one declared that the society "conducted itself brilliantly." It did not take long for the society's celebrations to become a tradition. Already in 1872, the *Jornal do Comércio* wrote that, "as always," the society "took a very active part in the public celebrations." By 1875, the Sociedade Comemorativa's celebrations had become so routine that this newspaper merely noted that they followed the program of previous years.[23]

It is difficult to determine what lay behind the Sociedade Comemorativa. Although Gamboa did not assume the presidency until after 1871's

7 September celebration, he soon became the society's heart and soul. In 1875, *Mephistopheles* (one of Rio de Janeiro's many short-lived illustrated newspapers) thanked Gamboa for his work and noted that he was, in fact, the only society member to take his task seriously. Most members had joined at his request and at best paid their dues casually. But the *cronista* could not resist a jibe at the unfashionably baggy pants that Gamboa habitually wore, implying that such commemorations were old fashioned.[24] In the early 1870s, the society regularly lamented its limited resources, but in 1871 a newspaper noted that the government had quietly subsidized its work.[25] Francisco Ferreira da Rosa later recalled that Gamboa seemingly spent all his time seeking funds for the Comemorativa; before each 7 September, he "went around with [a group] of girls dressed in green and yellow" to raise funds, reminiscent of the way that organizers took up collections for Church festivals. Another later account of society fund raising also described a girl, adorned with green-and-yellow ribbons and carrying a bag of the same colors, into which people tossed their nickels.[26]

Gamboa himself was hardly a prominent figure. He had enlisted in the cavalry as a second cadet in 1849; lacking the formal education required for promotion, he waited eleven years before his commission as an *alferes*. Ill health forced him into retirement at the outset of the Paraguayan War, and he worked for a few years as a civilian employee of the war ministry.[27] Very little is known about the other twenty-eight men who held office in the society from 1870 to 1886 (this figure excludes directors-at-large like Lorena, only rarely listed and apparently not very active members of the board).[28] Many of the society officers, like Gamboa, served in more than one year. Three held the title of doctor (but none of them appear among the medical doctors and lawyers in the *Almanaque Laemmert*), and one proudly noted that he was a *bacharel* (degree holder). Six of the men (including Gamboa) held military ranks (two captains, one lieutenant, and three *alferes*), but Captain João Mariano de Jesus (first secretary in 1882) was acting commander of the fire brigade. Carlos Clementino Carvalhaes (first secretary in 1873) was a retired artillery lieutenant,[29] while *Alferes* Wenceslau Vieira Armond (treasurer in 1881) must have been retired as well, for he resided in the old soldiers' home, an indication of his poverty. The limited information available on these men suggests that the Sociedade Comemorativa's leadership came mostly from the lower middle class.

The Comemorativa's connection to the Liceu also indicates ties to the working class. Founded in 1858, the Liceu provided free education in the arts and their application to trades and industry.[30] Manuel Duarte Moreira de Azevedo described it as "a popular institution, the working classes' school [and] the *povo*'s college." He also characterized the architect, Betencourt, as a "son of the *povo*" who had risen because of his merit and skill; he proudly wore his habit in the Ordem da Rosa on his "work shirt" (Betencourt's portrait, however, shows a thoroughly bourgeois gentleman). Betencourt was also later involved in labor organization, and the Liceu provided meeting space for many societies.[31] The most prominent member of the Sociedade Comemorativa was the Baron of Lorena, elected as one of the twelve directors-at-large for 1875, but he may well have considered it useful to become involved with a society that organized celebrations on his doorstep.[32] Moreover, as we will see, there was a tendency for prominent individuals to become involved in working-class and lower-middle-class organizations. Regardless of the society leadership's relatively modest social origins, newspapers and *cronistas* regularly praised its work, "which had the power to keep out of bed many people who saw the always pleasant tropical daybreak" or simply noted the "large concourse of *povo*" on the square.[33]

Some members of the Sociedade Comemorativa took their task seriously. In October 1872, Gamboa wrote to Alexandre José de Mello Moraes to request a set of the first series of his magazine, *Brasil Histórico* (Historical Brazil, 1864–68), which could no longer be found in bookstores, for society members had "on several occasions" engaged in heated debate about "the facts of Brazil's history, especially our political emancipation."[34] The historian obliged Gamboa with the magazine as well as the first volume of his *História do Brasil Reino e do Brasil Império* (History of Brazil as a Kingdom and as an Empire, 1871); the second volume was then in press. He also pointed out that a careful study of the book would show that the equestrian statue "amounts to no more than a garden ornament that evokes sad memories, because Pedro I imprudently demolished what the true patriots . . . had built." The statue of José Bonifácio should likewise be "viewed with indifference," for he was hardly a true patriot.[35] Gamboa's request is a rare indication that discussions of Brazilian history extended deeply into society. That the Sociedade Comemorativa did not accept Mello Moraes's advice and continued to celebrate around the statue suggests that its members drew their own conclusions about what was important, conclusions that the monarchy's critics found unwelcome.

In 1874, the society prepared statutes and submitted them for approval to the Council of State. The second article declared that the society's sole purpose was "to commemorate the empire's independence on 7 September of each year, with public festivities such as band shells, arches, illuminations, fireworks, etc., which will be done on Constitution Square and elsewhere if possible." It also pledged that the society would "make all efforts to ensure that these amusements were splendid." Annual dues were set at 6$000 (US$3.12), a level that corresponded to a tenth of an army *alferes*'s monthly base pay (or pension, in Gamboa's case), and all members were expected to wear a round medallion with the society's name, the date of independence, and the slogan "Independence or Death" during society functions. Most of the rest of the document dealt with routine administrative matters.[36] Councillors judged that the "society's purpose could not be more honorable" and recommended the statutes' approval after minor amendments to three clauses dealing with internal procedures.[37] Pedro approved this recommendation, but the society failed to respond, and its statutes were thus never officially registered. There is no indication that dues at that level were collected, but thirty-seven men met on 29 September 1874 to reelect the society's officers for 1875, perhaps following the procedures in the draft statutes.[38]

The society's failure to complete its registration may be an early indication of the problems that dogged it in the second half of the 1870s. They appear to have been related to an 1876 effort to wrest the street celebrations from the men of relatively modest social origins who controlled them. Gamboa and three other elected officers were removed from their posts early in the year; a new executive under Isidro Borges Monteiro oversaw a festival identical to that of previous years.[39] Monteiro was an honorary *desembargador* (supreme court judge) and had been Rio de Janeiro's chief of police in the 1850s, which may indicate a government attempt to take over the festival (he had also served on the equestrian statue commission). If so, the effort failed. The new officers remained in place for 1877, when the *Revista Ilustrada* reported that people preferred to "listen to the Santo Antônio Hill [cannon] blasts from their beds," an indication that Monteiro's board had failed to inspire much interest in the celebration. By 1878 they reportedly lacked the means to stage the festival "with the necessary brilliance." Gamboa, some of his friends, and residents of the neighborhood around Constitution Square stepped into the gap and took over the organization for that year, but rainy weather dampened the festivities.[40] The society's failure to list its directors in the *Almanaque Laemmert* for 1878, 1879, and 1880 suggests continuing difficulties.

At the same time that Gamboa was removed from the Sociedade Comemorativa's presidency, the Sociedade Independência (Independence Society) was founded to hold celebrations on São Francisco Square around the statue of José Bonifácio. This society's president, Conselheiro Dom Francisco Baltasar da Silveira, was a judge on the Supremo Tribunal da Justiça (the Supreme Court). Other officers included a doctor, a lieutenant-colonel (probably from the National Guard), and the city librarian (Afonso Herculano de Lima), which suggests a group of higher social standing than Gamboa's boards.[41] In addition to having the independence anthem sung at dawn by some ladies (members of the society), it held a Te Deum at the Santa Cruz dos Militares church, at which it freed five slaves (something that the

Comemorativa never did). For three evenings, the Independência arranged for music (navy bands) and the square's illumination. Despite the riot that disrupted this celebration in 1876 (see the following discussion), it conducted the same rituals in 1877 (freeing only three slaves, however).[42] The *Diário do Rio de Janeiro* happily reported that 1876's 7 September had been "more celebrated than in past years" thanks to the new society, and Joaquim Maria Machado de Assis expected that competition between it and the Comemorativa would stimulate greater celebrations in the future, but the Independência disappeared after 1877, leaving Gamboa and his society as the only organizers of street festivals on 7 September.[43]

The timing of the effort to remove Gamboa and to create a competing society suggests a connection to partisan politics. Both took place in the last years of the Conservative Duke of Caxias's cabinet (June 1875–January 1878), but João Lins Vieira Cansanção de Sinimbu's Liberal government (January 1878–March 1880) apparently left the society to its own devices; efforts to control the popular patriots would not resume until after the Conservatives returned to power in 1885. The short-lived Sociedade Independência and Monteiro's two-year presidency of the Sociedade Comemorativa indicate that not all were happy with Gamboa's control over street celebrations; the retired *alferes*'s ability to outlast them indicates that he enjoyed considerable prestige. Nevertheless, from the late 1870s, the celebrations came under increasing criticism, even though they were a sufficiently regular part of Rio de Janeiro life that the city's first tourist guide described them in detail.[44] *O Domingo* lamented in 1878 that the allegedly "enlightened" Rio de Janeiro celebrated independence so "ridiculously." Carlos de Laet wryly remarked in 1879 on the scrupulousness with which the society carried out its program, implying that political parties could learn a lesson or two from Gamboa and his fellow patriots' dedication to their program (*programa* also means political platform in Portuguese). But such regularity quickly degenerated into monotony. In 1881, one of the *Revista Ilustrada*'s *cronistas* wondered why "the festival committees have only one commemorative program: lamps in the two squares . . . and band music." The *Gazeta de Notícias*'s *cronista* developed this theme further, marveling at the "unchanging way" in which the program was repeated. The same men organized the celebration year after year; it always seemed to rain; electric lights almost always failed to work as promised (that year, "a very weak electric light . . . went out for good" at 12:15 am). Were it not for the artillery salutes, people would sleep right through the festival.[45]

Two years later, Ângelo Agostini gently satirized the celebrations, particularly the small wooden forts (the band shells) with cardboard cannon that real soldiers garrisoned during the day. Groups of men,

FIGURE IO.I.

The Sociedade Comemorativa da Independência do Império's celebrations,
7 September 1883.

Source: *Revista Illustrada*, 15 Sep. 1883.

representing the "brave Brazilian people," had gathered on the square, but with their peaceful attitude they "demonstrated no bravery" (Figure 10.1). To the right, "a sort of Otávio Hudson went around reciting some patriotic stuff in verse." The year before, while "a multitude of the *povo* crowded into Constitution Square" from the late afternoon of 6 September, one observer declared that the celebration was "ever more grotesque," especially now that real soldiers—perhaps even Paraguayan War veterans—were stationed on the mock forts.[46] The *Gazeta de Notícias*'s *cronista* made light of the forts and the artillery park on Santo Antônio Hill. They amounted to besiegers of the equestrian statue, and Pedro I had to decide, once again, whether he would declare "Fico" (I'll stay), as he did on 9 January 1822, or escape down Leopoldina Street, the only open route. Laet grumbled about the festival organizers' "lack of imagination" and wondered about Pedro I's boredom at the "classic celebrations of the great national day." Koseritz attributed a mixture of sadness and disdain to Pedro I as he watched the festival from his pedestal. Another *cronista* remarked that the patriots who sang the independence anthem actually "executed" it—a play on words that works equally in English and Portuguese—for their "good intentions are inversely related to their artistic talents."[47]

These critical comments about the festival also offer some details about the individuals associated with the Sociedade Comemorativa. We have already noted Gamboa's baggy pants and his undistinguished military career, to which a *cronista* snidely referred when he described him as the "*alferes* who never made lieutenant" and who never even got a knighthood in the Ordem de Rosa, the lowest condecoration bestowed by the empire.[48] Hudson, the poet in Figure 10.1, has been described as Brazil's first proletarian poet. He began his career as a typographer and gradually emerged as a journalist, poet, labor organizer, and advocate of popular education, although he apparently never abandoned his trade.[49] Antônio José Nunes Garcia, the poet of modest talent and old-fashioned taste, was also a regular sight at these festivities. Wrapped in a long scarf against the morning chill, he could always be counted on to hand out some colored pieces of paper which he claimed were "verses," recalled one *cronista*.[50]

To whom did the illuminations and the Sociedade Comemorativa's celebrations appeal? Laet expected in 1879 that 3,000 to 4,000 people would be on hand at dawn, although he would not attend himself, for he had no desire to catch bronchitis; the U.S. consul noted that, in 1884, "Constitution Park" had been "thronged with people all night."[51] Folklorist Luís Edmundo (1878–1961), the son of a municipal schoolteacher, later counted going from his home in Botafogo "to the city center to enjoy the illuminations" on days of national festivity as one of his earliest childhood memories, which he dated to 1883 or 1884.[52] Other than the streetcar fare, this was cheap entertainment for the family of a poorly paid civil servant, but the folklorist did not mention going to Constitution Square, which, according to Koseritz, stood out from the rest of the city in 1883 as a sort of "river of light" cast by "thousands of gas jets."[53] In fact, the press descriptions of those who spent the night at the square or arrived there early in the morning (always a large number), suggest that people like Luís Edmundo's family would not have spent much time there. Newspapers invariably noted that those on the square were part of the "*povo*"—the common people—a sharp contrast to the people of all classes who had spent time on the streets during the celebrations of the 1850s or during the festivities to welcome Pedro back in 1872 and 1877.[54] One old observer of changes in Rio de Janeiro society remarked in 1877 that nobody (of his class) went out to visit "festive illuminations" anymore and described the Sociedade Comemorativa as a group that struggled to keep alive rapidly disappearing old traditions.[55] In a dialogue between two fictional brothers-in-law published in *Distração*, one declared that, although he was Brazilian, he had "no obligation to be so foolish as to lose a whole night by going to the Rocio to listen to half a dozen idiots shout out something dull that simpletons call the *independence anthem*. . . . This nonsense doesn't belong here in this age. We now live in the century of knowledge! Nobody lives for such musical poetry."[56] In a telling 1884 report, the *Gazeta de Notícias* contrasted the "*povo*" who had gathered around the statue with the "*mocidade*"— middle- and upper-class youth—who had spent the night "happily dancing" to the tunes of carnival music in the clubs located in the vicinity of Constitution Square.[57] The following year, *O Mequetrefe*'s cartoon

FIGURE 10.2.
The *povo* celebrating independence, 7 September 1885.
Source: O Mequetrefe, 10 Sep. 1885.

likewise emphasized the lower-class and mixed-race social origins of the
street celebrants (Figure 10.2).

Koseritz, who judged the festival "more grotesque than magnificent,"
wondered why the "formidable human mass" had gathered around the
equestrian statue on the evening of 7 September 1884 for there was "absolutely nothing" to do except listen to the bands that played in the two
forts.[58] After Gamboa's death, Antônio Valentim da Costa Magalhães
declared that people no longer went to the square to see the tired decorations, hear the anthem, flirt, catch a cold, drink, or relieve others of
their wallets, indications of what took place in the crowds. Laet crypti-
cally alluded to prostitution and remarked critically on the "ingenuous
admirers of flags and fireworks" who crowded the square.[59] Of course,
most of these activities took place at any popular festival. Strikingly
absent from the accounts of the 7 September street celebrations are indications of the dancing that were an important part of popular festivities such as the Festival of the Holy Spirit and carnival. Nor did any
observer note the construction of temporary booths for the sale of food
and drink (although Laet described two old women selling cakes and
sweet bread in 1876, and a later *cronista* recalled sellers of *empadas* and
ice cream).[60] The area around the square may have been sufficiently well
provided with stores and bars that there was little need for foodsellers'
services.

In one of his early *crônicas*, Laet remarked of 1876's popular festivities: "There is in fact much poetry in this custom of the *povo*, [whose members] gather around their bronze heroes to hail the star of liberty."[61] It is impossible to know whether the *povo* really shared such sentiments, but after Gamboa's death in early 1886, commentators certainly attributed them to him. He had been "the unperceived strongbox into which we all deposited our patriotic spirit," explained the *Gazeta de Notícias*'s *cronista* after that year's celebration: "Faithful to his obligations, *Alferes* Gamboa died taking with him the precious deposit; hence the silent, melancholy, and unusual 7 September that we had."[62] Laet had some grudging words of praise for the late *alferes*'s enthusiasm for independence celebrations.[63] In this 1886 cluster of commentary about the late Gamboa, journalists underscored that, without him, no 7 September street celebrations took place, something that they viewed with ambivalence. Having no celebrations at all was worse than the hokey ones over which the *alferes* had presided.[64] Later that year, a very different group of men reorganized the Sociedade Comemorativa and its celebrations, to which we turn later in this chapter.

Gamboa's Comemorativa contrasts sharply in its social origins to the Sociedade Ipiranga of the 1850s. To be sure, the Comemorativa contemplated annual dues of 6$000, identical to those of the Ipiranga, but, unlike the latter, Gamboa's society never had more than a handful of paid-up members. While the Ipiranga's leadership came from the Liberal elite, the most visible Comemorativa leader was a humble army *alferes*; the press stressed that people of all classes attended the popular festivities of the late 1850s but emphasized that only the *povo* frequented the Comemorativa's commemorations. Maria Clementina Pereira da Cunha's work on Rio de Janeiro's carnival suggests an interpretation that can be applied to the Comemorativa, its relationship to the earlier societies like the Ipiranga, and the growing criticism of it in 1880s. She argues that the lower-class carnival societies founded in the late nineteenth century reflected the success of the pedagogical project of the elite carnival societies founded in the 1850s. However, when the new popular societies, with their unwelcome Afro-Brazilian rhythms, seemed to overwhelm the idealized European carnival promoted by the elite societies, they increasingly faced criticism.[65] In much the same way, Gamboa and the *povo* took over the street festivities of independence, ultimately to the dismay of those who could not accept these forms of popular patriotism, and especially the large contingent of *povo* that turned up, year after year, on Constitution Square.

Indeed, criticism of the Sociedade Comemorativa came from several quarters. As we have seen, Laet and other commentators tended to view its celebrations as old-fashioned and uncivilized. Self-proclaimed revolutionaries also saw little of virtue in the festival. After describing the "pharaonic pomp" of 7 September 1882, which included the Sociedade Comemorativa's celebration, *A Revolução* recommended that "every excited Brazilian go to the beach, crouch down, [and] expel his dose of independence from [his] belly onto the shining sand." True independence was not such artificial displays but building schools and factories, it added.[66] In 1885, one Oscar de Castro condemned those of the *povo* who celebrated "a monarchy that has a golden crown derived from the [slave] trade."[67] The following year, *O Farol*, the newspaper that had published Castro's lament, went further and declared that the 7 September celebrants were akin to the plantation slaves whose masters occasionally let them dance for a few hours before sending the overseer to drive them back to their quarters for the night; in 1874, a poet writing for a student newspaper called the celebrants "base slaves."[68] Other critical commentary of the 1870s focused on the *povo*'s failure to recognize the limits of the independence and sovereignty won on 7 September 1822, much as Mello Moraes had castigated Gamboa for celebrating around the equestrian statue. Veriano Fontino, author of an 1877 pamphlet that lamented the failure to remember Tiradentes and the other conspirators of 1789, condemned the "wretched *povo*" who would gather around the statue, "proof of *imperial power and tyranny*."[69]

By the 1880s, very few offered unqualified praise of the Comemorativa. *Distração*'s Manduca de Sá, a *cronista* who wrote in verse, declared in 1885: "You do well, ordinary Joe [*Zé miudo*] / When you see the dawn break / [And] shout enthusiastically / And then, happy, content / Take a stroll around / Hailing all and everything." The *Gazeta de Notícias*'s João Bigode declared that he would certainly be on the square at dawn to cheer independence.[70] These were, however, isolated voices among the critical chorus. The structural and conjunctural political questions that dominated the press discussion of 7 September's meaning scarcely intruded on the Sociedade Comemorativa's celebrations. By not spurning Pedro I's equestrian statue, however, the society implicitly accepted the monument's message about the origins of Brazilian independence, a message that had lost much of its resonance among the political class.

CAPOEIRAS AND THE 1876 BRAWL

Capoeiras' visibility on days of national festivity increased notably in the 1870s and 1880s. Far more so than in earlier decades, newspapers regularly reported the arrest of *capoeiras* who practiced their art in front of marching bands or honor guards returning to the barracks.[71] On Pedro's birthday in 1875, three *capoeiras* were arrested after a stabbing that took place in front of the honor guard after the official celebrations.

That same day, no fewer than fifteen (seven slaves, seven free men, and one who claimed to be free) were arrested on Dom Pedro II Square (the former Palace Square), perhaps in a police sweep to clear the area before the emperor's arrival for the levee and his grandson's baptism. Likewise, on 7 September 1887, six men were arrested on the square.[72] At 5:00 am on 7 September 1884, police arrested thirteen *capoeiras* on Constitution Square; they took custody of six more (three slaves and three free) later that day.[73] Carlos Eugênio Líbano Soares connects this surge in *capoeira* and in concern about it to the Paraguayan War's aftermath. Many *capoeiras* had been drafted to serve, and discontented veterans became heavily involved in the practice.[74]

Limited sources make it difficult to determine *capoeiras*' motives. Their displays in front of bands or parading troops likely amounted to swaggering that played a part in maintaining the internal hierarchy of the *capoeira maltas* (gangs) who gained prominence in these decades.[75] Rivalries between *maltas* often led to violence, and two travelers noted that they routinely pursued their vendettas on 7 September.[76] After a series of symbolic challenges involving the flags of the Nagoas and the Guaiamus (the two principal *maltas*) in early September 1885, a worried *Diário de Notícias* called on the police to clear their redoubts (respectively the areas around São Francisco Square and the Campo da Aclamação) before the upcoming celebrations. The Sociedade Comemorativa's festival on Constitution Square would, in fact, take place between the two gangs' headquarters, but there are no indications of *capoeira* violence on 7 September, although a few newspapers noted celebrants' worries early in the month.[77]

Although the evidence is episodic, it is clear that some *capoeiras* served as enforcers for political parties, most notably for a number of prominent Conservative politicians.[78] Liberals in opposition and Republicans complained that those who prevented their partisans from voting or who disrupted their meetings were *capoeiras* in government service, but Soares stresses that the *maltas* had "their own political view" and were more than mere party thugs; he goes so far as to speak of a "Capoeira Party" active in urban politics.[79] Others prefer to see *capoeiras* as engaged in a generic sort of resistance.[80] Based on the terse police arrest reports and the occasionally more extensive denunciations of *capoeira* activities on days of national festivity, however, it is very difficult to determine their motives.

There is no evidence that *capoeiras* ever deliberately intended to disrupt the celebration of days of national festivity. At most, they wanted to show off or use the occasion to settle scores with rivals, as is clear from the only time that *capoeiras*' actions actually put an end to a civic celebration. On 8 September 1876, two navy bands were assigned to the band shells that the new Sociedade Independência had erected on São

Francisco Square.[81] One band consisted of sailors, the other of marines. Another sailors' band, accompanying some members of the society on Ouvidor Street, attracted "a large gang of *capoeiras* causing their usual trouble." At the corner of Gonçalves Dias Street, urban guards (members of a civilian police force founded in 1866) arrested one of the *capoeiras*, who happened to be an off-duty sailor.[82] They tried to take him to their substation in an alley off São Francisco Square, but the other *capoeiras*, joined by the sailor-musicians who abandoned their band shell, attacked the guards and tried to free the prisoner. The guards made it to the substation, which then came under attack from as many as 300 *capoeiras* (mostly sailors and employees of the army arsenal, according to the *Jornal do Comércio*). Using the paving stones that had been removed to set up the band shells and the flags decorating the square, as well as broken flagpoles and bottles looted from a hotel and a pool hall, the mob attacked the substation, broke all its windows, and threatened to destroy the building's entire façade.

A military police patrol managed to force its way through the mob to protect the substation, but its commander was knocked senseless. The *capoeiras* assaulted the many guards who were returning to the station individually or in small groups after their shifts, insulting them and stripping them of their weapons and parts of their uniforms. The arrival of the police cavalry finally allowed authorities to clear the square; that the chief of police prevented the cavalry from charging the rioters with drawn swords ensured that no one was killed in the fracas, although seven police soldiers were hurt (one seriously), along with eleven urban guards; newspapers reported no information on casualties among the rioters. Before the cavalry arrived, many of the *capoeiras* escaped down Ouvidor Street bearing "police sabres, shakos, razors, and bits of banners . . . as victory trophies." The marine band watched from the safety of its band shell and left under discipline.

Both the *Diário do Rio de Janeiro* and the *Gazeta de Notícias* blamed the sailors and lamented that so many of them were involved in *capoeira*. The independence celebrations merely served as the occasion for this riot, which can be interpreted as a conflict between the two corporations—the police and the navy. The following day, police were out in force and arrested thirty-eight men. Both such conflicts among armed forces corporations and the penetration of police, army, and navy rank-and-file by *capoeiras* were common at this time.[83] Agostini's *Revista Ilustrada* made light of the whole affair with its cover picture that showed José Bonifácio energetically defending himself against all comers (Figure 10.3), and Machado de Assis remarked that this "*brawl*, a true *hors-d'oeuvre* to the celebration, amounted to a depiction of the Eastern War [the 1876–78 Serbian-Ottoman War]," with the police playing the part of Belgrade's defenders against the attacking Turks, the *capoeiras*.[84]

FIGURE 10.3.
The brawl between *capoeiras* and urban guards, 8 September 1876.
Source: *Revista Illustrada*, 9 Sep. 1876.

Given the large crowds that gathered at night to celebrate independence year after year, it is notable that the 1876 riot was the only instance of large-scale violence recorded during these celebrations. Frank Carpenter's characters saw the "densest masses of embodied patriotism" on 7 September 1877 and noted that the upper classes were "conspicuously courteous" while the "working people and slaves . . . were respectful even to servility." To be sure, these American visitors had slept in, despite the "fizz and bang of untimely pyrotechnics," and therefore missed what they were told was the best part of the celebration, the vigil from midnight to dawn, but they had nothing to fear from *capoeiras*.[85] Although later correspondents and *cronistas* recalled that "during the late Gamboa's time" citizens sometimes fell afoul of *capoeiras* during the Comemorativa's celebrations, there are no contemporary reports of this.[86] In short, the newspapers that frequently noted the peaceful nature of the popular festivals on Constitution Square were usually right.

FROM MANUMISSION TO ABOLITIONISM

The practice of freeing slaves in honor of days of national festivity, briefly pioneered by the Sociedade Ipiranga in the mid-1850s and revived during the celebrations at the end of the Paraguayan War, largely disappeared during the 1870s and early 1880s; it resumed on a large scale in the mid-1880s. Moderate abolitionists led the way in these manumissions, which were part of their strategy of gradually freeing Brazil's slaves. Their first victory came in Ceará on 25 March 1884 when they freed the last slave in the province. This achievement was widely hailed throughout Brazil; for the next years, few newspapers said anything about the charter on 25 March. In 1885, Rio de Janeiro's city council began organizing large-scale manumission ceremonies on the other two days of national festivity (and also on Isabel and Teresa Cristina's birthdays) through the so-called Livro de Ouro fund. In these ways, the great political question of how to accomplish the ending of slavery forced its way into the celebration of days of national festivity, and abolition became the principal question in these days' press coverage.

A handful of private individuals freed slaves to celebrate 7 September. In 1870, the scribe of the Colégio Dom Pedro II freed two slaves in honor of independence, while a certain Manoel Martins de Carvalho freed the thirteen-year-old creole, Belmira, in honor of Pedro's birthday and the prince's baptism in 1875. Two more such manumissions honored independence in 1882 and 1884.[87] The rarity with which references to such private patriotic manumissions were recorded in the press raises questions about Louis Couty's 1881 observation that "all the important domestic or national events serve as the pretext or reason for such liberations." If the number of private manumissions increased at this time, as one historian has suggested, this did not manifest itself in press coverage of the days of national festivity.[88]

Unlike the Comemorativa, the Sociedade Independência raised funds to purchase slaves' freedom—five women and children in 1876 and three more in 1877. Funds to free two of the children in 1876 came from the residents of São José parish, while society members bought the freedom of the other three slaves. To the three children freed in 1876, the society president added his forty-six-year-old slave woman, Benvinda.[89] The minutes of the directors' meetings from June to September 1876 offer no indication that the society saw this as contributing to the end of slavery.[90] The *Jornal do Comércio*'s *cronista* compared the Independência favorably to the Comemorativa, for the latter "spent its time shooting off fireworks and building band shells" while the former, "from its first day, produces good, dries tears, [and] breaks the chains of captivity." Laet likewise praised the Sociedade Independência in 1876 for freeing "five unhappy creatures, who were born into civilization on the same day as the *pátria*."[91] All of this was classic abolitionist rhetoric, which reduced slaves to helpless victims saved by heroic abolitionists.[92]

Standard histories of abolitionism date the start of the final campaign against slavery to 1879, when Deputies Jerônimo Sodré and Joaquim Nabuco attempted to place the issue on the legislative agenda. They founded a society to coordinate antislavery efforts, published a newspaper, *O Abolicionista* (1880–81), and drew support from Ferreira de Araújo's *Gazeta de Notícias* and the *Gazeta da Tarde*, which became the principal abolitionist periodical after José do Patrocínio took it over in mid-1881. In the 1881 elections, however, the Liberal government ensured the abolitionist deputies' defeat; Nabuco went into exile, and abolitionists shifted their focus to extraparliamentary activity.[93] With the founding of the Confederação Abolicionista (Abolitionist Confederation) in 1883, the campaign intensified, now on an increasingly popular footing. As many historians have observed, abolitionism became a mass political movement, one that mobilized many of the men disenfranchised by the 1881 electoral reform, as well as significant numbers of women.[94] The campaign also likely included people who participated in the Sociedade Comemorativa's celebrations, but Gamboa's society demonstrated no antislavery tendencies, and very few questioned this.

The resurgent abolition movement's first great victory came with the ending of slavery in Ceará on 25 March 1884, a local initiative apparently timed to coincide with the constitution's anniversary. Long anticipated as the final result of a carefully coordinated campaign, it sparked elaborate celebrations throughout the country.[95] While the usual official rituals in honor of the constitution took place in the capital, most of the press ignored the constitution in favor of celebrating this important abolitionist victory.[96] Typographers, medical students, Cearenses resident in the capital, and cadets at the Escola Militar all published special commemorative pamphlets or newspapers.[97] The military academy's commander did not, however, let his students join the celebration. Abolitionist students and teachers at the Escola Politécnica, which celebrated its tenth anniversary on 25 March 1884, were strictly enjoined not to associate this celebration with the abolitionist demonstrations taking place that day.[98] The *Folhinha Laemmert* later noted that no hasty observer should mistake the "bands, fireworks, torchlit processions, speeches, fairs, regattas, and widespread enthusiasm" for celebrations in honor of the constitution; all of this honored Ceará's abolition. *A Folha Nova*'s *cronista* observed a certain "exclusion of the official world . . . while the emperor was constantly involved in all of the demonstrations."[99] In this way, he recognized that Ceará's abolition had resulted from a popular movement—popular both in the sense of not led by the state and in the sense of drawing broad lower-class support—and that the imperial family was sympathetic to abolition, although most Liberal and Conservative parliamentarians, not to mention large slaveowners, preferred no further government intervention in the inevitable (but still distant) ending of slavery anticipated by the 1871 Free Womb Law.

In subsequent years, abolitionist societies commemorated their victory in Ceará with formal celebrations on 25 March that included speeches by movement leaders, music, and theatrical performances.[100] Speakers at the Confederação Abolicionista's celebration sometimes contrasted the constitution, which did not mention slavery yet forged the chains that kept millions in captivity, with the freedom won for Ceará's slaves, a first step toward final abolition.[101] Editorials rarely referred to the constitution's anniversary, as newspapers preferred to focus on the abolition movement; the ending of slavery in Ceará had, in short, completely changed the meaning of 25 March, and few lamented this.[102]

The rising tide of abolitionism forced further government action and, with strong support from Pedro, the cabinet of Manoel Pinto de Souza Dantas (June 1884–May 1885) drafted a bill to free elderly slaves (without indemnification) and to address problems with the national emancipation fund, which had freed very few slaves. Moderate Liberals and Conservatives in the chamber balked at a bill that failed to respect property rights; Dantas obtained a dissolution of parliament but could not win a majority in favor of the bill in the ensuing elections. He resigned in May 1885 and José Antônio Saraiva pushed a watered-down version of the bill through the chamber, before himself resigning in August. Pedro then had no option but to hand power to the Conservative Baron of Cotegipe, who secured the bill's passage in the Senate (28 September 1885) and then oversaw new elections that returned a large Conservative majority. The Saraiva-Cotegipe or Sexagenarian Law was "a complex and retrogressive act" that failed to satisfy abolitionists. To be sure, it freed slaves sixty years and older, but it required them to labor for another three years (a symbolic indemnity to their owners) and to remain in the municipality for five years; it set high maximum valuations for slaves freed by the emancipation fund and specified severe penalties for those who harbored fugitive slaves. Cotegipe's government enforced the legislation to the benefit of slaveowners and, in an important setback to abolitionists, resolved in 1886 to count the capital—then legally a "neutral municipality" administered by the imperial government—as part of Rio de Janeiro province for the enforcement of the ban on the interprovincial slave trade. This meant that the capital's slaves could again be legally sold to coffee plantations and made abolitionists' efforts to free the Corte's slaves more difficult.[103]

In this environment of police repression and harassment, radical abolitionists began to encourage slave flight or to assist runaways.[104] While moderate abolitionists may not have agreed with these tactics, they recognized that these efforts kept up the pressure on the government. The imperial family stood in a difficult position. While personally in favor of abolition, Pedro could not be seen as overly partisan in his approach; he had turned to Cotegipe and the Conservatives to force a watered-down sexagenarian law through parliament when Liberal cabinets proved unequal to the task. Declining health reduced his effectiveness and forced him to seek medical treatment in Europe in June 1887. Already in 1885, a commentator lamented that, at the age of sixty, Pedro lacked the vigor that he had displayed early in his reign (and wryly contrasted this with the expectation that sexagenarian slaves were perfectly capable of three more years of arduous labor for their masters).[105] Agostini frequently portrayed Cotegipe in royal robes and crown to underscore his power vis-à-vis Isabel, princess-regent for the third time from June 1887 to August 1888.[106] She, in turn, increasingly saw the ending of slavery as her moral and Christian duty, but she acted forcefully only in March 1888 by removing Cotegipe and installing João Alfredo Correia de Oliveira as president of a new Conservative council of ministers with a mandate to pass an abolition bill as soon as parliament convened in May.[107] In the last days of slavery, Isabel even sheltered fugitives on the grounds of her palace in Petrópolis.[108] At this point, José do Patrocínio abandoned his republicanism and cast his lot with the monarchy, recognizing that only the undemocratic moderating power could overcome the resistance to abolition in a parliament strongly dominated by slavocrat interests and even more unresponsive to popular concerns after the 1881 reform that had so dramatically reduced the electorate.[109]

This was the tense political environment during which the Livro de Ouro manumission ceremonies took place on days of national festivity and on Isabel and Teresa Cristina's birthdays. Through them, Rio de Janeiro's city council demonstrated its commitment to moderate abolitionism. The Livro de Ouro (Golden Book) was simply a manumission fund sponsored by the city council. Instituted in early 1884, its name derived from the luxurious register in which donors inscribed their names; Pedro and Eu were the first to do so. The money that it raised financed nine public manumission ceremonies between 28 July 1885 and 2 December 1887, during which 797 slaves—more than three-quarters of them women—received their freedom. The fund's stated goal was to free all of the capital's slaves, but it clearly fell far short, although on 7 September 1887 organizers still hoped to achieve their goal in 1890.[110] While historians have tended to dismiss such funds as insignificant efforts, Celso Castilho and Camillia Cowling have recently argued that they and the local mobilizations around them contributed to the broadening of Brazilian politics.[111]

Moreover, the six Livro de Ouro manumission ceremonies held on days of national festivity (7 September and 2 December in 1885, 1886, and 1887) provided the occasion for extensive debate in the capital's press about the Brazilian nation, abolition, and slavery's legacy. As José Ferreira Nobre, the city councilor who had taken the lead in organizing the fund, explained on 7 September 1887, "The *Livro de Ouro* is the peaceful solution to the great problem that worries all; liberty and rights unite in it; through it we free the slaves whose owners voluntarily bring them to this new baptism." The city council's president likewise emphasized the importance of order in his remarks on 2 December 1885: "We must not only occupy ourselves in freeing the slave; we must also tackle head on and with the maximum of energy the very difficult problems of the substitution, the utilization, and the moral uplift of the element that today is emancipated."[112] The organizers clearly intended that their patriotic manumissions respect the social and economic order, reflecting the concerns that guided the many deputies who insisted that the sexagenarian law include compensation to masters (the obligation to labor for three more years) and restrict the new freedpeople's movement.

The form of these ceremonies underscored these conservative understandings of emancipation. They took place amid considerable pomp in the city council building, lavishly decorated for the occasion. The 7 September 1887 ceremony was "extremely well attended" by officials and diplomats as well as by "many families from our best society," as was the one the year before.[113] Schoolchildren were also sometimes drafted to participate in the ceremony by forming honor guards; on 2 December 1886 they sang an anthem to liberty.[114] After music and speeches, Princess Isabel normally handed out the letters of liberty to the slaves who had been kept in a separate room until it was their turn to file in and humbly receive their papers (Figure 10.4).[115] Isabel's centrality in these ceremonies reflected both her personal rejection of slavery and her view of abolition as appropriate charitable work to undertake.[116] The rest of the imperial family remained in the background; after the ceremonies that he attended (he missed those of 1887 because he was in Europe for medical treatment), Pedro quietly proffered a few cryptic words of encouragement to the organizers, comments that quickly became the subject of speculation and sometimes mockery.[117] The one traveler who wrote about one of these ceremonies thought it "a humiliating spectacle, some twenty or thirty poor wretches, decked out for the occasion, being awarded their freedom."[118]

The Livro de Ouro ceremonies thus took place at a time when the monarchy stood in a relatively weak position against a strongly slavocrat cabinet. Rio de Janeiro's city council espoused a moderate abolitionism, while all had to contend with the radical abolitionists. The Cotegipe cabinet pointedly boycotted the 7 September and 2 December 1886 manumission ceremonies and "stood out, as always, by its absence" on 2 December 1887. It advised Isabel to take no part in the

FIGURE 10.4.
The Livro de Ouro manumission ceremony, 2 December 1886.
Source: Revista Illustrada, 8 Dec. 1886.

fund-raising campaigns.[119] Rumor had it that Pedro himself contributed the lion's share of the funds to the 2 December 1885 and 14 March 1886 ceremonies.[120] Critics remarked that the 2 December 1887 ceremony was scarcely advertised so as not to offend the cabinet. After the sixty-four slaves had been freed, Isabel suggested that the city council prepare an abolitionist festival for her father's return. As spokesman for the Instituto Histórico e Geográfico Brasileiro, the Viscount of Taunay presented a similar proposal during the levee; rumor had it that the cabinet was furious and intended to prevent the institute from electing this "revolutionary" as its representative for the next ceremony.[121]

Nevertheless, the early Livro de Ouro ceremonies generated considerable enthusiasm. The *Diário de Notícias* hailed 7 September 1885's ceremony as "the festival of freedom," a fitting way to celebrate "the day of liberty." On the 7th, 8th, and 9th, it published 30,000 copies of special abolitionist issues whose first two pages consisted of short statements by prominent abolitionists (its normal circulation was then 20,000). Many of the contributors remarked on the Livro de Ouro. Dr. José Antônio da Fonseca Lessa declared that "the freeing of slaves has always constituted Brazilian hearts' greatest desire" and expected that if all municipalities followed the capital's example, "it would produce, within the terms of the law, in a few years, the complete extinction of slavery."[122] Funds to free the 219 slaves at that independence-day ceremony came from parish subscriptions, private donations, and collections taken up in government departments. Even the city council's "laborers" came up with 100 mil-réis (US$38).[123]

While the press generally supported the Livro de Ouro manumissions, journalists frequently criticized aspects of the ritual. Artur Azevedo condemned the local subscriptions as little better than an illegal tax and speculated that many donors opened their wallets not out of abolitionist sentiment but because they hoped that a donation would help them get a license to open a kiosk. *Carbonário* went further and complained that the council was "doing good at someone else's expense"—using citizens' hard-earned money to celebrate the emperor's birthday. The councilors well knew that "the thing might produce a few baronetcies." Patrocínio, not yet converted to monarchism, thought that the 2 December 1887 manumissions had been "bought at a very high price" just to flatter Isabel. On 7 September 1886, Patrocínio sharply contrasted Pedro's participation in the manumission ceremony with the levee, during which the emperor would "receive homage from the nobility whose coats of arms were drawn from the mud of the [slave] trade. There, with Machiavellian skill, His Majesty will perceive that the collectivity's interests stand above those of the black [*negro*]."[124]

Many could not help but notice that the manumissions were insignificant in relation to the number of slaves in the country. In a brilliant *crônica*, Laet wrote about a figure reminiscent of the wandering Jew who visited Rio de Janeiro and attended the 2 December 1885 ceremony. After the 133rd and final slave received her freedom, he exclaimed: "Eight hundred and ninety-nine thousand, eight hundred and sixty-seven are missing . . . where are they?" For the indiscretion of subtracting the new freedpeople from the total of 900,000 slaves remaining in the country (a recent estimate given by the minister of agriculture), the police arrested him. Such "impatience does not sit well with the serious concerns about agricultural labor and [the] other ones on which national prosperity rests," remarked the *cronsista*.[125] At the end of that ceremony, Pedro expressed his desire to live to see the end of slavery, and João Capistrano de Abreu calculated that, even if all the country's municipalities emulated the capital, the monarch would have to live to the age of 105 to see his wish fulfilled![126] For his part, on 7 September 1885, Agostini expected that the last slave would gain his freedom only near the end of Isabel's long reign if abolition depended only on the Livro de Ouro.[127]

In 1886, the number of slaves freed in these ceremonies diminished notably from the peaks of 219 on 7 September 1885, 133 on 2 December 1885, and 173 on 14 March 1886 (the latter two figures likely the result of Pedro's personal contributions). On his birthday that year, when only fifty slaves were freed, Pedro quietly muttered that, since he had turned sixty-one that day, the council should at least have freed that many slaves. Widely reported in the press, his comment prompted the Count of São Salvador de Matosinhos, *O País*'s owner, to free enough slaves to make up the difference.[128] *O País*'s *cronista*, however, thought that the logical implication of Pedro's observation—that just sixty-two slaves should be freed next year—indicated his reluctance to embrace the abolitionist cause. The Livro de Ouro fund in fact freed sixty-two slaves on 2 December 1887, but a council member added two slaves of his own, so the total came to sixty-four.[129]

An embarrassing incident at the 7 September 1886 Livro de Ouro ceremony provided the occasion for a rare discussion about racial hierarchies. That day, two "correctly dressed" white men turned up among the sixty men and women who, two by two, were to receive their manumission papers. Isabel turned to her aides and asked, "Where are the people being freed?" When told that the two were, in fact, slaves, she visibly blushed; a lengthy frisson of shock and murmuring ran through the assembled dignitaries and journalists. Many lowered their eyes, and some of the spectators cried. An employee of the French legation was heard to mutter, "That's too much!" Isabel quickly composed herself and finished the ceremony, but Ferreira de Araújo later claimed that she continued to eye the two white men "with a look of profound pity."[130] That same day, the city council unveiled an expensive painting commemorating the first Livro de Ouro manumission ceremony of 29 July 1885. Observers noted that the artist, Pedro José Peres, had placed the emperor's face in shadows, which made him look like a "mulatto king" or "darker than any Caucasian should be."[131]

The press extensively debated the incidents' significance. Patrocínio condemned Isabel—and by extension, the rest of Brazilian society—for not being "shocked at the sight of slavery, the greatest of crimes, [when] it was imposed on dark skin" but for feeling great indignation at the sight of slavery stamped on "light skin." A *cronista* in another newspaper declared that Brazilians looked on enslaved blacks (*pretos*) as they viewed streetcar mules, while white slaves provoked feelings similar to those prompted by an outbreak of smallpox in the neighbor's house—a mixture of repugnance and relief that it was not happening at home.[132] A few days after the incident, Artur Azevedo defended the princess by reporting that she had later declared "that white slaves move me as much as yellow or black ones." An *O País cronista* remarked that white slaves should be no more surprising than the occasional "more or less dusky gentleman" among Brazil's nobility and added that the emperor should conclude from this incident "that it is time to stop haggling over freedom on the pretext of colors, and [to stop] celebrating political emancipation by giving such an ugly hue to civil emancipation." One wag suggested that, for lack of "free *pretos* with nothing to do," the two white men had been sent by "others even more clever" who sought to profit from the Livro de Ouro fund.[133] As far as the painting was concerned, a writer in *O País* expected that the artist would certainly touch it up (Peres claimed that the work was still unfinished); others thought that the problems with the painting derived from the council's choice of a foreigner (Peres had been born in Portugal), rather than the Brazilian artists Vítor Meireles de Lima or Pedro Américo de Figueiredo, both of whom had considerable experience with commemorative historical paintings. Peres had reportedly put in the lowest bid.[134] No one remarked that the painting shows only four slaves—a kneeling woman and three children receiving their manumission papers from Isabel—but fully a dozen white schoolchildren.

That white slaves were not supposed to exist of course only confirms the racial hierarchies of this society, and historians have noted that the final years of slavery and the immediate postabolition period were marked by an increasing "racialization" of society. As the end of slavery loomed, and with it the social hierarchies informed by it, racial rhetoric figured more prominently in Brazil. To be sure, this racialization coexisted with a liberal rhetoric of equality expressed in Azevedo's defence of Isabel or in radical abolitionists' hopes for more profound social transformations, but calls for European immigration and the worried debate about whether former slaves could be induced to work or whether Africans had been hopelessly corrupted by slavery soon dominated the political agenda.[135] That Peres focused his painting on white schoolchildren highlights the extent to which moderate abolitionism was about freeing a civilized white Brazil from the burden of slavery and not about aiding former slaves.

Amid the rapid collapse of slavery due to large-scale slave flight in São Paulo, parliament convened in May 1888 for its annual session and legislators quickly passed the so-called Golden Law, which Isabel signed on Sunday, 13 May.[136] As more than a few contemporary observers noted, slavery had already ended in practice, "revolutionarily," by the time that parliament finally acted.[137] For a week, Brazilians gave themselves over to "delirium" or seemingly "interminable celebrations," as abolitionist leaders put it.[138] These celebrations have been analyzed in some detail by Eduardo Silva, and they echoed many elements of Brazilian civic ritual culture, not to mention carnival as well.[139] The recently discovered collection of poetry distributed in the streets, printed on colored paper, looks much like the leaflets distributed at the equestrian statue's inauguration (they probably also resembled the pieces of colored paper that the poet, Garcia, called verses).[140] Silva notes that the celebrants sported the green-and-yellow "independence leaf" (the *croton variegatum*); such was the demand for this leaf that all of the city's croton bushes were stripped bare. This echoed, of course, the earlier use of the leaf in civic celebrations, but, curiously, there are no Brazilian references to its use on 7 September in the 1870s and 1880s. In 1873 and 1878, however, foreigners observed what they described the widespread wearing of these sprigs on 7 September, so this may have been a custom so common that Brazilians never mentioned it.[141] Large-scale demonstrations of electric light reflected the traditional custom of illuminations and celebrated modernity, while the emphasis on order in the press coverage repeated a standard trope in commentary on days of national festivity.[142] Talk of designating 13 May as a day of national festivity, however, came to naught when Deputy Afonso Celso de Assis Figueiredo Jr.'s proposal was buried in committee for the rest of the 1888 session.[143]

On 7 September, all of the city's newspapers connected abolition to independence, describing the end of slavery as the essential "complement to the work of national emancipation," as the *Diário de Notícias* put it the following day.[144] Editors however drew predictably different conclusions from this connection. The *Jornal do Comércio* celebrated abolition's peaceful nature and the fact that former slaves were now "free men."[145] Republicans called for a change in regime to complete the work of liberation.[146] Jacinto Heller's troupe put on an elaborate gala at the São Pedro Theater that began with a dramatic laudation by one Soares de Souza Júnior. Entitled *Libertas et Imperator* (Liberty and Emperor), it included characters representing Liberty, the Argentine Republic, Rio de Janeiro, and Brazil's provinces. *O País*'s reviewer judged this "novelty" a bit too long, but others praised this throwback to the midcentury repertoire. There is no indication of the plot, but the inclusion of Argentina, who declared that she wanted to join the celebrations, highlighted the change in Brazilian thinking about the neighboring republic, which could now be seen in a positive light thanks to its recent progress. The laudation ended with a tableau featuring the imperial portraits and the national anthem. The rest of the program was more conventional fare— *Faust*—but the intermission included a recitation of Soares de Souza's poem on three dates, 7 September, 13 May, and 22 August (independence, abolition, and Pedro's return).[147]

Abolition thus profoundly marked the celebration of days of national festivity in the mid-1880s. Ceará's abolition displaced the already limited attention paid to the constitution, while abolitionist demonstrations such as the Livro de Ouro manumissions came to dominate 7 September and 2 December. To associate independence with liberty for all was an easy rhetorical step, and to celebrate Pedro's birthday by freeing slaves recognized the imperial family's cautious support for abolition. Such moderate abolitionism, however, sat uncomfortably alongside the movement's many radical elements.

DISCIPLINING THE POPULAR PATRIOTS, 1885–1888

In 1885, Rio de Janeiro's city council did not just launch the Livro de Ouro manumissions; it also sponsored a popular festival that competed directly with the Sociedade Comemorativa's celebrations on Constitution Square. This marked the first step in a campaign to wrest control of the 7 September street festivals from the hands of Gamboa and his fellow popular patriots. Gamboa's death in 1886 cleared the way for a new group of men to take over the society and impose changes on the street celebrations. In some respects, this was nothing new, for the imperial government had long regulated popular organizations—from 1860 to 1882, societies like the Comemorativa required formal approval of their statutes by the Council of State[148]—and it frequently intervened in them through the subsidies that the Comemorativa occasionally received. The impending end of slavery, with all that abolition implied for social hierarchies, and the increasingly radical popular abolitionist movement that the Cotegipe government struggled to contain lent urgency to these efforts to discipline the *povo*, even though the Comemorativa had remained aloof from the campaign against slavery.

The city council displayed an unusual level of interest in 7 September 1885, and in addition to seeking to turn the day into an abolitionist demonstration through the Livro de Ouro, it promoted numerous other commemorations. The council archivist, José Ricardo Pires de Almeida, whose efforts to burnish Pedro I's image were noted in the last chapter, prepared an exhibition of documents and artifacts pertaining to independence, while the council called on residents to illuminate their façades (something that it had not done for some time).[149] It invited other institutions to join in the festivities, among them the Clube Regatas Guanabarense, which agreed to stage a regatta on the 8th, but it requested help from the council to put on a fireworks display on Botafogo beach.[150] The council asked for an artillery battery to fire salutes in front of the army headquarters, located across from the city council building on the Campo da Aclamação. It also raised an enormous arch-shaped band shell on São Francisco Square, illuminated by 3,000 candles and gas lights.[151] These efforts apparently motivated shopkeepers and others to join in, and there are indications of illuminations along Ouvidor and Constitution Streets.[152] These celebrations, as well as the official civic rituals, required so many bands that the adjutant-general could not satisfy all of the council's requests for martial music.[153]

The centerpiece of the council's initiative was the kermesse, a popular fair that it sponsored on the Campo da Aclamação to raise funds for abolition. It was an elaborate affair. The council constructed a "spacious and elegant pavillion," around which stood two rows of identical green-and-yellow booths with distinctive names, which sold trinkets and offered games of chance.[154] Such bazaars were common in the abolitionist movement during the mid-1880s; they apparently began in 1884, and the largest of them took place between August and October of 1885 (a very elaborate one in Porto Alegre on 7 September 1884 may have served as the inspiration for Rio de Janeiro's city council).[155] They also echoed older customs. As Laet observed, the kermesse resembled what "our forefathers did for the Holy Spirit festival," but he lamented that it had far more games of chance than the old Pentecost celebrations. Another critic also worried that the "temporary gambling dens" would attract all manner of riffraff.[156] There is, however, no evidence of disorder connected to the festival, despite the "great . . . concourse of *povo* at the booths,"[157] nor are there any indications of how much money the council managed to raise.

Divine Providence sought to reduce Brazilian patriotism to "reasonable proportions," according to Valentim Magalhães, and sent heavy rains that washed away so much of the enthusiasm that "only with much goodwill could one still perceive it."[158] Others saw larger crowds; aside from the criticism of gambling, journalists generally praised the council for its efforts to lend a "more magnificent character" to 7 September; one foreign observer judged that the celebration demonstrated "a new splendor."[159] When some of the published programs conflated the council's celebrations with those of the Sociedade Comemorativa, the society angrily protested, an indication that Gamboa considered the council's efforts to be unwelcome competition.[160] Certainly the Sociedade's traditional wooden forts and cardboard cannon paled in comparison to the council's arch and bazaar.

The city council did not repeat its efforts to promote independence celebrations in 1886. I have found no explanation for this, but when combined with the Sociedade Comemorativa's collapse after Gamboa death this meant that there were no popular festitivies on 7 September 1886. While many, as we have seen, commented that Gamboa's death was the main reason for this, the radical *Carbonário* concluded that the *povo* had finally learned "that the independence [won at] Ipiranga was nothing more than the suffocation of the republican effervescence that stirred up the free provinces"—an overly optimistic assessment.[161]

In 1887, the Sociedade Comemorativa da Independência do Império reappeared under a new board of directors headed by Senator Manoel Francisco Correia. It organized celebrations that looked very much like those of Gamboa's era, with band shells on Constitution Square, music and fireworks at night, the singing of the anthem at dawn around the statue—this time by music students and society members—followed by cheers, and a procession to the José Bonifácio statue to repeat the anthem and the cheers. The construction of a new street alongside Santo Antônio Hill made it impossible to place an artillery battery on its commanding heights, so the park was stationed in front of the barracks on the Campo da Aclamação, while fireworks would be lit on the hilltop. Later that afternoon, the society sponsored a parade of schoolchildren; in the evening, it held a *solenidade* (a formal meeting) in the city council chambers. Music and fireworks offered public entertainment on the nights of 7 and 8 September.[162]

The Comemorativa followed an almost identical program in 1888,[163] but it was clear to observers that this was no longer Gamboa's society. The *Diário de Notícias* declared in 1887 that "the traditional little angel [*anjinho*, an innocent deceased child] dressed in green and yellow"—in other words, Gamboa's Comemorativa—"gave way to the elegant representatives of Fluminense *high society*," or as the *Jornal do Comércio*'s *cronista* put it the following year, "citizens of high social standing."[164] In his keynote address at the 1887 *solenidade*, educator Joaquim Abílio Borges announced that the society's purpose was to restore the long-lost enthusiasm for 7 September celebrations, a curt dismissal of all that Gamboa had done.[165] In 1888, the *Gazeta de Notícias*'s *cronista* went further and declared that the society's efforts indicated the "ruling classes' desire to promote the means of awakening in the *povo* the sense of nationality, and in their hearts strengthen—if not implant—love of the *pátria*."[166]

The new Comemorativa's leadership came from a different class of men (and women) than in Gamboa's day.[167] Its new president, Correia, senator for Paraná since 1877, had served as minister of foreign affairs in the Conservative Rio Branco cabinet and had held important administrative positions, including the directorship of the 1872 census.[168] The vice president, Francisco Augusto de Almeida, a prominent homeopathic doctor, boasted a degree from the University of Pennsylvania and had held several government posts.[169] I have found no information on the remaining five men who held executive positions in 1887 and 1888, but Conservative party affiliations are clear from the membership in the 1887 subcommittee charged with organizing the celebrations. It included Senator Domingos José Nogueira Jaguaribe, Correia's cabinet colleague in 1871 (named the Viscount of Jaguaribe in 1888), and the prominent merchant and future senator, Manoel José Soares, a long-time Conservative activist.[170] The third member of this key committee was the second Baron of Ipanema, José Antônio Moreira Filho. The twenty directors-at-large for 1887 were a mixed lot. They included Garcia (the poet of questionable talent) and the architect, Betencourt. These throwbacks to Gamboa's era disappeared from the board in 1888, which now included ten women, perhaps schoolteachers.[171] The society's functions were not entirely restricted to Conservatives, and the keynote address at the 1888 *solenidade* was delivered by the Viscount of Ouro Preto (Afonso Celso de Assis Figueiredo), a Liberal who would preside over the empire's last cabinet. Now that slavery had been abolished, he called on Brazilians to develop their country's public education system.[172]

The society's new interest in pedagogy manifested itself in the promotion of schoolchildren's parades. These had first taken place in 1885, as part of the city council's effort to foster independence celebrations that year,[173] but they became a regular feature of the festivities only in 1887. That year the council refused to require municipal students and teachers to participate in the proposed parade, but the private Colégios Abílio (owned by Joaquim Abílio Borges) and Menezes Vieira dispatched their children for a late-afternoon parade.[174] The Abílio students, uniformed and regimented, carrying model rifles, impressed observers with their discipline and martial bearing. They also bore banners with the names of Tiradentes and Padre Roma (the martyrs of 1789 and 1817) and independence patriarchs including José Bonifácio and his brothers, José Clemente Pereira, and Gonçalves Ledo (a mix of names that included what were then republican heroes and traditional monarchist figures). Other banners featured the names of officers who had fought in the Paraguayan War, a rare allusion to the conflict in independence celebrations. The Menezes Vieira students marched in their white gymnastics uniforms, each sporting a green-and-yellow sash.[175] Six more schools joined the march, but the press scarcely took note of them. The Abílio students also distributed a pamphlet with patriotic poetry; thanks to the director's origins, it had a strongly Bahian flavor and invoked the province's independence day of 2 July alongside 7 September.[176]

Journalists hoped that more schools would participate in the future, and they were not disappointed.[177] A large number of municipal schools joined the 1888 parade; girls and boys alike participated, and they attracted large numbers of onlookers, no doubt many proud parents among them. The boys from the Colégio Italo-Brasileiro (Italian-Brazilian College) especially impressed journalists with their gymnastics demonstration.[178] The philosophy behind these parades appeared clearly in the commentary about the so-called Festa das Crianças (Children's Festival) to honor abolition. Held on 10 July 1888, this parade involved more than 2,000 students from twenty-eight municipal schools (close to a quarter of the 9,022 students enrolled in the city's ninety-four schools); it ended at the Imperial Teatro Dom Pedro II where, in Isabel's presence, the children sang anthems, recited poetry, and performed music. The *Diário de Notícias* explained that such festivals, widespread in Europe, instilled patriotism in students and "accustom[ed] them, future citizens, to life in community; [made] them more apt for social life; and regimented as they [were], instill[ed] in them the notion that in all events, in all things in life, it is necessary to maintain order."[179] These children's parades constituted the first steps on the long road that finally ended in the massed student choirs that filled soccer stadiums during independence-day celebrations under the Estado Novo dictatorship of 1937–45 (see the Conclusion).

The new Sociedade Comemorativa also had connections to other efforts to uplift and discipline the lower classes. Senator Correia had long promoted popular education in Rio de Janeiro.[180] From 1883 to 1886, he presided over the annual 7 September *solenidade* of the União Operária (Worker's Union), founded in 1882. These were rather stuffy affairs, consisting mostly of speeches by prominent men (often senators), music, and occasionally poetry readings or speeches by workers. The imperial family regularly attended these ceremonies, normally held in the afternoon in the São Pedro Theater's salon; in 1884, "the foreman of the government machine-shops" addressed the imperial family.[181] That year, the União also freed six slaves with funds raised by employees at the naval arsenal.[182] By the terms of its statutes, the União sought to "promote the general interests of the working class and of the country's trades"; not a mutual aid society, its main purpose was to break "the chains of ignorance" by promoting education among its members, mostly skilled workers in government employ.[183] In 1889, a *Gazeta de Notícias cronista* described the workers' 7 September meeting as a function "during which the festive meaning of the day was made known to the *povo.*"[184]

While one historian has described the União as a republican society, its close ties to the monarchy suggest otherwise.[185] In fact, the União's links to the official world drew regular criticism from the radical press. In 1882, Apulco de Castro condemned "a certain so-and-so Possidônio" and other "rascals, friends of easy jobs, . . . who go around pretending to be workers" and who sought government monies to celebrate 7 September on Constitution Square and in the São Pedro theater.[186] This connection between the União Operária and the Gamboa-era Comemorativa reinforces the other evidence about the latter's working-class origins, but Apulco's criticism also highlights the disdain that radicals felt for such societies' linkages to the monarchy. Three years later, Patrocínio's *Gazeta da Tarde* condemned Hudson for reading an address in verse to Princess Isabel at the União Operária *solenidade*, despite his well-known republican sympathies (he had signed the 1870 republican manifesto).[187] In 1889, *Carbonário* castigated the União for holding a ceremony from which members of the *povo* were excluded.[188]

The new Sociedade Comemorativa clearly enjoyed more resources than Gamboa's perpetually cash-strapped society. In 1888, it acquired a handsome silk banner for its parades and had the standard blessed in Sacramento Parish's church. It featured the equestrian statue, the Southern Cross, and an angel of liberty holding broken chains in one hand

and a crown for Pedro I in the other.[189] In both 1887 and 1888 it published a magazine to record its activities, in which it also reprinted the favorable press coverage. Both issues of the magazine listed extensive credits as the society thanked individuals and companies who had made cash donations or gifts-in-kind to support the festival. In both years, the Banco Mercantil rented the São Pedro Theater for the society's use, and streetcar companies transported students for free.[190] The society's *solenidades* attracted many "ladies and gentlemen" in 1888 and a "large number of distinguished families and gentlemen of high social position" in 1887.[191] By the society's own account, these worthies listened attentively to Borges's hour-long speech "on the important events in the history of this nation, for which Divine Providence reserves a brilliant future."[192]

While high society packed the city council building in 1887, "the extraordinary concourse of *povo*" in downtown streets and squares ensured that the day was "truly festive." As in Gamboa's day, crowds had started gathering on Constitution Square in the wee hours of the morning; so packed was the square that people had difficulty walking.[193] While some, including the society itself, repeated these assessments for 1888, others offered more critical views.[194] Raul Pompéia saw but a "small number of onlookers" at dawn and judged "the city absent from the national rejoicing." Likewise, a *Diário de Notícias cronista* observed only a cold "indifference." He went further and argued that the last real "popular celebration" on 7 September had taken place in 1848, when anti-Portuguese nativism and radical liberals' efforts to win the city elections had led to violence.[195] That these republicans should have dismissed the popular festivities and recalled the last great radical-liberal demonstrations on a day of national festivity is consistent both with their rejection of the monarchy and their evolution from radical liberalism.

A new design for the band shells on Constitution Square prompted much debate in 1888. Instead of the traditional forts, the society put up two octagonal pavilions, supported by sixteen columns, in which illuminated portraits of Pedro I and Pedro II faced the statue, surrounded by small shields that featured important dates in each emperor's reign.[196] Such ephemeral structures, common in earlier decades, now looked hopelessly old-fashioned. A writer in the *Diário de Notícias* called on the police to ban such "shameful manifestations of bad taste," while a *Gazeta de Notícias cronista* remarked that the illuminated emperor looked like he was suffering from "a neuralgia that inflame[d] his whole face and twist[ed] his features into an expression of pain that made him worthy of pity."[197] By contrast, Pompéia mustered some grudging words of praise for the new design (at least in comparison to the old traditional forts), but *Novidades* reported that one "old man" disliked the new decorations, an effective way of dismissing the previous years' decorations as old-fashioned.[198]

The reorganized Sociedade Comemorativa had clearly failed to satisfy all. While it marked a notable departure from the old society, it retained many of the forms of the traditional festivities, which can be read as evidence of an enduring tradition. However, it also reflected a suspicion of the popular classes, well captured by Laet's assessment of 1887's concluding fireworks display: "Thus it is once again proven that popular gatherings, always dangerous when it comes to listening to opposition speeches, are perfectly inoffensive when it comes to enjoying orderly fireworks."[199] These celebrations of independence furthermore raise the question of the monarchy's popularity, to which we now turn.

THE POPULAR MONARCHY, 1888–1889

During the final eighteen months of Brazil's imperial regime, the monarchy enjoyed unprecedented popularity in Rio de Janeiro. Already visible in the celebrations following the end of slavery, this popularity peaked later that winter, when Pedro returned from medical treatment in Europe.[200] Once again, the capital staged a traditional reception for its ruler, and even the planter-republican *Novidades* had to admit that, "regardless of the political leanings of each Brazilian citizen, his personal feeling is one of joy at seeing the Brazilian sovereign return to the *pátria*."[201] The degree to which this sentiment extended deeply into urban society was sharply revealed by the campaign to prepare the so-called popular album for presentation to Pedro on his birthday. A massive crowd of lower-class well-wishers thronged the downtown palace, much to the dismay of those who thought this an undignified spectacle and a dangerous example of street politics. The creation of the Guarda Negra and the celebrations of abolition's first anniversary further highlighted this popular political involvement, but there are indications that the monarchy's popularity was ebbing by mid-1889.

Pedro returned from his third journey to Europe on 22 August 1888. Once again, Rio de Janeiro had prepared an elaborate welcome for its emperor, one whose form closely resembled those of 1872 and 1877. The government decreed a holiday for civil servants, and newspapers eagerly anticipated the celebrations and filled many pages with descriptions of what one *cronista* described as "all that old-fashioned jubilation of magnificent days" and the "exaggerated rhetoric of great occasions" that constituted the "noisy and spectacular demonstration of national enthusiasm."[202] Warships, accompanied by numerous boats and launches, set out early in the morning to greet the *Congo*, the liner on which he was traveling. The emperor and empress landed at the navy yard to a tumultuous reception; crowds had been gathering there since 4:00 am and so packed the grounds that it was difficult for officials to force their way in. Isabel and Eu welcomed Pedro and Teresa Cristina and joined them for the short ride in an open landau through the crowded and decorated Primeiro de Março Street to the imperial chapel for a "short prayer." They lunched in the downtown palace and watched the Second Cavalry Regiment fire salutes. Three hundred municipal schoolchildren formed an honor guard at the navy yard and paraded past the palace; they then hurried to the Campo da Aclamação to form another honor guard.[203]

Once again, the city was elaborately decorated with arches, banners, and illuminations; band shells stood on all the major squares. Companies, corporations, and neighborhood commissions contributed to these decorations, which, according to *Novidades*, gave the city "a new celebratory air, an unusual feeling of profound contentment."[204] Among the decorations, the fire brigade's "seven beautiful arches of leaves" stood out, thanks to their clever incorporation of firefighting equipment. Granado Pharmacy on Primeiro de Março Street received special praise for its handsomely ornamented façade, which featured a portrait of Pedro, Teresa Cristina, and Prince Pedro Augusto (Figure 10.5).[205] I have found no indication of this celebration's cost, but the Chamber of Commerce alone reportedly spent 21 contos (US$10,710) on Primeiro de Março and its headquarters; a gust of wind on the 24th destroyed two candelabra alone worth 1,700 mil-réis (US$867).[206] As he had done in 1877, Pedro grumbled that the money could have been better spent on "a useful public institution" such as a maternity clinic.[207] Two *cronistas* heard rumors that more than 100 contos (US$51,000) had been collected but thought the decorations ridiculously old-fashioned, unworthy even of a country village. The illuminated imperial portraits at the Chamber of Commerce were so badly done that Laet, firmly monarchist, reportedly remarked that they must have been painted by Antônio da Silva Jardim, a well-known republican.[208]

One unusual demonstration took place on the morning of 22 August. Taking up a challenge issued by sixty-six "of the most distinguished high-society ladies," seventeen students at the Escola Militar scaled Sugar Loaf Mountain and hung a large banner with the word "*Salve*" (Hail) on the peak's sea side so that Pedro would see this greeting as his ship approached the bar. They had climbed up the day before and periodically launched fireworks during the night. At dawn, they raised the national flag, and when the *Congo* entered the harbor, they moved the banner to the bay side so that all could see it (Figure 10.6).[209] At the time, few had climbed Sugar Loaf, and the students' feat was often recalled later, but not without a sense of irony, given that many of them took part in the coup that overthrew Pedro fifteen months later.[210]

FIGURE 10.5.
Granado Pharmacy decorated for Pedro II's return, August 1888.

Source: "Homenagem da Drogaria Granado ao regresso de SS. MM. Imperiaes." *AIHGB*, IM, 1.1.68 foto. Courtesy Instituto Histórico e Geográfico Brasileiro.

As a *Jornal do Comércio cronista* put it, "the government organized an official reception worthy of the sovereigns, thus joining in the general jubilant feeling of the Corte's population." A *Novidades cronista*

FIGURE 10.6.
Cadets welcoming Pedro II from Sugar Loaf Mountain, 22 August 1888.
Note that this image is dated before the students accomplished
this feat on 20 Aug. 1888.
Source: Revista Illustrada, 18 Aug. 1888.

wrote more disdainfully about the government's role: "By its third directory, the ministry of empire regulates public rejoicing. Everying scheduled, ordered, carefully considered. Joy by program."[211] Other observers stressed that Pedro had been welcomed back with unprecedented
popular enthusiasm. Nabuco judged that the official festivities paled
in comparison to "the waves of *povo*" who dominated the festival. At
the navy yard's entrance, Raul Pompéia, no friend of monarchy, saw "a
poor old woman," overcome with emotion, "drying tears on the back
of her hand."[212] Eu perceptively noted however, that this was "a totally
personal homage," and he privately worried about republicanism's in-
roads; in its editorials leading up to Pedro's return, *Carbonário* likewise stressed that the festivities would honor Pedro personally.[213] Others
wondered whether Pedro was physically capable of assuming the reins
of government.[214] Most editorialists attributed the popular support for

Pedro to the recent abolition of slavery, but *Novidades* noted that Brazil was "a nation . . . in crisis" whose institutions were teetering on the brink of collapse thanks to the overhasty ending of slavery.[215]

Officially, the celebrations of Pedro's return would continue for three nights with the usual music, fireworks, parading, and illuminations, but they in fact lasted more than two weeks and merged into the independence celebrations. On 22 August, the União Operária, children from the orphanage and both public and private schools, and carnival societies paraded on Ouvidor Street. The Fenianos carnival club circulated more widely, "raising enthusiastic cheers to the imperial family."[216] The illuminated streets and squares were packed with people on the 22nd and the 23rd, but rain on the next night reduced the crowds.[217] Onze de Julho Square was especially well decorated by its residents for the three days of official celebrations, but São Cristóvão's committee resolved to delay its festivities until the 26th, likely to attract more people; because of bad weather, they were further delayed until 3 September.[218] On 25 August, the schoolchildren's battalion paraded in the neighborhoods around the Campo da Aclamação but could not demonstrate its skill at drill because of the "crowd of *povo*." For those who did not wish to rub elbows with the *povo* on the street, the Jockey and Derby Clubs held balls on the 23rd and the 24th.[219] A fireworks display on Botafogo beach on 2 September, paid for by the Chamber of Commerce's "central commission for the festivities," drew mixed assessments. A massive crowd—30,000 to 40,000 people—gathered, and Pedro arrived punctually at 7:00 pm; from the pavillion constructed for the occasion, he watched a flotilla of small ships salute him from the bay. The fireworks themselves only began after 9:00 pm, by which time the imperial family had already left. The *Diário de Notícias*'s *cronista* was unimpressed: "I saw nothing that I hadn't already admired in the village celebrations of my youth."[220]

An astonishing number of societies, corporations, and municipalities designated commissions to congratulate Pedro and Teresa Cristina. A "popular subscription" led by Captain Domingos da Silva Lisboa raised funds to prepare a diamond-encrusted "laurel crown" to be presented to the empress on 27 August.[221] Until well into September, the *Jornal do Comércio* listed such congratulations and presentations.[222] Among them were Africans. In mid-September, the Sociedade Vida Nova União da Nação Cabinda (New Life Union of the Cabinda Nation Society) planned a march to the palace to demonstrate their "profound love [for] and recognition of the father of the August Redeemer of the black race" and to congratulate him on his restored health and his "happy return to the *Pátria*."[223]

Such demonstrations of popular, Afro-Brazilian support for the monarchy presaged the dramatic events of Pedro's sixty-third birthday, the last that he would celebrate in Brazil. Thanks to Pompéia's *crônica*, some aspects of the incident are relatively well known. This republican described how the downtown palace was "surrounded and invaded by an immense mob of the popular classes, mostly men of color," who sought to present Pedro with a commemorative album in honor of his return. He added that Dom Obá II, an honorary army *alferes* and self-styled African ruler, was arrested for having dishonored his uniform by decorating it with "excessively African feathers." Moreover, the police had to force some "citizens" to don shirts before they entered the palace.[224] The press devoted considerable attention to this demonstration; its accounts reveal some of the nuances of this popular monarchism and allow us to go further than merely reading Pompéia's disdainful remarks against the grain.

The demonstration's origins lay in a "worker association's" campaign to prepare the popular album to honor the emperor's recent return from Europe.[225] Another example of the reciprocal relationship between elite or official and popular civic rituals, the album campaign echoed two earlier such presentations. On 2 December 1887, press representatives presented Isabel with a booklet that reprinted eleven classic poems in honor of her father.[226] For Pedro's return, the Barons of Loreto and Paranapiacaba, along with the city archivist, Pires de Almeida, prepared a polyanthea, a collection of autograph dedications to the monarch to be presented on 7 September. Eighty-seven leading political, literary, and cultural figures (the "country's enlightened classes" or the "national intelligentsia") contributed to this document, which in a later printed edition runs to 170 pages.[227]

The workers' association apparently sought to emulate the polyanthea contributors. It prepared a "popular album of congratulations for Their Imperial Majesties" to be presented by a "grand civic procession" from the Campo da Aclamação to the downtown palace on 2 December. I have not been able to identify with certainty any of the four men whose names appear on this printed invitation to corporations and societies to participate in the procession, but José Ponciano de Oliveira, the secretary, may be the same Ponciano de Oliveira listed as a founder of the União Operária and later described as a sometime fund-raiser for the Sociedade Comemorativa.[228] That the invitations were printed indicates that the society had at least some resources. Literary and cultural figures were not entirely excluded from this campaign, and Laet, who had contributed to the polyanthea, wrote a dedication in which he described the signatories as representing "all of this vast capital's social classes" who congratulated Pedro on his recovery and his safe return, as well as on slavery's abolition.[229] The signatures filled fully 554 manuscript pages, and *O País* reported that they numbered more than 9,000. Several journalists noted the attractive and ingeniously designed binding, no doubt the loving handiwork of a city artisan.[230]

To be sure, literacy limited participation in the album campaign, but this limit should not be exaggerated. The 1890 census revealed that 57.9 percent of Rio de Janeiro's male population claimed literacy, and there were other ways to participate besides signing the album, including joining the procession.[231] No observer offered any indication of how many people did so, but journalists listed some of the societies involved. They included labor organizations (the employees of a textile mill and the Associação dos Artistas Brasileiros Trabalho e Moralidade [Work and Morality Association of Brazilian Artisans]), students from the Colégio Italo-Brasileiro, a Paraguayan War veterans' association, mutual aid societies, the Clube Independência Dois de Julho (2 July Independence Club, perhaps a society of Bahian expatriates), music societies, and Afro-Brazilian carnival societies. The latter included the Sociedade F. J. C. C. I. dos Africanos, the União dos Lanceiros (Union of Lancers), the Triunfo dos Cucumbis (Triumph of the Cucumbis), and the Cucumbis Carnavalescos (Carnivalesque Cucumbis); resplendent in their colorful tunics and gleaming helmets, the Cucumbis danced at the procession's head. Cucumbis were, according to Mello Moraes Filho, musical societies recently created by Afro-Bahians who had migrated to Rio de Janeiro; he judged Lanceiros and Triunfo the most skilled and disciplined in their music and dance. The organizers had also obtained army, navy, and police bands to enliven the procession; all told, ten bands participated.[232]

That Pedro's birthday fell on a Sunday in 1888 no doubt helped to ensure that a "great mass of *povo*" joined the procession as it entered the downtown "with some disorder in its ranks, which made its appearance even more picturesque," according to a favorable *Gazeta de Notícias* reporter.[233] Most of the crowd waited outside while many society representatives went into the palace to offer the album to Pedro. The presentation "did not take place, however, with the regular pomp and the prescribed etiquette of official ceremonies," but the *Jornal do Comércio*'s *cronista* nevertheless judged it a sincere demonstration of popular affection for the emperor.[234] The album committee's spokesman was Joaquim Silvério de Azevedo Pimentel, a Paraguayan War veteran and minor writer, a detail which confirms Pompéia's pointed remark that none of the "contributors to the congratulatory literature," Laet among them, desired to associate themselves with the popular societies, much less the *povo* who had joined the parade.[235]

Although he apparently represented none of the societies involved in the album and the procession, Dom Obá II, dapperly dressed in his feather-bedecked uniform, also entered the palace and, according to *O Mequetrefe*'s *cronista*, led the crowd in cheers from one of the palace windows.[236] Valentim Magalhães watched Obá leave the palace in a tilbury, "after having held a *beija-mão* for some Mina blacks." Some of the "irreverent street children [*molecada*]" mocked Obá as his coach pulled away, and "a loyal subject of the prince protested furiously against the boos, requesting respect, with good reason, for the place and the day and shouting that the uproar was a national disgrace."[237] A few days later, army authorities arrested Obá for his failure to respect the uniform but not before he registered a complaint with *Carbonário*, the radical newspaper that most frequently published his paid articles.[238]

Thanks to Eduardo Silva's biography of Dom Obá II, the prince of the people is a well-known figure and is now understood to exemplify Rio de Janeiro's African and Afro-Brazilian street culture and its strong ties to the monarchy.[239] While Obá regularly attended Saturday public audiences at the São Cristóvão palace, no fewer than 125 times between June 1882 and December 1884, and, according to Mello Moraes Filho, often attended levees at the palace on days of national festivity, his presence at civic rituals is very rarely mentioned before the 2 December 1888 incident and never by the major newspapers.[240] *Corsário Júnior* saw him at the 2 December 1882 inauguration of the new city hall, and a fictional black man complained in patois that the uniform that Obá wore to the 2 December 1885 Livro de Ouro ceremony was so worn out that it was unworthy of the prince (he declared that he and his companions would raise funds to buy a new one).[241] Finally, it is possible that the third figure from the right in Figure 10.2 is meant to represent him. This lack of evidence may indicate that Obá's prominence was a phenomenon only of the very late 1880s, but it is also possible that the mainstream press simply ignored what most journalists must have considered an embarrassing and eccentric crank, despite (or because of) the respect that some Afro-Brazilians nurtured for him.

As the crowd dispersed after the album's presentation, part of the procession proceeded up Ouvidor Street to salute newspaper editorial offices. Wearing their Sunday best, some of the marchers sported flowers on their lapels, likely camellias, a symbol of the abolition movement. At night, according to Magalhães, Ouvidor Street—the traditional preserve of high society—was deserted, but wherever there were illuminations, "the concourse [of people] was large and the revelry not small," a rare indication of popular street celebrations on Pedro's birthday.[242]

A few journalists attempted to make sense of this unexpected popular incursion into the official civic ritual on Pedro's birthday. The *Jornal do Comércio*'s *cronista* thought that it exemplified the *povo*'s "profound esteem" for the monarch, while a *Diário de Notícias* commentator judged it a marked contrast to all of the "republican agitation."[243] We have already noted Pompéia's disdain for the shirtless black patriots; Filinto de Almeida judged their parade "so ridiculous, so burlesque," that only an accompaniment of Offenbach's music would do justice to his report for *A Província de São Paulo*. *O Mequetrefe* condemned the unspecified demagogues who described the procession as unworthy of the "civilized nations of the Old and New World." João Coelho Bastos, Rio de Janeiro's chief of police under the Cotegipe cabinet, known for his rough treatment of recaptured fugitive slaves, whose heads he ordered shaved, reportedly muttered: "If I had caught them in my day . . . I would have had to scrape many coconuts [*muito coco tinha que rapar*]," in other words, shave many heads. While criticizing Coelho Bastos, this illustrated periodical had nothing good to say about Obá's participation.[244]

No other celebration approached Pedro's birthday in the scale of its popular participation, but on 28 September, when the papacy conferred the Golden Rose on Isabel, Pompéia remarked on the "aristocracy's" sparse attendance and the "petty *povo*'s invasion" of the imperial chapel.[245] This decoration sealed her image as a fervent Catholic at odds with the liberal and secular Brazilian political class. The date of this ceremony, the anniversary of both the 1871 Free Womb Law and the 1885 liberation of sexagenarians, is also normally given as the day on which José do Patrocínio founded the Guarda Negra (Black Guard). Critics dismissed this association of black defenders of Isabel as thugs and *capoeiras* enlisted by the João Alfredo cabinet to intimidate republicans, none more bluntly than Rui Barbosa, who declared in March 1889, soon after he took over editorship of the *Diário de Notícias*, that "the grotesque African idols of the slave quarters . . . have given way to the fetishism of court idolatry, worthy of a nation of unwitting freedpeople."[246] More recent historians have tended to see the Guard as a legitimate expression of black political activism. Despite its prominence in violent incidents such as the disruption of a republican meeting on 30 December 1888 and its members' fervent support for the monarchy, and especially for Isabel, the Guard was not mentioned as a participant in the 2 December album popular presentation nor indeed in the coverage of any of the other days of national festivity after abolition.[247]

The constitution's anniversary in 1889 passed unnoticed by the press, save for routine reports on the official rituals for which Pedro and Teresa Cristina briefly came down from Petrópolis and the few brief editorials about the flexibility of Brazil's institutions that we noted in the last chapter.[248] By contrast, 13 May 1889 was a major festival.[249] The *Diário de Notícias* announced that the program was "exclusively popular," and indeed it did not include a levee at the palace, but other elements of official civic ritual took place, and the government decreed a one-day holiday.[250] At dawn, artillery salutes and fireworks announced the start of the celebrations, and bands were on hand to play the national anthem in major squares. Public buildings were decorated. Pedro and the rest of the imperial family arrived from Petrópolis late in the morning to attend mass at the Rosary church, a function organized by the Associação Comemorativa da Libertação (Association for the Commemoration of

Liberation) and the black brotherhood to which the church belonged. The bishop had ordered masses said in all parish churches, and the imperial family went from the Rosary church to the nearby São Francisco church for this service. They then attended the Confederação Abolicionista's *solendidade* in the Imperial Teatro Dom Pedro II. By late afternoon, Pedro was at the downtown palace to receive congratulations from civil society groups; he reviewed a small military parade and received repeated cheers from the crowds that thronged the palace environs. A lengthy series of processions completed the outdoor ceremonies.[251] That evening, all of the city's theaters put on galas, but the imperial family apparently returned to Petrópolis.

From late afternoon until well into the evening, numerous groups paraded down Ouvidor Street, among them children from the orphanage; municipal schoolchildren and students from the Liceu, led by Betencourt da Silva, who presented Isabel with a "rich civic crown"; and the Centro Tipográfico Treze de Maio (May Thirteenth Typographical Center), which included several allegorical floats, including one featuring a portrait of Gutenberg (the major newspapers joined this with floats that bore their standards).[252] At 6:00 pm, a group of "men of color" paraded; led by horsemen, they carried lanterns and marched in orderly ranks. Patrocínio's *Cidade do Rio* had announced that the men, "accompanied by their families," would carry a laurel crown and a spray of flowers to present to Isabel and João Alfredo.[253] "Upper-class youth" gathered in front of the *Diário de Notícias* building to protect the republican organ; to them, the marchers resembled the Guarda Negra. As the procession passed, a scuffle broke out, and people inside the offices heard a pistol shot but did not know whether anyone was hurt.[254] *Carbonário* later complained that the police had arrested some men for making republican statements in the crowd around the palace. The authorities did not, however, prevent other groups from daring republicans to show their faces so that they could be roughed up.[255] Nevertheless, the chief of police reported that nothing had disturbed public order.[256]

These incidents hint at the latent racial tensions that underlay the celebration. For some, the parade of black men was deeply worrisome. Indeed, all three republican newspapers had detected "grave indications of [impending] anarchy" in early May; Euclides da Cunha wrote to *A Província de São Paulo* that 13 May's celebration would amount to a "nineteenth-century barbarian invasion."[257] Merchants along Ouvidor Street apparently failed to illuminate the street's gaslight arches out of disdain for the "the little blacks' [*pretinhos*'] celebrations."[258] That day, Pedro pardoned just over 100 slaves sentenced to life in prison under the terms of an 1835 law that had stiffened penalties for violent slave resistance.[259] Although favorably received when it was first mooted, the pardon was soon condemned for freeing a "gang of bandits, assassins" who would only swell the ranks of Isabel's supporters and stimulate "race hatred."[260] Others, like Filinto de Almeida, condemned anything that smacked of racial identification, an effective way of silencing black claims, and accused abolitionists of promoting "race war."[261]

Editorials in two of the republican newspapers—Rui Barbosa's *Diário de Notícias* and the *Gazeta da Tarde*—emphasized the role of slaves and the *povo* in winning abolition in order to downplay the role of the monarchy; the *Gazeta* drew specific analogies to independence, also a popular victory in its view, and also one diverted by the monarchy. *Carbonário* lamented that, in the year that marked the centenary of the French Revolution, Brazilians were celebrating Isabel's role in abolition. *Novidades* went further and condemned the "official abolitionism" that sang "hosanas to the cabinet" and bemoaned the state of abandonment in which the government had left planters. As far as the newly freed people were concerned, government inaction had left them to be ruled by their "instincts."[262] In a signed editorial, Quintino Bocaiúva recalled the peaceful abolition and "noble resignation" of slaveowners who did not resist slavery's end but lamented the efforts "to transform the new citizens, still enslaved by ignorance, into political instruments," an allusion to the Guarda Negra; instead of an "honest force of laborers," these men had become a "terrorist legion designed to constrain the liberty of other citizens" who disagreed with them.[263]

The *Jornal do Comércio* took a considerably more generous view and argued that the Golden Law's beneficiaries "have not caused any worries nor any disorder that would inspire concern about national prosperity." So did the *Gazeta de Notícias*, which pointed out that the fears of "labor's disorganization" had largely been unfounded. Patrocínio's *Cidade do Rio* contrasted slaveowners' demands for compensation with ex-slaves' contentment at having received "merely liberty." The Liberal Party's *Tribuna Liberal* argued that it was impossible for ex-slaves and ex-masters to eye each other with hatred, for they were like family: "the black woman, always . . . ready to offer her strong and healthy blood via the milk of her breasts to her master's son," ensured feelings of "fraternity" between the grandsons of Europeans and Africans. After this Freyrean image of social harmony, the *Tribuna* went on to suggest that the *povo* would not be fooled by the government-funded celebrations and that all would remember that João Alfredo had been a late convert to abolitionism and had opposed the 1885 law. In the *Diário de Notícias*'s Republican Party column, Lopes Trovão explained that republicans' alliance with monarchist abolitionists had been a difficult tactical decision and now called on his "black brothers" to look past the monarchist celebrations to the republic, a regime of true liberty.[264]

On 11 May, exactly one year after his original proposal, Afonso Celso Jr. again requested that parliament take up his bill to declare the date of abolition a day of national festivity. After some procedural wrangling, the bill came to the floor on the 17th and was quickly quashed. Afonso Celso's fellow Liberal, Aristides de Sousa Espinola, argued that officially designated "celebrations" were "completely ridiculous"; counting Sundays and saints' days, the country had far too many holidays already, and "days of celebration" were actually "days of mourning and sadness, for they cause a notable diminution in production." Furthermore, given that the chamber was then debating a bill to suppress vagrancy, it made no sense to encourage idleness. "Those elaborate ceremonies," he concluded, referring to the traditional official rituals "that dazzled our grandparents, no longer move us; they leave us indifferent, if they don't provoke laughter."[265] The notorious antiabolitionist Domingos de Andrade Figueira, one of the few deputies who had voted against the Golden Law, shared Espinola's concerns and argued that it would be cruel for the government to mandate the official celebration of a measure that had harmed the material interests of so many people. Those who favored abolition had taken it on themselves to celebrate on the 13th, and it would be inappropriate for the government to get involved. A Ceará Liberal further questioned the cabinet on how much it had subsidized the celebrations of four days earlier.[266] The debate failed to hold deputies' attention, and the session lost quorum before a vote could be held; three days later, they rejected the bill.[267]

His earlier remarks about race war notwithstanding, Filinto de Almeida hoped that future anniversaries of abolition would be celebrated as enthusiastically and as peacefully as the day had been in 1889.[268] Nevertheless, the defeat of Afonso Celso's bill and the critical commentary on the celebrations revealed the conflicts over abolition's meaning and the struggles to construct a new and satisfactory social order. A proposal to erect a monument to abolition, designed by two Italian artists, went nowhere, despite some favorable press commentary on the maquette displayed on 13 May. On top of a large, octagonal column, a figure representing abolition or liberty holding the "diploma of redemption" stood, surrounded by slaves. The base of the pedestal featured bas-reliefs of commerce, industry, navigation, and agriculture, all presumably destined to progress as a result of slavery's end.[269] In short, the issues raised by abolition were far from resolved on the Golden Law's first anniversary; deputies could not stomach designating 13 May as a day of national festivity, much less agree on an interpretation to cast in bronze and to carve into stone.

The last day of national festivity celebrated under the empire came in a tense political context. In early June, João Alfredo's conservative cabinet fell; after much difficulty, the Viscount of Ouro Preto put together a Liberal cabinet that obtained a dissolution and used all means fair and foul to win the 31 August elections. The new cabinet, less closely connected to the São Paulo planter class than João Alfredo's ministry had been, pursued an aggressive expansionary monetary policy that "provoked a false boom" and led directly to the speculative bubble, the Encilhamento, of the early republic. This prosperity could not disguise the fact that Pedro was no longer able to manage the country's affairs, and few of the political class thought Isabel capable of governing in her own right.[270] The long-simmering military question—tensions between army officers and the government—gained a new dimension when the new cabinet moved to revitalize the old National Guard. Rumor had it that the Count of Eu was behind this measure, an alleged plot to replace the army with the Guard.[271] All of this was grist for the mill of the republican conspirators who joined with disaffected army officers to overthrow the monarchy on 15 November 1889.

Before this, however, the empire celebrated Brazil's independence one last time. Editorials on 7 September 1889 reflected deep political divisions. Progovernment and monarchist newspapers hailed the stability of Brazil's institutions, commended Brazilians for their love of the *pátria*, and celebrated the achievement of abolition, but the *Jornal do Comércio*'s editor had already been complaining about how difficult it was to defend an antirepublican position.[272] Republican newspapers, like *O País*, reminded readers that the nation's "democratic spirit and republican aspirations" had been thwarted back in 1822 and 1831 and called on citizens to take action in defence of liberty.[273] The Sociedade Comemorativa once again set to work decorating Constitution Square, and an extraordinarily large crowd was on hand to hear five military bands play the independence anthem at dawn. Most newspapers shared this favorable assessment by the *Jornal do Comércio*.[274] By contrast, Barbosa's republican *Diário de Notícias* declared in its editorial that "the legend of 7 September . . . in its glorification of the despot of the equestrian statue, is worth no more than the cardboard of the ridiculous castles that today surround" the monument; it also judged the square to have been deserted and saw little enthusiasm. *Novidades* admitted that the streets had a "cheerful appearance" but thought it all "inconsequential amusement."[275] The old pattern of politicized portrayals of civic celebrations, already visible in the coverage of 13 May, had reasserted itself with a vengeance.

The Sociedade Comemorativa, closely associated with Conservatives in 1887 and 1888, may have undergone changes in the three months between the appointment of the Ouro Preto cabinet and 7 September. The press coverage of its *solenidade* made no reference to the society's leadership; instead Prince Pedro Augusto presided over the session and gave his first public speech, in which he reviewed Brazil's history and "hailed the brilliant future reserved for Brazil." Deputy Afonso Celso Jr., son of the president of the council of ministers and author of the failed bill to make 13 May into a day of national festivity, then spoke about Brazil's peaceful history and the country's ability to achieve great things such as independence and abolition without serious conflict.[276] *Novidades* grudgingly acknowledged that the prince had made an effective public debut, but a radical republican weekly thought that putting him on the program was ridiculous, condemned his superficial understanding of history and his naïve respect for his forebears, and judged the whole session a fiasco.[277] For some time, the prince, the oldest son of Princess Leopoldina, raised in Brazil after his mother's untimely death, had been clumsily plotting to replace his aunt, Isabel, and his appearance at the ceremony may have been an effort to burnish his image.[278] The by now traditional parade of schoolchildren drew much favorable comment, and the imperial family again attended the União Operária's *solenidade*. *Carbonário* complained that this function—in its view, the only part of the festivities that might have had a "pronounced popular character"—amounted to a gathering of high society from which "the *povo* [stood] out by its absence."[279] Dom Obá II showed up at the levee but apparently remained in the palace lobby and caused no scandal.[280]

The parade of officers in the new National Guard attracted considerable attention. Resplendent in their colorful new uniforms, complete with Prussian-style helmets topped by red-and-white feather plumes, they marched up a crowded Ouvidor Street after the levee. At the intersection of Gonçalves Dias Street, some "lads" made fun of the officers. None of the many press accounts reported what they said, but the insults apparently involved the uniforms and the officers' physical attributes. Some officers took offence, drew their swords, and sought satisfaction. Others tried to arrest those responsible. No serious injuries resulted from the scuffle, mostly because the narrow street was too crowded for the officers to wield their weapons effectively.[281]

Were it not for the spectacle of National Guard officers descending from their dignity to win satisfaction from those who had insulted them and the efforts to burnish an erratic prince's reputation, journalists would have had little to write about on 7 September 1889. This day of national festivity offered neither the enthusiastic popular monarchism of Pedro's return, the previous year's independence day, and Pedro's birthday, nor the novelty of a Sociedade Comemorativa closely connected to the Conservative cabinet seeking to revitalize, update, and control traditional popular festivities, nor the lively celebrations of abolition and its first anniversary. It looked like the popular monarchism stimulated by slavery's end had run its course.

The popular festivities of independence suggest that the imperial state's ideology, the official view of independence as exemplified by the equestrian statue, resonated among Rio de Janeiro's free lower classes.

The *Jornal do Comércio* dismissed this in 1888 as the product of the *povo*'s failure to undertake "historical investigations," which would have led its members to realize that 1789 and 1817 were necessary precursors to 1822.[282] This concession to republican harping on the Inconfidência Mineira and the Pernambucan rebellion is telling evidence of the critics' success, while the denial that members of the *povo* could have their own view of history returns us to the issue of cultural interaction between elite and *povo*. The lessons of those who advocated the equestrian statue and celebrated Pedro I in the 1850s and 1860s had been learned—all too well, in fact—by the *povo*. To be sure, it is difficult to elucidate the views of the thousands who gave up hours of sleep to celebrate independence on Constitution Square, but their many critics and diminishing number of supporters reveal not just worries about the control of national symbols by members of the popular classes but also the *povo*'s stubborn loyalty to symbols already widely rejected among the elite. The efforts to bring the popular festivities under control— abortive in the mid-1870s and more successful in 1887–88—suggest a growing concern with the city's lower classes and their control over civic ritual, a concern that gained urgency in light of the impending end of slavery. The Conservative cabinets mostly sought to channel the popular patriotism and appear to have been more successful in this regard than the last Liberal cabinet on the sole day of national festivity that took place under its administration.

Even as the popular celebrations of the monarchy peaked in 1888–89, the press coverage demonstrated an undertone of disdain and worry. Just as the Sociedade Comemorativa looked more and more old-fashioned by the early 1880s, so too the custom of decorating façades, raising arches, and illuminating buildings looked out of date by the end of the decade. The popular demonstrations of support for Isabel and Pedro may have been acceptable in the aftermath of abolition and at the time of Pedro's return, but when they disrupted official rituals or took institutional form as the Guarda Negra, they were too dangerous. Those who did not want to see a popular monarchy moved to put an end to the imperial regime in November 1889.

Republican Innovations in the 1890s

On 15 November 1889, a military coup put an end to the empire and established a provisional republic. Within two days, Pedro II and his family were en route to exile, and the republican leadership turned to the task of consolidating the new regime. In short order, the provisional government designed new state symbols, instituted a new civic calendar, and changed street names associated with the monarchy to suitably republican ones. Enthusiastic republicans signed their correspondence with "Health and Fraternity [*Saúde e Fraternidade*]," a clumsy translation of the French Revolutionaries' "*Salut et Fraternité*," rather than the traditional "God keep your Excellency."[1] For a few years in the 1890s, republicans of various stripes promoted celebrations on the new days of national festivity to spread their message. Just as the French revolutionaries on whom the Brazilian republicans self-consciously modeled themselves discovered, it was not so easy to transform a society through ritual, and while much changed in Brazilian civic culture, later republican governments eventually made peace with the empire.[2] Twentieth-century Brazilian regimes, particularly the authoritarian ones, sought legitimacy through exalting independence heroes and linking themselves to the country's long history.

While republicans had long advocated the monarchy's overthrow, and tensions between the government and the army had long been simmering, the 15 November coup came as a surprise to many, including Pedro himself, who submitted quietly to the new state of affairs. The military coup had brought together a disparate group of discontents. Nominally under the leadership of Marshal Deodoro da Fonseca, an elderly officer who had had disagreements with the cabinet but had demonstrated no republican proclivities, the conspiracy was strongly influenced by Benjamin Constant Botelho de Magalhães, a positivist and mathematics teacher at the military academy; cadets and students at the academy were some of its keenest advocates. Liberal republicans such as Rui Barbosa, Quintino Bocaiúva, and Arístides Lobo were also involved and served for a time in the provisional government. Radical republicans, known as Jacobinos (Jacobins), advocated broader democracy and promoted anti-Portuguese nativism. The São Paulo planters who had been calling for decentralization under the banner of republicanism were not directly involved in the plot.[3]

Deodoro assumed the presidency and struggled to keep control of the fractious provisional government. A constituent assembly wrote a new constitution in 1890–91 and elected Deodoro as president for a term to last until 15 November 1894. The new republic would be a decentralized regime, with much more power and autonomy for the states (as the old provinces were now called) than the empire had allowed. By this time, positivist influence on the government had waned—Benjamin Constant died in January 1891—and an increasingly authoritarian Deodoro closed Congress in early November 1891, but the navy forced his resignation later that month. Vice President Marshal Floriano Vieira de Araújo Peixoto served out Deodoro's term but faced serious opposition from the navy, which revolted from September 1893 to March 1894, and from the Federalist Revolt in Rio Grande do Sul (1892–94). Floriano relied heavily on Jacobinos to mobilize the Rio de Janeiro population in defense of the republic, and many of them saw him as the strong leader who would break the old oligarchies' power. Financial difficulties dogged his government as the speculative boom of the early republic, the Encilhamento, gave way to a long economic crisis.[4] Prudente José de Morais e Barros, a representative of the São Paulo planter oligarchy, won the 1894 election and moved Brazil to civilian governance; he had to contend with ongoing Jacobino agitation, further inflamed by the perception that the Canudos Rebellion in Bahia (1896–97) constituted a monarchist threat to Brazil. He and his successor gradually put Brazil's finances in order and laid the foundation for the prewar Belle Époque during which major urban reforms turned much of Rio de Janeiro's downtown into a showcase capital city and dislocated large numbers of the urban poor.[5]

The lively popular support for the monarchy in 1888–89 contrasted sharply with most republicans' perception that, as Minister of the Interior Arístides Lobo put it three days after the coup, members of the *povo* watched it all stupefied, "like dumb beasts [*bestializados*]."[6] On 2 December 1889, a year after the enthusiastic album popular presentation to Pedro II, silence reigned: "No thunders of cannon are heard, no flags are waving in the streets and on the public buildings, no crowds are thronging the palace to offer congratulations, [and] no illuminations are in preparation for the night," reported *The Rio News*; the *Jornal do Comércio* quietly recalled "the respected old man who [had] presided over Brazil's destiny for many long years," as did the *Diário do Comércio*, which noted the "great Brazilian's" achievements.[7] One demonstration, however, took place. Dom Obá II led "a considerable crowd" from his home to the downtown palace, whose doors were of course fastened shut. They numbered more than 1,000 people, according to one *cronista*, but some were "*moleques* [street children]" making fun of the prince. Unable to celebrate Pedro II's birthday in the accustomed way, Obá and his followers shouted cheers before they were dispersed. Four days later, the government stripped him of his rank as honorary *alferes*.[8]

A more serious incident took place a few weeks later. Soldiers in the Second Artillery Regiment stationed in São Cristóvão mutinied in defense of a corporal who had quarreled with a sergeant. They drove the noncommissioned officer out of the barracks, hoisted the imperial flag, cheered the monarchy, and sought support from other units. Unsuccessful, they fortified themselves in their barracks where they were quickly surrounded by loyalist troops. Shooting broke out, and rumors of fifty dead and barracks walls "splashed with blood" soon circulated in the city, where panicked republican officials feared the worst. A secretary to the minister of the interior later recalled the tense atmosphere at army headquarters but was unimpressed at the first thirty or forty prisoners when they arrived: "Almost all blacks or mulattoes" wearing "disheveled and torn uniforms," they held their heads low, and only two or three cast threatening glances at their captors.[9] Most of the press hushed up key aspects of this incident, and only the *Tribuna Liberal* (the old imperial Liberal Party organ) reported the cheers to the emperor, but this was quickly accepted as true by *The Rio News* (which had reports from residents near the barracks that only nine were killed), a French foreign correspondent, and the U.S. and British ministers.[10] In February 1890, the ten soldiers condemned to death for this incident had their sentences commuted to life in prison; forty-eight others received shorter prison sentences. The provisional government smelled a larger monarchist plot and deported some key figures associated with the empire, including the last president of the council of ministers, the Viscount of Ouro Preto. For good measure, it also banned Pedro II and his family from ever returning to Brazil.[11]

Such indications of residual popular support for the monarchy—evidence that some of the *povo* had not passively accepted the new regime—facilitated the republican crackdown on the lower classes. A quick and brutally effective police campaign against *capoeiras* resulted in the deportation of more than 400 of them to the penal island of Fernando de Noronha as of mid-December.[12] The new regime intervened more heavily in daily life, as suggested by the sixty-four municipal bylaws approved from 15 November 1889 to the end of 1893; from the 1850s to the 1880s, the municipal government had issued an average of just over four per year.[13] In the longer term, the urban reforms epitomized by the construction of Central Avenue in the early 1900s and the creation of a showcase downtown district also implied the removal of many of the working class to more distant suburbs; the poorest of the poor could not afford this relocation and built makeshift housing on unoccupied hills, the first favelas. Violent resistance to a mandatory smallpox vaccination campaign in 1904 forced the government to back down but did not stop the larger transformation of Rio de Janeiro.[14] These developments highlighted the republican governments' authoritarian bent and their determination to foster progress as its leaders understood the concept.

The desire for progress also lay behind the provisional government's rapid institution of new symbols and new days of national festivity, with which this epilogue begins. In the heady days of 1890, new civic rituals flourished as different groups sought to present their understandings of the republic; the political unrest and economic crises of the rest of the decade made it difficult to sustain this enthusiasm, and many of the civic ritual innovations of 1890 did not endure. In the mid-1890s, the civilian government of Prudente de Morais secured the Jacobinos' marginalization and, much like 7 April 1831, 15 November 1889 amounted to a *"journée des dupes"* for those who sought radical change.[15] The abandonment of many of the civic-ritual innovations of the early 1890s highlighted these developments.

REPUBLICAN SYMBOLS AND NEW DAYS

OF NATIONAL FESTIVITY

As new regimes so often do, the provisional republican government moved quickly to efface its predecessor's more visible legacies and to institute its own symbols and civic calendar. These tasks took little more than two months to complete, and the well-organized positivists successfully introduced many of their ideas in the new flag and the new calendar of days of national festivity; even the preservation of the old national anthem was consistent with their belief in the importance of celebrating an enduring *pátria*.

Four days after the republic's proclamation, the provisional government decreed the adoption of a new flag. It resembled the old imperial flag in important ways, retaining the green background and the yellow lozenge, but replaced the imperial arms and the coffee and tobacco leaves with a blue circle emblazoned with the positivist slogan of "Order and Progress" and twenty-one stars to represent the states and the federal district of Rio de Janeiro. The decree declared that the old colors recalled the military victories won in defense of the *pátria* and symbolized its "perpetuity and integrity." The new flag, as José Murilo de Carvalho explains, resulted from the effective mobilization of positivists who blocked efforts of liberal republicans who had advocated a flag based on the U.S. stars and stripes. The republic's new flag remained controversial long after this period, but all efforts to change it failed.[16]

Changes to the names of government institutions came shortly after the new flag. On 21 November, the Colégio Dom Pedro II became the Instituto Nacional de Instrução Secundária (National Institute of Secondary Instruction), and several organizations had the word *imperial* removed from their names. *The Rio News* criticized this mania for name changes given that Pedro II had not been a tyrant.[17] The emperor's portraits disappeared from government offices, and Carlos de Laet recalled that clever civil servants took the paintings home as souvenirs, later selling them to collectors for a handsome profit.[18] Imperial coats of arms were removed from public structures, sometimes with incongruous results, such as on the gates to the park in the old Campo da Aclamação, which then bore (and today still bears) the republic's arms above the date of 1873. Municipal bylaws soon prohibited shops and other establishments from making reference to the empire, and enthusiastic republicans pressed for effective enforcement.[19] Vivaldo Coaracy recalled that the very word *imperial* became "taboo vocabulary," while Joaquim Maria Machado de Assis later satirized this in his novel *Esaú e Jacó* (Esau and Jacob, 1904). In one episode, Custódio, the owner of a confectionary, pays for a new sign with the word "*império* [empire]" in it just before the republic's proclamation. Fortunately, the painter has only reached the letter "d" in Confeitaria do Império, so there is time to change it. After contemplating calling his establishment Confeitaria da República or Confeitaria do Governo (the former risky, for there might be a restoration, and the latter dangerous because governments always have oppositions), he settles on Confeitaria do Custódio.[20] Streets and squares whose names recalled the old regime received new appellations. Dom Pedro II Square (the former Palace Square) now became 15 November Square (soon shortened to Praça XV), and Constitution Square became Tiradentes Square.[21]

A similar fate awaited the imperial palaces, which were stripped of their association with the old regime. São Cristóvão housed the republic's constituent assembly in 1890–91 and was then turned into a national historical museum. The galleries that linked the downtown palace to the old imperial chapel (now the diocesan cathedral) were demolished in 1890, symbolizing the separation of Church and state that the republic decreed in January 1890 and institutionalized in the 1891 constitution. The old building then served as the postal service's headquarters.

The summer palace at Petrópolis was converted into a school. Needless to say, republican presidents could not use the imperial palaces, and they established the seat of government in the Itamarati Palace, a former private residence adjacent to the army headquarters and just off the Campo da Aclamação, now dubbed the Praça da República (Republic Square).[22] In 1897, the presidency moved to the Catete Palace in a fashionable residential district south of downtown.

As Carvalho has shown, cartoonists in the illustrated newspapers portrayed the republic as a robust female figure, wearing classical robes and a Phrygian cap, and other artists also adopted this form of representing the new regime, which drew on the French Marianne, the symbol of that country's republic. This new symbol quickly displaced the Indian figure that had represented Brazil in the empire's illustrated press. By the early twentieth century, when republican enthusiasm had given way to disillusionment or even cynicism, critical cartoonists portrayed the regime as a debauched woman or an elderly and sick one, much as wags had earlier talked about the imperial constitution.[23]

The republic's proclamation, like the abdication of Pedro I and the Paraguayan War, sparked the publication of new "national hymns," as composers sought to capitalize on enthusiasm for the new regime. The provisional government quickly announced a competition for a new national anthem.[24] Some thirty compositions were submitted, but advocates of the old imperial anthem, composed by Francisco Manoel da Silva (which had no officially approved lyrics), mounted a press campaign to keep it on the grounds that it represented the enduring nation and *pátria*, not the transitory empire. At a function in the Itamarati Palace on 15 January 1890, the old anthem's champions arranged to have it played (with Deodoro's approval); a crowd outside first feared that the music heralded a counterrevolution, but they soon acclaimed the old and familiar tune. That night, the provisional government resolved to change the competition to one for a republic anthem.[25]

Four of the thirty submissions were performed at a special public concert at the Teatro Lírico (the old Imperial Teatro Dom Pedro II) on 20 January 1890. The winning composition—that of Leopoldo Miguez—with words by José Joaquim de Campos da Costa de Medeiros e Albuquerque became the "Anthem of the Proclamation of the Republic"; Medeiros e Albuquerque later recalled the considerable behind-the-scenes politicking that shaped the final outcome.[26] The evening ended with a stirring rendition of the national anthem, and several people later recalled that Deodoro reiterated his preference for Francisco Manoel's tune; *O País* reported, however, that one republican diehard shouted "Down with the monarchy's hymn!" from a box. This is the only indication of opposition to the decision to keep the old anthem; as far as positivists were concerned, something that symbolized the enduring *pátria* was well worth keeping. After a lengthy selection process, the current words to Brazil's national anthem were adopted in 1922.[27]

A few days before the anthem competition concluded, the provisional government decreed nine days of national festivity. The decree's text had reportedly been prepared in the Centro Positivista on the request of Demétrio Nunes Ribeiro, then briefly serving as minister of agriculture and public works, and it clearly betrays strong positivist influence.[28] The preamble declared that the republican regime rested on a "profound sense of universal fraternity" that would be developed by a "system of public celebrations designed to commemorate the continuity and solidarity of all human generations." The new days of national festivity began with 1 January, which commemorated "universal fraternity"; 21 April was dedicated to the "precursors of Brazilian independence, exemplified by Tiradentes"; 3 May recalled Brazil's "discovery" in 1500; 13 May celebrated "the brotherhood of Brazilians"; 14 July (the date of the Bastille's fall in 1789) commemorated "the Republic, Liberty, and the Independence of the American peoples"; 7 September was dedicated to Brazil's independence; 12 October recalled the "discovery of America"; 2 November was reserved for the "general commemoration of the dead"; and finally, 15 November would honor "the Brazilian *pátria*." In early 1891, the constituent assembly determined that 24 February, the date on which the new charter was signed, be added to the roster of days of national festivity.[29]

In contrast to the lively debate about the anthem, the new civic calendar apparently sparked no press discussion.[30] Luís Francisco da Veiga published an open letter to Benjamin Constant in which he called for the addition of 7 April, for the "great and truly national revolution" of 1831 was "irrefutably the culmination of all of Brazil's history." It won the country "constitutional liberties" and was certainly more worthy of celebration than 7 September 1822, for on that day, only part of Brazil had gained independence; moreover, this "independence" merely amounted to a change of masters. He recalled that 7 April had been a day of national festivity from 1831 to 1848 and lamented (incorrectly) that it had been revoked by executive decree. I have no indication that Veiga's proposal was seriously considered, but it is certainly consistent with his other efforts to burnish the reputation of his uncle, Evaristo da Veiga.[31]

In a well-received book published in early 1893, Rodrigo Otávio Langgaard de Menezes explained the meanings of the new days of national festivity to "the Brazilian youth," to whom he dedicated his work.[32] Otávio presented the dates in their historical order, therefore beginning with 12 October 1492. In rhetoric consistent with that of the Columbus fourth centenary celebrated around the Atlantic World the year before, he hailed the discovery of America as a great achievement that advanced science and religion.[33] Brazil's discovery by Pedro Álvares

Cabral's expedition on 3 May 1500 had given rise to the traditional use of the day as the opening of the imperial parliament, and the republican constitution continued this practice (which conveniently brought deputies and senators to Rio de Janeiro for the normally drier and cooler winter months). Otávio knew that the expedition's chronicler had dated the discovery to 22 April, but because of the adoption of the Gregorian calendar in 1582 the date was appropriately corrected to 3 May. It celebrated the beginnings of civilization brought to the "American savage."[34] To celebrate 14 July 1789 associated Brazil with what positivists saw as a universally relevant French revolution that, presumably, laid the groundwork for the "American peoples' liberty and independence," although Otávio did not connect it directly to Brazil.[35]

The inclusion of 21 April, the date of Tiradentes's execution in 1792, fulfilled a long-standing republican aspiration, and after reviewing the Inconfidência Mineira's history, Otávio held up Tiradentes as a "worthy example" of those who worked for "the *pátria*'s independence and liberty."[36] A republic would have followed independence, he argued, had not the "people's naïve generosity" toward Pedro I and the belief that he offered an easy route to liberty and national unity led to the imperial regime; thus, 7 September 1822 constituted merely a separation from Portugal and the 1822–89 period amounted to a "anachronistic gap in Brazil's history."[37]

To designate the date on which slavery was abolished as a day of fraternity among Brazilians sought to draw a veil over the many conflicts and struggles that had marked the abolition movement and may also have aimed to hide Isabel's role, as one historian has suggested. Otávio described slavery as Portugal's imposition on Brazil and abolition as the "generous aspiration of the Brazilian soul." He did, however, note that the abolitionist movement coincided with the "princess regent's good will" on 13 May 1888.[38]

Otávio described 15 November as the celebration of the republic and not of the *pátria* more generally, as the 1890 decree had done, an indication that this close identification of the republican regime with Brazil had failed to take root. He recounted the long history of Brazil's republican aspirations, already generalized in 1789, which expressed themselves in 1817 and 1824, and in the liberal revolts of 1842 and 1848. The Praieira Rebellion's defeat ushered in a "great degeneration of civic spirit, and the bastardization of the national character." The Paraguayan War distracted republican patriots as they turned their attention to the nation's defense, but the republican movement reawakened after the conflict and finally triumphed in 1889.[39] Recalling the dissolution of the 1823 constituent assembly, he hailed the new republic's charter as the product of a true "republican convention" elected by "universal suffrage"—no small exaggeration given the exclusion of women and most illiterates from voting but still an improvement over the late empire, which had also maintained an income requirement.[40]

Festas nacionais came with a curious preface by Raul Pompéia in which the Jacobino writer (and the Clube Jacobino's official "agitator") both praised Otávio's work and pointed out that Brazil's national days were not triumphs; rather, they revealed the cruel history of a "defeated *pátria*."[41] On 21 April, Brazil was "tortured and execrated along with Tiradentes"; independence amounted to "the perversion of our liberation by the simple and base tricks of a coarse autocrat"; and abolition actually constituted a defeat given the Portuguese imposition of a long-lasting "shameful labor regime" on the nation. It was too early to assess 15 November and 24 February, but "the bitter distresses of the present certainly do not herald glorious achievements." Pompéia concluded his essay with an analysis of what he saw as the domination of independent Brazil by Portuguese who controlled commerce, upheld racial prejudice (unknown to Brazilians), opposed abolition, and drove Benjamin Constant and Deodoro da Fonseca to early deaths (the first president passed away a few months after leaving office). They were responsible for the dismal state of "Brazilian patriotism," and Pompéia hoped that Otávio's book would inspire a third revolution, "the revolution of economic dignity, only after which we will be able to say that the Brazilian nation exists."[42]

These efforts to explain the meanings of the republic's national celebrations had already moved away from the more doctrinaire positivist rhetoric incorporated into the 1890 decree. By 1893, positivist influence on the republic had waned, but the Jacobinos, heirs to the radical liberal tradition of anti-Portuguese nativism, remained a potent force until 1897. Nonetheless, positivists' early influence shaped the republic's symbols and the concept of order and progress, shorn of its more metaphysical connotations, remained profoundly appealing to Brazil's dominant classes.

CELEBRATING THE REPUBLIC'S DAYS

OF NATIONAL FESTIVITY

Just as in 1831–33, the institution of a new regime, many aspects of which remained to be defined, sparked an intense round of civic rituals, during which Brazilians debated the nature of their polity and enacted their visions for the future. More authoritarian than the regency, the new republic soon restricted the press and kept political debate within narrower bounds than under the empire. Nonetheless, my partial reading of the press in the republic's first years and the few studies of early republican civic rituals reveal a burst of enthusiasm for new celebrations on the part of positivists and radical republicans in 1890, as well as the government's determination to celebrate the new regime's first anniversary. Too closely identified with the imperial regime, and perhaps also too closely associated with imperial popular festivities, 7 September fell by the wayside for several years. By the mid-1890s, the innovative forms of celebration had disappeared, as the republic's civic celebrations settled into a routine of official ritual that, according to critics, failed to inspire enthusiasm.

In the short space of three weeks from 21 April to 13 May 1890, Rio de Janeiro saw three rather different civic rituals, each of which featured civic processions heavily influenced by positivists and designed to teach suitably patriotic lessons to the populace. The Clube Tiradentes led the celebrations of its namesake and organized a "great civic procession" that retraced the condemned man's steps to the site of his execution. Artillery salutes from a battery on Santo Antônio Hill on 21 April marked its progress; members of the Apostolado Positivista (Positivist Apostolate) carried a bier with the bust of Tiradentes and distributed leaflets with his portrait. At 8:00 pm, they held a formal meeting at the Casino Fluminense (the club that had brought together the empire's elite); the president, the cabinet, and other officials attended. Bands played on São Francisco and Carioca Squares to entertain the populace.[43] Antônio da Silva Jardim gave the keynote address in which he reviewed what must have been to his audience the familiar history of Tiradentes and called on the "citizen, head of the Republic of the United States of Brazil," to lead the *pátria* to the "splendors of sociocracy," the positivist ideal.[44] When *Eco Popular* learned about the program, it remarked that this would be a celebration of Tiradentes unlike any of the previous ones. Certainly, no such public procession had taken place on 21 April under the empire, and positivists would participate in public commemorations until 1892. The choice of locations for the street entertainment ensured that nothing took place near the equestrian statue of Pedro I, and *O País* reminded its readers of the statue's significance by running Pedro Luís Pereira de Souza's critical 1862 poem. The *Jornal do Comércio*'s *cronista* observed that this procession was intended "for the *povo*'s education" and remarked on its similarity in form to the "sumptuous ecclesiastical ceremonies" to which members of the *povo* were accustomed. This time, however, instead of a saint, it was the "hero who let himself be hanged on the gallows to demonstrate his love of the *pátria*" who merited veneration.[45]

Two weeks later, a committee of army and navy officers organized a procession to commemorate Brazil's discovery on 3 May. The positivist artist Décio Villares designed all of the images. The first section of the parade was led by the navy minister and featured a model caravel escorted by sailors. A bust of Columbus was the principal object in the second section of the parade, the positivists' responsibility; it also featured a reproduction of Vítor Meireles de Lima's painting of the first mass held in Brazil. The third block focused on Brazil's indigenous peoples; sailors carried a pirogue and the portrait of an Indian. Other groups and societies joined the procession. According to historian Elisabete da Costa Leal, on whose work this account is based, newspapers emphasized that this procession celebrated the *pátria*'s birth. Honoring Columbus was consistent with the positivist stress on celebrating great men. It also avoided celebrating Cabral and thus giving undue attention to a Portuguese man, but some newspapers nevertheless reported that the bust represented Cabral, an indication that not all understood the organizers' message. *Revista Ilustrada*'s portrayal of the parade contrasted Indian savagery with modern, civilized celebration. Some newspapers raised the issue of whether 3 May was the actual date of Brazil's discovery, one that would be extensively discussed in the lead-up to the fourth centenary of Brazil's discovery.[46] The corrected date remained a holiday; abolished in 1930, it was restored during the constitutional regime (1934–37), but by the 1950s Brazilian schoolchildren were being taught that Brazil had been discovered on 22 April 1500.[47]

Ten days later came the second anniversary of slavery's abolition. The Confederaçao Abolicionista organized a civic procession that began at a grandstand constructed on the Praça da República. Deodoro and the cabinet attended the ceremonies there, and José do Patrocínio spoke. The procession, "composed of rather heterogeneous material"—*The Rio News*'s cryptic indication of its multiclass and multiracial character—began with the Confederação's float. It featured a globe emblazoned with the slogan, "Order and Progress," and a female figure representing the Republic. At her feet lay abolitionist society banners, camellias, and broken chains; in front of them two seated female figures represented the press and abolition. The float's sides were decorated with the names of abolitionist leaders and abolitionist *quilombos*. The next float included a three-meter bronze statue of an African woman, surrounded by a dozen children of color who scattered flowers on the crowds. The procession wound its way through the city until it dispersed at 15 November Square. Schoolchildren and a variety of other societies joined the procession, and residents were invited to illuminate their windows and to decorate their façades in honor of the two peaceful revolutions of 13 May and 15 November. This effort to associate abolition and the republic, which one historian sees as the key theme in these commemorations, did not quite work, and a passing reference to Isabel in Patrocínio's speech "was received with applause," according to *The Rio News*.[48]

Less celebration marked the next three days. Committees of French expatriates, businessmen, the army, the navy, and the press organized children's entertainment, a musical and literary matinee, and "popular dances" for 14 July.[49] Independence day was also scarcely celebrated. *The Rio News*, which usually mentioned civic celebrations in its "Local Notes" section, said nothing about the day in its 8 September issue, and a *cronista* in *O Porvir* lamented that not a single rocket was set off; the *caboclo* (Indian) figures around Pedro I's statue could only lament their abandonment on the traditionally festive day. The *Jornal do Comércio* noted that there was nothing to report; the commemorations had amounted to nothing more than some artillery salutes and the illumination of public buildings.[50] I have found no indication of public commemoration on 12 October 1890.[51]

The provisional government and the city government took the lead in organizing the celebrations on 15 November. Francisco Ferreira da Rosa described the day as "officially celebrated," and Carla Siqueira, the historian who has analyzed the press coverage of these commemorations, stresses the public rituals' predominantly military character.[52] The director of municipal public works received authorization to spend the hefty sum of fifty contos (US$23,000) on band shells and other decorations, most which apparently went to decorating and illuminating Republic Square and raising a column topped by a statue of liberty in the square's center. The municipality invited citizens to illuminate and decorate their façades for three days, and there are some indications that bands were stationed in squares throughout the city. There was a military parade, and Deodoro attended a special meeting of the city council during which his portrait was unveiled. The constituent assembly convened that day, and the Lyric Theater put on a concert conducted by Leopoldo Miguez.[53] Ferreira da Rosa also noted "popular celebrations," including a children's regatta in one of the Praça da República's ponds. An entrepreneur who expected that many would come into the city for the celebrations requested a license to construct four booths on Tiradentes Square at which the "popular masses" could enjoy "entertainment more suitable for their condition and [more to] their taste," namely "interesting games of chance and [other] popular games." The license was granted with the proviso that no gambling take place.[54]

The press commentary on these celebrations resembled the polarized discussions that we saw at many points during the imperial regime. Republican newspapers (*O País*, the *Gazeta de Notícias*, and the *Revista Ilustrada*) lauded the republic and described a city "taken over by the festivities" in which "an extraordinary mass of *povo*" eagerly celebrated the republican *pátria*. For *A Tribuna*, the fiercely monarchist organ, the republic was no more than the product of a "military rising" and the celebrations "exclusively official," unlike under the empire when ordinary people organized themselves to raise triumphal arches for their beloved monarch. During these three republican days, members of the *povo* were "mere spectator[s]."[55] All would have recognized these allusions to the late-imperial popular festivities of 7 September and Pedro's return in 1888. *The Rio News* concurred with *A Tribuna* and judged "that the three days of celebration decreed by the provisional government have aroused no exceptional popular manifestations of joy, and that the festivities have been very largely official and military in character." *O País* and *A Tribuna* also bickered over which regime— monarchy or republic—was more capable of progress. Siqueira notes, furthermore, that republicans and monarchists used the same rhetorical strategies to make their points; journalists in both camps distanced themselves from the *povo* and never mentioned the people when discussing political questions.[56]

Some of the innovations in 1890's celebrations endured for a few years, but the celebration of the republic's days of national festivity soon became more perfunctory and routine; many were strongly shaped by conjunctural political questions. A certain amount of official celebration took place on most days; even in the midst of the 1893 naval revolt, a traveler noted that government offices were closed "and the streets hung with flags" in honor of Columbus's discovery of America. No major civic rituals took place on 15 November that year, but the rebel ships "dressed with flags" and the Santa Cruz Fortress fired the customary dawn, noon, and dusk salutes, all practices unchanged from the monarchy, even if the flags looked a bit different. I have found no descriptions of 3 May celebrations, but in 1895 one *cronista* lamented that congress had failed to reach quorum and so did not begin its session that day as the constitution had mandated. By that year, French expatriates were the only ones who celebrated on 14 July.[57] The government chose 24 February 1897 to inaugurate the new presidential palace in Catete; some criticized the elaborate ceremonial that included a military parade and a costly state dinner, but one periodical recalled the "misanthropy and melancholy that were the characteristic tone of the late monarchy" and suggested that, "for the *povo*'s civic education," governments had to "demonstrate such grandeur, a preponderant part of their prestige and the influence that they must exert over the masses."[58]

The policy of investing in 15 November spectacle continued. In 1891, the municipal government received authorization to spend eighty contos (US$24,000) on "public festivities"; in the rush to complete band shells and other ephemeral decorations, the public works department went over budget (it did not help that a large quantity of lumber for the band shell in front of the Itamarati Palace had been pilfered); *Revista Ilustrada* was, however, unimpressed with the design (these public celebrations, it should be noted, took place during the tense interval between Deodoro's closing of congress and his resignation).[59] A radical republican chastised the government for not doing more to promote popular enthusiasm in 1892: "We saw nothing more than the parading troops, the illumination of public buildings, gala theater spectacles, [and] the customary flags on government and private establishments."[60] The Catholic periodical, *O Apóstolo*, likewise had little good to say about the "military parade" and mocked the Clube Tiradentes's civic march as a "carnivalesque procession"; members of the *povo* were "mere spectators." The commemorative photo album presented to Prudente de Morais after his inauguration and the 15 November 1894 celebrations reveals a carefully staged and heavily militarized civic ritual that in this case celebrated an orderly transition to civilian rule.[61] The following year, Machado de Assis described the republic's festivities as "the great military parade, congratulations to the president of the republic, the opening of the exposition, the gala theater spectacles, the fleet's maneuvers . . . well-chosen ceremonial" that the *povo* would enjoy. He suggested that they might be called "Novemberine Celebrations [*festas novembrinas*]," after Argentina's "*festas maias* [*fiestas mayas* or May celebrations]," but added that it was one thing to put on "brilliant" celebrations and quite another to make them truly "national and popular." In 1897, Quintino Bocaiúva's *O País*, then in opposition to Prudente de Morais's government, announced that it could not celebrate the republic while "the very nation sighed and sobbed" at its troubles.[62]

Independence remained difficult for republican governments to celebrate. Pedro I's centrality in the events of 1822 and the resulting monarchy, as well as the popular festivities of 7 September in the late empire, apparently discomfited republican leaders and activists. To be sure, the day could be defined as the date on which "a new American nationality" emerged, as *O País* declared in 1890, but the association with monarchy could not be so easily dispelled.[63] Laments about the limited celebration of 7 September recurred. In 1892, *O Mequetrefe* recalled *Alferes* Américo Rodrigues Gamboa, his fort-shaped band shells, and the enthusiastic dawn singing of the independence anthem but noted that this year's 7 September looked just like any other day. Two years later, Olavo Bilac also recalled the great celebrations of the Sociedade Comemoradora da Independência Nacional (he did not quite get the name right). He noted that the country now had a new day to celebrate, 15 November, that Pedro I was "demoralized," and that there were no more *capoeiras* to enliven civic celebrations; positivism, he concluded, had turned the day into a serious "religious commemoration" that did not allow for the "irreverent joy of popular commemorations."[64] Military parades on 7 September apparently began in 1895, an indication that the civilian government was moving to gain control of the day.[65] In 1898, a magazine noted the founding of the Sociedade Comemorativa das Datas Nacionais (Society for the Commemoration of National Days) and expected that 7 September would be "suitably" celebrated and that all "social classes" would take part. I know nothing more about this society, other than that it received eight contos (US$1,200) from the city to assist in its work, which the magazine praised, for "the population was in need of entertainment"; times had been hard, and such celebrations would help secure peace.[66]

The patterns of commemoration on 13 May remain to be established. In 1892, the city council received authorization to spend merely five contos (US$1,200) on "popular festivities," but there are indications that neighborhood associations and brotherhoods organized festivities as well in this year and in 1893. Organizers were too late to put together a schoolchildren's parade in 1895.[67] In 1892, a writer in *Revista Ilustrada* recommended that the government not get involved in 13 May celebrations for the "military parades or civic processions, formal meetings, [with their] vacuous, bombastic, and swinish [*suína*] oratory," amounted to a disgrace, as did the municipal decorations. Why not instead organize "*cateretês*, African sambas and public *maxixes*?" he asked, referring to popular dances of African and indigenous origins. This is likely an indication that lower-class Afro-Brazilians were marking abolition on their own and had turned their backs on official celebrations (in São Paulo, 13 May celebrations soon fell under the control of black organizations).[68] An 1898 program proposal signed by José Ponciano de Oliveira—the União Operária founder and possibly organizer of the 2 December 1888 album presentation to Pedro II—called for the "customary" artillery salutes and illuminations, a procession of social clubs on the evening of the 12th, a military parade, a formal meeting in the municipal council building to which the archbishop and the president would be invited. The president would also be asked to hold a reception at night, and there would be a special tribute to the press, "to which is due the glory for the liberation of the slaves." A simple band shell in front of the army headquarters would offer entertainment to the populace, and 250 "poor people" would receive charity in the form of two mil-réis (US$0.15) each at the Passeio Público. The proposed evening procession had all the marks of carnival, as it would culminate in a "confetti battle."[69]

The Sociedade Comemorativa das Datas Nacionais got involved in 1899, and the Baron of Loreto wrote to the exiled Princess Isabel that 13 May had been marked with "demonstrations of public joy [on a scale] never seen since [the start of] Your Imperial Highness's absence." He also sent her a copy of *Rua do Ouvidor* magazine, which featured the princess's portrait and published his article on abolition.[70] All of this indicates that most Brazilians were more interested in celebrating abolitionist heroes than in recalling former slaves, much less addressing the conditions under which the free poor (some recently freed) lived.[71] Radical republican efforts to claim abolition as "the glorious beginning of the strong and serene republic" defended by Floriano Peixoto, as one *cronista* put it in 1894, had but limited resonance. The view that abolition was "one of the monarchy's glories," a monarchist periodical's 1891 assessment, seems to have been widespread by the end of the decade, to judge by the accounts of the 1899 celebrations.[72] A disconcerting reminder of slavery's legacy came in 1892 with the widely reported discovery of one Ana, a São Paulo slave whose master had somehow contrived to keep her ignorant of abolition for four years![73] What is perhaps most striking about the press coverage of abolition celebrations in the 1890s is the absence of references to the participation of those who had had the most at stake—the former slaves. In this respect, republican civic ritual was clearly exclusionary.

The commemorations of 21 April followed the model of 1890, at least for a few years. Despite bad weather, the centenary of Tiradentes's death, described by *Revista Ilustrada* as "the greatest date of modern Brazil's history," was "celebrated in a worthy way" (*O Apóstolo*, not surprisingly, did not share this view). In one year, the city council paid for the Clube Tiradentes to have six theaters put on free shows for the populace.[74] It also marked the centenary with a commemorative plaque on the site of Tiradentes's execution, the exact location of which had been the cause of considerable debate. Critics of the equestrian statue had long juxtaposed the monument with the gallows on which Tiradentes had expired, but the municipality sided with those who held that the execution had actually taken place on the Campo da Polé, a site that in 1892 was located on Visconde do Rio Branco Street. This was where the council placed the plaque.[75]

Nevertheless, the equestrian statue continued to rankle radical republicans. In 1893, Jacobinos in the Clube Tiradentes sought to claim Tiradentes Square for their outdoor celebrations. The site would be "spectacularly decorated and illuminated," and a navy band would play in a large band shell; fireworks would be set off here after its *solenidade*.[76] The club received permission to build the band shell over and around the Pedro I statue, but in the face of widespread criticism Prefect (Mayor) Cândido Barata Ribeiro withdrew the authorization; according to *Revista Ilustrada*, the *povo* dismantled the "pine box" before the club could comply with the order. The club then canceled its parade.[77] The *povo*'s rejection of the attempt to hide the statue, furthermore, may indicate the popular monarchism that some found in the early twentieth century (see the Conclusion) or that, for some, this symbol was far from the "bronze lie" of republican rhetoric. Calls to remove the statue continued, but even sympathetic newspapers judged this iconoclastic enthusiasm to be excessive.[78]

That Pedro I's statue survived the Jacobino onslaught reveals the declining enthusiasm for instituting new forms of civic commemoration. To be sure, later that year came the authorization to raise a monument to Tiradentes on the site of his execution, but it was not inaugurated until 1926. This statue portrayed him as a martyr and offered no direct challenge to the first emperor's monument. Instead, it stood in front of the legislative assembly, approximately the site of the old city council building with the jail in which he had been held before his execution. Moreover, as Carvalho has shown, Tiradentes remained a polyvalent symbol; the military regime declared him to be the "Brazilian nation's civic patron" in 1965, and some of the armed left of the early 1970s imagined him as a revolutionary leader.[79]

In 1896, Artur Azevedo lamented the little effort to commemorate the martyr's execution:

> There were the classic flags
> And the ordinary artillery salutes
> And the old lamps
> There was nothing else!
> The republic looks like
> The fallen empire
> That never took seriously
> National celebrations.[80]

A few years earlier, *O Apóstolo* grumbled that, since 15 November 1889, no national celebration worthy of the name had taken place. Were it not for religious celebrations, Brazil "would look like a cemetery." National celebrations had been reduced to their military elements and to the illumination of public buildings.[81]

It is probably impossible to determine whether these contemporary assessments are correct, for they amount to traditional laments of opposition journalists that governments did not take civic ritual seriously or failed to elicit enthusiasm for them. That these laments came from opposite sides of the political spectrum is, however, significant. What Azevedo bemoaned was, in fact, the disappearance of the republican enthusiasm and the positivist pedagogic project so prominent in the new regime's early civic rituals. Presaged in the reorganized Sociedade Comemorativa da Independência do Império's celebrations of 1887 and 1888, this project briefly flourished as positivists and others sought to create a new civic culture and a new sense of republican patriotism starting in 1890. That it failed is hardly surprising; members of the *povo* no more desired positivist tutelage than did most members of the Brazilian political elite. To be sure, the latter might selectively adopt elements of the ideology—and aspects of it influenced the Brazilian elite and government until well into the twentieth century—but the orthodox Igreja Positivista Brasileira counted only fifty-three members in 1889.[82] *O Apóstolo* looked back at the empire through rose-colored glasses—as indeed monarchists would continue to do—but it is true that no civic celebration in the 1890s approached the popular resonance of the Sociedade Comemorativa's 7 September celebrations in the 1870s and early 1880s, not to mention the festivities of Pedro's return and his birthday in 1888. More important, none approached the Comemorativa's festivities in their autonomy and control by members of the lower-middle or working class. The Catholic periodical's argument about the importance of religious festivities, furthermore, is consistent with Carvalho's argument that the republic's *povo*, far from being bestialized, in fact spurned the limited benefits of republican citizenship in favor of constructing their own identities in popular festivals or in family and community life.[83] In short, the republicans of the 1890s failed to mobilize popular support for their regime. Like those who led the reorganized Sociedade Comemorativa, they sought to impose their vision of appropriate forms of patriotic celebration on the *povo*, most of whose members rejected this project.

Conclusion

The days of national festivity whose commemoration we have traced from Brazil's independence to the early 1890s served many purposes and had multiple meanings. As countless students of rituals and commemorations have observed, no festival has the same significance to all those involved in it. Year after year, imperial Brazil's civic rituals were an occasion for debate about the political institutions established in 1822–24, a time when those in power sought to impose their vision on the nation, an opportunity for some to claim status and membership in the nation, and a chance for many to celebrate and to enjoy spectacular sights and sounds. That Brazilians failed to agree on many things even as they joined in the commemorations of independence, the constitution, and the emperor may underscore what David Kertzer sees as one of political ritual's major purposes—to express and to demonstrate unity despite disagreement—but it also highlights that civic rituals provide an occasion to pursue political conflicts.[1] An analysis of imperial civic ritual reveals the very quick establishment of "Brazil" as the "nation" within which "Brazilians" would conduct their affairs, but nation building in this sense was not the issue on days of national festivity. Rather, the key questions concerned the institutions that governed Brazilians.

The imperial Brazilian civic rituals analyzed in this book raise numerous additional issues, among them the evolution of Brazilian civic rituals in the twentieth century and the changing attitudes toward the empire, the nature of civic rituals in the provinces, and the distinctiveness of Brazil in Latin American history. In the twentieth century, critics of the republic looked back favorably on the empire, while authoritarian regimes like the Estado Novo (New State, 1937–45) and the military dictatorship (1964–85) invested heavily in civic rituals to claim legitimacy and to foster loyalty. Largely abandoned by republican governments in the 1890s, 7 September regained prominence after 1900 and remains the country's principal civic holiday, a consequence of its firm establishment as the date of Brazil's independence during the empire.

This book's focus on Rio de Janeiro has left aside any consideration of civic ritual in the provinces, which remains to be studied systematically. The available evidence suggests that, during the empire, the commemoration of days of national festivity in provincial capitals closely followed the forms of the Corte's official rituals, as provincial elites and imperial government representatives sought to demonstrate their membership in the nation. Like so many other nineteenth-century states, the imperial government fostered the commemoration of days of national festivity throughout its far-flung territory. In these respects, imperial Brazil differed little from republican Spanish America, although the Brazilian empire's relative order and institutional continuity gave its civic ritual a stability unmatched elsewhere in the Americas. Even so, as we have seen, there were significant changes in how Brazilians celebrated their principal days of national festivity.

TWENTIETH-CENTURY CIVIC RITUAL

Much work remains to be done before we can speak with confidence about the evolution of twentieth-century Brazilian civic ritual and the commemoration of the country's national holidays. As the empire faded into the past and a restoration became an ever-more remote prospect, it became easier to treat 7 September as the nation's founding and to view the monarchy as a legitimate part of the nation's history. Likewise, disillusioned republicans held up the monarchy as a foil to what they saw as a failed republic. Authoritarian regimes heavily promoted civic rituals to foster nationalistic support, but little is known about the routine commemoration of national holidays during the longer periods of more or less democratic rule.

In the 1890s and early 1900s, the Instituto Histórico e Geográfico Brasileiro served as a refuge for monarchists. Its members held a special memorial after Pedro II's death; in silent commemoration, the institute closed its doors every 5 December, the date on which he died in 1891 in a Paris hotel room.[2] Prominent monarchist holdouts, such as Joaquim Nabuco and the Baron of Rio Branco, eventually reconciled themselves to the new regime and served it in distinguished capacities after 1900. A monument to Pedro was raised in Petrópolis in 1911 and inaugurated by President Hermes da Fonseca, Deodoro's nephew.[3] Calls to repatriate his body and to end the ban on the return of members of his family were occasionally heard, and in 1913 a bill to this effect passed in the chamber of deputies but failed in the senate.[4] World War I put a stop to the efforts to bring back the emperor's remains, and not until 7 September 1920 was a repatriation bill finally passed. Princess Isabel was too sick to travel, but the Count of Eu accompanied Pedro and Teresa Cristina's remains on their journey to Brazil in January 1921. They were interred in the national cathedral (the old imperial chapel) and transferred to Petrópolis in 1925. The ceremonies were carefully orchestrated, but Eu was surprised at the enthusiasm with which black Brazilians greeted him (Isabel and Eu's remains were repatriated in 1953).[5]

The popular response to Eu's visit is indicative of a strain of favorable recollection of the monarchy that some have detected in the urban lower classes. In 1908, folklorist and writer João do Rio found widespread monarchism, or at least much favorable recollection of the old regime, among the city's prison population; an old coachman declared that the empire had been "more beautiful . . . [and] more serious" than the republic. Others were surprised to find portraits of Pedro II in the homes of the poor and Afro-Brazilians.[6] No doubt much of this popular nostalgia for the empire reflected an idealization of the monarchy's role in abolition and fond recollections of the emperor. Republican governments' efforts to repress many aspects of popular culture and the urban reforms of the first decade of the new century that destroyed many downtown poor communities reinforced the positive view of the empire.

The return of Pedro II's and Teresa Cristina's remains, the independence centenary and the international exposition in honor of it, and the centenary of Pedro II's birth (1925) prompted new debate about the republic, the empire's legacy, and the appropriate form of government. The centralized empire, credited with achieving national unity, came off rather well in comparison to the decentralized republic, increasingly wracked by social and political unrest.[7] The many who sought authoritarian solutions to Brazil's crisis looked back favorably on the empire, and even the 1924 manifesto of the Tenentes, the junior officers who rebelled in São Paulo, called for a Brazil "like the one that the empire left, with the same principles of moral integrity, patriotic consciousness, administrative rectitude, and political wisdom."[8] A bill to make 2 December 1925 into a national holiday sparked a lively debate in the Rio de Janeiro press, and some wondered why the republic had been proclaimed at all, if the empire had been as marvelous a regime as its apologists were proclaiming. While the bill failed to pass, newly inaugurated President Artur Bernardes decreed a holiday anyway, and some judged that Pedro's birthday had sparked more enthusiasm than 15 November.[9]

How Brazilians commemorated and debated the Old Republic's eight civic holidays, to which 19 November (Flag Day) and 1 May (Labor Day) were added in 1908 and 1924 respectively, remains almost entirely unstudied. Flag Day's creation derived from a campaign to foster respect for this symbol, and Labor Day appears to have been a populist gesture on President Bernardes's part.[10] There are also indications of significant efforts to promote a militarized patriotic culture in São Paulo schools in the 1910s and 1920s, involving drill (in lieu of physical education) and parading on national holidays. These efforts were certainly connected to the campaign for obligatory military service led by Olavo Bilac's Liga de Defesa Nacional (National Defence League) in the 1910s.[11] As the army grew in size, large-scale military parades became a regular part of 7 September celebrations in Rio de Janeiro. In 1921, fully 13,000 troops showed off their skill in São Cristóvão.[12]

The 1930 Revolution, which brought Getúlio Vargas to power, accelerated some of these developments. The new regime initially did away with half of the Old Republic's holidays to encourage work and ushered in a period of significant flux in Brazil's civic calendar.[13] As Vargas's centralizing and development-minded government became more authoritarian—from 1937 to 1945 he ruled as dictator in the so-called Estado Novo—it consolidated a new civic calendar that retained 21 April, 1 May, and 12 October but focused its commemorations on two clusters of civic holidays. The Semana da Pátria (Week of the *Pátria*) stretched from Soldiers' Day (25 August, the Duke of Caxias's birthday) to 7 September. Celebrations of 10 November (the Estado Novo's founding), 15 November, and 19 November recalled key elements of his regime and connected it to the republic, while 27 November commemorated those killed in the 1935 communist revolt, a clearly political holiday that would long resonate in military circles.[14]

The Estado Novo's first flag day was commemorated with a symbolic burning of state flags that highlighted the new regime's centralization of power (bad weather, however, forced the ceremony's transfer to Sunday, 27 November, which allowed the regime to highlight its anticommunism). Estado Novo propaganda placed great emphasis on the flag as Brazil's principal national symbol.[15] Influenced by European fascist spectacle, Vargas's government staged enormous schoolchildren's parades during the Semana da Pátria and packed soccer stadiums with tens of thousands of students for the singing of patriotic songs, the so-called *canto orfeônico* championed by composer Heitor Villa-Lobos.[16] Radio and newsreels broadcast these ceremonies throughout the country, and there are indications that even remote towns staged small-scale versions of the dictatorship's Rio de Janeiro spectacles. In Santa Catarina, *canto orfeônico* assumed coercive forms as the state government used it to press for the assimilation of immigrant schoolchildren.[17] Vargas's Estado Novo also completed the mausoleum for Pedro and Teresa Cristina's remains in Petrópolis and oversaw the conversion of the old summer palace into the Museu Imperial (Imperial Museum).[18]

The liberal-democratic republic of 1945–64 brought few innovations to Brazil's civic calendar, save to remove the holidays that celebrated the Estado Novo; from 1945, Brazil had only two civic holidays, 7 September and 15 November; 21 April (the date of Tiradentes's execution) was restored in 1950.[19] The military regime of 1964–85 did not attempt to commemorate its origins with a new national holiday. Rather, it sought legitimacy through reinvigorating the celebration of established days such as 7 September, especially during its most repressive years from 1968 to the mid-1970s; one historian describes this as a "commemorative fever" that peaked in 1972, the sesquicentennial of independence.[20] That year, Brazil prevailed on Portugal, desperately in need of Brazilian diplomatic support to maintain its collapsing colonial position in Africa, to transfer Pedro I's remains to Brazil. They arrived in Brazil on 21 April and toured the country before finally being laid to rest at Ipiranga on 7 September.[21] By this time, 7 September celebrations in the form of military parades appeared to be such a well-established part of Brazilian culture that anthropologist Roberto DaMatta identified them as one of the three "fundamental forms by which the Brazilian social world is *ritualized*," alongside carnival and saints' processions.[22] In 1980, the military regime declared 12 October a holiday, but the day now celebrated Our Lady of Aparecida, Brazil's principal patron saint since 1930.[23]

While the twentieth-century commemoration of national holidays certainly reveals much about how Brazil's regimes, and particularly its authoritarian ones, have sought legitimacy in the past, it remains difficult to determine whether such celebrations had the impact that their promoters sought. A participant in an Estado Novo Semana da Pátria spectacle in Rio de Janeiro much later recalled it as "a giant parade to support the government" (his later careers as a sociologist and Brazil's president no doubt shaped this assessment), while those who participated in *canto orfeônico* in Santa Catarina have mixed recollections. Former teachers still take pride in their work training students to march and to sing; their charges recall the demanding drill and performances even in bad weather, while immigrants' children recall the slurs directed at them.[24]

More recently, civic ritual has largely lost its capacity to mobilize citizens. One of the military policemen detailed to the 21 April 1972 parade to welcome Pedro I's remains to Rio de Janeiro told a reporter for *Veja*, the principal Brazilian newsmagazine, that "if I weren't on duty, I swear that I'd be on my lounger at the beach."[25] On 15 November 2004, the *Jornal do Brasil* ran an editorial cartoon that quoted Henrique Bernardelli's well-known painting showing Deodoro da Fonseca proclaiming the republic. As he waves his hat to the cheers of other military men, the marshal muses: "I think I invented a long weekend!?" (that year,

15 November fell on a Monday).[26] Indeed, as in much of the rest of the world, twenty-first-century Brazilian national holidays have become days for family gatherings, a chance to go to the beach, and, if they fall in the beginning or the end of a week, an opportunity for a long weekend. The crowds at 7 September parades are normally sparse at best.

IMPERIAL CIVIC RITUAL IN THE PROVINCES

Just as the changes that the republic wrought in civic ritual remain to be studied in detail, so imperial civic ritual in the provinces needs further study. The empire was, in some respects, a strongly centralized regime, and the legislation that instituted its days of national festivity applied to the whole country. Provincial presidents (governors) marked days of national festivity with official civic rituals and sought to promote enthusiasm for the institutions celebrated on these days. There are indications that political mobilizations were central to provincial civic rituals, especially early in the imperial regime. In some provinces, particularly Bahia, local patriotism had an ambiguous relationship to the messages embodied in the days of national festivity.

Official civic ritual in provincial capitals looked much like that of Rio de Janeiro, with a few key differences. The days began with artillery salutes; ships and government offices raised flags; the available regular soldiers and the National Guard mustered for a parade. Officials and members of the local elite attended a Te Deum in the diocesan cathedral or the principal church, and then repaired to the provincial president's palace for a levee at which they paid their respects to the emperor's portrait, beside which the president and the bishop stood. The local newspapers published editorials about the day's meaning, and a theater gala or a ball might conclude the festivities. The theater gala began with cheers to the emperor's portrait, unveiled at the start of the program. Evening illuminations and sometimes music in the main square for the populace rounded out the celebrations.[27] As in Rio de Janeiro, provincial newspapers debated the days' meaning and viewed them through partisan political eyes. In 1855, *O Tocantins* declared that Goiás's population did not merely fulfill its obligations but that all shared in "the most vibrant and cordial demonstrations of satisfaction."[28] Seventeen years later, in Porto Alegre, the republican Francisco Xavier da Cunha condemned the "burlesque" custom of venerating the imperial portrait. The president's efforts to celebrate 25 March made him look like a *Kicumbi* (*cucumbi*) king, and the Guard parade reduced the citizen-soldiers to draft animals as they manhandled heavy field artillery. Nobody, he added, cheered.[29] Special occasions sometimes prompted presidents to arrange more elaborate celebrations, such as on 7–9 September 1867 when Belém had three days of celebrations to mark both independence's anniversary and the Amazon River's opening to international navigation.[30]

A memoirist from Minas Gerais and a commentator on Maranhão both emphasized the political nature of provincial civic ritual in the empire's first decades. They highlighted the partisan mobilizations of these years and suggested that, in the 1840s, civic rituals diminished notably.[31] Francisco de Paula Ferreira Rezende recalled the competing celebrations of Pedro II's majority and his coronation in Minas Gerais; Liberals led the former, while Conservatives took charge of the latter.[32] More generally, he stressed the centrality of illuminations, music, processions, and cheers in Minas Gerais political culture of the 1820s and 1830s, a view that heavily influenced Carla Simone Chamon's study of the partisan festivities after Pedro I's abdication and the proclamation of Pedro II's majority.[33] João Francisco Lisboa claimed that, by the 1850s, the only enthusiasm for days of national festivity in Maranhão could be found in election years when party leaders mobilized their clients and when partisan periodicals outdid each other in what he dismissed as exaggerated rhetoric.[34]

The imperial government encouraged provincial celebrations, and people in the provinces and the capital apparently paid attention to each other's activities on days of national festivity. The ministry of empire sometimes budgeted for subsidies to the provinces so that presidents could illuminate their palaces.[35] It also supplied portraits of the emperors; in 1857, Goiás's *O Tocantins* reported that the latest mule train had brought a new portrait of Pedro II, along with curtains, wallpaper, and carpet for the presidential palace's reception room.[36] News from Rio de Janeiro reached this remote provincial capital after about six weeks, so it was not until January 1856 that *O Tocantins*'s readers learned about how 2 December had been celebrated in the national capital.[37] A Goiás newspaper's Rio de Janeiro correspondent joined in the condemnation of the expenditure of 200 contos to celebrate the end of the Paraguayan War and added a typically provincial spin to his criticisms: The imperial government would not authorize forty contos for improving navigation on the Araguaia River, yet it could casually spend five times as much on ephemeral festivities![38] Reports from the provinces in Rio de Janeiro newspapers regularly noted that celebrations had taken place, and Altève Aumont, the French journalist enamored of 1858's 7 September enthusiasm, concluded that illuminations had taken place in every town and village of "the immense Brazilian empire," an enviable demonstration of the people's patriotism.[39] All of this underscores the importance of civic ritual to the imperial state and its efforts to foster loyalty.

Despite the emphasis on the national in imperial civic ritual, the empire apparently opened some space for the celebration of provincial civic identities. Starting in 1858, the *Almanaque Laemmert* began noting that the date on which each province joined independent Brazil was a holiday in that province.[40] I have been unable to find any indication of legislation that authorized this innovation, nor have I found any evidence that provinces instituted and commemorated new holidays as a result. In Maranhão, 28 July, the date of the province's adhesion to the imperial regime, was instituted as a provincial holiday in 1835.[41] Lisboa placed it alongside 7 September in his criticism of civic ritual customs in that province, but the extent of the 28 July celebrations in Maranhão remains to be established.[42] In Pernambuco, provincial patriotism had long highlighted the expulsion of the Dutch on 27 January 1654, and there are indications that the date was celebrated until 1830; in 1862, the newly founded provincial archeological and historical institute sought unsuccessfully to have the day proclaimed a holiday in the province.[43] Given the Pernambucan resistance to what many saw as a conservative independence imposed by Pedro I, it would have been difficult to identify a satisfactory day to commemorate joining Brazil in that province.

The only province that celebrated its independence on a large scale was Bahia, but its 2 July holiday (which commemorated the expulsion of Portuguese troops from Salvador back in 1823) had received legislative approval as a day of national festivity in 1831. Dois de Julho celebrations included the standard official rituals but also extensive popular festivities that frequently lasted for several days and that drew on the legacy of the popular mobilization required to win independence. Its symbols of the *caboclos* (the Indian statues that were and still are paraded each year) harked back to older representations of America and embodied newer radical readings of their meaning. The day outshone 7 September's celebration, and Dois de Julho rhetoric steered a careful course between loyalty to Brazil and to Bahia; as one journalist put it in 1867, Bahians were "surely Brazilians, but not Cariocas."[44] Rio de Janeiro newspapers sometimes drew comparisons between 7 September celebrations in the capital and 2 July's festival in Bahia, lamenting that enthusiasm for Brazilian independence did not match Bahians' spirited Dois de Julho festivities.[45]

The efforts to promote days of national festivity in the provinces can be read as evidence of a project to foster identification with the imperial nation-state. Association with the monarchy reinforced provincial elites' power, and their participation in civic rituals visibly affirmed social hierarchies.[46] Articles about civic rituals brought newspaper readers into a larger "imagined community" of Brazilians, much as Benedict Anderson would have it, but it also brought them into national politics as the debates about the empire's institutions and other political questions echoed in the provincial press.

THE BRAZILIAN EMPIRE IN CONTEXT

The Brazilian story of politicized civic ritual is certainly not unique. What distinguishes Brazil from Spanish America is, of course, the monarchy and the stability of its civic calendar; press freedom ensured that widely divergent views of the imperial regime appeared in print after 1830. The debate about the meanings of independence and the constitutional monarchy instituted in 1822–24 had its counterparts in Spanish America, and indeed elsewhere, as civic rituals provided some of the most public and visible fora in which to conduct politics.

For the Spanish-American republics that gained independence in the early 1820s, historical work on postindependence civic ritual has scarcely begun. Even more so than in Brazil, independence called into question the colonial regime's certainties. The new states quickly established civic holidays and sought to commemorate their founding and their institutions through annual celebrations, but profound political disagreements shaped the rituals. In Mexico, liberals and conservatives even failed to agree on which day to celebrate as the nation's founding. The date on which Miguel Hidalgo raised the standard of revolt against Spain in 1810 (16 September) appealed to liberals, while conservatives preferred to commemorate 27 September, the anniversary of Augustín Iturbide's triumphant entry into Mexico City in 1821. As William Beezley has pointed out, to celebrate the former meant seeing independence as a process to be completed by further liberal reforms, while the latter implied that independence was a fully consummated fact—in the form of a short-lived monarchy to boot.[47] Conservatives ultimately failed to dislodge 16 September from the civic calendar, and even Emperor Maximilian (1864–67) sought (unsuccessfully) to associate his regime with Hidalgo's memory in his bid to reconcile liberals to his rule.[48] In the 1890s, the authoritarian president Porfirio Díaz, whose birthday fell on 15 September, closely associated himself with independence by instituting a state dinner on the eve of the 16th; it enacted his regime's claim to progress and modernity.[49]

In Costa Rica, only sporadic municipal celebrations of Central America's declaration of independence (15 September 1821) are recorded for the first decades of the country's history. After the formal establishment of a separate Costa Rican republic in 1848, the centralizing regime of Juan Rafael Mora Porras (1849–55) instituted regular celebrations involving Te Deums, speeches, elite balls, and military music for the people of San José. Liberal regimes of the late nineteenth century fostered more elaborate celebrations and gradually secularized them; they constructed the 1856–57 war against William Walker's filibustering expeditions as a surrogate independence struggle. In the early twentieth century, military elements gave way to schoolchildren's parades on 15 September as official rhetoric highlighted the country's peaceful, orderly, hard-working vocations and contrasted these virtues with neighboring countries' failings.[50]

A smattering of work on other countries indicates similar patterns of politics and commemoration. In Venezuela, during his 1870–77 dictatorship, Antonio Guzmán Blanco invested heavily in civic rituals and closely associated himself with the image of Simón Bolívar, by then securely established as the patriarch of independence.[51] The Argentine government and members of the Buenos Aires elite, deeply worried about the influx of immigrants (just beginning on a large scale in the 1880s) and the rapidly growing urban population, heavily promoted large-scale patriotic celebrations and the commemoration of 25 May (the start of the independence struggle in the capital in 1810) and 9 July (the declaration of independence by the Congress of Tucumán in 1816) in schools as a way to instill nationalism.[52] Machado de Assis's 1895 remark about the "May festivals" apparently referred to these efforts. What is clear from this literature is that civic rituals were necessarily political. The deep divisions in most Spanish American republics in the first decades after independence meant that their civic rituals were probably even more contentious than those of the Brazilian empire.

In December 1889, the *Jornal do Comércio*'s *cronista* remarked that one of the reasons for the failure of "monarchical sentiments" to take root in Brazil was "the monarchy's lack of grandeur." João VI had apparently forgotten to bring "majesty" with him from Lisbon and Pedro II had thought that grandeur lay in charity.[53] Certainly there is much evidence for the Brazilian court's modesty, although the Regresso's investment in monarchical ritual from 1837 to 1841 and the midcentury decades more generally, when imperial weddings and Pedro's returns to Rio de Janeiro were celebrated with often considerable pomp and the government invested in theater galas, indicate that there were periods of something approaching majesty. The implicit counterfactual proposition in the *cronista*'s remarks—that the monarchy would have survived had it been more majestic and less bourgeois—is difficult to sustain. After all, the regime's more radical critics in the 1870s and 1880s thought it excessively devoted to costly and outdated ceremonial, and no amount of invention of tradition saved the continental European monarchies swept away by World War I.

To follow the Brazilian empire's commemoration of its days of national festivity from 1823 to 1889 is to trace the evolution of the imperial regime. Far from an exotic transplant to the Americas, as many republican critics characterized it, the Brazilian empire sank deep roots into Rio de Janeiro society. Its civic rituals certainly helped to create the nation, and they formed part of the annual cycle of popular and Church festivals by which Fluminenses marked their lives. To be sure, they celebrated a slavocrat and hierarchical regime, and many of the popular festivities were more about marking exclusions from the community imagined by the celebrants than about inclusion, but in this respect Brazilian patriots were no different from the nativist demonstrators on 4 July in the nineteenth-century United States, to mention one example.[54]

More important, imperial Brazil's days of national festivity were, as Condy Raguet perceptively put it back in 1826, days of political festivity. Through them, Brazilians debated the political institutions of the constitutional monarchy that governed them and regulated their political lives. Those in power had every reason to promote celebrations of the institutions through which they ruled as a way of demonstrating the legitimacy of their rule. The "loyal" opposition naturally saw things differently, but they tended to behave in the same way and to talk about civic rituals in the same way once in power. For most of the empire, few rejected the regime altogether, until republicans gained prominence in the 1870s and 1880s. They too fostered civic rituals and promoted symbols that challenged the official view of the beneficent constitutional monarchy founded by Pedro I in 1822–24.

What is striking is the extent to which the Brazilian empire's celebrations resonated among the free population. Alongside the official festivities, popular celebrations often also flourished. The political mobilizations on days of national festivity in the early 1830s indicate that many felt strongly about the institutions commemorated on these days. The surge of popular festivities on 7 September in the 1850s remains difficult to explain, but these celebrations represent an important form of politics linked to radical Liberals' mobilization in the 1856 and 1860 elections. The Sociedade Comemorativa da Independência do Império's celebrations of independence before 1886, as well as the large-scale lower-class mobilizations to celebrate Pedro's return and abolition in 1888–89, reveal that members of the *povo* were far from *bestializado*, as Aristides Lobo had dismissed them in 1889. This popular engagement with the imperial state and the apparent acceptance of its civic ritual messages prompted the takeover of the Comemorativa by members of Brazilian high society in 1887–88. Republicans' discomfort at the popular classes' limited engagement with their projects shares much with the late-imperial elite's efforts to instill what its members saw as a suitable patriotism in the benighted *povo*. Men like *Alferes* Américo Rodrigues Gamboa, Dom Obá II, José Ponciano de Oliveira, or Antônio José Nunes Garcia, along with the thousands who gathered around the equestrian statue of Pedro

I each night of 6–7 September, turned this site into what Manuel Duarte Moreira de Azevedo had wanted in 1867—a place for magnificent ceremonies of the nation—but neither the empire nor the republic could accept this popular form of marking days of national festivity, nor indeed the very people who constituted this nation. Popular celebration was too dangerous. The empire and the republic needed a *povo* to symbolically legitimize the messages of their civic rituals, but they could not accept a *povo* whose members celebrated the nation on their own.

Reference Matter

Abbreviations Used in the Notes

ABN	*Anais da Biblioteca Nacional*
ACD	*Anais da Câmara dos Deputados*
AGCRJ	Arquivo Geral da Cidade do Rio de Janeiro
AHEx	Arquivo Histórico do Exército
	RQ Requerimentos
AHMI	Arquivo Histórico do Museu Imperial
AIHGB	Arquivo do Instituto Histórico e Geográfico Brasileiro
AN	Arquivo Nacional
	GIFI Grupo de Identificação de Fundos Internos
	SPE Seção do Poder Executivo
AS	*Anais do Senado*
BN	Biblioteca Nacional
	DM Divisão de Música
	SI Seção de Iconografia
	SM Seção de Manuscritos
	DB Documentos Biográficos
	SOG Seção de Obras Gerais
	SOR Seção de Obras Raras
CLB	*Coleção das Leis do Brasil*
CM	*Correio Mercantil*
DRJ	*Diário do Rio de Janeiro*
JC	*Jornal do Comércio*
MHN	Museu Histórico Nacional
MJ	Ministro da Justiça
MI	Ministro do Império
NARS	National Archives and Records Service (USA)
OLL	Oliveira Lima Library
PRO	Public Record Office (Great Britain)
	FO Foreign Office
RIHGB	*Revista do Instituto Histórico e Geográfico Brasileiro*
Rio	Rio de Janeiro (City)
RSCII	*Revista da Sociedade Comemorativa da Independência do Império*

Notes

FRONT MATTER

1. Exchange rate data is drawn from Duncan, *Public and Private Operations*, 183.

2. The key sources for identifying pseudonyms are Gondim, *Pseudônimos*; Menezes, *Dicionário*, 785–800; Paiva, *Achêgas*; Reis, *Pseudonimos*.

INTRODUCTION

1. Lei, 9 Sep. 1826, *CLB*.

2. Hobsbawm and Ranger, *Invention*; Halbwachs, *On Collective Memory*; Nora, "Between Memory." For the case of Buenos Aires, see Acree, "Words," 47–50.

3. Pimenta Bueno, *Direito*, 20.

4. Anderson, *Imagined Communities*.

5. For a critique of Anderson's empirical work, see Guerra, "Forms."

6. For such an approach, see Burns, *Nationalism*. For more recent approaches, see Doyle and Pamplona, *Nationalism*.

7. Condy Raguet to Sec. of State, Rio, 23 Sep. 1826, NARS, M-121, roll 7.

8. I examine this debate and these days' meaning in Chapter One.

9. Kertzer, *Ritual*, 37–39, 72–73, 131–34.

10. Geertz, *Negara*, 13. See also his application of this model to other societies in Geertz, "Centers." Kertzer expands on this in his argument that ritual is central to all forms of politics, *Ritual*, passim.

11. Watanabe-O'Kelly, "Festival Books"; Buc, *Dangers*. For expositions of tropes in the accounts of Portuguese and colonial Brazilian civic rituals, see Megiani, *Rei*, 200–10, 225–81, 287–88; Schiavinatto, "Entre os manuscritos," 17–24.

12. On these questions, see the essays in Hüsken, *When Rituals Go Wrong*; Sax, Quack, and Weinhold, *Problem*.

13. For an introduction to these points, see Muir, *Ritual*, chap. 7. On Roman precedents, see Sumi, *Ceremony*.

14. Zaho, *Imago*; Mateos Royo, "All the Town," 177–78, 188. On Roman triumphs, see Beard, *Roman Triumph*.

15. Bryant, *King*, 22–23, 207–08.

16. Burke, *Fabrication*; Duindam, *Vienna*, 311.

17. Muir, *Ritual*, 294–97.

18. Himelfarb, "Versailles," 295–307; Smith, *Georgian Monarchy*, 95–104.

19. Schneider, *Ceremonial City*, 5; Jackson, *Vive le Roi!*

20. Curto, "Ritos"; Bebiano, *D. João V*; Araújo, "Ritualidade." On the iconography left by Portuguese monarchical ritual, see Mendonça et al., *Arte*.

21. Lopes Don, "Carnivals"; Curcio-Nagy, *Great Festivals*; Dean, *Inka Bodies*.

22. Osorio, *Inventing*, 57–79 (quote 58); Cañeque, *King's Living Image*.

23. Viqueira Albán, *Propriety*.

24. Ozouf, *Festivals*.

25. Mansel, *Court*; Agulhon, *Marianne into Battle*; Truesdell, *Spectacular Politics*; Hazareesingh, *Saint-Napoleon*; Agulhon, *Marianne au pouvoir*.

26. Burke, *Fabrication*, 201.

27. Travers, *Celebrating*, 11; O'Leary, *To Die For*, 16–20; Koschnik, "Political Conflict."

28. Waldstreicher, *In the Midst*, 352. For a similar approach to later periods, see Litwicki, *America's Public Holidays*.

29. Speech of Viscount of Nazareth, July 17, AS (1826), 3:129.

30. The pioneering works in this regard are Sean Wilentz, "Artisan Republican Festivals"; Davis, *Parades*. Many have followed in their footsteps: Heideking, Fabre, and Dreisbach, *Celebrating*; White, "It Was a Proud Day"; Schultz, *Ethnicity*; Clark, *Defining Moments*.

31. Major works on colonial celebrations include Jancsó and Kantor, *Festa*; Tinhorão, *Festas*; Priore, *Festas*; Schwartz, "Ceremonies"; Furtado, "Desfilar"; Gaeta, "Cortejo"; Santos, *Corpo*; Santiago, *Vila*.

32. Tinhorão, *Festas*, 116.

33. Moreira de Azevedo, *Rio*, 1:552; Vieira Fazenda, "Antiqualhas," *RIHGB* 86:140 (1919): 130 (originally published in 1901); Cruls, *Aparência*, 1:115, 197–98; 2:596–97; Mendonça, "Festas," 304, 306–09, 312.

34. Macedo, *Memórias da rua*, 66.

35. Oliveira Lima, *D. João VI*, 88; Schultz, *Tropical Versailles*, 1–2.

36. Debret, *Viagem*, 2:2. On the French artists, see Taunay, *Missão*; Lima, *J.-B. Debret*, 93–103.

37. On these celebrations, see Oliveira Lima, *D. João VI*, 65–69, 546–47, 605–22; Silva, *Cultura*, 57–67; Gazeta, 46–64; Malerba, *Corte*, 51–124, 263–72; Schultz, *Tropical Versailles*, 154–56; Souza, *Pátria*, 213–37, "Liturgia," and "D. João VI," 50–63; Schiavinatto, "Entre histórias" and "Entre os manuscritos"; Brand, "Sets"; Lopez, *Festas*; Assunção, *Ritmos*, 78–88, 107–19, 169–92, 199, 231–32; Schwarcz, Azevedo, and Costa, *Longa viagem*, 237–43, 251, 301–05, 321–30; Gouvêa, "Senado."

38. Henderson, *History*, 50–51; Cruls, *Aparência*, 1:283–84; Oliveira Lima, *D. João VI*, 63.

39. Thomas W. Sumter to Sec. of State, Rio, 8 and 29 Dec. 1815, NARS, M-121, roll 3; Decisão 46, 23 Dec. 1815, *CLB*. Travelers who reported this incident include Gendrin, *Récit*, 54–55; Freycinet, *Woman*, 13; Leithold, "Minha

excursão," 58. On João's attitude to ceremonies, see Oliveira Lima, *D. João VI*, 569.

40. Leithold, "Minha excursão," 58–59, 68; Rango, "Diário," 136; Varnhagen, *História geral*, 6th ed., 4:92; Schultz, *Tropical Versailles*, 156–58.

41. Lopez, *Festas*, 50, 56 (quote); Assunção, *Ritmos*, 155, 156. See also Slemian, *Vida*, 65. Schiavinnato speculates that more criticisms were expressed orally or in manuscript handbills but offers no direct evidence; "Entre histórias," 77–78,

42. Lopez, *Festas*, 186; Schiavinatto, "Entre histórias," 80.

43. The flood of recent literature on independence has deepened and broadened our understanding of the process. In English, the most reliable narrative is Barman, *Brazil*, 65–129. Good introductions to recent Brazilian work are found in Jancsó, *Brasil* and *Independência*, and Malerba, *Independência*. Key recent works on the changes in political culture wrought in the early 1820s include Oliveira, *Astúcia*; Lustosa, *Insultos*; Neves, *Corcundas*; Slemian, *Vida*. Older but still useful approaches include Costa, *Brazilian Empire*, 1–23; Rodrigues, *Independência*. For an important reconsideration of independence in Pernambuco, see Mello, *Outra Independência*. For an effort to elucidate the role of the popular classes, see Alves, "Plebeian Activism."

44. Barman, *Brazil*, 76–77. On José Bonifácio, see also Costa, *Brazilian Empire*, 24–52.

45. Lustosa, *Insultos*, 242–43.

46. Silva, *Gazeta*, 277; Lopez, *Festas*, 235–336; Souza, *Pátria*, 256–81; Ribeiro, *Símbolos*, 71–78; Schubert, *Coroação*.

47. On the issues raised by the coronation, see Oliveira, "Império"; Cardoso, "Ritual"; Araújo, "Ritualidade," 179–84; Schwarcz, Azevedo, and Costa, *Longa viagem*, 389–90, 392–93. On the consecration or unction's medieval origins, see Oakley, *Kingship*, 96–98.

48. On the Rio de Janeiro economy's autonomous development, see Fragoso, *Homens*; Fragoso and Florentino, *Aracaismo*.

49. For such approaches to the Brazilian state, see Mattos, *Tempo*; Graham, *Patronage* and "Constructing"; Carvalho, *Construção/Teatro*. See also the survey of these issues in Topik, "Hollow State."

50. Needell, *Party*, 5, 6–7.

51. For examples of the São Paulo group's work, see Jancsó, *Brasil*, and *Independência*, and its online journals, *Almanack Braziliense* (www.almanack. usp.br/) and *Almanack* (www.brasiliana.usp.br/almanack/); collections of the CEO's work include Carvalho, *Nação*; Carvalho and Neves, *Repensando*.

52. On this concept, see Corrigan and Sayer, *Great Arch*.

53. Important sources for the following paragraphs include Barreiros, *Atlas*; Ferrez, "O que ensinam."

54. Moreira de Azevedo, *Rio*, 2:359, 362; Coaracy, *Memórias*, 60–62.

55. Descriptions of the Palace Square and the market include Webster, *Narrative*, 1:41; Hill, *Fifty Days*, 3; Hall, *Around the Horn*, 74–75; Upham, *Notes*, 61–62; Brassey, *Voyage*, 43–44; Atchison, *Winter Cruise*, 127–28. On the palace's construction, see Coaracy, *Memórias*, 42.

56. Cruls, *Aparência*, 1:204–06; Varnhagen, *História geral*, 6th ed., 5:92–93.

57. Coaracy, *Memórias*, 50; Guimarães, "Nação," 10.

58. Cruls, *Aparência*, 2:423; La Salle, *Voyage*, 1:138; Biard, *Deux années*, 44, 47, 83–84; Expilly, *Brésil*, 250; Selys-Longchamps, *Notes*, 11; Macedo, *Memórias da rua*, 68–76.

59. Ursel, *Sud-Amérique*, 48. On Ouvidor Street, see also Needell, *Tropical Belle Époque*, 161–66.

60. Debret, *Viagem*, 2:261.

61. Ebel, *Rio*, 73–74; Webster, *Narrative*, 1:46–47; Burmeister, *Viagem*, 42; Expilly, *Brésil*, 62–63; Gaston, *Hunting*, 40.

62. Assumpção, *Narrativas*, 34–35; Morales de los Rios Filho, *Rio*, 210.

63. On the Valongo market, see Soares, "*Povo*," 29, 39, 41–44; Karasch, *Slave Life*, 29–50.

64. Sousa, *Teatro*, 1:291–92.

65. Cruls, *Aparência*, 1:316; Edmundo, *Rio*, 1:200–202.

66. Morales de los Rios Filho, *Rio*, 113, 141; Campos, *Caminhos*, 177, 78, 192–93.

67. For a sampling of these images, see Ferrez, *Iconografia*, 2:10, 60, 74, 78, 94, 160, 174–75, 187, 223–24, 250.

68. Silva, *Cultura*, 41–42, 54–55.

69. Coaracy, *Memórias*, 120; Morales de los Rios Filho, *Rio*, 199; Ewbank, *Life*, 140; Binzer, *Alegrias*, 55; Toussaint-Samson, *Parisian*, 38; Bennett, *Forty Years*, 83–84.

70. Eltis and Richardson, "New Assessment," 16.

71. Soares, "*Povo*," 376. These figures include the municipality's rural parishes.

72. Leitão, *Do civismo*, 311.

73. Guimarães, "Nação," 6–7, 14–18, 20–24; Wehling, *Estado*, 33–35.

74. Lamberg, *Brazil*, 292.

75. *Almanack Laemmert* (1844): 36–38; (1864): 168–78; (1884): 122–36.

76. Berger, *Bibliografia*.

77. Karasch, *Slave Life*; Soares, "*Povo*"; Frank, *Dutra's World*.

78. Graham, "Free African Brazilians."

79. Degler, *Neither Black nor White*; Skidmore, *Black into White*.

80. Dunlop, *Subsídios*, 40–55; Scherzer, *Narrative*, 1:125–26; Cunningham, *Notes*, 31–32.

81. Weid, "Bonde"; Needell, *Tropical Belle Époque*, 134–35, 151–53.

82. Hinchcliff, *Over the Sea*, 7. For a contemporary Brazilian assessment of the social changes wrought by streetcars, see França Júnior, *Folhetins*, 143–53.

83. C. Andrews, *Brazil*, 31 (quote); Dent, *Year*, 236–37; Coppin, *Quatre républiques*, 34–35; Rancourt, *Fazendas*, 42; Gallenga, *South America*, 382–83.

84. Moreira de Azevedo, *Rio*, 1:56, 2:545.

85. Biard, *Deux années*, 50–51; Elwes, *Sketcher's Tour*, 16. See also the analysis of Biard's experience in Araújo, *Romantisme*, 136–38; and Needell's analysis of dress, *Tropical Belle Époque*, 166–71.

86. Chalhoub, *Cidade*.

87. Magalhães, *Diário*, 126.

88. Gomes, "Dois séculos," 56–57.

89. Farias, Soares, and Gomes, *No labirinto*, 66; Soares, *Zungú*; Sampaio, *Juca Rosa*; Abreu, *Império*; Oliveira Lima, *D. João VI*, 595–600; Karasch, *Slave Life*, 254–301.

90. Holloway, "Healthy Terror"; Ferreira, *Inventando*; Cunha, *Ecos*.

91. Vianna, *Contribuição*; Sodré, *História*.

92. Waldstreicher, *In the Midst*, 10. See also Cardoso, "Ritual," 596.

93. Carvalho, *D. Pedro II*, 84; *Construção/Teatro*, 46–47; Holanda, "Do Império," 72.

94. Pratt, *Imperial Eyes*. For recent analyses of travelers, see Lima, *J.-B. Debret*; Araújo, *Romantisme*; Martins, *Rio*; Lisboa, "Olhares"; Sela, *Modos*.

95. A recent and accessible analysis for a very different society can be found in Beard, *Roman Triumph*, 31, 82, 101–02, 105, 167, 265.

CHAPTER ONE

1. On the post-1823 repression, see Morel, *Transformações*, 198; Macaulay, *Dom Pedro*, 193; Barman, *Brazil*, 123–29; Wisser, "Rhetoric," 9–10.

2. Oliveira, "Repercussão," 18–20.

3. Morel, *Transformações*, 157–59.

4. Mansel, *Court*, 149, 129 (quote).

5. William Tudor to Sec. of State, Rio, 6 Dec. 1828, NARS M-121, roll 8; Cochrane, *Narrative*, 2:13; Walsh, *Notices*, 1:487; Seidler, *Dez anos*, 44; Ebel, *Rio*, 152. See also Sousa, *Vida*, 2:84; Lustosa, *D. Pedro I*, 60–61, 64.

6. Walsh, *Notices*, 2:451.

7. Schultz, *Tropical Versailles*, 165–77.

8. Walsh, *Notices*, 2:447–49; Henderson, *History*, 50–51; Boelen, *Reize*, 1:74–75. See also Ebel, *Rio*, 38; Graham, "Escorço," 124.

9. Soares, *Capoeira*, 296.

10. Bösche, "Quadros," 167; Andrews, *Journey*, 2:246. See also Jacquemont, *Letters*, 1:40; Boelen, *Reize*, 1:73–74.

11. Armitage, *History*, 1:53–55 (quote 1:54), 2:2 (quote), 2:6–7.

12. Moreira de Azevedo, "Origem," 186; Morales de los Rios Filho, *Rio*, 465.

13. Moreira de Azevedo, "Origem," 190–91; Levasseur, *Brasil*, 117–18; Sandroni, *180 anos*, 37–41.

14. Levasseur, *Brasil*, 117. See also Graham's survey of the press in late October 1823, *Journal*, 322–23.

15. Armitage, *History*, 1:226.

16. Walsh, *Notices*, 1:427; João Loureiro to Manuel José Maria da Costa e Sá, Rio, 21 June 1829, *RIHGB* 76:2 (1914): 325; Moreira de Azevedo, "Origem," 192; Pereira da Silva, *Segundo periodo*, 167, 263–64.

17. Lei, 20 Sep. 1830, *CLB*.

18. Wisser, "Rhetoric," 21–39.

19. Rugendas, *Viagem*, 196. Pereira da Silva shared this assessment; *Segundo periodo*, 33.

20. Condy Raguet to Sec. of State, Rio, 20 March 1826, NARS, M-121, roll 6; 1 Sep. 1826, NARS, M-121, roll 7. For other such placards, see Pereira da Silva, *Segundo periodo*, 24–25, 36–37, 38–39.

21. Raguet to Sec. of State, Rio, 23 Sep. 1826, NARS, M-121, roll 7.

22. "Manifesto do Príncipe Regente aos Povos do Brasil" and "Manifesto do Príncipe Regente do Brasil aos governos e nações amigas," 1 and 6 Aug. 1822, in Mello Moraes, *História*, 2:414, 416.

23. Handelmann, *Historia*, 2:792n171; Lyra, "Memória," 177–89; Neves, *Corcundas*, 369–70; Oliveira, "Museu Paulista," 66–67; Neves, "Estado," 128; Schwarcz, Azevedo, and Costa, *Longa viagem*, 382, 388. For analysis closer to mine, see Macedo, "Independência," 57–59.

24. Lyra, "Memória," 198, 201.

25. Lisboa, *Historia*, part X, section I, 1; part X, section III, 53.

26. Lyra, "Memória," 191–97. On Cairu's interpretation, see also Neves, "Estado," 98; Oliveira, "Repercussão," 22–29.

27. Decreto, 21 Dec. 1822, *CLB*. This analysis follows Costa, *D. Pedro I*.

28. Decreto, 10 Dec. 1822, *CLB*.

29. "Falla com que Sua Magestade o Imperador abriu a Assembléa Geral Legislativa Constituinte no dia 3 de Maio de 1823," *CLB*.

30. Sessions of 5 and 9 Sep. 1823, Brazil, *Diario da Assembléa*, 1:722, 733.

31. Raguet to Sec. of State, Rio, 8 Sep. 1823, NARS, T-172, roll 2.

32. Baron Wenzel de Mareschal to Prince of Metternich, Rio, 30 Aug. 1823, *RIHGB* 314 (Jan.–March 1977): 346. See also Mareschal to Metternich, Rio, 20 Sep. 1823, *RIHGB* 315 (April–June 1977): 308.

33. "Soneto ao Faustissimo Anniversario da Independencia Brasileira," *O Sylpho*, 13 Sep. 1823.

34. Sessions of 7, 9, and 13 Oct. 1823, Brazil, *Diario da Assembléa*, 2:186–87, 214, 231–32.

35. Fernandes, *Elogio*, 4. Mareschal described the commemorations to Metternich, Rio, 21 Oct. 1823, *RIHGB* 315 (April–June 1977): 319.

36. Decisão 155 (Império), 23 Oct. 1823; Decisão 159 (Império), 10 Nov. 1823, *CLB*.

37. "Almanaque do Rio . . . 1824," 201.

38. "Anniversario da Gloriosa Coroação de SS. MM. II.," *Estrela Brasileira*, 3 Dec. 1823; Kotzebue, *New Voyage*, 1:47–54. Kotzebue dates this celebration to 19 Nov., but this is evidently an error, for he is clearly describing the same ceremony that the *Estrela* recounted; Cruls, *Aparência*, 1:330.

39. Raguet to Sec. of State, Rio, 20 Jan. 1824, NARS, T-172, roll 2; Mello Moraes, *Chronica*, 2:240.

40. Henry Chamberlain to George Canning, Rio, 10 Dec. 1823, PRO/FO 63, vol. 261, fol. 189.

41. "Ceremonial para o Juramento solemne . . . ," AHMI, I-POB 25.03.1824 PI.B.is; Mareschal to Metternich, Rio, 12 March 1824, *RIGHB* 319 (April–June 1978): 372.

42. Morel, *Transformações*, 227; Raguet to Sec. of State, Rio, 12 April 1824, NARS, T-172, roll 2.

43. "Extracto da Estrella Brasileira do Rio de Janeiro n.º 65, e 66," *Grito da Razão* (Salvador), 27 April 1824 (these issues of the *Estrella Brasileira* are missing from the BN's microfilm); Ebel, *Rio*, 109–17; Moreira de Azevedo, *Rio*, 2:163–64.

44. Chamberlain to Canning, Rio, 26 March 1824, PRO/FO 63, vol. 276, fol. 257v–58r; Raguet to Sec. of State, Rio, 12 April 1824, NARS, T-172, roll 2; Mareschal to Metternich, Rio, 31 March 1824, *RIHGB* 319 (April–June 1978): 376–77; Ebel, *Rio*, 118.

45. On this image's political purposes, see Santos, *Imagem*, 65, 68.

46. Carta de Lei, 25 March 1824, *CLB*. For analysis of the constitution's key terms, see Barman, *Brazil*, 123–26; Cunha, "Fundação," 253–62.

47. Schlichthorst, *Rio*, 110–11.

48. Twelve published works of the genre authored by Fernandes can be found in the AIHGB's library. On Fernandes, see Sacramento Blake, *Diccionario*, 5:117.

49. Graham, *Journal*, 319; Walsh, *Notices*, 1:519, 524.

50. Walsh, *Notices*, 1:525; Stewart, *Visit*, 1:61–62. The difficulty in walking backwards was also noted by Raguet to Sec. of State, Rio, 7 Jan. 1825, NARS, T-172, roll 3; [Ruschenberger], *Three Years*, 1:78; Robert C. Schenck to Daughters, Rio, 7 Sep. 1851, in Peskin and Ramos, "Ohio Yankee," 501; Stewart, *Brazil*, 110.

51. Boelen, *Reize*, 1:70; Walsh, *Notices*, 1:518; Bougainville, *Journal*, 1:624; Debret, *Viagem*, 2:127; Stewart, *Visit*, 1:56, 60 (quote).

52. Chamberlain to Canning, Rio, 13 Oct. 1824, PRO/FO 13, vol. 279, fol. 73r.

53. Bösche, "Quadros," 166; see also Walsh, *Notices*, 1:233; M. Graham, *Journal*, 232.

54. Graham, "Escorço," 89.

55. Kotzebue, *New Voyage*, 1:52–53.

56. Chamberlain to Canning, Rio, 13 Oct. 1824, PRO/FO 13, vol. 279, fols. 73r–74v; Raguet to Sec. of State, Rio, 8 Nov. 1824, NARS, T-172, roll 3; "Dia 12 de Outubro," *O Spectador Brasileiro*, 14 Oct. 1825; Mareschal to Metternich, Rio, 19 Oct. 1824, *RIHGB* 323 (April–June 1979): 206.

57. Raguet to Sec. of State, Rio, 12 Sep. 1824, NARS, T-172, roll 3; "Anniversario da Independencia Politica . . . ," *O Spectador Brasileiro*, 10 Sep. 1824; Mareschal to Metternich, Rio, 18 Sep. 1824, *RIHGB* 323 (April–June 1979): 200.

58. "Rio de Janeiro, 10 de Setembro 1822 [sic]," *O Spectador Brasileiro*, 10 Sep. 1824.

59. Decisão 210 (Guerra), 1 Oct. 1824, *CLB*.

60. *O Spectador Brasileiro*, 15 and 18 Oct. 1824.

61. Decisão 38 (Guerra), 7 March 1825; Decisão 187 (Guerra), 25 Aug. 1825; Decisão 198 (Guerra), 5 Sep. 1825 (Guerra), *CLB*. Costa analyzed the first two of these rulings but was unaware of the third, *D. Pedro I*, 23–27.

62. Chamberlain to Canning, Rio, 8 Sep. 1825, PRO/FO 13, vol. 10, fol. 48v; Schlichthorst, *Rio*, 197.

63. Raguet to Sec. of State, Rio, 15 Sep. 1825, NARS, T-172, roll 3.

64. Monteiro, *História*, 1:277–79, 281; Lyra, "Memória," 190–94; Sousa, *Vida*, 2:177, 186–89.

65. Mareschal to Metternich, Rio, 24 Oct. 1825, *RIHGB* 335 (April–June 1982): 157; Raguet to Sec. of State, Rio, 26 Oct. 1825, NARS, M-121, roll 6; Chamberlain to Canning, Rio, 15 Oct. 1825, PRO/FO 13, vol. 10, fol. 239.

66. Schlichthorst, *Rio*, 248.

67. This rhetorical trope was already widespread in 1822, "Manifesto do Príncipe Regente," 1 Aug. 1822, in Mello Moraes, *História*, 2:414; Veiga, "Poesias," *ABN* 33 (1911): 225, 244, 260. On colonial geography, see Magnoli, *Corpo*, 45–61, 71, 111, 296.

68. On the politics of this journey, see Macaulay, *Dom Pedro*, 190–91; Monteiro, *História*, 2:100–101.

69. "Noticias nacionaes," *Atalaia da Liberdade*, 15 March 1826.

70. *O Verdadeiro Liberal*, 4 April 1826. See also Silva, *Memórias*, 103.

71. Chamberlain to Canning, Rio, 15 April 1826, PRO/FO 13, vol. 22, fol. 411; Armitage, *History*, 1:227–29; Pereira da Silva, *Segundo periodo*, 83–85.

72. Raguet to Sec. of State, Rio, 12 April 1826, NARS, M-121, roll 6.

73. Mareschal to Metternich, Rio, 7 April 1826, *RIHGB* 346 (Jan.–March 1985): 247.

74. Henrique Garcez Pinto de Madureira to Francisco Gomes da Silva, Rio, 23 Feb. 1826, AHMI, I-POB-06.02.1826-Gar.c 1–6; "Noticias nacionaes," *O Verdadeiro Liberal*, 2 March 1826; "Juizo critico politico," *Atalaia da Liberdade*, 1 March 1826; *O Spectador Brasileiro*, 15 March 1826; Raguet to Sec. of State, Rio, 20 March 1826, NARS, M-121, roll 6; Sousa, *Teatro*, 1:286.

75. *Relação*, 5–7.

76. The literature on these entries is vast. See, among others, Bryant, *King*; Zaho, *Imago*; Beard, *Roman Triumph*; Megiani, *Rei ausente*. See also the literature on the reception of viceroys in Spanish America: Osorio, *Inventing Lima*, 57–79; Cañeque, *King's Living Image*, 119–55. For nineteenth-century Europe, see Unowsky, *Pomp*; Truesdell, *Spectacular Politics*, chap. 8. The Prince of Wales's 1860 reception in British North America echoed these older forms; Radforth, *Royal Spectacle*.

77. Chamberlain to Canning, Rio, 3 April 1826, PRO/FO 13, vol. 22, fol. 383r.

78. *Relação*, 13–14; Bougainville, *Journal*, 1:622–24.

79. "Rio de Janeiro, 2 de Abril," *O Spectador Brasileiro*, 3 April 1826.

80. Fernandes, *Homenagem*, 6–7.

81. *Relação*, 70–73, 94–97, 125–30; Schlichthorst, *Rio*, 185–86.

82. *Relação*, 14, 97.

83. Bougainville, *Journal*, 1:625–26; *Relação*, 30–37 (quote, 37).

84. "Aviso ao publico," *O Spectador Brasileiro*, 5 April 1826; *Relação*, 38; Bougainville, *Journal*, 1:626. Debret incorrectly dated this Te Deum to 4 April.

85. Souza, *Pátria*, 254.

86. Schlichthorst, *Rio*, 184–86. See also Monteiro, *História*, 2:111.

87. Raguet to Sec. of State, Rio, 12 April 1826, NARS, M-121, roll 6.

88. Lei, 9 Sep. 1826, *CLB*.

89. The following paragraphs are based on the debates in *AS* (1826), 1:85; 2:100–102; 3:14–16, 122–29; *ACD* (1826), 2:36; 3:262–65.

90. There is no indication that the Constituent Assembly proposed designating 9 January as a day of national festivity.

91. On Vergueiro's politics, see Rangel, *No rolar*, 158.

92. "Dia 7 de Setembro," *O Spectador Brasileiro*, 7 Sep. 1826; "Dia 12 de Outubro," *Aurora Fluminense*, 12 Oct. 1829. See also "Dia 12 de Outubro,"

O Spectador Brasileiro, 13 Oct. 1826; *Gazeta do Brasil*, 7 Sep. 1827; "Brésil," *L'Echo de l'Amérique du Sud*, 10 Sep. 1827; "Anniversaire du 12 octobre," *L'Echo de l'Amérique du Sud*, 13 Oct. 1827; *Astrea*, 14 Oct. 1828; "Jubilo Brasileiro," *A Luz Brasileira*, 13 Oct. 1829; *JC*, 13 Oct. 1829. Holman described the 12 Oct. 1829 celebrations, *Voyage*, 2:58–59.

93. Walsh, *Notices*, 2:419.

94. "Dia 25 de Março," *Aurora Fluminense*, 27 March 1829; *JC*, 28 March 1829.

95. Monteiro, *História*, 2:108. On Leopoldina's image, see "Oração funebre . . . ," in Monte Alverne, *Obras*, 4:235–53.

96. Raguet to Sec. of State, Rio, 22 Dec. 1826, NARS, M-121, roll 7; Debret, *Viagem*, 2:230–34; Macaulay, *Dom Pedro*, 202–03; Sousa, *Vida*, 2:229.

97. On Pedro's mistresses and illegitimate children, see Rangel, *Textos*, 101–295.

98. Tudor to Sec. of State, Rio, 26 Oct. 1829, NARS, M-121, roll 8.

99. Accounts of these celebrations include *Funcções*; "D. Pedro I e D. Amélia"; Debret, *Viagem*, 2:79, 271–73; *Folhinha d'algibeira, Supplemento*, 1–7; Armitage, *History*, 2:65; Sousa, *Vida*, 3:23–26.

100. *Funcções*, 43–45 (quote 43).

101. For additional descriptions, see Debret, *Viagem*, 2:272; *O Analista*, 2 Nov. 1829; *Folhinha d'algibeira, Supplemento*, 7.

102. For the poetry, see *Funcções*, 57–87; "D. Pedro I e D. Amélia," 103–35.

103. Marquis of Barbacena to Marquis of Palmela, Rio, 21 Oct. 1829, in "D. Pedro I e D. Amélia," 79.

104. Amaral, "Explicação," 247–48. On the coaches' origins see Oliveira Lima, *D. João VI*, 605, 747n846; Morales de los Rios Filho, *Rio*, 137.

105. The original source for this stage curtain is Debret's explanation of its imagery, *Viagem*, 2:268–70. For analyses of it, see Salles, *Nostalgia*, 98–100; Lopez, *Festas*, 330–36.

106. *Folhinha d'algibeira, Supplemento*, 7; *O Analista*, 2 Nov. 1829.

107. *O Analista*, 2 Nov. 1829; *Funcções*, 45; "D. Pedro e D. Amélia," 59–60, 65. On these dances, see Câmara Cascudo, *Diccionario*, 320–22, 905–06.

108. Debret, *Viagem*, 2:272–73. See also *Funcções*, 33–35.

109. *JC*, 5 Dec. 1829.

110. Letter from O Amigo do Bem Geral, *JC*, 4 Dec. 1829.

111. "Declarações," *DRJ*, 20 Feb. 1830; 30.ª sessão, 27 March 1830, "Actas," *Arquivo do Distrito Federal* 4 (1953): 162.

112. "Avisos," *Gazeta da Bahia* (Salvador), 19 June 1830. For an image with a similar message, see "Calendario perpetuo e allegorico . . . ," AIHGB, lata 403, doc. 12.

113. On this social unrest, see Soares, *Capoeira*; Ribeiro and Pereira, "Primeiro Reinado"; Alves, "Plebeian Activism."

114. Raguet to Sec. of Sate, Rio, 6 Oct. 1825, NARS, M-121, roll 6.

115. Armitage, *History*, 1:221; Walsh, *Notices*, 1:519.

116. Schlichthorst, *Rio*, 54, 184–85, 187.

117. Bösche, "Quadros," 166, 167.

CHAPTER TWO

1. For an analysis of the patterns of press commentary on these rituals, see Wisser, "Rhetoric," 118–20, 127–29.

2. Pereira da Silva, *Historia do Brazil*, vii.

3. Key modern works on this period include Ribeiro, *Liberdade*; Lima, *Cores*; Basile, "Império" and "Laboratório." Barman provides a reliable political narrative in *Brazil*, 150–88; as does Castro, "Experiência." These should be supplemented with Needell, *Party*, 30–72.

4. Morel, *Transformações*, chap. 5; Wisser, "Rhetoric."

5. Rezende, *Minhas recordações*, 67.

6. Little has been written on the vigorously contested civic rituals between March 1830 and March 1831, but see Wisser, "Rhetoric," 114–55, 158–64, 197–210; Lyra, "Memória," 201–02; Souza, *Pátria*, 342–50.

7. "Annuncio Constitucional," *A Luz Brasileira*, 24 March 1830; *Aurora Fluminense*, 22 March 1830.

8. *O Brasileiro Imparcial*, 27 March 1830; *Astrea*, 27 March 1830; *Aurora Fluminense*, 29 March 1830; "25 de Março," *JC*, 27 March 1830.

9. *O Brasileiro Imparcial*, 24 July 1830.

10. 25th Session, 13 March 1830, "Actas," *Arquivo do Distrito Federal* 4 (1953): 144. Article 74, Lei, 1 Oct. 1828, *CLB*. On this law's genesis, see Ricci, *Assombrações*, 352–57.

11. Emidio Antonini to Min. of Foreign Affairs, Rio, 27 March 1830, in Antonini, *Relatórios*, 64; "25 de Março," *JC*, 27 March 1830; *Astrea*, 27 March 1830; "Dia 25 de Março de 1830!!!" *Voz Fluminense*, 27 March 1830; *O Brasileiro Imparcial*, 27 March 1830; "Sobre o Dia 25 de Março," *A Luz Brasileira*, 31 March 1830.

12. *Aurora Fluminense*, 29 and 31 March 1830.

13. *Aurora Fluminense*, 1 Sep. 1830. See also "Dia 7 de Setembro," *Nova Luz Brasileira*, 7 Sep. 1830.

14. *Edital*, 4 Sep. 1830, quoted in Ribeiro, *Liberdade*, 244; *Nova Luz Brasileira*, 21 Sep. 1830; Letter to the Editor from Brasileiro, *Voz Fluminense*, 14 Oct. 1830.

15. Letter to the Editor from "Hum Parochiano de S. Rita," *Aurora Fluminense*, 10 Sep. 1830; *Nova Luz Brasileira*, 14 Sep. 1830.

16. *Astrea*, 15 March 1831. See also *O Tribuno do Povo*, 28 March 1831.

17. *CM*, 10 Sep. 1830; *O Moderador*, 11 Sep. 1830; *JC*, 9 Sep. 1830.

18. *Aurora Fluminense*, 10 Sep. 1830; *Nova Luz Brazileira*, 7 Sep. 1830.

19. 72nd Session, 25 Aug. 1830, "Actas," *Arquivo do Distrito Federal* 4 (1953): 309.

20. "Dia 7 de Setembro," *Nova Luz Brasileira*, 7 Sep. 1830; *Astrea*, 7 Sep. 1830.

21. *Aurora Fluminense*, 10 Sep. 1830.

22. *O Brasileiro Imparcial*, 7 Sep. 1830; Reis, *Oração*, 13.

23. *Voz Fluminense*, 15 Sep. 1830; *O Brasileiro Imparcial*, 16 Oct. 1830; *Nova Luz Brazileira*, 12 Oct. 1830.

24. Moreira de Azevedo, *Rio*, 2:270; *O Brasileiro Imparcial*, 16 Oct. 1830; *O Moderador*, 16 Oct. 1830; "Memoravel Dia Doze do Corrente Mez d'Outubro," *O Verdadeiro Patriota*, 13 Oct. 1830.

25. *O Verdadeiro Patriota*, 13 Oct. 1830; *O Moderador*, 13, 16, and 20 Oct. 1830; *CM*, 13 Oct. 1830; *JC*, 14 Oct. 1830; *O Brasileiro Imparcial*, 16 Oct. 1830.

26. *Voz Fluminense*, 14 and 21 Oct. 1830; *O Brasileiro Imparcial*, 12 and 16 Oct. 1830.

27. Petition of "Corpo de Commercio, e outras Corporações Civis, e Militares," ca. Feb. 1831, AGCRJ, 6-2-27, fol. 17; *CM*, 15 March 1831. On the amount raised by the subscription, see Monteiro, *História*, 2:193.

28. *CM*, 17 March 1831.

29. On Maia's death and the efforts of *O Verdadeiro Patriota*'s editor to provide for his family, see "Declarações," *DRJ*, 7 March 1831.

30. *O Verdadeiro Patriota*, 18 March 1831. See also *O Novo Censor*, 19 March 1831; *Diario Mercantil ou Novo Jornal do Commercio*, 16 March 1831; Moore, *Revolution*, 25 March 1831 (no pagination).

31. Arthur Aston to Viscount Palmerston, Rio, 17 March 1831, PRO/FO 13, vol. 81, fol. 179v.

32. On Borges da Fonseca, see Santos, *Homem*, 37–48; Ricci, *Atuação*, 133–60; Vianna, *Contribuição*, 535–95.

33. *O Republico*, 21 March 1831.

34. Armitage, *History*, 2:116; Faria, *Breve historia*, 33–34; [Barreto], *Historia*, 26; Ethan A. Brown to Sec. of State, Rio, 19 March 1831, NARS, M-121, roll 10.

35. Brazil, MJ, *Relatorio* (1831), 1; [Barreto], *Historia*, 20.

36. Moore, *Revolution*, 15 March 1831; Faria, *Breve historia*, 34; *Aurora Fluminense*, 18 March 1831; *O Tribuno do Povo*, 28 March 1831.

37. *O Novo Censor*, 19 March 1831. See also Bösche, "Quadros," 207; Armitage, *History*, 2:113.

38. Testimony of Domingos Ferreira Gomes, "Traslado do Processo a que deu moctivo os temultos das Garrafadas . . . ," BN/SM, 6, 3, 12.

39. Testimony of João Pedro da Veiga, "Traslado," BN/SM, 6, 3, 12.

40. Armitage, *History*, 2:114; *O Republico*, 16 March 1831; Borjes da Fonseca, *Manifesto*, 8–9; Faria, *Breve historia*, 27–30.

41. *O Novo Censor*, 19 March 1831; Verdadeiro Constitucional, *Defeza*, 2.

42. *Nova Luz Brazileira*, 18 March 1831; *Aurora Fluminense*, 18 March 1831; Moore, *Revolution*, 13 March 1831; Faria, *Breve historia*, 31–32.

43. Petition, 17 March 1831, *Aurora Fluminense*, 18 March 1831; "Analyze do Requerimento transcripto em a *Aurora* de 18 do corrente," *O Novo Censor*, 23 March 1831. Malheiros used the French "*sans-culotte.*"

44. Aston to Palmerston, Rio, 17 and 19 March 1831, PRO/FO 13, vol. 81, fols. 180r, 188r; Bösche, "Quadros," 212; Editais, 23 and 24 March 1831, *DRJ*, 28 and 30 March 1831; Faria, *Breve historia*, 46, 34–36.

45. *Aurora Fluminense*, 23 March 1831. For the subscription's accounts, see "A subscripção para os festejos do dia 25 de Março de 1831," *Aurora Fluminense*, 6 May 1831.

46. "Vinte e Cinco de Março," *O Tribuno do Povo*, 24 March 1831.

47. *CM*, 27 March 1831; *Astrea*, 26 March 1831; *O Verdadeiro Patriota*, 29 March 1831; *O Moderador*, 30 March 1831; "Festas nacionaes," *O Republico*, 30 March 1831; *O Brasileiro Offendido*, 30 March 1831; *Diario Mercantil ou*

Novo Jornal do Commercio, 26 March 1831. See also Brown to Sec. of State, Rio, 7 April 1831, NARS, M-121, roll 10; Brazil, MJ, *Relatorio* (1831), 2.

48. Bösche, "Quadros," 212; *O Brasileiro Offendido*, 26 and 30 March 1831.

49. Armitage, *History*, 2:125. Monteiro's account is based on these diplomats' reports; *Primeiro Reinado*, 2:198–99.

50. "Festas nacionaes," *O Repúblico*, 30 March 1831. See also *Diario Mercantil ou Novo Jornal do Commercio*, 28 March 1831; Moore, *Revolution*, 25 March 1831; Faria, *Breve historia*, 46; [Barreto], *Historia*, 29–30; Pereira da Silva, *Segundo periodo*, 444; Brazil, MJ, *Relatorio* (1831), 3. Borges da Fonseca later claimed that he had forestalled a regicidal plot that day, *Manifesto*, 4, 9.

51. *O Verdadeiro Patriota*, 29 March 1831.

52. Monte Alverne, *Oração*, 19, 20. The version of this sermon later published in Monte Alverne's collected works contains important differences in wording, *Obras*, 4:173–90. My reading of this sermon differs significantly from that of Monteiro, who sees it as an Exaltado declaration, *Primeiro reinado*, 2:198–99.

53. "Festas nacionaes," *O Repúblico*, 30 March 1831.

54. Moore, *Revolution of 1831*, 9 April 1831; *Aurora Fluminense*, 11 April 1831; Debret, *Viagem*, 2:274–75. A nineteenth-century historian offers an estimate of 30,000 people, Moreira de Azevedo, *Historia*, 8.

55. [Barreto], *Historia*, 54.

56. Nabuco, *Estadista*, 60.

57. Moore, *Revolution*, entries of 7 April; 1, 4, and 15 June 1831; Seidler, *Dez anos*, 300.

58. Ribeiro, *Liberdade*, 215, 279.

59. Ibid., 249–50 (quotes), 272–74. For a similar approach, see Wisser, "Rhetoric," 223–27. Some of this approach was anticipated by Martinho who stresses the class conflict between Portuguese-born clerks and native Brazilians, "Caixeiros," 28, 99, 102–31, 118–19.

60. Faria, *Breve historia*, 34.

61. Testimony of Victorino de Queiros Paiva, "Traslado," BN/SM, 6, 3, 12; Faria, *Breve historia*, 29–31; *Aurora Fluminense*, 18 March 1831; *O Brasileiro Vigilante*, 20 April 1831.

62. *O Novo Censor*, 19 March 1831. See also Hum Verdadeiro Constitucional's claim that patriot masters paid their slaves to join the Exaltados' demonstrations, *Defeza*, 2.

63. Ribeiro, *Liberdade*, 285–86; Flory, "Race."

64. Lima, *Cores*, 19–20, 71–75.

65. Schwartz, "Formation," 15; "Manifesto . . . ," *O Tribuno do Povo*, 14 April 1831. For similar language—"my *caibra* compatriots"—see *O Tribuno do Povo*, 28 March 1831.

66. *Astrea*, 17 March 1831.

67. William H. D. C. Wright to Sec. of State, Rio, 26 April 1830, NARS, M-121, roll 9; Brown to Sec. of State, Rio, 16 July 1831, NARS, M-121, roll. 10.

68. Macaulay, *Dom Pedro*, 226, 254–305.

69. Seidler, *História*, 177; Seidler, *Dez Anos*, 277.

70. Seidler, *História*, 186; Gardner, *Travels*, 10.

71. *O Brasileiro Offendido*, 30 March 1831. On this rhetorical practice, see Morel, *Transformações*, 97–98.

72. "Patria," *Nova Luz Brazileira*, 29 Jan. 1830. On changing understandings of *pátria*, see Barman, *Brazil*, 26–27, 58–60, 94–95; Jancsó and Pimenta, "Peças," 130–31, 136–37, 159–60; Lyra, "Pátria."

73. Testimony of ?, "Traslado," BN/SM, 6, 3, 12.

74. Testimony of José Maria Gomes, "Traslado," BN/SM, 6, 3, 12; Verdadeiro Constitucional, *Defeza*, 2.

75. *Aurora Fluminense*, 18 March 1831; Armitage, *History*, 2:116–17; Borjes da Fonseca, *Manifesto*, 10; *Edital*, Camara Municipal, 23 March 1831, *DRJ*, 30 March 1831; *O Tribuno do Povo*, 24 March 1831.

76. *Nova Luz Brazileira*, 18 March 1831; *Astrea*, 15 and 17 March 1831; Moore, *Revolution*, 14 March 1831; Traslado do Processo, BN/SM, 6, 3, 12.

77. *Nova Luz Brazileira*, 18 March 1831; *O Brasileiro Offendido*, 26 March 1831; *O Moderador*, 16 March 1830; Faria, *Breve historia*, 32. See also Ribeiro, *Liberdade*, 248–49; Morel, *Cipriano Barata*, 256.

78. *O Brasileiro Offendido*, 2 April 1831; [Barreto], *Historia*, 30; Borjes da Fonseca, *Manifesto*, 10. Cipriano Barata wore straw hats in Salvador in 1831; Morel, *Cipriano Barata*, 256.

79. Debret, *Viagem*, 1:150. See also Ribeiro, *Liberdade*, 249.

80. Moore, *Revolution*, 24 May 1831; *O Exaltado*, 15 Sep. 1831; *O Grito da Patria contra os Anarquistas*, 31 March 1832; *A Verdade*, 5 April 1832.

81. Wisser, "Rhetoric," 222–23.

82. *O Narcizo*, 2 April 1831. In Bahia, Cipriano Barata also wore homespun; Morel, *Cipriano Barata*, 256.

83. Bunbury, "Narrativa," 28; Brown to Sec. of State, Rio, 16 April 1831, NARS, M-121, roll 10; *O Republico*, 30 March 1831. Debret attributed the appellation "constitution tree" to Pedro I, *Viagem*, 2:275n298.

84. [Ruschenberger], *Three Years*, 1:74.

85. Debret, *Viagem*, 2:275n298; I. I. A. M., *Verdades*, 2.

86. Bandeira and Lago, *Debret*, 362.

87. The only other example of coffee leaves' use suggests that they were not uniformly patriotic symbols. In November 1823, the troops that closed the constituent assembly stuck coffee sprigs into their hats, and Pedro I wore a "lush bunch of coffee leaves," reportedly made by his mistress, Domitila de Castro. On this episode, see Macaulay, *Dom Pedro*, 158; Untitled and unattributed introduction to Pedro I, *Cartas*, 24; Antonio de Menezes Vasconcelos de Drummond, "Anotações," 83. Chamon suggests that coffee and tobacco leaves also alluded to the importance of agricultural labor as a source for the country's wealth, *Festejos*, 116–17.

88. *Aurora Fluminense*, 15 Sep. 1830.

89. Advertising, *Diario Mercantil ou Novo Jornal do Commercio*, 24 March 1831; Paula Brito, "Hymno offerecido à mocidade brasileira no dia 25 de março de 1831," in *Poesias*, 106–08.

90. E. Veiga, "Poesias," 251. He composed several other anthems in the following months, ibid., 252–65. On the issue of Evaristo's authorship, which was briefly questioned in 1833, see Vieira Fazenda, "Antiqualhas," *RIHGB* 93:147 (1923): 448–50.

91. On the much-debated question of the music's authorship, see Andrade, *Francisco Manuel da Silva*, 1:137–57; Lira, *História*, 25–47.

92. Andrade, *Francisco Manuel da Silva*, 1:156.

93. Bösche, "Quadros," 167.

94. Schlichthorst, *Rio*, 124.

95. Calmon, *História*, 129.

96. "Hymno ao Dia 7 de Setembro, Anniversario da Independência do Brasil," *Aurora Fluminense*, 15 Sep. 1830.

97. "Hymno offerecido à mocidade brasileira," in Paula Brito, *Poesias*, 108.

98. S. de S. O., "Hymno de Pedro II," BN/SOR, 89, 3, 1, n.º 33; Francisco de Paula Brito, "Hymno ao memoravel dia 7 d'abril de 1831," BN/SOR, 89, 3, 1, n.º 5.

99. Lira, *História*, 49–64; Andrade, *Francisco Manuel da Silva*, 1:158, 170–75; Pereira, "Hino," 22–24.

100. [Ovídio Saraiva de Carvalho e Silva], "Ao grande e heroico dia sete de abril de 1831," BN/SOR, 39, 19, 3.

101. "Ode ao Dia 25 de Março de 1831," in G[onçalves] de Magalhães, *Poesias*, 25.

102. Moniz, *Moniz Barretto*, 71, note *.

103. *Astrea*, 29 March 1831.

104. Seidler, *Dez anos*, 305.

105. Here I am following Basile's analysis of politics in civic rituals, "Império," 121. See also Basile, "Festas."

106. Barman, *Brazil*, 160–78; Needell, *Party*, 39–50; Basile, "Laboratório," 61, 63–64; Pereira da Silva, *Historia do Brazil*, 144.

107. Guimarães, "Liberalismo," 107–12; Basile, "Império," 83–109.

108. *JC*, 7 Sep. 1831.

109. "Conselho da Sociedade Defensora . . . ," *O Independente*, 6 Sep. 1831. See also *Aurora Fluminense*, 5 Sep. 1831.

110. "Sete de Setembro," *JC*, 7 Sep. 1831. See also *Astrea*, 6 Sep. 1831; *O Independente*, 9 Sep. 1831.

111. *Aurora Fluminense*, 5 Sep. 1831.

112. "Sete de Setembro de 1831," *JC*, 9 Sep. 1831.

113. *Aurora Fluminense*, 9 Sep. 1831.

114. *JC*, 9 Sep. 1831; *O Independente*, 9 Sep. 1831.

115. Aston to Palmerston, Rio, 28 Sep. 1831, PRO/FO 13, vol. 83, fol. 286r–v.

116. "Artigo communicado," *Astrea*, 17 Sep. 1831.

117. Basile, "Império," 90; Decreto, 5 Oct. 1831; Decisão 312 (Fazenda), 5 Oct. 1831, *CLB*.

118. Basile, "Império," 122.

119. Moreira de Azevedo, *Rio*, 1:493; Morales de los Rios Filho, *Rio*, 229.

120. Moreira de Azevedo, *Rio*, 1:554, 1:98–99, 1:520.

121. *O Nacional*, 27 Nov. 1832. A prominent deputy explained some years later that no formal government act had put an end to the *beija-mão*, speech of Honório Hermeto Carneiro Leão, 10 May 1838, *ACD* (1838), 1:78. According to Magda Ricci, Minister of Justice Diogo Antônio Feijó refused to let people kiss the young emperor's hand in 1831–32, *Assombrações*, 401.

122. *O Grito da Patria contra os Anarquistas*, 28 March 1832.

123. Sessions of 6, 10, and 12 Oct., *ACD* (1831), 2:220, 229–30, 231.

124. Session of 11 Oct., *AS* (1831), 2:259–65.

125. Decreto, 25 Oct. 1831, *CLB*; João Loureiro to Manuel José Maria da Costa e Sá, Rio, 15 Oct. 1831, *RIHGB* 76:2 (1914): 379.

126. "2 de Dezembro," *JC*, 2 Dec. 1831; *JC*, 5 Dec. 1831; *CM*, 4 Dec. 1831.

127. Needell, *Party*, 46–55 (quote 54); Barman, *Brazil*, 171–78; Basile, "Laboratório," 72–84; Castro, "Experiência," 22–38.

128. "Conta da despeza . . . ," 13 Sep. 1834, *RIHGB* 68:111 (1905): 246; "Receita e despeza . . . ," *RIHGB* 68:111 (1905): 245.

129. *Aurora Fluminense*, 28 March 1832.

130. "7 de Setembro," *Aurora Fluminense*, 10 Sep. 1832.

131. *O Independente*, 10 April 1833; *JC*, 27 March 1833.

132. *Aurora Fluminense*, 27 March 1833; *O Independente*, 27 March 1833.

133. *O Caramuru*, 28 March 1832.

134. *Aurora Fluminense*, 6 April 1832, 11 April 1834.

135. *Aurora Fluminense*, 11 April 1832, 10 April 1833; *O Independente*, 11 April 1832, 10 April 1833; *O Nacional*, 10 April 1833.

136. *O Sete de Abril*, 13 April 1833; *A Trombeta*, 23 April 1833. On the origin of the term *Chimango*, see Moreira de Azevedo, *Historia patria*, 115–16.

137. *Aurora Fluminense*, 10 Sep. 1832; *O Independente*, 5 Dec. 1832. See also *O Nacional*, 6 April 1833.

138. "O Dia 2 de Dezembro," *O Caramuru*, 5 Dec. 1832.

139. *O Grito da Pátria contra os Anarquistas*, 31 March 1832.

140. *O Nacional*, 23 March 1833.

141. Letter to the Editor from O Girante, *Aurora Fluminense*, 14 Sep. 1832; *O Independente*, 12 Sep. 1832; "Sete de Setembro de 1832," *O Conciliador Fluminense*, 11 Sep. 1832; *O Clarim da Liberdade*, 19 Sep. 1832.

142. *O Nacional*, 10 April 1833; "Ferroadas" and "Annuncios," *O Sete de Abril*, 13 April 1833; *O Imam*, 11 May and 12 Sep. 1833.

143. *O Clarim da Liberdade*, 19 Sep. 1832; *O Independente*, 12 Sep. 1832.

144. *Aurora Fluminense*, 11 Sep. 1833.

145. *A Loja de Belchior*, 16 Sep. 1833.

146. *O Catão*, 11 Sep. 1833. This newspaper was published by Francisco Gê Acaiaba Montezuma, then involved in a Caramuru-Exaltado alliance of convenience against Moderados; Vianna, *Contribuição*, 115.

147. *O Catão*, 10 Dec. 1832; *O Exaltado*, 10 Dec. 1832. See also *O Caramuru*, 5 Dec. 1832.

148. Seidler, *História*, 212.

149. *O Par de Tetas*, 29 March 1833; *Aurora Fluminense*, 27 March 1833.

150. *O Independente*, 7 April 1832.

151. *Astrea*, 7 April 1832.

152. *O Grito da Patria contra os Anarquistas*, 7 April 1832; *O Independente*, 7 April 1832; *O Brasileiro*, 7 April 1832.

153. *O Independente*, 11 April 1832; *O Nacional*, 10 April 1833.

154. *A Trombeta*, 23 April 1833; *O Imam*, 8 June 1833.

155. *O Independente*, 5 Dec. 1832; "Felicitação da Sociedade Defensora . . . ," *Aurora Fluminense*, 3 Dec. 1832; "Dia 2 de Dezembro," *Aurora Fluminense*, 6 Dec. 1832.

156. *D. Pedro I*, 7 Sep. 1833; *O Sete de Setembro*, 7 Sep. 1833; *A pedido*, *DRJ*, 9 Sep. 1833.

157. *O Catão*, 11 Sep. 1833.

158. *Aurora Fluminense*, 16 Sep. 1833.

159. *ACD* (1834), 1:68; Moreira de Azevedo, *Historia*, 144. For the political context, see Barman, *Brazil*, 175–77.

160. *O Verdadeiro Caramuru*, 3 Dec. 1833; "Auto de Averiguação . . . ," *JC*, 7 Dec. 1833.

161. Merolla, *Correspondencia*, 81; "Dia 2 de Dezembro," *Aurora Fluminense*, 6 Dec. 1833; *Arca de Noé*, 5 Dec. 1833; Brown to Sec. of State, Rio, 13 Dec. 1833, NARS, M-121, roll. 11; *O Verdadeiro Caramuru*, 3 Dec. 1833.

162. *Arca de Noé*, 5 Dec. 1833; *O Verdadeiro Caramuru*, 3 Dec. 1833.

163. José Ignacio Coimbra to MJ, Rio, 5 Dec. 1833, *Aurora Fluminense*, 9 Dec. 1833. On this incident, see also "Noticia das agressões populares . . . ," BN/SM, I-34, 16, 1.

164. *JC*, 9 Dec. 1833; *O Sete de Abril*, 10, 11, 14, 21 Dec. 1833; *Aurora Fluminense*, 11 Dec. 1833; João Antonio Rodrigues Carvalho to José Martiniano de Alencar, Rio, 19 Dec. 1833, *ABN* 86 (1966): 274.

165. Bösche, "Quadros," 219.

166. H. S. Fox to Viscount Palmerston, Rio, 18 Dec. 1833, PRO/FO 13, vol. 99, fols. 165–72v.

167. *Le Messager*, 29 March 1834; "Maravilhas da nossa idade" (variedades), O *Sete d'Abril*, 12 April 1834.

168. *O Sete de Abril*, 12 April 1834.

169. *Aurora Fluminense*, 11 April 1834. On the ball, see also *A Verdade*, 10 April 1834; "Programma da reunião festiva . . . ," *O Sete de Abril*, 29 March 1834; Merolla, *Correspondencia*, 108; Reynolds, *Voyage*, 517.

170. *O Sete de Abril*, 5 April 1834.

171. *Aurora Fluminense*, 16 April 1834. For the cost, see "Receita e despeza . . . ," 14 Feb. 1835, *RIHGB* 68:111 (1905): 246.

172. Moreira de Azevedo, *Historia*, 140–41.

173. Petition of Antonio Ribeiro Fernandes Torbes to Camara Municipal, Rio, 26 July 1834, AGCRJ, 43-3-64, fol. 1; *JC*, 9 Sep. 1834; *Aurora Fluminense*, 10 Sep. 1834; Rochette, *Relation*, 137.

174. *Aurora Fluminense*, 10 Sep. 1834.

175. Barman, *Brazil*, 183–88; Needell, *Party*, 59–72; Moreira de Azevedo, *Historia*, 210–11; Basile, "Laboratório," 85–90; Castro, "Experiência," 42–54.

176. "O Dia Sete de Setembro," *Jornal dos Debates Politicos e Litterarios*, 13 Sep. 1837. Torres Homem is identified as the editor of this newspaper by Macedo, *Memórias da rua*, 137. For similar rhetoric, see also *Pão d'Assucar*, 11 Sep. 1835. The relief at parties' disappearance was expressed in "União do Imperio," *DRJ*, 26 March 1835.

177. Hamond, *Diários*, 93, 56.

178. "Catastrophe," *O Sete d'Abril*, 5 Jan. 1835.

179. "Ainda o Dia Dois de Dezembro," *DRJ*, 5 Dec. 1836.

180. Hamond, *Diários*, 61, 112, 143.

181. "Dia Sete de Setembro," *Jornal dos Debates Politicos e Litterarios*, 13 Sep. 1837.

182. *JC*, 5 Jan. 1835.

183. "Discurso . . . ," *O Parlamentar*, 9 Sep. 1837. See also "O Dia 7 de Setembro de 1837," *Semanario do Cincinnato*, 9 Sep. 1837; Z. O. A. [Francisco Vilela Barbosa, Marquis of Paranaguá], *Saudade*.

184. *O Brasileiro Offendido*, 30 March 1837; "Vinte e Cinco de Março," *Pão d'Assucar*, 25 March 1836; "Honra ao Dia 25 de Março," *O Sete d'Abril*, 26 March 1836. See also *DRJ*, 8 Jan. 1835.

185. "Viva o Dia 25 de Março . . . ," *O Sete d'Abril*, 25 March 1837. See also "O Dia 25 de Março," *Pharol do Imperio*, 25 March 1837; "Dia Vinte Cinco de Março," *Semanario do Cincinnato*, 25 March 1837; *O Paquete do Rio*, 9 Sep. 1836.

186. Diogo Antonio Feijó to José Martiniano de Alencar, Rio, 3 July 1835, *ABN* 86 (1966): 229.

187. *O Novo Caramuru*, 7 Sep. 1835.

188. *O Chronista*, 8 April 1836; *O Pharol do Imperio*, 8 April 1837; "O Dia 7 de Abril!!" *O Sete d'Abril*, 7 April 1837.

189. "O Dia 2 de Dezembro," *O Sete d'Abril*, 2 Dec. 1836. See also "Ao muito alto e muito poderoso Senhor d. Pedro II," *O Sete d'Abril*, 7 Sep. 1836 (reprinted in *O Chronista*, 2 Dec. 1836); "O Dia Dois de Dezembro," *DRJ*, 2 Dec. 1836.

190. "Ao muito alto e muito poderoso Senhor D. Pedro II," *O Sete d'Abril*, 2 Dec. 1836.

191. Basile, "Império," 128. See also Basile, "Laboratório," 98.

CHAPTER THREE

1. Needell, *Party*, 55–80; Barman, *Brazil*, 189–216. More generally on the Regresso, see Flory, *Judge*, 131–80; Mattos, *Tempo*; Basile, "Laboratório," 84–90, 98; Parron, *Política*, chaps. 2–3.

2. Barman, *Citizen Emperor*, xvi. The image of the monarchy in iconography has been analyzed by Schwarcz, *Barbas*.

3. Schwarcz, *Império*, 20–21, 32–33. In this respect, she implicitly follows Mattos's interpretation of a hegemonic Saquarema-dominated ruling class, *Tempo*.

4. "Os festejos da coroação," *O Brasil*, 13 July 1841.

5. Hamond, *Diários*, 176.

6. Editais, 28 and 29 Nov. 1837, *JC*, 30 Nov. 1837.

7. *JC*, 1 Dec. 1837. For comments on the new carriages, see Hamond, *Diários*, 176; Hunter, *Diplomat's Lady*, 90; "Anniversario de S. M. o Imperador," *O Sete d'Abril*, 6 Dec. 1837; "O Dia Dous de Dezembro," *JC*, 4 Dec. 1837.

8. "O Dia Dous de Dezembro," *JC*, 4 Dec. 1837; Sr. Pereira da Silva, "O Dia Dous de Dezembro de 1837," *JC*, 5 Dec. 1837. The author of this text may be João Manoel Pereira da Silva, but nineteenth-century biographers provide conflicting information about whether he had returned to Rio by then; Santos, *Pantheon*, 483; Sacramento Blake, *Diccionario*, 3:479.

9. Hamond, *Diários*, 176. Other foreign diplomats concurred with this assessment; Barman, *Citizen Emperor*, 64.

10. Hamond, *Diários*, 176; Hunter, *Diplomat's Lady*, 90.

11. *O Chronista*, 2 Dec. 1837.

12. "Anniversario de S. M. o Imperador," *O Sete d'Abril*, 6 Dec. 1837; "Dous de Dezembro," *O Parlamentar*, 2 Dec. 1837. For hope for the future, see also the untitled article signed L. P. C. F., *DRJ*, 2 Dec. 1837.

13. Comandante Superior, Ordem do Dia, 1 Dec. 1837, *O Sete d'Abril*, 2 Dec. 1837; *DRJ*, 2 Dec. 1837.

14. "O Beija Mão e o Regresso," *O Cidadão*, 12 April 1838.

15. The dating of Araújo Lima's gesture derives from one of Justiniano José da Rocha's later newspapers, which called 1 Dec. 1860 the twenty-third anniversary of the custom's restoration, "Primeiro de dezembro e o beija-mão," *O Regenerador*, 1 Dec. 1860.

16. Rocha, "Ação," 185.

17. Speech of Teophilo Benedicto Ottoni, 10 May, *ACD* (1838), 1:75–76.

18. Speech of Honorio Hermeto Carneiro Leão, 10 May, *ACD* (1838), 1:77–78.

19. Speeches of Bernardo Pereira Vasconcelos and Ottoni, 10 May 1838, *ACD* (1838), 1:78, 79.

20. Speech of Antônio Carlos Ribeiro de Andrada Machado, 10 May 1838, *ACD* (1838), 1:80.

21. Speech of Vasconcelos, 11 Aug., *AS* (1840), 5:117.

22. On 25 January 1838, Justiniano's *O Chronista* questioned these "antiquated practices," cited in Barman, *Brazil*, 197.

23. Otoni, *Autobiografia*, 50.

24. Based on the invitations published in *DRJ*, 1838–1848. Between 1843 and 1848, only three announcements omitted reference to the *beija-mão*, those of the navy minister published on 4 Sep. 1846 and 8 Jan. 1847 and that of the army commander on 3 April 1844.

25. Wilkes, *Narrative*, 1:49; Horner, *Medical Topography*, 215 (7 April 1843); Radiguet, *Souvenir*, 285–86 (15 Oct. 1844, incorrectly described as Empress Teresa Cristina's birthday; it was, in fact, Pedro II's name day).

26. For an early exception, see "O Dia Sete de Setembro," *DRJ*, 9 Sep. 1840.

27. Otoni, *Autobiografia*, 48, 51; Chagas, *Teófilo Ottoni*, 28, 56–57, 138, 360.

28. Francisco de Lima e Silva to Pedro II, n.p., n.d., AHMI, 100-4941. The Museu Imperial dates this document to December 1835, but the reference to the *beija-mão* suggests that it was written after December 1837.

29. On the majority's politics, see Barman, *Brazil*, 198–211; Barman, *Citizen Emperor*, 68–73; Needell, *Party*, 80–95. On Pedro II's education, see Barman, *Citizen Emperor*, 39–41, 51–52, 55–56. For the assessment of this as a revolution, see William Hunter to Sec. of State, Rio, 31 July 1840, NARS, M-121, roll 14; Pereira da Silva, *Memorias*, 1:12.

30. "Canto ao Dia 23 de Julho de 1840," *A Mulher de Simplicio ou A Fluminense Exaltada*, 1 Dec. 1840.

31. *JC*, 25–26 July 1840; Hunter, *Diplomat's Lady*, 173.

32. Barman, *Brazil*, 209–11.

33. See the session of 24 July, *ACD* (1840), 2:357 58; Chagas, *Teófilo Ottoni*, 72.

34. See the debates of 8, 11, and 13 Aug., *AS* (1840), 5:80–86, 113–22, 142–77.

35. William Hunter to Sec. of State, Rio, 22 Dec. 1838, NARS, M-121, roll 13. Others shared this view, including Kidder, *Sketches*, 1:64; and the British minister, cited in Barman, *Princess Isabel*, 16.

36. Pereira da Silva, *Historia do Brazil*, 254.

37. "O Dia 2 de Dezembro," *O Despertador*, 3 Dec. 1838. For another Brazilian account of this festival, see "Festejos do dia 2 de dezembro," *JC*, 4 Dec. 1838. This festival was particularly well documented by U.S. visitors; Jenkins, *United States Exploring Expeditions*, 42–43; Wilkes, *Narrative*, 1:49; W. Reynolds, *Voyage*, 34–36; Coggeshall, *Thirty-Six Voyages*, 548–50.

38. For 1838, see Hunter, *Diplomat's Lady*, 117; "O Dia 2 de Dezembro," *O Sete d'Abril*, 5 Dec. 1838. For 1839, see João Loureiro to Manuel José Maria da Costa e Sá, Rio, 29 Nov. 1839, *RIHGB* 76:2 (1914): 444–45; "Anniversario natalicio de S. M. O Senhor D. Pedro II," *JC*, 1 Dec. 1839; "Festejos ao Dia 2 de Dezembro," *JC*, 4 Dec. 1839; "Os Festejos do Dia Dous de Dezembro," *O Despertador*, 4 Dec. 1839; Barman, *Citizen Emperor*, 69 (citing a French diplomat's assessment). For 1840, see Hunter, *Diplomat's Lady*, 184; "2 de Dezembro," *O Despertador*, 3 Dec. 1840.

39. "Os Festejos do Dia 2 de Dezembro," *A Regeneração*, 4 Dec. 1840. For another reference to popular subscriptions (lamenting their disappearance), see *O Constitucional*, 4 Dec. 1841.

40. Pedro II, *Diário*, 3 Dec. 1840.

41. "Os festejos do dia Dous de Dezembro," *O Despertador*, 4 Dec. 1839. For other accounts of the official routine on this day, see *O Despertador*, 3 Dec. 1839; "Festejo ao Dia 2 de Dezembro," *JC*, 4 Dec. 1839.

42. Pedro II, *Diário*, 2 and 4 Dec. 1840. For press accounts of these celebrations, see "Os Festejos do Dia 2 de Dezembro," *JC*, 2–3 Dec. 1840; "Os Festejos do Dia 2 de Dezembro," *A Regeneração*, 4 Dec. 1840.

43. Barman, *Citizen Emperor*, 74.

44. Rezende, *Minhas recordações*, 103–04.

45. Letter to the Editor, *O Filho do Sete d'Abril*, 4 Dec. 1838.

46. "Os festejos da coroação," *O Brasil*, 13 July 1841.

47. "O Dia 25 de Março de 1838," *Jornal dos Debates Politicos e Litterarios*, 29 March 1838.

48. "O Dia 9 de Janeiro," *Gazeta dos Domingos*, 6 Jan. 1839.

49. On the ritual of the session's opening, see Pereira da Silva, *Memorias*, 1:57.

50. "25 de Março," *O Sete d'Abril*, 26 March 1838. See also "Dia 25 de Março," *O Chronista*, 27 March 1838 and 26 March 1839; "O Dia 25 de Março," *O Despertador*, 23 and 26 March 1839, 26 March 1840; "O Dia Vinte Cinco de Março," *JC*, 25–26 March 1840; "O Dia 25 de Março," *JC*, 25–26 March 1841; "O Dia 25 de Março," *DRJ*, 26 March 1838 and 26 March 1839; "25 de Março," *DRJ*, 26 March 1840. On the Sabinada, see Kraay, "As Terrifying as Unexpected"; Souza, *Sabinada*.

51. See, for example, "O Dia 25 de Março de 1838," *Jornal dos Debates Politicos e Litterarios*, 29 March 1838; "Dia 25 de Março," *O Parlamentar*, 28 March 1838; "O Dia 25 de Março," *A Regeneração*, 30 March 1841.

52. "O Dia Sete de Abril," *O Despertador*, 7 April 1838. See also "O Dia Sete d'Abril," *O Chronista*, 7 April 1838; "O Dia 7 de Abril de 1838," *Jornal dos Debates Politicos e Litterarios*, 12 April 1838.

53. *O Despertador*, 7 April 1838; "Sete de Abril," *JC*, 9 April 1838; "O Dia 7 de Abril," *JC*, 7–8 April 1839; "O Dia 7 de Abril," *O Sete d'Abril*, 9 April 1838; "O Dia 7 de Abril," *DRJ*, 7 April 1838.

54. "O Dia 7 de Abril," *O Chronista*, 7 April 1838.

55. "O Dia Sete de Abril," *O Cidadão*, 11 April 1838; "Sétimo Anniversario da Memoravel Regeneração do Brasil," *O Parlamentar*, 7 April 1838.

56. "O Dia 7 de Setembro," *O Sete d'Abril*, 7 Sep. 1838; "O Dia Sete de Setembro," *O Despertador*, 6 Sep. 1838; "O Dia 7 de Setembro," *O Despertador*, 7 Sep. 1839; "O Dia Sete de Setembro de 1838," *JC*, 10 Sep. 1838; "O Dia 7 de Setembro," *JC*, 7 Sep. 1839; "Ao Dia 7 de Setembro," *O Chronista*, 11 Sep. 1838; "O Dia 7 de Septembro," *Jornal dos Debates Politicos e Litterarios*, 6 Sep. 1838; "O Dia Sete de Setembro," *O Parlamentar*, 12 Sep. 1838; "O Dia 7 de Setembro," *O Monarchista do Século 19*, 7 Sep. 1839; "O Dia Sete de Setembro," *A Regeneração*, 7 Sep. 1840; "O Dia 7 de Setembro," *A Trombeta Constitucional*, 7 Sep. 1840; "O Dia Sete de Setembro," *DRJ*, 7 Sep. 1838; "O Anniversario da Independencia," *DRJ*, 7 Sep. 1839.

57. Moreira de Azevedo, *Rio*, 1:520.

58. "Dia Sete de Setembro," *O Filho da Sentinella da Monarchia*, 11 Sep. 1840; "O Dia 7 de Setembro," *O Filho do Brasil*, 13 Oct. 1840; *O Filho do Brasil*, 19 Sep. 1840.

59. "O Dia 2 de Dezembro," *O Despertador*, 1 Dec. 1838, 3 Dec. 1839; "O Dia 2 de Dezembro" and "Os Annos do Imperador," *O Sete d'Abril*, 2 Dec. 1838; "O Dia Dous de Dezembro," *JC*, 3 Dec. 1838; "Anniversario Natalicio de S. M. O Senhor D. Pedro II," 1 Dec. 1839; "O Dia 2 de Dezembro de 1839," *O Instincto*, 3 Dec. 1839; "O Dia 2 de Dezembro," *DRJ*, 2 Dec. 1838; "Dia 2 de Dezembro," *DRJ*, 2 Dec. 1839; "O anniversario natalicio de S. M. I.," *DRJ*, 2 Dec. 1840.

60. "O Dia 2 de Dezembro," *O Parlamentar*, 5 Dec. 1838; "O dia 2 de Dezembro de 1838!" *O Filho do Sete d'Abril*, 4 Dec. 1838.

61. "O Dia 2 de Dezembro de 1839," *A Liga Americana*, 5 Dec. 1839.

62. "O Dia 2 de Dezembro" and "Ainda o Dia 2 de Dezembro," *A Regeneração*, 2 Dec. 1840.

63. Louzada, "Soneto," *JC*, 6 Dec. 1839.

64. Barman, *Brazil*, 212–13.

65. Schwarcz, *Barbas*, 83. For an uncritical description of the ritual that closely follows the contemporary newspaper coverage, see Santos, "Dom Pedro II."

66. Barman, *Citizen Emperor*, 78; Circular, 18 Aug. 1840, *CM* (Salvador), 1 Sep. 1840.

67. William Gore Ouseley to Viscount Palmerston, Rio, 1 March 1841, PRO/FO 13, vol. 169, fols. 154r–55r. See also Kidder, *Sketches*, 2:371; Hunter to Sec. of State, Rio, 21 April 1841, NARS, M-121, roll 14.

68. "Adiamento da Sagração . . . ," *O Despertador*, 3 May 1841; "Coroação de S. M. I.," *JC*, 10 May 1841.

69. Hunter, *Diplomat's Lady*, 195; "O Adiamento da Sagração de S. M. o Imperador," *O Despertador*, 7 May 1841.

70. "A Coroação," *O Brasil,* 12 June 1841; Ouseley to Palmerston, Rio, 14 June 1841 (confidential), PRO/FO 13, vol. 171, fol. 82.

71. Ouseley to Palmerston, Rio, 7 Aug. 1841, PRO/FO 13, vol. 171, fol. 265r.

72. Botafogo, *Balanço,* 18–22.

73. See the accounts in AN, cód. 569, fols. 143–58.

74. See the untitled document, dated 5 Feb. 1841, AGCRJ, 6-2-25, fol. 41.

75. Ouseley to Palmerston, Rio, 7 July 1841, PRO/FO 13, vol. 171, fol. 134r–v.

76. Hunter, *Diplomat's Lady,* 192.

77. Hunter to Sec. of State, Rio, 21 April 1841, NARS, M-121, roll 14; Ouseley to Palmerston, Rio, 1 March 1841, PRO/FO 13, vol. 169, fol. 153r–54r.

78. Hunter to Sec. of State, Rio, 15 Sep. 1841, NARS, M-121, roll 14.

79. Undated and untitled document, AGCRJ, 6-2-25, fol. 36.

80. *Fiscal,* Candelaria, to Camara, Rio, 1 July 1841, AGCRJ, 41-3-22, fol. 6r; "As testemunhas materiaes presenciadoras da coroação" (*comunicado*), JC, 6 May 1841.

81. "Os Festejos da Coroação," *A Mulher de Simplicio ou A Fluminense Exaltada,* 28 July 1841.

82. Mello Moraes Filho, *Historia,* 109, 112, 114.

83. See Neuville's petitions of June 1841 and the city council's responses in AGCRJ, 41-3-22, fols. 3–5 (quote fol. 4); 42-3-13, fols. 56 (quote), 57.

84. "Testemunhas materiaes," *JC,* 6 May 1841; Anuncios, *O Despertador,* 14 July 1841.

85. "Festejos da Coroação" (*correspondência*), JC, 14 July 1841.

86. Untitled Document, 3 July 1841, AGCRJ, 6-2-25, fol. 34; Mello Moraes Filho, *Historia,* 106.

87. *Edital,* 19 May 1841, JC, 9 July 1841; Declarações, *O Despertador,* 15 July 1841; Editaes, JC, 15 July 1841.

88. *Edital, O Despertador,* 13 July 1841.

89. *Fiscal,* Candelária, to Camara, Rio, 1 July 1841, AGCRJ, 41-3-22, fol. 6r; "Providencias policiaes . . . ," *O Despertador,* 10 July 1841.

90. Petitions of Gregorio Corelli to Camara, Rio, 18 Jan. and 1 Feb. 1841; and the *parecer* and *despacho,* AGCRJ, 42-3-13, fols. 49, 50, 51r–v.

91. Petition of Valli to Camara, Rio, May 1841; *Parecer, Fiscal,* Santana Parish, 21 May 1841, AGCRJ, 42-3-13, fol. 54r–v; Petition of Benard Irmãos to Camara, Rio, ca. May 1841, AGCRJ, 42-3-13, fol. 53. I do not know what these "hydraulic games" consisted of. See also Abreu, *Império,* 225–26.

92. "Os Convites," *O Maiorista,* 15 July 1841; "A Espada do Ypiranga," *O Maiorista,* 8 July 1841. The identification of Torres Homem as editor of this newspaper is by Magalhães Júnior, "Justiniano José da Rocha," 137.

93. "Relação das pessoas . . . para levarem as insignias," *JC,* 10 July 1841. For the political context of 1828–29, see Barman, *Brazil,* 152–56.

94. "Os Embaraços da Coroação," *O Brasil,* 24 April 1841; "Os Despachos pela Coroação de S. M. I.," *O Maiorista,* 20 July 1841; "O Descontentamento Geral," *O Maiorista,* 22–24 July 1841; "A Continuação dos Despachos," *O Maiorista,* 27 July 1841; "Ainda os Despachos da Coroação," *O Maiorista,* 29 July 1841; "Os Despachos da Coroação," *O Brasil,* 24 July 1841. For a defense of the *despachos,* see "As Graças por occasião da Coroação de S. M. o Imperador," *O Despertador,* 22 July 1841.

95. "Os festejos da coroação," *O Brasil*, 13 July 1841.

96. Araujo, *Opusculo*; Seixas, *Memoria*.

97. Hunter, *Diplomat's Lady*, 198. For other descriptions of the parade, see Ouseley to Palmerston, Rio, 7 Aug. 1841, PRO/FO 13, vol. 171, fol. 265r; "Coroação de S. M. o Imperador. Entrada na Cidade," *O Despertador*, 17 July 1841; *JC*, 16–17 July 1841.

98. Schwarcz, *Barbas*, 73.

99. The French ambassador complained of the "dreadful heat," cited in Morel, *Transformações*, 81.

100. Kidder, *Sketches*, 2:371; Barman, *Citizen Emperor*, 84.

101. The following account is based on *Disposições* and on "Coroação e Sagração de S. M. I.," *JC*, 20 July 1841. Schwarcz has analyzed *Disposições* in *Império*.

102. On the imperial insignia, see Schwarcz, *Barbas*, 78–80, and *Império*, 42–46.

103. The *Guia* was advertised for this price in the *JC*, 16–17 July 1841.

104. José de São Bento Damaso, "Oração gratulatória . . . ," *JC*, 21 July 1841.

105. On the sale of this lithograph, see Ferrez, *Muito leal e heróica cidade*, 150.

106. *DRJ*, 19 July 1841.

107. "Descrição do edificio construido para solemnidade da coroação e sagração . . . ," BN/SI, ARC.16.1.1(7); *DRJ*, 17 July 1841. See also Schwarcz, *Barbas*, 74–76, 569n13; Squeff, *Brasil*, 75, 117–18.

108. "Testemunhas materiaes," *JC*, 6 May 1841.

109. "Theatro de S. Pedro de Alcantara," *O Despertador*, 20 July 1841; "Theatro de S. Pedro d'Alcantara" (*folhetim*), *JC*, 21 July 1841; "O Baile da Coroação," *JC*, 26 July 1841.

110. Hunter, *Diplomat's Lady*, 200.

111. *JC*, 20 July 1841.

112. "O Incendio do Palacete . . . ," *O Despertador*, 23 July 1841.

113. "As Illuminações," *JC*, 18–19 July 1841.

114. The full series is reproduced in Santos, "Dom Pedro II," between pp. 86 and 87.

115. Squeff, *Brasil*, 116–19.

116. On the Roman triumphal arch, see Beard, *Roman Triumph*, 21, 45–46. For comparisons, see the many images in Mendonça et al., *Arte*; Megiani, *Rei*; Malerba, *Corte*; Bryant, *King*; Strong, *Splendour*.

117. Radforth, *Royal Spectacle*, 57–69 (quote 68). See also Truesdell, *Spectacular Politics*, 169.

118. "O Templo da Harmonia," *JC*, 18–19 July 1841.

119. "Arco da Rua Direita," *JC*, 18–19 July 1841.

120. See the descriptions in *JC*, 18–19, 22, 25 July 1841; *O Despertador*, 17 July 1841.

121. "Rocio da Cidade Nova," *O Despertador*, 17 July 1841; "Varanda do Rocio da Cidade Nova," *JC*, 18–19 July 1841. On *O Despertador* (1838–41) as the *JC*'s principal competitor, see Sandroni, *180 anos*, 96–97.

122. "As Illuminações," *O Maiorista*, 31 July 1841. The poem's text appears in "Pavilhão Chinez," *JC*, 21 July 1841.

123. Malta, *Ao muito alto e poderozo senhor*. For more typical poetry, see Pereira, *Votos*; "A Faustíssima Coroação," AIHGB, lata 222, doc. 8; "Oitava" and "Soneto," *JC*, 27 July 1841.

124. Quoted in Andrade, *Francisco Manuel da Silva*, 1:181.

125. Andrade attributes the new lyrics to Carvalho, *Francisco Manuel da Silva*, 1:182–83; a view accepted by Pereira, "Hino," 26–28.

126. Ouseley to Mr. Mandeville, Rio, 25 Aug. 1841, PRO/FO 13, vol. 171, fol. 276r.

127. Schwarcz, *Barbas*, 145.

128. Untitled Document, 5 Feb. 1841, AGCRJ, 6-2-25, fol. 38.

129. Santos, *Imagem*, 109.

130. Santos, "Dom Pedro II," 111–12. An image of the latter medallion appears in Schwarcz, *Barbas*, 81.

131. Cabral, *Selos*, 116–20, 122 (quote). The first stamps and low-denomination coins with Pedro's image were issued in 1866 and 1866–67, ibid., 128–34.

132. Bieber, "Visão." On this linkage between state and local elites, see also Graham, "Constructing."

133. "S. Pedro do Sul," *JC*, 4 July 1841; "Sergipe," *Diario de Pernambuco* (Recife), 1 July 1841.

134. *CM* (Salvador), 13 July 1841.

135. *Cidade do Rio*, 10 July 1888, quoted in *Festa*, 181. See also Coaracy, *Memórias*, 50.

136. Vieira Fazenda, "Antiqualhas," *RIHGB* 95:149 (1924): 42–45 (originally published in 1910).

137. Pereira da Silva, *Memorias*, 1:64; Oliveira, *Memorias*, 141–42, 146.

138. Soares, *Capoeira*, 410.

139. Lacombe, *Mordomo*, 296; Barman, *Citizen Emperor*, 85, 441n44.

140. Schwarcz, *Barbas*, chap. 10; Souza, *Pátria*, 230–32. See also Reis's discussion of Africans' understanding of kingship in Brazil, "Quilombos," 32–33.

141. Kidder, *Sketches*, 2:372.

142. "A Coroação e Sagração de S. M. I.," *O Brasil*, 22 July 1841.

143. Kidder, *Sketches*, 2:372.

144. Geertz, *Negara*.

CHAPTER FOUR

1. Barman, *Brazil*, 212–32; Needell, *Party*, 99–116; Mosher, *Political Struggle*, 206–48; Castro, "Política," 509–40.

2. Nabuco, *Estadista*, 139; Needell, *Party*, 117–66; Barman, *Brazil*, 232–35; Iglesias, "Vida," 9–38; Parron, *Política*, 232–39; 244–52.

3. Nabuco, *Estadista*, 161–63; Needell, *Party*, 168–80, 194–95; Barman, *Citizen Emperor*, 162–67; Iglesias, "Vida," 38–69.

4. Nabuco, *Estadista*, 364–66 (quote 365); Needell, *Party*, 200–19; Barman, *Citizen Emperor*, 188–92; Carvalho, *Construção/Teatro*, 185–86, 376; Iglesias, "Vida," 69–112.

5. Sandroni, *180 anos*, 106–16, 138.

6. These men's *crônicas* have been collected and published in modern editions; Martins Pena, *Folhetins*; Alencar, *Ao correr*; Paranhos, *Cartas*. Machado

de Assis's early *crônicas* in the *DRJ* and other newspapers can be found in "Machado de Assis: Obra completa," http://portal.mec.gov.br/machado/index .php (accessed July 2008).

7. "Chronica," *Revista Academica*, 15 March 1873. See also "Chronica da Quinzena," *Archivo Contemporaneo*, 15 Dec. 1872.

8. Chazkel, *"Crônica,"* no pagination; Chalhoub, "Arte," 67, 70–71.

9. Conde, "Film," 68. More generally, Resende, ed., *Cronistas*; and Cândido et al., *Crônica*.

10. Ramos, "Política," 115–16; José de Alencar to Redação do *CM*, Rio, 8 July 1855, in Alencar, *Cartas*, 42. See also Souza, *"Ao correr"*; and Needell, *Party*, 250–51.

11. Scherzer, *Narrative*, 1:134; Dabadie, *A travers l'Amérique*, 24–25; Ribeyrolles, *Brasil*, 2:100–101; Vicuña Mackenna, *Paginas*, 2:329.

12. Magalhães Júnior, "Justiniano José da Rocha," 150–54; Barman, "Justiniano José da Rocha," 12–21; Guimarães, "Ação," 80–81, 84–85; Needell, *Party*, 188–90. On the subsidies that Justiniano received for his *O Brasil*, see his letters to the Visconde do Uruguai, Rio, 4 June 1840, ca. June 1840, and ca. 1844, *RIHGB* 220 (July–Sep. 1953): 342, 344, 346. Nabuco also discussed press subsidies, *Estadista*, 183–85, 342n*.

13. Ribeyrolles, *Brasil*, 2:99–100. On the *JC*'s subscribers, see Moreira de Azevedo, "Origem," 191. On its business aspects, see Sandroni, *180 anos*, 123, 137, 147–49. On the name by which it was known, see ibid., 42.

14. Scherzer, *Narrative*, 1:134. Although the *Folhinha* appeared until well into the twentieth century and is briefly mentioned by memoirists and historians, I know of no scholarship on it; Edmundo, *Rio*, 4:740; Morales de los Rios Filho, *Rio*, 392. On earlier *folhinhas*, see Neves, "Folhinhas."

15. Advertising, *JC*, 14 Sep. 1863; *Folhinha Laemmert* (1889), title page.

16. "Festejo nacional," *O Paiz*, 26 March 1843. On the *JC*'s publication of government acts, see Sandroni, *180 anos*, 117.

17. "O 7 de abril," *Correio da Tarde*, 7 April 1848; *O Brado do Amazonas*, 20 April 1849; Stillman, *Seeking*, 66.

18. Martins Pena, *Folhetins*, 195.

19. Johnson, *Journals*, 33, 34, 37, 56–57, 89, 92, 143–44, 179, 180–84 (five references), 187, 190, 191, 193, 258 (quote). A U.S. Marines officer reported a similar frequency of artillery salutes in 1853–56; [Forde], *Our Cruise*, 38, 61, 74, 81, 100.

20. Radiguet, *Souvenir*, 250; Lavollée, *Voyage*, 20–21; Scherzer, *Narrative*, 1:179.

21. Adalbert, *Travels*, 1:270–79. See also *JC*, 8–9 Sep. 1842. Other travelers who described days of national festivity include Horner, *Medical Topography*, 215–26 (7 April 1843); Arnold, *Viaje*, 79 (2 Dec. 1847); Charles Williams, quoted in Ramirez, ed., *From New York*, 80–81 (25 March 1849); Stewart, *Brazil*, 150–53 (2 Dec. 1850).

22. For a few examples, see "Ministerio do Imperio," *JC*, 19 March 1845; Editais, *JC*, 6 Sep. 1847; "Repartição da Policia," *JC*, 1 Dec. 1850.

23. See the untitled document outlining preparations for 2 Dec. 1841, AGCRJ, 6-2-25, fol. 33.

24. For the parade's organization, see Ordem do Dia, *JC*, 1 Dec. 1843; Ordem do Dia N. 65, *JC*, 6 Sep. 1845.

25. *JC*, 3 Dec. 1849; *Correio da Tarde*, 3 Dec. 1849; "Interesting from Brazil," *The New York Herald*, 18 Oct. 1854; "Affairs in Brazil," *The New York Herald*, 13 Jan. 1855. Forde identifies himself as the *Herald* correspondent in *Our Cruise*, 103, and also describes these days' official ritual, ibid., 74, 81.

26. Declarações, *JC*, 8 April 1841; "Noticias diversas," *CM*, 28–29 March 1864; "Noticias diversas," *CM*, 24 March 1866.

27. "Noticiario," *DRJ*, 26 March 1860.

28. For three examples, see "8 de Setembro," *DRJ*, 9 Sep. 1850; [José Maria da Silva Paranhos], "Ao Amigo Ausente" (*comunicado*), *JC*, 30 March 1851; *CM*, 3 Dec. 1857.

29. *O Brasil*, 4 Dec. 1848; Hunter, *Diplomat's Lady*, 273; *O Grito Nacional*, 11 Sep. 1850.

30. *Folhetim*, *JC*, 9 Sep. 1855; "Revue de la semaine," *Courier du Brésil*, 9 Sep. 1855. On the cholera epidemic's start, see Moreira de Azevedo, *Rio*, 1:75, note cvii.

31. [Paranhos], "Ao amigo ausente" (*comunicado*), *JC*, 7 Sep. 1851. See also "Noticias e factos diversos," *Correio da Tarde*, 9 Sep. 1851; "10 de Setembro," *DRJ*, 11 Sep. 1851.

32. "Ao Sr. Manoel de Frias Vasconcellos, inspector-geral das obras publicas" (*a pedido*), *JC*, 3 Dec. 1854; *CM*, 2 Dec. 1857.

33. "Revista" (*folhetim*), *DRJ*, 28 March 1854; "Illuminação a gaz," *O Velho Brazil*, 28 March 1854.

34. *JC*, 3 Dec. 1854; *JC*, 3 Dec. 1861; "Chronica da Semana" (*folhetim*), *JC*, 9 Dec. 1861; "Chronica da Semana," [15 Dec. 1861], *Revista Popular* 3:12 (1861): 377. For other inaugurations on days of national festivity, see Moreira de Azevedo, *Rio*, 2:286, 293–95, 312–13, 370.

35. Rebouças, *Diario*, 15; Ordem do Dia 103, *CM*, 1 Dec. 1856.

36. For examples, see "O dia 2 de Dezembro," *Tres de Maio*, 4 Dec. 1858; "As graças," *Monitor Brasileiro*, 6 Dec. 1858; "As Graças do Dia Dous," *A Marmota*, 14 Dec. 1858; "O dia 2 de Dezembro de 1858 e as condecorações" (*a pedido*), *JC*, 22 Dec. 1858.

37. *Folhetim*, *JC*, 6 Dec. 1858. The pun on *cólera*, which means both cholera and choler (anger) in Portuguese, does not quite work in English; *colérico* can refer to both a cholera victim and an angry person.

38. *Correio da Tarde*, 3 Dec. 1851; Paulo Barbosa da Silva to Pedro II, Rio, 24 Oct. 1845, in Lacombe, *Mordomo*, 115; Barman, *Citizen Emperor*, 174.

39. "O Dia Dous de Dezembro," *A Marmota na Corte*, 4 Dec. 1849; "O dia 2 de Dezembro," *O Cosmorama na Bahia*, 8 Dec. 1849.

40. "O Dia 7 de Setembro de 1850," *O Grito Nacional*, 11 Sep. 1850; "Lembrança," *A Marmota na Corte*, 8 Oct. 1850; "O dia 2 de dezembro de 1850," *O Grito Nacional*, 4 Dec. 1850.

41. "O dia 2 de dezembro," *O Grito Nacional*, 6 Dec. 1851; [Paranhos], "Ao amigo ausente" (*comunicado*), *JC*, 7 Dec. 1851; "44.ª pacotilha, Carijó e Comp.ª" (*folhetim*), *CM*, 8 Dec. 1851.

42. *CM*, 10 Sep. 1848; William Hunter to Sec. of State, Rio, 12 Sep. 1838, NARS, M-121, roll 13.

43. Langsdorff, *Diário*, 155–56.

44. *JC*, 3 Dec. 1857; *A Tribuna Catholica*, 6 Dec. 1857.

45. Henry A. Wise to Sec. of State, Rio, 12 Jan. 1845, NARS, M-121, roll 15. In the 1850s, Belgian diplomats also complained about excessive ceremonial; Costa, *Visões*, 40.

46. Wise to Sec. of State, Rio, 27 Feb. 1847, NARS, M-121, roll 18.

47. James Watson Webb to Sec. of State, Petrópolis, 23 March (quote), 5 April, and 7 May 1862, NARS, M-121, roll 29. For another instance, see Robert C. Schenck to Daughters, Rio, 9 Jan. 1852, in Peskin and Ramos, "Ohio Yankee," 506.

48. "O Dia Dous de Dezembro," *A Marmota na Corte*, 4 Dec. 1849.

49. Bagehot, *English Constitution*, 4–5, 8.

50. Pedro II, *Diário*, 23 July 1842 (this entry has been translated and published in its entirety in Barman, *Citizen Emperor*, 89–92, whose translation I follow in the quotations); J. Carvalho, *D. Pedro II*, 25.

51. Barman, *Citizen Emperor*, 187–88; Pedro II, *Diário*, 2 Dec. 1862.

52. J. Carvalho, *D. Pedro II*, 90–96; Barman, *Citizen Emperor*, 139–40.

53. Mansel, *Court*, 188–90, 195; Baguley, *Napoleon III*, 160–62; Truesdell, *Spectacular Politics*, 67–74; Pani, "Proyecto," 426–35; Duncan, "Political Legitimization," 37–48.

54. Castelnau, *Expédition*, part 1, vol. 1, p. 58; Walpole, *Four Years*, 1:41 (quote); Skogman, *Viaje*, 25; McGillivray, *Narrative*, 18; Manet, *Lettres*, 53 (quote). The one exception is Colvocoresses, *Four Years*, 30.

55. Itier, *Journal*, 1:50; Charles Williams, quoted in Ramirez, *From New York*, 64.

56. Burmeister, *Viagem*, 50; Alberdi, *Obras*, 3:271.

57. Württemberg, "Viagem," 24; Barman, *Citizen Emperor*, 115–16. On Petrópolis, see Schwarcz, *Barbas*, 231–45; Needell, *Tropical* Belle Époque, 149–50.

58. Ribeyrolles, *Brasil*, 1:115; "Chronica da Quinzena," *Iris* (15 Sep. 1848): 475; Raffard, "Apontamentos," 514.

59. Schwarcz, *Barbas*, 319–43.

60. "O dia 25 de Março," *O Paiz*, 26 March 1843; "7 de Setembro," *O Mercantil*, 8 Sep. 1846.

61. "O 7 de Setembro," *O Maiorista*, 9 Sep. 1841; "O Dia Dous de Dezembro," *O Constitucional*, 4 Dec. 1841; "O Dia 2 de Dezembro," *O Maiorista*, 4 Dec. 1841.

62. *O Americano*, 8 Sep. 1849; "7 de Setembro," *O Social*, 9 Sep. 1845. See also "O Dia 7 de Setembro," *O Tempo*, 10 Sep. 1846; and "A Independencia do Brasil," *DRJ*, 9 Sep. 1841.

63. "O Dia 7 de Setembro," *O Mercantil*, 8 Sep. 1845.

64. Decreto 224, 24 Sep. 1842, *CLB*. The *Almanaque Laemmert* described the day as a "holiday" (1844): 15. Hunter noted the 1843 mourning, *Diplomat's Lady*, 267.

65. Wetherell, *Brazil*, 82; Almeida, *Oração funebre*, 4. See also the account of the commemorations in *Correio da Tarde*, 24 Sep. 1849.

66. "O Dia 7 de Setembro," *O Mercantil*, 8 Sep. 1845; *O Echo do Rio*, 9 Sep. 1843; "7 de Setembro," *O Mercantil*, 7 Sep. 1847.

67. "Dia 2 de Dezembro," *O Mercantil*, 3 Dec. 1844; "Dous de Dezembro," *O Social*, 2 Dec. 1845.

68. F. Pereira, *Ao muito alto e muito poderoso senhor*, 5.

69. "O dia 25 de Março," *O Paiz*, 26 March 1843; "O 25 de Março Bate a Porta!!!!" *O Constitucional*, 5 and 12 March 1842.

70. Ewbank, *Life*, 278–80 (quote 279). Other travelers who wrote about this ritual include Fletcher and Kidder, *Brazil*, 211–12; Schenk to Daughters, Rio, 5 May 1852, in Peskin and Ramos, "Ohio Yankee," 511–12. For a rare Brazilian account, see "Factos occorridos no dia 3 do corrente," *A Galeria*, 6 May 1845.

71. Horner, *Medical Topography*, 215; "Sete de Abril," *O Brasil*, 8 April 1845, 8 April 1848.

72. "A Maioridade," *O Brasil*, 23 July 1842; *CM*, 23 July 1848; "Noticiario," *DRJ*, 24 July 1848.

73. *AS* (1845), 3:81; (1846), 1:178; (1848), 2:216–17 (quotes from Paula Souza's speech), 3:102; *ACD* (1848), 2:201; Decreto 501, 19 Aug. 1848, *CLB*.

74. *JC*, 28 Aug. 1848; *DRJ*, 28 Aug. 1848. The *CM* did not mention the decree. Mattos considers the elimination of 7 April to have been a Luzia defeat, "Gigante," 15–17, 33.

75. Barreto, "À lei que reduziu a tres os feriados de grande gala, ou festa nacional," in *Classicos*, 2:234–36 (quote 236).

76. Barman, *Citizen Emperor*, 86–87, 95–99, 103–05.

77. "4 de setembro," *DRJ*, 5 Sep. 1843; "Chegada de S. M. a Imperatriz," *O Brazil*, 5 Sep. 1843. See also Schwarcz, *Barbas*, 91–98 (esp. 92).

78. On these aspects of Francisca and Joinville's wedding celebrations, see Johnson, *Journals*, 143–46; Hunter, *Diplomat's Lady*, 257. See also Joinville, *Vieux souvenirs*, 240; and Raffard, "Apontamentos," 482–98. For these aspects of Pedro and Teresa Cristina's wedding, see Johnson, *Journals*, 179–90; Rodriguez, *Viagem*, 37–40, 55.

79. Johnson, *Journals*, 181, 187; Parker, *Recollections*, 31; Castelnau, *Expédition*, part 1, vol. 1, pp. 62–63.

80. "Programma para o recebimento, desembarque e acompanhamento de Sua Magestade a Imperatriz," 7 Aug. 1843 (printed flyer), AN, cód. 573, fols. 18–21; Johnson, *Journals*, 176; "Nota de Divertimentos na occasião do feliz consorcio," n.d., AGCRJ, 6-2-25, fol. 57; João Baptista de Souza Velho to Camara, Rio, 19 Aug. 1843, AGCRJ, 6-2-25, fol. 62.

81. Johnson, *Journals*, 177; Hunter, *Diplomat's Lady*, 264.

82. Hunter, *Diplomat's Lady*, 264; *JC*, 5 Sep. 1843.

83. Castelnau, *Expédition*, part 1, vol. 1, p. 121. See also Rodriguez, *Viagem*, 40–41.

84. Johnson, *Journals*, 184; Rodriguez, *Viagem*, 41. For the procession route, see "Programma para o recebimento . . . ," art. 41, AN, cód. 573, fols. 18–21. See also "Chegada de S. M. a Imperatriz," *O Brazil*, 5 Sep. 1843; "4 de Setembro," *DRJ*, 5 Sep. 1843.

85. Johnson, *Journals*, 184–85; Hunter, *Diplomat's Lady*, 265.

86. Johnson, *Journals*, 185–86, 188–89. See also Rodriguez, *Viagem*, 42.

87. Johnson, *Journals*, 189–90. Johnson misdated this to 8 September, but it clearly was the same ritual described for the 7th by *JC*, 8–9 Sep. 1843; "Sete de

Setembro," *O Brasil*, 9 Sep. 1843; "8 de Setembro," *DRJ*, 9 Sep. 1843; Hunter, *Diplomat's Lady*, 266.

88. Johnson, *Journals*, 190, 191; "Camara Municipal," *O Pharol Constitucional*, 13 Sep. 1843.

89. Barman, *Citizen Emperor*, 99–100.

90. Wise to Sec. of State, Rio, 23 Feb. 1845, NARS, M-121, roll 15.

91. See Antonio Francisco de Paula e Hollanda Cav.ᶜ d'Albuquerque to Joaquim Marcellino de Brito, Rio, 11 June 1846; "Funcção do Nascimento da Serenissima Princesa Isabel" (draft), 6 July 1846, AN, cód. 566, docs. 19 and 22.

92. Ewbank, *Life*, 406; "Chronica da Quinzena," 31 July 1848, *Iris* (July–Dec. 1848), 376.

93. See the baptism programs in AN, cód. 567, fols. 180–84, 190–94, 233–36; Sena, *Rascunhos*, 422–31. Pfeiffer noted the opening of the chapel after the ceremony, *Woman's Journey*, 54.

94. *O Mercantil*, 2 April 1845; *JC*, 26 March 1845. "Chronica nacional (1845)," *Folhinha Laemmert* (1846), 105–19; "Interesting from Brazil," *Weekly Herald* (New York), 24 May 1845.

95. "Chronica Nacional," 11 Oct. 1848, *Folhinha Laemmert* (1850), 149.

96. "O Baptisado do Principe Imperial," *O Granadeiro*, 29 March 1845; *O Mercantil*, 2 April 1845; Petition of Manoel de Araujo Porto-Alegre to Emperor, 29 Nov. 1845, BN/SM, DB, C.693.24.

97. Hunter, *Diplomat's Lady*, 313 (quote); "Chronica nacional (1845)," *Folhinha Laemmert* (1846), 124–25; "Chronica da Quinzena," 15 Sep. 1848, *Iris* (July–Dec. 1848), 475.

98. Pfeiffer, *Woman's Journey*, 53–56. Her account closely matches the reports in *JC*, 26 March 1845; and *O Mercantil*, 26 March 1845.

99. Barbosa, *Oração*, 3, 10; Seixas, *Collecção*, 4:158.

100. For one example of each, see "Chronica da Quinzena," 31 July 1848, *Iris* (July–Dec. 1848), 376–77; Francisco Antonio Ribeiro et al. (Representatives of the Bahia Provincial Assembly) to Emperor, Rio, 3 April 1845, AN/SPE, IJJ⁹, vol. 605, no fol. numbers; "Soneto em solemnisação ao baptismo de sua alteza O PRINCIPE IMPERIAL offerecido a SS MM II pelos directores da illuminação da Praça da Constituição" (printed flyer), MHN, IM₅3.

101. Motion, Ezequiel, Camara, 21 July 1846, AGCRJ, 6-2-25, fol. 95. For another critique of civic rituals' noisy nature, see A. L. "Paginas menores" (*folhetim*), *CM*, 10 Sep. 1854.

102. "O dia 7 de Septembro," *O Brasil*, 9 Sep. 1847. For an account of this ritual, see "7 de Setembro," *O Mercantil*, 8 Sep. 1847.

103. Barman, *Citizen Emperor*, 111–14, 121–22.

104. Ewbank, *Life*, 269, 253.

105. *Edital*, 3 April 1846, *O Mercantil*, 8 April 1846; Ewbank, *Life*, 269–70; "A viagem de SS. MM. II. nas Provincias do Sul," *Folhinha Laemmert* (1847), 145–46; "26 de Abril," *DRJ*, 27 April 1846; *JC*, 27 April 1846. See also "Programma para o recebimento de Suas Magestades Imperiaes . . ." (printed flyer), AN, cód. 572, fols. 206–08.

106. Wise to Sec. of State, Rio, 14 April 1846, NARS, M-121, roll 17; *JC*, 1 May 1847; "Noticias diversas," *DRJ*, 1 May 1847; *JC*, 28 Feb. 1848, 1 March 1848.

107. James Hudson to Viscount Palmerston, Rio, 9 May 1848, PRO/FO 13, vol. 258, fol. 367r–69r (quote 367v). See also Lord Howden to Palmerston, Rio, 20 March 1848, PRO/FO 13, vol. 257, fol. 247r–v.

108. For the political interpretation of these events, see Pereira da Silva, *Memorias*, 1:172–73; Pinho, *Cotegipe*, 150; Mosher, *Political Struggle*, 201, 222–23. On José Clemente Pereira's political trajectory, see Needell, *Party*, 66–67, 115–16; Barman, *Brazil*, 153 (quote). Another condemnation of José Clemente appears in Timandro [Francisco de Sales Torres Homem], "Libelo," 73, 92.

109. See the routine reports on the official celebrations, *JC*, 9 Sep. 1848; *Correio da Tarde*, 9 Sep. 1848; *O Americano*, 20 Sep. 1848.

110. "A situação actual," *Correio da Tarde*, 9 Sep. 1848. See also *JC*, 9 Sep. 1848; *DRJ*, 9 Sep. 1848.

111. "À meia noite," *CM*, 9 Sep. 1848; "A tranquilidade publica," *CM*, 12 Sep. 1848; "E esta?" *O Farricoco*, 10 Nov. 1848.

112. Hudson to Palmerston, Rio, 12 Sep. 1848, PRO/FO 13, vol. 259, 264r–69r. Hudson incorrectly identified Nunes Machado as a senator.

113. Sessions of 11, 12, and 13 Sep., *ACD* (1848), 2:353–66, 368–69, 370; Sessions of 9, 11, and 12 Sep., *AS* (1848), 5:74–79, 121–34, 138–74.

114. Speech of José Pedro Dias de Carvalho, 11 Sep., *AS* (1848), 5:122–23.

115. Speech of Antônio Luis Dantas de Barros Leite, 12 Sep., *AS* (1848), 5:138–39.

116. Speech of José Joaquim Fernandes Torres, 12 Sep., *AS* (1848), 5:146, 150.

117. Speech of Urbano Sabino Pessoa de Melo, 11 Sep., *ACD* (1848), 2:364. See also speech of Bernardo de Souza Franco, 11 Sep., *ACD* (1848), 2:362.

118. "Festejos nacionaes," *O Brado do Amazonas*, 20 April 1849. Maranhense's editorship of this periodical is noted in "O Vate da Bacanga," *CM*, 26 March 1858. On him, see Machado, *Vida*, 106–08; Sacramento Blake, *Diccionario*, 3:274.

119. Morales de los Rios Filho, *Rio*, 471; Moreira de Azevedo, "Origem," 213–14.

120. "Fuzileiros e Permanentes, ou as fardas miguelistas," *O Farricoco*, 9 Dec. 1848. See also "Ainda os Permanentes, Fuzileiros e fardamento miguelista," *O Farricoco*, 23 Dec. 1848.

121. *O Brasil*, 26 March 1849; "Dia 25 de Março," *A Sentinela do Trono*, 28 March 1849 (quote).

122. "24 de Março," *CM*, 25 March 1849.

123. "O Dia Sete de Setembro," *O Grito Nacional*, 7 Sep. 1849; "O dia 2 de Dezembro," *O Grito Nacional*, 11 Dec. 1849.

124. "Ao Dia 7 de Setembro," *O Grito Nacional*, 7 Sep. 1850; "O que é o Dia 7 de Setembro para o Brasil," *O Grito Nacional*, 11 Sep. 1850. For additional examples of such criticism, see "O Dia Sete de Setembro," *A Marmota na Corte*, 4 Oct. 1850; "O Dia 7 de Setembro," *O Independente, Periodico Nacional*, 12 Sep. 1850.

125. "O dia 7 de Setembro," *O Brasil*, 10 Sep. 1850; "O dia 2 de Dezembro de 1850," *O Grito Nacional*, 4 Dec. 1850.

126. The subsidy is noted for March 1855 by Barman, "Justiniano," 27.

127. *Folhetim, JC*, 6 Dec. 1858.

128. "O dia 25 de março" (*comunicado*), *JC*, 25 March 1851.

129. "O dia 25 de março de 1824," *Correio da Tarde*, 24 March 1852. See also "O dia 25 de março," *JC*, 26 March 1855; "25 de Março," *DRJ*, 25 March 1858; "O dia 25 de março," *A Marmota na Corte*, 25 March 1851.

130. *JC*, 25 March 1858. For this view, see also Rocha, "Ação," 202. On criticisms of Brazil's neighbors, see Preuss, *Bridging*, 31.

131. Pimenta Bueno, *Direito*, iv, 560.

132. "O dia Dous de Dezembro," *Marmota Fluminense*, 2 Dec. 1852. The *JC* saw fit to reprint this article a few days later, 6 Dec. 1852. Pedro's biographers note that his reputation as a faithful husband has been exaggerated; Carvalho, *D. Pedro II*, 62–75; Barman, *Citizen Emperor*, 128, 148–49, 282–85.

133. "Um dia nacional," *A Epoca*, 17 Dec. 1853; *Correio da Tarde*, 2 Dec. 1857; "O dia dous de dezembro," *JC*, 2 Dec. 1858. For the latter theme, see also "Dous de dezembro," *Correio da Tarde*, 3 Dec. 1860; *JC*, 2 Dec. 1860.

134. "O dia Sete de Setembro," *JC*, 9 Sep. 1855. See also "7 de Setembro," *DRJ*, 7 Sep. 1853; "O Sete de Setembro," *CM*, 7 Sep. 1854; "Chronica," *A Saudade*, 7 Sep. 1862.

135. *JC*, 8–9 Sep. 1859; D. C., "Saudação ao dia 7 de setembro," *CM*, 7 Sep. 1859; *Folhetim*, *JC*, 7 Sep. 1856.

136. "A Sua Majestade Imperial," *CM*, 2 Dec. 1858; "A Sua Magestade o Imperador," *CM*, 2 Dec. 1860; "Dous de Dezembro," *DRJ*, 2 Dec. 1860; *DRJ*, 2 Dec. 1861.

137. "O Segundo Reinado," *A Actualidade*, 2 Dec. 1862.

138. Santos, *Homem*, 201–03; Vianna, *Contribuição*, 580–85; Pinho, *Cotegipe*, 472–75; Nabuco, *Estadista*, 296–301.

139. "O dia 2 de dezembro," *O Republico*, 10 Dec. 1854. See Paula Brito's signed editorial in *Marmota Fluminense*, 1 Dec. 1854.

140. "O dia 2 de dezembro," *O Grito Nacional*, 3 Dec. 1853.

141. "O dia 25 de março," *Correio da Tarde*, 30 March 1859; "Recordação historica," *Correio da Tarde*, 26 March 1860; "Vinte e cinco de março," *O Regenerador*, 27 March 1860; *DRJ*, 25 March 1861.

142. "O Imperio," *CM*, 27 March 1860. I do not know where *O Imperio* was published. This interpretation also appears in the 1849 pamphlet, Timandro [Torres Homem], "Libelo," 66–72.

143. [Paranhos], "Ao amigo ausente" (*comunicado*), *JC*, 30 March 1851; [José de Alencar], "Ao correr da pena" (*folhetim*), *CM*, 25 March 1855; *Folhetim*, *JC*, 1 April 1855; M., "Paginas menores" (*folhetim*), *CM*, 26 March 1856; *Folhetim*, *JC*, 30 March 1856; "Chronica da Quinzena," 31 March 1859, *Revista Popular* 1:2 (1859): 62.

144. Cartoon, *Bazar Volante*, 27 March 1864; Macedo, *Carteira*, first *folheto*, 18; references to the deceased constitution appear on 15, 16, 17, 104; and second *folheto*, 3, 43, 44, 67, 109, 126, 128, 136.

145. "O como se passou o dia 7 de setembro," *O Grito Nacional*, 10 Sep. 1851; "Sete de Setembro," *O Grito Nacional*, 7 Sep. 1854; "Como se passou o dia Sete de Setembro," *O Grito Nacional*, 9 Sep. 1854 (supplemento); "O Dia— Sete de Setembro . . . ," *O Grito Nacional*, 7 Sep. 1852.

146. *CM*, 7 Sep. 1857.

147. A S. M. o Imperador," *O Tyranno*, 12 Sep. 1857; "Ao dia 7 de Setembro (palavras de um sexagenario)," *O Carapuça*, 6 Sep. 1857; "7 de setembro," *7 de Setembro*, 7 Sep. 1859; "Independencia ou Morte" and "O Dia Sete de Setembro," *O Clamor Publico*, 7 Sep. 1860; *A Crença*, 6 Sep. 1863.

148. "O Dia 7 de Setembro," *Correio da Tarde*, 10 Sep. 1855.

149. On these movements, see Maxwell, *Conflicts*; Furtado, *Manto*; Mota, *Nordeste 1817*; Leite, *Pernambuco 1817*; Mello, *Outra Independência*, 25–63; Mosher, *Political Struggle*, 9–40.

150. Armitage, *History*, 1:10–11, 18–19.

151. On the 1839–40 research, see Haberly, "Mythification," 64–65; Southey, *History*, 3:678–86 (quote 679).

152. "O dia sete de setembro," *JC*, 6 Sep. 1840.

153. "Paginas menores" (*folhetim*), *CM*, 7 Sep. 1857. Justiniano also mentioned them as antecedents of independence in his 1855 pamphlet; Rocha, "Ação," 162.

154. "Vinte-Cinco de Março," *DRJ*, 24 March 1867.

155. Varnhagen, *Historia geral*, 1st ed., 2:269–82 (quote 282). For the Instituto Histórico e Geográfico Brasileiro's poor reception of the work, see Francisco Adolfo de Varnhagen to Pedro II, Madrid, 24 Sep. 1856, in Varnhagen, *Correspondência*, 235; and Araújo, *Experiência*, 181. On Varnhagen's political views, see also Wehling, *Estado*, 95, 102, 110–20, 184–85.

156. Varnhagen, *Historia geral*, 1st ed., 2:373, 392.

157. Barman, *Citizen Emperor*, 188.

158. "Programma para a recepção de SS. MM. II. . . . ," 19 Jan. 1860, AN/SPE, IJJ¹ 655, fols. 41r–43r.

159. *CM*, 12 Feb. 1860; *JC*, 12 Feb. 1860.

160. C. Linde, "Ao Feliz Regresso de SS. MM. II.," AHMI, MIII-19; "Chronica da quinzena," 16 Feb. 1860, *Revista Popular* 2:5 (1860): 251–52; "Echos de Rio de Janeiro," *Courier du Brésil*, 12 Feb. 1860.

161. "Chronica da quinzena," 16 Feb. 1860, *Revista Popular* 2:5 (1860): 252; *JC*, 12 Feb. 1860. See also "Noticias diversas," *CM*, 12 Feb. 1860.

162. For examples, see Machado de Assis's "A S. M. I.," AHMI, MIII-19; J[oaquim] Norberto de S[ouza] e S[ilva], "Ao Regresso de SS. MM. II," *Revista Popular* 2:5 (1860): 248.

163. Antonio José Nunes Garcia, "Cantata no glorioso dia da chegada de SS. MM. II. . . . ," MHN, IM_s 8.

164. Almeida, *Oração gratulatoria*, 10.

165. "Recepção de SS. MM. II.," *A Actualidade*, 18 Feb. 1860.

166. On the dynastic negotiations that led to these marriages, see Barman, *Citizen Emperor*, 152–58; Barman, *Princess Isabel*, 54–59; Daibert Júnior, *Isabel*, 47–51.

167. The programs are found in AN, cód. 565, fols. 153–56, 206–09. Isabel's wedding is described in Daibert Junior, *Isabel*, 53–61.

168. The hailstorm is mentioned by Taunay, *Memórias*, 311. The direction from which it came is mentioned in Albino José Barbosa de Oliveira to his children, Rio, 14 Oct. 1882, Oliveira, *Memórias*, 294. See also [Machado de Assis], "Ao acaso" (*folhetim*), *DRJ*, 17 Oct. 1864.

169. [Machado de Assis], "Ao acaso" (*folhetim*), *DRJ*, 1 Nov. 1864.

170. The pardons are noted in Daibert Júnior, *Isabel*, 58; the freeing of slaves is mentioned in Barman, *Princess Isabel*, 63; Barman, *Citizen Emperor*, 194.

171. *O Constitucional*, 17 Dec. 1864.

172. Webb to Sec. of State, Petrópolis, 20 Sep. 1864, NARS, M-121, roll 32; Rio, 23 Oct. 1864; Petrópolis, 23 Dec. 1864, NARS, M-121, roll 33.

CHAPTER FIVE

1. Enders, "O Plutarco"; Galvão, "Estátua"; Meghreblian, "Art," 76–81, 139; Green, "Emperor"; Ribeiro, "Memória"; Souza, *Pátria*, 351–65. See, however, the pioneering efforts to analyze the political discussions in Monteiro and Santos, "Celebrando," 59–63, and the important analysis by Cavallini, "Monumento."

2. Agulhon, "Statuomanie"; Savage, *Standing Soldiers*, 4. See also Bogart, *Public Sculpture*; Michalski, *Public Monuments*.

3. For examples of political monuments in different societies, see Rinke, "Pillars"; Driskel, *As Befits a Legend*; Cohen, "Symbols."

4. Manoel Dias de Oliveira, "Monumento dedicado ao dia nove de Janeiro de 1822 . . . ," AIHGB, DL 19.20.

5. Henry Chamberlain to George Canning, Rio, 14 May 1825, PRO/FO 13, vol. 9, fol. 77r–v. Moniz Barreto complained of his exclusion in "Inauguração da Estatua Equestre do Imperador," *Despertador Constitucional Extraordinario*, 24 May 1825. On him, see Sacramento Blake, *Diccionario*, 2:189–92; Silva, *Generais*, 2:57.

6. "Discurso feito perante S. M. I. . . . ," *Diario Fluminense*, 14 May 1825; Decisão 143, 6 July 1825, *CLB*.

7. "Estatua de D. Pedro 1.º . . . 1825–1827," AGCRJ, 43-1-57; "Lista dos dinheiros recebidos constantes da conta, 1825," AGCRJ, 43-1-55. For a few notices of donations, see *Diario Mercantil*, 14 Feb. and 18 March 1826; *Diario Fluminense*, 22 March 1826.

8. João José Vahia to Camara, Rio, 16 Nov. 1825, AGCRJ, 43-1-56, fol. 34; Ata, Camara, Salvador, 5 Nov. 1825 (copy), AGCRJ, 43-1-56, fol. 54r–55v; Condy Raguet to Sec. of State, Rio, 26 Oct. 1825, NARS, M-121, roll 5.

9. *Parecer*, Commissão . . . Plano da Estatua Equestre, c. 1825 (copy), AIHGB, lata 59, doc. 14; Porto Alegre, "Bellas Artes," 288; Herstal, *D. Pedro*, 1:219.

10. "Estatua equestre," *A Actualidade*, 19 March 1862; Porto Alegre, "Bellas Artes," 286; Moreira de Azevedo, *Rio*, 2:14.

11. "Demonstração das quantias com que subscreverão as Provincias do Imperio . . . ," 17 Jan. 1831, AGCRJ, 43-1-59, doc. 3C.

12. Secretario, Camara, to Vereadores, Rio, 17 Jan. 1831, AGCRJ, 43-1-59, doc. 3B; *O Narcizo*, 9 March 1831; Manoel Cavanha Quaresma to Camara, Rio, 20 June 1832, AGCRJ, 43-1-61, fol. 2.

13. *ACD* (1832), 2:144; (1835), 1:142; (1846), 2:394.

14. Procurador, Camara Municipal da Villa de S. Salvador dos Campos dos Goitacazes, to Camara, Rio, 4 Nov. 1834, AGCRJ, 43-1-61, fol. 4; *ACD* (1836), 2:76, 223.

15. "Ao memoravel dia 24 de Setembro de 1846 . . . ," in "Tributo de gratidão a Memoria do Snr. D. Pedro 1.º . . . ," BN/SM, I-35, 9, 11, p. 34. For a similar call, see *O Novo Despertador Constitucional*, 24 Sep. 1852.

16. Porto Alegre, "Estatua," 38; Porto Alegre, "Bellas Artes," 286, 288–91.

17. "Subscripção para os dous monumentos . . . ," ca. 1839, AIHGB, DL 59.15.

18. Petition of Humilanno José Batista Jardineiro to Camara, c. 1838, AGCRJ, 43-1-59, fol. 3.

19. See the documents in AIHGB, DL 59.5.

20. Porto Alegre, "Estatua equestre," 38; Manoel de Araujo Porto Alegre, "Memoria," Rio, 3 May 1839, BN/SM, I-46, 23, 1A.

21. The only contemporary references to this campaign are in Porto Alegre, "Estatua equestre," 38; Haddock Lobo, *Discurso*, 6. Moreira de Azevedo's brief remarks are apparently based on these sources, *Rio*, 2:14.

22. *ACD* (1846), 2:259; (1852), 2:389, 399 (Resende's speech); (1854) 3:291.

23. See the text of this proposal in *JC*, 10 Sep. 1854, and Frias Vasconcelos's motion, 25 Feb. 1853, AGCRJ, 43-1-62.

24. Souza, *Pátria*, 352.

25. "Camara Municipal, 30.ª Sessão, Extraordinária," 7 Sep. 1854 (printed flyer), AIHGB, lata 826, pasta 44. The minutes of this session are also reproduced in Moreira de Azevedo, *Rio*, 2:16–18.

26. *DRJ*, 8–9 Sep. 1854.

27. Letter to the Editor, Domingos de Azeredo Coutinho Duque-Estrada, *JC*, 10 Sep. 1854; "Uma estatua ao Sr. D. Pedro 1.º," *O Velho Brazil*, 12 Sep. 1854; "O monumento do Ypiranga," *O Brado do Amazonas*, 8 Oct. 1854; "A estatua equestre," *A Aurora Fluminense*, 9 June 1855.

28. Needell, *Party*, 232, 402n31. On Eusébio, see Sacramento Blake, *Diccionario*, 2:308–10.

29. Sacramento Blake, *Diccionario*, 3:326–27.

30. Santos, *Pantheon*, 509–13 (quote 510); Sisson, *Galeria*, 1:371–75.

31. Squeff, *Brasil*, 77, 232.

32. Manoel de Araujo Porto Alegre to [Francisco de Azevedo Monteiro] Caminhoá, Lisbon, 25 July 1871, AIHGB, lata 653, pasta 29; Silva, *Generais*, 2:484–503.

33. Sacramento Blake, *Diccionario*, 4:211–17.

34. *Almanaque Laemmert* (1859), 336, 504.

35. Sacramento Blake, *Diccionario*, 2:194–96. On the Duque Estrada family, see Needell, *Party*, 25.

36. Moreira de Azevedo, *Rio*, 2:44nXXVIII.

37. Sacramento Blake, *Diccionario*, 7:135–37, 3:314.

38. "Estatua equestre," *O Velho Brazil*, 26 Sep. 1854; Porto Alegre to Camara, Rio, 30 Sep. 1854, AGCRJ, 43-1-76.

39. "O monumento do Ypiranga," *O Brado do Amazonas*, 8 Oct. 1854.

40. Pierre Magni, "Projet du monument à eriger à Rio de Janeiro a S. M. Don Pedro I, Impereur du Brésil," BN/SI, Res.

41. F[rancisco] J[oaquim] Bittancourt da Silva, "A estatua equestre do Sr. D. Pedro 1.º," *O Brasil Illustrado*, 15 April 1855; Moreira de Azevedo, *Rio*, 2:215; Meghreblian, "Art," 80.

42. Moreira de Azevedo, *Rio*, 2:19. According to Herstal, all of the designs have been lost, but he indicates that they were reproduced in the 1877 edition of Moreira de Azevedo's *Rio*; Herstal, *D. Pedro I*, 1:255. There are, however, no images in the copy of this edition that was available on Google Books on 30 June 2009 (from Stanford University Library).

43. On Rochet, see Bénézit, *Dictionnaire*, 11:796; Rochet, *Louis Rochet.*

44. [Manoel de Araujo Porto Alegre], "Diario, 1856," in Galvão, "Manoel de Araujo Porto Alegre," 93–94.

45. "Annaes brasileiros," *Folhinha luso-brasileira*, 30.

46. *Estatua equestre*, 1–5; Louis Rochet to President and Members of Commission, Rio, 18 Sep. 1856, in Rochet, *Louis Rochet*, 162–166 (quote, 166); Moreira de Azevedo, *Pequeno panorama*, 5:22.

47. Eusébio de Queirós Coutinho Mattoso Camara to Camara, Rio, 10 July 1858, AGCRJ, 43-1-62; "A estatua equestre," *A Aurora Fluminense*, 9 June 1855.

48. "Conta do que tem recebido e dispendido . . . ," 30 Sep. 1864, AGCRJ, 43-1-59, no fol. number.

49. "Noticias diversas," *Guanabara* (1854): 408; Moreira de Azevedo, *Rio*, 2:35. See also "Estatua equestre," *JC*, 11 March 1862.

50. Camara Municipal to Sr. Graciano dos Santos Pereira, Rio, 29 Dec. 1860 (printed form letter), MHN, IMv5. See also the reports from two parish committees (Glória and São José) in AGCRJ, 43-1-59, fols. 9–16.

51. Iglesias, "Vida," 57–59; Needell, *Party*, 191–99.

52. On the 1856 election results, see F[rancisco] Otaviano [de Almeida Rosa] to [Francisco Inácio de Carvalho] Moreira, [Rio], 15 Dec. 1856 and 13 Jan. 1857, in Otaviano, *Cartas*, 107, 109.

53. Chagas, *Teófilo Otoni*, 285–95; Mendonça, "Cousas," 128 (quote); Barbosa, "Panfletos," 156–67.

54. Needell, *Party*, 201, 213–22; Barman, *Citizen Emperor*, 189–91; Barbosa, "Política," 300–12; Iglesias, "Vida," 79–81.

55. For a reference to the stipend, see Pedro II, *Diário*, 29 March 1862. The stipend appears to have been public knowledge, for the *Correio da Tarde* defended itself against accusations that it lived off government coffers; "Actualidade," *Correio da Tarde*, 5 March 1862.

56. Cavallini, "Monumento," 300; Mascarenhas, *Jornalista*, 257. Justiniano José da Rocha's *O Regenerador* had ceased publication in September 1861, and Firmino Rodrigues Silva's *Constitucional* only began publication on 1 July 1862. Nabuco's assessment is in *Estadista*, 370.

57. Guimarães, "Henrique Fleiüss," 165–74.

58. Rochet, *Louis Rochet*, 144.

59. "Estatua equestre de D. Pedro I," *JC*, 6 Sep. 1861; Moreira de Azevedo, *Rio*, 2:20.

60. "Programma para a ceremonia da collocação da pedra fundamental . . . ," AGCRJ, 43-1-62, fols. 31v–32r; "Relação historica," *Folhinha Laemmert* (1863), 28–37; Moreira de Azevedo, *Rio*, 2:21–23.

61. "Noticias diversas," *CM*, 2 Jan. 1862; "Estatua equestre do Sr. D. Pedro 1.º," *Correio da Tarde*, 1 Jan. 1862.

62. Pedro II, *Diário*, 1 Jan. 1862. See also *JC*, 2 Jan. 1862.

63. *Folhetim, JC*, 3 Jan. 1862; "Chronica da Quinzena," 15 March 1862, *Revista Popular*, 4:13 (1862): 380; "O que sahir" (*folhetim*), *JC*, 2 March 1862; "Estatua," *Semana Illustrada*, 1 Dec. 1861.

64. "Relação historica," *Folhinha Laemmert* (1863), 38; "Chronica da Semana," 15 Feb. 1862, *Revista Popular* 4:13 (1862): 252; "O que sahir" (*folhetim*) *JC*, 2 March 1862.

65. "Estatua," *Semana Illustrada*, 23 Feb. 1862.

66. For a description of the temporary structures, see Moreira de Azevedo, *Rio*, 2:23.

67. Pedro II, *Diário*, 13 March 1862; Moreira de Azevedo, *Rio*, 2:23.

68. Petition of Camara to Pedro II, 30 Dec. 1861 (draft), AGCRJ, 43-1-62, fol. 30; Commissão to Camara, Rio, 13 Jan. 1862, AGCRJ, 43-1-62; "Noticias diversas," *CM*, 1 Jan. 1862; "Noticias diversas," *A Actualidade*, 8 Jan. 1862.

69. "Programma para a inauguração da estatua equestre do Senhor D. Pedro 1.º," 17 Dec. 1861, AGCRJ, 43-1-62, fols. 43r–47v.

70. Ryan, "American Parade," 134. On U.S. parade culture, see also Davis, *Parades*. On Corpus Christi, see Santos, *Corpo*; Dean, *Inka Bodies*.

71. "Inauguração da Estatua Equestre de D. Pedro I" (*a pedido*), *CM*, 16 Jan. 1862; Um do povo, "A inauguração da estatua equestre no dia 25 de Março" (*a pedido*), *JC*, 6 March 1862; "O que sahir" (*folhetim*), *JC*, 2 March 1862.

72. "Estatua equestre do Sr. D. Pedro I," *JC*, 14 March 1862; "Noticias diversas," *CM*, 15 March 1862; "Noticias e avisos diversos," *Correio da Tarde*, 16 March 1862. For Pedro's insistence on holding the 25 March rituals, see Pedro II, *Diário*, 8 March 1862. For earlier worries about crowding in the square, see "Estatua equestre," *JC*, 7 March 1862. The final program appeared in "Inauguração da estatua equestre," *JC*, 24 March 1862, and is reprinted in Moreira de Azevedo, *Rio*, 2:24–29.

73. Vieira Fazenda, "Antiqualhas," *RIHGB* 142 (1920): 58–60 (originally published in 1903); 147 (1923): 447 (originally published in 1909). The schools are mentioned in "Agradecimentos" (*a pedido*), *CM*, 2 April 1862. On the rehearsals, see also "Contos do Rio de Janeiro," *Semana Illustrada*, 23 March 1862. The numbers of performers is given in "Noticiario," *DRJ*, 25 March 1862. Moreira de Azevedo presents slightly different figures: 242 instrumentalists and 653 singers, *Rio*, 2:33, 236.

74. "O que sahir" (*folhetim*), *JC*, 2 March 1862.

75. Starting in January 1862, the *JC*, the *DRJ*, and the *CM* regularly recorded these appointments. The doubts about the square's capacity appear in "Contos do Rio de Janeiro," *Semana Illustrada*, 2 March 1862.

76. The documents can be found in AN/SPE, IJJ^9, m. 605; IJJ^{11}, m. 62; IJ^6, m. 446. The ministry published these congratulations in nine issues of the *JC* between 4 and 28 April 1862. The *DRJ* also published many of them in the first week of April.

77. "Inauguração da estatua do Sr. D. Pedro I, Estrada de Ferro de D. Pedro II" (*declarações*), *CM*, 18 March 1862.

78. [Firmino Rodrigues Silva], "A estatua equestre" (*comunicado*), *JC*, 28 March 1862; advertisement in *DRJ*, 25 March 1862; Ribeiro, "Memória," 21–22.

79. "Noticiario," *DRJ*, 29 March 1862. Some of the lithographs have been reproduced in Herstal, *D. Pedro I*, 1:240–45, 247.

80. "Chronica da quinzena," [15 March 1862], *Revista Popular* 4:13 (1862): 379–80.

81. "Noticiario," *DRJ*, 14 March 1862. On the ubiquitous *frades de pedra* that protected buildings from vehicles, see Morales de los Rios Filho, *Rio*, 95, 203.

82. "E [sic] estatua equestre e as graças," *A Actualidade*, 25 March 1862. See also "Contos do Rio de Janeiro," *Semana Illustrada*, 30 March 1862; "Chronica da Quinzena," [15 April 1862]; *Revista Popular* 4:14 (1862): 126. On the decision not to issue decorations, see Pedro II, *Diário*, 14 March 1862.

83. "Noticias e avisos diversos," *Correio da Tarde*, 30 March 1862.

84. Pedro II, *Diário*, 19 March 1862; "Noticias e avisos diversos," *Correio da Tarde*, 22 April 1862.

85. "Publicações a pedido," *CM*, 29 and 30 March 1862; "Contos do Rio de Janeiro," *Semana Illustrada*, 6 April 1862; "Cousa estupenda," *O Charivari*, 27 April 1862; Pedro II, *Diário*, 26 April and 14 May 1862.

86. "A estatua equestre e a revolução," *A Actualidade*, 15 March 1862; *DRJ*, 15 March 1862; "Diario do Rio," *Correio da Tarde*, 16 March 1862; "Contos do Rio de Janeiro," *Semana Illustrada*, 23 March 1862. On the rumored plot, see also Cavallini, "Monumento," 316–18.

87. "A estatua equestre e a canalha," *A Actualidade*, 25 March 1862. See also "Noticiario," *DRJ*, 24 March 1862.

88. "Imprensa de Nichtheroy," *Correio da Tarde*, 26 March 1862; [Joaquim Maria Machado de Assis], "Commentarios da Semana" (*folhetim*), *DRJ*, 24 March 1862; "Ainda a inauguração," *O Charivari*, 27 April 1862.

89. "Inauguração da estatua equestre," *JC*, 26 March 1862; "Noticias diversas," *CM*, 26 March 1862; "Contos do Rio de Janeiro," *Semana Illustrada*, 30 March 1862. Moreira de Azevedo mentions the fallen arm, *Rio*, 2:29.

90. "Noticiario," *DRJ*, 26 March 1863; Taunay, *Memórias*, 79.

91. Pedro II, *Diário*, 25 March 1862; "Noticiario," *DRJ*, 26 March 1862.

92. James Watson Webb to Sec. of State, Petrópolis, 5 April 1862, NARS, M-121, roll 29; Vieira Fazenda, "Antiqualhas," *RIHGB* 142 (1920): 60–61; Pedro II, *Diário*, 30 March 1862; Albino José Barbosa de Oliveira to His Children, Rio, 27 July 1882, in A. Oliveira, *Memórias*, 269.

93. *Correio da Tarde*, 31 March 1862; "Noticias diversas," *CM*, 31 March 1862; "Noticiario," *DRJ*, 31 March 1862; "Inauguração da estatua equestre," *A Actualidade*, 3 April 1862.

94. "Contos do Rio de Janeiro," *Semana Illustrada*, 6 April 1862; Francisco Manoel Pereira to Emperor, [Rio], 25 March 1862, AN/SPE, IJJ[11], m. 62.

95. "Relação historica" and "Chronica nacional," *Folhinha Laemmert* (1863), 41–58, 186, 204–06; Moreira de Azevedo, *Pequeno panorama*, 5:40–43. See also Moreira de Azevedo, *Rio*, 2:31–35.

96. Moreira de Azevedo, *Rio*, 2:24; *Correio da Tarde*, 31 March 1862; "Relação historica," *Folhinha Laemmert* (1863), 44; "A revolução de 30 de março" (cartoon), *Semana Illustrada*, 6 April 1862.

97. Camara, *Discurso*, 4, 5. Pedro's assessment is in Pedro II, *Diário*, 30 March 1862. See also "El-rei Eusebio exautorado," *A Actualidade*, 3 April 1862. For the naming of Constitution Square, see Gerson, *História*, 121; Morales de los Rios Filho, *Rio*, 226; Coaracy, *Memórias*, 88. Eusébio's error has been repeated by some historians, M. Ribeiro, "Memória," 18; Green, "Emperor," 181–82.

98. Machado, *Vida*, 37n2. Three collections of these poems exist: AIHGB, lata 459, doc. 10; BN/SOG, III-75, 7, 22, nos. 1–37; OLL, Pamphlets 19th Cent. 199. The latter two collections were apparently compiled by Theotonio de Santa Humiliana, for both bear the same title page with the friar's declaration that the collection demonstrates "Brazilians' gratitude to their empire's founder."

99. "Poesia," *JC*, 31 March 1862.

100. [Joaquim] Hamvultando [de Oliveira], "Pedro Primeiro" (printed handbill), AIHGB, lata 459, doc. 10 (and also BN/SOG, III-75, 7, 22, no. 10).

101. Burgain, *Estatua*, 14.

102. Pedro II, *Diário*, 30 March 1862; "Theatros," *JC*, 31 March 1862; "Estatua equestre," *JC*, 2 April 1862.

103. "Ovação ao Sr. Rochet," *JC*, 3 April 1862; Moreira de Azevedo, *Pequeno panorama*, 5:44; "Contos do Rio de Janeiro," *Semana Illustrada*, 6 April 1862.

104. *Correio da Tarde*, 1 April 1862.

105. Pedro II, *Diário*, 8 March 1862.

106. *CM*, 27 March 1862.

107. Souza, *Pátria*, 365.

108. Some attribute the phrase "bronze lie [*mentira de bronze*]" to Otoni (Souza, *Pátria*, 359; Carvalho, *Formação*, 60; Milliet, *Tiradentes*, 79), but it does not appear in Otoni's pamphlet against the statue; Ottoni, *Estatua*. Otoni's biographer attributes it to Pedro Luís; Chagas, *Teófilo Otoni*, 313. On at least two occasions in late March 1862 writers in *A Atualidade* referred to the statue as a lie, but neither used the phrase "*mentira de bronze*": "We believe that the statue lies to posterity" ("Estatua equestre," *A Actualidade*, 22 March 1862); and "the bronze flattery that rises mendaciously" ("A estatua e Evaristo," *A Actualidade*, 30 March 1862). On 10 April, an *a pedido* published in two newspapers criticized the use of the word *mentira* to describe the statue; "O Mercantil, o Diário e o 1.º Reinado," *JC*, 10 April 1862; *Correio da Tarde*, 10 April 1862. Sandes suspects that the phrase circulated orally before entering the political lexicon; *Invenção*, 35.

109. The two pamphlets were, most likely, Pascual, *Rasgos*, 1862, a shamelessly adulatory biography of Pedro I by a Spanish émigré that the *Correio* acknowledged receiving a few days earlier ("Noticias diversas," *CM*, 18 March 1862); [Veiga], *Revolução*. The attribution of authorship is by Sacramento Blake, *Diccionario*, 5:406. On Pascual, see ibid., 1:148–50.

110. *CM*, 23 March 1862.

111. *CM*, 24 March 1862.

112. *CM*, 25 March 1862.

113. Ottoni, *Estatua*. Chagas dates the publication to 24 March 1862; *Teófilo Ottoni*, 314. It appeared on 25 March in *DRJ*, *CM*, and *A Actualidade*. The text of this pamphlet also apears in Chagas, *Teófilo Ottoni*, 314–18.

114. *DRJ*, 25 March 1862.

115. "Uma pagina de historia," *DRJ*, 25, 28, 29, and 30 March 1862.

116. "A estatua," *A Actualidade*, 25 March 1862.

117. Pedro II, *Diário*, 22 March 1862.

118. "A estatua equestre e o Mercantil," *JC*, 25 March 1862. The attribution to Firmino is by Mascarenhas, *Jornalista*, 249–50; Firmino probably drew on Varnhagen, *Historia geral*, 1st ed., 2:427, 439.

119. "O dia 25 de Março de 1862," *JC*, 25 March 1862. On the government's response, see also Cavallini, "Monumento," 320–22.

120. Pedro II, *Diário*, 25 March 1862. The assessment of Saião is by Iglesias, "Vida política," 81. See also Holanda, "Do Império," 15, 74.

121. Pedro II, *Diário*, 30 March 1862.

122. "A estatua equestre e o Mercantil" and "Juramento da Constituição" (*a pedidos*), *Correio da Tarde*, 26 March 1862.

123. "A estatua equestre e o Sr. Ottoni" (*a pedido*), *JC*, 26 March 1862. See also Soldado da Velha Guarda, *Appreciação*, 5.

124. [Silva], "A estatua equestre" (*comunicado*), *JC*, 28, 29, and 30 March 1862. The first installment also appeared in *Correio da Tarde*, 30 March 1862. The identification of Firmino as the author is by Pedro II; *Diário*, 30 March 1862.

125. Pedro II, *Diário*, 30 March 1862. The smile was noticed by Souza, *Prometeu*, 191.

126. "O Sr. D. Pedro de Bragança," *JC*, 30 March 1862; Pedro II, *Diário*, 30 March 1862.

127. "A estatua questre e o Sr. Theophilo Ottoni," *Correio da Tarde*, 30 March 1862; Pedro II, *Diário*, 30 March 1862. On Otoni's efforts to win a senate seat, see Cavallini, "Monumento," 304–06; Chagas, *Teófilo Ottoni*, 260–62, 267.

128. For these attacks, and some of Ottoni's responses, see the following *a pedidos*: O Monarchista, "O Sr. Ottoni, o Mucury e a estatua," *JC*, 2 and 6 April 1862; Ottoni, "A estatua equestre e o Mucury," *CM*, 3 and 4 April 1862. Chagas notes that Ottoni also published fully ten articles in his defense in the *DRJ* from 1 April to 24 May 1862; *Teófilo Ottoni*, 318n364.

129. [F. R. Silva], "A estatua equestre," *JC*, 28 March 1862; Um monarchista, "Um proscripto politico," *JC*, 30 March 1862.

130. "A voz da historia" (*a pedido*), *JC*, 29 March 1862. Other installments appeared on 30 March and 3, 6, and 12 April.

131. "Ingratidão nacional" (*a pedido*), *CM*, 29 March 1862.

132. "Juizo de Armitage e de Timandro sobre a estatua equestre," *A Actualidade*, 25 March 1862. Armitage's *History* had been published in Portuguese in Rio in 1837.

133. "D. Pedro julgado por Evaristo," *A Actualidade*, 13 April 1862. Evaristo's obituary of Pedro I, dated 3 Nov. 1834, was reprinted in "D. Pedro I julgado por Evaristo Ferreira da Veiga" (*a pedido*), *JC*, 28 March 1862; *Correio da Tarde*, 30 March 1862.

134. "Juizo de Armitage e de Timandro sobre a estatua equestre," *A Actualidade*, 25 March 1862. On Torres Homen's political evolution, see Nabuco, *Estadista*, 337; Magalhães Júnior, "Salles Torres Homem," 31; Iglesias, "Vida política," 13–14.

135. "Coherencia," *A Actualidade*, 3 April 1862.

136. "O 7 de Abril," *DRJ*, 7 April 1862; "O 7 de Abril de 1831," *A Actualidade*, 7 April 1862; "7 de abril," *Jornal do Povo*, 7 April 1862. The comments about 7 April's elimination as a day of national festivity appear in "Estatua Equestre" (*a pedido*), *Correio da Tarde*, 10 April 1862; "O Mercantil, o Diário e o 1.º reinado" (*a pedido*), *JC*, 10 April 1862.

137. Dr. França Leite, "Pedro I e a estatua equestre" (*a pedido*), *JC*, 30 March 1862.

138. "A estatua e João Guilherme Ractcliff," *A Actualidade*, 30 March 1862; "Ractcliff" and "O 7 de Abril de 1831," *A Actualidade*, 7 April 1862. On the Confederação, see Bernardes, "Pernambuco"; Leite, *Pernambuco 1824*; Mosher, *Political Struggle*, 62–77; Mello, *Outra Independência*, 163–237.

139. [Veiga], *Revolução de 7 de abril*, 3 (quote), 7.

140. "O que sahir" (*folhetim*), *JC*, 2 March 1862; "Estatua equestre" (*comunicado*) and "A estatua e Evaristo," *A Actualidade*, 22 and 30 March 1862; "Vinte e cinco de março de 1862" (*a pedido*), *JC*, 25 March 1862. One defense of Veiga appeared a few days later, "A revolução de 7 de Abril de 1831" (*a pedido*), *JC*, 28 March 1862.

141. J. Carvalho, *Formação*, 60–61; Ribeiro, "Memória," 25; Enders, "Plutarco," 58; Haberly, "Mythification," 66.

142. Dr. N. J. M., "Aos martyres da Independencia do Brazil," *DRJ*, 25 March 1862; "Inconfidencia de Minas," *DRJ*, 26 March 1862.

143. [Pedro Luiz Pereira de Souza], "Tira-dentes," *A Actualidade*, 25 March 1862. That there was no granite in the monument apparently did not affect the poem's reception.

144. Mendonça, "Cousas," 129. Romero made the same point, *Historia*, 2:1197.

145. Carvalho, *Formação*, 61. See also Milliet, *Tiradentes*, 80. Needless to say, Pedro Luís's poem was not included in the collections of verse compiled after the inauguration.

146. Póvoa, *Annos*, 220. It was later reprinted in *Tiradentes* (1885): 4; Romero, *Historia*, 2:1191–97.

147. "O Tiradentes e sua estatua," *Revista Popular* 4:14 (1862): 242; Ribeyrolles, *Brasil*, 1:47–95.

148. Chagas, *Teófilo Ottoni*, 12.

149. "Noticias diversas," *A Actualidade*, 10 May 1862; "Chronica nacional," *Folhinha Laemmert* (1868), 253. On Tiradentes's use as a Liberal symbol, see also Cavallini, "Monumento," 324.

150. Luiz Vicente De-Simoni, "À inauguração da estatua equestre em bronze do imperador D. Pedro Primeiro no lugar em que está collocado," AIHGB, lata 459, doc. 10. Souza reads this sonnet as a having a more radical message; *Pátria*, 358–59.

151. [Silva], "A estatua equestre" (*comunicado*), *JC*, 28 March 1862.

152. O Soldado de Cezar, "O protesto Ottoni" (*a pedido*), *JC*, 30 March 1862. This article was also reprinted as an *a pedido* in *Correio da Tarde*, 3 April 1862; it probably drew on Varnhagen, *Historia geral*, 1st ed., 2:373–92.

153. Veterano, *Estátua*, 2, 24–25, 28, 30–31, 33–34. See also Souza, *Pátria*, 361–63. On the Inconfidência as, among other things, an attempt by tax farmers to escape their obligations, see Maxwell, *Conflicts*, 131–32, 140. On the Instituto Histórico's disdain for the 1817 movement, see Guimarães, "Entre a Monarquia e a República," 152–56.

154. "Novo projecto para uma estatua patriotica," *Semana Illustrada*, 13 April 1862; Milliet, *Tiradentes*, 107–17, 139–81.

155. Feitola, "A estatua de D. Pedro 1.°," *A Mocidade*, 31 Jan. 1862.

156. "O que sahir" (*folhetim*), *JC*, 31 March 1862; Pedro II, *Diário*, 31 March 1862.

157. See the *a pedidos* entitled "Perguntas innocentes ao Sr. L. Rochet," *CM*, 2, 3, 5, 6, and 7 April 1862. These issues are also raised in A. D. Hubert, "La statue equestre de D. Pedro I. par M. Rochet," *Courier du Brésil*, 13 April 1862.

158. "O cavallo de bronze" (*a pedido*), *CM*, 6 April 1862; [Machado de Assis], "Commentarios da Semana" (*folhetim*), *DRJ*, 24 March 1862.

159. Macedo, *Memórias do sobrinho*, 258.

160. "Monumento equestre do Sr. D. Pedro I . . . ," *Brasil Historico*, 24 July 1864.

161. Moreira de Azevedo, *Pequeno panorama*, 5:50–55; he retained this view in 1877, *Rio*, 2:39–41.

162. [Machado de Assis], "Commentarios da Semana" (*folhetim*), *DRJ*, 1 April 1862.

163. On this bill's progress, see *ASB* (1861), 3:231, 246, 289–90, 342–44; (1862), 1:5, 8–9. There is no indication that the chamber considered this bill after receiving it on 16 May 1862, *ACD* (1862), 1:21.

164. Barbosa, *Obras*, 2:256; Alves, *José do Patrocínio*, 60.

165. "Contos do Rio de Janeiro," *Semana Illustrada*, 13 April 1862.

166. [Machado de Assis], "Commentarios da semana" (*folhetim*), *DRJ*, 1 April 1862.

167. Fletcher and Kidder, *Brazil*, 38; Maurício, *Algo*, 106.

168. Moreira de Azevedo, *Pequeno panorama*, 5:44–45, 49 (quote). Compare the equivalent passage in *Rio*, 2:33–34.

169. Coaracy, *Memórias*, 99–102; Morales de los Rios Filho, *Rio*, 71–72; Cruls, *Aparência*, 2:417; Green, *Beyond Carnival*, 18–20; Green, "Emperor," 198, 199; Soares, *Rameiras*, 41–49. A Portuguese traveler who visited Rio in 1895 repeatedly mentioned the prostitution openly conducted in the bars and nightclubs surrounding the square; J. Chagas, *De bond*, 68–69, 72–73, 75–82, 85.

170. "O Anno Novo," *Folhinha Laemmert* (1867), lxi.

CHAPTER SIX

1. Pereira da Silva, *Memorias*, 1:255–56.

2. Alencastro, "Vida"; Schwarcz, *Barbas*, 101–24; Borges, "Em busca"; Needell, *Tropical* Belle Époque, chaps. 4–5.

3. Porto Alegre, "Angélica e Firmino," in *Teatro*, 2:50, 49.

4. "Chronica" (*folhetim*), *DRJ*, 11 Sep. 1853; "Album" (*folhetim*), *DRJ*, 10 Sep. 1854.

5. For accounts of 2 December celebrations that follow this form, see "2 de Dezembro," *Correio do Brazil*, 3 Dec. 1852; "Chronica da semana" (*folhetim*), *JC*, 9 Dec. 1861. On the French "official shouters," see Truesdell, *Spectacular Politics*, 8–9, 152.

6. "O *Jornal do Commercio*, o *Mercantil* e o dia 25 de março," *A Actualidade*, 2 April 1859. Compare the two newspapers' accounts: *CM*, 26–27 March 1859; *JC*, 26–27 March 1859.

7. "A parada do dia 2," *O Republico*, 7 Dec. 1855; F[rancisco] de Paula Brito, "Dous de Dezembro," *Marmota Fluminense*, 2 Dec. 1855.

8. "Sette de Setembro," *O Regenerador*, 10 Sep. 1861.

9. "O Dia 7 de Setembro," *O Velho Brasil*, 14 Sep. 1854. I have not been able to identify the specific article in *O Repúblico* to which Justiniano referred.

10. "O dia 7 de Setembro," *O República*, 18 Sep. 1854. On the popular 2 July celebrations in Salvador, which commemorated the expulsion of Portuguese troops from the city in 1823, see Kraay, "Between Brazil and Bahia." It is not clear what Borges da Fonseca knew of 4 July celebrations.

11. "Noticias diversas," *CM*, 7 Sep. 1854.

12. Manoel de Araújo Porto Alegre to Paulo Barbosa da Silva and Francisca de Paula Barbosa, Rio, 28 Nov. 1853, in Porto Alegre, *Correspondência*, 87. This passage is difficult to translate: "asneira, porque ela me fala ao coração em uma época onde a pátria está na algibeira, e o coração na gaveta, e a nacionalidade na latrina."

13. *Folhetim*, *JC*, 9 Sep. 1855.

14. "Relatorio dos trabalhos da directoria provisoria . . . ," 30 Aug. 1855–30 Sep. 1856, *CM*, 23 March 1857. For one of the printed invitations, see José Candido Gomes to Marquis of Olinda, Rio, 15 July 1856, AIHGB, lata 215, doc. 31.

15. *Almanack Laemmert* (1857): 336.

16. See the advertisements in *JC*, 6 Sep. 1855, 7 Sep. 1856, 6 Sep. 1857.

17. "Programma dos festejos que a Sociedade 'Ypiranga' tem deliberado fazer . . . ," [1856], AGCRJ, 43-3-64, fol. 3r–v; "Programma dos festejos que a Sociedade Ypiranga pertende [sic] fazer no dia 7 de Setembro de 1857," BN/SM, II-31, 33, 19; "Sociedade Ypiranga," *Correio da Tarde*, 9 Sep. 1856.

18. "O Sete de Setembro," *A Marmota*, 16 Sep. 1859; "Noticias à mão (Chronica da Semana)," *O Espelho*, 4 Sep. 1859. On the Sociedade Petalógica, see Machado, *Vida*, 56–58; Coaracy, *Memórias*, 97–99.

19. Sociedade Independencia Brazileira to Camara Municipal, Rio, 29 July 1857, 31 July 1858, 18 July 1859, AGCRJ, 43-3-64, fols. 6, 10, 19; "Chronica da semana" and "Chronica da quinzena," 1 and 20 Sep. 1859, *Revista Popular*, 1:3 (1859): 333, 396. The assessment of its membership appears in "A Sociedade Independencia Brazileira," *DRJ*, 6 Sep. 1857, while the number of members appears in "Chronica Diaria," *DRJ*, 10 Sep. 1857.

20. Petition of Associação Nacional dos Artistas to Camara, Rio, 20 July 1858, AGCRJ, 43-3-64, fol. 9; "Os Festejos do dia Sete de Setembro pela Associação Nacional dos Artistas," *A Sentinella do Inferno*, 7 Aug. 1857.

21. *Almanaque Laemmert* (1866): 378. See its programs published in "Noticiario," *DRJ*, 6 Sep. 1862, 6 Sep. 1863, 6 Sep. 1864.

22. "Noticias diversas," *CM*, 8–9 Sep. 1859; "Festejos," *JC*, 8–9 Sep. 1859; "Dia 7 de Setembro," *JC*, 7 Sep. 1861.

23. "Sociedade Setembrista Castellense," *JC*, 6 Sep. 1862; "Noticias diversas," *CM*, 8–9 Sep. 1863.

24. "Chronica diaria," *DRJ*, 8–9 Sep. 1857; 6 and 7 Sep. 1858.

25. On Amaral, see Sacramento Blake, *Diccionario*, 5:35–37. On Porto Alegre's politics, see Squeff, *Brasil*, 75–78.

26. Moreira de Azevedo, *Rio*, 2:462; Squeff, *Brasil*, 77.

27. Sacramento Blake, *Diccionario*, 5:391–92.

28. Basile, *Ezequiel Corrêa dos Santos*, 129–34.

29. Sacramento Blake, *Diccionario*, 3:37–39, 4:4–5; Silva, *Generais*, 2:364–66.

30. Speech of Joaquim Pinto de Campos, 19 Aug., *ACD* (1871), 4:192. On Dias da Motta's politics in the 1840s, see Gouvêa, "Política," 129–30, 135.

31. On Campos, see Sacramento Blake, *Diccionario*, 4:224–29.

32. The six are Bento da Silva Lisboa, Bernardo de Souza Franco, João da Silva Carrão, José Bonifácio de Andrada e Silva (the younger), José Pedro Dias de Carvalho, and Pedro de Alcântara Bellegarde. On their careers and that of Macedo, see Sacramento Blake, *Diccionario*, 1:400–401, 1:417–18, 4:48–49, 4:183–90, 4:350–51, 5:116–17, 7:8–11.

33. William Stafford Jerningham to Earl of Clarendon, Rio, 12 Sep. 1856, PRO/FO 13, vol. 340, fols. 84r.

34. "Appello ao patriotismo," *O Relampago*, 7 Sep. 1856.

35. "Album" (*folhetim*), *DRJ*, 10 Sep. 1854.

36. "Felicitações," *CM*, 8–9 Sep. 1858.

37. The two are the Sociedade Festival Sete de Setembro and the Sociedade Sete de Setembro; "Noticias diversas," *CM*, 9 and 20 Jan. 1862.

38. "A Sociedade—Independencia Brazileira . . . ," *Correio da Tarde*, 10 Sep. 1857; "Descripção da festa da Sociedade Independencia Brazileira . . . ," *CM*, 8–9 Sep. 1857.

39. "Associação Nacional dos Artistas," *Correio da Tarde*, 10 Sep. 1857.

40. On Brandão's parliamentary activities, see *ACD* (1857), 3:227–29, 232–39, 3:252, 4:29 (the Sunday closing bill); 3:167–69, 190 (the food prices commission); *ACD* (1855), 4:205–07; (1856), 1:58–59, 2:84–87, 2:100–04 (the nationalization of retail commerce). Apparently these bills all died in parliamentary committees. They may have been related to earlier efforts at the municipal level to restrict working hours, Popingis, *Proletários*, 108, 112–13, 155n3; Martinho, "Caixeiros," 114–15.

41. As far back as 1848–49, some Liberals had contemplated encouraging the "working population" to vote; Carvalho, "Conferências," 20–21.

42. Jesus, "Associativismo," 145, 149–55. For comparisons, see Sabato, *Many*; Forment, *Democracy*.

43. *Folhetim*, *JC*, 9 Sep. 1855; "Noticias artisticas," *A Semana*, 28 Sep. 1856; *JC*, 9 Sep. 1856; *Folhetim*, *JC*, 14 Sep. 1856; M., "Paginas Menores" (*folhetim*),

CM, 7 Sep. 1856; A. D. Hubert, "Chronique de la semaine," *Courier du Brésil,* 7 and 14 Sep. 1856; "Interesting from Brazil," Rio, 14 Sep. 1856, *North American* (Philadelphia), 5 Nov. 1856.

44. "O anniversario da Independencia," *DRJ,* 9 Sep. 1856.

45. "A semana" *(folhetim), JC,* 14 Sep. 1857. See also *JC,* 8–9 Sep. 1857; "Livro do Domingo" *(folhetim), DRJ,* 13 Sep. 1857; Théodore Casaubon, "Brésil," *Revue Espagnole, Portuguaise, Brésilienne et Hispano-Américaine* (Paris) (5 Nov. 1857): 192.

46. "Paginas Menores" *(folhetim), CM,* 14 Sep. 1857; "Chronica diaria," *DRJ,* 8–9 Sep. 1857.

47. "A semana" *(folhetim), JC,* 13 Sep. 1858. See also "Chronica Diaria," *DRJ,* 8–9 Sep. 1858; and "Paginas sem titulo" *(folhetim), DRJ,* 12 Sep. 1858.

48. Altève Aumont, "Courrier d'Amérique," 9 Oct. 1858, *Revue des Races Latines* (Paris) (10 Dec. 1858): 588 (this correspondence was quoted in "Dias 25 de Março e 7 de Setembro," *Correio da Tarde,* 29 March 1859); Biard, *Deux années,* 97.

49. "Chronica da Quinzena," 20 Sep. 1859, *Revista Popular* 1:3 (1859): 394–95; "Noticias diversas," *CM,* 8–9 Sep. 1859; "O dia 7 de Setembro," *JC,* 8–9 Sep. 1859; "Festejos do dia 7," *Correio da Tarde,* 9 Sep. 1859.

50. "Echos de Rio de Janeiro," *Courier du Brésil,* 11 Sep. 1859; "Noticias à mão (chronica da semana)," *O Espelho,* 18 Sep. 1859. Unfortunately, no copies of Leuzinger's lithograph have survived.

51. See the petitions in AGCRJ, 43-3-64, fols. 11, 15, 16, 20; and "O dia 7 de Setembro," *Correio da Tarde,* 15 July 1858, 5 Sep. 1859; "Noticias diversas," *CM,* 5 and 6 Sep. 1859.

52. O Oprimido, "O dia 7 de setembro e as subscripções para os festejos," *O Tyranno,* 12 Sep. 1857.

53. "Paginas Menores" *(folhetim), CM,* 14 Sep. 1857; *A Marmota,* 14 Sep. 1858; "Noticias frescas," *O Charivary Nacional,* 4 Sep. 1859.

54. "Labyrintho" *(folhetim), JC,* 8–9 Sep. 1860; "Noticiario," *DRJ,* 7 Sep. 1860. See also "Noticiario," *DRJ,* 8–9 Sep. 1860; and *CM,* 8–9 Sep. 1860.

55. "Chronica da Quinzena," 10 Sep. 1860 [sic = 1861], *Revista Popular,* 3:11 (1861): 377. Morales de los Rios Filho lists *"fogo de palha"* (literally, straw blaze) as a nineteenth-century expression for a love that does not last, *Rio,* 88. On the decline, see also "Sete de Setembro," *A Marmota,* 6 Sep. 1861; "Sete de Setembro," *DRJ,* 7 Sep. 1861.

56. *O Barco dos Traficantes,* 12 Sep. 1862, "Noticias diversas," *A Actualidade,* 9 Sep. 1862; Pedro II, *Diário,* 7 Sep. 1862; "Noticiario," *DRJ,* 8–9 Sep. 1862; *DRJ,* 7 Sep. 1862. See also *A Semana Illustrada,* 14 Oct. [sic = Sep.] 1862.

57. *O Espectador da América do Sul,* 10 Sep. 1863; "Sociedade Ypiranga" *(a pedido), JC,* 3 Sep. 1863. See also *O Constitucional,* 7 Sep. 1863. The fact that Francisco de Sales Torres Homem was president in 1862 indicates a significant change in the society's political linkages, for as we saw in Chapter Five, this erstwhile radical liberal had become a Saquarema by this time.

58. "7 de Setembro," *DRJ,* 7 Sep. 1857.

59. Campos, *Discurso,* 13–14 (quote), 28–30.

60. On these changes in carnival, see, most recently, Ferreira, *Inventando*, 55–77.

61. "A Semana" (*folhetim*), *JC*, 1 March 1857.

62. Abreu, *Império*, 250, 252.

63. "Paginas sem titulo" (*folhetim*), *DRJ*, 12 Sep. 1858; "Paginas Menores" (*folhetim*), *CM*, 7 Sep. 1857.

64. "Chronica Diaria," *DRJ*, 10 Sep. 1857; "Associação Nacional dos Artistas," *Correio da Tarde*, 10 Sep. 1857.

65. "O Anniversario da Independencia," *Correio da Tarde*, 9 Sep. 1857.

66. On Christie's poor relations with fellow diplomats, other British citizens, and even his household staff, see James Watson Webb to Sec. of State, Petrópolis, 9 Nov. 1862, NARS, M-121, roll 30. On the crisis, see Graham, "Fundamentos."

67. Cerqueira, *Reminiscências*, 207; clippings from the *JC* enclosed in Webb to Sec. of State, Petrópolis, 7 Jan. 1863, NARS, M-121, roll 30; Mattoso, *Cousas*, 61.

68. Pereira da Silva, *Memorias*, 1:311. See also Webb to Sec. of State, Petrópolis, 7 Feb. 1863, NARS, M-121, roll 30.

69. See, for a few examples, Varela, *Estandarte*; J. J. Teixeira, "Hymno patriotico," BN/DM, M-II-43; Brazileiro, "Ao dia 7 de setembro" (*a pedido*), *JC*, 7 Sep. 1863. On literary responses to the Christie Question, see Forman, "Harbouring Discontent." The volunteering and the plan to attack the British ships is described in Guilhereme Schüch de Capanema to Antônio Gonçalves Dias, Rio, 24 Jan. 1863, *ABN* 91 (1971): 278–79.

70. On the donations, see "Offerecimentos patrioticos," a regular column in the *JC* in early 1863. Otoni's role is described in Chagas, *Teofilo Ottoni*, 326–40.

71. Barman, *Citizen Emperor*, 191; Iglesias, "Vida," 8. See also Needell, *Party*, 217–19.

72. *DRJ*, 25 March 1863.

73. *DRJ*, 7 Sep. 1863; F. S. Dias da Motta, "Viva a independencia da nação brasileira," *CM*, 7 Sep. 1863 (also in *JC*, 7 Sep. 1863).

74. "Dia 7 de Setembro," *JC*, 7 Sep. 1864; "Noticias diversas," *CM*, 8 Sep. 1864. See also "Noticiario," *DRJ*, 8–9 Sep. 1864.

75. "Noticias diversas," *Constitucional*, 10 Sep. 1864; [Joaquim Maria Machado de Assis], "Ao acaso" (*folhetim*), *DRJ*, 11 Sep. 1864.

76. Mello Moraes Filho, *Festas*, 147–51. The chapter was originally published as "O Sete de Setembro (tradicionalismo)," *Gazeta de Noticias*, 7 Sep. 1887.

77. "O Dia da Independencia," *Correio da Tarde*, 6 Sep. 1858.

78. This perception of the streets draws on DaMatta's interpretation of "house" and "street" in Brazilian culture, *Casa*.

79. França Júnior, *Folhetins*, 133.

80. Radforth, *Royal Spectacle*, 78–81.

81. "Noticias diversas," *CM*, 5 Sep. 1858.

82. Coaracy, *Memórias*, 175. For another recollection of *copinhos*, see Reis, "Rio," 24.

83. "Luz electrica," *JC*, 12 Sep. 1858; "Festejos de 7 de Setembro," *JC*, 7 Sep. 1859; "Illuminação electrica," *JC*, 7 Sep. 1860; "Illuminação electro-magnetica," *JC*, 7 Sep. 1861; "Noticias diversas," *CM*, 7 Sep. 1860.

84. Letter from "O cego que vê, o surdo que ouve," *JC*, 2 Sep. 1856. On the bonfire plans, see "Noticias diversas," *CM*, 6 Sep. 1856; and "Paginas menores" (*folhetim*), *CM*, 7 Sep. 1856.

85. "Illuminações," *JC*, 10 Sep. 1856; "Chronica Diaria," *DRJ*, 9 Sep. 1856.

86. Fletcher and Kidder, *Brazil*, 99; Forde, *Our Cruise!*, 38; Andrews, *Brazil*, 40.

87. For one rare example, see "S. M. o Imperador," *Diario de Noticias*, 5 Sep. 1888.

88. For fireworks regulations, see Decisão 75 (Fazenda), 23 April 1829, *CLB*; and the bylaws issued between 1838 and 1883 in *Codigo*, 20, 83, 97–98, 122–23 (quote 122), 279, 260. On the U.S. campaigns against fireworks, see Litwicki, *America's Public Holidays*, 191–92, 207–9; Cohn, "Popular Culture," 170–78.

89. Bennett, *Forty Years*, 187–88.

90. "Pertence a Todos" (*comunicado*), *JC*, 9 Sep. 1845; "Policia da Corte," *DRJ*, 10 Sep. 1854; "Noticias diversas," *CM*, 10 Sep. 1857; "Parte," *Correio da Tarde*, 9 and 10 Sep. 1859; "Prisões," *CM*, 4 Dec. 1863, 9 Sep. 1864.

91. "Capoeiras," *DRJ*, 3–4 Dec. 1864; "Ferimento," *JC*, 27 March 1852.

92. "44.ª pacotilha, Carijó e comp." (*folhetim*), *CM*, 8 Dec. 1851; "Quitandeiras," *JC*, 5 Sep. 1858; "O Largo do Capim e o Campo da Acclamação," *Correio da Tarde*, 9 Sep. 1858.

93. "Noticias artisticas," *A Semana*, 28 Sep. 1856.

94. "Attenção," *CM*, 8–9 Sep. 1857.

95. Observadores, "Alerta" (*a pedido*), *CM*, 8–9 Sep. 1857.

96. There are two different accounts of this incident: "Desordens," *JC*, 11 Sep. 1859; "Noticias diversas," *CM*, 11 Sep. 1859. The condemnation of the police appeared in "Festejos nacionaes," *7 de Setembro*, 18 Sep. 1859, on which Jesus bases his analysis, *Visões*, 60–61.

97. For a recent examination of this practice, see McGraw, "Spectacle," 269, 272–76, 282.

98. Bethell, *Abolition*, 313; Conrad, *Destruction*, 27.

99. "Espelho," *Correio da Tarde*, 1 Sep. 1856; "Boas tardes," *Correio da Tarde*, 5 Sep. 1856.

100. "Alforria," *JC*, 7 and 9 Sep. 1856; "Relatorio dos trabalhos . . . ," *CM*, 23 March 1857; Karasch, *Slave Life*, 345.

101. "Carta de João Fernandes a seu compadre Manoel Mendes" (*folhetim*), *Correio da Tarde*, 6 Sep. 1856; "Paginas menores" (*folhetim*), *CM*, 7 and 21 Sep. 1856; "O anniversario da Independencia," *DRJ*, 9 Sep. 1856.

102. Conrad, *Destruction*, 73n6.

103. *Folhetim*, *JC*, 14 Sep. 1857. See also "Sociedade Ypiranga," *Correio da Tarde*, 15 July 1857; "Sociedade Ypiranga," *CM*, 12 Sep. 1857; "Saudação ao dia 7 de Setembro de 1857 . . . ," *A Marmota*, 11 Sep. 1857.

104. "Discurso recitado pelo Sr. Visconde de Sapucahy," *Correio da Tarde*, 10 Sep. 1857; Campos, *Discurso*, 30–31.

105. "Noticias diversas," *CM*, 8–9 Sep. 1857. On Teixeira e Souza, see Treece, *Exiles*, 104; Sacramento Blake, *Diccionario*, 1:184–86.

106. *A Marmota,* 14 Sep. 1858; *O Constitucional,* 10 Sep. 1862; "Noticiario," *DRJ,* 7 Sep. 1862. The boy's color is mentioned in "Dia 7 de Setembro," *JC,* 7 Sep. 1862.

107. "Viva o dia 7 de setembro" (*a pedido*), *CM,* 8–9 Sep. 1863.

108. "Carta de João Fernandes . . ." (*folhetim*), *Correio da Tarde,* 10 Sep. 1855.

109. Adalbert, *Travels,* 1:275.

110. João Pandiá Calógeras to His Son, Rio, 2 Dec. 1864, in Calógeras, *Ministério,* 144.

111. "O dia 2 de dezembro," *O Grito Nacional,* 3 Dec. 1853; Advertising, *CM,* 25 March 1852.

112. "Viva o dia 7 de Setembro" (*a pedido*), *CM,* 5 Sep. 1857.

113. See, for example, "Noticias diversas," *CM,* 2 Dec. 1858; *A Actualidade,* 24 March 1863; S. W. P., "Insurrectionary Movement in Rio . . . ," *Weekly Herald* (New York), 21 Oct. 1854.

114. For some lighthearted remarks about this, see "Folhetim do *Diario do Rio,*" *DRJ,* 7 Sep. 1873; "Fantasias" (*folhetim*), *JC,* 14 Sep. 1879.

115. Speech of José Martins da Cruz Jobim, 12 Sep., *ASB* (1861), 3:344.

116. Taunay, *Memórias,* 16; Porto Alegre to Silva and Barbosa, Rio, 28 Nov. 1853, in Porto Alegre, *Correspondência,* 87.

117. Advertising, *JC,* 31 March and 1 Dec. 1852; Assier, *Brésil,* 223–34; "Visita das priminhas," *Periodico dos Pobres,* 4 Dec. 1852.

118. "Noticias diversas," *CM,* 8–9 Sep. 1862; Assier, *Brésil,* 223. He did not indicate whether anyone was hurt, and I have found no press reference to this accident.

119. The earliest criticism of this that I found is "As salvas officiaes," *Gazeta de Notícias,* 25 March 1877. For examples of pensions (all for men from outside of Rio), see *ACD* (1861), 2:101; (1866), 3:48; (1874), 2:5; (1880), 1:312.

120. For a few examples, see "O dia Dous de Dezembro," *A Marmota na Corte,* 4 Dec. 1849; "Parada de 25 de março," *DRJ,* 26–27 March 1863; "Guarda Nacional da Côrte" (*a pedido*), *CM,* 27 March 1863.

121. [José Maria da Silva Paranhos], "Ao amigo ausente" (*folhetim*), *JC,* 7 Dec. 1851; Pfeiffer, *Woman's Journey,* 51.

122. Stewart, *Brazil,* 151; "8.ª pacotilha, Carijó" (*folhetim*), *CM,* 30–31 March 1851.

123. "Vales ao portador," *A Verdade sem Rebuço,* 12 Dec. 1864.

124. "Carta de D. Mathias ao seu compadre Pitorra," *Periodico dos Pobres,* 7 Sep. 1850; "Visita das priminhas," *Periodico dos Pobres,* 9 Sep. 1854; 9 Sep. 1851. On meat consumption, see *JC,* 3 Dec. 1854; Campos, *Nos caminhos,* 61–62.

125. Advertising, *JC,* 4 Sep. 1856; Morison, *By Sea,* 11; Carpenter, *Round about Rio,* 240.

126. "Carta de D. Mathias . . . ," *Periodico dos Pobres,* 7 Sep. 1850.

127. See the notices and advertisements in *JC,* 5 Sep. 1851; 6 Sep. 1856; 7 Sep. 1856; 6 Sep. 1864; *CM,* 7 Sep. 1855; 8–9 Sep. 1859; *DRJ,* 7 Sep. 1862, 6 Sep. 1863; and Moreira de Azevedo, *Rio,* 2:58.

128. "O pai e o filho," *O Guaracyaba,* Jan. 1851. I have not been able to identify Quintana, who does not appear in Sacramento Blake's *Diccionario.*

129. Hunter, *Diplomat's Lady*, 335–36; "Interesting from Brazil," *North American* (Philadelphia), 5 Nov. 1856; "Demonstrations in Rio," *The Anglo-Brazilian Times*, 24 Nov. 1865.

130. Hunter, *Diplomat's Lady*, 200. Ewbank saw something similar during the 1846 celebrations of Pedro's return, although he did not mention a disparity between the number of men and women; *Life*, 274.

131. "Noticias diversas," *CM*, 7 Sep. 1862; "Passeio Publico," *JC*, 7 Sep. 1862; Moreira de Azevedo, *Rio*, 1:555, 559; Gaston, *Hunting*, 20–21; Keyes, "Our Life," 308–09.

132. Machado de Assis, "A Semana," *Gazeta de Noticias*, 14 May 1893, in *Obra*, 3:584. On the street's name change, see Coaracy, *Memórias*, 365.

133. Advertising, *JC*, 3 May 1846, 1 Dec. 1850, 5 Sep. 1857; 4 Sep. 1859; *CM*, 6 Sep. 1856, 3 Sep. 1857; *Periodico dos Pobres*, 3 Dec. 1850.

134. Alencastro, "Vida," 45–51; Magaldi, *Music*, 8–12; Needell, *Tropical Belle Époque*, 144. For foreigners' remarks on pianos, see Ribeyrolles, *Brasil*, 1:171; Canstatt, *Brasil*, 213, 214; Binzer, *Alegrias*, 55; Néry, *Aux Etats-Unis*, 34; Biard, *Deux années*, 83.

135. Vieira Fazenda, "Antiqualhas," *RIHGB* 95:149 (1924): 183 (originally published in 1911).

136. "Paginas menores" (*folhetim*), *CM*, 21 Sep. 1856; Vieira Fazenda, "Antiqualhas," *RIHGB* 93:147 (1923): 447 (originally published in 1909). On this issue, see also Andrade, *Francisco Manuel da Silva*, 1:156–58.

137. Kidder, *Sketches*, 1:191; Pfeiffer, *Woman's Journey*, 53; Stewart, *Brazil*, 152; Expilly, *Brésil*, 137.

138. Advertising, *JC*, 2 Sep. 1856.

139. Custodio de Oliveira Lima, "À Sua Magestade Imperial o Sr. D. Pedro II . . ." (*a pedido*), *JC*, 2 Dec. 1856; *CM*, 3 Dec. 1856.

140. Brief biographies of these men appear in Sacramento Blake, *Diccionario*, 2:345 and 5:117–18; Unowsky, *Pomp*, 129. Another such "professional patriot" is identified by Silva, Gazeta, 202–03.

141. Souza, *Promotheu*, 171–81; Barman, *Citizen Emperor*, 137; Machado, *Vida*, 91.

142. "O Dia Dous de Dezembro," *A Marmota na Corte*, 4 Dec. 1849; Gondim, *Vida*, 27.

143. A. L., "Paginas menores" (*a pedido*), *CM*, 10 Sep. 1854.

144. Morales de los Rios Filho, *Rio*, 475. See also the satire of this custom in Macedo, *Memórias do sobrinho*, 278.

145. "Livro do Domingo" (*folhetim*), *DRJ*, 28 March 1858.

146. "Illuminação," *JC*, 30 Nov. 1856; "Festejo" and "Illuminação do Arsenal da Guerra," *JC*, 1 and 4 Dec. 1860; M., "O dia dous de Dezembro de 1862," *Semana Illustrada*, 7 Dec. 1862.

147. *CM*, 3 Dec. 1864.

148. "Te Deum," *JC*, 2 Dec. 1861.

149. Calógeras to Son, Rio, 2 and 15 Dec. 1864, in Calógeras, *Ministério*, 144, 160.

CHAPTER SEVEN

1. Duarte, *Noites*, 147.

2. On the theater as a political space in the 1810s, see Malerba, *Corte*, 91–124; Mammi, "Teatro," 48–49; Magaldi, *Music*, 12–13; Oliveira Lima, *D. João VI*, 549, 617–19; Schwarcz, Azevedo, and Costa, *Longa viagem*, 294–95, 365.

3. Hessel and Raeders, *Teatro*, 118.

4. Marzano, *Cidade*, 17–19; S. Souza, *Noites*, 231, 297; Magaldi, *Music*, 8–12; Mencarelli, *Cena*, 27, 36–37, 61, 176–80, 307.

5. Souza, *Carpinteiros*; Augusto, *Questão*, 207–47; Marzano, *Cidade*; Mencarelli, *Cena*.

6. Turner, *From Ritual*, 112–13.

7. "Theatros," *JC*, 23 March 1839. The rest of this paragraph is based on Villela, "Theatro de S. Januario," *JC*, 31 March–2 April 1839.

8. Morales de los Rios Filho describes *Exemplar caridade*, *Rio*, 363. I have not been able to identify the other play. Their 7 April 1838 performances were advertised in *JC*, 6 April 1838.

9. On the renovations, from October 1838 to 7 September 1839, see Paixão, *Theatro*, 157.

10. For surveys of Rio's theaters, see Sousa, *Teatro*, 1:281–95; Augusto, *Questão*, 112–34.

11. Souza, *Carpinteiros*, 85–86; Souza, *Noites*, 50–51, 279–82; Augusto, *Questão*, 115.

12. "Carta de D. Mathias ao seu compadre Pitorra," *Periodico dos Pobres*, 10 Sep. 1850.

13. "O Theatro Lyrico e a policia da corte," *JC*, 9 Sep. 1867.

14. "Theatro, e Modas," *A Marmota na Corte*, 28 March 1851. For additional comments on this problem, see Martins Pena, *Folhetins*, 83; [José Maria da Silva Paranhos], "Ao amigo ausente," *JC*, 30 March 1851; *Folhetim*, *JC*, 29 March 1852; ***, "A directoria do Theatro Lyrico e a policia," *CM*, 8 Sep. 1855; O Brasileiro, "Theatro Lyrico," *Correio da Tarde*, 10 Sep. 1855.

15. *JC*, 1 Dec. 1837; Hamond, *Diários*, 176. Justiniano José da Rocha recalled similar prices for boxes on the emperor's birthday in 1838 and 1839; "Factos Notaveis," *O Brasil*, 30 July 1840.

16. William Gore Ouseley to Viscount Palmerston, Rio, 7 Aug. 1841, PRO/FO 13, vol. 171, fol 265.

17. "Visita das priminhas," *Periodico dos Pobres*, 4 Dec. 1851.

18. Ebel, *Rio*, 85; Schlichthorst, *Rio*, 120; Seidler, *Dez Anos*, 47.

19. Theater advertising, *JC*, 25 March 1852; Sena, *Rascunhos*, 412–14. On the Provisório's seat arrangement, see Gordon, "New Opera House," 53, 56–57. The complaint about excessive prices appeared in *folhetim*, *JC*, 29 March 1852. Raised prices are confirmed in "Informações dadas pela commissão diretora do Theatro da Corte . . . ," in Brazil, MI, *Relatório* (1851), *anexo*, 6.

20. Theater advertising, *JC*, 25 March 1852.

21. I have not been able to identify Furtado Coelho's play.

22. Theater advertising, *JC*, 30 Nov. 1866.

23. *Folhetim*, *JC*, 10 Dec. 1844.

24. "8.ª pacotilha, Carijó e Comp.ª," *CM*, 30–31 March 1851; "Theatro de S. Januario" (*folhetim*), *DRJ*, 9 Dec. 1851; Boelen, *Reize*, 1:72–73; Toussaint-Samson, *Parisian*, 93.

25. Schlichthorst, *Rio*, 123–24, 187 (quotes); "O Dia 2 de Dezembro," *O Sete d'Abril*, 5 Dec. 1838; *folhetim*, *JC*, 7 Dec. 1840; Altève Aumont, "Courrier d'Amérique," 7 Sep. 1858, *Revue des Races Latines* (Paris) (10 Nov. 1858): 279.

26. Ebel, *Rio*, 85; MacDouall, *Narrative*, 23; Brand, *Journal*, 302; [Ruschenberger], *Three Years*, 1:63; Kotzebue, *New Voyage*, 1:52–53.

27. "Carta de D. Mathias . . . ," *Periodico dos Pobres*, 10 Sep. 1850.

28. Giron, *Minoridade*, 186; Andrade, *Francisco Manuel da Silva*, 2:69.

29. Koseritz, *Imagens*, 127.

30. Ribeyrolles, *Brasil*, 1:172.

31. Souza, *Noites*, 62–63, 128n68; Marzano, *Cidade*, 42–45, 63–66; Augusto, *Questão*, 130–33. On army pay, see Schulz, *Exército*, 211. Magaldi vacillates between stressing the socially exclusive nature of theatergoing and its social breadth, *Music*, xxi, 13, 17, 31n45, 38–39, 54, 60n13–14. Ticket prices suggest that even the popular annual reviews of the 1890s were directed at the "middle sectors"; Mencarelli, *Cena aberta*, 158–60.

32. Kotzebue, *New Voyage*, 1:52–53; [Ruschenberger], *Three Years*, 1:63.

33. For classic comments on this issue, see Costa, *Brazilian Empire*, 240–42; more generally, Graham, "Free African Brazilians," 30–58.

34. "Consideração à farda," *CM*, 9 Sep. 1852.

35. Moreira de Azevedo, *Rio*, 2:159; Henderson, *History*, 58.

36. "Theatro de S. Pedro d'Alcantara," *Ostensor Brasileiro* (1845–46): 59; Magaldi, *Music*, 14; Walsh, *Notices*, 1:167; Pfeiffer, *Woman's Journey*, 48; Castelneau, *Expédition*, part 1, vol. 1, p. 63. Schlichthorst indicates that the boxes each held five seats, *Rio*, 120.

37. Gordon, "New Opera House," 56.

38. Cabral, *Guia*, 371.

39. Souza, *Noites*, 61; Maurício, *Algo*, 28–29.

40. Schlichthorst, *Rio*, 123. On singing the independence anthem at theater galas, see also Vieira Fazenda, "Antiqualhas," *RIHGB* 147 (1923): 274 (originally published in 1908).

41. Tiradentes, "National Independence Day," *New York Times*, 25 Oct. 1873.

42. M., "Paginas menores," *CM*, 8 Sep. 1855.

43. *CM*, 8–9 Sep. 1856; "Paginas menores," *CM*, 21 Sep. 1856; "O anniversario da Independencia," *DRJ*, 9 Sep. 1856.

44. Martins Pena, *Folhetins*, 364.

45. J. N. de S. S., "Hymno da Independencia," *Gazetinha dos Sabados*, 9 Sep. 1876.

46. *O Brasil*, 10 Sep. 1850; *L'Echo de l'Amérique du Sud*, 13 Oct. 1827; Adalbert, *Travels*, 1:279; "O dia 2 de Dezembro," *O Novo Tempo*, 5 Dec. 1844.

47. "Carta de João Fernandes . . . ," *Correio da Tarde*, 10 Sep. 1855; "O Dia Sete de Setembro," *Jornal dos Debates Politicos e Litterarios*, 13 Sep. 1837; Altève Aumont, "Courrier d'Amérique," 7 Sep. 1858, *Revue des Races Latines* (Paris) (10 Nov. 1858): 279.

48. *Edital, O Spectador Brasileiro,* 3 Dec. 1824; A. Andrade, *Francisco Manuel da Silva,* 1:194–95; Paixão, *Theatro,* 466, 470.

49. "O Dia Sete de Setembro," *Jornal dos Debates Politicos e Litterarios,* 13 Sep. 1837; Pedro II, *Diário,* 2 Dec. 1840. The author of a theater *crônica* heartily concurred with Pedro, *JC,* 7 Dec. 1840. See also "Os poetas no theatro" (*correspondências*), *DRJ,* 2 Dec. 1842.

50. *Folhetim, JC,* 5 Dec. 1851; "44.ᵃ pacotilha . . . ," *CM,* 8 Dec. 1851; Pedro II, *Diário,* 23 July 1842.

51. [José de Alencar], "Ao correr da pena," *CM,* 4 Dec. 1854. For the same image of a rain of paper, see "Theatro Provisório," *Correio do Brazil,* 3 Dec. 1852. The AIHGB has preserved some poetry leaflets distributed on 2 December 1861, lata 222, doc. 8; lata 444, doc. 1.

52. *Correio da Tarde,* 3 Dec. 1851; "44.ᵃ pacotilha . . . ," *CM,* 8 Dec. 1851.

53. Altève Aumont, "Courier d'Amérique," 9 Oct. 1858, *Revue des Races Latines* (Paris) (10 Dec. 1858): 589; "Visita das priminhas," *Periodico dos Pobres,* 4 Dec. 1851. For the poem's full text, see "À S. M. O Imperador," *JC,* 6 Dec. 1851.

54. Machado, *Vida,* 128–29; "Relatorio do Chefe de Polícia da Corte," in Brazil, MI, *Relatorio* (1877), *anexo,* 40; "Rio de Janeiro," *A Provincia de São Paulo* (São Paulo), 30 Sep. 1877.

55. Adalbert, *Travels,* 1:280.

56. "Carta de D. Mathias . . ." and "Soneto recitado no theatro na noite de Sete de Setembro," *Periodico dos Pobres,* 10 Sep. 1850.

57. Schlichthorst, *Rio,* 124; Brand, *Journal,* 304; Langsdorff, *Diário,* 185–86; Vincent, *Around and about South America,* 222; Marzano, *Cidade,* 46, 50; Machado, *Vida,* 282–83.

58. Schlichthorst, *Rio,* 120; Douville, *30 mois,* 237; "Chronica," *A Saudade,* 9 Feb. 1862; Ferrière Le Vayer, *Ambassade,* 39; Ribeyrolles, *Brasil,* 1:172.

59. "Os festejos do Dia Dous de Dezembro," *O Despertador,* 4 Dec. 1839; *JC,* 9 Sep. 1835; *Folhetim, JC,* 1 April 1855; Hamond, *Diários,* 143.

60. "Edital de 29 de novembro de 1824," in Sousa, *Teatro,* 1:327–30; Paixão, *Theatro,* 465, 469.

61. "Visita das priminhas," *Periodico dos Pobres,* 9 Sep. 1852. On *pateadas,* see Souza, *Noites,* 289–91.

62. "Carta de João Fernandes . . . ," *Correio da Tarde,* 10 Sep. 1855; Letters to the Editor, *CM,* 8, 10, and 11 Sep. 1855; *JC,* 9 and 11 Sep. 1855. On the theater "parties" or "factions" and police efforts to control them, see Giron, *Minoridade,* 14, 73–75, 82–83, 89, 97–99, 134, 147; Souza, *Noites,* 58–59, 279–80; Magaldi, *Music,* 47; Andrade, *Francisco Manuel da Silva,* 2:13–14, 47–51.

63. *Correio da Tarde,* 3 Dec. 1855. For another indication, see "O 25 de março," *Correio da Tarde,* 26 March 1859.

64. *Folhetim, JC,* 5 Dec. 1851; *Folhetim, CM,* 11 Dec. 1849.

65. Needell, *Tropical Belle Époque,* 77–80.

66. Fulcher, *Nation's Image,* 2, 6, 8, 104, 125–29, 170, 201; Johnson, *Backstage,* 23, 63, 78–80, 181–83; Barbier, *Opera,* 11, 17, 36–39.

67. On the importance of lotteries to theaters' financial viability, see the petition of José Bernardino de Sá, president of the Sociedade Theatral de S. Pedro

d'Alcantara, to Pedro II, requesting that cancelled lotteries be restored, Rio, 13 Dec. 1850, BN/SM, II-34, 25, 31.

68. Brazil, MI, *Relatorio* (1856), 80; Paixão, *Theatro*, 184.

69. Iglesias, "Vida," 23.

70. "Carta de D. Mathias . . . ," *Periodico dos Pobres*, 3 Dec. 1850. See also Magaldi, *Music*, 52–55.

71. "Miscellanea," *JC*, 15 Oct. 1828; "Theatro de S. Pedro d'Alcantara" (*folhetim*), *JC*, 5 Dec. 1839; "2 de Dezembro," *O Mercantil*, 3 Dec. 1846.

72. "O dia 2 de dezembro," *O Novo Tempo*, 5 Dec. 1844.

73. "Visita das priminhas," *Periodico dos Pobres*, 6 Dec. 1853; "Theatro S. Pedro de Alcantara," *Periodico dos Pobres*, 28 March 1854.

74. Speech of Fernando Sebastião Dias da Motta, 30 Aug., *ACD* (1845), 2:796.

75. Martins Pena, *Folhetins*, 307.

76. Jacquemont, *Letters*, 1:40; "Imperial Theatro," *O Spectador Brasileiro*, 11 Sep. 1826. On Rossini's reception in Rio, see Kühl, "Chegada."

77. In this regard, Rosselli's comments on the quality of operatic talent in nineteenth-century Buenos Aires applies equally to Rio de Janerio, where many of those who appeared in the Argentine capital also had engagements; "Opera Business," 161, 163–64.

78. Giron, *Minoridade*, 119; Magaldi, *Music*, 39–42; Andrade, *Francisco Manuel da Silva*, 1:196–98.

79. Calculated from theater advertising in the newspapers. On operatic tastes, see Magaldi, *Music*, 39–44. This repertoire also prevailed in Buenos Aires and Montevideo; Rosselli, "Opera Business," 167–68; Salgado, *Teatro*, 8–13, 23–42, 50–69.

80. "96.ª pacotilha . . . ," *CM*, 5 Dec. 1852; *Folhetim*, *JC*, 29 March 1852; "Visita das priminhas," *Periodico dos Pobres*, 9 Sep. 1852; "Semana Lyrica" (*folhetim*), *JC*, 7 Dec. 1852. See also "O Theatro Italiano," *JC*, 4 Dec. 1852.

81. *Folhetim*, *JC*, 11 Sep. 1853; *JC*, 10 Sep. 1854. For negative reviews, see "Theatro Lyrico Fluminense" (*folhetim*), *JC*, 7 Dec. 1854 (Giacomo Meyerbeer's *Robert le Diable*); "Theatro Lyrico," *A Semana*, 30 March 1856 (Verdi's *Attila*); *CM*, 8–9 Sep. 1863 (Donizetti's *Maria di Rohan*).

82. *Folhetim*, *CM*, 11 Dec. 1849.

83. Aguilar, "National Opera," 84. See also Dolkart, "Elitelore"; Needell, *Tropical Belle Époque*, 78, 179.

84. Gondim, *Vida*, 84–116. For the sale of a libretto in the lobby on an opera's opening night, see "Obras publicadas," *DRJ*, 6 Sep. 1844.

85. M., "Paginas menores," *CM*, 8 May 1855.

86. Andrade, *Francisco Manuel da Silva*, 2:83–85, 87–88, 178.

87. De-Simoni, *Marília*. On this libretto, see also Andrade, *Francisco Manuel da Silva*, 2:86–87, 189; Kühl, "Luiz Vicente De-Simoni"; Wehrs, "Neukomm," 106, 110, 111–15.

88. "Programma sobre a creação de uma opera nacional," in Brazil, MI, *Relatorio* (1856), *anexo* O; (1858), 20. On this project, see also Azevedo, *150 anos*, 65–68; Sousa, *Teatro*, 1:197–203; Paixão, *Theatro*, 274–306; Andrade, *Francisco Manuel da Silva*, 2:91–109. On Porto Alegre's project for the academy, see Squeff, *Brasil*, 181–82; Meghreblian, "Art," 25–32.

89. "Opera nacional," *JC*, 4 Sep. 1861; *Correio da Tarde*, 8 Sep. 1861; Reis, *Noite*. On the reception of this opera, see "Opera Nacional," *DRJ*, 6 Sep. 1861; "Noticiario," *DRJ*, 9 Sep. 1861; "A Noite do Castello do maestro Antonio Carlos Gomes," *Semana Illustrada*, 8 Sep. 1861; Giron, *Minoridade*, 197–200.

90. Almeida, "Dois amores." On this opera's reception, see ibid., 191n*; Andrade, *Francisco Manuel da Silva*, 1:101–2; "Dous Amores," *A Semana Illustrada*, 8 Dec. 1861.

91. Brazil, MI, *Relatorio* (1861): 39–40; (1862): 29–30.

92. Gomes, *Joanna*; *CM*, 8–9 Sep. 1863. On the controversies, see Azevedo, *150 anos*, 68, 75; Mariz, *História*, 64; Andrade, *Francisco Manuel da Silva*, 2:107–08.

93. Only a partial manuscript libretto has survived, Henrique Alves de Mesquita, "O vagabundo ou a infidelidade, sedução e vaidade punidas," Biblioteca Alberto Nepomuceno, Universidade Federal do Rio de Janeiro, M-III-14 (*Libretos*).

94. *CM*, 9 Sep. 1864; "Revista Theatral," *Esperança*, 11 Sep. 1864. See also "Theatro Lyrico," *DRJ*, 8–9 Sep. 1864; "Theatrologia," *Bazar Volante*, 8 Sep. 1864; Andrade, *Francisco Manuel da Silva*, 2:108–09.

95. Giron, *Minoridade*, 162–63. For a similar assessment, see Paixão, *Theatro*, 306.

96. Brazil, MI, *Relatorio* (1864), 24.

97. For examples of this moniker, see "Cronica Teatral," *Revista Teatral*, 19 Feb. 1860, quoted in Giron, *Minoridade*, 384; M., "O dia dous de Dezembro de 1862," *Semana Illustrada*, 7 Dec. 1862.

98. [Joaquim Maria Machado de Assis], "Ao acaso," *DRJ*, 10 Jan. 1865.

99. Sousa, *Teatro*, 1:222–25; Paixão, *Theatro*, 240–41; Magaldi, *Music*, 48–49; Souza, *Noites*, 254–55; Machado, *Vida*, 191–93; Needell, *Tropical* Belle Époque, 162–63, 165, 172, 175, 289n24. For contemporary criticisms of the Alcazar, see Macedo, *Memórias da rua*, 111–12.

100. Manoel de Araujo Porto Alegre, "Peço venia," no date (draft), AIHGB, lata 653, doc. 16; França Júnior, *Política*, 278; Taunay, *Memórias*, 98; Mattoso, *Cousas*, 272–74.

101. Codman, *Ten Months*, 176–77. In 1865, William James found the Alcazar to be the only entertainment regularly available, and he quickly tired of it; William James to Henry James, Rio, 23 July 1865, in James, *Brazil*, 65–66. D[illon] had much the same reaction, *Twelve Month's Tour*, 18.

102. On these issues, see Needell, *Tropical* Belle Époque, 171–77.

103. Alcazar Lyrico Advertisements, *JC*, 7 Sep. 1859, 2 Dec. 1863, 7 Sep. 1864, 2 Dec. 1864. See also the favorable *a pedido*, "Alcazar Lyrico," *Correio da Tarde*, 9 Sep. 1859.

104. *Freischütz* was also the first German romantic opera staged on a day of national festivity.

105. Mariz, *História*, 67; Azevedo, *150 anos*, 77–78.

106. "Il Guarany," *Jornal da Tarde*, 3 Dec. 1870; Guimarães Júnior, "Revista do Domingo," *DRJ*, 4 Dec. 1870.

107. Magaldi, *Music*, 140–42.

108. Andrews, "Carlos Gomes's *Il Guarany*," 41; Magaldi, *Music*, 140.

109. Faria, *Idéias*, 57, 78, 81. See also Machado, *Vida literária*, 294; Sousa, *Teatro*, 1:172–73; the much older assessment of Levasseur et al., *Brasil*, 129.

110. For general discussions of Romanticism in Brazil, see Schwarcz, *Barbas*, 126–55; Ricupero, *Romantismo*; Rodrigues, *José de Alencar*, 83–92; Treece, *Exiles*; Salles, *Nostalgia*, 75–113; Newcomb, "José de Alencar's Critical Writing"; Ventura, *Estilo*, 30–42; Araújo, *Experiência*; Kodama, *Índios*; Needell, *Tropical* Belle Époque, 181–88.

111. Schwarcz, *Barbas*, 131–38; Ricupero, *Romantismo*, 153–78; Treece, *Exiles*, 160–207; Machado, *Vida*, 249–51.

112. Squeff, *Brasil*, 224–31; Francisco Adolfo de Varnhagen to Pedro II, Madrid, 24 Sep. 1856, in Varnhagen, *Correspondência*, 235. On Varnhagen's views, see Puntoni, "Sr. Varnhagen." See also Wehling, *Estado*, 52, 64–66, 113–14, 164–65, 195–97; Ricupero, *Romantismo*, 138–41; Schwarcz, *Barbas*, 140–41; Haußer, "Civilização"; Kodama, *Índios*, 176–82.

113. Treece, *Exiles*, 3. On policy toward Indians, see Cunha, "Política."

114. Adet, "Empire," 1084; "Theatro de S. Pedro d'Alcantara" (*folhetim*), *JC*, 5 Dec. 1839. On this point, see also Machado, *Vida*, 43. For another example, see Graham, *Journal*, 245.

115. "A noite de hoje," *A Marmota na Corte*, 25 March 1851; theater advertising, *JC*, 24 March 1851. The play was likely one of the stage versions that appeared soon after the publication of Eugène Sue's *Les mystères de Paris* (1842–43).

116. *O Verdadeiro Liberal*, 6 April 1826.

117. "Espectaculos," *O Constitucional*, 6 May 1831; *O Brasileiro Vigilante*, 7 May 1831. On this play and its context, see also Prado, *João Caetano*, 12–13. No script is known to exist.

118. Souza, *Noites*, 31.

119. G[onçalves] de Magalhães, *Tragédias*, 5; Faria, *Idéias*, 30–37; Sousa, *Teatro*, 1:169–70; Albuquerque, "Brazilian Theatre," 112–13; Machado, *Vida*, 284; Souza, *Noites*, 35–37.

120. Albuquerque, "Brazilian Theater," 114–16; Martins Pena, *Comédias*.

121. Souza, *Noites*, 38. I have not been able to locate this contract, and Souza offers no reference to it.

122. Quoted in Prado, *João Caetano*, 54.

123. Letter from Hum Irmão da Caridade, *JC*, 10 Sep. 1840. Neither the play nor the playwright appear in Sousa's dictionary of Brazilian theater, *Teatro*, vol. 2. Sacramento Blake tentatively identifies him as Gaspar José de Mattos Pimentel, *Diccionario*, 3:505. On the Botocudo war, see Langfur, *Forbidden Lands*, 262–87.

124. Treece, *Exiles*, 98–141.

125. Sousa, *Teatro*, 1:330. On the Conservatório, see Sousa, *Teatro*, 1:309–20; Paixão, *Theatro*, 463–64; Souza, *Noites*, 139–201.

126. Brazil, MI, *Relatorio* (1862): 28.

127. Davis, "Opera."

128. Viqueira Albán, *Propriety*, 35, 39–42, 46–51, 64–75, 90–95.

129. Decisão 141 (Império), 21 July 1830, *CLB*; "Theatro, e modas," *A Marmota na Corte*, 28 March 1851.

130. Souza, *Noites*, 154.

131. Decreto 1307, 30 Dec. 1853, *CLB*.

132. "Noticias diversas," *CM*, 4 Sep. 1858; Sousa, *Teatro*, 1:177; Faria, *Idéias*, 80. I have not been able to locate this script.

133. Prado, *João Caetano*, 129–30.

134. Macedo, "Cobé," in *Teatro*, 2:9–80; M—as. [Machado de Assis], "Revista de theatros," *O Espelho*, 11 Sep. 1859. For modern readings of *Cobé*, see Treece, *Exiles*, 93–94, 161–64; Ricupero, *Romantismo*, 174.

135. Macedo, "Amor e pátria," in *Teatro*, 1:171, 172. See also Sandes, *Invenção*, 44–49.

136. Alencar, "O jesuíta," in *Obra*, 4:477–536). On this play, see Lehnen, "Foundational Mission"; Sandes, *Invenção*, 49–58; Fleck and Tavares, "Apóstolo." Incidentally, *O jesuíta* is the only nineteenth-century Brazilian play translated into English; Alencar, *Jesuit*.

137. Prado, *João Caetano*, 131, 139, 173–76.

138. Porto Alegre, "Angélica e Firmino," in *Teatro*, 2:25–122.

139. João Caetano dos Santos, "Memória tendente à necessidade de uma Escola Dramática . . . ," in Ferreira, *Ator*, 14–21; J[osé] M[aria] da S[ilv]a Paranhos to Marquis of Olinda, Rio, 15 July 1863, AIGHB, lata 216, doc. 62.

140. Toussaint-Samson, *Parisian*, 94.

141. On Realism, see Souza, *Noites*, 31–120; Faria, *Idéias*, 85–144; Sousa, *Teatro*, 1:188–97; Paixão, *Theatro*, 186, 193.

142. Alencar, "Mãe," in *Obra*, 4:291–348. For contemporary assessments of *Mãe*, see "Notícias diversas," *CM*, 26 March 1860; "Paginas menores," *CM*, 1 April 1860; Frederico Zuccaro, "Theatro," *JC*, 24 March 1860. For modern assessments of *Mãe*, see Souza, *Noites*, 113–15; Treece, *Exiles*, 176–78; Ricupero, *Romantismo*, 175–77.

143. Lopes, *Sete de Setembro*, 52, 53. For a favorable contemporary review, see L-a., "Litteratura Dramatico," *Revista Popular* (15 Aug. 1862), 221–23. See also Sandes, *Invenção*, 59–61.

144. Joaquim Manuel de Macedo, "*Folhetim*," *JC*, 19 Aug. 1861, in Faria, *Idéias*, 532.

145. Souza, *Noites*, 275, 293–97. On the emergence of popular theater, see Marzano, *Cidade*, 31–32, 72, 101–03, 125; Mencarelli, *Cena aberta*, 36–37, 61, 105, 128–29; Augusto, *Questão*, 207–46; Souza, *Carpinteiros*, 67–91, 127–62.

146. For typical contemporary remarks on Brazilian theater's decadence, see Moreira de Azevedo, *Rio*, 2:177–78. For historians who repeat these views, see Sousa, *Teatro*, 1:230–35; Paixão, *Theatro*, 506–55.

147. On such laudations, see Malerba, *Corte*, 100–11; Mammi, "Teatro," 46–47. To my knowledge, they have never been systematically analyzed.

148. On the Brazilian-born Stockmeyer, see Giron, *Minoridade*, 161; Magaldi, *Music*, 65–66; Andrade, *Francisco Manuel da Silva*, 2:238–39. Bosoni and Bussmeyer were expatriates who spent time in Rio; Andrade, *Francisco Manuel da Silva*, 2:150, 152. On the Bahian Rebouças, see *Enciclopédia*, 2:645. I have not been able to identify Santos Neves.

149. "Os Festejos do Dia Dous de Dezembro," *O Despertador*, 4 Dec. 1839.

150. "Theatro Constitucional Fluminense," *JC*, 2 Dec. 1836; Hamond, *Diários*, 143; "Theatro Constitucional Fluminense," *JC*, 21 March 1837; "13°

Anniversario do Juramento da Constituição em—25 de março—," *Pharol do Imperio*, 28 March 1837; *Pharol do Imperio*, 10 April 1837; "Theatro Constitucional Fluminense," *JC*, 8 April 1834, 6 April 1837, 6 Sep. 1837; "O Dia Sete de Setembro," *Jornal dos Debates Politicos e Literarios*, 13 Sep. 1837.

151. Martins Pena, *Folhetins*, 364.

152. "Theatro Constitucional Fluminense," *DRJ*, 1 Dec. 1835.

153. "Chronica Nacional," *Folhinha Laemmert* (1853), 135–36. On the fire losses, see also Moreira de Azevedo, *Rio*, 2:172–73.

154. Porto Alegre, *Prologo*. Albuquerque identifies Porto Alegre's *Prologo dramatico* as the first Brazilian play, for it appeared some months before Gonçalves de Magalhães's *Antonio José*; "Brazilian Theater," 113. However, *Prologo* belongs to a completely different genre, and numerous such works antedated it. Incidentally, *Prologo* was not included in Porto Alegre's collected works, *Teatro*.

155. Porto Alegre, *Prologo*, 5.

156. Pereira da Silva, "O dia dous de dezembro de 1837," *JC*, 5 Dec. 1837.

157. "Anniversario de S. M. o Imperador," *O Sete d'Abril*, 6 Dec. 1837.

158. "Theatro da Praça da Constituição," *O Chronista*, 6 Dec. 1837.

159. "Prologo Infernal," *O Chronista*, 13 Dec. 1837.

160. "Prologo Infernal," *O Chronista*, 16 Dec. 1837. On Porto Alegre's notorious pride and vanity, see Machado, *Vida*, 250.

161. *O Chronista*, 16 Dec. 1837; Squeff, *Brasil*, 95–96, 121n6. In mid-December, Porto Alegre published a lithograph, considered the first Brazilian cartoon, in which he accused Justiniano of corruption; Lima, *História* 1:71–73, 82; Magalhães Júnior, "Justiniano José Rocha," 146. This cartoon and the debate about *Prologo* are certainly connected.

162. Domingos de Azevedo Coutinho Duque Estrada, *Parecer*, 21 Nov. 1857, BN/SM, I-8, 14, 61.

163. Thomaz J[os]é Pinto de Sirqueira, *Parecer*, 31 Aug. 1851, BN/SM, I-8, 10, 36.

164. Thomas José Pinto de Cerqueira, *Parecer*, 4 Feb. 1852; André Pereira Lima, *Parecer*, 5 Feb. 1851; João Caetano dos Santos to [Conservatório Dramático], Rio, 13 Feb. 1851, BN/SM, I-8, 7, 52; Antonio José de Araujo, *Parecer*, Feb. 1851, BN/SM, I-8, 7, 58; Petition of Florindo Joaquim da Silva to Conservatorio Dramatico, Rio, 16 Aug. 1851 (with *despacho* by Bivar, 18 Aug. 1851), BN/SM, I-2, 25, 95; Luiz G. S. de Biraio, *Parecer*, 8 March 1851, BN/SM, I-8, 2, 18.

165. "A cantata allegorica do dia 2 de dezembro," *CM*, 2 Dec. 1851; Giannini, *Harmonia*.

166. "44.ª pacotilha . . . ," *CM*, 8 Dec. 1851. For another favorable view, see "Visita das priminhas," *Periodico dos Pobres*, 4 Dec. 1851.

167. "A semana," *Album Semanal*, 7 Dec. 1851; *folhetim*, *JC*, 5 Dec. 1851.

168. "137.ª pacotilha . . . ," *CM*, 11 Sep. 1853. For the variant title, see the Teatro Provisório's advertisement, *JC*, 5 Sep. 1853.

169. "Chronica da Quinzena," *Revista Popular*, 2 Aug. 1860.

170. "A União do Imperio," *A Marmota*, 4 Dec. 1860; Vecchy, *União*.

171. Vecchy, *União*, 5; Valle, *Elogio*; Burgain, *Vaticínio*.

172. Giannini, *Harmonia*, 9.

173. *JC*, 6 Sep. 1840; Letter from Hum Irmão da Caridade, *JC*, 10 Sep. 1840. See also *O Brasil*, 7 Sep. 1840.

174. Valle, *Elogio*, 6; Garcia, *Elogio*.

175. G[onçalves] de Magalhães, "A queda do despotismo," in *Poesias*, 243–56; *Elogio dramatico*; Garcia, *Elogio*.

176. Martins Pena, *Folhetins*, 224. The author and title are listed in the advertisement in *JC*, 30 April 1847.

177. Fernandes, *Alliança*, 15.

178. Valle, *Elogio*, 12; Garcia, *Elogio*, 11. In addition to the ones previously noted, see the references to portraits in Ultra, *Gloria*, 12; G[onçalves] de Magalhães, "Queda," 255; idem, "Elogio drammatico em applauso do anniversario do memoravel dia sete de setembro," in *Poesias*, 240; *Elogio*; Burgain, *Vaticinio*, 4.

179. "Theatro de S. Pedro de Alcantara," *JC*, 6 Sep. 1840; Letter from Hum Irmão de Caridade, *JC*, 10 Sep. 1840.

180. Valle, *Elogio*, 4; Garcia, *Elogio*, 5.

181. *Folhetim*, *JC*, 5 Dec. 1851; "A semana," *Album Semanal*, 7 Dec. 1851. For similar criticisms, see "Theatro de S. Januario" (*folhetim*), *DRJ*, 9 Dec. 1851. Giannini had made the costume decisions, "Theatro de S. Januário" (*correspondência*), *JC*, 7 Dec. 1851.

182. "137.ª pacotilha . . . ," *CM*, 11 Sep. 1853; "Theatro de S. Pedro," *CM*, 5 Dec. 1857.

183. Belluzzo, *Brasil*, 76–85; Earle, *Return*, 27; V. Araújo, *Experiência*, 160–70; Haußer, "Civilização," 237–41; Langer, "Enigmas."

184. Mendonça, "Festas," 307; Oliveira Lima, *D. João VI*, 607; Schwarcz, *Barbas*, 41.

185. Kraay, "Between Brazil," 265–66.

186. *O Grito Nacional*, 7 Sep. 1853.

187. "O Dia 7 de Setembro de 1850," *O Grito Nacional*, 11 Sep. 1850.

188. Lima, *História*, 2:754, 782. An 1840 lithograph calling on the Brazilian government take a firmer stance in a dispute over the border with French Guiana prefigured the imagery of the 1860s; Santos, *Imagem*, 93.

189. Needell, "Domestic Civilizing Mission."

190. Forman, "Harbouring Discontent," 236.

CHAPTER EIGHT

1. Cunha, *Chama*. Most recent literature takes a more critical view: Doratioto, *Maldita guerra*; Whigham, *Paraguayan War*; Kraay and Whigham, eds., *I Die*; Beattie, *Tribute*, 38–63.

2. Barman, *Citizen Emperor*, 199 (quote), 202, 211–23; Needell, *Party*, 239–49; Iglesias, "Vida," 103–12; Holanda, "Do Império," 7–10, 105. For a criticism of the view that this was a coup, see Pinho, *Politica*, 55–128; Carvalho, *D. Pedro II*, 193.

3. Nabuco, *Estadista*, 666–69; Holanda, "Do Império," 116–19; Carvalho, "Radicalismo," 26–35, 43–47 (quote 26); Iglesias, "Vida política," 111–12; Barbosa, "Panfletos," 176–78; Carvalho, "Conferências," 26–30.

4. Centeno, *Blood*, 55–56, 77, 87, 228, 232.

5. Taunay, *Memórias*, 91. On this patriotic mobilization, see also Schwarcz, *Barbas*, 304; Kraay, "Patriotic Mobilization," 62–65.

6. Codman, *Ten Months*, 185; Pafuncio Semicupio Pechincha, "O anno novo de 1870," *Folhinha Laemmert* (1870), x.

7. João Pandiá Calógeras to Son, Rio, 2 and 22 Jan. 1865, in Calógeras, *Ministério*, 186, 202.

8. Silva, *Prince*, 21–23; Fluminense, *Traços*. The circumstances of her death are noted in "Chronica nacional," *Folhinha Laemmert* (1869), 151. See also Ipsen, "Delicate Citizenship," 22–74.

9. Silva, "Príncipe," 70.

10. "Venit, vidit, vicit," *Semana Illustrada*, 12 Nov. 1865; Barman, *Citizen Emperor*, 202; Schwarcz, *Barbas*, 300.

11. See the program, "Recepção de S. M. o Imperador," *JC*, 5 Nov. 1865.

12. "Chegada de Suas Magestades," *DRJ*, 10 Nov. 1865 (quote); *JC*, 10 Nov. 1865; "Noticias diversas," *CM*, 10 Nov. 1865.

13. "Noticias Diversas," *CM*, 11 Nov. 1865; William Van Vleck Lidgerwood to James Watson Webb, Rio, 1 Dec. 1865, NARS, M-121, roll 33.

14. "Noticias Diversas," *CM*, 12 Nov. 1865; "Festejos," *JC*, 11 Nov. 1865. The critic's remarks appear in Argus, "Illuminações" (*a pedido*), *JC*, 12 Nov. 1865.

15. Theater Advertising, *JC*, 11 Nov. 1865; *JC*, 12 Nov. 1865.

16. Edward Thornton to Earl Russell, Rio 15 Nov. 1865, PRO/FO 13, vol. 428, fol. 87 (quote); "Festejos," *JC*, 13 Nov. 1865; "Festejos," *DRJ*, 14 Nov. 1865; "Demonstrations in Rio," *The Anglo-Brazilian Times*, 24 Nov. 1865.

17. "Poesia" (*a pedido*), *JC*, 14 Nov. 1865.

18. "Frequesia de S. José" (*a pedido*), *JC*, 10 Nov. 1865; "Festejos na rua do Porto" (*a pedido*), *JC*, 13 Nov. 1865.

19. "Chronica nacional," *Folhinha Laemmert* (1867), 153.

20. Um commissionado, "A camara municipal e os festejos" (*a pedido*), *JC*, 8 Nov. 1865; "Festejos" (*a pedido*), *CM*, 10 Nov. 1865.

21. Carne verde, "Os festejos e a camara municipal" (*a pedido*), *JC*, 10 Nov. 1865; "Festejos" (*a pedido*), *JC*, 8 Nov. 1865.

22. "Noticias diversas," *CM*, 8 Nov. 1865; "Recepção de S. M. o Imperador," *JC*, 5 Nov. 1865; *JC*, 10 Nov. 1865.

23. Paulo Barbosa da Silva to Marquis of Olinda, [Rio], 2 Nov. 1865, AIHGB, lata 213, doc. 53.

24. "7 de Setembro," *Diario do Povo*, 7 Sep. 1867; *A Guarda Nacional*, 9 Sep. 1866; "Chronica," *O Futuro*, 9 Sep. 1869.

25. "Anniversario," *DRJ*, 8 Sep. 1869. The day off in 1868 can be inferred from "Anniversario," *DRJ*, 9 Sep. 1868.

26. [Joaquim Maria] M[achado de] A[ssis], "Ao acaso (revista da semana)," *DRJ*, 28 March 1865.

27. "Festejos," *DRJ*, 12 Nov. 1865; "Noticias diversas," *CM*, 12 Nov. 1865; "Festjos," *JC*, 11 Nov. 1865. On guardsmen's views of garrison service, see "Guarda Nacional" (*a pedido*), *JC*, 13 May 1870; "Guarda nacional" (*a pedido*), *JC*, 24 June 1870.

28. França Júnior, *Política*, 88. On the winding down of theater subventions, see Augusto, *Questão*, 103.

29. "Theatro Lyrico Fluminense," *JC*, 9 Sep. 1868.

30. Andrade, *Francisco Manoel da Silva*, 2:76–77.

31. Albernoz, *Primeiro voluntario*. The *JC* noted the publication of at least three other piano works in honor of Pedro's return in its issue of 10 Nov. 1865.

32. "Noticias diversas," *CM*, 4 Dec. 1865; "Hoje 2 de dezembro de 1865," *JC*, 2 Dec. 1865. On the lack of time to rehearse it in November, see "Festejos," *JC*, 11 Nov. 1865.

33. Gottschalk, *Voyages*, 485; Starr, *Louis Moreau Gottschalk*, 426–27, 431–35. My interpretation of Gottschalk's "Grande fantasia" differs from that of Carvalho, who argues that this composition popularized the national anthem; *Formação*, 126–27. Incidentally, to my knowledge, Gottschalk's "Grande fantasia" is the only bit of patriotic music from this period that continues to be recorded, most recently by Brazilian pianist Carla Sverner, *Piano*, track 1.

34. Vasques, *Brasil*; theater advertising, *DRJ*, 25 March 1865. On Vasques's comic scenes, see Marzano, *Cidade*, 40, 139, 153–57; Souza, *Carpinteiros*, 27, 39–40, 74–75, 81.

35. Theater advertising, *JC*, 6 Sep. 1865; Machado, *Vida*, 29–30.

36. Theater advertising, *JC*, 1 Dec. 1865, 25 March and 7 September 1868.

37. "Noticias diversas," *CM*, 7 Sep. 1865; "Noticiario," *DRJ*, 6 Sep. 1866; "Noticias Diversas," *CM*, 6 Sep. 1866.

38. *Almanak Laemmert* (1868): 413; (1869): 412; (1870): 405; "Dia 7 de setembro," *JC*, 6 Sep. 1865; "Noticias diversas," *CM*, 6 Sep. 1865; "Dia 7 de setembro," *JC*, 6 Sep. 1867; "Chronique," *Ba-Ta-Clan*, 14 Sep. 1867; "Dia 7 de Setembro," *JC*, 7 Sep. 1867.

39. "Dia 7 de setembro," *JC*, 6 Sep. 1865; Augusto Ferreira dos Santos Varginha to Camara, Rio, 23 Aug. 1867, AGCRJ, 43-3-64, fol. 21. See the advertising in the *JC* in the first week of September, 1865–69.

40. "S. P. M. Monarchista Brasileira," *JC*, 7 Sep. 1866, 1867 and 1869; "S. P. E. Litterarios," *JC*, 9 Sep. 1866; "Sociedade Brazileira Ensaios Litterarios," *JC*, 9 Sep. 1867; "Sociedade Ensaios Litterarios," *CM*, 7 Sep. 1867; "Sociedade brasileira Ensaios Litterarios," *DRJ*, 7 Sep. 1867.

41. "Dia 2 de Dezembro," *JC*, 29 Nov. 1865; "Festejos," *DRJ*, 4 Dec. 1868.

42. *CM*, 7 Sep. 1867; "Novidades da semana," *A Pacotilha*, 15 Sep. 1866; "Chronique," *Ba-Ta-Clan*, 14 Sep. 1867.

43. "Jornal de Confucio—7 de Setembro," *Opinião Liberal*, 13 Sep. 1866.

44. "O dia 25 de março," *DRJ*, 25 March 1869.

45. "25 de março de 1865," *Brasil Historico*, 2 April 1865; *CM*, 25 March 1867.

46. *CM*, 25 March 1868; *Diario do Povo*, 25 March 1868; *Opinião Liberal*, 4 April 1868. On the origins and meaning of *imperialismo*, see Holanda, "Do Império," 63–64.

47. "7 de setembro e o futuro," *Opinião Liberal*, 13 Sep. 1866; *A Pacotilha*, 7 Sep. 1866; *A Guarda Nacional*, 9 Sep. 1866.

48. *CM*, 7 Sep. 1866; "O dia 7 de setembro," *CM*, 7 Sep. 1868.

49. *DRJ*, 7 Sep. 1868.

50. "Sete de Setembro," *Diario do Povo*, 7 Sep. 1868.

51. "Anniversario natalicio de S. M. o Imperador," *Semana Illustrada*, 3 Dec. 1865. See also *A Regeneração*, 10 Dec. 1866 and 30 Nov. 1867; "Dous de Dezembro," *DRJ*, 2 Dec. 1867.

52. *Diario do Povo*, 2–3 Dec. 1867.

53. *CM*, 2 Dec. 1866; "Novidades da semana," *O Pandokeu*, 9 Dec. 1866; H., "Dous de Dezembro" (*a pedido*), *JC*, 3 Dec. 1866.

54. *DRJ*, 2 Dec. 1868 and 2 Dec. 1869; *Sentinella da Liberdade*, 5 and 12 Dec. 1869.

55.   Oh! excelso monarca, eu vos saudo!
    Bem como vos sauda o mundo inteiro;
    O mundo, que conhece as vossas glorias. . . .
    Brasileiros, erguei-vos, e de um brado
    O monarca saudae,—saudae com hinos
    Do dia de Dezembro o dois faustoso
    O dia que nos trouxe mil venturas!
    Ribomba ao nascer d'alva a artilharia
    E parece dizer em som festivo
    Imperio do Brasil, cantae, cantae!
    Festival harmonia reina em todos;
    As glorias do monarca, as sãs virtudes,
    Zelemos, decantando-as sem cessar.
    A excelsa Imperatriz, a mae dos pobres,
    Não olvidamos também de festejar
    Neste dia imortal que é para ela
    O dia venturoso em que nascêra
    Sempre grande o imortal Pedro II.

Um monarchista, "Hymno dedicado a S. M. I. o Senhor D. Pedro II, no dia 2 de dezembro de 1868" (*a pedido*), *JC*, 2 Dec. 1868.

56. "Chronique," *Ba-Ta-Clan*, 5 Dec. 1868. The reference was apparently to "Interesse Publico n.° 40" (*a pedido*), *DRJ*, 3 Dec. 1868. A young journalist later insisted that the *JC* had been unaware of the acrostic; Mattoso, *Cousas*, 19–20.

57. *Opinião Liberal*, 3 Dec. 1868; "Variante do hymno publicado no dia 2 . . . , *DRJ*, 4 Dec. 1868.

58. Mattoso, *Cousas*, 19–20; Magalhães Júnior, *Império*, 80–81. Ferreira Vianna's pamphlet is "Conferência." On his politics, see also Magalhães Júnior, "Ferreira Vianna"; Needell, *Party*, 422n64; Carvalho, *D. Pedro II*, 61, 236. In 1880, an ephemeral newspaper attributed the poem to Otaviano, "Excavações," *Tagarella*, 3 Dec. 1880. Nabuco noted that, in the 1867 election, both Historical Liberals and Conservative Saquaremas "denounced *imperialismo* with equal bitterness"; *Estadista*, 593.

59. Machado, *Vida*, 111–12, 118n9; Vicente, "Bobo," 132–39.

60. Barman, *Citizen Emperor*, 230. See also Carvalho, *Cidadania*, 78–80; Carvalho, *D. Pedro II*, 122; Doratioto, *Maldita Guerra*, 461.

61. "Sete de Setembro," *DRJ*, 7 Sep. 1865. For the one other example of similar rhetoric that I have located, see "Ao dia 7 de setembro de 1866" (*a pedido*), *JC*, 9 Sep. 1866.

62. Luiz Guimarães Jr., "Revista do Domingo" (*folhetim*), 10 Sep. 1871, *DRJ*, 11 Sep. 1871.

63. These are key themes in the recent literature on the Paraguayan War; Doratioto, *Maldita guerra*; Whigham, *Paraguayan War*; Kraay and Whigham, *I Die*; Beattie, *Tribute*, 38–63.

64. Mello Moraes Filho, *Festas*, 152, 450.

65. França Júnior, *Política*, 191, 197–98; Pedro II to Condessa de Barral, Rio, 10 March 1868, in *D. Pedro II e a Condessa*, 132.

66. James Watson Webb to Sec. of State, Boa Viagem, 7 Aug. 1868, NARS, M-121, roll 35; Taunay, *Memórias*, 301.

67. "Estatua Equestre do Sr. D. Pedro II," *DRJ*, 19 March 1870; "Estatua equestre do Sr. D. Pedro II," *JC*, 19 March 1870; "Estatua equestre a S. M. o Imperador," *JC*, 20 March 1870; "Estatua Equestre a Sua Magestade o Imperador," *DRJ*, 21 March 1870; "Estatua Equestre à S. M. o Imperador," *Jornal da Tarde*, 21 March 1870.

68. "Assumpto de varias cores," *A Vida Fluminense*, 26 March 1870; *Illustração Americana*, 27 March 1870; *DRJ*, 7 Sep. 1870; "O imperador, a estatua equestre e a instrucção publica," *Opinião Liberal*, 26 March 1870.

69. Rodrigues, "Guerra," 27–55.

70. For a few accounts of these parades, see "Voluntarios da Patria," *JC*, 22 March 1870; "Chronica geral," *A Reforma*, 22 March 1870; *A Vida Fluminense*, 26 March and 2 April 1870; "Chronique," *Ba-Ta-Clan*, 26 March 1870; "Voluntarios da Patria" and "Desembarque de voluntarios," *JC*, 30 April–1 May 1870; Lester, "Brazil," *Hartford Daily Courant*, 14 May 1870. See also Rodrigues, "Guerra," chap. 2.

71. Balaban, *Poeta*, 207–10.

72. *A Vida Fluminense*, 30 April 1870; "The Returned Volunteers," *The Anglo-Brazilian Times*, 23 May 1870.

73. Ipsen, "Delicate Citizenship," 166–210; Ipsen, "*Patrícias*," 313–23.

74. Henry T. Blow to Sec. of State, Petrópolis, 24 March 1870, NARS, M-121, roll 38. Blow's account closely conforms to the press coverage, "Regosijo nacional," *DRJ*, 18 March 1870; "Festejos pela terminação da guerra," *DRJ*, 19 March 1870; "Regosijo publico," *DRJ*, 20 March 1870; "Regosijo nacional," *Jornal da Tarde*, 18 and 19 March 1870; "Chronica geral," *A Reforma*, 20 March 1870.

75. "Regozijo publico," *JC*, 20 March 1870.

76. "Grande e solemne Te-Deum," "Te-Deum," and "Festa municipal em S. Francisco de Paula," *JC*, 25, 26, and 27 March 1870.

77. *A Vida Fluminense*, 9 and 30 April 1870 (quote). See also the illustrations in the issues of 30 April and 7 and 14 May.

78. Povo Agradecido, "A chegada do Sr. Conde d'Eu" (*a pedido*), *JC*, 27 April 1870; George Buckley Mathew to Earl of Clarendon, Rio, 30 April 1870, PRO/FO, vol. 469, fol. 111v.

79. "A S. M. o Imperador" (*a pedido*), *JC*, 27 April 1870.

80. A. de A., "Assumpto de varias cores," *A Vida Fluminense*, 7 May 1870; *A Comédia Social*, 21 April 1870. For descriptions of the structures, see "Festejos," *JC*, 28 and 29 April 1870.

81. Keyes, "Our Life," 329; "The Arrival of the Comte d'Eu," *The Anglo-Brazilian Times*, 6 May 1870; Rebouças, *Diario*, 120.

82. "Recepção de S. A. o Sr. Conde d'Eu," *JC*, 30 April–1 May 1870; *DRJ*, 30 April 1870; *A Reforma*, 1 May 1870; "Regosijo nacional," *Jornal da Tarde*, 30 April 1870; "Recepção do General Gastão de Orleans," *A Reforma*, 1 May 1870.

83. "Theatro Lyrico," *Jornal da Tarde*, 4 May 1870; "Manifestações patrioticas," *JC*, 4 May 1870. The complaint about price gouging appeared in Um Brazileiro, "Theatro Lyrico Fluminense" (*a pedido*), *JC*, 30 April–1 May 1870.

84. "Manifestações patrioticas," *JC*, 4 and 6 May 1870; "Felicitações," *JC*, 8, 15, and 16 May 1870; "Veteranos da Independencia," *JC*, 8 June 1870.

85. "Baile," *JC*, 13 May 1870. For examples of neighborhood celebrations, see "Festejos," *JC*, 10 May 1870 (Principe dos Cajueiros Street), 24 May 1870 (Cais da Imperatriz), 5 June 1870 (Botafogo). For examples of Te Deums, see "Te-Deum," *JC*, 7 May 1870 (Irmandade de Santa Cruz), 11 May 1870 (Venerável Ordem Terceira da Penitência), 12 May 1870 (Campinho), 3 June 1870 (Ilha do Governador).

86. Beattie, *Tribute*, 59. See also Izecksohn, "Guerra," 416.

87. Speech of José de Alencar, 19 May, *ACD* (1870), 1:44.

88. "Festejos da rua dos Ourives entre as ruas do Ouvidor e S. Pedro" (*a pedido*), *JC*, 16 May 1870. The bickering about the quality of decorations can be followed in a series of paid articles entitled "Festejos da rua dos Ourives," *JC*, 30 April–1 May, 2 and 3 May 1870.

89. "Festejo do largo de Estacio de Sá" (*a pedido*), *JC*, 31 May 1870.

90. On these points, see the following *a pedidos* in the *JC*: "Rua da Assembléa," 2 May 1870 (quote); "Para a commissão dos festejos da praça do commercio ler e avaliar," 28 April 1870; "À commissão dos festejos na freguezia de Santa Rita. Protesto em tempo," 29 April 1870; "1.º districto da frequesia de Santa Rita," 30 April–1 May 1870; "Festejos da rua do Livramento," 3 May 1870.

91. "Summary of News," *The Anglo-Brazilian Times*, 6 May 1870.

92. "Recepção de S. A. o Sr. Conde d'Eu," *JC*, 30 April–1 May 1870; "Recepção do General Gastão de Orleans," *A Reforma*, 1 May 1870; "Regosijo nacional," *Jornal da Tarde*, 30 April 1870; "The Arrival of the Comte d'Eu," *The Anglo-Brazilian Times*, 6 May 1870. *A Reforma* announced the reason for not publishing in its issue of 29 April 1870.

93. "Liberdade," *JC*, 30 April–1 May, and 2 and 3 May 1870.

94. "Liberdade" (*a pedido*), *JC*, 30 April–1 May 1870.

95. "Festejo do largo de Estacio de Sá" (*a pedido*), *JC*, 31 May 1870.

96. "Chronica geral," *A Reforma*, 3 May 1870.

97. See the notices entitled "Emancipação," *JC*, 24 and 26 May, 11 and 12 June, and 8 July 1870. See also Ipsen, "Delicate Citizenship," 202–03.

98. "Summary of News," *The Anglo-Brazilian Times*, 23 May and 23 July 1870.

99. Conrad, *Destruction*, 70–89; Needell, *Party*, 248–71.

100. Doratioto, *Maldita guerra*, 455; Rodrigues, "Guerra," chap. 6.

101. J. Julio de Barros, "O Duque de Caxias," *A Reforma*, 3 May 1870. The responses appeared in the *JC*: "A Reforma" and "Manifestação dos Officiaes," 4 May 1870; Sotero de Castro, "Ao meu amigo o Sr. Dr. J. Julio de Barros," 7 May 1870.

102. "Quem é o Conde d'Eu," *O Gavroche*, 1889; Daibert Júnior, *Isabel*, 64–66; Barman, *Princess Isabel*, 107–09.

103. These events, but not the political context, have been described by Beattie, *Tribute*, 59–61; Ipsen, "Delicate Citizenship," 192–94. A fuller account appears in Rodrigues, "Guerra," chaps. 4–5, but it contains several key errors.

104. Proposta, Baron of Muritiba (Minister of War), 18 May; speech of Alencar, 19 May, *ACD* (1870), 1:39, 1:44–46. On Alencar's disagreements with the cabinet, see Needell, *Party*, 257.

105. Speech of Muritiba, 19 May, *ACD* (1870), 1:46–48.

106. *ACD* (1870), 1:50, 70; "Festejos," *JC*, 22 May 1870; *ASB* (1870), 1:16–17.

107. "Assumptos de varias côres," *A Vida Fluminense*, 21 May 1870. This was an exaggeration, for the forty contos was also intended to cover the cost of decorations, musicians, and singers. For similar criticisms, see Solon, "Festejos nacionaes!!!" (*a pedido*), *JC*, 16 May 1870. On the press criticisms, see also Ipsen, "Delicate Citizenship," 194–96.

108. *Vida Fluminense*, 21 May 1870.

109. Ypiranga, "Os Brazileiros prescriptos no anno da graça de 1870!" (*a pedido*), *JC*, 20 May 1870. See also the response to this critique by Um cidadão plebeu, "Festejos officiaes" (*a pedido*), *JC*, 29 May 1870. Itaboraí's alleged nepotism is noted in "Festejos," *A Reforma*, 6 July 1870.

110. "Festança official" (*a pedido*), *JC*, 22 May 1870.

111. Speeches of Antonio Luiz Dantas de Barros Leite, 15 June, *ASB* (1870), 1:176–77; José Inácio Silveira da Mota and Bernardo de Souza Franco, 20 June, *ASB* (1870), 1:208–14, 215–16; Muritiba, 27 June, *ASB* (1870), 1:248–50.

112. Speech of José Tomás Nabuco de Araújo, 27 June, *ASB* (1870), 1:250–52 (quotes 252). On Nabuco de Araújo's leadership, see Nabuco, *Estadista*, 680.

113. Lei 1766, 8 July 1870, *CLB*.

114. For descriptions of the temple, see "Festa Official," *JC*, 11 July 1870; "Festejos officiaes," *DRJ*, 11 July 1870.

115. For images of the side structures, see Ferrez, "O que ensinam," plate 46; Salles, *Guerra*, 197, 200.

116. Os Gratos Habitantes Supra Mencionados, "Festejos no campo de Sant'Anna" (*a pedido*), *JC*, 20 May 1870. On the fire, see Sena, *Rascunhos*, 415.

117. "Ministro da Guerra" and "Archibancadas," *DRJ*, 10 July 1870; "Archibancadas" (*aviso*), *JC*, 10 July 1870; "Exame das archibancadas," *Diario Official do Imperio do Brasil*, 10 July 1870.

118. "Archibancadas no Campo da Acclamação," *Jornal da Tarde*, 9 July 1870; "Ministerio da Guerra," *A Reforma*, 9 July 1870; "Prevenção!" *A Reforma*, 10 July 1870.

119. The announcement of the date appeared in "Festejos," *JC*, 3 July 1870. The program was published the following day; "Diario Official," *DRJ*, 4 July 1870; "Festejos Officiaes," *Jornal da Tarde*, 4 July 1870; "Festejos," *JC*, 4 July 1870.

120. Alencar, "A festa macarrônica," in *Obra*, 4:1196–1203. Pedro's refusal of this statue is mentioned in speech of José Inácio Silveira da Mota, 20 June, *ASB* (1870), 1:209. On Alencar's criticisms of Pedro, see Barman, *Citizen Emperor*, 259–61.

121. "O jesuitismo de um jornal de grande circulação da corte" and "Festa macarronica," *A Reforma*, 10 and 12 July 1870; *Roleta italiana*; Antônio Tibúrcio Ferreira de Sousa to João Brígido, Rio, 18 July 1870, in Câmara, *Soldado*, 235.

122. "Ao publico," *A Reforma*, 8 July 1870; "Ministerio da Guerra," *A Reforma*, 9 July 1870; "Parte não editorial," *A Reforma*, 6 July 1870. For this criticism, see also "Aos officiaes do 1.º de infantaria" (*a pedido*), *JC*, 10 July 1870.

123. "Ministerio da Guerra," *JC*, 9 July 1870; "Festa official," "A festa," and *folhetim*, *A Reforma*, 10 July 1870.

124. See the advertising for seats in the bleachers and the theater gala in *JC*, 10 July 1870.

125. Etelvino, "O que vai por ahi," *A Comedia Social*, 7 July 1870; "Uma idéa grandiosa" and "Um pensamento patriotico" (*a pedidos*), *JC*, 10 July 1870; "Festejos officiaes" (*a pedido*), *JC*, 30 June 1870.

126. Tibúrcio to Brígido, Rio, 8 June 1870, in Câmara, *Soldado*, 231.

127. "Festejos officiaes," *DRJ*, 11 July 1870; "Festa official," *JC*, 11 July 1870; "Festejos officiaes," *Jornal da Tarde*, 11 July 1870; "Noticias do dia," *Diario Official do Imperio do Brasil*, 12 July 1870.

128. "A opiniao," *A Reforma*, 12 July 1870; "O cantor official," *A Reforma*, 13 July 1870; "The 'Official Rejoicing,' " *The Anglo-Brazilian Times*, 23 July 1870; Etelvino, "O que vai por ahi," *Comédia Social*, 14 July 1870; Hadfield, *Brazil*, 35.

129. *Roleta*, 3–4, 15–16 (quote 4).

130. Etelvino, "O que vai por ahi," *Comédia Social*, 14 July 1870; *Semana Illustrada*, 17 July 1870; *Vida Fluminense*, 16 July 1870.

131. See, in *A Reforma*, "Parte Não Editorial," 13 July 1870; "Parte Não Official" and "Esbanjamento (Parte não editorial)," 16 July 1870; "Como foi a festa," 12 July 1870; "Folhetim," 17 July 1870. The *JC*'s assessment of the decorations appears in "Festa official," *JC*, 11 July 1870. For a halfhearted attempt to rebut the opposition criticisms, see *Diario Official do Imperio do Brasil*, 14 July 1870.

132. Etelvino, "O que vai por ahi," *Comedia Social*, 14 July 1870; "O cantor official," *A Reforma*, 13 July 1870; "Os officiaes do exercito e o povo apreciados pelo—*Diario Official*," *A Reforma*, 15 July 1870; "A opinião," *A Reforma*, 12 July 1870; "A falsidade official," *A Reforma*, 15 July 1870; *Roleta*, 10–11; Tibúrcio to Brígido, Rio, 18 July 1870, in Câmara, *Soldado*, 234. On these protests, see also Dória, "Cousas," 267. Correspondents for São Paulo and Santa Catarina newspapers also noted them; Rodrigues, "Guerra," 172–75.

133. "A opinião," *A Reforma*, 12 July 1870; Tibúrcio to Brígido, Rio, 18 July 1870, in Câmara, *Soldado*, 234.

134. Beattie, *Tribute*, 59; Beattie, "Illustrating Race," 190–91.

135. Coaracy, *Memórias*, 333–68; Morales de los Rios Filho, *Rio*, 235; Moreira de Azevedo, *Rio*, 1:247, 2:499–500.

CHAPTER NINE

1. For an analysis that dates the decline to 1868, see Holanda, "Do Império."

2. On the illustrated newspapers, see Silveira, *Batalha*; Távora, *D. Pedro II*; Andrade, *História*; Sodré, *História*, 234–37, 247–53; Balaban, *Poeta*; Lima, *História*, 1:96–131, 2:748; Guimarães, "Henrique Fleiüss"; Maringoni, *Angelo Agostini*.

3. On the *Revista Ilustrada*'s circulation, see Lima, *História*, 1:122. Agostini's independence is noted in Balaban, *Poeta*, 346, 348. For indications of the press's competition, see the memoirs of a journalist in the 1880s, Mattoso, *Cousas*, 128–34.

4. On the fine print, see Albuquerque, *Quando eu era vivo*, 19. On the *JC*'s politics, see Sandroni, *180 anos*, 188. Circulation figures are from Canstatt, *Brasil*, 220n*; Mulhall, *Handbook*, 81 (quote); Levasseur et al., *Brasil*, 121.

5. Needell, *Party*, 293; Binzer, *Alegrias*, 75.

6. Sodré, *História*, 257; Machado, *Vida*, 41. The general 1881 circulation figures are noted by Machado, "Imprensa," 249. The *Gazeta de Notícias* circulation figures are for 1881; Galvão, *Catálogo*, 1:382. *O Paiz* published circulation figures in its masthead in 1886 and 1889; the remark about its ranking appeared in its issue of 1 Sep. 1889. I know of no data on total newspaper circulation.

7. "Typos e costumes," *Brazil Illustrado* 7 (1887): 112.

8. Sodré, *História*, 265–67; Magalhães Júnior, *Império*, 209–13; Araújo, "Pasquins," 50, 98–100. On Apulco's death, see Holloway, "Defiant Life."

9. Allain, *Rio*, 195; Mac-Érin, *Huit mois*, 119; Montet, *Brésil*, 111–14; Selys-Longchamps, *Notes*, 24; James R. Partridge to Sec. of State, Petrópolis, 22 Sep. 1874, NARS, M-121, roll 43. See also Machado, *Vida*, 239–40; Carvalho, *D. Pedro II*, 84–86.

10. Andrews, *Brazil*, 238; Levasseur et al., *Brasil*, 124.

11. Nabuco, *Estadista*, 677–79, 703–04; Carvalho, *Construção / Teatro*, 186–88; Needell, *Party*, 239–48, 252–53; Barman, *Citizen Emperor*, 211–13, 217–24, 241–43.

12. On the 1871 law, see Needell, *Party*, 272–314; Holanda, "Do Império," 112–15, 125–32, 136–45; Costa, *Da senazla*, 387–93; Conrad, *Destruction*, 90–105; Chalhoub, *Visões*, 26, 141–43, 160–61; Chalhoub, *Machado de Assis*, 139–55, 163–92, 203–06; Pena, *Pajens*; Salles, "Águas."

13. Reform and its limits are key themes in Costa, "1870–1889."

14. Barros, "Questão religiosa"; Groot, *Brazilian Catholicism*, 59–63. Agostini paid much attention to this question; Balaban, *Poeta*, 229–335.

15. Holanda, "Do Império," 176–92, 195–245; Carvalho, *Construção/Teatro*, 359–60; Barman, *Citizen Emperor*, 251–53, 269–73, 285–86, 288–90, 296–97; Carvalho, *D. Pedro II*, 180–85; Graham, *Patronage*, 182–206.

16. Holanda, "Do Império," 18, 258–63.

17. Barman, *Citizen Emperor*, 275–334.

18. For criticisms of the Indian symbol, see França Júnior, *Política*, 280–81; "O Symbolo do Brazil," *Brazil Americano*, 7 July 1875; Koseritz, *Imagens*, 37–38; Beattie, "Illustrating," 195–96.

19. Mello, *República*, 71–76, 94–147. On the Generation of 1870, see also Alonso, *Idéias*; Mota, *Silvio Romero*, 24–35, 54–56; Ventura, *Estilo tropical*, esp. 10–12.

20. Pereira da Silva, *Historia do Brazil*, 155–56; "A Sua Majestade Imperador" (*a pedido*), *JC*, 28 Feb. 1885, quoted in Silva, *Dom Obá II*, 198.

21. *Diario de Noticias*, 9 Sep. 1870; "O Dia Nacional," *A Reforma*, 8 Sep. 1870.

22. "Um anniversario" *A Reforma*, 2 Dec. 1871. The newspaper kept the original Latin: "*Ave Cesar, morituri te salutant.*"

23. "Chronica da quinzena," *Archivo Contemporaneo*, 15 Dec. 1872; Lei 2395, 10 Sep. 1873, *CLB*.

24. Decreto 132, 27 April 1872, *CLB*.

25. Cunha, *Propaganda*, 477, 425, 427; "Beija-mão abolido," *A Republica*, 29 April 1872.

26. Partridge to Sec. of State, Petrópolis, 16 May 1872, NARS, M-121, roll 41.

27. Barman, *Citizen Emperor*, 308–12. For a Brazilian critique of the downtown palace, see Moreira de Azevedo, *Rio*, 1:19. Foreigners' critical comments about the palaces include Canstatt, *Brasil*, 207; North, *Recollections*, 1:185; Kennedy, *Sporting Sketches*, 232; Binzer, *Alegrias*, 60, 63; Koseritz, *Imagens*, 39, 44–45; Hübner, *Diplomata*, 36–38, 51; Carpenter, *Round about Rio*, 245. For a rare favorable comment, see Hilliard, *Politics*, 364.

28. On these cartoons, see Távora, *D. Pedro II*, 40–47; Schwarcz, *Barbas*, 409–14. See also *Corsario*, 27 March 1883; Koseritz, *Imagens*, 41–44; "Marmota da semana," *Diario de Noticias*, 22 April 1887; *Folhinha Laemmert* (1885): 11, 55; (1887): 57; (1888): 36.

29. For examples, see "Anniversario da Constituição do Império," *DRJ*, 26 March 1873; "Corte" and "Audiencia imperial," *JC*, 25 March 1882; "Suas Magestades e Altezas Imperiaes," *JC*, 25 March 1883; "Corte," *JC*, 26 March 1884; "Vinte e cinco de Março," *JC*, 26 March 1886; "Noticiario," *O Paiz*, 26 March 1885; "Local Notes," *The Rio News*, 5 April 1885; "Varias Noticias," *JC*, 24 March 1889. On the Rio–Petrópolis connection, see Carvalho, *D. Pedro II*, 95; Barman, *Princess Isabel*, 164.

30. Pedro II to João Alfredo Correia de Oliveira, 17 March 1875; João Alfredo to Pedro, Andaraí, 21 March 1875; Pedro to João Alfredo, 21 March 1875, *RIHGB* 274 (1967): 185–86.

31. "Grande gala," *DRJ*, 3 Dec. 1873.

32. Cannadine, "Context"; Hull, "Prussian Dynastic Ritual"; Fujitani, *Splendid Monarchy*; Wortman, *Scenarios*.

33. Schwarcz, *Barbas*, 410 (quote), 427.

34. *A Vida Fluminense*, 7 Nov. [sic = Dec.] 1872. On the French Second Empire's celebrations, see Truesdell, *Spectacular Politics*; Hazareesingh, *Saint-Napoleon*, 31–36. On European royalty's view of Pedro, see Barman, *Citizen Emperor*, 238, 282.

35. "Sete de Setembro," *Gazeta da Tarde*, 7 Sep. 1881; *Atirador Franco*, 27 March 1881. See also Botafogo, *Balanço*, a series of articles first published in *A Republica* in 1877.

36. "Theatro Lyrico," *JC*, 8–9 Sep. 1872; "Theatro Lyrico," *Gazeta de Noticias*, 9 Sep. 1878; "Theatros e . . . ," *Gazeta de Noticias*, 25 March 1879; *O Espectador*, 7 Dec. 1884; "Sete de Setembro," *Gazeta de Noticias*, 8 Sep. 1886.

37. Paixão, *Theatro*, 487–88; Sousa, *Teatro*, 1:319–20. For concerns about theater behavior, see "Relatorio do Chefe da Policia da Corte," *anexos* to Brazil, MJ, *Relatorio* (1873): 183–84; (1874): 191; (1875): 263–64; (1880–81): 39; Brazil, MJ, *Relatorio* (1880–81): 203.

38. "Chronica," *A Vida Fluminense*, 10 Sep. 1870.

39. See José Rodrigues Teixeira's *a pedidos* in *JC*, 2 Dec. 1866; 2 Dec. 1867; 7 Sep. and 1 Dec. 1868; 7 Sep. and 2 Dec. 1869; 10 July, 7 Sep., and 2 Dec. 1870; 2 Dec. 1872; 7 Sep. 1874; 6 Sep. and 12 Dec. 1875; 2 Dec. 1877; 2 Dec. 1878. He mentioned his occupation on 2 Dec. 1866 and on 7 Sep. and 1 Dec. 1868.

40. Garcia, *Censor*, 11–13; Antonio José Nunes Garcia, "A luz da verdade," BN/SOR, 084, 5, 12, n.° 15; Lulú Senior [José Ferreira de Sousa Araújo], "Balas de estalo," *Gazeta de Noticias*, 3 Dec. 1885.

41. Price, *Two Americas*, 21; Mac-Érin, *Huit mois*, 115; Lemay, *A bord de la Junon*, 140; Verbrugghe and Verbrugghe, *Forêts vierges*, 113.

42. For a cadet's memoir of service in this detachment, see Barros, "Reminiscências," 89–98.

43. Edmundo, *De um livro*, 1:187; Fort, *Récit*, 289–90; Burke and Staples, *Business*, 41, 60 (for the estimate of 1815); Lamberg, *Brazil*, 281; "Os annos do rei," *Corsario*, 5 Dec. 1882. See also Barman, *Citizen Emperor*, 306.

44. "Topicos do Dia," *O Paiz*, 2 Dec. 1886. On Irajá, see Sacramento Blake, *Diccionario*, 6:164.

45. Tiradentes, "Brazil," *New York Times*, 31 Oct. 1872; Mac-Érin, *Huit mois*, 120; Serbin, *Needs*, 26; Groot, *Brazilian Catholicism*, 25–26.

46. Hadfield, *Brazil*, 172.

47. "Boatos," *A Reforma*, 3 Dec. 1871. For another critical comment on rented coaches, see C[arlos Maximiliano Pimenta] de L[aet], "Microcosmo" (*folhetim*), *JC*, 3 Dec. 1882. On the Fábrica de Cerveja, see Cabral, *Guia*, 364; Coaracy, *Memórias*, 133–34; Reis, "Rio," 55. On *A Reforma*'s readership, see Sodré, *História*, 232, 246.

48. "Pingos e chingos," *O Mequetrefe*, 6 Dec. 1879. On Pedro's insistence on his routines, see Barman, *Citizen Emperor*, 134, 287–88, 297.

49. *Folhetim*, *A Reforma*, 3 Dec. 1876; NEC [Laet], "Folhetim," *DRJ*, 9–10 Sep. 1876.

50. Quesada, *Mis memorias*, 1:123. The *Gazeta da Tarde* made similar observations, "2 de Dezembro," 2 Dec. 1880; "Cortejo no Paço," 25 March 1881. See also "Topicos do Dia," *O Paiz*, 2 Dec. 1886.

51. "Dia 2 de Dezembro," *JC*, 3 Dec. 1875, 1877, and 1878.

52. *Gazeta de Noticias*, 26 March 1881; "Chronica politica," *Brazil Americano*, 11 Sep. 1875; *A Lanterna*, 9 Dec. 1876; *O Intrujão*, 4 Dec. 1883.

53. "Carta independente," *Corsario*, 7 Sep. 1883.

54. Zig-Zag, "Balas de estalo," *Gazeta de Noticias*, 8 Sep. 1883; Otoni, *Autobiografia*, 5; "De noite e de dia," *Gazeta de Noticias*, 2 Dec. 1882.

55. "Outro cortejo," *Carbonario*, 27 March 1882. See also "O cortejo," *Carbonario*, 6 Sep. 1881; "De domingo a domingo (revista semanal)," *O Paiz*, 6 Dec. 1885.

56. Braz, "Muitos parabens," *O Besouro*, 7 Dec. 1878. See also Compadronico, "Ao correr da pena," *Jornal do Povo*, 8 Dec. 1878. On the rumors, see "Dizia-se hontem," *Gazeta de Noticias*, 3 Dec. 1879.

57. "Sete de Setembro," *JC*, 7 Sep. 1870; Sysipho, "Chronica," *A Vida Fluminense*, 5 Dec. 1874; "Exposição Nacional," *Gazeta de Noticias*, 3 Dec. 1875; *Gazeta de Noticias*, 2 Dec. 1881; "Jardim do Campo da Acclamação," *JC*, 8 Sep. 1880; *A Folha Nova*, 2 Dec. 1882.

58. Koseritz, *Imagens*, 187.

59. The baptism's program appeared in *JC*, 1 Dec. 1875; *Gazeta de Noticias*, 1 Dec. 1875. The Belgian diplomat was Ursel, *Sud-Amérique*, 186–87. The U.S. minister likewise judged this an "especial fete"; William A. Purrington to Sec. of State, Rio, 6 Dec. 1875, NARS, M-121, roll 44.

60. *A Vida Fluminense*, 4 Dec. 1875; *Semana Illustrada*, 5 Dec. 1875.

61. Courier, "Chronica," *O Mequetrefe*, 4 Dec. 1875.

62. "Chronica local," *Brazil Americano*, 4 Dec. 1875; "O dia 2 de Dezembro de 1875," *Brazil Americano*, 11 Dec. 1875. The prince's full name appears in "Baptizado," *JC*, 3 Dec. 1875. *O Republicano* also condemned the closing of the doors; 21 Dec. 1875.

63. Rio de Janeiro's first tourist guide gave an official capacity of 1,944 in 1883 but noted that more people could be packed in (Cabral, *Guia*, 371), while the *Almanak Laemmert* reported a capacity of 2,500 in 1883 (Augusto, *Questão*, 118–19). Travelers regularly noted the much larger figure: Koseritz, *Imagens*, 126, 208; Ballou, *Equatorial America*, 165; Vincent, *Round and About in South America*, 237–38; "South American Theatres," *New York Times*, 30 Sep. 1888; Maurício, *Algo*, 188–90. The role of this theater as an elite institution is noted by Coaracy, *Memórias*, 130 (quote), and analyzed for a slightly later period by Needell, *Tropical* Belle Époque, 77–80.

64. "Relatorio do Chefe de Policia da Corte," 41; appendix to Brazil, MJ, *Relatório* (1877). For criticism of the theater closure, see *Mephistopheles*, 27 March 1875; Assumpção, *Narrativas*, 69–77.

65. On the anthems, see the theater advertising in the major newspapers. The audience participation is mentioned in Tiradentes, "Brazil," 26 Sep. 1873; *New York Times*, 25 Oct. 1873.

66. The chief of police is mentioned in this role in *Gazeta de Noticias*, 9 Sep. 1876; "Factos diversos," *A Reforma*, 23 March 1878; "Sete de Setembro," *Gazeta de Noticias*, 8 Sep. 1880.

67. "Theatros e . . . ," *Gazeta de Noticias*, 3 Dec. 1880 (quote); "Dizia-se hontem," *Gazeta de Noticias*, 2 and 4 Dec. 1880; "Como isto é vergonhoso," *Gazeta da Tarde*, 2 Dec. 1880; "Excavações," *Tagarella*, 3 Dec. 1880; Chronica, *Gazeta de Noticias*, 5 Dec. 1880. The only earlier reference to this practice that I know of is "A verdade acerca da festa," *A Republica*, 8 Sep. 1872.

68. *Gazeta de Noticias*, 7 Sep. 1885; "Local Notes," *The Rio News*, 15 Sep. 1885. For other examples, see Zig-Zag, "Balas de estalo," *Gazeta de Noticias*,

8 Sep. 1883; "Sete de Setembro," *Gazeta de Noticias*, 8 Sep. 1884; José Telha [José Ferreira de Sousa Araújo], "Macaquinhos no sotão," *Gazeta de Noticias*, 7 Sep. 1886; "As festas de ante-hontem à noite," *Novidades*, 9 Sep. 1889.

69. *Brazil Americano*, 11 Sep. 1875.

70. Decreto 4,666, 4 Jan. 1871, *CLB*.

71. Pedro to Barral, Rio, 7 Sep. 1880, in *D. Pedro II e a Condessa*, 360. The data on gala programs in this and the following paragraphs are compiled from advertisements in the major dailies.

72. "Noticias locaes," *A Nação*, 1 Dec. 1874; Amorim, "O Cedro Vermelho," in *Teatro*, 167–467. On the play's submission to the competition, see Francisco Gomes do Amorim to Antônio Gonçalves Dias, Lisbon, 27 Aug. 1858, *ABN* 91 (1971): 197–98. For the review, see "Theatro Lyrico," *JC*, 4 Dec. 1874. The advice appears in "A Semana" (*folhetim*), *JC*, 6 Dec. 1874.

73. I have not been able to locate this script, which was apparently not published.

74. "Anniversario da constituição do Imperio," *DRJ*, 26 March 1873; "Theatros e . . . ," *Gazeta da Noticias*, 2 Dec. 1881.

75. "Theatros e . . . ," *Gazeta de Noticias*, 3 Dec. 1880; Pedro to Barral, Rio, 2 Dec. 1880, *D. Pedro II e a Condessa*, 383; *Diario do Brazil*, 4 Dec. 1883; *O Espectador*, 9 Dec. 1883.

76. "Palcos e bastidores," *Gazeta da Tarde*, 25 March 1881.

77. "Dia 2 de Dezembro," *JC*, 3 Dec. 1871.

78. "Noticias locaes," *A Nação*, 1 Dec. 1873. It is not clear whether this was Vasques, *Brasil*, described in Chapter Eight, which ended with an allegory with this title.

79. Campos, *Brasil*; "Noticias locaes," *A Nação*, 1 Dec. 1873.

80. Caminhoá, *Documentos*, 7 (quote), 31–154 (the press debate), 156–66 (the budget and the contract), 33 (the description).

81. Pedro to Barral, Rio, 14 March 1876, in *D. Pedro II e a Condessa*, 160; Moreira de Azevedo, *Rio*, 1:57; Francisco de Azevedo Monteiro Caminhoá to Camara, Rio, 1 May 1890, AGCRJ, 44-1-49, fol. 56r. For a lament about the failure to raise the monument, see "Monumento no Campo da Acclamação" (*a pedido*), *JC*, 23 April 1886.

82. Thomas A. Osborn to Sec. of State, Rio, 27 March 1882, NARS, M-121, roll 47 (quotes); Henry W. Hilliard to Sec. of State, Rio, 3 and 19 Dec. 1878, and 10 May 1879, NARS, M-121, roll 45.

83. Zig-Zag, "Balas de estalo," *Gazeta de Noticias*, 8 Sep. 1883.

84. On the nickname, see Edmundo, *De um livro*, 1:219; Albuquerque, *Quando eu era vivo*, 27; Barman, *Citizen Emperor*, 318; Schwarcz, *Barbas*, 416; Holanda, "Do Império," 236; Jesus, *Visões*, 137.

85. For editorials that articulated these themes, see "Dous de Dezembro," *Diario de Noticias*, 2 Dec. 1870; "2 de Dezembro," *A Nação*, 3 Dec. 1873; "2 de Dezembro," *A Nação*, 1 Dec. 1874; "O dia 2 de dezembro," *A Nação*, 3 Dec. 1875; "Chronica da Semana," *Mephistopheles*, 5 Dec. 1874; *Gazeta de Noticias*, 2 Dec. 1875, 2 Dec. 1876; *DRJ*, 2 Dec. 1875; "Dous de Dezembro," *Illustração Popular*, 2 Dec. 1876; *Jornal da Tarde*, 3 Dec. 1877; "Dous de Dezembro," *O Cruzeiro*, 2 Dec. 1878.

86. *DRJ*, 2 Dec. 1877.

87. Cunha, *Propaganda*, 475–77 (quote 477); "O anniversario," *A Republica*, 2 Dec. 1871.

88. "O Imperador," *A Reforma*, 2 Dec. 1870 (quote); "O natalicio imperial," *A Reforma*, 2 Dec. 1874; "Anniversario imperial," *A Reforma*, 2 Dec. 1875; "Chronica politica," *A Reforma*, 2 Dec. 1876 (quote).

89. Barman, *Citizen Emperor*, 258–61, 314–15; Holanda, "Do Império," 19.

90. "O dia 2 de Dezembro," *A Consciencia Nacional*, 2 Dec. 1877; "Dous de Dezembro," *O Conservador*, 9 Dec. 1879.

91. See, for instance, "2 de dezembro," *Brazil*, 2 Dec. 1883; [José Ricardo] Pires de Almeida, "2 de Dezembro," *Diario de Noticias*, 2 Dec. 1886.

92. "Dous de Dezembro," *JC*, 2 Dec. 1887; "O Sr. D. Pedro II," *JC*, 2 Dec. 1888. See also "O Imperador," *Gazeta da Tarde*, 2 Dec. 1887; "Dois de Dezembro," *Diario de Noticias*, 2 Dec. 1886.

93. "Topicos do Dia," *A Folha Nova*, 2 Dec. 1883; "Anniversario," *Diario do Brazil*, 2 Dec. 1885 (quote).

94. "2 Dezembro," *Gazeta da Tarde*, 3 Dec. 1883; "Ave Cezar!" (*folhetim*), *Gazeta da Tarde*, 2 Dec. 1880; "Excavações," *Tagarella*, 3 Dec. 1880; *Corsário*, 2 Dec. 1880. Tagarela's editor is identified by Araújo, "Pasquins," 87.

95. *Corsario*, 2 Dec. 1882. On Corsário's readership, see Holloway, "Defiant Life," 82. I have not been able to identify King Simon XL.

96. "25 de Março," *JC*, 25 March 1878; "O dia 25 de Março," *A Nação*, 26 March 1873; "Vinte e Cinco de Março," *A Nação*, 24 March 1874; "Vinte e Cinco de Março," *A Nação*, 24 March 1876; *Jornal da Tarde*, 25 March 1870.

97. *DRJ*, 25 March 1870. See also *DRJ*, 25 March 1877.

98. "Boatos," *A Reforma*, 25 March 1871; Dr. Semana, "Badaladas," *Semana Illustrada*, 24 March 1872 (both Joaquim Maria Machado de Assis and Antônio Valentim da Costa Magalhães contributed to this column). For other personifications of the constitution as a woman, see the untitled *a pedido* in *DRJ*, 25 March 1873; L[aet], "Microcosmo," *JC*, 27 March 1881. For one exceptional portryal of the constitution as a sick man, see *O Mequetrefe*, 25 March 1875.

99. "O juramento da Constituição," *A Reforma*, 25 March 1871; "Approximação de Datas," *A Republica*, 25 March 1872.

100. *A Evolução*, 25 March 1886; "Juramento da Constituição," *Brazil*, 25 March 1884; "Festa da Constituição," *Gazeta da Tarde*, 25 March 1881; Hugo Leal, "Homens e factos" (*folhetim*), *Gazeta da Tarde*, 28 March 1881.

101. "25 de Março," *JC*, 25 March 1889. See also "25 de Março," *Gazeta da Tarde*, 26 March 1889; "Anniversario da Constituição," *O Municipio Neutro*, 25 March 1889.

102. "25 de Março," *Tribuna Liberal*, 25 March 1889. See also "A Constituição," *O Paiz*, 25 March 1889.

103. "Sete de Setembro," *JC*, 7 Sep. 1881.

104. For examples of this view, see "O dia de hontem," *A Nação*, 8 Sep. 1872; "7 de Setembro," *O Figaro*, 8 Sep. 1877; "Sete de Setembro," *Diario Fluminense*, 7 Sep. 1884; "Commemoração à Independencia do Brasil," *Gazeta Suburbana*, 7 Sep. 1884.

105. See the editorials, all entitled "Sete de Setembro," in the *JC*'s 7 Sep. issues of 1878, 1880, 1881, 1882, and 1883.

106. *DRJ*, 7 Sep. 1876; "Chronica Fluminense," 9 Sep. 1876, *A Provincia de São Paulo* (São Paulo), 13 Sep. 1876. See also the untitled editorial on 7 Sep. 1877 and "7 de Setembro," *DRJ*, 7 Sep. 1878.

107. *Correio do Brazil*, 9 Sep. 1872; "Sete de Setembro," *Gazeta de Noticias*, 7 Sep. 1881; "Sete de Setembro," *A Folha Nova*, 7 Sep. 1883.

108. Visconde de Porto Seguro [Varnhagen] to Pedro II, Vienna, 16 June 1875, in Varnhagen, *Correspondência*, 432–33; Varnhagen, *Historia da Independencia*, 349–50; Pereira da Silva, *Historia da fundação*, 7:333–36; Pereira da Silva, *Historia do Brazil*, 161–62; Pereira da Silva, *Segundo periodo*, vi–vii, 21–22; Moreira de Azevedo, *Historia*, 12, 149–50.

109. "Sete de Setembro," *Gazeta da Tarde*, 7 Sep. 1887; "Sete de Setembro," *O Paiz*, 7 Sep. 1887.

110. See the editorials entitled "O Dia 7 de Setembro," *Gazeta de Noticias*, 7 Sep. 1875; "Sete de Setembro," *Gazeta de Noticias*, 7 Sep. 1877, 1878, 1879, 1882, 1884, 1886. For other 7 Sep. editorials that celebrated progress, see "Independencia do Brazil," *Diario de Noticias*, 7 Sep. 1870; *O Tupy*, 7 Sep. 1877; *O Cruzeiro*, 7 Sep. 1878; "Sete de Setembro," *Diario do Commercio*, 7 Sep. 1889.

111. *Gazeta da Noite*, 6 Sep. 1879; "Sete de Setembro," *O Rio de Janeiro*, 7 Sep. 1886.

112. "Espectaculo repugnante," *Brazil Americano*, 11 Sep. 1875; "Sete de Setembro," *A Reforma*, 7 Sep. 1877; *Folhetim*, *A Reforma*, 5 Sep. 1875; Frederico Rego, "Sete de Setembro," *A Reforma*, 7 Sep. 1873.

113. "Os 59 annos de existencia nacional," *Diario do Brazil*, 7 Sep. 1881; "Sete de Setembro," *Gazeta da Tarde*, 7 Sep. 1882.

114. "Sete de Setembro," *Gazeta de Noticias*, 7 Sep. 1885. For similar criticisms, see "Sete de Setembro," *A Folha Nova*, 7 Sep. 1883.

115. "O Dia Nacional," *A Reforma*, 8 Sep. 1870; "Sete de Setembro," *A Reforma*, 7 Sep. 1876. See also "Sete de Setembro," *O Paiz*, 7 Sep. 1886.

116. "A Independencia do Brazil," *O Trabalho*, 5 Oct. and 11 Nov. 1879; "Conferencia," *Corsario*, 7 Sep. 1883; [Silvio Romero and Tristão de Alencar Araripe Júnior], *Lucros e Perdas* (Sep. 1883), 1–5; *O Meio*, 7 Sep. 1889.

117. *Revista Illustrada*, 7 Sep. 1878; "A Independencia do Brazil," *O Trabalho*, 7 Sep. and 12 Oct. 1879.

118. [F. Cunha], "Anniversario," *A Republica*, 7 Sep. 1873. This editorial is reprinted in his *Propaganda*, 687–88, where it is incorrectly dated to 1874. See also *Brazil Americano*, 11 Sep. 1875; "O dia 7 de Setembro," *Revolução*, 12 Sep. 1882; "Sete de Setembro," *Corsario*, 7 Sep. 1881; "Sete de Setembro," *Corsario*, 7 Sep. 1883.

119. "Sete de Setembro," *Carbonario*, 6 Sep. 1881.

120. "Sete de Setembro," *Novidades*, 7 Sep. 1888. On *Novidades*'s politics, see Alves, *José do Patrocínio*, 141, 203, 214.

121. Mello Moraes, *Independencia*, 287, 223–27; Tralgabadas [Joaquim Maria Serva Sobrinho], "Ao acaso (chronica semanal)," *Gazeta de Noticias*, 9 Sep. 1877; Veiga, *Primeiro Reinado*, 60–61.

122. Pires de Almeida, *Elogio*.

123. "Uma data memoravel," *A Reforma*, 7 Sep. 1871.

124. [Machado de Assis], "Ao acaso (cronica da semana)," *DRJ*, 25 April 1865.

125. Pedro to Barral, Rio, 24 March 1881, in *D. Pedro II e a Condessa*, 406; A. Torres, "A viagem imperial" (*folhetim*) *Atirador Franco*, 10 April 1881; Gama, *Minhas memorias*, 186–91.

126. Pereira da Silva, *Historia da fundação*, 1:224–25, 4:137–41 (quotes 138), 175–76.

127. "Sete de Setembro," *Gazeta de Noticias*, 7 Sep. 1881.

128. "Seis de março," *O Republico*, 6 March 1854. For another example of this, see "O Septe de Setembro," *Chronica do Imperio* 2 (1876): 3–10.

129. "21 de abril," *Gazeta da Tarde*, 21 April 1882; "7 de Setembro," *Diario de Noticias*, 7 Sep. 1889.

130. "A Independencia do Brazil," *O Trabalho*, 7 Sep. 1879; Mello Moraes, *Independencia*, 64. Varnhagen condemned the movement, *Historia geral*, 1st ed., 2:292–93.

131. Carvalho, *Formação*, 55–73.

132. "O precursor," *A Republica*, 21 April 1872.

133. Souza e Silva, *Historia*, 429–30 (quote on unity), 416 (quote on Tiradentes). On this book, see also McNab, "Decanonização."

134. Romero, *Historia*, 2:771. For an explicit rebuttal of the Instituto's views, already well known before the publication of Joaquim Norberto's book, see Esqueiros, *Processo*, 1, 196–97.

135. Souza e Silva, "Tiradentes," 135–37.

136. Speech and bill of José Mariano Carneiro da Cunha, 25 April 1879, *ACD* (1878), 4:697. The 1878 parliamentary session was delayed and took place during the first months of 1879. For press references to José Mariano's proposal, see "Chronica Nacional," *Folhinha Laemmert* (1880): 102; "Tiradentes!" *Jornal da Noite*, 21 April 1882. In 1883, the Clube Tiradentes petitioned the chamber of deputies to take up the bill, *ACD* (1883), 5:92, but nothing came of this.

137. Thimoteo Antunes, "Nome desconhecido," *Tiradentes* (1883): 1.

138. R[aimundo] T[eixeira] Mendes, "Uma pagina da nossa historia," *A Crença*, 10 June 1875; Mendes, *Patria*, 28, 104–05. On Postivism in Brazil, see Costa, *History*, 82–175; Alonso, *Idéias*, 120–46, 205–22; Fragale Filho, *Aventura*.

139. Silva Jardim, *Salvação*, 19, 21; Silva Jardim, *Tradições*, 8–12, 17–18. For other references to the historically necessary republic, see H. L., "21 de Abril de 1792," *Tiradentes* (1886): 8; C. M., "No dia de hoje," *Tiradentes* (1888): 1.

140. "Cartas de um caipira: Carta 418" (*folhetim*) *JC*, 22 April 1881; "Tiradentes," *Revolução*, 21 April 1881.

141. "Tiradentes," *Atirador Franco*, 29 April 1881 (quote); "A Festa de Tira-Dentes," *Gazeta da Tarde*, 22 April 1881 (which noted the flag without the crown). See also "Anniversario do Tira-Dentes," *A Revelação*, 22 April 1881. On the Clube Tiradentes's founding, see "Acto da installação do Clube Tiradentes em 21 de abril de 1881," *Tiradentes* (1890): 6.

142. "A festa de Tira-dentes," *Gazeta da Tarde*, 22 April 1881.

143. "Tiradentes," *Gazeta da Tarde*, 22 April 1882; "Tiradentes," *Gazeta de Noticias*, 22 April 1882; "Tiradentes," *O Progresso*, 27 April 1882.

144. *Tiradentes* (1882). The BN also holds issues for 1883–86, 1888, 1890, 1893, and 1894.

145. "Tiradentes," *Mequetrefe*, 30 April 1883; *A Folha Nova*, 21 April 1884; "Tiradentes," *Gazeta da Tarde*, 22 April 1885; "21 de abril," *Gazeta da Tarde*, 22 April 1886.

146. "Tiradentes," *Gazeta da Tarde*, 22 April 1885; "Club Tiradentes," *JC*, 21 and 23 April 1885. On the republican deputies, see Pereira da Silva, *Memorias*, 2:285.

147. Filindal [Francisco Filinto de Almeida], "Historia dos Sete Dias," *A Semana*, 25 April 1885; "Tiradentes," *O Paiz*, 21 April 1887.

148. Publicola, "Balas de estalo," *Gazeta de Noticias*, 7 Sep. 1883; Milliet, *Tiradentes*, 82–83.

149. Kirkendall, *Class Mates*, 156–65.

150. "21 de Abril," *Gazeta da Tarde*, 21 April 1886.

151. B. G., "Elle!" (*folhetim*), *Atirador Franco*, 21 April 1881; "O mez de Abril," *Labaro Academico*, 30 April 1874; "Homenagem a Tiradentes," *Corsario*, 21 April 1883.

152. "Tiradentes," *Phalange*, 30 April 1883; Matheus Arrar, "Libertas quae sera tamen," *O Adversario*, 21 April 1884; Musa do Povo [Otávio Hudson], "Joaquim José da Silva Xavier (o Tira-dentes)," *JC*, 21 April 1881; *O Mequetrefe*, 12 Sep. 1876; "21 de Abril," *Gazeta da Tarde*, 21 April 1882; "Tiradentes," *Gazeta de Noticias*, 21 April 1882; "Uma homenagem," *Cruzada*, 1 May 1883; Lannes Costa, "Tiradentes," *O Porvir*, 13 Oct. 1882; "A Independencia do Brasil," *O Trabalho*, 14 Sep. 1879.

153. T. B. M. Castro, "Joaquim José da Silva Xavier (Tiradentes)," *O Adversario*, 21 April 1884. For similar views, see Braulio Cordeiro, "Sete de Setembro," *Echo Popular*, 7 Sep. 1884; Letter from J. A. Pinto Junior, *Gazeta de Noticias*, 10 Sep. 1876.

154. A. V. [Ernesto da Cunha de Araújo Viana], "Tiradentes," *O Esboço*, 21 April 1889. See also Silvestre de Lima, "Tiradentes," *A America* (20 Oct. 1879): 13–15; Lima, *Episodios*, 8–12; *O Tiradentes*, 20 Oct. 1888.

155. *O Tentamen*, 21 April 1883; Jeronymo de Cerqueira, Untitled Article, *Atirador Franco*, 21 April 1881.

156. Ernesto Coutinho, Untitled Article, *Atirador Franco*, 21 April 1881; C. Moreira, Untitled Article, *Atirador Franco*, 21 April 1881; B. Guimarães, "Hymno a Tira-Dentes," *Relampago*, 17 May 1882.

157. "Tiradentes," *O Paiz*, 21 April 1889 (precursor to liberty); "21 de abril," *Gazeta da Tarde*, 21 April 1887 (precursor to independence); "Tiradentes," *O Paiz*, 21 April 1885 (precursor to liberty, independence, and the republic).

158. Haberly, "Mythification," 67–68.

159. Carvalho, *Formação*, 61.

160. Fontino, *Sete de Setembro*, 5; "O Tiradentes," *Gazeta da Tarde*, 21 April 1884. For other examples of this trope, see Cunha, *Propaganda*, 687; "Tiradentes," *O Artista*, 21 April 1883; "Tiradentes," *Gazeta da Tarde*, 21 April

1885; *Labaro Academico*, 30 Sep. 1874; "Sete de Setembro," *Carbonario*, 7 Sep. 1885.

161. *Folhetim*, *A Revelação*, 17 April 1881; "Topicos do Dia," *A Folha Nova*, 8 Sep. 1883.

162. "Viva," *O Besouro*, 7 Sep. 1878.

163. Carvalho, *D. Pedro II*, 27.

164. "A verdade acerca da festa," *A Republica*, 8 Sep. 1872.

165. "Recepção de SS. MM. Imperiaes," *JC*, 25 March 1872.

166. Luiz Guimarães J.^{or}, "Revista do Domingo," *DRJ*, 30–31 March 1872.

167. North, *Recollections*, 1:117; Luiz Guimarães J.^{or}, "Revista do Domingo," *DRJ*, 30–31 March 1872; "South America," 4 April 1872, *Boston Daily Globe*, 25 May 1872 (the US$50,000 profit); "Return of the Emperor . . . ," 25 April 1872, *New York Times*, 21 May 1872 (the US$150,000 gas bill). For a Brazilian critique of gas company profits, see "A quem a festa agradou mais" (cartoon), *O Mosquito*, 6 April 1872.

168. "South America," 4 April 1872, *Boston Daily Globe*, 25 May 1872; C. Ferreira, "Sem título" (*folhetim*), *Correio do Brazil*, 31 March 1872; Partridge to Sec. of State, Petropólis, 8 April 1872, NARS, M-121, roll 41.

169. "Festejos para a recepção de Suas Magestades Imperiaes," *DRJ*, 30–31 March 1872; "Regresso de SS. MM. Imperiaes," *JC*, 1–2 April 1872. On the monuments, see also "Supplemento commemorativa dos principaes festejos . . . ," AIHGB, Icon., M4, Gav. 1, n.° 9.

170. "Noticiario," *DRJ*, 4 April 1872.

171. Z, Untitled Editorial, *A Vida Fluminense*, 6 April 1872; *O Mosquito*, 6 April 1872.

172. "Viagem de SS. MM. Imperiaes," *JC*, 1–2 April 1872; "Festejos," *JC*, 4 April 1872.

173. "Vivão SS. MM. Imperiaes," *JC*, 1–2 April 1872.

174. "Theatro," *Correio do Brazil*, 5 April 1872; *Semana Illustrada*, 7 April 1872 (which published Rozendo Moniz's poem, "Ave Imperator"); "Theatro Lyrico," *JC*, 5 April 1872; Luiz Guimarães Jr., "A volta do imperador" (*folhetim*), *DRJ*, 5 April 1872; A. de A., "Assumpto de varias côres," *A Vida Fluminense*, 6 April 1872. The worries about the play's reception appear in C. Ferreira, "Festas de Recepção e o 'Avarento' " (*folhetim*), *Correio do Brazil*, 7 April 1872. On the yawns, see "Um espectaculo de grande gala," *A Republica*, 5 April 1872.

175. Cartoon, *A Vida Fluminense*, 20 April 1872; "Altos e baixos" (*folhetim*), *JC*, 31 March 1872; Cunha, *Propaganda*, 414–17.

176. C. Ferreira, "Festas . . . ,' " *Correio do Brazil*, 7 April 1872; "Um espectaculo de grande gala," *A Republica*, 5 April 1872.

177. "Inauguração da estátua de José Bonifácio," *Folhinha Laemmert* (1874): 3–8; O Oyapock e o Amazonas, "Estatua de Jose Bonifacio" (*a pedido*), *JC*, 10 April 1862.

178. Commissão to Camara, Rio, 28 Jan. 1862, AGCRJ, 43-1-69, fol. 2r.

179. "Revista da quinzena," *A Mocidade*, 15 Feb. 1863; "A estatua de José Bonifacio," *A Crença*, 6 Sep. 1863.

180. On the composition of the new committee, see "Estatua de José Bonifácio," *JC*, 3 Sep. 1872. On Bom Retiro, see Barman, *Citizen Emperor*, 54; on Homem de Mello and Macedo, see Sacramento Blake, *Diccionario*, 2:463–67, 4:183–90.

181. "Inauguração . . . ," *Folhinha Laemmert* (1874): 10–12; Ferreira, *Guia*, 50.

182. "Estatua de José Bonifacio," *A Republica*, 6 April 1872.

183. "Estatua de José Bonifacio" (avisos), *JC*, 6 Sep. 1872; "Programma . . . ," *Diario de Noticias*, 3 Sep. 1872; "Estatua de José Bonifacio," *JC*, 3 Sep. 1872.

184. Tiradentes, "Brazil," *New York Times*, 31 Oct. 1872. The rest of this account is compiled from *JC*, 8–9 Sep. 1872; "Estatua de José Bonifacio," *Correio do Brazil*, 9 Sep. 1872; "Inauguração," *A Nação*, 8 Sep. 1872; "Farça oficial," *A Republica*, 8 Sep. 1872.

185. "Estatua de José Bonifacio" (*a pedido*), *JC*, 7 Sep. 1872; *JC*, 8–9 Sep. 1872; F. J. Betencourt da Silva, "A inauguração da estatua de Jose Bonifacio, e o pardo Adão" (*a pedido*), *JC*, 12 Sep. 1872; "Chronica nacional," *Folhinha Laemmert* (1874): 161.

186. "Inauguração . . . ," *Folhinha Laemmert* (1874): 17–21 (quote 19). The text of the speech also appears in Aguiar, *Apontamentos*, 28–31 (quote, 29–30).

187. "Sete de Setembro," *JC*, 7 Sep. 1872. For much the same argument, see the untitled editorial and "Chronica" in *A Vida Fluminense*, 7 Sep. 1872; "Sete de Setembro e José Bonifácio," *O Mosquito*, 7 Sep. 1872; "Sete de Setembro," *O Movimento*, 7 Sep. 1872; "A José Bonifacio de Andrada e Silva," *D. Pedro II*, 7 Sep. 1872; Moreira de Azevedo, *Historia*, 301; *Correio do Brazil*, 7 Sep. 1872; *Diario de Noticias*, 10 Sep. 1872. See also Aguiar, *Apontamentos*, 6–27. Aguiar was José Bonifácio's son-in-law.

188. Machado de Assis, "À inauguração da estatua de José Bonifacio," *JC*, 7 Sep. 1872; Homem de Mello, *Discursos*, 17–21 (quote 20).

189. "A farça imperial," *A Republica*, 7 Sep. 1872. See also Esqueiros [Pinto], *Processo*, 1.

190. "Noticias," *Centro Academico*, 6 Sep. 1872; "Estatua," *A Republica*, 8 Sep. 1872; "Farça official," *A Republica*, 8 Sep. 1872.

191. Esqueiros [Pinto], *Martyres*, 7, 111. On Pinto, see Sacramento Blake, *Diccionario*, 1:60.

192. Pereira da Silva, *Historia da fundação*, 7:279–80, 282–83, 292–93, 305–06; "Proh Pudor!" *A Crença*, 20 March 1875.

193. "A farça imperial," *A Republica*, 8 Sep. 1872; "A verdade acerca da festa," *A Republica*, 8 Sep. 1872.

194. "As duas estatuas" and "Jose Bonifacio de Andrada e Silva," *A Reforma*, 7 Sep. 1872.

195. *A Vida Fluminense*, 15 Sep. 1872; G. de A., "A estatua de José Bonifacio de Andrada e Silva," *O Futuro*, 15 Sep. 1872; Argesilio, "Folhetim da *Nação*," *A Nação*, 9 Sep. 1872; "Cartas de um caipira, carta XIV" (*folhetim*), *JC*, 12 Sep. 1872.

196. "Estatua de Tiradentes," *A Republica*, 13 Sep. 1872.

197. Um democrata, "Mais estatua!" (*a pedido*), *JC*, 13 Sep. 1872.

198. "Monumento a Tira-dentes," *Semana Illustrada*, 15 Sep. 1872; "Estatua de Tiradentes," *D. Pedro II*, 25 Sep. 1872; "Estatua a Tira-dentes," *O Futuro*, 1 Oct. 1872; "Tiradentes," *O Tupy*, 5 Oct. 1872; Gouvea, *Ao povo*.

199. "Chronica," *Archivo Contemporaneo*, 15 Feb. 1873; Souza e Silva, "Tiradentes," 138.

200. Sacramento Blake, *Diccionario*, 7:24; Aquino Fonseca, "Um graveto . . . de historia patria," *Tiradentes* (1883): 3; L. L., "A justiça da posteridade," *Tiradentes* (1883): 3. Curiously, the laments in the 1880s about the lack of a Tiradentes statue rarely refer to Gouveia's campaign: "Tiradentes," *Gazeta de Noticias*, 21 April 1881; Cantumirim, "Ephemerides," *Gazeta de Noticias*, 21 April 1887; "Tiradentes," *Gazeta da Tarde*, 21 April 1888; "Tiradentes," *O Paiz*, 21 April 1889.

201. "Folhetim," *A Reforma*, 7 Sep. 1873; "Folhetim," *DRJ*, 14 Sep. 1873. For later references to the darkened statue, see *O Mequetrefe*, 9 Sep. 1875; Zig-Zag, "Balas de estalo," *Gazeta de Noticias*, 8 Sep. 1883; Julio X. S. Moura, "José Bonifacio de Andrada e Silva," *Gazeta Suburbana*, 7 Sep. 1884.

202. "Monumento historico no Largo de S. Francisco . . . ," *Brazil Historico*, 5 Aug. 1873; Mello Moraes, *Independencia*, 100–37, 180–223, 299–305. The quotation is from the book's unpaginated preface. See also Veiga's 1877 criticisms, *Primeiro Reinado*, 55–56.

203. The daily press extensively covered the ceremonies, *DRJ*, *Gazeta de Noticias*, and *JC*, 26, 27, and 28 Sep. 1877. Carpenter reported on the ceremony in "Brazil," *Chicago Daily Tribune*, 8 Nov. 1877 (in which he estimated the cost); he also wrote about it in his novel, *Round about Rio*, 240–44. Texeira's *a pedido* is "Chegada de SS. MM. Imperiaes," *JC*, 26 Sep. 1877. The criticism of the Guarda Velha arch appears in *Revista Illustrada*, 22 Sep. 1877; it is also described in "Festejos," *DRJ*, 26 Sep. 1877.

204. Cartoon, *Revista Illustrada*, 22 Sep. 1877.

205. On the drought and relief efforts, see Greenfield, *Realities*.

206. *JC*, 27 Sep. 1877; "Noticiario," *Jornal da Tarde*, 27 Sep. 1877; "Chegada de SS. MM. Imperiaes," *Gazeta de Noticias*, 27 Sep. 1877; "Desembarque de Suas Magestades Imperiaes," *DRJ*, 27 Sep. 1877. On the later Te Deums and levee, see "Noticiario," *DRJ*, 28 Sep. 1877; "Regresso de SS. MM. Imperiaes," *JC*, 29 Sep. 1877.

207. C[arpenter], "Brazil," *Chicago Daily Tribune*, 8 Nov. 1877; França Júnior, *Folhetins*, 136–41.

208. Um Negociante, "Festejos" (*a pedido*), *JC*, 2 Oct. 1877. For criticisms of the cost, see A. Gil, Untitled editorial, *Revista Illustrada*, 1 Sep. 1877; Tancredo, "A cidade adorna-se," *Comedia Popular*, 22 Sep. 1877; "Carnaval áulico," *Revista Illustrada*, 22 Sep. 1877; E. V. S., "O regresso do rei," *A Republica*, 16 Sep. 1877.

209. "O regresso de suas magestades," *A Republica*, 16 Sep. 1877.

210. Ille, "Revista semanal" (*folhetim*), *JC*, 30 Sep. 1877; "Manumissões," *JC*, 28 Sep. 1877.

211. Caption to cover cartoon, *Revista Illustrada*, 13 Sep. 1877; Bastos, "Tam-Tam," *Comédia Popular*, 3 Oct. 1877.

212. "Cartas de um caipira, carta 275° (1.ª carta)" (*folhetim*), *JC*, 28 Sep. 1877. See also A. Gil, untitled editorial, *Revista Illustrada*, 29 Sep. 1877.

213. "Dono e Senhor," *A Republica*, 27 Sep. 1877; *DRJ*, 27 Sep. 1877 (quote); "O Cidadão Imperial," *Jornal da Tarde*, 26 Sep. 1877.

214. "De domingo a domingo (revista semanal)," *O Paiz*, 27 March 1887. For similar analysis, see Souvenir, "Na Rua do Ouvidor," *Diario de Noticias*, 3 Dec. 1887.

215. "De domingo a domingo (revista semanal)," *O Paiz*, 27 March 1887. The Offenbach reference is to *La Belle Hélène* (1864), which parodies Helen's elopment with Paris. The seer, Colchas (Calchas), advised the Greeks in the ensuing Trojan War.

CHAPTER TEN

1. Barman, *Citizen Emperor*, 346; Schwarcz, *Barbas*, 438, 448, 450; Carvalho, *D. Pedro II*, 178.

2. Chalhoub, *Visões*, 179–86.

3. Jesus, *Visões*, 36–39.

4. Abreu, *Império*, 334, 385; Schwarcz, *Barbas*, 519–25.

5. Mello, *República*, 185–88.

6. Schwarcz, *Barbas*, 518. See also Mello, *República*, 189.

7. On the Vintem Riot, see Jesus, *Visões*, 123–38; Graham, "Vintem Riot"; Balaban, *Poeta*, 363–91. On Pedro's reaction, see Carvalho, *D. Pedro II*, 176; Barman, *Citizen Emperor*, 290; Holanda, "Império," 237.

8. *Gazeta de Noticias*, 26 March 1881.

9. On street politics, see Mello, *República*, 19–44.

10. Hübner, *Diplomata*, 86–87, 163–64; Barman, *Citizen Emperor*, 352.

11. The last indication of this society's activities are "Chronica geral," *A Reforma*, 7 Sep. 1870; "Sociedade Festival Sete de Setembro," *DRJ*, 7 Sep. 1870.

12. On the Castelo celebrations, see "Revista diaria," *Diario da Tarde*, 6 Sep. 1878; *Gazeta de Noticias*, 6 Sep. 1878; petition of Moradores do Morro do Castello to Camara, Rio, 28 Aug. 1878, AGCRJ, 43-3-68, fol. 20. On the Glória celebrations, see *Gazeta de Noticias*, 9 Sep. 1876; "Festejos no dia 7 de Setembro," *JC*, 7 Sep. 1877.

13. "Festejos em S. Christovão," *JC*, 10 Sep. 1888; "O Sete de Setembro em S. Christovão," *Diario de Noticias*, 10 Sep. 1888.

14. "Passeio Publico," *Gazeta de Noticias*, 2 Dec. 1877.

15. A. de A., "Assumptos de varias cores," *A Vida Fluminense*, 9 Sep. 1871; "Festejos," *DRJ*, 8 Sep. 1873; "Sete de Setembro," *Gazeta da Tarde*, 7 Sep. 1881.

16. Mello Moraes Filho, *Festas*, 151.

17. Advertisement, *JC*, 6 Sep. 1870. On the gas lighting, see the society's petition to Camara, 18 Aug. 1870, AGCRJ, 43-1-64, fol. 28; Manager, Rio de Janeiro Gas Company, to Camara, 18 Aug. 1870, AGCRJ, 43-3-64, fol. 23; Gamboa to Camara, Rio, 18 Jan. 1873, AGCRJ, 43-3-68, fol. 2.

18. "Sete de setembro," *JC*, 8 Sep. 1870.

19. "Sete de setembro," *JC*, 6 Sep. 1871; "Sete de Setembro," *Jornal da Tarde*, 5 Sep. 1871; "Festejos," *Jornal da Tarde*, 6 Sep. 1871.

20. "Dia 7 de Setembro," *JC*, 4 Sep. 1872; "Noticias locaes," *A Nação*, 9 Sep. 1873.

21. Advertising, *JC*, 6 Sep. 1874; "Sete de Setembro," *JC*, 8 Sep. 1874.

22. "Sete de Setembro," *JC*, 8 Sep. 1883; "Sete de Setembro," *JC*, 8 Sep. 1885. A later *cronista* also recalled that Gamboa regularly led the cheers; "Chronica da semana," *Gazeta de Noticias*, 9 Sep. 1888.

23. "Sete de setembro," *JC*, 8–9 Sep. 1871; "Anniversario da Independencia," *Correio do Brazil*, 9 Sep. 1872; *JC*, 8–9 Sep. 1872; "Sociedade Commemorativa da Independencia do Imperio," *JC*, 6 Sep. 1875; "Sete de setembro," *DRJ*, 8 Sep. 1875.

24. "Chronica da semana," *Mephistopheles*, 11 Sep. 1875. For other comments on Gamboa's baggy pants, see "Chronica da Semana," *Gazeta de Noticias*, 11 Sep. 1887; "Collaboração," *Corsario*, 7 Sep. 1881. Others also noted later that he did most of the society's work; "Chronica da Semana," *Gazeta de Noticias*, 8 Sep. 1889.

25. Advertising, *Diario de Noticias*, 5 Sep. 1872; Advertising, *JC*, 6 Sep. 1873; "S. C. da Independencia do Imperio," *Jornal da Tarde*, 9 Sep. 1871. For a later accusation of a government subsidy, see "7 de setembro," *Corsario*, 3 Sep. 1882.

26. Ferreira da Rosa, "Memorial," 88; Ferreira da Rosa, *Prosa*, 6:24–25; "7 de Setembro," *O Mequetrefe*, Sep. 1892.

27. See his petitions and service record in AHEx/RQ, A-58-1815.

28. The list of directors' names was compiled from the *Almanak Laemmert* (1872–77, 1881–86) and from the society's newspaper advertisements.

29. Sacramento Blake, *Diccionario*, 2:60.

30. A. Barros, *Liceu*, 15–17, 34.

31. Moreira de Azevedo, *Rio*, 2:107, 109, and plate between 2:184–85; Sacramento Blake, *Diccionario*, 3:3–4; Hahner, *Poverty*, 97; Barros, *Liceu*, 111–12.

32. *Almanak Laemmert* (1875): 511.

33. *Folhetim, DRJ*, 13 Sep. 1874; "Festejos," *A Nação*, 8 Sep. 1872. See also *Gazeta de Noticias*, 8 Sep. 1875; "Chronica," *Vida Fluminense*, 12 Sep. 1874.

34. Américo Rodrigues Gamboa to Alexandre José de Mello Moraes, [Rio], 21 Oct. 1872, in Mello Moraes, *Independencia*, 353.

35. Mello Moraes to Gamboa, [Rio, 23 Oct. 1872], in Mello Moraes, *Independencia*, 353–54. It is not clear how Gamboa and his companions were to draw these conclusions from the disorganized *História do Brasil*, which consists mostly of documents interspersed with Mello Moraes's sparse comments; Mello Moraes, *História*. There are a few criticisms of Pedro and José Bonifácio in the second volume, 2:47, 48, 335–36, 440.

36. "Estatutos da Sociedade Comemorativa da Independencia do Imperio," AN/GIFI, Conselho de Estado, Seção de Negócios do Império, cx. 552, pac. 2, env. 2, doc. 27, fols. 7, 8, 11. On army pay, see Schulz, *Exército*, 211.

37. Viscount of Souza Franco, Marquis of Baependy, and Viscount Bom Retiro to Pedro, 22 Aug. 1874, AN/GIFI, Conselho de Estado, Seção Negócios do Império, cx. 552, pac. 2, env. 2, doc. 27, fol. 2r.

38. "Sociedade Commemorativa da Independencia do Imperio," *JC*, 1 Oct. 1874.

39. Compare the listing in *Almanak Laemmert* (1876): 538 with the program published in *Gazeta de Noticias*, 6 Sep. 1876 (which mentioned the new officers).

40. *Revista Illustrada*, 8 Sep. 1877; "Festejos da Independencia," *DRJ*, 6 Sep. 1878; "Festejos," *DRJ*, 7 Sep. 1878. The rain is noted in D. Filho, "A viagem imperial," *O Besouro*, 14 Sep. 1878.

41. *Almanak Laemmert* (1877), 545. Silveira is listed with the other judges, *Almanak Laemmert* (1877), 144. Lima's biography appears in Sacramento Blake, *Diccionario*, 1:14.

42. First Secretary, Sociedade Independencia, to Camara, Rio, 29 Aug. 1876, AGCRJ, 43-3-68, fol. 16; *Gazeta de Noticias*, 6 Sep. 1876; "Independência do Imperio," *DRJ*, 6 Sep. 1876; "Sete de Setembro," *JC*, 6 Sep. 1876; *Diario de Noticias*, 6 Sep. 1877.

43. "Independencia do Imperio," *DRJ*, 8 Sep. 1876; [Joaquim Maria Machado de Assis], "Historia de quinze dias," *Illustração Brasileira*, 15 Sep. 1876.

44. Cabral, *Guia*, 366–67.

45. "Noticiario," *O Domingo*, 15 Sep. 1878; C[arlos Maximiliano Pimenta] de L[aet], "Microcosmo" (*folhetim*), *JC*, 7 Sep. 1879; Alter, "Chronicas fluminenses," *Revista Illustrada*, 10 Sep. 1881; "Chronica," *Gazeta de Noticias*, 11 Sep. 1881.

46. "Sete de Setembro," *Gazeta de Noticias*, 8 Sep. 1882; Cont. Oscar, "Reclamação," *O Mequetrefe*, 10 Sep. 1882. For similar complaints, see A., Letter to the Editor, Botafogo, 7 Sep., *Gazeta Suburbana*, 7 Sep. 1884; Ferreira da Rosa, *Prosa*, 6:25.

47. "Chronica," *Gazeta de Noticias*, 17 Sep. 1882; L[aet], "Microcosmo," *JC*, 10 Sep. 1882; Koseritz, *Imagens*, 187; "Chronica da Semana," *Gazeta de Noticias*, 7 Sep. 1884.

48. "Dia a dia," *Gazeta da Tarde*, 7 Sep. 1886.

49. Menezes, *Dicionário*, 331; Sacramento Blake, *Diccionario*, 6:321; Hahner, *Poverty*, 76.

50. "Chronica da Semana," *Gazeta de Noticias*, 9 Sep. 1888. For other references to Garcia, see "Chronica da Semana," *Gazeta de Noticias*, 8 Sep. 1889; Violino, "Reportagem parnasiana," *Diario de Noticias*, 6 Sep. 1886. Garcia did not rate an entry in Sacramento Blake's *Diccionario*.

51. L[aet], "Microcosmo," *JC*, 7 Sep. 1879; Andrews, *Brazil*, 57.

52. Edmundo, *Livro*, 1:66.

53. Koseritz, *Imagens*, 187.

54. In addition to the references to "*povo*" above, see *Diario de Noticias*, 9 Sep. 1870; "Sete de Setembro," *JC*, 8 Sep. 1870; *JC*, 8–9 Sep. 1872; *A Nação*, 10 Sep. 1875; "As duas mentiras (7 de Setembro)," *O Mequetrefe*, 9 Sep. 1875; *Gazeta de Noticias*, 9 Sep. 1877; Mariani, "Cousas e lousas," *O Trabalho*, 14 Sep. 1879; "Sete de Setembro," *Gazeta de Noticias*, 8 Sep. 1881; "A festa da Independencia," *Gazeta da Tarde*, 7 Sep. 1882; "Sete de Setembro," *Gazeta de Noticias*, 8 Sep. 1883; "Sete de Setembro," *Gazeta de Noticias*, 8 Sep. 1884.

55. "Em familia," *Illustração do Brazil*, 15 Sep. 1877.

56. *Distracção*, 12 Sep. 1885.

57. "A Noite de Ante-Hontem," *Gazeta de Noticias*, 8 Sep. 1884.

58. Koseritz, *Imagens*, 186, 187. Historians who have commented on Koseritz's account have been unaware of this festival's nature, and therefore, misinterpret it as a pretext for celebrating or as an example of government-provided entertainment; Schwarcz, *Barbas*, 257; Mota, *Sílvio Romero*, 58–59.

59. Marcos Valente [Antônio Valentim da Costa Magalhães], "Historia dos quinze dias," *A Semana*, 11 Sep. 1886; L[aet], "Microcosmo," *JC*, 13 Sep. 1885. For other references to pickpockets, see "Carta," *Corsario*, 11 Sep. 1883; "Ecos da Corte," *A Provincia de São Paulo* (São Paulo), 10 Sep. 1886.

60. NEC [Laet], "Folhetim," *DRJ*, 9–10 Sep. 1876; Fantasio, "Chronica," *A Cigarra*, 12 Sep. 1895.

61. NEC [Laet], "Folhetim," *DRJ*, 9–10 Sep. 1876.

62. "Chronica da Semana," *Gazeta de Noticias*, 12 Sep. 1886; see also José Telha [José Ferreira de Araújo], "Macaquinhos no sotão," *Gazeta de Noticias*, 7 Sep. 1886; "Dia a dia," *Gazeta da Tarde*, 7 Sep. 1886; Ferreira da Rosa, *Prosa*, 6:26–27; "Ecos da Corte," *A Provincia de São Paulo* (São Paulo), 10 Sep. 1886.

63. L[aet], "Microcosmo," *JC*, 12 Sep. 1886.

64. In addition to the previous notes, see Box, "Cogitemos," *Distracção*, 4 Sep. 1886; "Dia a dia," *Gazeta da Tarde*, 7 Sep. 1886; "Chronica da semana," *Gazeta de Noticias*, 8 Sep. 1889; D. Demetrio, "Chronica," *Rua do Ouvidor*, 10 Sep. 1898.

65. Cunha, *Ecos*, 154–55, 159–60.

66. "O dia 7," *Revolução*, 12 Sep. 1882. This article has also been analyzed by Jesus, *Visões*, 47–48. See also "Sete de Setembro," *Corsario*, 7 Sep. 1881.

67. Oscar de Castro, "Viva a Independencia," *O Pharol*, 7 Sep. 1885.

68. "Sete de Setembro," *O Pharol*, 7 Sep. 1886; T. Tupy, "Sete de Setembro," *Labaro Academico*, 15 Sep. 1874.

69. Carlos Ferreira, "Folhetim Sem Titulo," *Correio do Brazil*, 9 Sep. 1872; "As duas mentiras," *O Mequetrefe*, 9 Sep. 1875; Fontino, *Sete de Setembro*, 4, 8.

70. Manduca de Sá, "Sete de Setembro," *Distracção*, 5 Sep. 1885; João Bigode, "Balas de estalo," *Gazeta de Notícias*, 7 Sep. 1885.

71. For three examples, one from each day of national festivity, see "Diversas occurencias," *JC*, 4 Dec. 1872; "Capoeiras," *JC*, 8 Sep. 1874; *Gazeta de Noticias*, 26 March 1882.

72. "Capoeiras," *JC*, 3 Dec. 1875; "Ainda e sempre os capoeiras," *JC*, 9 Sep. 1887; "Capoeiras," *Gazeta da Tarde*, 7 Sep. 1887.

73. "Capoeiras," *JC*, 8 and 9 Sep. 1884.

74. Soares, *Negregada instituição*, 212–17, 290–92.

75. Holloway, "Healthy Terror," 665, 670; Soares, *Negregada instituição*, 79–83; Assunção, *Capoeira*, 87–93.

76. Verbrugghe and Verbrugghe, *Forêts*, 113.

77. "Guerra aos capoeiras!" *Diario de Noticias*, 5 Sep. 1885; "Fêtes au 7 Septembre," *Le Sud-Américaine*, 13 Sep. 1885; "Já sei, já sei," *Já Sei, Já Sei* 3 ([Sep.] 1885); A. R., "Sete de Setembro," *Distracção*, 5 Sep. 1885; Filindal [Filinto de Almeida], "Historia dos sete dias," *A Semana*, 12 Sep. 1885. On capoeira challenges, see Abreu, *Capoeiras*, 3–4.

78. Soares, *Negregada institutição*, 295–66; Assunção, *Capoeira*, 82–83; Talmon-Chvaicer, *Hidden History*, 80–86.

79. Soares, *Negregada instituição*, 207, 241–46.

80. Talmon-Chvaicer, *Hidden History*, 68; Desch-Obi, *Fighting*, 165, 189–90.

81. The following composite account is based on "Independencia do Imperio," *DRJ*, 9–10 Sep. 1876; "Conflicto serio," *JC*, 9–10 Sep. 1876; "Grave conflicto," *Gazeta de Noticais*, 10 Sep. 1876. This incident has also been analyzed by Jesus, *Visões*, 61–62.

82. On the urban guard, see Holloway, *Policing*, 231–40.

83. *Gazeta de Noticias*, 11 Sep. 1876. On military personnel involved in *capoeira* and conflicts among corporations, see Holloway, *Policing*, 140–52, 266–70; Assunção, *Capoeira*, 84–85; Soares, *Negregada instituição*, 83–87, 210.

84. [Machado de Assis], "Historia de Quinze Dias," *Illustração Brasileira*, 15 Sep. 1876.

85. Carpenter, *Round about Rio*, 207, 203, 204.

86. "Ecos da Corte," *A Provincia de São Paulo* (São Paulo), 10 Sep. 1886; "Chronica da Semana," *Gazeta de Noticias*, 9 Sep. 1888 (quote); Fantasio, "Chronica," *A Cigarra*, 12 Sep. 1895.

87. *Diario de Noticias*, 9 Sep. 1870; "Emancipação," *JC*, 10 Sep. 1870; "Liberdade," *JC*, 3 Dec. 1875; "Manumissões," *Gazeta de Noticias*, 9 Sep. 1882; "Manumissão," *JC*, 8 Sep. 1884.

88. Couty, *Esclavage*, 23; Costa, *Da senzala*, 402.

89. "Sete de Setembro," *JC*, 8 Sep. 1876; "Noticiario," *DRJ*, 8 Sep. 1877; *Gazeta de Noticias*, 8 Sep. 1877.

90. "Atas, Sociedade para Conservação da Data da Independência Nacional" [sic], copy, AGCRJ, 44-4-50, fols. 1–4v.

91. "A semana" (*folhetim*), *JC*, 17 Sep. 1876; NEC [Laet], "Folhetim," *DRJ*, 9–10 Sep. 1876.

92. On this aspect of abolitionism, see Schwarcz, "Dos males," 26, 32–40.

93. Moraes, *Campanha*, 13, 16–19; Conrad, *Destruction*, 135–69; Toplin, *Abolition*, 60–62, 67–69; Bergstresser, "Movement."

94. Costa, *Da senzala*, 387, 404, 412, 429–34; Carvalho, *Construção/ Teatro*, 294; Prado, *Memorial*, 149–53; Machado, *Plano*, 17, 147–58, 166, 243; Castilho, "Abolition," 89, 267; Kittleson, "Campaign," 84, 91, 100–01; Kittleson, "Women," 100, 114; Moraes, *Campanha*, 41.

95. On Ceará's final abolition and the celebrations throughout the country, see Girão, *Abolição*, 179–81; Toplin, *Abolition*, 97–99; Conrad, *Destruction*, 170–82, 186–88; Castilho, "Abolition," 74, 106–14; Ferreira, "Nas asas," 44–59.

96. "25 de Março," *JC*, 26 March 1884; *Gazeta de Noticias*, 25 March 1884; "O dia 25 de março de 1884," *O Imparcial*, 26 March 1884; "Topicos do dia," *A Folha Nova*, 25 March 1884; "Homenagem ao Ceará," *Gazeta da Tarde*, 25 March 1884; *Revista Illustrada*, 29 March 1884; "Summary of News," *Anglo-Brazilian Times*, 1 April 1884; *The Rio News*, 5 April 1884.

97. *Vinte e Cinco de Março*, [25 March] 1884; *O Acarapé*, 25 March 1884; *A Terra da Redempção*, 25 March 1884; *Ceará*, 25 March 1884.

98. Bergstresser, "Movement," 67; Speech of Francisco Antunes Maciel, 9 May, *ACD* (1884), 1:100.

99. "Ano Novo," *Folhinha Laemmert* (1885): 24; "Lapsos de lapis de Friburgo" (*folhetim*), *A Folha Nova*, 30 March 1884.

100. For descriptions of these events, see "25 de Março," *O Correio Familiar*, 28 March 1886; "25 de Março," *O Paiz*, 26 March 1887; "Festival Abolicionista," *Diario de Noticias*, 26 March 1888; "Festival Abolicionista," *Gazeta da Tarde*, 26 March 1888; "Festival Abolicionista," *O Paiz*, 25 March 1888.

101. "25 de Março," *Gazeta da Tarde*, 26 March 1886.

102. For laments about the lack of attention to the charter, see "Chronica da Semana," *Gazeta de Noticias*," 28 March 1886; "Boletim," *O Paiz*, 26 March 1886; "De Domingo a Domingo," *O Paiz*, 28 March 1886.

103. On the 1885 law and its implementation, see Moraes, *Campanha*, 45–147; Mendonça, *Entre a mão*, 29–36; Conrad, *Destruction*, 210–29 (quote 210), 233–37, 263–64; Toplin, *Abolition*, 101–10, 182–85; Costa, *Da senzala*, 417–25, 442–43; Needell, "Brazilian Abolitionism," 238–41, 243–48.

104. Silva, *Camélias*, 11–40.

105. "Topicos do Dia," *O Paiz*, 2 Dec. 1885.

106. Cartoons of Cotegipe as emperor are reproduced in Patrocínio, *Campanha*, 145, 190, 209.

107. Barman, *Princess Isabel*, 178–82; Barman, *Citizen Emperor*, 333–34, 341–42.

108. Rebouças, *Diario*, 312; Silva, *Camélias*, 28–30, 36–38; Daibert, *Isabel*, 122.

109. Silva, *Camélias*, 36; U. Alves, *José do Patrocínio*, 205, 207, 210, 225–26.

110. On the Livro de Ouro's organization, see *The Rio News*, 5 March 1884; Moraes, *Campanha*, 43; Ferreira da Rosa, "Memorial," 66. The hope to end slavery by 1890 appears in "Sete de Setembro," *JC*, 8 Sep. 1887.

111. Castilho and Cowling, "Funding," 89–120. Compare Conrad, *Destruction*, 196–97.

112. "Sete de Setembro," *JC*, 8 Sep. 1887; "[2] de Dezembro 1885," *Diario de Noticias*, 3 Dec. 1885.

113. "7 de Setembro," *Gazeta da Tarde*, 7 Sep. 1887; "Noticiario," *O Paiz*, 3 Sep. 1886.

114. "Sete de Setembro," *JC*, 8 Sep. 1885; "Festa municipal," *Gazeta de Noticias*, 3 Dec. 1885; "Dous de Dezembro," *JC*, 3 Dec. 1886.

115. "Camara Municipal," *O Paiz*, 3 Dec. 1885; "A Festa de Liberdade," *Gazeta de Noticias*, 8 Sep. 1886.

116. Barman, *Princess Isabel*, 170–75; Daibert, *Isabel*, 110–12, 116–17, 125–27, 130–31; Cowling, "Debating," 288–90.

117. For one example, see "Chronica da Semana," *Gazeta de Noticias*, 5 Dec. 1886.

118. Kennedy, *Sporting Sketches*, 227.

119. Castilho and Cowling, "Funding," 95–97; Proudhomme [José do Patrocínio], "Semana Politica," *Gazeta da Tarde*, 4 Dec. 1886; "Em vez de chronica," *Gazeta de Noticias*, 4 Dec. 1887; Otoni, *Autobiografia*, 235–36.

120. Andrews, *Brazil*, 83; "Secção Complexa," *A Nova Politica*, 20 March 1886; *The Rio News*, 5 Dec. 1885.

121. "As alforrias," *Carbonario*, 5 Dec. 1887; "Dous de Dezembro," *Novidades*, 3 Dec. 1887; Barman, *Princess Isabel*, 179; "De Domingo a Domingo," *O Paiz*, 4 Dec. 1887.

122. "Sete de Setembro de 1822," *Diario de Noticias*, 7 Sep. 1885. Lessa's statement appeared on 9 Sep. 1885.

123. These donations were widely reported in the major dailies in early September 1885: *JC*, *Diario de Noticias*, *Gazeta de Noticias*, *O Paiz*, and *Gazeta da Tarde*.

124. Arthur Azevedo, "Chronica Fluminense," *Vida Moderna*, 11 Sep. 1886; "Libertos," *Carbonario*, 4 Dec. 1885; "Interior," *Cidade do Rio*, 3 Dec. 1887; "7 de setembro," *Gazeta da Tarde*, 7 Sep. 1886.

125. L[aet], "Microcosmo," *JC*, 6 Dec. 1885.

126. Blick [João Capistrano de Abreu], "Historietas," *Revista Illustrada*, 12 Dec. 1885.

127. Cartoon, *Revista Illustrada*, 12 Sep. 1885.

128. On the number of slaves freed in previous ceremonies and Pedro's comment, see "Dous de Dezembro," *Gazeta de Noticias*, 3 Dec. 1886. The later manumissions are noted in "Libertação de escravos," *JC*, 3 Dec. 1886; "Noticiario," *O Paiz*, 3 Dec. 1886.

129. "De Domingo a Domingo," *O Paiz*, 5 Dec. 1886; "Dous de Dezembro," *Gazeta de Noticias*, 3 Dec. 1887.

130. The first reports did not editorialize about the incident: "Festa de Liberdade," *Gazeta da Tarde*, 7 Sep. 1886; "Camara Municipal," *Diario de Noticias*, 8 Sep. 1886; "A Festa de Libertação," *Gazeta de Noticias*, 8 Sep. 1886. On Isabel's extra compassion for the white slaves, see José Telha [Ferreira de Araújo], "Macaquinhos no sotão," *Gazeta de Noticias*, 9 Sep. 1886.

131. "Ecos da Corte," *A Provincia de São Paulo* (São Paulo), 10 Sep. 1886; "Topicos do Dia," *O Paiz*, 9 Sep. 1886. A reproduction of this painting appears in Daibert, *Isabel*, plate vi. On its cost, see Castillo and Cowling, "Funding," 99.

132. "Semana politica," *Gazeta da Tarde*, 11 Sep. 1886; José Telha [Ferreira de Araújo], "Macaquinhos no sotão," *Gazeta de Noticias*, 9 Sep. 1886.

133. Arthur Azevedo, "Chronica Fluminense," *Vida Moderna*, 11 Sep. 1886; "De Domingo a Domingo," *O Paiz*, 12 Sep. 1886; Box, "Cogitemos," *Distracção*, 11 Sep. 1886.

134. "Topicos do Dia," *O Paiz*, 9 Sep. 1886; A. Azevedo, "Chronica Fluminense," *Vida Moderna*, 11 Sep. 1886; "Semana Politica," *Gazeta da Tarde*, 11 Sep. 1886. Machado de Assis criticized the council for accepting the lowest bid, "Balas de estalo," *Gazeta de Noticias*, 8 Sep. 1885. On Meireles and Pedro Américo's reputations, see Moreira de Azevedo, *Rio*, 2:209.

135. Albuquerque, *Jogo*, 34–39; Azevedo, *Onda*, 37, 87, 103–04, 139–53, 159; Skidmore, *Black*, 27–64.

136. On the politics of final abolition, see Moraes, *Campanha*, 299–353; Conrad, *Destruction*, 230–73; Needell, "Brazilian Abolitionism," 252–58.

137. Otoni, *Autobiografia*, 278; Andrews, *Blacks*, 39–42.

138. Rebouças, *Diario*, 313; Nabuco, *Diários*, 1:293.

139. Silva, "Law," 451–62; Silva, "Sobre versos," 16–40; Silva, "Integração," 114; Daibert, *Isabel*, 141–60. For photographs of these celebrations, see Lago and Lago, *Coleção*, 292–303. Jesus downplays the popular participation, *Visões*, 165–68, 172–74.

140. Venâncio, *Panfletos*; Moraes, "Abolição," 87–98.

141. Silva, "Law," 452; Tiradentes, "Brazil," *New York Times*, 25 Oct. 1873; Verbrugghe and Verbrugghe, *Forêts*, 112–13. Carpenter described the leaf but did not indicate that it was worn in 1877; *Round about Rio*, 213–14.

142. Silva, "Sobre versos," 28; Silva, "Law," 457; Silva, "Integração," 113; Prado, *Memorial*, 153n560.

143. *ACD* (1888), 1:62, 68; 6:370.

144. "Sete de Setembro," *Diario de Noticias*, 8 Sep. 1888.

145. "Sete de Setembro," *JC*, 7 Sep. 1888. See also "Sete de Setembro," *A Pilheria*, 7 Sep. 1888; Julio Verim, "Sete de Setembro de 1888," *Revista Illustrada*, 8 Sep. 1888.

146. *Carbonario*, 7 Sep. 1888; Personne, "Cousas do Dia," *Cidade do Rio*, 7 Sep. 1888.

147. "Theatros," *O Paiz*, 9 Sep. 1888; "Theatros e . . . ," *Gazeta de Noticias*, 9 Sep. 1888; "Theatro de S. Pedro de Alcantara," *JC*, 9 Sep. 1888; "Echos e notas," *Diario de Noticias*, 9 Sep. 1888. The author was probably Antonio Soares de Souza Júnior, a poet and long-time republican activist; Sacramento Blake, *Diccionario*, 1:318. On changing Brazilian views of Spanish America, see Preuss, *Bridging*, 47–74.

148. Batalha, "Sociedades," 45; Jesus, *Visões*, 93, 106.

149. Proposta, 10 July 1885 (copy), AGCRJ, 44-4-51, fol. 22; *Edital*, *JC*, 5 Sep. 1885. On Pires de Almeida, see Sacramento Blake, *Diccionario*, 5:152.

150. President, Club Regatas Guanabarense, to President, Camara, Rio, 28 July 1885, AGCRJ, 43-3-69, fols. 1–2.

151. "Sete de Setembro," *Diario de Noticias*, 7 Sep. 1885; "Sete de Setembro," *JC*, 8 Sep. 1885.

152. "Dia Sete de Setembro," *Campeão Lusitano*, 12 Sep. 1885; "Sete de Setembro," *Gazeta de Noticias*, 8 Sep. 1885; "Aspecto da cidade," *Diario de Noticias*, 8 Sep. 1885.

153. Informação, Repartição de Ajudante General, Rio, 20 Aug. 1885 (copy), AGCRJ, 43-3-68, fol. 28.

154. "Sete de Setembro," *JC*, 8 Sep. 1885; "Praça da Acclamação," *Diario de Noticias*, 8 Sep. 1885.

155. Jesus, *Visões*, 150–52. On the Porto Alegre *kermesse*, see Kittleson, "Campaign," 93–34; Kittleson, "Women," 104.

156. L[aet], "Microcosmo," *JC*, 13 Sep. 1885; Filindal [Almeida], "Historia dos sete dias," *A Semana*, 5 Sep. 1885. On Pentecost celebrations, see Abreu, *Império*.

157. "Sete de Setembro," *Gazeta de Noticias*, 8 Sep. 1885.

158. Valentim Magalhães, "Independencia . . . e morte," *Diario de Noticias*, 10 Sep. 1885.

159. "O anniversario da Independencia," *O Paiz*, 7 Sep. 1885 (quote); "Sete de Setembro," *JC*, 8 Sep. 1885; L[aet], "Microcosmo," *JC*, 13 Sep. 1885; Fil-

indal [Almeida], "Historia dos sete dias," *A Semana*, 5 Sep. 1885; "Aspecto da cidade," *Diario de Noticias*, 8 Sep. 1885; Allain, *Rio*, 193.

160. "Sociedade Commemorativa da Independencia e do Imperio" (declarações), *JC*, 7 Sep. 1885.

161. "Sete de Setembro," *Carbonario*, 10 Sep. 1886.

162. *RSCII* (1887): 2–3. The problem of the artillery park's location is discussed in "Festejos do dia 7 de Setembro," *JC*, 3 Sep. 1887; L[aet], "Microcosmo," *JC*, 11 Sep. 1887. For a description of this celebration that closely follows the program, see Ferreira da Rosa, *Prosa*, 6:26–34.

163. *RSCII* (1888): 9–11.

164. "Notas do dia," *Diario de Noticias*, 6 Sep. 1887 (French in original); "A Semana" (*folhetim*), *JC*, 10 Sep. 1888.

165. "Discurso . . . ," *RSCII* (1887): 6. On Borges, see Sacramento Blake, *Diccionario*, 4:73, 514.

166. "Chronica da Semana," *Gazeta de Noticias*, 9 Sep. 1888.

167. The names of the society's executive appear in *RSCII* (1887): 1–2; (1888): 5–6.

168. Sacramento Blake, *Diccionario*, 6:84–85.

169. Sacramento Blake, *Diccionario*, 2:404.

170. *RSCII* (1887): 2; Sacramento Blake, *Diccionario*, 2:222, 6:144.

171. *RSCII* (1887): 1–2; (1888): 6. I have not been able to identify any of these women.

172. "Discurso . . . ," *RSCII* (1888): 21–25.

173. "Sete de Setembro," *JC*, 8 Sep. 1885; "Sete de Setembro," *Gazeta de Noticias*, 8 Sep. 1885; "Aspecto da Cidade," *Diario de Noticias*, 8 Sep. 1885.

174. See the *despacho* on Sociedade Commemorativa da Independencia do Imperio to Camara, Rio, 12 Aug. 1887, AGCRJ, 44-4-48, fol. 16v.

175. "Descripção . . . ," *RSCII* (1887): 38–39; "Procissão civica," *Gazeta de Noticias*, 8 Sep. 1887; L[aet], "Microcosmo," *JC*, 11 Sep. 1887; "Procissão civica," *Diario de Noticias*, 8 Sep. 1887.

176. "Como se executou o programma . . . " and "Independencia ou Morte," *RSCII* (1887): 3, 20–32.

177. "Sete de Setembro," *JC*, 8 Sep. 1887; "Chronica da Semana," *Gazeta de Noticias*, 11 Sep. 1887.

178. "Sete de Setembro," *Gazeta de Noticias*, 8 Sep. 1888; "Chronica da Semana," *Gazeta de Noticias*, 9 Sep. 1888; "Sete de Setembro," *JC*, 8 Sep. 1888; "Sete de Setembro," *O Paiz*, 8 Sep. 1888; "Na rua do Ouvidor," *Diario de Noticias*, 8 Sep. 1888; "Sete de Setembro," *Carbonario*, 10 Sep. 1888.

179. *Festa das creanças*, 172–74 (the number of schools), and 165 (transcription from *Diario de Noticias*, 10 July 1888). The statistics on enrolment appear in Brazil, MI, *Relatorio* (1888): 19. For contemporary photographs of schoolchildren's parades, probably taken in May 1888, see Lago and Lago, *Coleção*, 294–95, 306–07.

180. Mello Moraes, *Chronica*, 2:430; Carvalho, "Conferências," 35.

181. For União Operária programs that include Correia, see "Corpo Collectivo União Operária," *Gazeta de Noticias*, 7 Sep. 1883; "Sete de Setembro," *Gazeta de Noticias*, 8 Sep. 1884; "União Operaria," *JC*, 8 Sep. 1885; "Festas e

saráos," *O Paiz*, 7 Sep. 1886. The worker spokesman's occupation is noted by Andrews, *Brazil*, 58.

182. *A Folha Nova*, 6 Sep. 1884; "Manumissões," *Gazeta de Noticias*, 6 Sep. 1884.

183. "Estatutos do Corpo Collectivo União Operária," approved by Decreto 8766, 18 Nov. 1882, *CLB*; *Gazetinha Aguia de Ouro*, 15 Sep. 1882. On the União's social composition, see Hahner, *Poverty*, 91.

184. "Chronica da Semana," *Gazeta de Noticias*, 8 Sep. 1889.

185. Batalha, "Sociedades," 64.

186. "7 de setembro," *O Corsario*, 5 Sep. 1882. In his next issue, he again dismissed Possidônio as an ersatz "artisan"; "O dia 7," *O Corsario*, 11 Sep. 1882. I have not been able to identify Possidônio.

187. "A Independencia," *Gazeta da Tarde*, 9 Sep. 1885; Batalha, *Dicionário*, 79.

188. "As festas de sabbado," *Carbonário*, 10 Sep. 1889.

189. *RSCII* (1888): 29, 31–32.

190. *RSCII* (1887): 35–37; (1888): 39–48.

191. "Sete de Setembro," *JC*, 8 Sep. 1888; "Festas da Independencia," *O Paiz*, 8 Sep. 1887.

192. "Como se executou o programma . . . ," *RSCII* (1887): 4.

193. "Sete de Setembro," *Gazeta da Noticias*, 8 Sep. 1887; "Como se executou o programma . . . ," *RSCII* (1887): 3. See also "Sete de Setembro," *Gazeta de Noticias*, 8 Sep. 1887; "Sete de Setembro," *JC*, 8 Sep. 1887.

194. "Como de executou o programma . . . ," *RSCII* (1888): 12; "Sete de Setembro," *Diario de Noticias*, 8 Sep. 1888; "De Palanque," *Diario de Noticias*, 8 Sep. 1888; "A semana" (*folhetim*), *JC*, 10 Sep. 1888; "Sete de Setembro," *O Paiz*, 8 Sep. 1888.

195. Pompéia, *Crônicas*, 39; Lucano, "Chronica Semanal," *Diario de Noticias*, 10 Sep. 1888.

196. For descriptions of these structures, see "Sete de Setembro," *JC*, 8 Sep. 1888; "Sete de Setembro," *Diario de Noticias*, 8 Sep. 1888.

197. "De palanque," *Diario de Noticias*, 8 Sep. 1888; "Chronica da Semana," *Gazeta de Noticias*, 9 Sep. 1888.

198. Pompéia, *Crônicas*, 39; "A independencia," *Novidades*, 7 Sep. 1888.

199. L[aet], "Microcosmo," *JC*, 11 Sep. 1887.

200. Carvalho, *D. Pedro II*, 200; Schwarcz, *Barbas*, 443–44; Barman, *Citizen Emperor*, 343.

201. "SS. MM. Imperiaes," *Novidades*, 22 Aug. 1888.

202. Lauro, "De monoculo," *Diario de Noticias*, 21 Aug. 1888.

203. For the program, see "Regresso de SS. MM. Imperiaes," *JC*, 21 Aug. 1888. For detailed accounts of the day, see *Gazeta da Tarde*, 22 Aug. 1888; *JC*, 23 Aug. 1888. For a photograph of this ritual, see Lago and Lago, *Coleção*, 304. On the schoolchildren, see Pompéia, *Crônicas*, 33; "Chegada de Suas Magestades Imperiaes," *Novidades*, 22 Aug. 1888.

204. "Chegada de Suas Magestades Imperiaes," *Novidades*, 22 Aug. 1888. For additional descriptions, see "Regresso de SS. MM. Imperiaes," *JC*, 21 Aug. 1888; "Recepção de Suas Magestades," *JC*, 24 Aug. 1888.

205. On the fire brigade's arches, see "Recepção de SS. MM. Imperiaes," *Novidades*, 24 Aug. 1888. Granado Pharmacy is praised in "A chegada de SS. MM. Imperiaes"; "Recepção de Suas Magestades," *JC*, 23 Aug. 1888; "Recepção de SS. MM. Imperiaes," *Novidades*, 23 Aug. 1888.

206. "Regresso de Suas Magestades Imperiaes," *JC*, 25 Aug. 1888.

207. "A subscripção popular do Rio de Janeiro," *JC*, 23 Aug. 1888.

208. Jack, "Notas de um simples," *Novidades*, 27 Aug. 1888; V[alentim] M[agalhães], "Notas à margem," *Gazeta da Tarde*, 23 Aug. 1888; Eloy, o Heróe, "De palanque," *Diario de Noticias*, 24 Aug. 1888.

209. Dr. Allemão, "Chronica," *Revista da Familia Academica* 1:11 (Sep. 1888): 349; "Chegada de Suas Magestades," *Gazeta da Tarde*, 22 Aug. 1888; "A chegada de SS. MM. Imperiaes," *JC*, 23 Aug. 1888; Raul, "A chegada do Imperador," *Revista Illustrada*, 25 Aug. 1888. The names of the ladies and the students are given in "Recepção de Suas Magestades," *JC*, 24 Aug. 1888; "Regresso de Suas Magestades," *JC*, 25 Aug. 1888.

210. Laet, "Entre Montes," *Jornal do Brasil*, 3 April 1913, in *Crônicas*, 292; Vieira Fazenda, "Antiqualhas," *RIHGB* 95:149 (1924): 673 (originally published in 1913); Ferreira da Rosa, "Memorial," 103.

211. "Sem rumo" (*folhetim*), *JC*, 27 Aug. 1888; Gyp., "Lanterna," *Novidades*, 21 Aug. 1888.

212. Joaquim Nabuco, "O Imperador," *O Paiz*, 23 Aug. 1888; Pompéia, *Crônicas*, 33. For other assessments of the popular enthusiasm, see Néry, *Aux Etats-Unis du Brésil*, 264; Raul, "A chegada do Imperador," *Revista Illustrada*, 25 Aug. 1888; "A Chegada de SS. MM. Imperiaes," *JC*, 23 Aug. 1888; "A semana" (*folhetim*), *JC*, 27 Aug. 1888; Thomas J. Jarvis to Sec. of State, Rio, 31 Aug. 1888, NARS, M-121, roll 50.

213. Cited in Barman, *Citizen Emperor*, 343; "Preparativos da festa" and "Recepção Imperial," *Carbonário*, 17 and 20 Aug. 1888. See also Holanda, "Do Império," 353.

214. Pompéia, *Crônicas*, 33; V[alentim] M[agalhães], "Notas a margem," *Gazeta da Tarde*, 22 Aug. 1888.

215. "A Chegada de SS. MM. Imperiaes," *JC*, 23 Aug. 1888; "D. Pedro Segundo," *Gazeta da Tarde*, 22 Aug. 1888; "O Imperador," *Novidades*, 23 Aug. 1888.

216. "A Chegada de SS. MM. Imperiaes," *JC*, 23 Aug. 1888; "Recepção de SS. MM. Imperiaes," *Novidades*, 23 Aug. 1888.

217. "Recepção de SS. MM. Imperiaes," *Novidades*, 23 Aug. 1888; "O regresso de SS. Magestades . . . ," *Gazeta da Tarde*, 23 Aug. 1888; "Chegada de SS. Magestades," *Novidades*, 24 Aug. 1888; "Regresso de Suas Magestades Imperiaes," *JC*, 25 Aug. 1888.

218. On the Onze de Julho festival, see "Recepção de SS. MM. Imperiaes," *Novidades*, 23 Aug. 1888; "Recepção de Suas Magestades," *JC*, 23 Aug. 1888. São Cristóvão's festival is also noted in "Regresso de SS. MM. Imperiaes," *JC*, 5 Sep. 1888.

219. "Regresso de Suas Magestades Imperiaes," *JC*, 25 and 26 Aug. 1888.

220. "Recepção de Suas Magestades," *JC*, 23 Aug. 1888; "Regresso de SS. MM. Imperiaes," 2 Sep. 1888; "A Praia de Botafogo," *Gazeta da Tarde*, 3 Sep.

1888; "De palanque," *Diario de Noticias*, 4 Sep. 1888. The crowd's size is mentioned in "S. M. o Imperador," *Diario de Noticias*, 4 Sep. 1888.

221. "Homenagem a S. M. a Imperatriz," *JC*, 25 Aug. 1888; "Echos e noticias," *Novidades*, 27 and 28 Aug. 1888.

222. See *JC*, 21, 23, 30, and 31 Aug. 1888; 1 and 2 Sep. 1888.

223. *Cidade do Rio*, 19 Sep. 1888, quoted in Farias, Soares, and Gomes, *Labirinto*, 19; Gomes, "No meio," 84.

224. Pompéia, *Crônicas*, 61–62. For analysis based solely on Pompéia's *crônica*, see Silva, *Prince*, 1; Carvalho, *Bestializados*, 28.

225. "A semana" (*folhetim*), *JC*, 9 Dec. 1888. This is the only reference to the organizing association and the *cronista* failed to provide its name.

226. *Ao Senhor D. Pedro II*; "Noticiario," *O Paiz*, 2 Dec. 1887.

227. *Polyanthea*. The characterizations of its contributors appear in "Polyanthea historica do Segundo Reinado," *Gazeta de Noticias*, 7 Sep. 1888; "Album de Autographos," *Diario de Noticias*, 7 Sep. 1888.

228. Comissão Executiva to Camara," [Rio], 12 Nov. 1888, AGCRJ, 6-2-31, fol. 24; Batalha, *Dicionário*, 252; "7 de Setembro," *O Mequetrefe*, Sep. 1892.

229. "Album popular," *JC*, 3 Dec. 1888. Laet's contribution appears in *Polyanthea*, 38–39.

230. "Album popular," *JC*, 3 Dec. 1888; "Album popular," *O Paiz*, 3 Dec. 1888. For descriptions of the album, see "2 de Dezembro," *Diario de Noticias*, 3 Dec. 1888; "Cortejo," *Gazeta de Noticias*, 3 Dec. 1888.

231. On literacy rates, see Hahner, *Emancipating*, 22.

232. "Album Popular," *O Paiz*, 3 Dec. 1888; "2 de Dezembro," *Diario de Noticias*, 3 Dec. 1888; "Cortejo," *Gazeta de Noticias*," 3 Dec. 1888. The Cucumbis Carnavalescos are mentioned in "Album Popular," *Novidades*, 3 Dec. 1888, while the description of their costume and performance is from Filindal [Almeida], "Rio de Janeiro," 9 Dec. 1888, *A Provincia de São Paulo* (São Paulo), 14 Dec. 1888. I have not been able to identify the acronym in the African society's name. On Cucumbis, see Mello Moraes Filho, *Festas*, 167–71.

233. "Cortejo," *Gazeta de Noticias*, 3 Dec. 1888.

234. "A semana" (*folhetim*), *JC*, 9 Dec. 1888.

235. "Cortejo," *Gazeta da Tarde*, 3 Dec. 1888; Sacramento Blake, *Diccionario*, 4:243–44; Pompéia, *Crônicas*, 61.

236. "Chronica," *O Mequetrefe*, Dec. 1888. This appears to be the incident to which Mello Moraes Filho alludes; *Festas*, 546–47.

237. V[alentim] M[agalhães], "O dia de hontem," *Tribuna Liberal*, 3 Dec. 1888.

238. "O Principe Obá," *Gazeta de Noticias*, 5 Dec. 1888; "Obá—o principe," *Cidade do Rio*, 5 Dec. 1888; "A injustiça para com o Sr. D. Oba," *Carbonario*, 3 Dec. 1888.

239. Silva, *Prince*. See, however, Jesus's suggestion that Obá should be seen as an exceptional figure, particularly in his self-assured relationship with Pedro II, *Visões*, 81, 88.

240. Silva, *Prince*, 73–76; Koseritz, *Imagens*, 159–60; Mello Moraes Filho, *Festas*, 546, 547. I have, furthermore, found no evidence to confirm Mello Moraes Filho's account of Obá forcing himself into the reception for the

diplomatic corps on a 7 September "about twenty years ago," or around 1870; *Festas*, 547.

241. "Inauguração do novo paço municipal," *Corsario Junior*, 3 Dec. 1882; *Distracção*, 5 Dec. 1885.

242. V[alentim] M[agalhães], "O dia de hontem," *Tribuna Liberal*, 3 Dec. 1888.

243. "Sem rumo," *JC*, 6 Dec. 1888; "De Palanque," *Diario de Noticias*, 3 Dec. 1888.

244. Filindal [Almeida], "Rio de Janeiro," 9 Dec. 1888, *A Provincia de São Paulo* (São Paulo), 14 Dec. 1888; *O Mequetrefe*, Dec. 1888. On Coelho Bastos, see Silva, *Camélias*, 26–27; Moraes, *Campanha*, 155–56; Reis, "Rio," 81.

245. Pompéia, *Crônicas*, 46. On this ceremony and Isabel's Catholicism, see Barman, *Princess Isabel*, 190; Barman, *Citizen Emperor*, 346; Daibert, *Isabel*, 89–100.

246. *Diario de Notícias*, 19 March 1889, quoted in Albuquerque, *Jogo*, 184; Gomes, "No meio das águas," 86.

247. On the Guarda Negra, see Bergstresser, "Movement," 175–85; Ricci, *Guarda Negra*; Soares, *Negregada*, 251–64; Gomes, "No meio"; Trochim, "Brazilian Black Guard"; Albuquerque, *Jogo*, 183–94.

248. "Corte," *Diario do Comercio*, 25 March 1889.

249. There is no scholarship on this celebration, but see Daibert's analysis of the efforts to promote Isabel's image; *Isabel*, 169–83.

250. "13 de maio," *Diario de Noticias*, 12 May 1889; "Treze de maio," *JC*, 12 May 1889; "13 de maio," *Diario do Commercio*, 13 May 1889; "Treze de Maio," *Cidade do Rio*, 11 May 1889.

251. "Treze de Maio," *JC*, 13 May 1889; "13 de maio," *Diario do Commercio*, 14 May 1889; "Treze de Maio," *Novidades*, 14 May 1889; "Treze de Maio," *JC*, 14 May 1889.

252. "Treze de Maio," *JC*, 13 May 1889; "Treze de Maio," *JC*, 14 May 1889.

253. "Treze de Maio," *Novidades*, 14 May 1889; "Festas de 13 de Maio," *Diario de Noticias*, 14 May 1889; "Treze de Maio," *Cidade do Rio*, 11, 13, and 14 May 1889.

254. "Episodios do dia 13 de maio" and "Tiro de rewolwer na rua do Ouvidor," *Carbonario*, 15 May 1889; "Treze de Maio," *Novidades*, 14 May 1889; "Festas de 13 de Maio," *Diario de Noticias*, 14 May 1889.

255. "Episodios do dia 13 de maio," *Carbonario*, 15 May 1889.

256. "A ordem nas festas da Abolição," *JC*, 15 May 1889.

257. "13 de maio," *Diario de Noticias*, 11 May 1889; Euclydes da Cunha, "Da Corte," *A Provincia de São Paulo* (São Paulo), 17 May 1889.

258. "13 de maio," *Carbonario*, 15 May 1889.

259. "Perdões," *JC*, 13 May 1889; "Perdões," *O Paiz*, 14 March 1889.

260. Filindal [Almeida], "Historia dos sete dias," *Diario do Commercio*, 21 April 1889; G. H., "Dia a dia," *Gazeta da Tarde*, 14 May 1889; "Cousas da semana," *Gazeta da Tarde*, 20 May 1889.

261. Filindal [Almeida], "Historia dos sete dias," *Diario do Commercio*, 13 May 1889; "Rio de Janeiro," 11 May 1889, *A Provincia de São Paulo* (São Paulo), 14 May 1889.

262. "O dia maximo," *Diario de Noticias*, 13 May 1889; "Treze de Maio," *Gazeta da Tarde*, 13 May 1889; "13 de Maio," *Carbonario*, 13 May 1889; "13 de maio," *Novidades*, 13 May 1889.

263. Q. Bocayuva, "Primeiro Anniversario," *O Paiz*, 13 May 1889.

264. "Treze de Maio," *JC*, 13 May 1889; "13 de Maio," *Gazeta de Noticias*, 13 May 1889; "Treze de Maio," *Cidade do Rio*, 13 May 1889; "Treze de Maio," *Tribuna Liberal*, 13 May 1889; Lopes Trovão, "13 de Maio," *Diario de Noticias*, 13 May 1889.

265. Speech of Afonso Celso Jr., *ACD* (1889), 1:21; speech of Aristides de Sousa Espinola, 17 May, *ACD* (1889), 1:67–68, 164–65.

266. Speeches of Domingos de Andrade Figueira and Leandro Chaves de Melo Ratisbona, 17 May, *ACD* (1889), 1:68–69. On Andrade Figueira's consistent antiabolitionism, see Moraes, *Campanha*, 337–39; Pena, *Pajens*, 323.

267. *ACD* (1889), 1:77.

268. Filindal [Almeida], "Historia dos sete dias," *Diario do Commercio*, 20 May 1889.

269. "Treze de Maio," *JC*, 14 May 1889; "Monumento," *Gazeta da Tarde*, 14 May 1889; "Monumento," *Novidades*, 14 May 1889; "Local Notes," *The Rio News*, 24 Aug. 1888.

270. Barman, *Citizen Emperor*, 344–46; 350–53; Schulz, *Financial Crisis*, 73–78 (quote 75); Colson, "On Expectations."

271. Barman, *Citizen Emperor*, 353–56; Mattoso, *Cousas*, 30, 169.

272. "Sete de Setembro," *JC*, 7 Sep. 1889; "O dia do Brazil," *Tribuna Liberal*, 8 Sep. 1889; "Sete de Setembro," *Gazeta da Tarde*, 7 Sep. 1889; João Carlos de Souza Ferreira to Antonio Picot, Rio, 18 June 1889, in Sandroni, *180 anos*, 243.

273. "Sete de Setembro," *O Paiz*, 7 Sep. 1889.

274. "Sete de Setembro," *JC*, 8 Sep. 1889; "A Semana" (*folhetim*), *JC*, 9 Sep. 1889; "A festa nacional," *Diario do Commercio*, 8 Sep. 1889; "Sete de Setembro," *O Paiz*, 8 Sep. 1889; "Chronica da semana," *Gazeta de Noticias*, 8 Sep. 1889.

275. "7 de Setembro," *Diario de Noticias*, 7 Sep. 1889; "O dia de hontem," *Diario de Noticias*, 8 Sep. 1889; "A semana passada," *Diario de Noticias*, 9 Sep. 1889; "As festas de ante-hontem," *Novidades*, 9 Sep. 1889.

276. "Sete de Setembro," *O Paiz*, 8 Sep. 1889; "Sete de Setembro," *JC*, 8 Sep. 1889; "7 de Setembro," *Tribuna Liberal*, 8 Sep. 1889.

277. "Sete de Setembro," *Novidades*, 7 Sep. 1889; *O Meio*, 7 and 14 Sep. 1889.

278. Barman, *Citizen Emperor*, 344, 347–48, 366; Schwarcz, *Barbas*, 433.

279. "Batalhão escolar," *Gazeta da Tarde*, 7 Sep. 1889; "Sete de Setembro," *O Paiz*, 8 Sep. 1889; "Sete de Setembro," *JC*, 8 Sep. 1889; "As festas de sabbado," *Carbonario*, 9 Sep. 1889.

280. "As festas de ante-hontem no paço da cidade," *Novidades*, 9 Sep. 1889; "Notas do dia," *Diario do Commercio*, 8 Sep. 1889.

281. "Desacatos—Conflitos," *O Paiz*, 8 Sep. 1889; "Conflicto na Rua do Ouvidor," *Diario do Commercio*, 8 Sep. 1889; "O dia de hontem," *Diario de Noticias*, 8 Sep. 1889; "A semana passada," *Diario de Noticias*, 9 Sep. 1889;

"Corre como certo . . . ," *Diario de Noticias*, 9 Sep. 1889; "As festas de ante-hontem," *Novidades*, 9 Sep. 1889; Gil, "Linhas por baixo," *Novidades*, 9 Sep. 1889; "Aos domingos" (*folhetim*), *JC*, 15 Sep. 1889; Flamino, "Chronica," *Archivo Contemporaneo Illustrado*, 16 Sep. 1889; "Local Notes," *The Rio News*, 9 Sep. 1889.

282. "Sete de Setembro," *JC*, 7 Sep. 1888.

EPILOGUE

1. Ferreira Neto, "Elaboração," 84; Fragale Filho, *Aventura*, 47–48.

2. Ozouf, *Festivals*.

3. Barman, *Citizen Emperor*, 356–63. On the republican conspiracy's development and ideology, see Lemos, "Alternativa"; Carvalho, *Formação*, 17–33; Costa, *Brazilian Empire*, 202–33. Its military connections are examined in Castro, *Militares*; Schulz, *Exército*; Holanda, "Do Império," 306–47; Lemos, *Benjamin Constant*, 333–411.

4. For useful political narratives of the early republic, see Bello, *History*, 46–138; Hahner, *Civilian-Military Relations*. On the Jacobinos, see Hahner, *Poverty*, 131–56; Queiroz, "Reflections"; Gomes, "Monarquistas."

5. Bello, *History*, 138–84; Hahner, *Poverty*, 157–84; Meade, "*Civilizing*," 17–101; Needell, "Revolta," 249–62.

6. Carvalho, *Bestializados*, 9.

7. *The Rio News*, 2 Dec. 1889; *JC*, 2 Dec. 1889; "2 de Dezembro," *Diario do Commercio*, 2 Dec. 1889.

8. The incident is described in Silva, *Prince*, 1–2, whose source is "Foguetes," *O Paiz*, 3 Dec. 1889. Mello Moraes Filho also mentioned Obá's demonstration but was uncertain whether it had actually happened; *Festas*, 548. The other accounts of this episode include "Chronica," *Cidade do Rio*, 3 Dec. 1889 (the estimate of 1,000 people); "Actualidades," *Cidade do Rio*, 7 Dec. 1889; "Obá II," *Diario do Commercio*, 7 Dec. 1889; "Chronica da Semana," *Gazeta de Noticias*, 8 Dec. 1889.

9. Hugh Wyndham to Marquis of Salisbury, Rio, 20 Dec. 1889, PRO/FO 13, vol. 658, fols. 307–08 (quote 308r); Albuquerque, *Quando eu era vivo*, 119–21 (quotes 121). On this incident, see also Castro, "Revoltas," 303–07.

10. "Mutiny or Conspiracy," *The Rio News*, 23 Dec. 1889; Leclerc, *Lettres*, 17–18, 21–23; Robert Adams Jr. to Sec. of State, Rio, 28 Dec. 1889, NARS, M-121, roll 51; Wyndham to Salisbury, Rio, 22 Dec. 1889 (confidential), PRO/FO 13, vol. 658, fols. 315–18.

11. *The Rio News*, 24 Feb. 1890; Decretos 78 and 78A, 21 Dec. 1889, *CLB*.

12. "Local Notes," *The Rio News*, 16 Dec. 1889; Dominó Sobrinho, "Pequenos Echos," *Revista Illustrada*, 14 Dec. 1889; Assunção, *Capoeira*, 93–95.

13. Calculated from *Codigo*, i–x. On this issue, see also Chazkel, *Laws*.

14. Carvalho, *Bestializados*, 91–139; Meade, "*Civilizing*"; Needell, "Revolta."

15. Costa, *Brazilian Empire*, 233.

16. Decreto 4, 19 Nov. 1889, *CLB*; Carvalho, *Formação*, 111–15; Lemos, *Benjamin Constant*, 434, 438–40; Fragale Filho, *Aventura*, 44–45.

17. Decretos 9 and 10, 21 Nov. 1889, *CLB*. More such changes came in January, Decretos 112A and 113, 11 Jan. 1890, *CLB*. *The Rio News*'s criticism appeared on 25 Nov. 1889.

18. Laet, "História antiga," *Jornal do Brasil*, 23 May 1907; "Microcosmo," *O País*, 15 Sep. 1915, in *Crônicas*, 84, 77.

19. Sena, *Rascunhos*, 418; Police Chief to President of Intendencia Municipal, Rio, 10 July 1890, AGCRJ, 50-1-88; Deocleciano Martyr to President of Intendencia Municipal, Rio, 15 June 1892, AGCRJ, 50-1-90; Petition of J. J. Lopes Nazareth et al. to President of Intendencia Municipal, ca. 1892, AGCRJ, 50-1-89.

20. Coaracy, *Todos contam sua vida*, 175; Machado de Assis, *Esaú e Jacó*, in *Obra*, 1:1025–28.

21. Gerson, *História*, 28, 121. Many more such changes were proposed; Lemos, *Benjamin Constant*, 442–45.

22. Coaracy, *Memórias*, 171; Ferreira da Rosa, "Memorial," 153; Decreto 119A, 7 Jan. 1890, *CLB*; Gerson, *História*, 32, 199–200.

23. Carvalho, *Formação*, 75–96; Schwarcz, *Barbas*, 574–79, 501, 507; Lima, *História*, 1:xvii, 3:1020. The last representations of Brazil as an Indian in *Revista Illustrada* appeared on 18 Jan. and 8 Feb. 1890.

24. "Local Notes" and "Revolutionary Incidents," *The Rio News*, 25 Nov. 1889.

25. Lira, *História*, 124–29; "Hymno nacional," *JC*, 16 Jan. 1890; Lira, *História*, 130–32, 136–40; Pereira, "Hino," 28–33; Carvalho, *Formação*, 124–25. Sena misdates this episode to 15 Nov. 1890, *Rascunhos*, 476–77.

26. "O Hymno da Proclamação," *JC*, 21 Jan. 1890; Decreto 171, 20 Jan. 1890, *CLB*; Ferreira da Rosa, "Memorial," 149–50; Albuquerque, *Quando eu era vivo*, 117.

27. Lira, *História*, 141–50 (quote 148), 155–212; Pereira, "Hino nacional," 33, 34.

28. A critic of the decree noted its provenance; L. Veiga, *7 de abril*, 2n*. Raimundo Teixeira Mendes later claimed authorship; Leal, "Calendário," 68–69. Ferreira Neto judges it a collaboration between the two; "Elaboração," 81.

29. Decreto 115B, 14 Jan. 1890, *CLB*; Sessions of 23 and 24 Feb. 1891; Brazil, *Annaes do Congresso Constituinte*, 3:869, 911–12; Decreto 3, 28 Feb. 1891, *CLB*.

30. Leal, "Calendário," 64.

31. Veiga, *7 de abril*, iii, 4, 10, 14, 38–40. The pamphlet is a brief version of his 1877 *Primeiro Reinado*. In 1891, the *Gazeta de Noticias* took up this issue; Motta, *Nação*, 15. On Veiga, see Sacramento Blake, *Diccionario*, 5:406–09; his 1862 efforts on behalf of his uncle are noted in Chapter Six and appeared in much more detail in *Primeiro Reinado*, 489–518.

32. Octavio, *Festas*, frontispiece. For the book's favorable reception, see "Festas Nacionaes," *O Album* (April 1893): 141. It received two more editions by 1905, and extracts of it were reprinted as pamphlets; Oliveira, "Festas," 182, 188n6.

33. Octavio, *Festas*, 3–20. For examples of the 1892 Columbus rhetoric, see Almeida, "Há cem anos," 19–21.

34. Octavio, *Festas*, 23–39 (quote 34).

35. Ibid., 41–59.

36. Ibid., 61–95 (quote 95).

37. Ibid., 99–126 (quotes, 117, 125).

38. Daibert Júnior, *Isabel*, 185–200; Octavio, *Festas*, 128–67 (quotes 167).

39. Octavio, *Festas*, 171–207 (quote 195).

40. Ibid., 211–33 (quote 233). On voter eligibility for the constituent assembly elections, see Decreto 200a, 8 Feb. 1890, *CLB*. Illiterates registered to vote under the empire, however, could cast ballots for the assembly, Nicolau, *História*, 26–27.

41. Pompéia, "Introdução," in Octavio, *Festas*, iii–iv. The separate publication is Pompéia, *Carta*. On Pompéia, see also Oliveira, "Festas," 179–80. His function in the club is noted in Hahner, *Poverty*, 139.

42. Pompéia, "Introdução," in Octavio, *Festas*, v–vi, xix–xxi.

43. Milliet, *Tiradentes*, 89–95. For the program, see *Tiradentes* (1890): 8; "Tiradentes," *JC*, 20 April 1890. For descriptions of the day's celebrations, see "Homenagem a Tiradentes," *JC*, 22 April 1890; Ferreira da Rosa, "Memorial," 154; Julio Verim, "Tiradentes," *Revista Illustrada*, 26 April 1890. The leaflet is reproduced in Carvalho, *Formação*, 66; Milliet, *Tiradentes*, 141. See also Christo, "Esquartejamento," 146. On the Casino Fluminense, see Needell, *Tropical* Belle Époque, 64–72.

44. Silva Jardim, *Tiradentes*, 42.

45. "Tiradentes," *Echo Popular*, 19 April 1890; Leal, "Calendário," 74–75; Milliet, *Tiradentes*, 80n118; Y. "Aos domingos," *JC*, 27 April 1890.

46. Leal, "Calendário," 78–87; *Revista Illustrada*, 3 May 1890; Oliveira, "Imaginário," 188–89.

47. Williams, "Civicscape," 60; Coaracy, *Memórias*, 260.

48. The description of the procession is drawn from Fulano de Tal, "Festas," *Revista Illustrada*, no. 590, May 1890; and the centerfold lithograph in this issue, which focused on the first float. The cheer to Isabel is mentioned in "Local Notes," *The Rio News*, 19 May 1890. See also Daibert Júnior, *Isabel*, 188–90.

49. Commissão dos Festejos Populares to Cidadão . . . , Rio, 9 July 1890 (unaddressed printed form letter), AGCRJ, 43-3-70, fol. 1; Fulano de Tal, "14 de Julho," *Revista Illustrada*, no. 597, July 1890; Reporter, "14 de Julho," *Revista Illustrada*, no. 598, July 1890.

50. "Local Notes," *The Rio News*, 8 Sep. 1890; G. S., "Notas da Quinzena," *O Porvir*, 10 Sep. 1890; "Sete de Setembro," *JC*, 8 Sep. 1890. *Revista Illustrada* also failed to note any celebrations of 7 Sep. 1890, nos. 601–602, Sep. 1890.

51. Likewise, for Columbus's fourth centenary, there were no significant public celebrations, Almeida, "Há cem anos," 21.

52. Ferreira da Rosa, "Memorial," 168; Siqueira, "Imprensa comemora a República: Memórias," 161–62.

53. Director das Obras to President of Intendencia Municipal, Rio, 18 Oct. 1890, AGCRJ, 43-3-73, fol. 2; "Festejos," *JC*, 16 Nov. 1890; "Intendencia Municipal," *JC*, 17 Nov. 1890; "Festejos," *JC*, 15 Nov. 1890; "Festejos," *JC*, 18 Nov. 1890; "Varias Noticias," *JC*, 15 Nov. 1890; "Festejos," *JC*, 16 Nov. 1890.

54. Ferreira da Rosa, "Memorial," 69; Petition of Alvaro Fróes to President of Intendencia Municipal, Rio, 4 Nov. 1890, AGCRJ, 43-3-71, fol. 1.

55. Quoted in Siqueira, "Imprensa comemora a República: Memórias," 167–69, 170–71.

56. *The Rio News*, 17 Nov. 1890; Siqueira, "Imprensa comemora a República: Memórias," 172–73, 178–79.

57. Vincent, *China*, 25; Neeld, *Diary*, 22; Pinto, "Pequenos Echos," *Revista Illustrada*, no. 694, May 1895; Thome Jr., "Pequenos Echos," *Revista Illustrada*, no. 691, July 1895.

58. M. S., "A festa do Cattete," and the cartoon entitled "No dia 24 de fevereiro," *Don Quixote*, 6 March 1897; Testis, *Traços*, 51–56. See also a Portuguese journalist's account, Leitão, *Do civismo*, 49–51.

59. Order from Minister of Interior, Rio, 14 Oct. 1891, AGCRJ, 43-3-73, fol. 7; C. A. Nascimento Silva to Intendente de Obras, Rio, 30 Nov. 1891, AGCRJ, 43-3-73, fol. 84r–85r; Thomé, "Pequenos Echos," *Revista Illustrada*, no. 633, Nov. 1891.

60. P. de Gouvea [Alexandre Fernandes], "Chronica," *O Mequetrefe*, Nov. 1892. The same view appeared in S. Thomé, "Pequenos Echos," *Revista Illustrada*, no. 652, Nov. 1892.

61. *O Apostolo*, 15 Nov. 1892, quoted in Almeida, "Há cem anos," 24; "Dias Festivos, 15 de Novembro de 1894," BN/SI, cofre.

62. Machado de Assis, "A Semana," *Gazeta de Noticias*, 17 Nov. 1895, in *Obra*, 3:684–85; *O Paiz*, 15 Nov. 1897, quoted in Siqueira, "Imprensa comemora a República: O 15 de novembro," 110.

63. *O Paiz*, 7 Sep. 1890, quoted in Motta, *Nação*, 15.

64. "7 de Setembro," *O Mequetrefe*, Sep. 1892; Fantasio [Olavo Bilac], "Chronica," *A Cigarra*, 12 Sep. 1895.

65. Motta, *Nação*, 16.

66. "7 de setembro," *Rua do Ouvidor*, 3 Sep. 1898; Director-Geral Interino, 1.ª Seção, to Sr. Director Geral da Fazenda, Prefeitura do Districto Federal, Rio, 13 Oct. 1898, AGCRJ, 43-3-80, fol. 2r; "Festas nacionaes," *Rua do Ouvidor*, 10 Sep. 1898.

67. Fernando Lobo to Candido Bento Ribeiro, Rio, 12 May 1892, AGCRJ, 43-4-12, fol. 13; Adriano da Costa Pereira et al. to Intendencia Municipal, Rio, 12 May 1892, AGCRJ, 43-4-12, fol. 14; Petition of Veneravel Irmandade do Senhor Jesus do Bonfim e N. S. do Paraiso to Prefeito Municipal, 1 May 1893, AGCRJ, 43-3-75, fol. 1; Professores Publicos Primarios Municipaes to Prefeito, Rio, 11 May 1895, AGCRJ, 43-3-77, fol. 1.

68. Farfarello, "Echos e notas," *Revista Illustrada*, no. 644, May 1892; Andrews, *Blacks*, 213–16.

69. José Ponciano de Oliveira, "13 de Maio," 4 May 1898, AGCRJ, 43-4-12, fols. 18r–22r.

70. "Echos e Factos," *Rua do Ouvidor*, 13 May 1899; Franklin Doria [Baron of Loreto] to Isabel, Rio, 13 May 1899, AIHGB, lata 304, pasta 7, doc. 1; Baron of Loreto, "A Abolição no Brazil," *Rua do Ouvidor*, 13 May 1899.

71. For examples of this rhetoric, see "Chronica," *O Mequetrefe*, May 1891; "13 de Maio," *Rua do Ouvidor*, 14 May 1898.

72. "Chronica Fluminense," *O Album*, May 1894; *O Apostolo*, 15 May 1891, quoted in Abreu, "Pensamento," 87n23. On the failure of republican abolitionism, see also Daibert Júnior, *Isabel*, 191–94.

73. Machado de Assis, "A Semana," *Gazeta de Noticias*, 15 May 1892; available at http://machado.me.gov.br (accessed January 2011). This *crônica* does not appear in his *Obra completa*.

74. Programs, *Tiradentes* (1893): 8; (1894): 4; "O Centenario" and "Festejos," *Revista Illustrada*, no. 643, April 1892; Almeida, "Há cem anos," 17; *Alferes* Augusto de Faria to President of Conselho da Intendencia, n.d., ARCRJ, 40-4-84, fol. 10.

75. On this debate, see Americo Vespucci, "O logar do supplicio," *Tiradentes* (1890): 6; Miguel Lemos, "Determinação do Lugar em que foi suppliciado o Tiradentes," *JC*, 11, 13, 14, and 16 April 1892 (clippings in AN, cod. 725, fols. 1–6); Vieira Fazenda, "Antiqualhas," *RIHGB* 95:149 (1924): 451–55 (originally published in 1912). On the plaque, see the draft program for its unveiling, 7 April 1892, AGCRJ, 40-4-86, fols. 1r–2v; Cruls, *Aparência*, 1:189; Morales de los Rios Filho, *Rio*, 226–27.

76. "Club Tiradentes," *Tiradentes* (1893): 8.

77. This incident is outlined in Carvalho, *Formação*, 61, 69; Milliet, *Tiradentes*, 109–10. Neither author mentions the *povo*'s role, which is noted in an article entitled "Justo," *Revista Illustrada*, no. 659, April 1893; and in the centerfold cartoon, *Revista Illustrada*, no. 660, May 1893. Machado de Assis captures the incident's impact in "A Semana," *Gazeta de Notícias*, 23 April 1893, in *Obra*, 3:582–83.

78. Untitled text by Lucio de Mendonça; Badaré, "A mentira de bronze," in *Tiradentes* (1893): 1, 7; "21 de abril de 1894," *Tiradentes* (1894): 2. See also the many 1894 articles cited in Oliveira, "Monumentalização," 37–41. Critics of the band shell and the calls to remove the statue include "Chronica Fluminense," *O Album*, April 1893; "A Estatua," *A Ilustração Sul-Americana*, July 1894; Fantasio [Bilac], "Chronica," *A Cigarra*, 12 Sep. 1895; Werneck, *D. Pedro I*; Edmundo, *Rio*, 1:147–48.

79. Milliet, *Tiradentes*, 111–12, 207–12; Carvalho, *Formação*, 71.

80. Gavroche [Artur Azevedo], "Festejos oficiais," *O Paiz*, 22 April 1896, quoted in Milliet, *Tiradentes*, 112.

81. Almeida, "Há cem anos," 21 (quote), 26–27.

82. Holanda, "Do Império," 302.

83. Carvalho, *Bestializados*, chap. 5.

CONCLUSION

1. Kertzer, *Ritual*, 67–76.

2. Instituto Histórico e Geográfico Brasileiro, *Homenagem*; Barman, *Citizen Emperor*, 401–02; Schwarcz, *Barbas*, 496.

3. Barman, *Citizen Emperor*, 404.

4. Mattoso, *Cousas*, 44–55.

5. Barman, *Citizen Emperor*, 405–06; Sandes, *Invenção*, 206–14; Daibert Júnior, *Isabel*, 206, 240–47; Guimarães, "Primeira República."

6. Rio [Barreto], *Alma*, 81 (quote), 157, 161; E. Silva, *Queixas*, 62–63, 75–76.

7. On this debate, see Sandes, *Invenção*, 139–76; Motta, *Nação*, 23–31; Siqueira, "Imprensa comemora a República: O 15 de novembro," 129–49.

8. Quoted in Silva, "República," 69. On this point, see also Sandes, *Invenção*, 215–18.

9. Silva, "República," 60–69; Sandes, *Invenção*, 199–204.

10. Ferreira da Rosa, *Prosa*, 6:106–11; Decreto 4,859, 26 Sep. 1924, in Carvalho, *Feriados*, 244.

11. Souza, "Militarização"; Lambert, "Festa"; Bittencourt, "Tradições"; Beattie, *Tribute*, 232–33; Skidmore, *Black*, 154, 147, 160.

12. Ferreira da Rosa, *Prosa*, 2:59–68.

13. González, "Conmemoraciones," 200; Williams, "Civicscape," 59–60.

14. Williams, "Civicscape," 60–64; Parada, *Educando*, 20–21; Castro, *Invenção*, 49–67.

15. Parada, *Educando*, 30–36; Brazil, Serviço de Divulgação, *Bandeira*.

16. Parada, *Educando*, 59–65, 69–92, 108–48; Williams, "Civicscape," 63–66.

17. Parada, *Educando*, 81; Rangel, "Festas"; Unglaub, "Prática."

18. Williams, *Culture Wars*, 150–56.

19. Williams, "Civicscape," 61; Lei 662, 6 April 1949; Lei 1,266, 18 Dec. 1950, *CLB*.

20. Chirio, "Fêtes," 89–108 (quote, 97). The fullest study of 1972's commemorations is Almeida, "Regime."

21. Schiavinatto, "Praça," 92–98; Dávila, *Hotel*, 148–50; Catroga, "Culto," 470; Cerri, "1972," 193–97; Almeida, "Regime," 211–43.

22. DaMatta, *Carnivals*, 26–60 (quote 26).

23. Lei 6.802, *CLB*. On Aparecida, see Souza, "Mãe."

24. Cardoso with Winter, *Accidental President*, 39; Unglaub, "Prática," 109, 112, 113, 116, 121, 122–23.

25. Quoted in Schiavinatto, "Praça," 93.

26. *Jornal do Brasil*, 15 Nov. 2004. The painting appears in Carvalho, *Formação*, 97.

27. Kidder, *Sketches*, 2:145 (7 Sep. 1840, Recife); Vauthier, *Diário*, 114–15 (2 December 1840, Recife); Chavanges, "Brésil," 87 (2 Dec. 1842, Ouro Preto); Avé-Lallemant, *Viagem*, 276–77 (7 Sep. 1858, Curitiba); Agassiz and Agassiz, *Journey*, 293–94 (2 Dec. 1865, Manaus). The only analysis of routine days of national festivity in a province is Kraay, "Definindo."

28. "O dia 2 de dezembro," *O Tocantins* (Goiás), 8 Dec. 1855.

29. "Festas officiaes," "A parada," and "Anniversario," in Cunha, *Propaganda*, 362–63, 369–71, 477. The references to *kicumbis* appear on 362, 370.

30. Moreira de Azevedo, *Curiosidades*, 101–08.

31. Rezende, *Minhas recordações*, 228; Lisboa, *Jornal*, 189.

32. Rezende, *Minhas recordações*, 131–32. Similar patterns also appeared in São Paulo; Ricci, *Assombrações*, 435.

33. Rezende, *Minhas recordações*, 67–69; Chamon, *Festejos*.

34. Lisboa, *Jornal*, 189–204.

35. *ACD* (1858), 5:46; (1882), 3:205.

36. *O Tocantins* (Goiás), 30 Sep. 1857. On the dispatch of portraits to Bahia, see Kraay, "Definindo," 70–71.

37. *O Tocantins* (Goiás), 23 Jan. 1856.

38. "Correspondência da Prov. de Goyaz," Rio, 27 May 1870, *Provincia de Goyaz*, 2 July 1870. For another such complaint, see *O Alabama* (Salvador), 15 July 1870.

39. Altève Aumont, "Courrier d'Amérique," *Revue des Races Latines* (Paris) (10 Dec. 1858): 589.

40. *Alamanak Laemmert* (1858): 15.

41. Marcelo Cheche Galves, e-mail communication, 17 Feb. 2011. In 1831, the senate rejected this proposal after the chamber had approved it, *ACD* (1831), 1:128; *ASB* (1831), 2:172.

42. Assunção, "Popular Culture," 281; Lisboa, *Jornal*, 189, 194–204. Galves notes that, before 1826, the date was not celebrated, which he attributes to "Portuguese" political dominance; "Aderir," 117.

43. Mello, *Rubro veio*, 51.

44. Kraay, "Between Brazil and Bahia," 278; Kraay, "Definindo," 79.

45. In addition to Antônio Borges da Fonseca's remarks cited in Chapter Six, see "Carta de João Fernandes a seu compadre Manoel Mendes," *Correio da Tarde*, 15 Sep. 1856; "O Dia 7 de Setembro," *Correio da Tarde*, 10 Sep. 1855; "Dizia-se hontem . . . ," *Gazeta de Noticias*, 8 Sep. 1879.

46. Graham, "Constructing," 35–37.

47. Beezley, *Mexican National Identity*, 56–57. More generally, see also the essays in Beezley and Lorey, *¡Viva Mexico!*

48. Pani, "Proyecto," 445–54; Duncan, "Independence Celebrations" and "Political Legitimation," 54–58.

49. Beezeley, *Mexican National Identity*, 79–85; Esposito, *Funerals*, 86–97.

50. Díaz Arias, *Fiesta*. See also Palmer, "Getting."

51. Calzadilla, "Olor"; Salvador, *Efímeras efemérides*, 150–53, 167–88, 189–243.

52. Bertoni, "Construir." Earlier commemoration of these days remains little studied, but Garavaglia stresses the continuity between colonial celebrations and the early *fiestas mayas* (25 May celebrations); *Construir*, 57–88.

53. Y., "Aos domingos" (*folhetim*), *JC*, 8 Dec. 1889.

54. Davis, *Parades*, 150–51.

Bibliography

ARCHIVES AND LIBRARIES

Arquivo Geral da Cidade do Rio de Janeiro (AGCRJ)
Arquivo Histórico do Exército (AHEx)
    Requerimentos (RQ)
Arquivo Histórico Estadual de Goiás
Arquivo Histórico do Museu Imperial (AHMI)
Arquivo do Instituto Histórico e Geográfico Brasileiro (AIHGB)
Arquivo Nacional (AN)
    Grupo de Identificação de Fundos Internos (GIFI)
    Seção do Poder Executivo (SPE)
Biblioteca Alberto Nepomuceno, Universidade Federal do Rio de Janeiro
Biblioteca da Associação Comercial do Rio de Janeiro
Biblioteca Nacional (BN)
    Divisão de Música (DM)
    Seção de Iconografia (SI)
    Seção de Manuscritos (SM)
    Seção de Obras Gerais (SOG)
    Seção de Obras Raras (SOR)
Biblioteca Pública do Estado da Bahia
Fundação Casa de Rui Barbosa
Library of Congress
Museu Histórico Nacional (MHN)
National Archives and Records Service (NARS)
    Microcopy T-172 ("Despatches from United States Consuls in Rio de Janeiro, 1811–1906")
    Microcopy M-121 ("Despatches from United States Ministers to Brazil, 1809–1906")
Oliveira Lima Library (OLL)
Public Record Office (PRO)
    Foreign Office (FO) 13 ("General General Correspondence before 1906: Brazil, 1825–1905", microfilm)
University of California, Berkeley

NEWSPAPERS

Most of the newspapers cited in this work are available in microfilm at Rio de Janeiro's Biblioteca Nacional, and are listed in its *Catálogo de periódicos brasileiros microfilmados*. A small number of newspapers not available at the BN were consulted at the Fundação Casa de Rui Barbosa and are listed in its *Catálogo dos periódicos da Coleção Plínio Doyle*. Roderick Barman kindly shared his copy of *O Grito Nacional*. A small number of cited periodicals not held by these institutions were consulted at other archives and libraries:

Courier du Brésil, 1854–62 (University of California, Berkeley)
Diario Official do Imperio do Brasil, 1870 (Biblioteca Pública do Estado da Bahia)
O Farricoco, 1848–49 (AN)
Folhinha Laemmert, 1830–89 (AIHGB)
A Ilustração Sul-Americana, 1894 (AIHGB)
Iris, 1848–49 (AIHGB)
Ostensor Brasileiro, 1845–46 (AIHGB)
Província de Goyaz (Goiás), 1855–57 (Arquivo Histórico Estadual de Goiás)
A Provincia de São Paulo (São Paulo), 1875–89 (University of California, Berkeley)
Revue Française, 1839–40 (OLL)
Revue des Races Latines (Paris), 1857–58 (Library of Congress)
Revue Espagnole, Portugaise, Brésilienne et Hispano-Américaine, 1857 (Library of Congress)
O Tocantins (Goiás), 1870 (Arquivo Histórico Estadual de Goiás)

PRINTED SOURCES

Abreu, Martha. *O império do divino: Festas religiosas e cultura popular no Rio de Janeiro, 1830–1900*. Rio: Nova Fronteira; São Paulo: FAPESP, 1999.
———. "Pensamento católico, abolicionismo e festas religiosas no Rio de Janeiro, 1870–1890." In *Escravidão, exclusão e cidadania*, ed. Marco Pamplona, 75–105. Rio: Access Editora, 2001.
Abreu, Placido de. *Os capoeiras*. Rio: Tip. Seraphim Alves de Brito, 1886.
Acree, William G. Jr. "Words, Wars, and Public Celebrations: The Emergence of Rioplatense Print Culture." In *Building Ninteenth-Century Latin America: Re-Rooted Cultures, Identities and Nations*, ed. William G. Acree Jr. and Juan Carlos González Espitia, 32–58. Nashville, TN: Vanderbilt University Press, 2009.
"Actas das sessões da Ill.ma Camara Municipal, 1830–1831." *Arquivo do Distrito Federal* 4 (1953): 92–463; 5 (1954): 67–372.
Adalbert, Prinz van Preussen. *Travels of His Royal Highness Prince Adalbert of Prussia*, 2 vols. London: David Bogue, 1849.

Adet, Émile. "L'empire du Brésil et la société brésilienne en 1850." *Revue des Deux Mondes* 9 (1851): 1082–1105.

Agassiz, Elizabeth Cabot Cary, and Jean Louis Rodolphe Agassiz, *A Journey in Brazil, by Professor and Mrs. Louis Agassiz*. Boston: Ticknor and Fields, 1868.

Aguiar, Antonio Augusto da Costa. *Apontamentos historicos à respeito do grande ministro da independência José Bonifacio de Andrada e Silva*. Rio: Typ. do Apostolo, 1872.

Aguilar, Gonzalo. "The National Opera: A Migrant Genre of Imperial Expansion." *Journal of Latin American Cultural Studies* 12:1 (2003): 83–94.

Agulhon, Maurice. *Marianne au pouvoir: L'imagerie et la symbolique républicaines de 1880 à 1914*. Paris: Flammarion, 1989.

———. *Marianne into Battle: Republican Imagery and Symbolism in France, 1789–1880*, trans. Janet Lloyd. London and New York: Cambridge University Press, 1981.

———. "La 'statuomanie' et l'histoire." *Ethnologie Française* 8 (1978): 145–72.

Alberdi, J[uan] B[autista]. *Obras selectas*, new ed., 18 vols., ed. Joaquín V. González. Buenos Aires: La Facultad, 1920.

Albernoz, J. A. A. *O primeiro voluntario da patria: Himno dedicado a S. M. o Imperador por. . . .* Rio: Nicasio Garcia, 1865.

Albuquerque, [José Joaquim de Campos da Costa de] Medeiros e. *Quando eu era vivo: Memórias, 1867 a 1934*, ed. póstuma e definitiva. Rio: Record, 1982 [1942].

Albuquerque, Severino João. "The Brazilian Theatre up to 1900." In *Cambridge History of Latin American Literature*, 3 vols., ed. Roberto González-Echeverria and Enrique Pupo-Walker, 3:105–25. Cambridge, UK: Cambridge University Press, 1996.

Albuquerque, Wlamyra R. de. *O jogo da dissimulação: Abolição e cidadania negra no Brasil*. São Paulo: Companhia das Letras, 2009.

Alencar, José de. *Ao correr da pena*, ed. João Roberto Faria. São Paulo: Martins Fontes, 2004.

———. *Cartas e documentos de . . .* , ed. Raimundo de Menezes. São Paulo: Conselho Estadual de Cultura, 1967.

———. *Obra completa*, 4 vols. Rio: José Aguilar, 1958–60.

———. *The Jesuit*, trans. Edgardo R. de Brito. Boston: Richard G. Badger, 1919.

Alencastro, Luiz Felipe de. "Vida privada e ordem privada no Império." In *História da vida privada no Brasil*, 4 vols., ed. Fernando A. Novais, 2:11–93. São Paulo: Companhia das Letras, 1997.

Allain, Émile. *Rio de Janeiro: Quelques données sur la capitale et sur l'administration du Brésil*. Paris: L. Frinzine; Rio: Lachaud, 1886.

Almanak Laemmert. Rio: Laemmert, 1844–1889.

"Almanaque do Rio de Janeiro para o ano de 1824." *RIHGB* 278 (Jan.–Mar. 1968): 197–360.

"Almanaque do Rio de Janeiro, [1827]." *RIHGB* 300 (July–Sep. 1973): 137–260.

Almeida, Adjovanes Thadeu Silva de. "O regime militar em festa: A comemoração do Sesquicentenário da Independência brasileira." PhD dissertation, Universidade Federal do Rio de Janeiro, 2009.

Almeida, Antônio do Coração de Maria e. *Oração funebre do augusto fundador do Imperio, o Senhor D. Pedro Primeiro que nas exequias celebradas a 24 de Setembro de 1849, 15.° anniversario da sua infausta morte, pela irmandade de N. S. da Gloria na sua capella do Rio de Janeiro, recitou.* . . . Rio: Typ. F. de Paula Brito, 1849.

———. *Oração gratulatoria que no solemne Te-Deum mandado celebrar pela Illustrissima Camara Municipal da Corte na Igreja dos Terceiros de N. S. do Carmo no dia 13 de Fevereiro de 1860 por occasião do Feliz Regresso de SS. MM. II. das Provincias do Norte recitou perante os mesmos Augustos Senhores.* . . . Rio: Typ. F. de Paula Brito, 1860.

Almeida, Jaime de. "Há cem anos, o Quarto Centenário: Dos horríveis sacrilégios às santas alegrias." *Estudos Históricos* 5:9 (1992): 14–28.

Almeida, Manuel Antônio de. "Dois amores." In *Obra dispersa: Crítica, crônica,* ed. Bernardo de Mendonça, 191–223. Rio: Rios Graphica, 1991.

Alonso, Angela. *Idéias em movimento: A Geração de 1870 na crise do Brasil-Império.* Rio: Civilização Brasileira, 2002.

Alves, José Celso de Castro. "Plebeian Activism, Popular Constitutionalism: Race, Labor, and Unrealized Democracy in Rio de Janeiro, Brazil, 1780s–1830s." PhD dissertation, Yale University, 2006.

Alves, Uelinton Farias. *José do Patrocínio: A imorredoura cor de bronze.* Rio: Garamond, 2009.

Amaral, Francisco Pedro de. "Explicação alegórica (impressa) da decoração dos coches de estado de D. Pedro I." *Publicações Historicas do Arquivo Nacional* 17 (1917): 243–48.

Amorim, Francisco Gomes de. *Teatro: Ódio de Raças—Cedro Vermelho,* ed. Maria Aparecida Ribeiro and Fernando Matos Oliveira. Braga: Angelus Novus Editora, 2000.

Anderson, Benedict. *Imagined Communities: Reflections on the Origins and Spread of Nationalism.* London: Verso, 1996.

Andrade, Ayres de. *Francisco Manuel da Silva e seu tempo: Uma fase do passado musical do Rio de Janeiro à luz de novos documentos,* 2 vols. Rio: Edições Tempo Brasileiro, 1967.

Andrade, Joaquim Marçal Ferreira de. *História da fotoreportagem no Brasil: A fotografia na imprensa no Rio de Janeiro de 1839 a 1900.* Rio: Elsevier, 2004.

Andrews, Christopher Columbus. *Brazil: Its Condition and Prospects,* 3rd ed. New York: D. Appleton and Co., 1891 [1887].

Andrews, George Reid. *Blacks and Whites in São Paulo, Brazil, 1888–1988.* Madison: University of Wisconsin Press, 1991.

Andrews, Jean. "Carlos Gomes's *Il Guarany*: The Frontiers of Miscegenation in Nineteenth-Century Grand Opera." *Portuguese Studies* 16 (2000): 26–42.

Andrews, Joseph. *Journey from Buenos Aires through the Provinces of Cordova, Tucuman, and Salta, to Potosi . . . ,* 2 vols. London: John Murray, 1827.

Antonini, Emidio. *Relatórios sobre o Brasil, 1828–1831.* São Paulo: Instituto Cultural Italo-Brasileiro, 1962.

Ao senhor Dom Pedro II: Homenagem da imprensa nacional. Rio: Imprensa Nacional, 1887.

Araújo, Ana Cristina. "Ritualidade e poder na corte de D. João V." *Revista de História das Idéias* 22 (2001): 175–208.

Araújo, Ana Lúcia. *Romantisme tropical: L'aventure d'un peintre français au Brésil*. Québec: Les Presses de l'Université Laval, 2008.

Araujo, Manuel do Monte Rodrigues de [Conde de Irajá]. *Opusculo sobre a questão que tivéra o excellentissimo Arcebispo da Bahia e Metropolitano do Brasil, D. Romualdo de Seixas com o bispo capellão-mor do Rio de Janeiro, Manoel do Monte Rodrigues de Araujo a respeito do ministro, à quem competia fazer a cerimonia da benção e coroação de S. M. o Imperador do Brasil*. Rio: Typ. de M. J. Cardoso, 1841.

Araújo, Rodrigo Cardoso Soares de. "Pasquins e o submundo da imprensa na Corte imperial (1880–1883)." MA thesis, Universidade Federal do Rio de Janeiro, 2009.

Araújo, Valdei Lopes. *A experiência do tempo: Conceitos e narrativas na formação nacional brasileira (1813–1845)*. São Paulo: Hucitec, 2008.

Armitage, John. *The History of Brazil from the Period of the Arrival of the Braganza Family in 1808, to the Abdication of Don Pedro the First in 1831*. London: Smith, Elder, and Co., 1836.

Arnold, Samuel Greene. *Viaje por America del Sur*, trans. Clara de la Rosa. Buenos Aires: Emecé, 1951.

Assier, Adolphe d'. *Le Brésil contemporain: Races, moeurs, institutions, paysages*. Paris: Durand e Lauriel, 1867.

Assumpção, [Thomaz] Lino d'. *Narrativas do Brazil (1876–1880)*. Rio: Livraria Contemporanea de Faro & Lino, 1881.

Assunção, Matthias Röhrig. *Capoeira: The History of an Afro-Brazilian Martial Art*. London: Routledge, 2005.

———. "Popular Culture and Regional Society in Nineteenth-Century Maranhão, Brazil." *Bulletin of Latin American Research* 14:3 (Sep. 1995): 265–86.

Assunção, Paulo de. *Ritmos da vida: Momentos efusivos da família real portuguesa nos trópicos*. Rio: Arquivo Nacional, 2008.

Atchison, Charles C. *A Winter Cruise in Summer Seas: "How I Found" Health*. London: S. Low, Marston & Co., 1891.

Augusto, Antonio José. *A Questão Cavalier: Música e sociedade no Império e na República*. Rio: Folha Seca and Funarte, 2010.

Avé-Lallemant, Robert. *Viagem pelo Sul do Brasil no ano de 1858*, trans. Teodoro Cabral. Rio: Instituto Nacional do Livro, 1953.

Azevedo, Célia Maria Marinho de. *Onda negra, medo branco: O negro livre no imaginário das elites—século XIX*. Rio: Paz e Terra, 1987.

Azevedo, Luiz Heitor Corrêa de. *150 anos de música no Brasil*. Rio: José Olympio, 1956.

———. *Bibliografia musical brasileira, 1820–1950*. Rio: Instituto Nacional do Livro, 1952.

Bagehot, Walter. *The English Constitution*. London: Kegan Paul, Trench, Trubner & Co., Ltd., 1925.

Baguley, David. *Napoleon III and His Regime: An Extravaganza*. Baton Rouge: Louisiana State University Press, 2000.

Balaban, Marcelo. *Poeta do lápis: Sátira e política na trajetória de Ângelo Agostini no Brasil imperial (1864–1888)*. Campinas: Ed. UNICAMP, 2009.

Ballou, Maturin M. *Equatorial America: Descriptive of a Visit to St. Thomas, Martinique, Barbadoes, and the Principal Capitals of South America*. Boston: Houghton, Mifflin, and Co., 1892.

Bandeira, Júlio, and Pedro Correia do Lago. *Debret e o Brasil: Obra completa (1816–1831)*. Rio: Capivara, 2008.

Barbier, Patrick. *Opera in Paris, 1800–1850: A Lively History*, trans. Robert Luono. Portland, OR: Amadeus Press, 1995.

Barbosa, Januario da Cunha. *Oração de acção de graças celebradas na imperial capela no dia 30 de Março do corrente ano pelo nascimento e baptismo de S. A. I. o Senhor Principe Primogenito D. Affonso Pedro Christino Leopoldo Felippe Eugenio Miguel Gabriel Raphael Gonzaga*. Rio: Typographia Nacional, 1845.

Barbosa, Rui. *Obras Completas*, 49 vols. Rio: Ministério de Educação e Cultura and Fundação Casa de Rui Barbosa, 1951–82. Electronic edition available at www.docvirt.no-ip.com/ObrasRui/STF_Biblioteca.htm (accessed August 2009).

Barbosa, Silvana Mota. "'Panfletos vendidos como *canela*': Anotações em torno do debate político nos anos 1860." In *Nação e cidadania no Império: Novos horizontes*, ed. José Murilo de Carvalho, 153–83. Rio: Record, 2007.

———. "A política progressista: Parlamento, sistema representativo e partidos nos anos 1860." In *Repensando o Brasil do Oitocentos*, ed. José Murilo de Carvalho and Lúcia Maria Bastos Pereira das Neves, 293–324. Rio: Civilização Brasileira, 2009.

Barman, Roderick J. *Brazil: The Forging of a Nation, 1798–1852*. Stanford, CA: Stanford University Press, 1988.

———. *Citizen Emperor: Pedro II and the Making of Brazil, 1825–1891*. Stanford, CA: Stanford University Press, 1999.

———. "Justiniano José da Rocha e a época da Conciliação: Como se escreveu 'Ação, Reação, Transação.'" *RIHGB* 301 (Oct.–Dec. 1973): 3–32.

———. *Princess Isabel of Brazil: Gender and Power in the Nineteenth Century*. Wilmingon, DE: Scholarly Resources, 2002.

Barreiros, Eduardo Canabrava. *Atlas da evolução urbana da cidade do Rio de Janeiro—Ensaio, 1565–1965*. Rio: IHGB, 1965.

Barreto, Francisco Muniz. *Classicos e romanticos: Exercicios poéticos*, 2 vols. Salvador: Tip. de Camillo Lellis Masson, 1855.

[Barreto, Joaquim Francisco Alves Branco Moniz]. *História da revolução do Brasil, com peças officiaes e facsimile da propria mão de Dom Pedro, por hum membro da Camara dos Deputados*. Rio: Typ. Imperial de Seignot Plancher, 1831.

Barros, Alvaro Paes de. *O Liceu de Artes e Ofícios e seu fundador: Depoimento histórico no primeiro centenário da grande instituição*. Rio: n.p., 1956.

Barros, João do Rego. "Reminiscências de há cinqüenta anos: Um cadete do 1.° Regimento de Cavalaria." *RIHGB* 93:152 (1925): 89–98.

Barros, Roque Spencer M. de. "A questão religiosa." In *História geral da civilização brasileira. Tomo 2: O Brasil monárquico*, 5 vols., ed. Sérgio Buarque de Holanda, 4:338–66. São Paulo: Difel, 1966–71.

Basile, Marcello Otávio Neri de Campos. *Ezequiel Corrêa dos Santos: Um jacobino na Corte imperial*. Rio: Editora FGV, 2001.

———. "Festas cívicas na Corte regencial." *Varia História* 22:36 (Jul.–Dec. 2006): 494–516.

———. "O Império em construção: Projetos de Brasil e ação política na Corte regencial." PhD dissertation, Universidade Federal do Rio de Janeiro, 2004.

———. "O laboratório da nação: A era regencial." In *O Brasil Imperial*, 3 vols., ed. Keila Grinberg and Ricardo Salles, 2:53–119. Rio: Civilização Brasileira, 2009.

Batalha, Claudio H. de M. *Dicionário do movimento operário: Rio de Janeiro do século XIX aos anos 1920, militantes e organizações*. São Paulo: Fundação Perseu Abramo, 2008.

———. "Sociedades de trabalhadores no Rio de Janeiro no século XIX—Algumas reflexões em torno da formação da classe operária." *Cadernos AEL* 6:10–11 (1999): 43–66.

Beard, Mary. *The Roman Triumph*. Cambridge, MA: The Belknap Press of Harvard University Press, 2007.

Beattie, Peter M. "Illustrating Race and Nation in the Paraguayan War Era: Exploring the Decline of the Tupi Guarani Warrior in the Embodiment of Brazil." In *Military Struggle and Identity Formation in Latin America: Race, Nation, and Community during the Liberal Period*, ed. Nicola Foote and René D. Harder Horst, 174–203. Gainesville: University Press of Florida, 2010.

———. *The Tribute of Blood: Army, Honor, Race, and Nation in Brazil, 1864–1945*. Durham, NC: Duke University Press, 2001.

Bebiano, Rui. *D. João V: Poder e espectáculo*. Aveiro: Livraria Estante, 1987.

Beezley, William H. *Mexican National Identity: Memory, Innuendo, and Popular Culture*. Tucson: University of Arizona Press, 2008.

Beezley, William H., and David E. Lorey, eds. *¡Viva Mexico! ¡Viva la Independencia! Celebrations of September 16*. Wilmington, DE: Scholarly Resources, 2001.

Bello, José Maria. *A History of Modern Brazil, 1889–1964*, trans. James L. Taylor. Stanford, CA: Stanford University Press, 1966.

Belluzzo, Ana Maria de Moraes. *O Brasil dos viajantes*, 2nd ed., 3 vols. in 1. São Paulo: Metalivros; Rio: Objetiva, 1999.

Bénézit, Emmanuel. *Dictionnaire critique et documentaire des peintres, sculpteurs, dessinateurs et graveurs de tous les temps*, rev. ed., 14 vols. Paris: Grund, 1999.

Bennett, Frank. *Forty Years in Brazil*. London: Mills & Boon, 1914.

Berger, Paulo. *Bibliografia Rio de Janeiro de viajantes e autores estrangeiros, 1531–1900*. Rio: Livraria São José, 1964.

Bergstresser, Rebecca Baird. "The Movement for the Abolition of Slavery in Rio de Janeiro, Brazil, 1880–1889." PhD dissertation, Stanford University, 1973.

Bernardes, Denis Antônio de Mendonça. "Pernambuco e o Império (1822–1824): Sem constituição soberana não há união." In *Brasil: Formação do Estado e da nação*, ed. István Jancsó, 219–49. São Paulo: Hucitec; Ijuí: Unijuí, 2003.

Bertoni, Lilia Ana. "Construir la nacionalidad: Héroes, estatuas y fiestas patrias, 1887–1891." *Boletin del Instituto de Historia Argentina y Americana—Dr. E. Ravignani*, 3rd ser. 5 (First Semester 1992): 77–110.

Bethell, Leslie. *The Abolition of the Brazilian Slave Trade: Britain, Brazil, and the Slave Trade Question*. Cambridge, UK: Cambridge University Press, 1970.

Biard, [Auguste] F[rançois]. *Deux années au Brésil*. Paris: Hachette, 1862.

Bieber, Judy. "A 'visão do sertão': Party Identity and Political Honor in Late Imperial Minas Gerais, Brazil." *Hispanic American Historical Review* 81:2 (May 2001): 309–42.

Binzer, Ina von [Ulla von Eck]. *Alegrias e tristezas de uma educadora no Brasil*. São Paulo: Anhembi, 1965.

Bittencourt, Circe Maria Fernandes. "As 'tradições nacionais' e o ritual das festas cívicas." In *O ensino de história e a criação do fato*, ed. Jaime Pinsky, 43–72. São Paulo: Contexto, 1988.

Boelen, J[acobus]. *Reize naar Oost- en Westkust van Zuid Amerika. . . .* 3 vols. Amsterdam: Ten Brink en de Vries, 1835.

Bogart, Michele. *Public Sculpture and the Civic Ideal in New York City, 1890–1930*. Chicago: University of Chicago Press, 1989.

Borges, Valdeci Rezende. "Em busca do mundo exterior: Sociabilidade no Rio de Machado de Assis." *Estudos Históricos* 28 (2001): 49–69.

Borjes da Fonseca, Antonio. *Manifesto político, apontamentos da minha vida política e da vida politica do Dr. Urbano Pessoa de Melo*. Recife: Typ. Commercial de G. H. de Mira, 1867.

Bösche, Eduardo Theodoro. "Quadros alternados de viagens terrestres e maritimas, aventuras, acontecimentos politicos, descripção de usos e costumes de povos durante uma viagem ao Brasil," trans. Vicente de Sousa Queirós. *RIHGB* 83:137 (1918): 133–241.

Botafogo, Antonio Joaquim de Sousa, *O balanço da dynastia*. Rio: Imprensa Nacional, 1890.

Bougainville, Baron Hyacinth, Yves Philippe Potentin de. *Journal de la navigation autour du globe de la frégate* La Thétis *et de la corvette* L'Espérance *pendant les années 1824, 1825 et 1826*, 2 vols. Paris: Arthus Bertrand, 1837.

Brand, Charles. *Journal of a Voyage to Peru: A Passage across the Cordillera of the Andes, in the Winter of 1827. . . .* London: Henry Colburn, 1828.

Brand, Diane. "Sets and Extras: Ephemeral Architecture and Urban Ceremony in Rio de Janeiro (1808-1821)." *Journal of Latin American Cultural Studies* 15:3 (Dec. 2006): 263–79.

Brassey, Annie. *A Voyage in the "Sunbeam": Our Home on the Ocean for Eleven Months*, 2nd ed. London: Longman's, Green, and Co., 1879.

Brazil. *Anais da Camara dos Deputados*. Rio: 1826–89.

———. *Anais do Senado*. Rio: 1826–89.

———. *Annaes do Congresso Constituinte da República*, 2nd ed., 3 vols. Rio: Imprensa Nacional, 1924.

———. *Coleção das Leis do Brasil*. Rio: 1822–90.

———. *Diario da Assembléa Geral Constituinte e Legislativa do Império do Brasil, 1823*, 4 vols. in 2, facsimile ed. Brasília: Senado Federal, 1972.

Brazil. Fundação Biblioteca Nacional. *Catálogo de periódicos brasileiros microfilmados*. Rio: Fundação Biblioteca Nacional, 1994.

———. *Música no Rio de Janeiro imperial, 1822–1870: Exposição comemorativa do primeiro decênio da Seção de Música e Arquivo Sonoro*. Rio: Biblioteca Nacional, 1962.

Brazil. Ministerio da Justiça. *Relatorios*. Rio: 1825–89.

Brazil. Ministério da Justiça e Negócios Interiores. Arquivo Nacional. *Organizações e programas ministeriais: Regime parlamentar no Império*, 2nd ed. Rio: Departamento de Imprensa Nacional, 1962.

Brazil. Ministerio do Imperio. *Relatorios*. Rio: 1832–88.

Brazil. Serviço de Divulgação. *Uma só bandeira para toda a Pátria*. Rio: Serviço de Divulgação do Gabinete do Chefe de Policia do Districto Federal, n.d. [ca. 1938–45].

Bryant, Lawrence M. *The King and the City in the Parisian Royal Entry Ceremony: Politics, Ritual, and Art in the Renaissance*. Geneva: Droz, 1986.

Buc, Philippe. *The Dangers of Ritual: Between Early Medieval Texts and Social Scientific Theory*. Princeton, NJ: Princeton University Press, 2001.

Bunbury, Charles James Fox. "Narrativa de viagem de um naturalista inglês ao Rio de Janeiro e Minas Gerais (1833–1835)," trans. Helena Garcia de Sousa. *Anais da Biblioteca Nacional* 62 (1940): 5–135.

Burgain, L[uis] A[ntonio]. *A estatua do Imperador Dom Pedro I por . . . traduzido em Portuguez por *****. Rio: Typographica Imp. e Const. de J. Villeneuve e C., 1862.

———. *O vaticínio: Drama allegorico em applauso ao glorioso dia da Coroação e Sagração de Sua Magestade D. Pedro II*. Rio: Typ. da Ass. do Despertador, 1841.

Burke, Peter. *The Fabrication of Louis XIV*. New Haven, CT: Yale University Press, 1992.

Burke, Ulick Ralph, and Robert Staples Jr. *Business and Pleasure in Brazil*. London: Field and Tuer; New York: Scribner and Welford, 1884.

Burmeister, Hermann. *Viagem ao Brasil através das províncias do Rio de Janeiro e Minas Gerais*, trans. Manoel Salvaterra and Hubert Schoenfelt. São Paulo: Martins, 1952 [1853].

Burns, E. Bradford. *Nationalism in Brazil: A Historical Survey*. New York: Frederick A. Praeger, 1968.

Cabral, Alfredo do Vale. "Anais da Imprensa Nacional, 1823–1831." *ABN* 73 (1953): 39–115.

———. *Guia do viajante no Rio de Janeiro*. Rio: Typ. da Gazeta de Noticias, 1882.

Cabral, Luciano Mendes. *Selos, moedas e poder: O Estado Imperial brasileiro e seus símbolos*. Rio: Apicuri, 2009.

Calmon, Pedro. *Historia do Brasil na poesia do povo*. Rio: A Noite, 1943.

Calógeras, João Batista. *Um ministério visto por dentro: Cartas inéditas de João Batista Calógeras, alto funcionário do Império*, ed. Antonio Gontijo de Carvalho. Rio: José Olympio, 1959.

Calzadilla, Pedro Enrique. "El olor de la pólvora: Fiestas patrias, memorias y nación en la Venezuela guzmancista, 1870–1877." *Cahiers du Monde Hispanique et Luso-Brésilienne* 73 (Dec. 1999): 111–30.

Camara, Euzebio de Queiroz Coutinho Mattoso. *Discurso dirigido a S. M. o Senhor Dom Pedro II pelo conselheiro de Estado . . . presidente da Commissão encarregada de erigir a estatua equestre do Fundador do Imperio*. Rio: Typ. de Paula Brito, 1862.

Câmara, José Auréliano Saraiva. *Um soldado do Império: O General Tibúrcio e seu tempo*. Rio: José Olympio, 1978.

Câmara Cascudo, Luís da. *Dicionário do folclore brasileiro*, 9th ed. Rio: Ediouro, n.d.

Caminhoá, F[rancisco] de A[zevedo] M[onteiro]. *Documentos, juizo critico e orçamento relativos ao monumento patriotico do Brasil destinado ao Campo d'Acclamação no Rio de Janeiro*. Rio: Typ. Perseverança, 1874.

Campos, Joaquim Jacome de Oliveira, *O Brasil e o Paraguay, ou, A rendição da Uruguayana; quadro allegorico*. Rezende: M. Nunes Fernandes, 1873.

Campos, Joaquim Pinto de. *Discurso sagrado recitado em commemoração da Independencia do Brasil no solemnissimo Te Deum que a Sociedade Ypiranga fez celebrar no dia 7 de setembro de 1857, na igreja do Carmo desta capital*. Rio: Typ. Universal de Laemmert, 1857.

Campos, Pedro Henrique Pedereira, *Nos caminhos da acumulação: Negócios e poder no abastecimento de carnes verdes para a cidade do Rio de Janeiro (1808–1835)*. São Paulo: Alameda, 2010.

Cândido, Antônio, et al. *A crônica: O gênero, sua fixação e suas transformações no Brasil*. Campinas: Ed. da UNICAMP; Rio: Fundação Casa de Rui Barbosa, 1992.

Cañeque, Alejandro. *The King's Living Image: The Culture and Politics of Viceregal Power in Colonial Mexico*. London: Routledge, 2004.

Cannadine, David. "The Context, Performance and Meaning of Ritual: The British Monarchy and the 'Invention of Tradition,' c. 1820–1977." In *The Invention of Tradition*, ed. Eric Hobsbawm and Terence Ranger, 101–64. Cambridge, UK: Cambridge University Press, 1983.

Canstatt, Oskar. *Brasil: A terra e a gente, 1871*, trans. Eduardo de Lima Castro. Rio: Conquista, 1975.

Cardoso, Ângela Miranda. "Ritual: princípio, meio e fim. Do sentido do estudo das cerimônias de entronização brasileiras." In *Brasil: Formação do Estado e da nação*, ed. István Jancsó, 549–602. São Paulo: Hucitec; Ijuí: Unijuí, 2003.

Cardoso, Fernando Henrique, with Brian Winter. *The Accidental President of Brazil: A Memoir*. New York: Public Affairs, 2006.

Carpenter, Frank de Yeux. *Round about Rio*. Chicago: Jansen, McClurg & Co., 1884.

Carvalho, [Antonio dos] Reis. *Os feriados brasileiros: Sumárias apreciações sôbre os dias de festa nacional considerados como datas de celebração do

Culto Cívico, da Religião da Pátria, preâmbulo da Religião da Humanidade. Rio: Pimenta de Mello e C., 1926.

Carvalho, José Murilo de. *Os bestializados: O Rio de Janeiro e a República que não foi,* 3rd ed. São Paulo: Companhia das Letras, 1999.

———. *Cidadania no Brasil: O longo caminho.* Rio: Civilização Brasileira, 2001.

———. "As conferências radicais do Rio de Janeiro: Novo espaço de debate." In *Nação e cidadania no Império: Novos horizontes,* ed. José Murilo de Carvalho, 17–41. Rio: Record, 2007.

———. *A construção da ordem: A elite política imperial/Teatro de sombras: A política imperial,* rev. ed. Rio: Ed. UFRJ and Relume Dumará, 1996.

———. *D. Pedro II: Ser ou não ser.* São Paulo: Companhia das Letras, 2007.

———. *A formação das almas: O imaginário da República no Brasil.* São Paulo: Companhia das Letras, 1990.

———. ed. *Nação e cidadania no Império: Novos horizontes.* Rio: Record, 2007.

———. "Radicalismo e republicanismo." In *Repensando o Brasil do Oitocentos: Cidadania, política e liberdade,* ed. José Murilo de Carvalho and Lúcia Maria Bastos Pereira das Neves, 19–48. Rio: Civilização Brasileira, 2009.

Carvalho, José Murilo de, and Lúcia Maria Bastos Pereira das Neves, eds. *Repensando o Brasil do Oitocentos: Cidadania, política e liberdade.* Rio: Civilização Brasileira, 2009.

Castelnau, Francis, Comte de. *Expedition dans les parties centrales de l'Amérique du Sud, de Rio de Janeiro à Lima, et de Lima au Pará. . . .* 7 parts, 15 vols. Paris: P. Bertrand, 1850–59.

Castilho, Celso Thomas. "Abolition Matters: The Politics of Antislavery in Pernambuco, Brazil, 1869–1888." PhD dissertation, University of California, Berkeley, 2008.

Castilho, Celso Thomas, and Camillia Cowling. "Funding Freedom, Popularizing Politics: Abolitionism and Local Emancipation Funds in 1880s Brazil." *Luso-Brazilian Review* 47:1 (Spring 2010): 89–120.

Castro, Celso. *A invenção do Exército brasileiro.* Rio: Zahar, 2002.

———. *Os militares e a República: Um estudo sobre cultura e ação política.* Rio: Jorge Zahar, 1995.

———. "Revoltas de soldados contra a República." In *Nova História Militar Brasileira,* ed. Celso Castro, Vitor Izecksohn, and Hendrik Kraay, 301–13. Rio: Editora FGV and Bom Texto, 2004.

Castro, Paulo Pereira. "A 'experiência republicana,' 1831–1840." In *História geral da civilização brasileira.* Tomo 2: *O Brasil monárquico,* 5 vols., ed. Sérgio Buarque de Holanda, 2:9–67. São Paulo: Difel, 1966–71.

———. "Política e administração de 1840 a 1848." In *História geral da civilização brasileira.* Tomo 2: *O Brasil monárquico,* 5 vols., ed. Sérgio Buarque de Holanda, 2:509–40. São Paulo: Difel, 1966–71.

"Catálogo de jornais e revistas do Rio de Janeiro (1808–1889) existentes na Biblioteca Nacional." *ABN* 85 (1965): 7–208.

"Catálogo dos manuscritos sobre o Rio de Janeiro existentes na Biblioteca Nacional." *ABN* 102 (1982): 5–220; 104 (1984): 1–170; 196 (1986): 53–233.

Catroga, Fernando. "O culto cívico de D. Pedro IV e a construção da memória liberal." *Revista de História das Idéias* 12 (1990): 445–70.

Cavallini, Marco Cícero. "Monumento e política: Os 'comentários da semana' de Machado de Assis." In *História em cousas miúdas: Capítulos de história social da crônica no Brasil,* ed. Sidney Chalhoub et al., 299–340. Campinas: Ed. UNICAMP, 2005.

Centeno, Miguel Angel. *Blood and Debt: War and the Nation-State in Latin America.* University Park: Pennsylvania State University Press, 2002.

Cerqueira, Dionísio. *Reminiscências da campanha do Paraguai, 1865–1870.* Rio: Biblioteca do Exército Editora, 1980.

Cerri, Luís Fernando. "1972: 'Sete bandeiras do setecentenário por mil cruzeiros velhos.'" *Estudos Ibero-Americanos* 25:1 (June 1999): 193–208.

Chagas, João. *De bond: Alguns aspectos da civilisação brasileira.* Lisbon: Livraria Moderna, [1897].

Chagas, Paulo Pinheiro. *Teófilo Ottoni: Ministro do povo.* Belo Horizonte: Itatiaia, 1978.

Chalhoub, Sidney. "A arte de alinhavar histórias: A série 'A + B' de Machado de Assis." In *História em cousas miúdas: Capítulos de história social da crônica no Brasil,* ed. Sidney Chalhoub et al., 67–85. Campinas: Ed. UNICAMP, 2005.

———. *Cidade febril: Cortiços e epidemias na corte imperial.* São Paulo: Companhia das Letras, 1996.

———. *Machado de Assis, historiador.* São Paulo: Companhia das Letras, 2003.

———. *Visões da Liberdade: Uma história das últimas décadas de escravidão na Corte.* São Paulo: Companhia das Letras, 1990.

Chamon, Carla Simone. *Festejos imperiais: Festas cívicas em Minas Gerais (1815–1845).* Bragança Paulista: EDSF, Universidade São Francisco, CDAPH, 2002.

Chavagnes, M. L. de. "Le Brésil en 1844—Sa situation morale, politique, comerciale et financière—La société brésilienne." *Revue des Deux Mondes.* New Ser. 7 (July–Dec. 1844): 66–106; (Oct.–Dec. 1844): 849–909.

Chazkel, Amy. "The Crônica, the City, and the Invention of the Underworld: Rio de Janeiro, 1889–1922." *Estudios Interdisciplinares de América Latina y el Caribe* 12:1 (Jan.–June 2001). Available at www1.tau.ac.il/eial/ (accessed June 2007).

———. *Laws of Chance: Brazil's Clandestine Lottery and the Making of Urban Public Life.* Durham, NC: Duke University Press, 2011.

Chirio, Maud. "Fêtes nationales et régime dictatorial au Brésil." *Vingtième Siècle* 90 (April 2006): 89–108.

Christo, Maraliz de Castro Vieira. "O esquartejamento de uma obra: A rejeição ao Tiradentes de Pedro Américo." *Locus* (Juiz de Fora) 4:2 (1998): 143–67.

Clark, Kathleen Ann. *Defining Moments: African-American Commemoration and Political Culture in the South, 1863–1913.* Chapel Hill: University of North Carolina Press, 2005.

Coaracy, Vivaldo. *Memórias da cidade do Rio de Janeiro,* 3rd ed. Belo Horizonte: Itatiaia; São Paulo: EdUSP, 1988 [1955].

———. *Todos contam sua vida: Memórias de infância e juventude.* Rio: José Olympio, 1959.

Cochrane, Thomas, Earl of Dundonald. *Narrative of Services in the Liberation of Chili, Peru, and Brazil from Spanish and Portuguese Domination,* 2 vols. London: James Ridgway, 1859.

Codigo de posturas, leis, decretos, editaes e resoluções da Intendencia Municipal do Districto Federal. Rio: Papeleria e Typographia Mont'Alverne, 1894.

Codman, John. *Ten Months in Brazil: With Incidents of Voyages and Travels, Descriptions of Scenery and Character, Practices of Commerce and Productions, etc.* Boston: Lee and Shepard, 1867.

Coggeshall, George. *Thirty-Six Voyages to Various Parts of the World, Made between the Years 1799 and 1841,* 3rd ed. New York: Published by and for the Author, 1858.

Cohen, William. "Symbols of Power: Statues in Nineteenth-Century Provincial France." *Comparative Studies in Society and History* 31:3 (July 1989): 491–513.

Cohn, William H. "Popular Culture and Social History." *Journal of Popular Culture* 11:1 (1977): 167–79.

Colson, Frank. "On Expectations: Perspectives on the Crisis of 1889 in Brazil." *Journal of Latin American Studies* 13:2 (May 1981): 265–92.

Colvocoresses, George Musalas. *Four Years in a Government Exploration Expedition. . . .* New York: Cornish, Lamport & Co., 1852.

Conde, Maite. "Film and the Crônica: Documenting New Urban Experiences in Turn-of-the-Century Rio de Janeiro." *Luso-Brazilian Review* 42:2 (2005): 66–88.

Conrad, Robert. *The Destruction of Brazilian Slavery, 1850–1888.* Berkeley: University of California Press, 1972.

Coppin, Henry. *Quatre républiques de l'Amérique du Sud.* Paris, 1890.

"Correspondência de D. Pedro II com o conselheiro João Alfredo." *RIHGB* 274 (Jan.–Mar. 1967): 87–202.

"Correspondência do barão de Mareschal." *RIHGB* 313–49 (1976–85).

"Correspondencia passiva de Antônio Gonçalves Dias." *ABN* 91 (1971): 9–356.

"Correspondencia passiva do senador José Martiniano de Alencar." *ABN* 86 (1966): 3–468.

Corrigan, Philip, and Derek Sayer. *The Great Arch: English State Formation as Cultural Revolution.* Oxford, UK: Blackwell Publishers, 1985.

Costa, Emilia Viotti da. "1807–1889." In *Brazil: Empire and Republic, 1822–1930,* ed. Leslie Bethell, 161–213. Cambridge, UK: Cambridge University Press, 1989.

———. *The Brazilian Empire: Myths and Histories.* Chicago: University of Chicago Press, 1985.

———. *Da senzala à colônia.* São Paulo: Difusão Européia do Livro, 1966.

Costa, João Cruz. *A History of Ideas in Brazil: The Development of Philosophy in Brazil and the Evolution of National History,* trans. Suzette Macedo. Berkeley: University of California Press, 1964.

Costa, Luiz Monteiro da. *D. Pedro I entre o 7 de setembro e o 12 de outubro.* Salvador: Imprensa Official da Bahia, 1956.

Costa, Milton Carlos. *Visões políticas do Império: Diplomatas belgas no Brasil (1834–1864)*. São Paulo: Annablume, 2011.

Couty, Louis. *L'esclavage au Brésil*. Paris: Guillaumin, 1881.

Cowling, Camillia. "Debating Womanhood, Defining Freedom: The Abolition of Slavery in 1880s Rio de Janeiro." *Gender and History* 22:2 (Aug. 2010): 284–301.

Cruls, Gastão. *Aparência do Rio de Janeiro (noticia histórica e descritiva da cidade)*, 2 vols. Rio: José Olympio, 1952 [1949].

Cunha, Francisco Xavier da. *Propaganda contra o império: Reminiscencias na imprensa e na diplomacia, 1870 a 1910*. Rio: Imprensa Nacional, 1914.

Cunha, Manuela Carneiro da. "Política indigenista no século XIX." In *História dos índios no Brasil*, 2nd ed., ed. Manuela Carneiro da Cunha, 133–54. São Paulo: Companhia das Letras, 1998.

Cunha, Marco Antonio. *A chama da nacionalidade: Ecos da Guerra do Paraguai*. Rio: Biblioteca do Exército Editora, 2000.

Cunha, Maria Clementina Pereira da. *Ecos da folia: Uma história social do carnaval carioca entre 1880 e 1920*. São Paulo: Companhia das Letras, 2001.

Cunha, Pedro Octávio Carneiro da. "A fundação de um império liberal." In *História geral da civilização brasileira*. Tomo 2: *O Brasil monárquico*, 5 vols., ed. Sérgio Buarque de Holanda, 1:135–78, 238–62, 379–404. São Paulo: Difel, 1966–71.

Cunningham, Robert O. *Notes on the Natural History of the Strait of Magellan and the West Coast of Patagonia*. Edinburgh: Edmonston and Douglas, 1871.

Curcio-Nagy, Linda A. *The Great Festivals of Colonial Mexico City: Performing Power and Identity*. Albuquerque: University of New Mexico Press, 1994.

Curto, Diogo Ramada. "Ritos e cerimónias da monarquia em Portugal (séculos XVI a XVIII)." In *A memória da nação*, ed. Francisco Bethencourt and Diogo Ramada Curto, 201–65. Lisbon: Sá da Costa, 1991.

"D. Pedro I e D. Amélia." *Documentário Histórico* 1 (1950): 1–214.

Dabadie, F. *A travers l'Amérique du Sud*. Paris: Ferdinand Sartorius Editeur, 1859.

Daibert Júnior, Robert. *Isabel, a "Redentora" dos escravos: Uma história da princesa entre olhares negros e brancos (1846–1988)*. Bauru: EDUSC, 2004.

DaMatta, Roberto. *A casa e a rua: Espaço, cidadania, mulher e morte no Brasil*. São Paulo: Brasiliense, 1985.

———. *Carnivals, Rogues, and Heroes: An Interpretation of the Brazilian Dilemma*, trans. John Drury. Notre Dame, IN: University of Notre Dame Press, 1991.

Dávila, Jerry. *Hotel Trópico: Brazil and the Challenge of African Decolonization, 1950–1980*. Durham, NC: Duke University Press, 2010.

Davis, John A. "Opera and Absolutism in Restoration Italy, 1815–1860." *Journal of Interdisciplinary History* 36:4 (Spring 2006): 569–94.

Davis, Susan G. *Parades and Power: Street Theatre in Nineteenth-Century Philadelphia*. Berkeley: University of California Press, 1988.

Dean, Carolyn. *Inka Bodies and the Body of Christ: Corpus Christi in Colonial Cuzco, Peru*. Durham, NC: Duke University Press, 1999.

Debret, Jean-Baptiste. *Viagem pitoresca e histórica ao Brasil*, 3 vols. in 2, trans. Sergio Milliet. São Paulo: Livraria Martins and Editora da Universidade de São Paulo, 1972.

———. *Voyage pittoresque et historique au Brésil*. . . . 3 vols. Paris: Firmin Didot Frères, 1834–39.

Degler, Carl N. *Neither Black nor White: Slavery and Race Relations in Brazil and the United States*. Madison: University of Wisconsin Press, 1971.

Dent, Hastings Charles. *A Year in Brazil with Notes on the Abolition of Slavery, the Finances of the Empire, Religion, Meteorology, Natural History*. London: Kegan Paul, Trench, and Co., 1884.

Desch-Obi, T. J. *Fighting for Honor: The History of African Martial Art Traditions in the Atlantic World*. Columbia: University of South Carolina Press, 2008.

De-Simoni, Luiz Vicente. *Marília de Itamaracá ou a Donzela da Mangueira*. Rio: Typ. Dous de Dezembro, 1854.

Díaz Arias, David. *La fiesta de la independencia en Costa Rica, 1821–1921*. San José: Editorial Universidad de Costa Rica, 2007.

D[illon], L. *A Twelve Months' Tour in Brazil and the River Plate with Notes on Sheep Farming*. Manchester, UK: Alexander Ireland, 1867.

Disposições para a sagração de S. M. o Imperador. Rio: Typographia Nacional, 1841.

Dolkart, Ronald H. "Elitelore at the Opera: The Teatro Colon of Buenos Aires." *Journal of Latin American Lore* 9:2 (1983): 231–50.

Doratioto, Francisco. *Maldita Guerra: Nova história da Guerra do Paraguai*. São Paulo: Companhia das Letras, 2002.

Dória, Luiz Gastão d'Escragnolle. "Cousas do passado." *RIHGB* 71:118 (1908): 183–403.

Douville, J[ean] B. *30 mois de ma vie, quinze mois après mon voyage au Congo . . . suivis de details . . . sur les moeurs . . . des habitans du Brésil*. Paris: Imprimerie d'Éverat, 1830.

Doyle, Don H., and Marco Antonio Pamplona, eds. *Nationalism in the New World*. Athens: University of Georgia Press, 2006.

Driskel, Michael Paul. *As Befits a Legend: Building a Tomb for Napoleon, 1840–1861*. Kent, OH: Kent State University Press, 1995.

Drummond, Antonio de Menezes Vasconcellos de. "Annotações de A. M. V. de Drummond à sua biographia publicada em 1836 na *Biographie universelle et portative des contemporains*." *ABN* 13:3 (1885–86): 1–149.

Duarte, Regina Horta. *Noites circenses: Espetáculos de circo e teatro em Minas Gerais no século XIX*. Campinas: Ed. da UNICAMP, 1995.

Duindam, Jeroen. *Vienna and Versailles: The Courts of Europe's Dynastic Rivals, 1550–1780*. Cambridge, UK: Cambridge University Press, 2003.

Duncan, Julian Smith. *Public and Private Operations of Railways in Brazil*. New York: Columbia University Press, 1932.

Duncan, Robert H. "Embracing a Suitable Past: Independence Celebrations under Mexico's Second Empire, 1864–6." *Journal of Latin American Studies* 30:2 (May 1998): 249–77.

————. "Political Legitimization and Maximilian's Second Empire in Mexico, 1864–1867." *Mexican Studies* 12:1 (Winter 1996): 27–66.

Dunlop, C[harles] J[ulius], *Subsídios para a história do Rio de Janeiro*. Rio: Imperial Novo Milênio, 2008 [1957].

Earle, Rebecca. *The Return of the Native: Indians and Myth-Making in Spanish America, 1810–1930*. Durham, NC: Duke University Press, 2007.

Ebel, Ernst. *O Rio de Janeiro e seus arredores em 1824*, trans. Joaquim de Sousa Leão Filho. São Paulo: Editora Nacional, 1972.

Edmundo, Luiz. *De um livro de memorias*, 5 vols. Rio: n.p., 1958.

————. *O Rio de Janeiro do meu tempo*, 5 vols. Rio: Conquista, 1938.

Elogio dramatico intitulado: Gloria do Brasil, offerecido á S. M. I. o Senhor D. Pedro II, por occasião de solemnisar-se a posse do Exm.º Regente, que teve lugar no dia 12 de Outubro de 1835, pela companhia do Theatro Constitucional Fluminense. Rio: Typ. Imperial de F. P. Brito, 1835.

Eltis, David, and David Richardson. "A New Assessment of the Transatlantic Slave Trade." In *Extending the Frontiers: Essays on the New Transatlantic Slave Trade Database*, ed. David Eltis and David Richardson, 1–60. New Haven, CT: Yale University Press, 2008.

Elwes, Robert. *A Sketcher's Tour Round the World*. London: Hurst and Blackett, 1854.

Enciclopédia da música brasileira: Erudita, folclorica, popular. São Paulo: Arte Editora, 1977.

Enders, Armelle. "'O plutarco brasileiro': A produção de vultos nacionais no Segundo Reinado." *Estudos Históricos* 14:25 (2000): 41–62.

Esposito, Matthew D. *Funerals, Festivals, and Cultural Politics in Porfirian Mexico*. Albuquerque: University of New Mexico Press, 2010.

Esqueiros [Alfredo Moreira Pinto]. *Martyres da liberdade: Às sagradas cinzas de João Guilherme Ratcliffe e de seus companheiros de martirio e à heroica Provincia de Pernambuco, theatro da gloriosa revolução de 1824*. Rio: Typ. de J. D. Oliveira, n.d.

————. *Processo do primeiro martyr da liberdade brasileira, Joaquim José da Silva Xavier, por antonomasia o Tira-dentes, filho da provincia de Minas-Geraes*. Rio: Typ. de J. L. Vianna, 1872.

Estatua equestre do Senhor D. Pedro I: Contracto do Sr. Rochet, estatuario, e proposta apresentada por elle à commissão em 1856. Rio: Typ. Dous de Dezembro de Paula Brito, 1856.

Ewbank, Thomas. *Life in Brazil: Or, a Journal of a Visit to the Land of the Cocoa and the Palm*. New York: Harper, 1856.

Expilly, [Jean] Charles [Marie]. *Le Brésil tel qu'il est*. Paris: E. Dentu, 1862.

Faria, João Roberto. *Idéias teatrais: O século 19 no Brazil*. São Paulo: Perspectiva, 2001.

Faria, Silverio Candido de. *Breve historia dos felizes acontecimentos politicos no Rio de Janeiro em os sempre memoraveis dias 6, e 7 de Abril de 1831, remontada à epocha da viagem do Ex-Imperador à Provincia de Minas Gerais*. Rio: Typ. de Thomaz B. Hunt e C., 1831.

Farias, Juliana Barreto, Carlos Eugênio Líbano Soares, and Flávio dos Santos Gomes. *No labirinto das nações: Africanos e identidades no Rio de Janeiro, século XIX.* Rio: Arquivo Nacional, 2005.

Fernandes, José Pedro. *Alliança da Virtude, e da Fortuna: Drama para se representar no Imperial Theatro de S. Pedro d'Alcantara no Faustissimo Anniversario de S. M. I. a Imperatriz do Brasil.* Rio: Typ. de Gueffier & C., 1830.

———. *Elogio no muito fausto natalicio e anniversario da gloriosa acclamação de sua magestade imperial o Senhor D. Pedro Primeiro, Imperador Constitucional e defensor perpetuo do Brasil, recitado no Theatro de S. João. . . .* Rio: Typ. de Silva Porto, 1823.

———. *Homenagem consagrada ao Imperador do Brasil D. Pedro I no seu feliz regresso da Cidade da Bahia à Capital do Imperio.* Rio: Imprensa Imperial e Nacional, 1826.

Ferreira, Felipe. *Inventando carnavais: O surgimento do carnaval no século XIX e outras questões carnavalescas.* Rio: UFRJ Editora, 2005.

Ferreira, Felix. *Guia do estrangeiro no Rio de Janeiro. . . .* Rio: B. L. Garnier, 1873.

Ferreira, Lusirene Celestino França. "Nas asas da imprensa: A repercussão da abolição da escravatura na província do Ceará nos periódicos do Rio de Janeiro (1884–1885)." MA Thesis, Universidade Federal de São João del-Rei, 2010.

Ferreira, Procópio. *O ator Vasques.* Rio: Serviço Nacional do Teatro, 1979.

Ferreira da Rosa, [Francisco]. "Memorial de [sic] Rio de Janeiro: Personagens—fatos—narrativa de acontecimentos—vida e progresso da cidade em meio século (1878–1928)." *Arquivo do Distrito Federal* 2 (1951): 5–634.

———. *Prosa sadia (pequeno extrato de uma antiga coleção de escritos),* 9 vols. Rio: Grafica Sauer, 1936–46.

Ferreira Neto, Edgard Leite. "A elaboração positivista da memória republicana." *Tempo Brasileiro* 87 (Oct.–Dec. 1986): 79–103.

Ferreira Vianna, Antonio. "A conferência dos Divinos." In *Três panfletários do Segundo Reinado,* ed. R[aimundo] Magalhães Junior, 257–64. Rio: ABL, 2009 [1885].

Ferrez, Gilberto. *Iconografia do Rio de Janeiro, 1530–1890: Catálogo analítico,* 2 vols. Rio: Casa Jorge Editorial, 2000.

———. *A muito leal e heróica cidade de São Sebastião do Rio de Janeiro: Quatro séculos de expansão e evolução.* Rio: Banco Boavista S.A., 1965.

———. "O que ensinam os antigos mapas e estampas do Rio de Janeiro." *RIHGB* 268 (July–Sept. 1965): 27–42; 278 (Jan.–March 1968): 87–104.

Ferrière le Vayer, Théophile de. *Une ambassade française en Chine: Journal de voyage.* Paris: Librairie d'Amyot, 1854.

A Festa das Creanças: Commemoração da Lei de 13 de Maio que aboliu a escravidão no Brazil. Rio: Imprensa Nacional, 1888.

Fleck, Eliane Cristina Deckman, and Mauro Dillman Tavares. "Um apóstolo da Independência do Brasil: O projeto de Estado-nação em *O Jesuita* de José de Alencar." *Anos 90* 29 (July 2009): 315–48.

Fletcher, James C., and Daniel P. Kidder. *Brazil and the Brazilians Portrayed in Historical and Descriptive Sketches*, 8th ed. Boston: Little, Brown, and Co., 1868.

Flory, Thomas. *Judge and Jury in Imperial Brazil, 1808–1871: Social Control and Political Stability in the New State*. Austin: University of Texas Press, 1981.

———. "Race and Social Control in Independent Brazil." *Journal of Latin American Studies* 9:2 (Nov. 1977): 199–224.

———. *Traços biográficos da heroina brasileira Jovita Alves Feitosa, ex-sargento do 2.º Corpo de Voluntarios do Piauhy, natural do Ceará*. Rio: Typ. Imparcial de Brito & Irmão, 1865.

Folhinha d'algibeira ou diario civil e ecclesiastico do anno de 1830. Rio: P. Plancher-Seignot, 1829.

Folhinha luso-brasileira para o anno de 1857. . . . Rio: Livraria de D. J. Gomes Brandão, [1856].

Fonseca, Gondim da. *Biografia do jornalismo carioca (1808–1908)*. Rio: Quaresma Editora, 1941.

Fontino, Veriano. *Sete de Setembro*. Rio: n.p., 1877.

Forde, P. J. *Our Cruise! The Inns and Outs of It, Being a Journal of U.S. Ship Savannah's Cruise on the Coast of Brazil from 1853 to 1856*. New York: n.p., 1856.

Forman, Ross G. "Harbouring Discontent: British Imperialism through Brazilian Eyes in the Christie Affair." In *An Age of Equipoise? Reassessing Mid-Victorian Britain*, ed. Martin Hewitt, 225–43. Aldershot, UK: Ashgate, 2000.

Forment, Carlos A. *Democracy in Latin America, 1760–1900*. Vol. 1: *Civic Selfhood and Public Life in Mexico and Peru*. Chicago: University of Chicago Press, 2003.

Fort, Joseph-Auguste Aristide. *Le récit de ma vie avec la description d'un voyage et d'un séjour dans l'Amérique du Sud*. Paris: Chez L. Bataille, 1893.

Fragale Filho, Roberto da Silva. *A aventura política positivista: Um projeto republicano de tutela*. São Paulo: LTR, 1998.

Fragoso, João Luis Ribeiro. *Homens da grossa aventura: Acumulação e hierarquia na praça mercantil do Rio de Janeiro (1790–1830)*. Rio: Arquivo Nacional, 1992.

Fragoso, João Luis Ribeiro, and Manolo Florentino. *O arcaísmo como projeto: Mercado atlântico, sociedade agrária e elite mercantil em uma economia colonial tardia, Rio de Janeiro, c. 1790–c. 1840*, 4th ed. Rio: Civilização Brasileira, 2001.

França Júnior, J[oaquim] J[osé] de. *Folhetins*. Rio: Typ. da *Gazeta de Noticias*, 1878.

———. *Política e costumes: Folhetins esquecidos (1867–1868)*. Rio: Civilização Brasileira, 1957.

Frank, Zephyr L. *Dutra's World: Wealth and Family in Nineteenth-Century Rio de Janeiro*. Albuquerque: University of New Mexico Press, 2004.

Freycinet, Rose. *A Woman of Courage: The Journal of Rose de Freycinet on Her Voyage around the World, 1817–1820*, ed. Marc Serge Rivière. Canberra: National Library of Australia, 2003.

Fujitani, T[akashi]. *Splendid Monarchy: Power and Pageantry in Modern Japan*. Berkeley: University of California Press, 1996.

Fulcher, Jane. *The Nation's Image: French Grand Opera as Politics and Politicized Art*. New York: Cambridge University Press, 1987.

Funcções do casamento de Sua Magestade Imperial o Senhor Dom Pedro I.º com a serenissima Senhora Princeza Amelia de Leuchtenberg. Rio: Typ. Imperial de P. Plancher-Seignot, 1830.

Fundação Casa de Rui Barbosa. *Catálogo dos periódicos da Coleção Plínio Doyle*. Rio: Edições Casa de Rui Barbosa, 2000.

Furtado, João Pinto. *O manto de Penélope: História, mito e memória da Inconfidência Mineira de 1788–9*. São Paulo: Companhia das Letras, 2002.

Furtado, Júnia Ferreira. "Desfilar: A procissão barroca." *Revista Brasileira de História* 33 (1997): 251–79.

Gaeta, Mara Aparecida Junqueira da Veiga. "O cortejo de Deus e a imagem do rei: A procissão de Corpus Christi na capitania de São Paulo." *História* (São Paulo) 13 (1994): 109–20.

Gallenga, Antonio Carlo Napoleone. *South America*, 2nd ed. London: Chapman and Hall, 1889.

Galvão, Alfredo. "A estátua eqüestre de D. Pedro I." *Arquivos da Escola Nacional de Belas Artes* 8 (1962): 33–43.

———, ed. "Manuel de Araújo Pôrto Alegre: Sua influência na Academia Imperial de Belas Artes e no meio artístico do Rio de Janeiro." *Revista do Patrimônio Histórico e Artístico Nacional* 14 (1959): 1–106.

Galvão, B[enjamin] F[ranklin] Ramiz. *Catálogo da Exposição de História do Brasil*, 3 vols., facsimile ed. Brasília: Editora da Universidade de Brasília, 1981.

Galves, Marcelo Cheche. " 'Aderir', 'jurar' e 'aclamar': O Império no Maranhão (1823–1826)." *Almanack* 1 (Nov. 2010): 105–18.

Gama, Nicolau Antonio Nogueira Vale da, Visconde de Nogueira da Gama. *Minhas memorias*. Rio: Magalhães e Comp., 1893.

Garavaglia, Juan Carlos. *Construir el estado, inventar la nación, siglos XVIII–XIX*. Buenos Aires: Prometeu Libros, 2007.

Garcia, Antonio José Nunes. *Elogio dramatico allegorico: O triumpho do Brasil, ou A queda da inveja*. Rio: Typ. Brasiliense de F. M. Ferreira, 1851.

———. *O censor fluminense*, 2nd ed., rev'd. Rio: n.p., 1889 [1879].

Gardner, George. *Travels in the Interior of Brazil, Principally through the Northern Provinces and the Gold and Diamond Districts during the Years 1836–1841*, 2nd ed. London: Reeve, Benham, and Reeve, 1841.

Gaston, J[ames] McF[adden]. *Hunting a Home in Brazil: The Agricultural Resources and Other Characteristics of the Country*. Philadelphia: King and Baird, 1867.

Geertz, Clifford. "Centers, Kings, and Charisma: Reflections on the Symbolics of Power." In *Culture and Its Creators*, ed. Joseph Ben-David and Terry Nichols Clark, 150–71. Chicago: University of Chicago Press, 1977.

————. *Negara: The Theatre State in Nineteenth-Century Bali*. Princeton, NJ: Princeton University Press, 1980.

Gendrin, Victor-Athanase. *Récit historique, exact et sincère, par mer et par terre, de quatre voyages faits au Brésil, au Chili, dans les Cordillères des Andes, à Mendoza, dans le désert, et à Buenos Aires*. Versailles: M. Gendrin, 1856.

Gerson, Brasil. *História das ruas do Rio*, 5th ed., ed. Alexei Bueno. Rio: Lacerda Ed., 2000.

Giannini, Gioacchino. *A harmonia celestial no Brasil: Representação theatral lyrica e allegorica em um só acto para festejar o Faustissimo dia 2 de Dezembro do Anno de 1851*. Rio: Typ. de F. de Paula Brito, 1851.

Girão, Raimundo. *A abolição no Ceará*, 2nd ed. Fortaleza: Secretaria de Cultura do Ceará, 1969.

Giron, Luis Antonio. *Minoridade crítica: A ópera e o teatro nos folhetins da Corte*. São Paulo: Editora da Universidade de São Paulo, 2004.

Gomes, Amanda Muzzi. "Monarquistas restauradores e jacobinos: Ativismo político." *Estudos Históricos* 21:42 (2008): 284–302.

Gomes, Antonio Carlos. *Joanna de Flandres ou A Volta do Cruzado: Drama lyrico em quatro actos*. Rio: Typ. da Actualidade, 1863.

Gomes, Flávio dos Santos. "No meio das águas turvas: Racismo e cidadania no alvorecer da República, A Guarda Negra na Corte, 1888–1889." *Estudos Afro-Asiáticos* 21 (Dec. 1991): 75–96.

Gomes, Isabelle Macedo. "Dois séculos em busca de uma solução: Esgotos sanitários e meio ambiente na cidade do Rio de Janeiro." In *Formas, movimentos, representações: Estudos de geografia histórica carioca*, ed. Maurício de Almeida Abreu, 56–71. Rio: Da Fonseca Comunicação, 2005.

G[onçalves] de Magalhães, D[omingos] J[osé]. *Poesias de. . . .* Rio: Typ. de R. Ogier, 1832.

————. *Tragedias: Antonio José, Olgiato e Othelo*. Rio: B. L. Garnier, 1865.

Gondim, Eunice Ribeiro. *Pseudônimos e rúbricas de autores brasileiros*. Rio: Estado de Guanabara, Secretaria da Educação e Cultura, Biblioteca Estadual, 1961.

————. *Vida e obra de Paula Brito*. Rio: Livraria Brasiliana Editora, 1965.

González, Luis Arnaldo. "Conmemoraciones de la Libertad: El 13 de mayo en el discurso varguista." *Op. Cit.: Revista del Centro de Investigaciones Historicas* 16 (2005): 179–219.

Gordon, Eric A. "A New Opera House: An Investigation of Elite Values in Mid-Nineteenth-Century Rio de Janeiro." *Inter-American Institute for Musical Research Yearbook* 5 (1969): 49–66.

Gottschalk, Louis Moreau. *Les voyages extraordinaires de L. Moreau Gottschalk, pianiste et aventurier*. Paris: Editions Pierre-Marcel Favre, 1985.

Gouvêa, Maria de Fátima Silva. "Política provincial na formação da monarquia constitucional brasileira, Rio de Janeiro, 1820–1850." *Almanack Braziliense* 7 (May 2008): 119–37.

————. "O Senado da Câmara do Rio de Janeiro no contexto das cerimônias de aclamação de D. João VI." In *Anais do Seminário Internacional D. João*

VI, um rei aclamado na América, 249–59. Rio: Museu Histórico Nacional, 2000.

Gouvea, Pedro Bandeira da. *Ao povo brasileiro: Estatua de Tira-Dentes, subscripção popular.* Rio: Typ. da América, 1872.

Graham, Maria Dundas [Callcott]. "Escorço biográfico de Dom Pedro I, com uma noticia do Brasil e do Rio de Janeiro em seu tempo." *ABN* 60 (1938): 67–176.

———. *Journal of a Voyage to Brazil and Residence There during Part of the Years 1821, 1822, 1823.* London: Longman, Hurst, Rees, Orme, Brown, and Green, 1824.

Graham, Richard. "Constructing a Nation in Nineteenth-Century Brazil: Old and New Views on Class, Culture, and the State." *The Journal of the Historical Society* 1:2–3 (Winter 2000): 17–66.

———. "Free African Brazilians and the State in Slavery Times." In *Racial Politics in Contemporary Brazil,* ed. Michael Hanchard, 30–58. Durham, NC: Duke University Press, 1999.

———. "Os fundamentos da ruptura de relações diplomáticas entre o Brasil e a Grã-Bretanha em 1863: 'A Questão Christie.'" *Revista de História* 24 (Jan.–Jun. 1962): 117–38, 379–42.

———. *Patronage and Politics in Nineteenth-Century Brazil.* Stanford, CA: Stanford University Press, 1990.

Graham, Sandra Lauderdale. "The Vintem Riot and Political Culture: Rio de Janeiro, 1880." *Hispanic American Historical Review* 60:3 (August 1980): 431–49.

Green, James N. *Beyond Carnival: Male Homosexuality in Twentieth-Century Brazil.* Chicago: University of Chicago Press, 1999.

———. "The Emperor and His Pedestal: Pedro I and Disputed Views of the Brazilian Nation, 1860–1900." In *Brazil in the Making: Facets of National Identity,* ed. Carmen Nava and Ludwig Lauerhass Jr., 181–202. Lanham, MD: Rowman and Littlefield, 2006.

Greenfield, Gerald M. *The Realities of Images: Imperial Brazil and the Great Drought.* Philadelphia: American Philosophical Society, 2001.

Groot, C. F. G. de. *Brazilian Catholicism and Ultramontane Reform, 1850–1930.* Amsterdam: CEDLA, 1995.

Guerra, François-Xavier. "Forms of Communication, Political Spaces, and Cultural Identities in the Creation of Spanish-American Nations." In *Beyond Imagined Communities: Reading and Writing the Nation in Nineteenth-Century Latin America,* ed. John Charles Chasteen and Sara Castro-Klarén, 3–32. Baltimore: Johns Hopkins University Press, 2003.

Guimarães, Lúcia Maria Paschoal. "Ação, reação e transação: A pena de aluguel e a historiografia." In *Nação e cidadania no Império: Novos horizontes,* ed. José Murilo de Carvalho, 71–91. Rio: Record, 2007.

———. "Entre a Monarquia e a República: A Revolução Pernambucana de 1817 e suas representações no Instituto Histórico e Geográfico Brasileiro." In *Entre a Monarquia e a República: Imprensa, pensamento político e historiografia (1822–1889),* ed. Maria Leite Lessa and Silvia Carla Pereira de Brito Fonseca, 152–61. Rio: EdUERJ, 2008.

————. "Henrique Fleiüss: A função cívica e pedagógica da caricatura nas páginas da *Semana Illustrada* (1860–1876)." In *Repensando o Brasil do Oitocentos*, ed. José Murilo de Carvalho and Lúcia Maria Bastos Pereira das Neves, 153–74. Rio: Civilização Brasileira, 2009.

————. "Liberalismo moderado: Postulados ideológicos e práticas políticas no período regencial (1831–1837)." In *O liberalismo no Brasil imperial: Origens, conceitos e prática*, ed. Lúcia Maria Paschoal Guimarães and Maria Emília Prado, 103–26. Rio: Revan, 2001.

————. "A Primeira República e as representações de d. Pedro II." In *História: Narrativas plurais, múltiplas linguagens*, ed. Heloísa Helena Pacheco Cardoso and Maria Clara Thomaz Machado, 143–59. Uberlândia: Ed. UFU, 2005.

Guimarães, Manoel Luis Salgado. "Nação e civilização nos trópicos: O IHGB e o projeto de uma história nacional." *Estudos Históricos* 1:1 (1988): 5–27.

Haberly, David T. "The Mythification of Tiradentes: Two Brazilian Literary Legends." *Romance Quarterly* 52:1 (Winter 2005): 64–78.

Haddock Lobo, Roberto Jorge. *Discurso dirigido a S. M. o Snr. D. Pedro II Imperador Constitucional e Defensor Perpetuo do Brazil pelo Dr. . . . secretario da commissão encarregada de erigir a estatua equestre do Fundador do Imperio*. Rio: Typographia de Paula Brito, 1862.

Hadfield, William. *Brazil and the River Plate, 1870–76*. Sutton, UK: W. R. Church, 1877.

Hahner, June E. *Civilian-Military Relations in Brazil, 1889–1898*. Columbia: University of South Carolina Press, 1969.

————. *Emancipating the Female Sex: The Struggle for Women's Rights in Brazil, 1850–1940*. Durham, NC: Duke University Press, 1990.

————. *Poverty and Politics: The Urban Poor in Brazil, 1870–1920*. Albuquerque: University of New Mexico Press, 1986.

Halbwachs, Maurice. *On Collective Memory*, trans. Lewis A. Coser. Chicago: University of Chicago Press, 1992.

Hall, L[inville]. J[ohn]. *Around the Horn in '49: Journal of the Hartford Union Mining and Trading Company*. Wethersfield, CT: L. J. Hall, 1898 [1849].

Hallewell, L. *Books in Brazil: A History of the Publishing Trade*. Metuchen, NJ: The Scarecrow Press, 1982.

Hamond, Graham Eden. *Os diários do almirante . . . , 1825–1834/38*, trans. Paulo F. Geyer. Rio: Editora J. B., 1984.

Handelmann, Gottfried Heinrich. *Historia do Brasil*, 2 vols., trans. IHGB. Rio: IHGB, 1931 [1860].

Haußer, Christian. "Civilização e nação: O índio na historiografia brasileira oitocentista." *Jahrbuch für Geschichte Lateinamerikas* 44 (2007): 235–57.

Hazareesingh, Sudhir. *The Saint-Napoleon: Celebrations of Sovereignty in Nineteenth-Century France*. Cambridge, MA: Harvard University Press, 2004.

Heideking, Jürgen, Geneviève Fabre, and Kai Dreisbach, eds. *Celebrating Ethnicity and Nation: American Festive Culture from the Revolution to the Early 20th Century*. New York: Berghan Books, 2001.

Henderson, James. *A History of Brazil Comprising Its Geography, Commerce, Colonisation, Aboriginal Inhabitants, etc. etc. etc.* London: Longman, Hurst, Rees, Orme and Brown, 1821.

Herstal, Stanislaw. *D. Pedro: Estudo iconográfico*, 3 vols. São Paulo and Lisbon: n.p., 1972.

Hessel, Lothar Francisco, and Georges Raeders. *O teatro no Brasil da Colônia à Regência*. Porto Alegre: Universidade Federal do Rio Grande do Sul, 1974.

Hill, Pascoe Grenfell. *Fifty Days on Board a Slave Vessel in the Mozambique Channel, in April and May, 1843*. London: John Murray, 1844.

Hilliard, Henry W. *Politics and Pen Pictures at Home and Abroad*. New York: G. P. Putnam's Sons, 1892.

Himelfarb, Hélène. "Versailles: Functions and Legends." In *Rethinking France: Les Lieux de Mémoire*. Vol. 1: *The State*, ed. Pierre Nora, trans. Mary Trouille, 269–333. Chicago: University of Chicago Press, 2001.

Hinchcliff, Thomas Woodbine. *Over the Sea and Far Away: Being a Narrative of Wanderings around the World*. London: Longman's, Green, and Co., 1876.

Hobsbawm, Eric J., and Terence Ranger, eds. *The Invention of Tradition*. Cambridge, UK: Cambridge University Press, 1988.

Holanda, Sérgio Buarque de. "Do Império à República." In *História geral da civilização brasileira*. Tomo 2: *O Brasil monárquico*, 5 vols., ed. Sérgio Buarque de Holanda, 5:7–435. São Paulo: Difel, 1966–71.

Holloway, Thomas H. "'A Healthy Terror': Police Repression of *Capoeiras* in Nineteenth-Century Rio de Janeiro." *Hispanic American Historical Review* 69:4 (Nov. 1989): 637–76.

———. "The Defiant Life and Forgotten Death of Apulco de Castro: Race, Power, and Historical Memory." *Estudios Interdisciplinares de América Latina* 191 (Jan.–June 2008): 81–102.

———. *Policing Rio de Janeiro: Repression and Resistance in a 19th-Century City*. Stanford, CA: Stanford University Press, 1993.

Holman, James. *A Voyage Round the World, Including Travels in Africa, Asia, Australia, America, etc., etc. from MDCCCXXVII to MDCCCXXXII.* 4 vols. London: Smith, Elder, and Co., 1834.

Homem de Mello, Francisco Inacio Marcondes, Barão. *Discursos pronunciados pelo . . . , um na sessão cívica em homenagem a José Bonifácio em 8 de dezembro de 1886, e outro, por occasião da inauguração da estatua de José Bonifacio de Andrada e Silva no dia 7 de setembro de 1872*. São Paulo: Typographia King, 1887.

Horner, Gustavus R. B. *Medical Topography of Brazil and Uruguay*. Philadelphia: Lindsay and Blakiston, 1845.

Hübner, Baron Alexander von. *Um diplomata austríaco na corte de São Cristóvão (à margem do diário do barão Hubner): Brasil—Uruguai—Argentina de 1882*, ed. Roberto Mendes Gonçalves. Rio: Conselho Federal de Cultura, 1976.

Hull, Isabel V. "Prussian Dynastic Ritual and the End of Monarchy." In *German Nationalism and the European Response, 1890–1945*, ed. Carole Fink,

Isabel V. Hull, and MacGregor Knox, 13–41. Norman: University of Oklahoma Press, 1985.

Hunter, Mary Robinson. *A Diplomat's Lady in Brazil: Selections from the Diary of Mary Robinson Hunter, 1834–1848*, ed. Evelyn M. Cherpak. Newport, RI: Newport Historical Society, 2001.

Hüsken, Ute. *When Rituals Go Wrong: Mistakes, Failure, and the Dynamics of Ritual*. Leiden: Koninklijke Brill NV, 2007.

I. I. A. M. *Verdades puras sobre as consequencias do dia sete d'abril, pelo cidadão brasileiro*. . . . Rio: Typ. do *Diario*, 1833.

Iglesias, Francisco. "Vida política, 1848–1866." In *História geral da civilização brasileira. Tomo 2: O Brasil monárquico*, 5 vols., ed. Sérgio Buarque de Holanda, 3:9–112. São Paulo: Difel, 1966–71.

Instituto Histórico e Geográfico do Brasil. *Homenagem do . . . : Sessão extraordinaria em commemoração do fallecimento de S. M. o Snr. D. Pedro II celebrada a 4 de Março de 1892*. Rio: Companhia Typ. do Brazil, 1892.

Ipsen, Wiebke. "Delicate Citizenship—Gender and Nationbuilding in Brazil, 1865–1891." PhD dissertation, University of California, Irvine, 2005.

———. "*Patrícias*, Patriarchy, and Popular Demobilization: Gender and Elite Hegemony in Brazil at the End of the Paraguayan War." *Hispanic American Historical Review* 92:2 (May 2012): 303–30.

Itier, Jules, *Journal d'un voyage en Chine en 1843, 1844, 1845, 1846*. 3 vols. Paris: Chez Dauvin et Fontaine, 1848.

Izecksohn, Vitor. "A Guerra do Paraguai." In *O Brasil imperial*, 3 vols., ed. Keila Grinberg and Ricardo Salles, 2:385–424. Rio: Civilização Brasileira, 2009.

Jackson, Richard. *Vive le Roi! A History of the French Coronation from Charles V to Charles X*. Chapel Hill: University of North Carolina Press, 1984.

Jacquemont, Victor. *Letters from India, Describing a Journey in the British Dominions . . .* , 2 vols. London: Edward Churton, 1834.

James, William. *Brazil through the Eyes of . . . : Diaries, Letters, and Drawings, 1865–1866*, trans. John M. Monteiro, ed. Maria Helena P. T. Machado. Cambridge, MA: Harvard University Press, 2006.

Jancsó, István, ed. *Brasil: Formação do Estado e da nação*. São Paulo: Hucitec; Ijuí: Unijuí 2003.

———. *Independência: História e historiografia*. São Paulo: Hucitec and FAPESP, 2005.

Jancsó, István, and Iris Kantor, eds. *Festa: Cultura e sociabilidade na América portuguesa*, 2 vols. São Paulo: Hucitec, 2001.

Jancsó, István, and João Paulo G. Pimenta. "Peças de um mosaíco (ou apontamentos para o estudo da emergência da identidade nacional brasileira)." In *Viagem incompleta, a experiência brasileira (1500–2000), formação: Histórias*, ed. Carlos Guilherme Mota, 129–75. São Paulo: Editora Senac, 2000.

Jenkins, John S. *United States Exploring Expeditions . . . in 1838, 1839, 1840, 1841, and 1842*. Auburn, NY: James. M. Alden, 1850.

Jesus, Ronaldo Pereira de. "Associativismo no Brasil do século XIX: Repertório crítico dos registros de sociedades no Conselho de Estado (1860–1889)." *Locus* 13:1 (Jan.–June 2007): 144–70.

———. *Visões da monarquia: Escravos, operários e abolicionismo na Corte.* Belo Horizonte: Argumentum, 2009.

Johnson, Daniel Noble. *The Journals of . . . (1822–1853), United States Navy,* ed. Mendel L. Peterson. Washington, DC: Smithsonian Institution, 1959.

Johnson, Victoria. *Backstage at the Revolution: How the Royal Paris Opera Survived the End of the Old Regime.* Chicago: University of Chicago Press, 2008.

Joinville, Prince de. *Vieux souvenirs de Mgr. le Prince de Joinville, 1818–1848,* ed. Daniel Meyer. Paris: Mercure de France, 1970.

Karasch, Mary C. *Slave Life in Rio de Janeiro, 1800–1850.* Princeton, NJ: Princeton University Press, 1987.

Kennedy, William Robert. *Sporting Sketches of South America.* London: R. H. Porter, 1892.

Kertzer, David I. *Ritual, Politics, and Power.* New Haven, CT: Yale University Press, 1988.

Keyes, Julia L. "Our Life, in Brazil." *Alabama Historical Quarterly* 28 (1966): 129–339.

Kidder, Daniel P. *Sketches of Residence and Travels in Brazil, Embracing Historical and Geographical Notices of the Empire and Its Several Provinces,* 2 vols. Philadelphia: Sorin and Ball, 1845.

Kirkendall, Andrew J. *Class Mates: Male Student Culture and the Making of a Political Class in Nineteenth-Century Brazil.* Lincoln: University of Nebraska Press, 2002.

Kittleson, Roger A. "'Campaign All of Peace and Charity': Gender and the Politics of Abolitionism in Porto Alegre, Brazil, 1879–88." *Slavery and Abolition* 22:3 (2001): 83–108.

———. "Women and Notions of Womanhood in Brazilian Abolitionism." In *Gender and Slave Emancipation in the Atlantic World,* ed. Pamela Scully and Diana Paton, 99–120. Durham, NC: Duke University Press, 2005.

Kodama, Kaori. *Os índios e o Império do Brasil: A etnografia do IHGB entre as décadas de 1840 e 1860.* São Paulo: EdUSP, 2009.

Koschnik, Albrecht. "Political Conflict and Public Contest: Rituals of National Celebration in Philadelphia, 1788–1815." *Pennsylvania Magazine of History and Biography* 98 (1994): 209–48.

Koseritz, Carl von. *Imagens do Brasil,* trans. Afonso Arinhos de Melo Franco. São Paulo: Martins, 1943.

Kossoy, Boris. *Dicionário histórico-fotográfico brasileiro: Fotógrafos e ofício da fotografia no Brasil (1833–1910).* São Paulo: Instituto Moreira Salles, 2002.

Kotzebue, Otto von. *A New Voyage Round the World, in the Years 1823, 24, 25, and 26.* London: Henry Colburn and Richard Bentley, 1830.

Kraay, Hendrik. "'As Terrifying as Unexpected': The Bahian Sabinada, 1837–38." *Hispanic American Historical Review* 72:4 (Nov. 1992): 501–27.

———. "Between Brazil and Bahia: Celebrations of Dois de Julho in Nineteenth-Century Salvador." *Journal of Latin American Studies* 31:2 (May 1999): 255–86.

———. "Definindo a nação e o Estado: Rituais cívicos na Bahia pós-Independência (1823–1850)." *Topoi* 3 (Sep. 2001): 64–90.

———. "Patriotic Mobilization in Brazil: The Zuavos and Other Black Companies." In *I Die With My Country: Perspectives on the Paraguayan War*, ed. Hendrik Kraay and Thomas L. Whigham, 61–80. Lincoln: University of Nebraska Press, 2004.

Kraay, Hendrik, and Thomas L. Whigham, eds. *I Die with My Country: Perspectives on the Paraguayan War*. Lincoln: University of Nebraska Press, 2004.

Kühl, Paulo Mugayar. "A chegada das óperas de Rossini no Rio de Janeiro." *Rotunda* 4 (April 2006): 59–70.

———. "Luiz Vicente De-Simoni e uma pequena poética de ópera em português." *Rotunda* 3 (Oct. 2004): 36–48.

La Salle, A. de. *Voyage autour du monde exécuté pendant les années 1836 et 1837 . . .* , 3 vols. Paris: Arthus Bertrand, 1851.

Lacombe, Américo L. Jacobina. *O mordomo do Império*. Rio: Biblioteca do Exército, 1994.

Laet, Carlos de. *Crônicas*, 2nd ed., ed. Homero Senna. Rio: Academica Brasileira de Letras, 2000.

Lago, Laurênio. *Brigadeiros e generais de D. João VI e D. Pedro I no Brasil: Dados biográficos, 1808–1831*. Rio: Imprensa Militar, 1938.

———. *Os generais do Exército brasileiro de 1860 a 1889: Traços biográficos*. Rio: Imprensa Nacional, 1942.

Lago, Pedro Corrêa do, and Bia Corrêa do Lago. *Coleção Princesa Isabel: Fotografia do século XIX*. Rio: Capivara, 2008.

Lamberg, Mauricio. *O Brazil illustrado com gravuras*, trans. Luiz de Castro. Rio: Lombaerts, 1896.

Lambert, Hercidia Maria Facuri Coelho. "Festa e participação popular (São Paulo—início do século XX)." *História* (São Paulo) 13 (1994): 121–29.

Langer, Johnni. "Enigmas arqueológicos e civilizações perdidas no Brasil oitocentista." *Anos 90* 6:9 (1998): 165–85.

Langfur, Hal. *The Forbidden Lands: Colonial Identity, Frontier Violence, and the Persistence of Brazil's Eastern Indians, 1750–1830*. Stanford, CA: Stanford University Press, 2006.

Langsdorff, E. de, Baroness of. *Diário da Baronesa E. de Langsdorff: Relatando sua viagem ao Brasil por ocasião do casamento de S. A. R. o Príncipe de Joinville, 1842–1843*, trans. Patrícia Chittoni Ramos et al. Florianópolis: Editora Mulheres, 1999.

Lavollée, Charles Humbert. *Voyage en Chine-Ténériffe-Rio de Janeiro. . . .* Paris: Just Rouvier; A. Ledoyen, 1852.

Leal, Elisabete da Costa. "O Calendário republicano e a festa cívica do descobrimento do Brasil em 1890: Versões de história e militância positivista." *História* 25:2 (2006): 64–93.

Leclerc, Max. *Lettres du Brésil*. Paris: E. Plon, Nourrit et Cie, 1890.

Lehnen, Leila. "Foundational Mission: José de Alencar's *O Jesuita* and the Making of the Nation." *Espéculo* 30 (July–Oct. 2005); available at www.ucm.es/info/especulo/numero30.

Leitão, Joaquim. *Do civismo e da arte no Brasil*. Lisbon: Liv. Editora Tavares Cardoso e Irmão, 1900.

Leite, Glacyra Lazzari. *Pernambuco 1817*. Recife: Fundação Joaquim Nabuco and Editora Massangana, 1988.

———. *Pernambuco 1824*. Recife: Fundação Joaquim Nabuco and Editora Massangana, 1989.

Leithold, Theodor Von. "Minha excursão ao Brasil ou viagem de Berlim ao Rio de Janeiro e volta. . . ." In *O Rio de Janeiro visto por dois prussianos em 1819*, ed. and trans. Joaquim de Sousa Leão Filho, 1–121. São Paulo: Companhia Editora Nacional, 1966.

Lemay, Gaston. *A bord de la* Junon. . . . Paris: G. Charpentier, 1881.

Lemos, Renato. "A Alternativa republicana e o fim da monarquia." In *O Brasil imperial*, 3 vols., ed. Keila Grinberg and Ricardo Salles, 3:401–44. Rio: Civilização Brasileira, 2009.

———. *Benjamin Constant: Vida e história*. Rio: Topbooks, 1999.

Levasseur, É[mile], et al. *O Brasil*, trans. Luiz Cavalcanti de M. Guerra and José Augusto de Carvalho. Rio: Bom Texto and Letras e Expressões, 2001 [1889].

Lima, Herman. *História da caricatura no Brasil*, 4 vols. Rio: José Olympio, 1963.

Lima, Ivana Stolze. *Cores, marcas e falas: Sentidos da mestiçagem no Império do Brasil*. Rio: Arquivo Nacional, 2003.

Lima, José Fernandes de Barros. *Episodios da conspiração mineira; Tiradentes, poemeto realista*. Maceió: Tip. M. Rocha, 1884.

Lima, Valéria. *J.-B. Debret: Historiador e pintor*. Campinas: Editora UNICAMP, 2007.

Lira, Mariza. *História do hino nacional brasileiro*. Rio: Biblioteca do Exército Editora, 1954.

Lisboa, João Francisco. *Jornal de Timon: Partidos e eleições no Maranhão*, ed. José Murilo de Carvalho. São Paulo: Companhia das Letras, 1995.

Lisboa, José da Silva. *Historia dos principaes successos politicos do Imperio do Brazil*. Rio: Typographia Imperial e Nacional, 1825–30.

Lisboa, Karen Macknow. "Olhares estrangeiros sobre o Brasil do século XIX." In *Viagem incompleta, 1500–2000: Formação, histórias*, ed. Carlos Guilherme Mota, 265–99. São Paulo: Editora Senac, 2000.

Litwicki, Ellen M. *America's Public Holidays, 1865–1920*. Washington, DC: Smithsonian Institution Press, 2000.

Lopes, Valentim José da Silveira. *Sete de Setembro: Drama em 2 actos por . . . representado pela primeira vez no Theatro do Gymnasio Dramatico do Rio de Janeiro no dia 7 de Setembro de 1861*. Rio: Typ. e Livraria de B. X. Pinto de Souza, 1861.

Lopes Don, Patricia. "Carnivals, Triumphs, and Rain Gods: A Civic Festival in the City of Mexico-Tenochtitlán in 1539." *Colonial Latin American Review* 6:1 (June 1997): 17–40.

Lopez, Emilio Carlos Rodrigues. *Festas públicas, memória e representação.* São Paulo: Humanitas, 2004.

Loureiro, João. "Cartas de . . . escritos do Rio de Janeiro ao Conselheiro Manuel José Maria da Costa e Sá, de 1828 a 1842." *RIHGB* 76 (1914): 271–468.

Lustosa, Isabel. *D. Pedro I.* São Paulo: Companhia das Letras, 2006.

———. *Insultos impressos: A guerra dos jornalistas na Independência, 1821–1823.* São Paulo: Companhia das Letras, 2000.

Lyra, Maria de Lourdes Viana. "Memória da Independência: Marcos e representações simbólicas." *Revista Brasileira de História* 15:29 (1995): 173–206.

———. "'Pátria do cidadão': A concepção de pátria/nação em Frei Caneca." *Revista Brasileira de História* 18:36 (1998): 395–420.

Macaulay, Neill. *Dom Pedro: The Struggle for Liberty in Brazil and Portugal, 1798–1834.* Durham, NC: Duke University Press, 1986.

MacDouall, John. *Narrative of a Voyage to Patagonia and Tierra del Fuego.* London: Renshaw and Rush, 1833.

Macedo, Francisco Riopardense de. "Independência ou morte—uma nova visão." *Revista do Instituto Histórico e Geográfico do Rio Grande do Sul* 133 (1998): 57–64.

Macedo, Joaquim Manuel de. *Anno biographico brazileiro*, 3 vols. Rio: Typographica e Lithographia do Imperial Instituto Artistico, 1876.

———. *A carteira do meu tio.* Rio: Typ. Dous de Dezembro, 1855.

———. *Memórias da rua do Ouvidor.* Brasília: Universidade de Brasília, 1988 [1878].

———. *Memórias do sobrinho do meu tio*, ed. Flora Sussekind. São Paulo: Companhia das Letras, 1995 [1867–68].

———. *Teatro completo*, 3 vols.. Rio: MEC, Fundação Nacional de Arte, Serviço Nacional de Teatro, 1979.

Mac-Érin, U. *Huit mois sur les deux océans: Voyage d'études et d'agrément.* Tours: Cattier; Paris: Larcher, [1885].

Machado, Humberto Fernandes. "Imprensa abolicionista e censura no Império do Brasil." In *Entre a monarquia e a República: Imprensa, pensamento político e historiografia (1822–1889)*, ed. Monica Leite Lessa and Silvia Carla Pereira de Brito Fonseca, 243–59. Rio: EdUERJ, 2008.

Machado, Maria Helena. *O plano e o pânico: Os movimentos sociais na década da abolição.* Rio: Editora UFRJ and EDUSP, 1994.

Machado, Ubiratan. *A vida literária no Brasil durante o romantismo.* Rio: EdUERJ, 2001.

Machado de Assis, Joaquim Manoel. *Obra completa*, 2nd ed., 3 vols., ed. Afrânio Coutinho. Rio: Editora José Aguilar, 1962.

———. "Machado de Assis: Obra completa," http://portal.mec.gov.br/machado/index.php (accessed July 2008).

Magaldi, Cristina. *Music in Imperial Rio de Janeiro: European Culture in a Tropical Milieu.* Lanham, MD: Scarecrow Press, 2004.

Magalhães, [José Vieira] Couto de. *Diário íntimo*, ed. Maria Helena Pereira Toledo. São Paulo: Companhia das Letras, 1998.

Magalhães Júnior, R[aimundo]. "Ferreira Vianna e *A conferência dos divinos*." In *Três panfletários do Segundo Reinado*, ed. R[aimundo] Magalhães Júnior, 209–56. Rio: ABL, 2009.

———. *O Império em chinelos*. Rio: ABL, 1957.

———. "Justiniano José da Rocha e *Ação; Reação; Transação*." In *Três panfletários do Segundo Reinado*, ed. R[aimundo] Magalhães Júnior, 125–58. Rio: ABL, 2009.

———. "Salles Torres Homem e *O libelo do povo*." In *Três panfletários do Segundo Reinado*, ed. R[aimundo] Magalhães Júnior, 7–51. Rio: ABL, 2009.

Magnoli, Demétrio. *O corpo da pátria: Imaginação geográfica e política externa no Brasil (1808–1912)*. São Paulo: Editora da Universidade Estadual Paulista and Moderna, 1997.

Malerba, Jurandir. *A corte no exílio: Civilização e poder no Brasil às vésperas da Independência (1808–1821)*. São Paulo: Companhia das Letras, 2000.

Malerba, Jurandir, ed. *A Independência brasileira: Novas dimensões*. Rio: FGV Editora, 2006.

Malta, I[gnacio] J[osé]. *Ao muito alto e poderozo senhor D. Pedro II Imperador Constitucional e Defensor Perpetuo do Brazil, em 18 de Julho de 1841, faustissimo dia de sua coroação*. . . . Rio: Typ. do Diario de N. L. Vianna, 1841.

Mammi, Lorenzo. "Teatro em música no Brasil monárquico." In *Festa: Cultura e sociabilidade na América portuguesa*, 2 vols., ed. István Jancsó and Iris Kantor, 1:37–52. São Paulo: EdUSP, 2001.

Manet, Édouard. *Lettres de jeunesse, 1848–1849*. Paris: Louis Rouart et Fils, [1928].

Mansel, Philip. *The Court of France, 1789–1830*. Cambridge, UK: Cambridge University Press, 1988.

Maringoni, Gilberto. *Angelo Agostini: A imprensa ilustrada da Corte à Capital Federal, 1864–1910*. São Paulo: Devir, 2011.

Mariz, Vasco. *História da música no Brasil*, 2nd ed. Rio: Civilização Brasileira, 1983.

Martinho, Lenira Menezes. "Caixeiros e pés-descalços: Conflitos e tensões em um meio urbano em desenvolvimento." In Lenira Menezes Martinho and Riva Gorenstein, *Negociantes e caixeiros na sociedade da Independência*, 21–124. Rio: Secretaria Municipal da Cultura, 1993.

Martins, Luciana de Lima, *O Rio de Janeiro dos viajantes: O olhar britânico (1800–1850)*. Rio: Jorge Zahar Editora, 2001.

Martins Pena, [Luiz Carlos]. *Comédias*, ed. Darcy Damasceno. Rio: Edições de Ouro, 1966.

———. *Folhetins: A Semana Lírica*. Rio: INL, 1965.

Marzano, Andrea. *Cidade em cena: O ator Vasques, o teatro e o Rio de Janeiro, 1839–1892*. Rio: FAPERJ and Folha Seca, 2008.

Mascarenhas, Nelson Lage. *Um jornalista do Império (Firmino Rodrigues Silva)*. São Paulo: Companhia Editora Nacional, 1961.

Mateos Royo, José Antonio. "All the Town Is a Stage: Civic Ceremonies and Religious Festivities in Spain during the Golden Age." *Urban History* 26:2 (Aug. 1999): 165–89.

Mattos, Ilmar Rohloff. "O gigante e o espelho." In *O Brasil imperial*, 3 vols., ed. Keila Grinberg and Ricardo Salles, 2:13–51. Rio: Civilização Brasileira, 2009.

———. *O tempo saquarema*. São Paulo: Hucitec, 1987.

Mattoso, Ernesto. *Cousas do meu tempo (reminiscencias)*. Bordeaux: Imprimeries Gounouilhou, 1916.

Maurício, Augusto. *Algo do meu velho Rio*. Rio: Editora Brasiliana, 1966.

Maxwell, Kenneth R. *Conflicts and Conspiracies: Brazil and Portugal, 1750–1808*. Cambridge, UK: Cambridge University Press, 1973.

McGillivray, John. *Narrative of the Voyage of H. M. S. Rattlesnake*. London: T. W. Boone, 1852.

McGraw, Jason. "Spectacles of Freedom: Public Manumissions, Political Rhetoric, and Citizen Mobilisation in Mid-Nineteenth-Century Colombia." *Slavery and Abolition* 32:2 (June 2011): 269–88.

McNab, Gregory. "A decanonização da Inconfidência Mineira e a história de Joaquim Norberto." In *Toward Socio-Criticism*, ed. Roberto Reis, 197–218. Tempe: Center for Latin American Studies, Arizona State University, 1991.

Meade, Teresa A. *"Civilizing" Rio: Reform and Resistance in a Brazilian City*. University Park: Pennsylvania State University Press, 1997.

Megiani, Ana Paula Torres. *O rei ausente: Festa e cultura política nas visitas dos Filipes a Portugal (1581 e 1619)*. São Paulo: Alameda, 2004.

Meghreblian, Caren Ann. "Art, Politics, and Historical Perception in Imperial Brazil, 1854–1884." PhD dissertation, University of California, Los Angeles, 1990.

Mello, Evaldo Cabral de. *A outra independência: O federalismo pernambucano de 1817 a 1824*. São Paulo: Ed. 34, 2004.

———. *Rubro veio: O imaginário da restauração pernambucana*, 2nd ed. Rio: Topbooks, 1997.

Mello, Maria Tereza Chaves de. *A república consentida: Cultura democrática e científica do final do Império*. Rio: ANPUH, 2007.

Mello Moraes, A[lexandre] J[osé] de. *Chronica geral do Brazil*, 2 vols. Rio: B. L. Garnier, 1886.

———. *História do Brasil-Reino e do Brasil-Império*, 2 vols. Belo Horizonte: Itatiaia, 1982 [1871–73].

———. *A Independencia e o Imperio do Brazil ou A Independencia comprada por dous milhões de libras esterlinas e o Império do Brazil com dous imperadores no seu reconhecimento, e cessão; seguido da historia da constituição politica do patriarchado, e da corrupção governamental, provado com documento authenticos*. Rio: Typ. do Globo, 1877.

Mello Moraes Filho, [Alexandre José de]. *Festas e tradições populares do Brasil*, 3rd ed. Rio: F. Briguiet, 1946 [1895].

———. *Historia e costumes*. Rio: B. L. Garnier, 1904.

Mencarelli, Fernando Antônio. *Cena aberta: A absolvição de um bilontra e o teatro de revista de Arthur Azevedo*. Campinas: Editora da UNICAMP, 1999.

Mendes, Raimundo Teixeira. *Patria brazileira: Discurso lido na sessão sociolatrica da Sociedade Positivista do Rio de Janeiro, celebrada na noite de 26 de Guttemberg de 93*. Rio: Sociedade Positivista, 1881.

Mendonça, Isabel Mayer Godinho. "Festas e arte efêmera em honra da família real portuguesa no Brasil colonial." In *Arte efêmera em Portugal*, ed. Isabel Mayer Godinho Mendonça et al., 300–20. Lisbon: Fundação Calouste Gulbenkian, 2001.

Mendonça, Isabel Mayer Godinho, et al., eds. *Arte efêmera em Portugal*. Lisbon: Fundação Calouste Gulbenkian, 2001.

Mendonça, Joseli Maria Nunes. *Entre a mão e os anéis: A lei dos sexagenários e os caminhos da abolição no Brasil*. Campinas: Editora UNICAMP, 1999.

Mendonça, Salvador de. "Cousas do meu tempo." *Revista do Livro* 20 (Dec. 1960): 107–98.

Menezes, Raimundo de. *Dicionário literário brasileiro*, 2nd ed. Rio: Livros Técnicos e Científicos, 1978.

Merolla, Gennaro. *Correspondência brasileira (1832–1834)*. São Paulo: Instituto Cultural Italo-Brasileiro, 1963.

Michalski, Sergiusz. *Public Monuments: Art in Political Bondage*. London: Reaktion Books, 1998.

Milliet, Maria Alice. *Tiradentes: O corpo do herói*. São Paulo: Martins Fontes, 2001.

Moniz, Rozendo. *Moniz Barretto: O repentista*. Rio: B. L. Garnier, 1886.

Monte Alverne, Francisco de. *Obras oratórias do padre mestre fr. Francisco do Monte Alverne*, 4 vols. Rio: Eduardo & H. Laemmert, 1853–54.

———. *Oração d'acção de graças, que no dia 25 de Março de 1831 anniversario do solemne juramento da Constituição, celebrado na Igreja de S. Francisco de Paula, por o Povo Fluminense. Recitou Fr. . . . *Rio: Typ. de R. Ogier, 1831.

Monteiro, Fernanda Fonseca, and Gisele Cunha dos Santos. "Celebrando a fundação do Brasil: A inauguração da estátua eqüestre de D. Pedro I." *Revista Eletrônica de História do Brasil* 4:1 (Jan.–June 2000): 53–64.

Monteiro, Tobias. *História do Império: O Primeiro Reinado*, 2 vols. Belo Horizonte and São Paulo: EDUSP, 1982 [1939–46].

Montet, Édouard. *Brésil et Argentine: Notes et impressions de voyage*, 2nd ed. Geneva: Ch. Eggimann & Cie, [1897].

Moore, Joseph William. *The Revolution of 1831*, ed. J. M. Harvey. São Paulo: Sociedade Brasileira de Cultura Inglesa, 1962.

Moraes, Evaristo de. *A campanha abolicionista, 1879–1888*, 2nd ed. Brasília: Editora UNB, 1986 [1924].

Moraes, Renata Figueiredo. "A abolição da escravidão: História, memória e usos do passado na construção de símbolos e heróis no maio de 1888." In *Mitos, projetos e práticas políticas: Memória e historiografia*, ed. Rachel Soihet et al., 83–102. Rio: Civilização Brasileira, 2009.

Morales de los Rios Filho, Adolfo. *O Rio de Janeiro imperial*, 2nd ed. Rio: Topbooks, 2000 [1946].

Moreira de Azevedo, Manuel Duarte. *Curiosidades, noticias e variedades historicas brasileiras*. Rio: B. L. Garnier, 1873.

———. *Historia patria: O Brazil de 1831 a 1840*. Rio: B. L. Garnier, 1884.

———. "Origem e desenvolvimento da imprensa no Rio de Janeiro." *RIHGB* 28:2 (1865): 169–224.

———. *Pequeno panorama, ou, Descripção dos principaes edifícios da cidade do Rio de Janeiro*, 5 vols. in 2. Rio: Typ. de F. de Paula Brito, 1861–67.

———. *O Rio de Janeiro: Sua história, monumentos, homens notaveis, usos e curiosidades*, 2 vols., 3rd ed., ed. Elysio de Oliveira Belchior. Rio: Livraria Brasiliana Editora, 1969 [1877].

Morel, Marco. *Cipriano Barata na sentinela da liberdade*. Salvador: Academia de Letras da Bahia and Assembléia Legislativa do Estado da Bahia, 2001.

———. *As transformações dos espaços públicos: Imprensa, atores políticos e sociabilidades na cidade imperial*. São Paulo: Hucitec, 2005.

Morison, James. *By Sea to San Francisco, 1849–1850: The Journal of Dr. . . ,* ed. Lonnie J. White and William D. Gillespie. Memphis: Memphis State University Press, 1977.

Mosher, Jeffrey C. *Political Struggle, Ideology, and State Building: Pernambuco and the Construction of Brazil, 1817–1850*. Lincoln: University of Nebraska Press, 2008.

Mota, Carlos Guilherme. *Nordeste 1817*. São Paulo: Perspectiva, 1972.

Mota, Maria Aparecida Rezende. *Sílvio Romero: Dilemas e combates no Brasil da virada do século XIX*. Rio: Ed. FGV, 2000.

Motta, Marly Silva da. *A nação faz 100 anos: A questão nacional no centenário da Independência*. Rio: Fundação Getúlio Vargas, CPDOC, 1992.

Muir, Edward. *Ritual in Early Modern Europe*, 2nd ed. Cambridge, UK: Cambridge University Press, 2005.

Mulhall, M[ichael] G[eorge]. *Handbook of Brazil*. Buenos Aires: n.p., 1877.

Museu Histórico Nacional. *Catálogo da coleção iconográfica do Arquivo Histórico*. Brasília, 1992.

Nabuco, Joaquim. *Diários*, 2 vols., ed. Evaldo Cabral de Mello. Rio: Bem-Te-Vi; Recife: Fundação Joaquim Nabuco, 2005.

———. *Um estadista do Império*. Rio: Editora Nova Aguilar, 1975 [1897].

Needell, Jeffrey D. "Brazilian Abolitionism, Its Historiography, and the Uses of Political History." *Journal of Latin American Studies* 42:2 (May 2010): 231–61.

———. "The Domestic Civilizing Mission: The Cultural Role of the State in Brazil." *Luso-Brazilian Review* 36:1 (Summer 1999): 1–18.

———. *The Party of Order: The Conservatives, the State, and Slavery in the Brazilian Monarchy, 1831–1871*. Stanford, CA: Stanford University Press, 2006.

———. "The 'Revolta contra Vacina' of 1904: The Revolt against 'Modernization' in 'Belle Époque' Rio de Janeiro." *Hispanic American Historical Review* 67:2 (May 1987): 233–69.

———. *A Tropical* Belle Époque: *Elite Culture and Society in Turn-of-the-Century Rio de Janeiro*. Cambridge, UK: Cambridge University Press, 1987.

Neeld, [Reginald Russell]. *Diary of the Revolution at Rio de Janeiro*. Portsmouth: Charpentier & Co., 1895.

Néry, M. F.-J. de Santa-Anna. *Aux États-Unis du Brésil: Voyages de M. T[héodore] Durand avec illustrations.* Paris: Librairie Ch. Delgrave, [1890].

Neves, Lúcia Maria Bastos Pereira das. *Corcundas e constitucionais: A cultura política da Independência (1820–1822).* Rio: FAPERJ and Revan, 2003.

———. "Estado e política na Independência." In *O Brasil imperial,* 3 vols., ed. Keila Grinberg and Ricardo Salles, 1:95–136. Rio: Civilização Brasileira, 2009.

———. "Folhinhas e almanaques: História política no Império do Brasil (1824–1836)." In *Linguagens e práticas da cidadania no século XIX,* ed. Gladys Sabina Ribeiro and Tânia Maria Tavares Bessone da Cruz Ferreira, 231–46. São Paulo: Alameda, 2010.

Newcomb, Robert Patrick. "José de Alencar's Critical Writing: Narrating National History in the Romantic Era." *Luso-Brazilian Review* 44:1 (2007): 1–19.

Nicolau, Jair. *História do voto no Brasil.* Rio: Jorge Zahar, 2002.

Nora, Pierre. "Between Memory and History: *Les Lieux de Mémoire.*" *Representations* 26 (Spring 1989): 7–25.

North, Marianne. *Recollections of a Happy Life: Being the Autobiography of . . . ,* ed. Mrs. John Addington Symonds, 2 vols. London: Macmillan and Co., 1892.

O'Leary, Cecilia Elizabeth. *To Die For: The Paradox of American Patriotism.* Princeton, NJ: Princeton University Press, 1999.

Oakley, Francis. *Kingship: The Politics of Enchantment.* Malden, MA: John Wiley, 2006.

Octavio [de Langgaard de Menezes], Rodrigo. *Festas nacionaes: Com uma introdução de Raul Pompeia.* Rio: F. Briguiet & C., 1893.

Oliveira, Albino José Barbosa de. *Memorias de um magistrado do Império,* ed. Americo Jacobina Lacombe. São Paulo: Nacional, 1943.

Oliveira, Cecília Helena L. de Salles. *A astúcia liberal: Relações de mercado e projetos políticos no Rio de Janeiro (1820–1824).* Bragança Paulista: EDUSF and ÍCONE, 1999.

———. "O Museu Paulista da USP e a memória da Independência." *Cadernos CEDES* 22:58 (Dec. 2002): 65–80.

———. "Repercussão da revolução: Delineamento do império do Brasil, 1808/1831." In *O Brasil imperial,* 3 vols., ed. Keila Grinberg and Ricardo Salles, 1:15–54. Rio: Civilização Brasileira, 2009.

Oliveira, Eduardo Romero. "O império da lei: Ensaio sobre o cerimonial de sagração de D. Pedro I (1822)." *Tempo* 13:20 (Jan. 2009): 133–59.

Oliveira, Ilda Centeno de, and Ronaldo Menegaz. "Índice dos *Anais da Biblioteca Nacional,* v. 1–99." *ABN* 100 (1980): 1–143

Oliveira, Lúcia Lippi. "As festas que a República manda guardar." *Estudos Históricos* 2:4 (1989): 172–89.

———. "Imaginário histórico e poder cultural: As comemorações do descobrimento." *Estudos Históricos* 14:26 (2000): 183–202.

Oliveira, Rodrigo Perez. "A monumentalização de Manoel Luís Osório: A construção de uma memória militar nos últimos dias do governo do Marechal

Floriano Peixoto (1887–1894)." *Militares e Política* 7 (July–Dec. 2010): 23–50.

Oliveira Lima, [Manoel de]. *D. João VI no Brasil.* 3rd ed. Rio: Topbooks, 1996 [1908].

Osorio, Alejandra B. *Inventing Lima: Baroque Modernity in Peru's South Sea Metropolis.* New York: Palgrave Macmillan, 2008.

Otaviano, Francisco. *Cartas de . . . coligidas, anotadas e prefaciadas por Wanderley Pinho.* Rio: Civilização Brasileira, 1977.

Otoni, Cristiano Benedito. *Autobiografia.* Brasília: Ed. UNB, 1983 [1908].

Ottoni, Theophilo Benedicto. *A estatua equestre, carta.* Rio: Typ. do Diario do Rio, 1862.

Ozouf, Mona. *Festivals and the French Revolution,* trans. Alan Sheridan. Cambridge, MA: Harvard University Press, 1988.

Paiva, Tancredo de Barros. *Achêgas de um diccionario de pseudonymos, iniciais, abreviaturas e obras anonymas de auctores brasileiros e de estrangeiros, sobre o Brasil ou no mesmo impressas.* Rio: J. Leite, 1929.

Paixão, Múcio da. *O theatro no Brazil: Obra pósthuma.* Rio: Ed. Moderna, 1930.

Palmer, Steven. "Getting to Know the Unknown Soldier: Official Nationalism in Liberal Costa Rica, 1880–1900." *Journal of Latin American Studies* 25:1 (Feb. 1993): 45–72.

Pani, Erika. "El proyecto de Estado de Maximiliano a través de la vida cortesana y del ceremonial público." *Historia Mexicana* 178 (Oct.–Dec. 1995): 423–60.

Parada, Mauricio. *Educando corpos e criando a nação: Cerimônias cívicas e práticas disciplinares no Estado Novo.* Rio: Editora PUC-Rio, 2003.

Paranhos, José Maria da Silva. *Cartas ao amigo ausente.* Rio: Ministério das Relações Exteriores, Instituto Rio Branco, 1953.

Parker, William Harwar. *Recollections of a Naval Officer, 1841–1865.* New York: Charles Scribner's, 1885.

Parron, Tâmis. *A política da escravidão no Império do Brasil, 1826–1865.* Rio: Civilização Brasileira, 2011.

Pascual, Antonio Deodoro do. *Rasgos memoraveis do senhor D. Pedro I° Imperador do Brasil, excelso Duque de Bragança.* Rio, 1862.

Patrocínio, José do. *Campanha abolicionista: Coletânea de artigos.* Rio: Fundação Biblioteca Nacional, 1996.

Paula Brito, Francisco de. *Poesias de Francisco de Paula Brito.* Rio: Typ. P. Brito, 1863.

Pedro I. *Cartas do Imperador D. Pedro I a Domitilla de Castro, Marqueza de Santos.* Rio: Typ. Moraes, 1896.

Pedro II. *D. Pedro II e a Condessa de Barral através da correspondência íntima do imperador, anotada e comentada,* ed. R[aimundo] Magalhães Júnior. Rio: Civilização Brasileira, 1956.

———. *Diário do imperador, 1840–1891.* CD-ROM. Petrópolis: Museu Imperial, [1999].

Pena, Eduardo Spiller. *Pajens da casa imperial: Jurisconsultos, escravidão e a lei de 1871.* Campinas: Editora da UNICAMP, 2001.

Pereira, Avelino Romero Simões. "Hino nacional brasileiro: Que história é esta?" *Revista do Instituto de Estudos Brasileiros* 38 (1995): 21–42.

Pereira, Fidelis Honorio da Silva dos Santos. *Ao muito alto e muito poderoso Senhor D. Pedro II Imperador Constitucional e Defensor Perpetuo do Brasil O. D. C. em Dois de Dezembro de 1847, dia de seus faustos e preciosos annos.* Rio: Typographia Nacional, 1847.

————. *Votos a Deos na Gloriosa Sagração, e Coroação de Sua Magestade Imperial o Senhor Dom Pedro II, Imperador Constitucional.* Rio: Typographia Nacional, 1841.

Pereira, Paulo Roberto, ed. *Brasiliana da Biblioteca Nacional: Guia de fontes sobre o Brasil.* Rio: Fundação Biblioteca Nacional and Nova Fronteira, 2001.

Pereira da Silva, J[oão] M[anuel]. *Historia da fundação do imperio brazileiro,* 7 vols. Rio: B. L. Garnier, 1864–68.

————. *Historia do Brazil durante a menoridade de d. Pedro II° (1831 a 1840),* 2nd ed. Rio: B. L. Garnier, 1888 [1878].

————. *Memorias do meu tempo,* 2 vols. Rio: n.p., 1895–96.

————. *Segundo periodo do reinado de D. Pedro I no Brazil: Narrativa historica.* Rio: B. L. Garnier, 1871.

Perez, Eliana, Maria José Fernandes, and Paulo Homeniuk. "Bibliografia de viajantes." *ABN* 120 (2000): 273–321.

Peskin, Allan, and Donald Ramos. "An Ohio Yankee at Dom Pedro's Court: Notes on Brazilian Life in the 1850's by an American Diplomat, Robert C. Schenck." *The Americas* 38:4 (April 1982): 497–517.

Pfeiffer, Ida. *A Woman's Journey around the World.* London: Plain Label Books, 1850.

Pimenta Bueno, José Antônio. *Direito público brasileiro e análise da Constituição do Império.* Brasília: Senado Federal, 1978 [1857].

Pinho, Wanderley. *Cotegipe e seu tempo: Primeira Phase, 1815–1867.* São Paulo: Companhia Editora Nacional, 1937.

————. *Política e políticos no Império: Contribuições documentaes.* Rio: Imprensa Nacional, 1930.

Pires de Almeida, [José Ricardo]. *Elogio historico de D. Pedro I, egregio fundador do Imperio do Brazil.* Rio: Typ. de G. Leuzinger & Filhos, [1885].

Polyanthea: Album de autographos offerecido a sua magestade o senhor Dom Pedro II Imperador do Brazil por occasião de seu regresso a patria em Setembro de 1888. Voirom: Typ. e Lithographia A. Molloret, 1892.

Pompéia, Raul. *Carta ao autor das festas nacionaes.* Rio: Typ. de Leuzinger & Filhos, 1893.

————. *Crônicas do Rio,* ed. Virgílio Moretzsohn Moreira. Rio: Prefeitura da Cidade do Rio de Janeiro, 1996.

Popingis, Fabiane. *Proletários de casaca: Trabalhadores do comércio carioca (1850–1911).* Campinas: Editora UNICAMP, 2007.

Porto Alegre, Manoel de Araújo. "Bellas Artes: A estatua equestre do fundador do Império." *Guanabara* 3 (1854): 284–92.

————. *Correspondência com Paulo Barbosa da Silva,* ed. Américo Jacobina Lacombe. Rio: Academia Brasileira de Letras, 1991.

———. "A estátua eqüestre do Senhor D. Pedro I." *Revista Popular* 1:2 (1859): 37–40.

———. *Prologo dramatico representado no Theatro Constitucional Fluminense, no faustissimo dia Dous de Dezembro de 1837. Composto por. . . . Musica do Mestre Candido José da Silva.* Rio: Typ. Imperial de F. P. Brito, 1837.

———. *Teatro completo*, 2 vols., eds. Renata Guerra and Edwaldo Cafezeiro. Rio: INACEN, 1988.

Póvoa, Pessanha, *Annos academicos: São Paulo, 1860–1864.* Rio: Typ. Perseverança, 1870.

Prado, Décio de Almeida. *João Caetano: O ator, o empresário, o repertório.* São Paulo: EDUSP and Perspectiva, 1972.

Prado, Maria Emília. *Memorial das desigualdades: Os impasses da cidadania no Brasil, 1870–1902.* Rio: Revan, 2005.

Pratt, Mary Louise. *Imperial Eyes: Travel Writing and Transculturation*, 2nd ed. New York: Routledge, 2008.

Preuss, Ori. *Bridging the Island: Brazilians' Views of Spanish America and Themselves, 1865–1912.* Madrid and Frankfurt: Iberoamericana and Vervuert, 2011.

Price, Sir Rose Lambert. *The Two Americas: An Account of Sport and Travel, with Notes on Men and Manners in North and South America.* Philadelphia: J. B. Lippincott and Co., 1877.

Priore, Mary del. *Festas e utopias no Brasil colonial.* São Paulo: Brasiliense, 1994.

Puntoni, Pedro. "O Sr. Varnhagen e o patriotismo caboclo: O indígena e o indianismo perante a historiografia brasileira." In *Brasil: Formação do Estado e da nação*, ed. István Jancsó, 633–75. São Paulo: Hucitec; Ijuí: Unijuí, 2003.

Queiroz, Suely Robles Reis de. "Reflections on Brazilian Jacobins of the First Decade of the Republic (1893–1897)." *The Americas* 48:2 (Oct. 1991): 181–205.

Quesada, Vicente Gregorio. *Mis memorias diplomaticas: Misión ante el gobierno del Brasil*, 2 vols. Buenos Aires: Coni Hermanos, 1907.

Radforth, Ian. *Royal Spectacle: The 1860 Visit of the Prince of Wales to Canada and the United States.* Toronto: University of Toronto Press, 2004.

Radiguet, Max. *Souvenir de l'Amérique espagnole: Chili-Pérou-Brésil*, new ed. Paris: Calman Lévy, 1890.

Raffard, Henri. "Apontamentos acerca de pessoas e cousas do Brazil." *RIHGB* 61:98 (1898): 5–567.

Ramirez, Salvador A. *From New York to San Francisco via Cape Horn in 1849: The Gold Rush Voyage of the Ship "Pacific," an Eyewitness Account.* Carlsbad: Tentacled Press, 1985.

Ramos, Ana Flávia Cernic. "Política e humor nos últimos anos da monarquia: A série 'Balas de Estalo'." In *História em cousas miúdas: Capítulos de história social da crônica no Brasil*, ed. Sidney Chalhoub, 87–121. Campinas: Ed. UNICAMP, 2005.

Rancourt, Etienne de. *Fazendas et estancias: Notes de voyage sur le Brésil et la République Argentine.* Paris: Plon, 1901.

Rangel, Alberto. *No rolar do tempo*. Rio: José Olympio, 1937.

———. *Textos e pretextos: Incidentes da chronica brazileira à luz de documentos conservados na Europa*. Tours: Arrault, 1926.

Rangel, Carlos Roberto da Rosa. "Festas entre bandeiras." *Cadernos do CHDD* 6:1 (Special Issue, 2007): 173–95.

Rango, Ludwig von. "Diário de minha viagem até o Rio de Janeiro no Brasil e volta nos anos de 1819 e 1820." In *O Rio de Janeiro visto por dois prussianos em 1819*, ed. and trans. Joaquim de Sousa Leão Filho, 113–66. São Paulo: Companhia Editora Nacional, 1966.

Rebouças, André. *Diario e notas autobiograficas*, ed. Ana Flora and Inácio José Verissimo. Rio: José Olympio, 1938.

Reis, A[ntonio] J[osé] Fernandes de. *A noite do castello: Opera lyrico em 3 actos por . . . musica de A. Carlos Gomes, dedicado a S. M. I*. Rio: Typ. e Livraria de B. X. Pinto de Sousa, 1861.

Reis, Antonio Simões dos. *Pseudonimos brasileiros: Pequenos verbetes para um dicionario*, 2 vols. Rio: Z. Valverde, 1941.

Reis, João José. "Quilombos e revoltas escravas no Brasil." *Revista USP* 28 (Dec. 1995–Jan. 1996): 14–39.

Reis, Joaquim Pereira dos. *Oração de acção de graças recitada na igreja parochial de N. Senhora da Candelaria no dia 7 de Setembro de 1830 anniversario da Independencia brasileira*. Rio: Typ. Imperial e Nacional, 1830.

Reis, Vicente [Torres da Silva]. "O Rio de Janeiro no crepúsculo da monarquia—aspectos de sua vida social e comercial." *RIHGB* 345 (Oct.–Dec. 1984): 7–84.

Relação dos publicos festejos que tiverão lugar do 1. de abril até 9. pelo feliz regresso de SS. MM. II. e A. I. voltando da Bahia à Corte Imperial. Rio: Imperial Typographia de Plancher, 1826.

Resende, Beatriz, ed. *Os cronistas do Rio*. Rio: José Olympio, 1995.

Reynolds, Jeremiah N. *Voyage of the United States Frigate Potomac . . . during the Circumnavigation of the Globe in the Years 1831, 1832, 1833, and 1834*. New York: Harper and Brothers, 1835.

Reynolds, William. *Voyage to the Southern Ocean: The Letters of Lieutenant . . . from the U.S. Exploring Expedition, 1838–1842*, ed. Anne Hoffman Cleaver and E. Jeffrey Stann. Annapolis: Naval Institute Press, 1988.

Rezende, Francisco de Paula. *Minhas recordações*. Rio: José Olympio, 1944.

Rheingantz, Carlos G. *Titulares do Império*. Rio: Ministério da Justiça e Negócios Interiores, Arquivo Nacional, 1960.

Ribeiro, Gladys Sabina. *A liberdade em construção: Identidade nacional e conflitos antilusitanos no Primeiro Reinado*. Rio: Relume-Dumará, 2002.

Ribeiro, Gladys Sabina, and Vantuil Pereira. "O Primeiro Reinado em revisão." In *O Brasil imperial*, 3 vols., ed. Keila Grinberg and Ricardo Salles, 1:137–73. Rio: Civilização Brasileira, 2009.

Ribeiro, Maria Eurydice de Barros. "Memória em bronze: Estátua eqüestre de D. Pedro I." In *Cidade vaidosa: Imagens urbanas do Rio de Janeiro*, ed. Paulo Knauss, 15–28. Rio: Sette Letras, 1999.

———. *Os símbolos do poder: Cerimônias e imagens do Estado monárquico no Brasil*. Brasília: UNB, 1995.

Ribeiro, Roberto Feijó. *Dicionário de pseudônimos, cognomes e títulos famosos*. Fortaleza: Gráfica Editorial Cearense, 1983.

Ribeiro Filho, J. S. *Dicionário biobibliográfico de escritores cariocas*. Rio: Brasiliana, 1965.

Ribeyrolles, Charles. *Brasil pitoresco: História-descrições-viagens-colonização-instituições*, trans. Gastão Penalva, 3 vols. in 2. São Paulo: Martins, 1941 [1859–61].

Ricci, Magda. *Assombrações de um padre regente: Diogo Antônio Feijó (1784–1843)*. Campinas: Ed. UNICAMP, 2001.

Ricci, Maria Lúcia de Souza Rangel. *A atuação de um publicista: Antônio Borges da Fonseca*. Campinas: Pontifícia Universidade Católica de Campinas, 1995.

———. *Guarda Negra: Perfil de uma sociedade em crise*. São Paulo: Campinas, 1990.

Ricupero, Bernardo. *O romantismo e a idéia de nação no Brasil (1830–1870)*. São Paulo: Martins Fontes, 2004.

Rinke, Stefan H. "Pillars of the Republics: Early Monuments and the Politics of Memory in the Post-Colonial Americas." *Iberoamericana*. New Ser. 1:4 (Dec. 2001): 91–111.

Rio, João do [João Paulo Barreto]. *A alma encantadora das ruas*. Niterói: Imprensa Oficial do Estado do Rio de Janeiro, 2007 [1908].

Rocha, Justiniano José da. "Ação; reação; transação: Duas palavras acerca da atualidade." In *Três panfletários do Segundo Reinado*, ed. Raimundo Magalhães Junior, 159–205. Rio: ABL, 2009 [1855].

Rochet, André. *Louis Rochet: Sculpteur sinologue, 1813–1878*. Paris: A. Bonne, 1978.

Rochette, Joseph de. *Relation d'un voyage à Fez en 1825 et extrait d'un voyage au Brésil et à La Plata en 1834. . . .* Chambéry: Ménard, 1888.

Rodrigues, Antônio Edmilson Martins. *José de Alencar: O poeta armado do século XIX*. Rio: FGV Editora, 2001.

Rodrigues, José Honório. *Independência: Revolução e contra-revolução*, 5 vols. Rio: Livraria Francisco Alves Editora, 1975.

Rodrigues, Marcelo Santos. "Guerra do Paraguai: Os caminhos da memória entre a comemoração e o esquecimento." PhD dissertation, Universidade de São Paulo, 2009.

Rodriguez, Eugenio. *A viagem da imperatriz*, ed. and trans. Gastão Penalva. Rio: Imprensa Nacional, 1936.

Roleta italiana: Governo e povo. Rio: Typ. Industria Nacional J. J. C. Cotrim, 1870.

Romero, Sylvio. *Historia da literatura brazileira*, 2 vols. Rio: B. L. Garnier, 1888.

Rosselli, John. "The Opera Business and the Italian Immigrant Community in Latin America, 1820–1930: The Example of Buenos Aires." *Past and Present* 127 (1990): 155–82.

Rugendas, Johann Moritz. *Viagem pitoresca através do Brasil*, trans. Sérgio Milliet. São Paulo: Círculo do Livro, n.d. [1835].

[Ruschenberger, William S. W.] *Three Years in the Pacific, Containing Notices of Brazil, Chile, Bolivia, Peru, &c. in 1831, 1832, 1833, 1834, by an Officer in the United States Navy,* 2 vols. London: Richard Bentley, 1835.

Ryan, Mary. "The American Parade: Representations of the Nineteenth-Century Social Order." In *The New Cultural History,* ed. Lynn Hunt, 131–53. Berkeley: University of California Press, 1989.

Sabato, Hilda. *The Many and the Few: Political Participation in Republican Buenos Aires.* Stanford, CA: Stanford University Press, 2001.

Sacramento Blake, Augusto Victorino Alves do. *Diccionario bibliographico brazileiro,* 7 vols. Rio: Typographia Nacional, 1883–1902.

Salgado, Susana. *The Teatro Solís: 150 Years of Opera, Concert, and Ballet in Montevideo.* Middletown, CT: Weslyan University Press, 2003.

Salles, Ricardo. "As águas do Niagara: Crise da escravidão e o ocaso saquarema." In *O Brasil imperial,* 3 vols., ed. Keila Grinberg and Ricardo Salles, 3:39–82. Rio: Civilização Brasileira, 2009.

———. *Guerra do Paraguai: Memórias e imagens.* Rio: Edições Biblioteca Nacional, 2003.

———. *Nostalgia imperial: A formação da identidade nacional no Brasil do Segundo Reinado.* Rio: Topbooks, 1996.

Salvador, José María. *Efímeras efemérides: Fiestas cívicas y arte efímero en la Venezuela de los siglos XVII–XIX.* Caracas: Universidad Católica Andrés Bello, 2001.

Sampaio, Gabriela. *Juca Rosa: Um pai de santo no Rio de Janeiro imperial.* Rio: Arquivo Nacional, 2009.

Sandes, Noé Freire. *A invenção da nação: Entre a Monarquia e a República.* Goiânia: UFG and AGEPEL, 2000.

Sandroni, Cícero. *180 anos do Jornal do Commercio, 1827–2007, de D. Pedro I a Luiz Inácio Lula da Silva.* Rio: Quorum, 2007.

Santiago, Camila Fernandes Guimarães. *A vila em ricas festas: Celebrações promovidas pela câmara de Vila Rica, 1711–1744.* Belo Horizonte: C/ Arte, FACE-FUMEC, 2003.

Santos, Beatriz Catão Cruz. *O corpo de deus na América: A festa de* Corpus Christi *nas cidades da América portuguesa, século XVIII.* São Paulo: Annablume, 2005.

Santos, Francisco Marques dos. "Dom Pedro II e a preparação da maioridade." *Estudos Brasileiros* 3:7 (July–Dec. 1941): 7–140.

Santos, Lery. *Pantheon fluminense: Esboços biographicos.* Rio: Typ. Leuzinger & Filhos, 1880.

Santos, Mário Márcio de A. *Um homem contra o Império: Vida e lutas de Antônio Borges da Fonseca.* Recife: Fundação do Patrimônio Histórico e Artístico de Pernambuco, 1995.

Santos, Renata. *A imagem gravada: A gravura no Rio de Janeiro entre 1808 e 1853.* Rio: Casa da Palavra, 2008.

Sarthou, Carlos. *Relíquias da cidade do Rio de Janeiro.* Rio: Gráfica Olímpica Editora, 1961.

Savage, Kirk. *Standing Soldiers, Kneeling Slaves: Race, War, and Monument in Nineteenth-Century America*. Princeton, NJ: Princeton University Press, 1997.

Sax, William S., Johannes Quack, and Jan Weinhold, eds. *The Problem of Ritual Efficacy*. Oxford, UK: Oxford University Press, 2010.

Scherzer, Karl. *Narrative of the Circumnavigation of the Globe by the Austrian Frigate Novara . . . in the Years 1857, 1858, and 1859*, 3 vols. London: Saunders, Otley, and Co., 1861.

Schiavinatto, Iara Lis. "Entre histórias e historiografias: Algumas tramas do governo joanino." In *O Brasil imperial*, 3 vols., ed. Keila Grinberg and Ricardo Salles, 1:55–93. Rio: Civilização Brasileira, 2009.

———. "Entre os manuscritos e os impressos." In *Entre a Monarquia e a República: Imprensa, pensamento político e historiografia (1822–1889)*, ed. Monica Leite Lessa and Silvia Carla Pereira de Brito Fonseca, 13–34. Rio: Eduerj, 2008.

———. "A praça pública e a liturgia política." *Cadernos CEDES* 22:58 (Dec. 2002): 81–99.

Schlichthorst, C. O. *O Rio de Janeiro como é, 1824–1826 (huma vez e nunca mais)*, trans. Emmy Dodt and Gustavo Barroso. Rio: Ed. Getúlio Costa, 1943 [1829].

Schneider, Robert A. *The Ceremonial City: Toulouse Observed, 1730–1780*. Princeton, NJ: Princeton University Press, 1995.

Schubert, Guilherme. *A coroação de d. Pedro I*. Rio: Arquivo Nacional, 1973.

Schultz, April R. *Ethnicity on Parade: Inventing the Norwegian American through Celebration*. Amherst: University of Massachusetts Press, 1994.

Schultz, Kirsten. *Tropical Versailles: Empire, Monarchy, and the Portuguese Royal Court in Rio de Janeiro, 1808–1821*. London: Routledge, 2001.

Schulz, John. *O Exército na política: Origens da intervenção militar, 1850–1894*. São Paulo: EdUSP, 1994.

———. *The Financial Crisis of Abolition*. New Haven, CT: Yale University Press, 2008.

Schwarcz, Lilia Moritz. *As barbas do Imperador: D. Pedro II, um monarca nos trópicos*, 2nd ed. São Paulo: Companhia das Letras, 1999.

———. "Dos males da dádiva: Sobre ambigüidades no processo da Abolição brasileira." In *Quase-cidadão: Histórias e antropologias da pós-emancipação no Brasil*, ed. Olívia Maria Gomes da Cunha and Flávio dos Santos Gomes, 23–54. Rio: FGV Editora, 2007.

———. *O Império em procissão*. Rio: Jorge Zahar, 2001.

Schwarcz, Lilia Moritz, with Paulo Cesar de Azevedo and Angela Marques da Costa. *A longa viagem da biblioteca dos reis: Do terremoto de Lisboa à Independência do Brasil*, 2nd ed. São Paulo: Companhia das Letras, 2002.

Schwartz, Stuart B. "Ceremonies of Public Authority in a Colonial Capital: The King's Processions and the Hierarchies of Power in Seventeenth-Century Salvador." *Anais de História de Além-Mar* 5 (2004): 7–26.

———. "The Formation of a Colonial Identity in Brazil." In *Colonial Identity in the Atlantic World, 1500–1800*, ed. Nicholas Canny and Anthony Pagden, 15–50. Princeton NJ: Princeton University Press, 1987.

Seidler, Carl [Friedrich Gustav]. *Dez anos no Brasil*, 3rd ed., trans. Bertoldo Klinger. São Paulo, Martins, and Brasília, INL, 1976 [1835].

———. *História das guerras e revoluções do Brasil em 1825 a 1835*, trans. Alfredo de Carvalho. São Paulo: Companhia Editora Nacional, 1939 [1837].

Seixas, Romualdo Antonio de. *Collecção das obras do Excellentissimo Senhor Dom Romualdo de Seixas*, 4 vols. Salvador: Typ. de Epiphanio Pedrozo, 1839–52.

———. *Memoria apologetica do arcebispo da Bahia, Metropolitana e primaz do Brasil; em resposta a uma opusculo do Exm.° e Rem.° d. Manoel do Monte Rodrigues e Araujo, bispo do Rio de Janeiro e Capellão-mor de S. M. o Imperador. . . .* Salvador: Typ. de Galdino José Bizerra e Comp, 1842.

Sela, Eneida Maria Mercadante. *Modos de ser, modos de ver: Viajantes europeus e escravos africanos no Rio de Janeiro (1808–1850)*. Campinas: Editora UNICAMP, 2008.

Selys-Longchamps, Walthère. *Notes d'un voyage au Brésil*. Brussells: Librairie C. Muquardt, 1875.

Sena, Ernesto. *Rascunhos e perfis*. Brasília: Editora Universidade de Brasília, 1983.

Serbin, Kenneth P. *Needs of the Heart: A Social and Cultural History of Brazil's Clergy and Seminaries*. Notre Dame, IN: University of Notre Dame Press, 2006.

Silva, Alfredo Pretextato Macıal da. *Os generais do Exército brasileiro de 1822 a 1889 (traços biographicos)*, 2nd ed., 2 vols. Rio: Americana, 1940.

Silva, Eduardo. *As camélias do Leblon e abolição da escravatura*. São Paulo: Companhia das Letras, 2003.

———. *Dom Obá II d'África, o príncipe do povo: Vida, tempo e pensamento de um homem livre de cor*. São Paulo: Companhia das Letras, 1997.

———. "Integração, globalização e festa: A abolição da escravatura como história cultural." In *Escravidão, exclusão e cidadania*, ed. Marco Pamplona, 107–18. Rio: Access Editora, 2001.

———. "Law, Telegraph and Festa: A Revaluation of Abolition in Brazil." In *Pour l'histoire du Brésil: Melanges offerts à Kátia de Queirós Mattoso*, ed. François Crouzet et al., 451–62. Paris: L'Harmattan, 2000.

———. *Prince of the People: The Life and Times of a Free Man of Colour*, trans. Moyra Ashford. London: Verso, 1993.

———. "O Príncipe Obá, um voluntário da pátria." In *Guerra do Paraguai, 130 anos depois*, ed. Maria Eduardo Castro Magalhães Marques, 65–76. Rio: Relume Dumará, 1995.

———. *As queixas do povo*. Rio: Paz e Terra, 1988.

———. "A República comemora o Império—Um aspecto ideológico da crise dos anos 20." *Revista Rio de Janeiro* 1:2 (1986): 59–70.

———. "Sobre versos, bandeiras e flores." In *Panfletos abolicionistas: O 13 de maio em versos*, ed. Renato Pinto Venâncio, 16–40. Belo Horizonte: Arquivo Público Mineiro, 2007.

Silva, Francisco Gomes da. *Memórias*, 2nd ed., ed. Noronha Santos. Rio: Editora Souza, 1959 [1831].

Silva, Maria Beatriz Nizza da. *Cultura e sociedade no Rio de Janeiro, 1808–1821*, 2nd ed. São Paulo: Nacional, 1978.

———. *A Gazeta do Rio de Janeiro (1808–1822): Cultura e sociedade*. Rio: EdUERJ, 2007.

Silva Jardim, Antonio da. *Salvação da patria (Governo republicano): Conferencia realizada no Club Republicano de São Paulo, em a noite de 7 de abril de 1888*. Santos: Typ. do *Diario de Santos*, 1888.

———. *Tiradentes: Discurso lido por . . . na sessão solemne do Club Tiradentes em homenagem ao patriota martir na noite de 21 de abril de 1890*. Rio: Typ. G. Leuzinger e Filhos, 1890.

———. *Tradições republicanas: Tiradentes, discurso lido no corrente anno no Club Republicano de Santos, na noite de 21 de Abril, anniversario do martyrio do Patriota*. . . . Rio: n.p., 1888.

Silveira, Mauro Cesar. *A batalha de papel: A Guerra do Paraguai através da caricatura*. Porto Alegre: L&PM, 1996.

Siqueira, Carla. "A imprensa comemora a República: Memórias em luta no 15 de novembro de 1890." *Estudos Históricos* 7:14 (1994): 161–81.

———. "A imprensa comemora a República: O 15 de novembro nos jornais cariocas, 1890–1922." MA thesis, Pontifícia Universidade Católica do Rio de Janeiro, 1995.

Sisson, S. A. *Galeria dos brasileiros ilustres*, 2 vols., 2nd ed. Brasília: Senado Federal, 1999 [1861].

Skidmore, Thomas E. *Black into White: Race and Nationality in Brazilian Thought*. New York: Oxford University Press, 1974.

Skogman, C[arl Johann Alfred]. *Viaje de la fragata sueca "Eugenia" (1851–1853): Brasil-Uruguay-Argentina-Chile-Peru*, trans. Kyell Henrichsen. Buenos Aires: Ediciones Argentinas Solar, 1942.

Slemian, Andréa. *Vida política em tempo de crise: Rio de Janeiro (1808–1824)*. São Paulo: Hucitec, 2006.

Smith, Hannah. *Georgian Monarchy: Politics and Culture, 1714–1760*. Cambridge, UK: Cambridge University Press, 2006.

Soares, Carlos Eugênio Líbano. *A capoeira escrava e outras tradições rebeldes no Rio de Janeiro (1808–1850)*. Campinas: Editora da UNICAMP, 2001.

———. *A negregada instituição: Os capoeiras na corte imperial, 1850–1890*. Rio: Access, 1999.

———. *Zungú: Rumor de muitas vozes*. Rio: Arquivo Público do Estado do Rio de Janeiro, 1998.

Soares, Luís Carlos, *"O Povo de Cam" na capital do Brasil: A escravidão urbana no Rio de Janeiro do século XIX*. Rio: 7Letras, 2007.

———. *Rameiras, ilhoas, polacas: A prostituição no Rio de Janeiro do século XIX*. São Paulo: Ática, 1992.

"Sociedade Defensora da Liberdade e Independencia Nacional." *RIHGB* 68:111 (1905): 225–47.

Sodré, Nelson Werneck. *História da imprensa no Brasil*, 2nd ed. Rio: Graal, 1977.

Soldado da Velha Guarda de 1831, Um. *Appreciação da estatua equestre do Senhor D. Pedro*. Rio: Typ. de Paula Brito, 1862.

Sousa, J. Galante de. *O teatro no Brasil*, 2 vols. Rio: MEC/INL, 1960.

Sousa, José Antônio Soares de, ed. "Cartas de Justiniano José da Rocha ao Visconde do Uruguai." *RIHGB* 220 (Jul.–Sep. 1953): 339–48.

Sousa, Octavio Tarquínio de. *A vida de D. Pedro I*, 3 vols. Belo Horizonte and São Paulo: EdUSP, 1988.

Southey, Robert. *History of Brazil*, 3 vols. London: Longman, Hurst, Rees, Orme and Brown, 1817–22.

Souza, Iara Lis Carvalho. "D. João VI no Rio de Janeiro: Entre festas e representações." In *Anais do Seminário Internacional D. João VI, um rei aclamado na América*, 50–63. Rio: Museu Histórico Nacional, 2000.

———. "Liturgia real: Entre a premência e o efêmero." In *Festa: Cultura e sociabilidade na América portuguesa*, 2 vols, ed. István Jancsó and Iris Kantor, 2:545–66. São Paulo: Hucitec, 2001.

———. *Pátria coroada: O Brasil como corpo político autônomo, 1780–1831*. São Paulo: Editora UNESP, 1998.

Souza, João Cardoso de Menezes e, Barão de Paranapiacaba. *Prometeu acorrentado*. Rio: Imprensa Nacional, 1907.

Souza, Juliana Beatriz A. de. "Mãe negra de um povo mestiço: Devoção a Nossa Senhora Aparecida e identidade nacional." *Estudos Afro-Asiáticos* 29 (March 1996): 85–102.

Souza, Paulo Cesar. *A Sabinada: A revolta separatista da Bahia (1837)*. São Paulo: Brasiliense, 1987.

Souza, Rosa Fátima de. "A militarização da infância: Expressões do nacionalismo na cultura brasileira." *Cadernos CEDES* 20:52 (Nov. 2000): 104–21.

Souza, Silvia Cristina Martins de. "*Ao correr da pena*: Uma leitura dos folhetins de José de Alencar." In *A história contada: Capítulos de história social da literatura no Brasil*, ed. Sidney Chalhoub and Leonardo Affonso Miranda Pereira, 123–43. Rio: Nova Fronteira, 1998.

———. *Carpinteiros teatrais, cenas cômicas e diversidade cultural no Rio de Janeiro oitocentista: Ensaios de história social da cultura*. Londrina: EdUEL, 2010.

———. *As noites do Ginásio: Teatro e tensões culturais na Corte (1823–1868)*. Campinas: Editora da UNICAMP, 2002.

Souza e Silva, Joaquim Norberto de. *Historia da conjuração mineira: Estudo sobre as primeiras tentativas para a independencia nacional, baseados em numerosos documentos impressos ou originais existentes em varias repartições*. Rio: B. L. Garnier, 1873.

———. "O Tiradentes perante os historiadores oculares do seu tempo." *RIHGB* 44:1 (1881): 131–39.

Squeff, Leticia. *O Brasil nas letras de um pintor: Manuel de Araújo Porto Alegre*. Campinas: Editora da UNICAMP, 2004.

Starr, S. Frederick. *Louis Moreau Gottschalk*. Urbana: University of Illinois Press, 1995.

Stewart, Charles Samuel. *Brazil and La Plata: The Personal Record of a Cruise*. New York: G. P. Putnam and Co., 1856.

———. *A Visit to the South Seas, in the United States Ship* Vincennes, *during the Years 1829 and 1830*, 2 vols. London: Henry Colburn and Richard Bentley, 1832.

Stillman, J. D. B., *Seeking the Golden Fleece: A Record of Pioneer Life in California*. San Francisco: A. Roman and Co., 1877.

Strong, Roy. *Splendour at Court: Renaissance Spectacle and the Theatre of Power*. London: Weidenfield and Nicholson, 1973.

Sumi, Geoffrey S. *Ceremony and Power: Performing Politics in Rome between Republic and Empire*. Ann Arbor: University of Michigan Press, 2005.

Sverner, Clara. *O piano nas Américas*. CD-ROM. Rio: Rob Digital, 2000.

Talmon-Chvaicer, Maya. *The Hidden History of Capoeira: A Collision of Cultures in the Brazilian Battle Dance*. Austin: University of Texas Press, 2008.

Taunay, Afonso de E. *A missão artística de 1816*. Brasília: Ed. Universidade de Brasília, 1983 [1912].

Taunay, Alfredo d'Escragnolle, Visconde de. *Memórias*. Rio: Biblioteca do Exército, 1960.

Távora, Araken. *D. Pedro II e o seu mundo através da caricatura*. Rio: Editora Documentária, 1976.

Testis [Vicente Cândido de Figueiredo Saboia, Visconde Saboia]. *Traços da política republicana no Brazil*. N.p., 1897.

Timandro [Francisco de Sales Torres Homem]. "O libelo do povo." In *Três panfletários do Segundo Reinado*, ed. R[aimundo] Magalhães Junior, 53–121. Rio: ABL, 2009 [1849].

Tinhorão, José Ramos. *As festas no Brasil colonial*. São Paulo: Editora 34, 2000.

Topik, Steven. "The Hollow State: The Effect of the World Market on State-Building in Brazil in the Nineteenth-Century." In *Studies in the Formation of the Nation-State in Latin America*, ed. James Dunkerley, 112–32. London: Institute of Latin American Studies, 2002.

Toplin, Robert Brent. *The Abolition of Slavery in Brazil*. New York: Atheneum, 1972.

Toussaint-Samson, Adèle. *A Parisian in Brazil: The Travel Account of a Frenchwoman in Nineteenth-Century Rio de Janeiro*, ed. June E. Hahner. Wilmington, DE: Scholarly Resources, 2001 [1883].

Travers, Len. *Celebrating the Fourth: Independence Day and the Rites of Nationalism in the Early Republic*. Amherst: University of Massachusetts Press, 1997.

Treece, David. *Exiles, Allies, Rebels: Brazil's Indianist Movement, Indigenist Politics, and the Imperial Nation-State*. Westport, CT: Greenwood, 2000.

Trochim, Michael R. "The Brazilian Black Guard: Racial Conflict in Post-Abolition Brazil." *The Americas* 44:3 (Jan. 1988): 285–300.

Truesdell, Matthew. *Spectacular Politics: Louis-Napoleon Bonaparte and the "Fête Impériale," 1849–1870*. New York: Oxford University Press, 1997.

Turner, Victor. *From Ritual to Theatre: The Human Seriousness of Play*. New York: Performing Arts Journal Publications, 1982.

Ultra, João Francisco da Silva. *A gloria do Brasil: Elogio dramatico representado em noute de 2 de dezembro de 1848, anniversario natalicio de S. M. I. o Senhor D. Pedro Segundo, no Theatro de S. Salvador pela Sociedade Dramatica Particular Instrucção e Recreio*. Campos: Typ. Patriotico de Eugenio Bricolens, 1848.

Unglaub, Tânia Regina da Rocha. "A prática do canto orfeônico e cerimônias cívicas na consolidação de um nacionalismo ufanista em terras catarinenses." *Revista Linhas* 10:1 (Jan.–June 2009): 105–27.

Unowsky, Daniel L. *The Pomp and Politics of Patriotism: Imperial Celebrations in Habsburg Austria, 1848–1916.* West Lafayette, IN: Purdue University Press, 2007.

Upham, Samuel C. *Notes of a Voyage to California via Cape Horn together with Scenes in El Dorado, in the Years 1849–50.* Philadelphia: The Author, 1878.

Ursel, Charles d'. *Sud-Amérique: Séjours et voyages au Brésil, à la Plata, au Chili, en Bolivie et au Péru.* Paris: E. Plon, 1879.

Vainfas, Ronaldo, ed. *Dicionário do Brasil Imperial (1822–1889).* Rio: Objetiva, 2002.

Valle, José Antonio do. *Elogio dramatico ao faustissimo baptisado do principe imperial Dom Pedro augustissimo herdeiro do solo do Brazil . . . (Levado á scena no theatro do Salão da Floresta pela Senhora Clara Delmastro, emprezaria do mesmo theatro).* Rio: Typ. de M. A. da Silva Lins, 1848.

Varela, Luis Nicolau Fagundes, *O estandarte auri-verde: Cantos sobre a questão anglo-brazileira.* Salvador: Typ. Imparcial de J. R. de A. Marques, 1863.

Varnhagen, Francisco Adolfo de. *Correspondência ativa,* ed. Clado Ribeiro de Lessa. Rio: INL, 1961.

———. *Historia da Independencia do Brazil.* Rio: Livraria Castilho, 1919.

———. *História geral do Brasil: Antes da sua separação e independência de Portugal,* 6th ed., 5 vols. São Paulo: Melhoramentos, 1959.

———. *Historia geral do Brazil, isto é do descobrimento, colonização, legislação e desenvolvimento deste Estado, hoje imperio independente, escripta em presença de muitos documentos autenticos recolhidos nos archivos do Brazil, de Portugal, da Hespanha e da Hollanda,* 1st ed., 2 vols. Rio: E. & H. Laemmert, 1854–57.

Vasques, Francisco Correia. *O Brasil e o Paraguai: Scena patriotica O. D. C. aos defensores da patria pelo artista. . . .* Rio: Typ. Popular de Azevedo Leite, 1865.

Vauthier, Louis Léger. *Diário íntimo do engenheiro Vauthier (1840–1846),* ed. Gilberto Freyre. Rio: Serviço Geográfico do Ministério da Educação e Saúde, 1940.

Vecchy, José de. *A união do imperio, allegoria ao dia 2 de dezembro de 1860, anniversario natalicio de S. M. o Imperador Senhor D. Pedro II: Mimica e baile postos em scena no theatro S. Pedro d'Alcantara no dia . . . pelo coreographo. . . .* Rio: Typographia de F. de Paula Brito, 1860.

Veiga, Evaristo Ferreira da. "Poesias de Evaristo da Veiga." *ABN* 33 (1911): 145–331.

Veiga, Luiz Francisco da. *O 7 de Abril não contemplado entre os dias de festividade nacional, pelo Decreto de 14 de Janeiro de 1890, promulgado pelo governo provisório, do Brazil: Carta Dirigida ao Eminente Brazileiro Ministro da Guerra Dr. Benjamim Constant Botelho de Magalhães.* Rio: Imprensa Nacional, 1890.

————. *O Primeiro Reinado estudado a luz da sciencia, ou A revolução do 7 de abril de 1831 justificada pelo direito e pela historia.* Rio: Leuzinger, 1877.

————. *A revolução de 7 de abril de 1831 e Evaristo Ferreira da Veiga por um fluminense amante da constituição.* Rio: Villeneuve, 1862.

Venâncio, Renato Pinto de, ed. *Panfletos abolicionistas: O 13 de Maio em versos.* Belo Horizonte: Secretaria do Estado de Cultura de Minas Gerais, Arquivo Público Mineiro, 2007.

Ventura, Roberto. *Estilo tropical: História cultural e polêmicas literárias no Brasil, 1870–1914.* São Paulo: Companhia das Letras, 1991.

Verbrugghe, Louis, and Georges Verbrugghe. *Forêts vierges: Voyage dans l'Amérique du Sud et l'Amérique Centrale.* Paris: Calman Lévy, 1880.

Verdadeiro Constitucional, Hum. *Defeza, ou fiel, e verdadeira exposição dos acontecimentos que tiverão lugar no Rio de Janeiro por occasião da chegada de SS. MM. II. as noites de 11 a 15 de março. Que ao respeitaval corpo do commercio offerece.* . . . Rio: Tipographia do Diario, 1831.

Veterano, Um. *A Estatua Equestre: Opusculo-politico-historico sobre factos da Independencia do Brazil nos reinados de SS. MM. El Rei o Sr. D. João VI, e o imperador o Sr. D. Pedro I, por.* . . . Salvador: Typ. de Antonio Olavo da França Guerra, 1862.

Vianna, Hélio. *Contribuição à história da imprensa brasileira (1812–1869).* Rio: Imprensa Nacional, 1945.

Vicente, Vicente de Paula. "O bobo do rei faz anos." *RIHGB* 325 (Oct.–Dec. 1979): 132–39.

Vicuña Mackenna, Benjamin. *Paginas de mi diario durante tres años de viaje, 1853–1854–1855.* Santiago: Universidad de Chile, [1936].

Vieira Fazenda, José. "Antiqualhas e memorias do Rio de Janeiro." *RIHGB* 86:140 (1919): 5–463; 88:142 (1920): 3–560; 89:143 (1921): 5–491; 93:147 (1923): 5–601; 95:149 (1924): 1–691.

Vincent, [Ethel Gwendoline], Mrs. Howard. *China to Peru, over the Andes: A Journey through South America.* London: Sampson, Low, Marston & Company, 1894.

Vincent, Frank. *Around and about in South America.* New York: D. Appleton, 1890.

Viqueira Albán, Juan Pedro. *Propriety and Permissiveness in Bourbon Mexico,* trans. Sonya Lipsett-Rivera and Sergio Rivera Ayala. Wilmington, DE: Scholarly Resources, 1999.

Waldstreicher, David. *In the Midst of Perpetual Fetes: The Making of American Nationalism, 1776–1820.* Chapel Hill: University of North Carolina Press, 1997.

Walpole, Frederick. *Four Years in the Pacific in Her Majesty's Ship "Collingwood" from 1844 to 1848,* 2 vols. London: Richard Bentley, 1849.

Walsh, Robert. *Notices of Brazil in 1828 and 1829,* 2 vols. London: Frederick Westley and A. H. Davis, 1830.

Watanabe-O'Kelly, Helen. "Festival Books in Europe from Renaissance to Rococo." *The Seventeenth Century* 3:2 (1988): 181–201.

Webster, William Henry Bayley. *Narrative of a Voyage to the Southern Atlantic Ocean in the Years 1828, 29, 30, performed in the H. M. Sloop* Chanticleer . . . , 2 vols. London: Richard Bentley, 1834.

Wehling, Arno. *Estado, história, memória: Varnhagen e a construção da identidade nacional.* Rio: Nova Fronteira, 1999.

Wehrs, Carlos. "Neukomm e A. Maersch, músicos, e De Simoni, libretista, precursores do nacionalismo musical brasileiro." *RIHGB* 380 (July–Sep. 1993): 104–17.

Weid, Elizabeth van der. "O bonde como elemento de expansão urbana no Rio de Janeiro." *Siglo XIX*, 2nd Ser. 16 (July–Dec. 1994): 78–103.

Werneck, André Peixoto de Lacerda. *D. Pedro I e a independência: A proposito da demolição da estatua da Praça Tiradentes.* Rio: Typ. da Empreza Democratica, 1895.

Wetherell, James. *Brazil: Stray Notes from Bahia: Being Extracts from Letters, &c., during a Residence of Fifteen Years*, ed. William Hadfield. Liverpool: Webb and Hunt, 1860.

Whigham, Thomas L. *The Paraguayan War.* Vol. 1: *Causes and Early Conduct.* Lincoln: University of Nebraska Press, 2002.

White, Shane. " 'It Was a Proud Day': African-American Festivals and Parades in the North, 1741–1834." *Journal of American History* 81:1 (June 1994): 13–50.

Wilentz, Sean. "Artisan Republican Festivals and the Rise of Class Conflict in New York City, 1788–1837." In *Working-Class America: Essays on Labor, Community, and American Society*, ed. Michael H. Frisch and Daniel J. Walkowitz, 37–77. Urbana: University of Illinois Press, 1983.

Wilkes, Charles. *Narrative of the United States Exploring Expedition during the Years 1838, 1839, 1840, 1841, 1842*, 5 vols., new ed. New York: George P. Putnam, 1851.

Williams, Daryle. "Civicscape and Memoryscape: The First Vargas Regime and Rio de Janeiro." In *Vargas and Brazil: New Perspectives*, ed. Jens R. Hentschke, 55–82. New York: Palgrave MacMillan, 2006.

———. *Culture Wars in Brazil: The First Vargas Regime, 1930–1945.* Durham, NC: Duke University Press, 2001.

Wisser, William M. "Rhetoric and Riot in Rio de Janeiro, 1827–1831." PhD dissertation, University of North Carolina at Chapel Hill, 2006.

Wortman, Richard S. *Scenarios of Power: Myth and Ceremony in Russian Monarchy from Peter the Great to the Abdication of Nicholas II.* Princeton, NJ: Princeton University Press, 2006.

Württemberg, Paul Alexander von. "Viagem do Príncipe Alexandre de Württemburg à América do Sul." *RIHGB* 171 (1936): 3–30.

Z. O. A. [Francisco Vilela Barbosa, Marquês de Paranaguá]. *A saudade pela sentidissima morte do Senhor D. Pedro Primeiro, ex.º Imperador do Brazil, gloza offerecida aos coraçoens sensiveis por . . .* , 2nd ed. Rio: Typ. do Diario de N. L. Vianna, 1835.

Zaho, Margaret Ann. *Imago Triumphalis: The Function and Significance of Triumphal Imagery for Italian Renaissance Rulers.* New York: Peter Lang Publishing, 2004.

Index